RR AMERICAN INDIANS

AMERICAN INDIANS

Volume III
Pueblo tribes, Western – Zuni language

A Magill Book
from the **Editors of Salem Press**

Consulting Editor
Harvey Markowitz
**D'Arcy McNickle Center for the History
of the American Indian, Newberry Library**

Salem Press, Inc.
Pasadena, California   Englewood Cliffs, New Jersey

Editor in Chief: Dawn P. Dawson

Consulting Editor: Harvey Markowitz   *Project Editor:* McCrea Adams
Research Supervisor: Jeff Jensen   *Photograph Editor:* Valerie Krein
Proofreading Supervisor: Yasmine A. Cordoba   *Production Editor:* Janet Long
Layout: James Hutson   *Illustrations:* Craig Attebery
Maps: Moritz Design

Library of Congress Cataloging-in-Publication Data

American Indians / consulting editor, Harvey Markowitz
    p.   cm. — (Ready reference)
"A Magill Book"
Includes bibliographical references and index.
ISBN 0-89356-757-4 (set : alk. paper) — ISBN 0-89356-760-4 (vol 3 : alk. paper)
1. Indians of North America—Encyclopedias.   2. Indians of Mexico—Encyclopedias.   I. Markowitz, Harvey.
II. Series.
E76.2.A45   1995
970.004'97—dc20
                                                                                    94-47633
                                                                                    CIP

First Printing

PRINTED IN THE UNITED STATES OF AMERICA

CONTENTS

Alphabetical List of Entries li

Pueblo tribes, Western 643
Pushmataha 645
Puyallup 646

Quapaw 647
Quechan 647
Queen Anne 648
Quetzalcóatl 648
Quileute 648
Quillwork 648
Quinault 649
Quinney, John W. 650

Railroads 651
Rain in the Face 651
Ranching 652
Red Bird 653
Red Cloud 653
Red Jacket 654
Red River War 654
Red Shoes 655
Reifel, Ben 655
Religion 655
Religious specialists 659
Relocation 662
Removal 664
Renville, Joseph 665
Reservation system of the United
    States 666
Reserve system of Canada 670
Resource use, pre-contact 671
Resources 672
Ridge, John Rollin 673
Ridge, Major 674
Riel, Louis, Jr. 674
Riel Rebellions 676
Riggs, Lynn 677
Rite of Consolation 677
Rites of passage 677
Rocky Boy 679
Rogers, Will 679
Roman Nose 679
Rosebud Creek, Battle of 679
Ross, John 680

Sacagawea 682
Sachem 684
Sacred, the 684
Sacred narratives 686
Salinan 687

Salish 688
Salishan language family 688
Salmon 689
Salt 689
Samish 689
Samoset 691
San Lorenzo 691
Sand Creek Massacre 691
Sand Painting 693
Sanpoil-Nespelem 694
Santa Fe Trail 695
Sarsi 695
Sassacus 696
Satanta 696
Sauk 696
Saybrook, Battle of 698
Scalps and scalping 698
Scarface Charlie 699
Scholder, Fritz 700
Sculpture 700
Seattle 701
Secotan 701
Secret societies 702
Sekani 702
Semiahmoo 703
Seminole 703
Seminole Wars 704
Seneca 706
Sequoyah 706
Seri 708
Serpent mounds 708
Serrano 709
Shábona 710
Shaker Church 710
Shaking Tent Ceremony 711
Shalako 711
Shasta 711
Shawnee 712
Shells and shellwork 712
Shikellamy 713
Shinnecock 713
Short Bull 713
Shoshone 714
Shuswap 715
Sign language 715
Siletz 715
Silko, Leslie Marmon 716
Sinagua 716
Siouan language family 717
Sioux 718
Sioux uprisings 723
Sitting Bull 724

Siuslaw 726
Skagit 726
Slave 727
Slavery 727
Slocum, John 729
Smohalla 729
Snake Dance 729
Snake War 730
Snaketown 730
Snohomish 731
Snoqualmie 731
Social control, traditional 731
Societies, non-kin-based 732
Society of American Indians . . . 735
Sooke 735
Southeast 736
Southern Cult 740
Southwest 740
Sovereignty 743
Spirit dancing 745
Spiro 745
Spokane 746
Spotted Tail 746
Spybuck, Ernest 747
Squamish 747
Squanto 748
Squash 748
Standing Bear 748
Standing Bear, Luther 749
Stereotypes 749
Stomp Dance 751
Stumbling Bear 751
Subarctic 752
Subsistence 754
Suicide 759
Sun Dance 760
Suquamish 762
Susquehannock 762
Swallah 763
Sweatlodges and sweatbaths . . . 763
Sweezy, Carl 764
Syllabaries 764
Symbolism in art 765

Tahltan 767
Tall Bull 767
Tallchief, Maria 767
Tammany 767
Tanaina 768
Tanana 768
Tanning 768
Tarhe 769

Tattoos and tattooing 769
Tavibo 769
Tawaquaptewa 769
Technology 770
Tecumseh 773
Tecumseh's Rebellion 774
Teedyuscung 775
Tekakwitha, Kateri 775
Ten Bears 776
Tendoy 776
Tenino 776
Tenochtitlán 777
Tenskwatawa 778
Teotihuacán 778
Termination policy 778
Texas 779
Texas Rangers 779
Thames, Battle of the 780
Thompson 780
Thorpe, Jim 781
Thule 781
Tiger, Jerome R. 782
Tikal 782
Tillamook 783
Timucua 783
Timucua language 783
Tiou 784
Tipi 784
Tippecanoe, Battle of 785
Tlingit 786
Tobacco 787
Tobacco Society and Dance 788
Tohome 788
Tohono O'odham 788
Tolowa 789
Toltec 789
Tomah 789
Tomahawks 790
Tomochichi 790
Tonkawa 790
Tonkawa language 791
Tools 791
Torture 793
Totem poles 794
Totems 795
Toys 795
Trade 796
Trade and Intercourse Acts 797
Trading posts 797
Trail of Broken Treaties 799
Trail of Tears 799
Transportation modes 802
Treaties and agreements in
    Canada 804
Tres Zapotes 807

Tribe 807
Tricksters 809
Tsatoke, Monroe 810
Tsetsaut 810
Tsimshian 811
Tubatulabal 811
Tula 812
Tule 812
Tunica 812
Tunica language 813
Turquoise 813
Tuscarora 813
Tuskegee 814
Tutchone 814
Tutelo 814
Tututni 815
Twana 815
Twins 815
Two Leggings 815
Two Moon 816
Two Strike 816
Tyigh 816

Umatilla 819
Umpqua 819
Uncas 819
Urban Indians 820
Ute 822
Uto-Aztecan language family . . . 824
Uxmal 825

Veracruz 827
Victorio 827
Visions and vision quests 828
Vizenor, Gerald R[obert] 829
Voting Rights—Canada 829
Voting Rights—United States . . . 830

Waban 832
Wabash, Battle of the 832
Waccamaw 833
Waco 833
Wagon Box Battle 833
Wakashan language family 834
Walam Olum 834
Walapai 835
Walla Walla 835
Walla Walla Council 835
Wampanoag 836
Wampum 836
Wanapam 837
Wapasha 837
Wappinger 838
Wappo 838
War bonnets 838

Ward, Nancy 839
Warfare and conflict 839
Warren, William W. 842
Wasco 843
Washakie 843
Washita River, Battle of the 843
Washoe 844
Water and water rights 845
Watie, Stand 846
Wattle and daub 848
Weapons 848
Weatherford, William 849
Weaving 849
Weetamoo 851
Weirs and traps 852
Welch, James 852
Wenatchi 852
Whales and whaling 853
White Bird 853
White Buffalo Society 853
White Cloud 854
White Deerskin Dance 854
White Eyes 854
White Man Runs Him 854
White Paper of Canada 856
Wichita 856
Wickiup 857
Wigwam 857
Wild rice 858
Wild west shows 858
Wildcat 859
Williams, Eleazar 860
Windigo 860
Winema 860
Winnebago 860
Winnebago Uprising 863
Winnemucca, Sarah 864
Wintun 864
Wishram 864
Witchcraft and sorcery 865
Wiyot 865
Wolf Mountains, Battle of 865
Women 865
Women of All Red Nations 868
Wooden Leg 869
Woodland 869
Wounded Knee Massacre 870
Wounded Knee occupation 871
Wovoka 872
Wright, Allen 873

Yahi 874
Yakima 874
Yakima War 875
Yakonan language family 876

CONTENTS

Yamasee 876
Yamasee War 877
Yana 877
Yaqui 878
Yaquina 878
Yavapai 879
Yaxchilan 879
Yazoo 879
Yellow Wolf 880
Yellowknife 880
Yokuts 880
Yonaguska 881
Young Bear 881
Young Man Afraid of His
    Horses 881

Yuchi 882
Yuki 882
Yuman language family 882
Yurok 883

Zapotec 884
Zotom 885
Zuni language 885

Educational Institutions and
    Programs 887
Festivals and Pow-wows 892
Museums, Archives, and
    Libraries 895

Organizations, Agencies, and
    Societies 907
Populations of U.S.
    Reservations 911
Reservations: United States . . . 914
Reserves and Bands: Canada . . . 917
Time Line 921
Tribes by Culture Area 930
Glossary 932
Mediagraphy 937
Bibliography 944

List of Entries by Category XIX
Index XXV

ALPHABETICAL LIST OF ENTRIES

Volume I

Abenaki 1
Achumawi 2
Acoma, Battle of 2
Acorns 3
Activism 3
Adair, John L. 6
Adario 6
Adena 7
Adobe 8
Adobe Walls, Battles of 8
Adoption 8
African American-American Indian
    relations 9
Agriculture 12
Ahtna 16
Ais 16
Alabama 16
Alaska Native Brotherhood and
    Alaska Native Sisterhood . . . 17
Alaska Native Claims Settlement
    Act 17
Alcatraz Island occupation 18
Alcoholism 19
Aleut 20
Alford, Thomas Wildcat 22
Algonquian language family 22
Algonquin 23
All-Pueblo Council 24
Allen, Paula Gunn 24
Allotment system 24
Alsea 27
American Horse 27
American Indian 27
American Indian Civil Rights
    Act 28
American Indian Defense
    Association 28
American Indian Higher Education
    Consortium 29
American Indian Movement 29
American Indian Policy Review
    Commission 31
American Indian Religious Freedom
    Act 32
American Indian studies programs
    and archives 32
Amerind 35
Anadarko 36
Anasazi 36

Annawan 38
Antonio, Juan 38
Apache 38
Apache Tribe of Oklahoma 41
Apache Wars 42
Apalachee 43
Apalachicola 44
Apes, William 44
Appliqué and ribbonwork 44
Arapaho 45
Arapoosh 49
Archaic 49
Architecture—Arctic 50
Architecture—California 51
Architecture—Great Basin 52
Architecture—Northeast 53
Architecture—Northwest
    Coast 53
Architecture—Plains 55
Architecture—Plateau 56
Architecture—Southeast 56
Architecture—Southwest 57
Architecture—Subarctic 59
Arctic 59
Arikara 63
Arpeika 63
Art and artists, contemporary . . . 64
Articles of Agreement 65
Arts and crafts—Arctic 66
Arts and crafts—California 67
Arts and crafts—Great Basin . . . 68
Arts and crafts—Northeast 70
Arts and crafts—Northwest
    Coast 70
Arts and crafts—Plains 72
Arts and crafts—Plateau 73
Arts and crafts—Southeast 74
Arts and crafts—Southwest 75
Arts and crafts—Subarctic 77
Asah, Spencer 78
Assiniboine 78
Astronomy 80
Atakapa 81
Atakapa language family 81
Athapaskan language family 82
Atlatl 82
Atotarho 82
Atsina 83
Atsugewi 84

Auchiah, James 84
Awa Tsireh 85
Awatovi 85
Aztalan 85
Aztec 86

Bacon's Rebellion 88
Bad Heart Bull, Amos 88
Ball game and courts 89
Banks, Dennis 89
Banner stones 89
Bannock 90
Bannock War 90
Barboncito 91
Basketmaker 91
Baskets and basketry 92
Bat Cave 94
Bayogoula 95
Beads and beadwork 95
Beans 97
Bear Hunter 97
Bear River Campaign 97
Bear's Heart, James 98
Beaver 98
Beaver Wars 98
Bella Bella 100
Bella Coola 100
Beothuk 100
Beothuk language 101
Beringia 101
Big Bear 101
Big Bow 102
Big Foot 102
Big Tree 102
Big Warrior 103
Biloxi 103
Birchbark 103
Black Drink 104
Black Elk 104
Black Hawk 105
Black Hawk War 107
Black Hills 109
Black Kettle 110
Blackfoot and Blackfeet
    Confederacy 110
Blacksnake 113
Bladder Festival 114
Blankets 114
Bloody Knife 115

Blue Eagle, Acee 115
Boats and watercraft 116
Bonnin, Gertrude Simmons 117
Booger Dance 118
Boudinot, Elias 118
Boudinot, Elias Cornelius 119
Bowl 120
Bowlegs, Billy 120
Bows, arrows, and quivers 120
Bozeman Trail wars 121
Brant, Joseph 122
Brant, Molly 124
Bronson, Ruth Muskrat 124
Bruce, Louis R. 125
Buffalo 125
Buffalo Dance 126
Buffalo Hump 127
Bull Bear 127
Bundles, sacred 127
Bureau of Indian Affairs 128
Burke Act 129
Bushyhead, Dennis Wolf 130

Cacique 131
Caddo 131
Caddoan language family 134
Cahokia 135
Cahuilla 135
California 136
Calumets and pipe bags 139
Calusa 139
Campbell, Ben Nighthorse 140
Canonchet 140
Canonicus 141
Canyon de Chelly 141
Cape Fear 141
Captain Jack 142
Captivity and captivity
    narratives 142
Carib 143
Carlisle Indian School 143
Carrier 145
Catahecassa 145
Catawba 145
Cayuga 146
Cayuse 146
Cayuse War 148
Certificate of Degree of
    Indian Blood 148
Chaco Canyon 149
Chantways 149
Charlot 150
Chasta Costa 151
Chehalis 151
Chemakum 151

Cheraw 151
Cherokee 151
Cherokee Tobacco case 157
Cherokee War 157
Cheyenne 158
Chiaha 160
Chichén Itzá 160
Chichimec 161
Chickasaw 161
Chickee 162
Chilcotin 163
Children 163
Chilkat blankets 165
Chinook 166
Chipewyan 167
Chisholm, Jesse 167
Chitimacha 167
Chitimacha language 168
Choctaw 168
Chumash 170
Cíbola, Seven Cities of 171
Civil rights and citizenship 172
Clallam 177
Clans 177
Clatskanie 178
Cliff dwellings 178
Cloud, Henry Roe 179
Clovis 180
Clowns 180
Coast Yuki 180
Cochise 181
Cocopa 182
Codices 182
Coeur d'Alene 183
Colorow 184
Columbia 184
Colville 184
Comanche 185
Comcomly 187
Comox 187
Conquering Bear 187
Coos 187
Coos language 188
Copalis 188
Copan 189
Copway, George 189
Corn 189
Corn Woman 192
Cornplanter 192
Cornstalk 193
Costanoan 193
Cotton 194
Council of Energy Resource
    Tribes 194
Councils, tribal 194

Coup sticks and counting 196
Courts, tribal 196
Coushatta 196
Cowichan 197
Cowlitz 197
Crashing Thunder 197
Crazy Horse 198
Crazy Snake 199
Cree 199
Creek 201
Creek War 204
Crow 204
Crow Dog 207
Crowfoot 209
Cuello 209
Culture areas 210
Cupeño 214
Curly 214
Curtis, Charles 214

Dances and dancing 217
Dancing Rabbit Creek,
    Treaty of 220
Danger Cave 220
Dating methods 221
Datsolalee 222
Death and mortuary customs . . . 222
Declaration of First Nations 223
Decora, Spoon 223
Deer, Ada Elizabeth 223
Deer Dance 224
Deganawida 224
Dekanisora 224
Delaware Prophet 225
Delgadito 225
Deloria, Ella Cara 225
Deloria, Vine, Jr. 227
Delshay 227
Demography 227
Department of Indian Affairs and
    Northern Development 231
Desert culture 232
Determined Residents United for
    Mohawk Sovereignty 232
Diegueño 233
Diseases, post-contact 233
Dodge, Henry Chee 236
Dogrib 237
Dogs 237
Dohasan 237
Donnaconna 238
Dorset 238
Dozier, Edward Pasqual 238
Dragging Canoe 239
Dress and adornment 239

Drums 243
Dull Knife 244
Duwamish 245

Earthlodge 246
Eastman, Charles Alexander 246
Education, post-contact 247
Education, pre-contact 252
Effigy mounds 253
Elderly 254
El Tajín 255
Emerald Mound 256
Employment and
    unemployment 256
Erdrich, Louise 260
Erie 260
Eskiminzin 261
Eskimo-Aleut language
    family 261
Esselen 261
Ethnophilosophy and
    worldview 262
Etowah 265

Fallen Timbers, Battle of 266
False Face Ceremony 267
Feast of the Dead 267
Feasts 267
Feathers and featherwork 269
Federally recognized tribes . . . 270
Fernandeño 270
Fifteen Principles 271
Fire and firemaking 271
Fish and fishing 272
Flat Mouth 272

Flathead 274
Flutes 275
Folsom 276
Food preparation and cooking . . . 276
Foreman, Stephen 278
Fort Atkinson, Treaty of 278
Fort Greenville, Treaty of 278
Fort Laramie Treaty of 1851 . . . 280
Fort Laramie Treaty of 1868 . . . 281
Fort Mims, Battle of 282
Fort Stanwix, Treaty of 283
Fort Wayne, Treaty of 283
Fox 284
Francis, Josiah 287
Francis, Milly Hayo 288
Fremont 288
French and Indian Wars 288
Friends of the Indian
    organizations 289

Gabrielino 290
Gadsden Purchase 290
Gall 290
Gambling 291
Games and contests 292
Ganado Mucho 294
Garakontie, Daniel 295
Garra, Antonio 295
Garry, Spokane 295
Gender relations and roles 296
General, Alexander 299
General Allotment Act 299
Geronimo 300
Ghost Dance 302
Gifts and gift giving 303

Gilcrease, William Thomas . . . 303
Gitksan 304
Godfroy, Francis 304
Gold and goldworking 304
Gorman, R. C. 305
Gosiute 305
Gourd Dance 305
Grass, John 306
Grass Dance 306
Grass house 306
Great Basin 306
Great Sun 308
Green Corn Dance 309
Guadalupe Hidalgo,
    Treaty of 309
Guale 310
Guardian spirits 310
Guns 311

Hagler 312
Haisla 312
Hako 312
Half-King 314
Hamatsa 314
Han 314
Hancock 315
Hand games 315
Handsome Lake 315
Hare 316
Harjo, Joy 316
Harper, Elijah 317
Harris, LaDonna 317
Havasupai 317
Hayes, Ira Hamilton 318

Volume II

Headdresses 319
Heat-Moon, William Least 320
Hewitt, John N. B. 320
Hiawatha 321
Hidatsa 321
Hides and hidework 323
Hitchiti 323
Hogan 324
Hogan, Linda 324
Hohokam 324
Hokan language family 325
Hokeah, Jack 325
Hole-in-the-Day 326
Hollow Horn Bear 326
Hooker Jim 328

Hopewell 328
Hopocan 329
Horses 329
Horseshoe Bend, Treaty of 330
Howe, Oscar 330
Howling Wolf 330
Huchnom 331
Hudson's Bay Company 331
Humor 331
Hump 332
Hunt, George 332
Hunting and gathering 332
Hupa 333
Huron 333
Husk Face Society 334

Igloo 335
Ignacio 335
Illinois 335
Incest taboo 336
Indian 336
Indian Act of 1876 (Canada) . . . 337
Indian Act of 1951 (Canada) . . . 337
Indian Act of 1989 (Canada) . . . 338
Indian Arts and Crafts Board . . . 338
Indian Child Welfare Act 339
Indian Citizenship Act 340
Indian Claims Commission . . . 340
Indian Education Acts 341
Indian police and judges 342
Indian Removal Act 342

Indian Reorganization Act 343
Indian Rights Association 343
Indian Self-Determination and
    Education Assistance Act . . . 344
Indian Territory 344
Indian-white relations—
    Canadian 346
Indian-white relations—Dutch
    colonial 350
Indian-white relations—English
    colonial 351
Indian-white relations—French
    colonial 355
Indian-white relations—
    Norse 358
Indian-white relations—Russian
    colonial 360
Indian-white relations—Spanish
    colonial 361
Indian-white relations—Swedish
    colonial 364
Indian-white relations—U.S.,
    1775-1830 365
Indian-white relations—U.S.,
    1831-1870 368
Indian-white relations—U.S.,
    1871-1933 371
Indian-white relations—U.S.,
    1934-1995 375
Ingalik 378
Inkpaduta 378
Institute of American Indian
    Arts 379
International Indian Treaty
    Council 379
Inuit 380
Iowa 383
Irateba 383
Iroquoian language family 383
Iroquois Confederacy 385
Irrigation 388
Isatai 388
Ishi 388
Isparhecher 389

Johnson, Emily Pauline 390
Joking relations 390
Jones, Peter 391
Joseph the Younger 391
Journalism 393
Journeycake, Charles 395
Juaneño 395

Kachinas 396
Kalapuya 397

Kalispel 397
Kamia 398
Kamiakin 398
Kansa 399
Karankawa 400
Karankawa language 400
Karok 401
Kaska 402
Katlian 402
Kawaiisu 402
Keeler Commission 402
Keetoowah Society 403
Kennekuk 403
Keokuk 403
Keresan language family 405
Key Marco 405
Kichai 406
Kickapoo 406
Kickapoo Resistance 407
Kickapoo uprisings 407
Kicking Bear 407
Kicking Bird 408
King Philip's War 408
Kinnikinnick 410
Kinship and social
    organization 410
Kiowa 413
Kiowa-Tanoan language
    family 414
Kivas 415
Klah, Hosteen 415
Klamath 416
Klikitat 417
Knives 418
Konkapot, John 418
Koster 418
Koyukon 418
Kuksu rituals and society 419
Kutchin 420
Kutenai 420
Kutenai language 421
Kwakiutl 421

Lacrosse 423
La Flesche, Francis 423
La Flesche, Susan 423
La Flesche, Susette or
    Josette 423
Lake 424
Lame Deer 424
Lances and spears 424
Land claims 425
Language families 426
La Venta 429
Lawyer 429

Lean Bear 430
Lean-to 430
Left Hand the First 431
Left Hand the Second 431
Lehner 431
Lenni Lenape 431
Lillooet 434
Little Bighorn, Battle of the 434
Little Crow 435
Little Priest 436
Little Raven 436
Little Robe 436
Little Turtle 437
Little Wolf 437
Logan, James 439
Lone Wolf 439
Lone Wolf v. Hitchcock 439
Long Walk 440
Longest Walk 442
Longhouse 442
Longhouse religion 443
Looking Glass 445
Lord Dunmore's War 446
Luiseño 447
Lumbee 447
Lummi 448

McGillivray, Alexander 449
McIntosh, William 449
McNickle, D'Arcy 449
McQueen, Peter 450
Mahican 450
Maidu 451
Makah 451
Maliseet 452
Manahoac 453
Mandan 453
Mangas Coloradus 454
Manhattan 454
Manibozho 455
Mankato 455
Mankiller, Wilma Pearl 455
Manuelito 456
Maple syrup and sugar 457
Marriage and divorce 458
Martínez, Crescencio 459
Martínez, Julián 459
Martínez, María Antonía 459
Maru Cult 460
Masks 460
Massachusett 462
Massasoit 463
Mathematics 463
Mato Tope 464
Matonabbee 464

Mattaponi 464
Mattole 465
Maya 465
Means, Russell 467
Medicine and modes of curing,
    post-contact 469
Medicine and modes of curing,
    pre-contact 472
Medicine bundles 475
Medicine Lodge, Treaties of 476
Medicine wheels 477
Meech Lake Accord 477
Menewa 477
Menominee 478
Menses and menstruation 480
Meriam Report 481
Mesa Verde 481
Metacomet 482
Metalwork 483
Methow 483
Metis 483
Miami 484
Miantonomo 485
Micanopy 485
Micmac 485
Middens 486
Midewiwin 486
Midland 487
Midwinter Ceremony 487
Migrations 487
Military societies 490
Mimbres 490
Minnesota Uprising 491
Missions and missionaries 491
Mississippian 492
Missouri 493
Mitla 493
Miwok 494
Mixtec 494
Mobile 495
Moccasins 495
Modoc 495
Modoc War 496
Mogollon 497
Mohawk 498
Mohegan 499
Mojave 499
Molala 501
Momaday, N. Scott 501
Moneton 501
Money 501
Montagnais 502
Montauk Confederacy 502
Monte Albán 503
Montezuma, Carlos 504

Mopope, Stephen 504
Morning Star Ceremony 505
Mosaic and inlay 505
Moses 505
Mother Earth 506
Mounds and mound builders 506
Moundville 507
Mountain 508
Mountain Wolf Woman 508
Mourning Dove 508
Muckleshoot 509
Multnomah 509
Murie, James 509
Musgrove, Mary 510
Music and song 510
Muskogean language family 514

Nabedache 516
Na-Dene language family 516
Naiche 516
Nakaidoklini 517
Names and naming 517
Nampeyo 517
Nana 518
Nanticoke 519
Narragansett 519
Naskapi 520
Natawista 520
Natchez 520
Natchez Revolt 521
National Congress of American
    Indians 521
National Council of American
    Indians 522
National Indian Association 522
National Indian Youth
    Council 523
Natiotish 523
Native American 524
Native American Church 524
Native American Rights Fund . . . 524
Nauset 525
Navajo 525
Navajo-Hopi Land Settlement
    Act 530
Navajo Rehabilitation Act 531
Navajo War 531
Neutral 532
Nez Perce 532
Nez Perce War 535
Niantic 536
Ninham, Daniel 537
Ninigret 537
Nipissing 537
Nipmuck 537

Nisqually 538
Nooksack 538
Nootka 538
Northeast 540
Northwest Coast 542
Northwest Ordinance 545
Nottaway 545

Oaxaca 546
Ocaneechi 547
Occom, Samson 547
Oconostota 547
Ofo 548
Ojibwa 548
Okanagan 550
Okeepa 551
Oklahoma Indian Welfare
    Act 551
Old Briton 551
Old Copper culture 552
Olmec 552
Omaha 553
Oneida 555
Oneota 555
Onondaga 556
Opechancanough 556
Opothleyaholo 557
Oral literatures 557
Oratory 560
Oregon Trail 561
Ornaments 562
Ortiz, Simon 562
Osage 562
Osceola 564
Oshkosh 565
Otherday, John 565
Oto 566
Ottawa 566
Ouray 567
Ozette 568

Paints and painting 569
Paiute, Northern 569
Paiute, Southern 570
Palenque 572
Paleo-Indian 572
Palouse 573
Pamlico 573
Pan-Indianism 574
Parfleche 575
Parker, Ely Samuel 575
Parker, Quanah 577
Passaconaway 580
Passamaquoddy 580
Patayan 580

Patents 581
Patwin 581
Pavonia Massacre 581
Pawhuska 582
Pawnee 582
Paxton Riots 584
Peach Wars 585
Pemmican 585
Peña, Tonita 586
Pennacook 586
Penobscot 586
Penutian language family 587
Pequot 588
Pequot War 588
Petalésharo 590
Petroglyphs 590
Petun 592
Peyote and peyote religion 592
Pima 593
Pima uprisings 594
Pine Ridge shootout 594
Pipestone Quarries 594
Pit house 595
Pitchlynn, Peter Perkins 595

Plains 596
Plank house 599
Plano 599
Plateau 600
Plenty Coups 603
Pocahontas 603
Pochteca 605
Pokagon, Leopold 605
Pokagon, Simon 605
Political organization and
    leadership 605
Pomo 609
Ponca 610
Pontiac 611
Pontiac's Conspiracy 612
Poospatuck 613
Popé 613
Popovi Da 614
Porter, Pleasant 614
Posey, Alexander Lawrence 614
Potawatomi 614
Potlatch 615
Pottery 616
Poundmaker 618

Poverty Point 619
Powhatan 619
Powhatan Confederacy 620
Powhatan Wars 621
Pow-wows and contemporary
    celebrations 622
Praying Indians 624
Prehistory—Arctic 624
Prehistory—California 625
Prehistory—Great Basin 625
Prehistory—Northeast 626
Prehistory—Northwest Coast . . . 626
Prehistory—Plains 627
Prehistory—Plateau 629
Prehistory—Southeast 630
Prehistory—Southwest 630
Prehistory—Subarctic 632
Proclamation of 1763 633
Projectile points 633
Puberty and initiation rites 634
Public Law 280 636
Pueblo 636
Pueblo (Popé's) Revolt 637
Pueblo tribes, Eastern 637

Volume III

Pueblo tribes, Western 643
Pushmataha 645
Puyallup 646

Quapaw 647
Quechan 647
Queen Anne 648
Quetzalcóatl 648
Quileute 648
Quillwork 648
Quinault 649
Quinney, John W. 650

Railroads 651
Rain in the Face 651
Ranching 652
Red Bird 653
Red Cloud 653
Red Jacket 654
Red River War 654
Red Shoes 655
Reifel, Ben 655
Religion 655
Religious specialists 659
Relocation 662
Removal 664

Renville, Joseph 665
Reservation system of the United
    States 666
Reserve system of Canada 670
Resource use, pre-contact 671
Resources 672
Ridge, John Rollin 673
Ridge, Major 674
Riel, Louis, Jr. 674
Riel Rebellions 676
Riggs, Lynn 677
Rite of Consolation 677
Rites of passage 677
Rocky Boy 679
Rogers, Will 679
Roman Nose 679
Rosebud Creek, Battle of 679
Ross, John 680

Sacagawea 682
Sachem 684
Sacred, the 684
Sacred narratives 686
Salinan 687
Salish 688
Salishan language family 688

Salmon 689
Salt 689
Samish 689
Samoset 691
San Lorenzo 691
Sand Creek Massacre 691
Sand Painting 693
Sanpoil-Nespelem 694
Santa Fe Trail 695
Sarsi 695
Sassacus 696
Satanta 696
Sauk 696
Saybrook, Battle of 698
Scalps and scalping 698
Scarface Charlie 699
Scholder, Fritz 700
Sculpture 700
Seattle 701
Secotan 701
Secret societies 702
Sekani 702
Semiahmoo 703
Seminole 703
Seminole Wars 704
Seneca 706

Sequoyah 706
Seri 708
Serpent mounds 708
Serrano 709
Shábona 710
Shaker Church 710
Shaking Tent Ceremony 711
Shalako 711
Shasta 711
Shawnee 712
Shells and shellwork 712
Shikellamy 713
Shinnecock 713
Short Bull 713
Shoshone 714
Shuswap 715
Sign language 715
Siletz 715
Silko, Leslie Marmon 716
Sinagua 716
Siouan language family 717
Sioux 718
Sioux uprisings 723
Sitting Bull 724
Siuslaw 726
Skagit 726
Slave 727
Slavery 727
Slocum, John 729
Smohalla 729
Snake Dance 729
Snake War 730
Snaketown 730
Snohomish 731
Snoqualmie 731
Social control, traditional 731
Societies, non-kin-based 732
Society of American Indians 735
Sooke 735
Southeast 736
Southern Cult 740
Southwest 740
Sovereignty 743
Spirit dancing 745
Spiro 745
Spokane 746
Spotted Tail 746
Spybuck, Ernest 747
Squamish 747
Squanto 748
Squash 748
Standing Bear 748
Standing Bear, Luther 749
Stereotypes 749
Stomp Dance 751

Stumbling Bear 751
Subarctic 752
Subsistence 754
Suicide 759
Sun Dance 760
Suquamish 762
Susquehannock 762
Swallah 763
Sweatlodges and sweatbaths 763
Sweezy, Carl 764
Syllabaries 764
Symbolism in art 765

Tahltan 767
Tall Bull 767
Tallchief, Maria 767
Tammany 767
Tanaina 768
Tanana 768
Tanning 768
Tarhe 769
Tattoos and tattooing 769
Tavibo 769
Tawaquaptewa 769
Technology 770
Tecumseh 773
Tecumseh's Rebellion 774
Teedyuscung 775
Tekakwitha, Kateri 775
Ten Bears 776
Tendoy 776
Tenino 776
Tenochtitlán 777
Tenskwatawa 778
Teotihuacán 778
Termination policy 778
Texas 779
Texas Rangers 779
Thames, Battle of the 780
Thompson 780
Thorpe, Jim 781
Thule 781
Tiger, Jerome R. 782
Tikal 782
Tillamook 783
Timucua 783
Timucua language 783
Tiou 784
Tipi 784
Tippecanoe, Battle of 785
Tlingit 786
Tobacco 787
Tobacco Society and Dance 788
Tohome 788
Tohono O'odham 788

Tolowa 789
Toltec 789
Tomah 789
Tomahawks 790
Tomochichi 790
Tonkawa 790
Tonkawa language 791
Tools 791
Torture 793
Totem poles 794
Totems 795
Toys 795
Trade 796
Trade and Intercourse Acts 797
Trading posts 797
Trail of Broken Treaties 799
Trail of Tears 799
Transportation modes 802
Treaties and agreements in
    Canada 804
Tres Zapotes 807
Tribe 807
Tricksters 809
Tsatoke, Monroe 810
Tsetsaut 810
Tsimshian 811
Tubatulabal 811
Tula 812
Tule 812
Tunica 812
Tunica language 813
Turquoise 813
Tuscarora 813
Tuskegee 814
Tutchone 814
Tutelo 814
Tututni 815
Twana 815
Twins 815
Two Leggings 815
Two Moon 816
Two Strike 816
Tyigh 816

Umatilla 819
Umpqua 819
Uncas 819
Urban Indians 820
Ute 822
Uto-Aztecan language
    family 824
Uxmal 825

Veracruz 827
Victorio 827

Visions and vision quests 828
Vizenor, Gerald R[obert] 829
Voting Rights—Canada 829
Voting Rights—
    United States 830

Waban 832
Wabash, Battle of the 832
Waccamaw 833
Waco 833
Wagon Box Battle 833
Wakashan language family 834
Walam Olum 834
Walapai 835
Walla Walla 835
Walla Walla Council 835
Wampanoag 836
Wampum 836
Wanapam 837
Wapasha 837
Wappinger 838
Wappo 838
War bonnets 838
Ward, Nancy 839
Warfare and conflict 839
Warren, William W. 842
Wasco 843
Washakie 843
Washita River, Battle of the 843
Washoe 844
Water and water rights 845
Watie, Stand 846
Wattle and daub 848
Weapons 848

Weatherford, William 849
Weaving 849
Weetamoo 851
Weirs and traps 852
Welch, James 852
Wenatchi 852
Whales and whaling 853
White Bird 853
White Buffalo Society 853
White Cloud 854
White Deerskin Dance 854
White Eyes 854
White Man Runs Him 854
White Paper of Canada 856
Wichita 856
Wickiup 857
Wigwam 857
Wild rice 858
Wild west shows 858
Wildcat 859
Williams, Eleazar 860
Windigo 860
Winema 860
Winnebago 860
Winnebago Uprising 863
Winnemucca, Sarah 864
Wintun 864
Wishram 864
Witchcraft and sorcery 865
Wiyot 865
Wolf Mountains, Battle of 865
Women 865
Women of All Red Nations 868
Wooden Leg 869

Woodland 869
Wounded Knee Massacre 870
Wounded Knee occupation 871
Wovoka 872
Wright, Allen 873

Yahi 874
Yakima 874
Yakima War 875
Yakonan language family 876
Yamasee 876
Yamasee War 877
Yana 877
Yaqui 878
Yaquina 878
Yavapai 879
Yaxchilan 879
Yazoo 879
Yellow Wolf 880
Yellowknife 880
Yokuts 880
Yonaguska 881
Young Bear 881
Young Man Afraid of His
    Horses 881
Yuchi 882
Yuki 882
Yuman language family 882
Yurok 883

Zapotec 884
Zotom 885
Zuni language 885

RR AMERICAN INDIANS

—

Pueblo tribes, Western

TRIBES AFFECTED: Acoma, Hopi, Laguna, Zuni
CULTURE AREA: Southwest
LANGUAGE GROUPS: Keresan, Tewa, Uto-Aztecan, Zuni
PRIMARY LOCATION: Southwest
POPULATION SIZE: 28,884 (1990 U.S. Census)

The Western Pueblos are considered to be a part of the cultural pattern known as the Desert culture, a migration that extended southward from the Great Basin and covered most of the Southwest, dating the earliest human inhabitants of this region some ten thousand years ago. During this long history, most changes in Pueblo culture have occurred since the time of contact with Europeans, specifically with the Spanish. The Pueblos have managed to control these changes, especially in their ceremonial life, through persistence and protection.

The Pueblo Revolt of 1680. As did most Indians of the Southwest, Pueblo peoples experienced the impact of three Western European cultures: Spanish, Mexican, and Anglo-American. One of the most disruptive qualities of contact for the Pueblos was Western European religion, which was intolerant of competing beliefs and ceremonies. By the middle of the seventeenth century, after almost a hundred years of forced labor and European religion, the Pueblos planned to put an end to the suffering that resulted from Spanish oppression. Aware of the strengths and weaknesses of their adversary, the Pueblo communities decided that a united resistance would be the most successful. Careful planning produced what is generally called the Pueblo Revolt of 1680. Although the Pueblos outnumbered the Spanish, the Spanish had an advantage because of their weaponry.

The Northern Pueblos laid siege to the Spanish capital of Santa Fe, where more than a thousand colonists and missionaries had taken refuge. Other Pueblos, including Acoma, Hopi, and Zuni, contributed to the revolt by killing the Spaniards and missionaries living in or near these pueblos. Spanish houses, churches, church records, and furniture were burned or destroyed. Through the later testimony of captured Indians, it became clear that the leaders of the revolt (Popé among them) wanted to obliterate all representations of Spanish culture and religion. Success of this objective was realized but was short-lived. Don Diego de Vargas reconquered the area in the winter of 1691-1692; all of New Mexico was reconquered by 1696. Faced with a conquer-and-destroy attitude for hundreds of years, it is a testimony to the strength of the people of the Western Pueblos that they survived and retained many of their customs and beliefs.

Although the Acoma, Hopi, Laguna, and Zuni tribes share many similar customs and beliefs, they should be viewed as separate, independent societies.

Acoma. The Pueblos of Acoma and Laguna share the same language, Keresan, and are closely related. Laguna lies about 40 miles west of Albuquerque. Fifteen miles west-southwest of Laguna is Acoma. The word Acoma means "place that always was." Archaeologists have generally agreed that Acoma has been inhabited at least from 1200 C.E. to the present. Little is known about the origins of the Acomas, but they claim to have always lived on their mesa.

Acoma, as most pueblos, is structured by clans that are always matrilinear in descent. A clan comprises all the descendants of a traditional maternal ancestor. Males go to live with the clan of their wife at marriage. The difference between clans and families is that clans are a ceremonial institution of membership. Acoma society is matriarchal; Acoma women own the houses and everything in them, even if an item is brought there by their husbands. Women also have claim to all domestic animals, such as sheep and chickens. Certain ceremonial rights, however, such as entrance into a kiva (ceremonial chamber), are open only to men.

Elections for officials at Acoma are held yearly during the winter solstice. The government consists of a cacique (governor), who nominates those who will run for office. To assist the governor are two lieutenant governors, three war chiefs and their two cooks, along with ten *principales*. Aside from the cacique and the principales, who serve life terms, offices are held for one year.

The cacique sets the date for ceremonies that may vary chronologically—for example, those ceremonies held on the solstices. Rabbit hunts are held before almost all important occasions. Some dances, such as the corn dance, are recreational rather than sacred or ceremonial. Anyone can observe or participate in these dances. The most important communal ceremony is that of the K'atsina (Kachina) dancers. K'atsinas are spirit rainmakers. It is said that in the old days, the K'atsina used to come to the village bringing the people gifts and cheering them when they were sad. There was a great fight between the spirits and the people, however; the spirits refused to come to the village anymore, but they told the people they could wear masks and pretend they were K'atsinas and all would be well; rain would come.

Pottery is the main form of art pursued by the Acomas. It is less durable than Zuni pottery but more various in its designs, which include trees, leaves, birds, flowers, and geometrical patterns. Pottery serves both utilitarian and ceremonial functions and has historically been a cultural indicator of what was acceptable or fashionable.

Potters hold a special place of respect at both Acoma and Laguna. Often today, because of the commercial value of Acoma pottery, a potter may be the primary wage earner of the family. Pottery produced for simple household means maintains a special significance because it was made from materials of the earth to support some type of life activity. Observers of Acoma have remarked that a pot has a "conscious existence," and Wanda Aragon, an Acoma potter, has said that "when you're finished with a pot you flow life into it and it is given life."

Regardless of culture, potters produce interpretations that reflect changing values and cultural demands. This may explain the emphasis on pottery at Acoma, a village that has emphasized pottery in its economy more than Laguna. Laguna has three times the population of Acoma, but Acoma has many more potters.

Laguna. The Laguna migration to their present village is even more mysterious than that of the Acoma. Tribal traditions and pottery found in ruins can trace Laguna culture back to the last decade of the seventeenth century, but no one can say where they lived before that. There is no reference to the tribe by Spanish historians, who confused them with the Acomas, a tribe having one central village and who spoke the same language as the Lagunas. Many historians date the founding of Laguna between 1697 and 1699 by a combination of settlers from various groups, including Jemez, Santo Domingo, Zia, and a few disgruntled Acoma.

The Lagunas also have a matriarchal, clan-based social structure. They have their own calendar, recognizing twenty-eight days to a moon, but there are no year designations. Events or phenomena are used to keep track of time. According to this calendar, the winter solstice begins the yearly ceremonies. Migration and the journey from the north are recounted in songs. The Keres words for winter solstice are *Kú wa mi Shu ko* (*Kú wa mi*, "south"; *Shu ko*, "corner") meaning "the south corner time." There are also K'atsina (Kachina) dances during planting and harvesting seasons, the importance of rain having a significant role at Laguna.

Hopi. Rain is of major importance for the Hopis as well. Two general characteristics appear repeatedly in pottery motifs; a respect and desire for rain and a belief in the unity of all life. Pottery making for Hopis, as with most Pueblo communities, is an art that exists in the mind of the potter. There are no permanent patterns set down for design layouts. Sand paintings made on the floors of kivas are derived from clan traditions and, like pottery, the designs are carried only in the memory of the artists.

Hopi society is complex, consisting of thousands of people, each of whom is affiliated with one of thirteen villages. Oraibi, once the largest Hopi village, was one of the most determined to reject religious and political imposition during the time of the Pueblo Revolt. Much later, at the beginning of the nineteenth century, the Oraibi split occurred. The village divided into two factions, termed "hostiles" and "friendlies" by the United States government. The hostiles resented policies that would forcibly educate their children. The friendlies saw advantages to American education. The disagreement escalated, and the hostiles were forced from the village in September of 1906. Other theories emphasize the importance of internal, social instability in causing the split. Whatever the case, a well-established society had fragmented.

Hopi villages are matrilineal; women own the houses and, therefore, the economy, if they distribute items such as produce from their homes. For ceremonies and politics, men have the most influence, with the major focus of rituals being concentrated in the kiva. These tendencies are generalized, however, and many exceptions occur.

There are several clans among the Hopi, serving as a source of social identity and performing what has become the most important modern function, regulating marriage. The modern government has for the most part become secular-ized, although some religious overtones still emerge. The board of directors' meetings can be open or closed and can discuss everything from land disputes to the writing of village history.

Zuni. Tribal traditions and history are also a major concern for the Zuni Pueblo. During the 1980's, the Zunis established their own public school system, which promoted and emphasized Zuni culture. A staff of experts frequently visit classes to explain tribal traditions. Every August there is a tribal fair, including a rodeo, a parade complete with floats, and social dances. The crowning of Miss Zuni takes place during this event; the young woman is not chosen for her beauty, but rather for her knowledge of Zuni culture. She must be fluent in the Zuni language, and she is tested on the history of the tribe, ensuring that the culture will be passed on.

Prior to 1934, members of the government, the Zuni Tribal Council, had been appointed by the Council of High Priests. Since 1934, elections of officers have been open to the tribe, but, ironically, it was not until 1965 that women were able to vote in this matriarchal society.

The present-day Zuni pueblo is settled at the location of the village of Halona wa, one of six villages existing before the eighteenth century. The other five villages were abandoned, probably because of Apache and Navajo raids, diseases introduced at the time of contact, and the Spanish reconquest. The legend of the "Seven Cities of Cíbola," reported to be large, rich cities, may have been based on the six Zuni villages. Hearing of the legend prompted Francisco Vásquez de Coronado to explore the area in 1540. He was disappointed to find some rather poor farmers supplementing their agricultural base with hunting. Spanish chroniclers would later write of the Zuni that "what they worshiped most was water."

The Zuni language is still the language of social discourse, with most Zunis also being fluent in English. The social structure is similar to that of the other Western Pueblos; it is a matriarchal, clan-based culture. Clan divisions and names of clans at Zuni are reflected among other Pueblos—Eagle, Sun, Badger, Turkey, and so on—with each clan having a specific religious function. Zuni priests act as mediators between the people and the Kachinas, the spirits who bring rain.

Most tribes in the Southwest make and use fetishes, but of all the Pueblos the Zuni have the reputation for being the most skillful at carving them. The purposes for which a fetish may be used varies. There are fetishes for hunting, curing diseases, war, gambling, and initiations. Hunting fetishes are the kind most often seen for sale. The fetish most highly prized by a Zuni is one of the natural concretation bearing resemblance to an animal. Shell, stone, wood, plant, or animal material may be used to carve a fetish; their purpose in assisting humans remains the same, regardless of the material. Fetishes are regarded as living things and must be carefully attended.

—Kimberly Manning

See also Anasazi; Arts and crafts—Southwest; Corn Woman; Gadsden Purchase; Guadalupe Hidalgo, Treaty of; Indian-white relations—Spanish colonial; Keresan language family; Kivas; Mesa Verde; Pottery; Prehistory—Southwest; Pueblo; Pueblo tribes, Eastern; Southwest.

BIBLIOGRAPHY

Cushing, Frank. *Zuni Fetishes*. Facsimile ed. Flagstaff, Ariz.: KC Publications, 1966. A description of Zuni fetishes, their significance, and the shapes and materials used. Accompanied by some black-and-white photographs.

Dillingham, Rick. *Acoma and Laguna Pottery*. Santa Fe, N.Mex.: School of American Research Press, 1992. An excellent source of photographs and sensitive descriptions of both Acoma and Laguna pottery. A detailed account of the function, form, and design of the pottery.

Dozier, Edward P. *The Pueblo Indians of North America*. New York: Holt, Rinehart and Winston, 1970. A mostly historical accounting of the Western and Rio Grande Pueblos, with an overview of culture and ceremonies.

Dutton, Bertha P., and Miriam A. Marmon. *The Laguna Calendar*. Albuquerque: University of New Mexico Press, 1936. Dutton gives some insights into the Laguna system of time, noting when special ceremonies are held and translating Keresan words into English.

Minge, Ward Alan. *Acoma: Pueblo in the Sky*. Albuquerque: University of New Mexico Press, 1976. Minge follows the Acoma people from prehistory to the modern day. Includes some information on Laguna, illustrations of Acoma, and tables covering population, livestock, and land holdings.

Scully, Vincent. *Pueblo: Mountain, Village, Dance*. 2d ed. Chicago: University of Chicago Press, 1989. Scully provides numerous photographs and descriptions of various Pueblos, their plazas, structures, surrounding terrain, and dances.

Sedgwick, Mary K. *Acoma, the Sky City: A Study in Pueblo Indian History and Civilization*. Cambridge, Mass.: Harvard University Press, 1926. An examination of both the Acoma and Laguna tribes that covers history, ceremonies, social structure, and Spanish influence.

Whiteley, Peter M. *Deliberate Acts: Changing Hopi Culture Through the Oraibi Split*. Tucson: University of Arizona Press, 1988. An exploration of the Oraibi split, its history, and its effects on Hopi society today. Whiteley also examines ritual, politics, and anthropological data.

Young, M. Jane. *Signs from the Ancestors: Zuni Cultural Symbolism and Perceptions of Rock Art*. Albuquerque: University of New Mexico Press, 1988. Young gives commentary on Zuni culture in her discussion of Zuni rock art. Drawings and illustrations are provided.

Pushmataha (June, 1764, British Indian territory in present-day Noxubee County, Miss.—Dec. 24, 1824, Washington, D.C.): Tribal chief

ALSO KNOWN AS: Apushamatahubib (Warrior's Seat Is Finished)

TRIBAL AFFILIATION: Choctaw

SIGNIFICANCE: The most powerful Choctaw leader of the early nineteenth century, Pushmataha allied his people with

the United States during the Creek War (1813-1814) and the War of 1812

Few hard facts are known about Pushmataha's early life. He fostered the legend that he had sprung fully grown from an oak tree split by lightning. This story may have been a way of covering up his relatively humble origins. His position among his fellow Choctaws was attributable to his personal achievements as a warrior, hunter, athlete, and orator. He became the chief of the Six Towns district of the Choctaw Nation, and by the early nineteenth century was the most influential of the Choctaw leaders.

Pushmataha greatly influenced the course of Choctaw relations with the United States. In 1804, he met with President Thomas Jefferson, signing a treaty that ceded a small tract of Choctaw land in return for guarantees of friendship and assistance. Within the tribe, he emphasized the need for education.

Pushmataha proved himself to be a loyal ally of the United States. In 1811, he used his considerable oratorical abilities to blunt Tecumseh's appeal for a pan-Indian alliance against American expansion. He raised a large contingent of Choctaws for service in the Creek War of 1813-1814. He and his warriors later fought against the British at New Orleans. As a reward, he was made a brigadier general in the United States Army.

As Choctaw lands came under increasing white pressure, Pushmataha continued to seek accommodation. In 1820, at the Treaty of Doak's Stand, he agreed to the cession of a large portion of tribal lands in western and central Mississippi; in

Choctaw leader Pushmataha was made a brigadier general in the U.S. Army for his service in the Creek War and the War of 1812. (Library of Congress)

return the Choctaws received extensive lands west of the Mississippi River. In late 1824, hoping to prevent further cessions, he visited Washington to meet directly with President James Monroe. He became ill, however, and died. He was buried there with the honors due his military rank.

See also Choctaw; Creek War; Dancing Rabbit Creek, Treaty of; Indian-white relations—U.S., 1775-1830; Tecumseh.

Puyallup: Tribe

CULTURE AREA: Northwest Coast
LANGUAGE GROUP: Salishan
PRIMARY LOCATION: Puget Sound basin
POPULATION SIZE: 1,281 (1990 U.S. Census)

The name Puyallup comes from the Indian name for the Puyallup River, sometimes written *pwiya'lap*. The Puyallup were one of several tribes collectively called the Southern Coast Salish, living in the Puget Sound basin. The Puyallup lived at the mouth of the Puyallup River and along the neighboring Washington coastline. There were twelve subdivisions and villages; the Steilacoom, for example, lived on Steilacoom Creek and the adjacent beach. The Puyallup were hunters, fishers, and gatherers.

The Puyallup lived in villages in the winter and camps in the summer. A village consisted of large wooden houses occupied by several families. Puyallup society was divided into three social classes: upper-class freeman, lower-class freeman, and slaves. Upper-class Puyallup were from good families, possessed wealth, and had the means to participate in certain ceremonies. The wealthiest male was usually the village headman. The lower class lacked these requisites, and slaves and their descendants were captives of war who were kept by wealthy masters. Each village was closely tied to neighboring villages by means of marriages between prominent families, kinship, mutual use of the same land, and joint participation in various ceremonies. In addition, individual status was determined in part by how well an individual was known in other villages. Within the freeman class was a group of professional warriors. They occasionally led raiding parties for slaves but were primarily called upon to defend their village from attack by outside tribes, primarily the Lekwiltok.

Guardian spirits were a central part of Puyallup life. Every individual ability and accomplishment (such as wealth, war, gambling, and hunting) was facilitated by the appropriate spirit. Training began in childhood so that by age eight a child was able to seek out the appropriate guardian spirit, which came in a vision.

By the 1850's whites had established settlements on Puyallup land, and in 1854 and 1855 treaties set aside land for the Puyallup near Tacoma, Washington. Their involvement in the white economy (selling furs, fishing and logging commercially, and working in hopyards) became extensive. Attempts to Christianize the Puyallup and minimize the influence of tribal customs were only partially successful. More critically, the Puyallup were economically exploited by whites. Families sold their allotted reservation land, and by the late 1970's, the entire Puyallup reservation occupied only 33 acres. This occurred on top of epidemics of smallpox and malaria in the 1850's which significantly reduced the population.

Puyallup fortunes were reversed, however, beginning in the mid-1960's. The population had increased significantly, and they were permitted greater control over their own affairs. The Boldt Decision in 1974 reaffirmed the early treaties guaranteeing fishing rights. Tribal members became adept in business management; some established and learned to manage fisheries. They also formed a tribal government with a strong business orientation, which developed a network of stores, marinas, and restaurants on the reservation.

See also Northwest Coast; Salishan language family.

Quapaw: Tribe
CULTURE AREA: Southeast
LANGUAGE GROUP: Siouan
PRIMARY LOCATION: Oklahoma
POPULATION SIZE: 1,538 (1990 U.S. Census)

Unlike many other American Indian tribes, the Quapaws (or Arkansas) have not preserved elaborate traditions explaining their origins. They say only that their Ancient Ones came forth from the water. Because of this, the history of the tribe is difficult to uncover. The Quapaws, or "Downstream People," migrated from the Ohio Valley to the Arkansas River near where it joins the Mississippi River in the mid 1600's. Since the Quapaws went downstream, their kindred tribes called them Ugaxpa, or "drifted downstream." Their principal villages were on the west bank of the Mississippi River in what is now Arkansas. The forests and rivers supplied plenty of berries, game, and other food. They had large, well-tilled fields and cultivated gourds, pumpkins, sunflowers, beans, squash, and corn. Corn was considered the most important agricultural product. They hunted buffalo, which was a substantial part of their diet, and preserved what was not needed immediately for winter.

The focus of Quapaw life was the permanent village, which was actually a cluster of multiple family dwellings. Their faith played a role in every aspect of tribal life; the central force of the universe was Wah-kon-tah, who was all and in all. They believed in life after death and in a judgment that would lead to a life of joy or perpetual torment. They often traded with the Caddoes on the Red River and had established a trade route between the two settlements. The manufactured goods of white society, which the people wanted, brought about establishment of trade with eastern tribes who had contact with the Europeans. The first Europeans to encounter the Quapaws were the French explorers Jacques Marquette and Louis Jolliet in 1673. The trading done with whites was ultimately detrimental to the Downstream People; by 1699 smallpox had killed so many that only three hundred warriors remained.

Only a thousand Quapaws were left in 1818 when they ceded 30 million acres to the United States for $4,000 and annuities. A remaining million acres were ceded in 1824. In 1925 the Quapaws moved to the Caddo Reservation in Louisiana, where they were plagued by disease and floods. Most of the tribe left and returned to Arkansas. A treaty in 1833 gave these people land in northwest Oklahoma (then Indian Territory). They scattered during the Civil War, but in the late 1800's survivors gathered on the reservation in Indian Territory to reestablish tribal life. The Downstream People remained a poor tribe until nickel and zinc were discovered on the reservation in the 1920's; then they prospered. The population dropped to 236 in 1895 but had risen to 929 in 1980 and 1,538 in 1990. Of those listed in the census as Quapaw, probably no more than 20 percent are more than one-fourth Quapaw, yet the tribe maintains its unique identity.

See also Indian Territory; Siouan language family; Southeast.

Quechan: Tribe
CULTURE AREA: Southwest
LANGUAGE GROUP: Yuman
PRIMARY LOCATION: Southwestern Arizona, southeastern California
POPULATION SIZE: 1,972 (1990 U.S. Census)

The Quechan, or Yuma, tribe is one of the few that have never been relocated away from their ancestral land. Quechan territory lies around the confluence of the Gila and Colorado rivers. The Quechan came to this area between 1540 and 1700. (Although "Yuma" is essentially synonymous with Quechan, the term "Yuman" applies to a language group and to a number of tribes, including the Quechan, Maricopa, and Cocopa.)

The Quechan derived their subsistence from cultivating the rivers' floodplains and from gathering wild fruits, nuts, and seeds. A popular wild food was mesquite, which they ground into flour for cakes or fermented to make an intoxicating beverage.

Apart from shamans, the spiritual leaders, there was a *kwaxot*, or civil leader, and a *kwanami*, or war leader. The primary leader was probably the *paipataxan*, or "real person," who made the majority of decisions about issues that affected the tribe.

The Quechan were occasionally in conflicts with the Cocopa, Maricopa, and Pima. Sometimes the Quechan would ally themselves with the Mojave and Sand Papago (Tohono O'odham) tribes. Attacks were initiated to steal supplies and obtain captives that could be traded for horses and other necessities. In the 1770's, Europeans and Mexicans attempted to control the area where the Gila and Colorado rivers join by trying to "civilize" the Quechan. Eventually, the Quechan tired of their new allies' cultural impositions and destroyed the Mexican and European settlements.

In 1852, the United States was able to establish a garrison on a cliff overlooking the rivers. Fort Yuma's dealings with the Quechan were relatively peaceful. This peace was further ensured when the commander of the fort had a Quechan named Pasqual made "tribal chief."

Between the 1850's and the 1900's, the U.S. government tried to bargain land away from the group, but in 1912, the Fort Yuma Reservation was established, temporarily stabilizing Quechan landholdings. By the 1960's, however, the Quechans had sold much of their land because of economic stress. They ceased most of their farming activities and became wage earners. They were forced to adopt the federally accepted form of local government called the "tribal council." After several nonviolent protests in the 1960's and 1970's, the U.S. government finally restored 25,000 acres to the Quechan in 1978.

As of 1990, the majority of Quechans lived on this land, working as farmers, laborers, artisans, and craftspeople. They remained closely tied to their land and continued to celebrate many of their traditions.

See also Cocopa; Prehistory—Southwest; Southwest; Yuman language family.

Queen Anne (c. 1650, junction of Pamunkey and Mattapony rivers, present-day Va.—c. 1725): Tribal leader
TRIBAL AFFILIATION: Pamunkey Powhatan
SIGNIFICANCE: As leader of the Pamunkey tribe, a member of the Powhatan Confederacy, Queen Anne aided white Virginia settlers against hostile tribes

Queen Anne's husband, Totopotomoi, was principal chief of the Pamunkey tribe. With his death in battle as an ally of whites against other Indian tribes in 1656, Queen Anne assumed leadership of the Pamunkeys. In 1675 she traveled to Williamsburg to respond to governor William Berkeley's request for her aid in suppressing Bacon's Rebellion—a rebellion within Virginia ostensibly caused by Berkeley's failure to protect western Virginians from hostile Indians.

In full Indian attire, Queen Anne appeared at the Colonial Council, where she initially refused Berkeley's request, citing his earlier failure to protect her husband and her tribe. After promises of future aid, she reluctantly provided the governor with assistance. Afterward, in tribute, she was presented with a silver-inscribed medal (now in the collection of the Association for the Preservation of Virginia Antiquities).

See also Bacon's Rebellion; Indian-white relations—English colonial; Opechancanough; Powhatan Confederacy; Pohatan Wars.

Quetzalcóatl

TRIBES AFFECTED: Aztec, Maya
SIGNIFICANCE: Quetzalcóatl, one of the three great Aztec gods, was a benevolent deity who presided over learning and the priesthood

Quetzalcóatl, commonly referred to as the Feathered or Plumed Serpent, was one of the three Aztec "great gods." These gods ranked in importance immediately under the four creative deities and above the various gods of fertility, nature, the planets, and constellations. The other two great gods were Huitzilopochtli, Hummingbird Wizard or Hummingbird of the South, war and sun god, the chief god of Tenochtitlán (present-day Mexico City), and Tezcatlipoca, Smoking Mirror, chief god of the pantheon, often described in solar terms, the chief god of Texcoco.

Quetzalcóatl, the third great god, was the god of learning and the priesthood and the chief god of Cholula (where the ruins of a temple dedicated to him may still be seen). Aztec myth held that Quetzalcóatl had once been a man, presiding over a golden age in the state of Anahuac. He is generally depicted in sculpture, fresco, and carvings as a man of tall stature with a light complexion, long, dark hair and a substantial beard. Quetzalcóatl somehow angered one of the principal gods and was exiled. He left his followers at the Gulf of Mexico, departing in a wizard skiff made of serpent skins, promising to return. Given Quetzalcóatl's physical characteristics and his gallant promise to return as recorded in Aztec folk myth, the Spaniards cannot have understood their phenomenal luck in chancing to approach the Mexican coast from the same Gulf of Mexico waters whence Quetzalcóatl left.

In an interesting expression of crosstribal influence, Laguna Pueblo novelist Leslie Marmon Silko uses the Aztec Quetzalcóatl in *Almanac of the Dead* (1991) as one of the recurring symbols of the text (a stone serpent that appears overnight) and in the retelling of the Aztec cosmogony myth (similar to the Osiris limb-gathering creation myth).

See also Aztec; Indian-white relations—Spanish colonial; Maya; Silko, Leslie Marmon; Tenochtitlán; Teotihuacán.

Quileute: Tribe

CULTURE AREA: Northwest Coast
LANGUAGE GROUP: Chimakuan
PRIMARY LOCATION: Western Washington
POPULATION SIZE: 580 (1990 U.S. Census)

The Quileute, a maritime people, dwelled in permanent split-cedar-roofed longhouses that accommodated several extended families or even a lineage. They were dependent primarily upon fishing, which was reflected in their ceremonies, settlement patterns, technology, and mythology. Quileute society was internally stratified with hereditary chiefs, commoners, and slaves. Status was gained through oratory, warfare, birth, and accumulation and redistribution of traditional forms of wealth (usually in the forms of copper, slaves, obsidian blades, pileated red woodpecker scalp capes, and dentalium shells). Kinship was bilateral. Residence tended to be patrilocal. They had a shamanistic religion; polygyny; complex ceremonies, including the potlatch; house and totem pole-raising; rites of passage; and the launching of hollowed red cedar canoes for trading. Raven was a cultural hero, and art was typified by geometric and representational thunderbird-whale motifs.

First European American contact was with the Spanish in 1775 and with the British in 1787. The Quileute signed a reservation treaty in 1855 with Governor Isaac I. Stevens, but through a misunderstanding the Quileute remained in their territory until 252 were removed in 1889 to a one-mile-square reservation at La Push, on the western coast of Washington. In 1893, the remaining 71 inhabitants moved to the Hoh River. In 1882, a school was established at La Push. The syncretic Indian Shaker Church was introduced to the Quileute in 1895.

In 1936, the Quileute adopted a constitution and bylaws, and in 1937 they became an independent and self-governing sovereign people governed by a five-member elected council. Today, their main sources of income are a fish-buying company, a tourists' trailer park, a cooperative store, and a fishing gear store that supplies local fishermen and tourists. Many Quileute are self-employed in logging and fishing. There are numerous successful efforts at revitalizing certain aspects of Quileute traditional culture, particularly with the teaching of woodworking skills.

See also Northwest Coast; Shaker Church.

Quillwork

TRIBES AFFECTED: Pantribal throughout the porcupine's native habitat
SIGNIFICANCE: Quillwork is a form of decoration that was used across the northeastern United States and Canada and

as far west as the western slopes of the Rockies and through the central Plains south and east to the coast—the area where porcupines are native; it is still used today by artists from these areas

Porcupine quills provided many tribes with material that could be dyed a variety of bright colors. Several methods were used, and the quillwork of the Plains may be differentiated from that of the eastern nations. In both cases the quills were taken from the porcupine by rolling it in a soft robe. The quills would stick and could be removed individually; the barbs were cut off and the quills were cleaned. Quills are tubular in shape but could be flattened by pulling them between the teeth. Plant and animal dyes were used to dye them bright colors. Popular colors were bright pink, bright yellow, purple, green, and red. Some northern nations used quills in their natural color, off-white with dark brown ends.

After dyeing, they were ready to be plaited together, often in rows creating both geometric designs and pictorial representations. Plains nations preferred geometric designs, whereas those of the Eastern Woodlands tended to be floral in pattern. Good quillwork was tiny, tight, and colorful, and it created beautiful decorations on any article of clothing. Several techniques were used. The quills could be wrapped around a narrow strip of stiff rawhide or one that had been cut into symbolic shapes, such as medicine wheels. These small strips of wrapped rawhide could also be sewn onto any article of clothing, often in adjoining rows as decoration. Another technique was to quill directly onto the garment, weaving the quills together; they were then secured by sinew threads. This was a more common technique for larger pictures or whole areas of clothing that were quilled.

Quality quillwork was greatly valued, and girls were taught the art carefully by loving and talented relatives. A talented quillworker was revered for her artistry, and her creations were highly valued by those lucky enough to wear items of her handiwork. Quilled moccasins, shirts, bandoliers, gloves, hats, jackets, breechcloths, leggings, dresses, and robes were all valued exchange items in giveaways and other acts of generosity, necessary in demonstrating a family's goodness. Quillwork was a lightweight decoration that was both durable and flexible. It could get wet and retain its shape, so it was an exceptionally practical form of ornamentation.

Quillwork was later replaced by beadwork as Europeans poured into the continent, disrupting and influencing the native peoples. Like any new item, beads were desired. Beadmaking with European glass beads replaced native beadmaking from seashells. Because the European beads from Czechoslovakia and eastern Europe were colorful and small, they could be used to replicate quillwork decorations. The colors, however, were different. No longer were the bright pinks, yellows, and purples of quillwork common; now, reds, blues, yellows, and greens became more popular. The best quillworkers continued as long as they could find quills. Their work can be seen in many museums, still beautifully durable.

See also Beads and beadwork; Dress and adornment.

Quinault: Tribe

CULTURE AREA: Northwest Coast
LANGUAGE GROUP: Salishan
PRIMARY LOCATION: Mouth of the Quinault River, Washington
POPULATION SIZE: 967 (Quinault Reservation, per 1990 U.S. Census); 2,491 (Quinault Nation office at Taholah, Washington, 1994)

The name Quinault (sometimes spelled Quinaielt) is derived from *kwi' nail*, the name of their largest settlement, located at the site of the present-day village of Taholah at the mouth of the Quinault River. The Quinault are one of several tribes referred to as Southwestern Coast Salish. Traditionally, the Quinault were primarily fishers and hunters and, to a lesser extent, gatherers. Salmon was the basic staple. The Quinault were excellent canoemen, and in their large ocean-going canoes, they were the southernmost coastal tribe to hunt whales.

The Quinault lived in large houses, holding from two to ten families, in about twenty villages. Social class was divided into slave and free, with free divided into nobility and commoners. Nobility consisted of those with inherited status and wealth. The Quinault extensively traded and intermarried with neighboring tribes, and these regional networks also contributed to status. Commoners lacked these perquisites. Slaves were obtained in raids or in trades.

The village leader or chief was chosen by village members from among those males with enough wealth to ensure that some of that wealth could be distributed to others at potlatches. The potlatch in turn served to enhance the leader's prestige. The leader advised and mediated disputes but otherwise had no prescribed powers.

Religion focused on acquisition of guardian spirits, which were necessary for a successful life. Particular spirits conveyed particular powers to their recipient (such as wealth or success at gambling, curing illness, or whaling). Other important mythical spirits were Misp, creator and caretaker of the world, and Xwoni Xwoni, the trickster buffoon. Salmon were the focus of several taboos and ceremonies.

Whites had established trading settlements in the area by the early 1800's. In the early 1830's a malaria epidemic reduced the population from 1,250 (in 1805) to 158 by 1857. In 1855 the Quinault signed the Treaty of Olympia with the United States. They kept a large reservation on the mouth of the Quinault River, where they were subject to the machinations of whites to Christianize them and make them give up their traditional lifestyle and customs.

The reservation economy centered on fishing and government jobs but never provided sufficient employment. It was estimated in 1985 that 30 percent of the adults living there were unemployed. As a result, many have left the reservation permanently to seek employment in urban locations. Beginning in 1907, and over the opposition of the Quinault, Congress authorized allotment of Quinault land to other tribes. By the 1980's the Quinault Indian Nation was composed of the

Robert Pope, a Quinault, awaits the beginning of a religious ceremony before the casket of his grandfather, a Quinault medicine man, can be moved to higher ground. (AP/Wide World Photos)

Quinault and six affiliated tribes. About a third of the 190,000-acre Quinault reservation is owned by non-Indians.

See also Northwest Coast; Potlatch; Salishan language family; Salmon.

Quinney, John W. (1797, New Stockbridge, N.Y.—July 21, 1855, Stockbridge, N.Y.): Tribal spokesman, translator

ALSO KNOWN AS: Quinequan

TRIBAL AFFILIATION: Mahican (Stockbridge)

SIGNIFICANCE: Quinney was a Mahican leader at the time the tribe relocated from the East to the Great Lakes area

As a young man, John W. Quinney was taught to read and write English. He assisted Moravian missionaries in translating religious works into printed, phonetic Mahican (Stockbridge).

White encroachment in the early 1800's pushed the Mahicans from the Hudson River valley, and Quinney was instrumental in purchasing Menominee land in Wisconsin. The U.S. government was willing to grant citizenship to the Stockbridge, since the vast majority were Christianized. This would have effectively ended their existence as a separate tribe and ended their need for their own land. Quinney resisted American citizenship for his tribe.

Quinney was appointed grand sachem in 1852, although his family was not of the hereditary line of sachems; the appointment may have been largely honorary. He served until his death in 1855. Quinney was hostile to the Mohawk throughout his life and was resentful that his people were removed and the Mohawk were not.

See also Mahican; Menominee; Mohawk; Relocation.

BIBLIOGRAPHY

LePoer, Barbara Leitch. *A Concise Dictionary of Indian Tribes of North America.* Edited by Kendall T. LePoer. Algonac, Mich.: Reference Publications, 1979.

Skinner, Alanson. "Mahican Ethnology." *Bulletin of the Public Museum of the City of Milwaukee* 2, no. 1 (1912): 87-116.

Trigger, Bruce, ed. *Northeast.* Vol. 15 in *Handbook of North American Indians*, edited by William C. Sturtevant. Washington, D.C.: Smithsonian Institution Press, 1978.

Railroads

TRIBES AFFECTED: Pantribal

SIGNIFICANCE: Nineteenth century railroads, especially transcontinental lines, signaled an end to the isolation of Indian lands and the destruction of traditional Indian economies, military capabilities, and cultural integrity

Through the early 1860's, American railroads were granted rights-of-way across Indian lands east of the Mississippi by treaties or by virtue of Indian removals such as occurred with the Cherokee, Chickasaw, Choctaw, Creek, and Seminole peoples that began in the early 1800's. By the 1850's, because of sectional politics, the lobbying of private businesses, a popular belief in Manifest Destiny, and a general desire to end Indian problems, proposals emerged at the federal level for construction of transcontinental lines. The Gadsden Purchase (1853) was based on visions of a southerly rail route to California, while additional proposals argued for more northerly lines crossing the United States and Canada.

These proposals came to fruition between the early 1860's and the 1890's, as Americans built the world's densest railway network, the centerpieces of which were the American (and one Canadian) transcontinental railroads: the Union Pacific-Central Pacific; the Atchison, Topeka, and Santa Fe; the Southern Pacific; and the Canadian Pacific. Construction of these railways and their ancillary lines was partially subsidized by federal and state land grants that totaled 139 million acres west of the Mississippi. By design, the transcontinental railroads cut through the heart of Indian lands. This situation resulted in the destruction of the buffalo upon which Indian livelihoods depended, facilitated American military campaigns against dozens of western tribes, and accelerated white settlement. By the mid-1880's, hastened by railroads, effective Indian resistance to white incursions had collapsed. Subsequently, railroads helped expose nearly all Indian peoples to white culture—its products, settlers, tourists, scientists, government officials, and businesses—and wrought profound changes in traditional tribal ways.

See also Buffalo; Gadsden Purchase; Indian-white relations—U.S., 1831-1870; Indian-white relations—U.S., 1871-1933.

Rain in the Face (c. 1835, forks of the Cheyenne River, N.Dak.—Sept. 14, 1905, Standing Rock, N.Dak.): Chief

ALSO KNOWN AS: Amarazhu, Iromagaja

TRIBAL AFFILIATION: Hunkpapa Sioux

SIGNIFICANCE: During the Sioux Wars of the 1860's and 1870's, Rain in the Face was a leading war chief

His name came from childhood incidents in which blood, along with red and black war paint, streaked his face. Not a hereditary chief, Rain in the Face earned his reputation and status in war. During the war for the Bozeman Trail (1866-1868), Rain in the Face was a leading war chief, participating

This engraving of people shooting buffalo from a train symbolizes the changes wrought by railroads. (Library of Congress)

Hunkpapa Sioux war chief Rain in the Face is said to have been the warrior who killed Custer at the Battle of the Little Bighorn. (National Archives)

in numerous raids. At Fort Trotten, North Dakota, he was severely wounded.

Arrested in 1873 for the murder of a white surgeon, Rain in the Face, though admitting his guilt, was aided by a white guard, who permitted his escape. He thereafter participated in the war for the Black Hills (1876-1877) and in the last great Indian victory, the Battle of the Little Bighorn, during which he was reputed to have killed George Armstrong Custer. At war's end, he retreated with Sitting Bull to Canada, returning with him to Montana in 1880 and surrendering at Fort Keogh. Rain in the Face had seven wives and numerous children.

See also Black Hills; Bozeman Trail wars; Crazy Horse; Little Bighorn, Battle of the; Red Cloud.

Ranching

Tribes affected: Pantribal

Significance: Many Native American tribes adopted the cattle and sheep ranching practices of European Americans, which gave them a steady food supply and a means of livelihood

North American Indians' experience with ranching may be dated back to the appearance of the Spanish in the Southwest during the sixteenth century. Although at first the Indians captured stock for food and consumed the stolen animals quickly, eventually they began to breed animals acquired as gifts or through further raiding.

When the Spanish established settlements in the Southwest, their *rancherías* of cattle and sheep became targets for stock raids to supplement the desert fare of local Indians. Cattle were as yet not tended but were butchered and prepared for food as was native wild game, such as buffalo, the only "cattle" the Indians had known.

The Navajo learned the value of ranching early, and sheep herds became a focal point of their lifestyle. The sheep provided them with a manageable food source in the arid Southwest, and the wool provided material for superior clothing and blankets. The nomadic lifestyle of sheepherders suited the Navajo people, who had earlier been raiders of the Pueblo tribes.

Eastern Indians subdued by European invasion attempted to assimilate themselves into the dominant society by taking up farming and the management of livestock. The Cherokee, in particular, did very well until they were forced westward by the pressure of white settlers.

Western Indians who found their reservation lands unsuitable for farming often attempted ranching to survive. Sometimes these ventures were successful, but often grazing lands were instead leased to European Americans to provide some income for the tribe or individual.

Modern American Indians continue to engage in ranching as a means of livelihood. The Navajo, for example, raise sheep, horses, and cattle, and their colorful rugs woven from animal

LIVESTOCK ON AMERICAN INDIAN LANDS, 1989

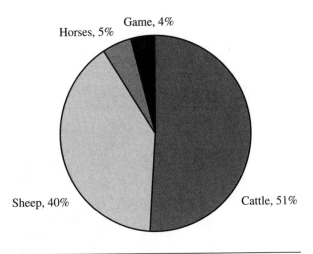

Source: United States Department of the Interior, *Bureau of Indian Affairs Natural Resource Information System Inventory and Production Report, 1989.*

Note: Includes only land under BIA jurisdiction, not privately owned lands.

fibers command high prices. In Arizona, the San Carlos Apaches operate five cattle associations on their reservation. As an additional source of revenue, the tribe owns two herds, one of which is designated as the "old folks herd" and benefits elderly Apaches.

See also Agriculture; Apache; Navajo; Pueblo tribes, Eastern; Pueblo tribes, Western; Weaving.

Red Bird (c. 1788, near Prairie du Chien, Wis.—Feb. 16, 1828, Prairie du Chien, Wis.): War Chief

ALSO KNOWN AS: Wanig Suchka, Zitkaduta

TRIBAL AFFILIATION: Winnebago

SIGNIFICANCE: Leader of the brief Winnebago Uprising, Red Bird was war chief of a small, militant group of Winnebagos

Born at the forks of the Mississippi and Wisconsin rivers, Red Bird succeeded his father as war chief of the Prairie La Crosse Winnebagos. As lead prices rose in the 1820's, federal officials seeking to obtain rich Indian lands attempted to discourage Indians from mining and selling lead to traders. Consequently, tensions escalated, and in 1826 warriors killed members of a French trading family. In 1827, two warriors were accused of murder; rumors of their imminent execution reached Red Bird's village. Authorized by tribal council, Red Bird and two other warriors killed two white settlers and scalped an infant. On June 30, Red Bird also attacked a Mississippi boatman who had kidnapped and raped several Indian women. Subsequently, federal troops, Illinois volunteers, and white volunteer miners massed at Fort Snelling. When other Winnebagos failed to join the uprising, Red Bird surrendered to white forces, expecting immediate execution. His trial met with several delays, however, and Red Bird died of dysentery shortly before charges against him were dropped because of a lack of witnesses.

See also Winnebago; Winnebago Uprising.

Red Cloud (Sept. 20, 1822, fork of the Platte River, Nebr.—Dec. 10, 1909, Pine Ridge Reservation, S.Dak.): Chief

ALSO KNOWN AS: Makhpia-sha

TRIBAL AFFILIATION: Sioux (Lakota or Teton group, Oglala band)

SIGNIFICANCE: Red Cloud's uniformly brilliant achievements on the battlefield and as a leader, diplomat, and negotiator distinguish him as one of the greatest of Sioux chiefs and most illustrious of nineteenth century Indians

Red Cloud was a member of the Snake family, the most distinguished and forceful family of his tribe. Red Cloud had no claim to hereditary chieftainship. He accomplished what he did through personal resourcefulness, intelligence, skill, and force of character.

Red Cloud grew up aware of the friction between Indians and whites. His father died of drunkenness from liquor introduced into the tribe by whites. Red Cloud developed an abiding distrust of white intentions and an uncompromising attitude toward them. He became a bitter enemy of the whites and predicted disaster if they were allowed into Sioux country.

Oglala Sioux leader Red Cloud was both a brilliant war leader and a masterful negotiator. (National Archives)

The encroachment by whites into Sioux territory following the discovery of gold in California in 1849 led to warfare. In 1855, the army soundly defeated the Teton. From the ashes of this defeat, Red Cloud emerged as the new Teton chief.

Red Cloud did not sign the Harney-Sanborne Treaty in 1865, which assured whites safe passage through Sioux territory over the Bozeman Trail. He maintained his attacks on the whites and always rebuffed peace offerings. From August 1, 1866, to year's end, the Sioux killed more than 150 people (eighty alone in the Fetterman Massacre), wounded twenty, and captured almost seven hundred horses and mules.

The Sioux incurred two significant defeats and casualties on August 1 and 2, 1867, partly because of the use of the new breech-loading rifles by the soldiers. Hundreds of Sioux decided against further fighting and left camp; however, Red Cloud held the others together, arguing that continued fighting would force the whites to leave. Red Cloud proved prophetic. No further major battles occurred, but Sioux harassing tactics convinced the government of their determination to defend their territory. A peace conference was arranged at Fort Laramie on April 29, 1868. Red Cloud proved to be a masterful negotiator, and by November, all his terms had been met:

The forts were abandoned, the Bozeman Trail was closed to whites, and whites were not permitted in Indian Territory.

Red Cloud retired to life on the reservation for his remaining days. Although he never fought again, he remained an effective negotiator and diplomat for his people. For example, in 1870, the government wanted to move the Sioux to new agencies. Red Cloud went to Washington, D.C., and effectively resisted government demands. In a stirring speech in New York, he accused whites of betrayal and deception. Public outcry forced the government to recant. Red Cloud's only blemishes were his poor relations with another great Sioux chief, Crazy Horse, and his possible involvement in Crazy Horse's death.

See also Bozeman Trail wars; Crazy Horse; Fort Laramie Treaty of 1868; Sioux.

Red Jacket (c. 1756, near Canoga, N.Y.—Jan. 20, 1830, Seneca Village, N.Y.): Tribal chief, orator

ALSO KNOWN AS: Sagoyewatha (He Causes Them to Be Awake)

TRIBAL AFFILIATION: Seneca

SIGNIFICANCE: An eloquent speaker known for his great wit and memory, Red Jacket participated in numerous treaty conferences, arguing against Seneca assimilation into white society

Red Jacket was born about 1756 near Canoga, New York. His original name was Otetiani (Always Prepared), but upon his election as a merit chief shortly after the American Revolution he was given the Wolf Clan title Sagoyewátha (He Causes Them To Be Awake). To the whites, he was known as Red Jacket because of his fondness for red coats (first provided by the British).

At the Council at Oswego (1777), he and Cornplanter urged Iroquois neutrality in the revolution. When the council decided to join the British cause, he followed the Iroquois custom of unanimity and joined the war effort at Oriskany (1777) and Cherry Valley (1778), but he fled both encounters. He later participated in the Schoharie Valley campaign (1780). His undistinguished war record did not prevent recognition of his oratorical skills, and he served as speaker for the women and chiefs at Buffalo Creek. From 1790 to 1794, he was present at seven major negotiations between Iroquois and U.S. officials. In 1792, George Washington presented him with a silver medal.

Initially he was open to the adoption of some white ways, but land sales, fraud, and frontier evangelists made him wary of whites. He took an increasingly conservative cultural position. At the same time, he signed treaties selling land and negotiated secretly with federal commissioners, receiving six hundred dollars and a hundred-dollar annuity at Big Tree in 1797. This apparent hypocrisy earned him the enmity of the prophet Handsome Lake, who declared that Red Jacket would be undergoing eternal punishment for his role in the sale of Seneca land.

Red Jacket's harshest attacks were reserved for missionaries. Noting the absence of beneficial effects of preaching in white communities, he wondered why Christians were unable to reach agreement on their religion. He was so humiliated when his wife converted to Christianity that he left her briefly. Deposed as chief in 1827 by a minority of chiefs (all Christians), he was reinstated the following year. As leader of the pagan faction, he objected to tactics used to obtain Seneca acquiescence to land sales to the Ogden Land Company and Seneca removal to Kansas. Red Jacket sent remonstrances to the governor of New York and President John Quincy Adams, and he personally visited Adams, securing an investigation that upheld charges of fraud.

As vain as he was eloquent, and with a reputation for intemperance, he was disappointed in never being named a confederacy chief. This may have been a result of his conflict with Handsome Lake, or perhaps reflected the Winnebagos' fear of concentrating too much authority in such a wily individual. He died on January 20, 1832, ironically receiving a Christian burial. His remains were reburied in 1884 (along with those of other prominent Senecas) by the Buffalo Historical Society.

See also Brant, Joseph; Cornplanter; Handsome Lake; Iroquois Confederacy; Seneca.

Red River War

DATE: 1874-1875

PLACE: Oklahoma, Texas

TRIBES AFFECTED: Comanche, Kiowa

SIGNIFICANCE: The Red River War brought an end to effective Indian resistance on the southern Plains and marked the end of the Quaker peace policy toward the Indians

The Treaty of Medicine Lodge in 1867 assigned the Comanche and Kiowa to reservations in the western Indian Territory, but the tribes also believed that it guaranteed them the exclusive use of the panhandle in Texas as their hunting grounds. Most of the Kiowa moved to the reservation, but small groups remained in the panhandle, as did a large band of Comanche led by Quanah Parker.

Controversy quickly arose over the use of the panhandle. Indians were alarmed when government survey parties began working in the area; they assumed that white settlers would soon follow, and also were outraged when white hunters began slaughtering the buffalo herds. Quaker administrators supported the Comanche and Kiowa in protests, while Major General Phillip H. Sheridan, commanding the Department of the Missouri, supported the whites and sent his troops to skirmish with raiding parties of warriors.

General William T. Sherman, as commander of the army, delayed his decision while trying to resolve the conflicting reports. Unfortunately for the Indians, he was on an inspection trip in north Texas in 1871 when a party of Comanche and Kiowa attacked a nearby army wagon train, killing six teamsters. Sherman ordered Sheridan to suppress all Indians outside of the reservations.

After smaller expeditions failed to establish order, as evidenced by the Indian attack at Adobe Walls, Sheridan organized a large-scale push into the panhandle in 1874, which developed into the Red River War. Casualties were relatively light on both sides, but there was great destruction of Indian property. The principal engagement took place when troops destroyed an encampment of Comanche and Kiowa in Palo Duro Canyon. Drought and hunger brought a quick end to the Red River War. By the early summer of 1875, most Indian leaders, including Parker, had surrendered, and twenty-six were sent to prison in Florida. The Red River War ended effective Indian resistance on the southern Plains and convinced Sherman that a harsher policy toward other tribes was necessary.

See also Adobe Walls, Battles of; Medicine Lodge, Treaties of; Parker, Quanah.

Red Shoes (c. 1700, New Stockbridge, N.Y.—June 22, 1748): Peacemaker

ALSO KNOWN AS: Shulush Homa

TRIBAL AFFILIATION: Choctaw

SIGNIFICANCE: Red Shoes was an advocate of peace and trade with whites

Red Shoes rose to prominence during the period of factionalism in the Choctaw tribe that culminated in civil war between 1746 and 1750. The Choctaw were allied with the French, fighting against the English and their Chickasaw allies. Red Shoes was awarded a French medal for his loyal service soon after the Natchez Revolt of 1729. Soon afterward, however, he became an advocate of peace with the Chickasaw and trade with English merchants from South Carolina. His reasons may have included a chronic shortage of trade goods from the French, his marriage connections with the Chickasaw, or the fact that his wife suffered a rape at the hands of the French. Whatever the reason, Red Shoes was received with ceremony by the English at Charleston in 1738.

Red Shoes attempted to sway other Choctaw towns away from their dependence on the French, and ultimately contributed to serious political divisions in the tribe. French diplomats, desperate to reestablish their influence before losing their loyal allies to either an English alliance or unpredictable neutrality, conspired to induce other Choctaw war chiefs to assassinate Red Shoes. He was murdered on June 22, 1747 while escorting an English trader from the Creek towns to Choctaw territory.

Red Shoes was probably from the village of Couechitto. His name derives from the Choctaw title for war chief, *soulouche oumastabe*, or red shoe killer.

See also Chickasaw; Choctaw; Indian-white relations—English colonial.

Reifel, Ben (Sept. 19, 1906, Parmelee, S.Dak.—Jan. 2, 1990, Sioux Falls, S.Dak.): Politician

TRIBAL AFFILIATION: Rosebud Sioux

SIGNIFICANCE: Reifel served five terms in Congress after several years in various capacities in the Bureau of Indian Affairs

Ben Reifel, who would become a congressman from South Dakota, was born in Parmelee, South Dakota, son of a German father and a Sioux mother. Reifel did not pass the eighth grade until he was sixteen and did not go to high school. His father could "see no reason for it," and he told Ben that he was needed on the farm. The young man read whatever he could find, and his passion for education grew. Finally the young man ran away from home, hiking 250 miles to enroll in high school.

Despite his late start in formal education, Reifel earned a B.S. degree from South Dakota State University in 1932. He joined the army reserves as a commissioned officer while in college and was called to duty in World War II. At the end of the war, he was appointed Bureau of Indian Affairs (BIA) superintendent at the Fort Berthold Agency, North Dakota.

Reifel returned to college at Harvard University for a masters in public administration and then became one of the first American Indians to earn a Ph.D., also at Harvard. When he returned to the Dakotas, he held several BIA posts including the superintendency at Pine Ridge, where he was the first head Indian agent of native blood. His career at the BIA culminated when he was appointed area director of the office in Aberdeen, South Dakota.

In 1960, Reifel retired from the BIA to run for Congress. He won on his first run for public office (as a Republican) and served five terms before retiring in 1970. On his retirement, Reifel, who had fought so hard to get a formal education, was awarded an honorary degree from the University of South Dakota.

See also Bureau of Indian Affairs (BIA).

Religion

TRIBES AFFECTED: Pantribal

SIGNIFICANCE: American Indian religions are varied, but they generally contain concepts that stress harmony and the interrelatedness of all life and existence; a wide range of activities may be considered religious, because American Indian religions are not based on the division into sacred and secular realms that is characteristic of many modern religions

Until relatively recently, descriptions of American Indian religions have been written from the perspective of Europeans and their American descendants, ranging from the earliest explorers and missionaries to twentieth century anthropologists. Discussions tended to be framed by a number of questions that reflected the European tradition, including whether American Indians had religion at all, what type of religion they had, and what they held sacred. Another problematic aspect to the study of Indian religions is that there is no way to determine what American Indian religions were truly like before contact with Europeans; there is no way to recover the stories, rituals, norms of behavior, and organizational norms as they existed before they were influenced—sometimes subtly, sometimes radically—by Europeans.

Pre-Contact. The first written details of American Indian religion were recorded by French and Spanish Catholics or English Protestants. For them "religion" meant the Christian religion, and specifically their own version of it. One either had this religion or did not. Clearly the American Indians did not. Thus they were called pagans and were criticized for their superstitions; sometimes they were feared as agents of the devil. For these European Christians, religion dealt with God, the supernatural, an invisible world, and sacred books, rites, and people. Religion was thought to be able to move beyond ethnic or national borders without losing its validity.

They found little of this type of religion among American Indians. One reason was that there was not one single American Indian religion. There were many American Indian religions. In a sense, each tribe *was* its own religion; some tribes had no word or idea equivalent to the Western notion of "religion." The concept as presented by Europeans was foreign to their way of life; the typical religious institutions, stories, and rituals of Christianity did not stand out as religiously distinct from nonreligious ones. Europeans looked for religious stories and activity which resembled their own. An Indian's entire life was religious: Constructing a canoe among the Nootka was a religious act, a treaty discussion among the Iroquois was religious, farming among the Hopi was a religious act, the rabbit drive among the Rappahannock was a religious act. These acts were not considered religious from the perspective of Europeans and thus they saw no religion in them. On the other hand, they heard stories which sounded like some of their own religious stories and saw rituals that seemed somewhat like theirs. These they described as the Indian religion.

The French missionaries were most acute among the Europeans in showing respect for what they considered the religion of the Indians. The Great Spirit became God. The vision quest was viewed as the search for one's call by God. The French saw in their versions of American Indian religions hints of the ancient Roman and Greek religions to which they wished to bring, as a complement, Catholicism.

The American Indians, however, saw little of religious import in the European way of life. The things that gave the Indians' lives direction and purpose seemed lacking in the Europeans' way of life. Europeans did not honor and respect equally the material and immaterial world, and they did not seek to keep a balance between their inner and outer life. They viewed the afterlife as a horrible place for those who disobeyed religious law, and they were unable to speak, chant, sing, dance, and celebrate their life without written words. The Europeans, from the Indian perspective, lacked coherence and direction to their life. At the same time there were many attractive aspects to European life. Surrounded by the European way of life, of which its religion was a part, the Indian religions were overwhelmed and changed but not destroyed.

Post-Contact. From the moment of first contact, Indian religions changed. All religions change when they encounter powerful new cultural traditions. When these religions have a written history, scholars can trace how they change. Since Indian religions are not based on a written tradition, however, there is no clear idea of how much they have subtly changed in

accepting European Christian ideas, items of worship, rituals, and images.

It has been suggested that many Christian Indians kept their tribal religions alive while adopting and practicing Christianity without realizing that they were also maintaining their traditional religions—in other words they adopted the Christian view of what was "religious" and did not consider that the tribal traditions they were maintaining were in fact religious ones. Christianity never considered, for example, making a canoe to be religious; therefore, European Christianity had nothing "religious" to say about it. Many aspects of American Indian religions were retained because the nature of Indian religion itself is dynamic. An oral tradition is able to adapt and change in a way that a literate tradition is not. Because Indian religions kept their inherent vitality and practical qualities, Indians were many times able to accept Christianity and keep their own religion.

Animistic Approach. When cultural anthropologists have studied the religions of various cultures, they have frequently employed the views and descriptions of a field of study known as comparative religion. One example is the classification of types of religious systems, one of which is called animism. Another is the concept that religion involves the realm of the sacred, which is contrasted with the secular or profane realm of everyday life.

Animism is a theory of religious origins which claims that early humans believed that everything that exists has its own spirit or living power which governs its existence. Thus the first humans heard the wind howl and thought that it must possess a life like the lives of animals that howl. They found themselves surrounded by spirits: rain spirits, tree spirits, pond spirits, sun and moon spirits. As small children talk to trees and flowers—and wait for an answer—so these first, primitive people did the same. The conversation among the spirits, human and otherwise, became the first prayers, rituals, rules, and institutions known as religion.

A theory of origins is nothing unless it also describes what comes afterward. What eventually came after the "primitive," according to this theory, was the modern Western world of writing, mathematics, and science. In this classification system, since American Indians did not write and had not developed the other "advanced" aspects of European societies, they were primitive peoples. Therefore, it was assumed, they probably had a spirit religion, or animistic religion. It did not take long for a significant body of literature to develop which described the animistic world of Indian religion. The Lakota *wakan* and the Algonquian *manitou* were understood to belong to the world of the spirits. The Pawnee Indians of the Plains were seen to have a hierarchy of star spirits, all subservient to the great spirit in the sky, Tirawa. The Plains Indians' Sun Dance was seen as a dance to win support from the Great Spirit. Buffalo Spirit, Caribou Spirit, and Corn Spirit were seen to direct the coming or growth of these animals or plants. There are guardian spirits won in fasting visions by youths of the Plateau and the Northeast Woodlands. The hunting tribes were described as depending on their hunters' ability to be possessed by one or several of these spirits in order to be able to have the power of that spirit. The tribe itself was seen to have a deep relation with its guardian spirit, or totem, which appeared in the form of an animal. Many books written about Indian religion have used the theory of animism to describe that religion.

The Sacred. Throughout most of the twentieth century, the sacred and its various manifestations were understood to be central to religious life by most scholars of religion. Although they disagreed about details, they agreed that the sacred was separate from the profane or ordinary, was a manifestation of eternal realities, was known in ways different from those by which ordinary reality was known, and existed before and after those who experienced it. From this perspective, Indian life was surrounded by the sacred. It was manifested in all nature, in special people such as the shamans and medicine men and women, in rituals in which sacred objects and sacred sounds enabled people to be in contact with the power of the surrounding spirits, and in sacred poles which held up the sky.

Their sacred stories or myths enabled them to reach back to the beginning of time and to re-create time and life itself. They could reach back to the creation of a sacred reality that gave direction and purpose to all life; this reality was the people themselves. A number of scholars exploring American Indian religion from the perspective of religion's sacred realm have found it an attractive alternative to the way modern Western religion divides the sacred and secular into two realms, thereby helping make possible the repetitive boredom of industrialized societies.

Influence of Lifestyles. Recently Indian religion has been described in terms of hunting and agricultural lifestyles. The religion of the Paleolithic hunting culture of Eurasia is seen reflected in such common American Indian beliefs and practices as Thunderbird, Mother Earth, the bear ritual, hunting taboos, and certain shamanic rituals. This religion was gradually replaced (7000-5000 B.C.E.) by religions reflective of specialized regional farming cultures in which maize and tobacco became central parts of religious rituals.

The religion of the hunter centers on the hunt: going into the field and tracking, then killing, the animal. This religion sees a symbiosis between the hunter and the hunted. They share the same life energies or spirit. The intricate rearrangement of bones after a kill found among some tribes reflected this shar-

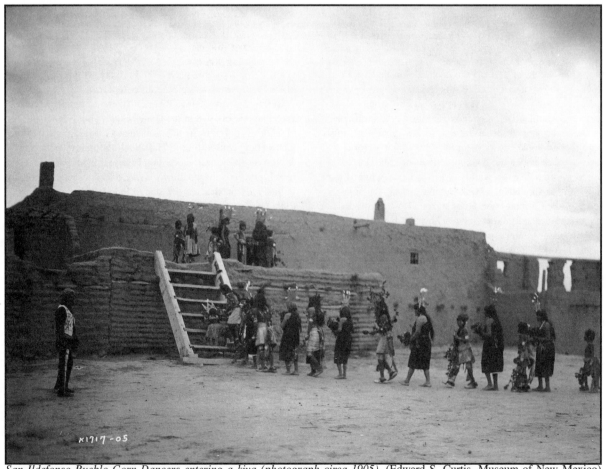

San Ildefonso Pueblo Corn Dancers entering a kiva (photograph circa 1905). (Edward S. Curtis, Museum of New Mexico)

CHRISTIAN AFFILIATIONS OF AMERICAN INDIANS, 1979

Church or Denomination	Ordained Ministers		Total Indian Membership	Active Communicants
	Male	Female		
American Baptist			1,200	1,000
Assemblies of God	3	1	3,300	2,980
Church of the Nazarene	11	3	2,652	1,557
Cumberland Presbyterian	10		500	209
Episcopal	36	13	19,674	10,364
Friends, California Yearly Meeting	6	2	775	725
American Lutheran	1		1,758	—
Mennonite	3		195	156
Orthodox Church in America	10		2,200	2,000
Roman Catholic	11		177,651	—
Southern Baptist	248		36,000	28,444
United Methodist	79	1	14,360	11,969
United Presbyterian	27		8,190	6,826
Wesleyan	35		500	500
Independent churches	5		8,000	6,950
Other	56	5	43,244	14,823
Total	**541**	**25**	**320,199**	**106,523**

Source: Beaver, R. Pierce, ed., *The Native American Christian Community: A Directory of Indian, Aleut, and Eskimo Churches.* Monrovia, Calif.: MARC, 1979. Dash (—) indicates unavailable data.

ing. The placing of a small piece of salmon underneath the floor of a snowhouse by the Netsilik Inuit was a sign of respect for the salmon's "soul." Chants to a dead bird or animal were common. Another common feature among hunting religions is the belief that animal species have a "master spirit" that, under, certain conditions, allows them into the hunter's world. The Caribou Man among the Naskapi Indians of Labrador, for example, is said to live in a world of caribou hair as white as snow and deep as mountains. These mountains are the immense house of the Caribou Man. He is surrounded by thousands of larger-than-life spiritual caribou, who pass in and out of his caribou paradise along paths which he controls for his purposes. The animals' spirits circulate, waiting to be sent back to the hunter's world in new fleshly bodies. If the bones and the animal are treated properly, the enfleshed animal will return.

The religion of the farmer focused on earth, seasons, life, and death. While in many parts of the world farming religions seem to have led to an increase in animal, human, and plant sacrifice, this does not seem to have been the case in North America. Sacrifice did occur, however: White dogs were sacrificed by the natives of Northeast Woodlands; self-mutilation occurred in the Sun Dance of the Lakota and in the Mandan Okeepa (Okipa) ceremony; the Pawnee sacrificed a young captive girl to Morning Star. This latter example is expressive of the major life-death-life theme found in farming religions, for the young girl was a personification of the vegetation whose necessary death promotes the growth of plants. Farmers' cultures are more settled, and their religions reflect the complexity of living all

year long in the same place. The intricate religious hierarchy of the Pueblo Indians reflects this complexity.

Religion Today. Passage of the American Indian Religious Freedom Act in 1978 in the United States and the recognition of aboriginal rights in the Canadian constitution have had far-reaching consequences. The search for identity now occurring among American Indians is also a search for religion. This search proceeds in two directions: one which seeks to find an Indian religion that can be shared among all tribes—a pan-Indian religion—and another which attempts to affirm the religious distinctiveness and variety found in each tribe before the first encounters with the Europeans. Current writings take strong stands in support of either of these positions.

Indian religion has always been a vital part of Indian life, and it continues to be. Since the beginning, missionaries and scholars alike have tried to impose their questions and answers on Indian ways of life, which always contained more than they saw. Therefore, Indians have always had to struggle to retain Indian spirituality, Indian sacrality, Indian Christianity, and Indian lifestyles.

Indian religions began as oral traditions. They were sung, danced, spoken, and lived. The written investigations of non-Indians, while valuable in recording a tradition, abstracted that tradition from the people who enlivened it. This orality is still present, contextualizing the everyday religious life of American Indians.

Harmony. Harmony is found in a deep sense of connectedness with the entire universe. Harmony and balance are to be expected and considered normal. One's life (individual and social) is to sustain this harmony among creatures and within space and time. There is harmony among all creatures, living and dead. Names such as Grandmother Spider, Corn Mother, and Coyote the Trickster help indicate this. The entire universe is like an intricate network of family members, each dependent upon each.

There are stories that connect the past and present in such a way that the listener becomes aware of how alive this present world is to its past. When one hears the Inuit story of Sedna the unwilling bride, one becomes aware of how the game animals of the sea grew from the joints of her fingers. When one hears the Pueblo stories of Corn Woman, one sees them reflected in the four colors of corn. The best-known stories of the various Tricksters such as Coyote, Raven, Mink, and Blue Jay help one realize that each of these reorders the universe through its actions and thus returns the surrounding world to the harmony necessary for it to continue. These are not stories that attempt only to connect one to an ancient past; they are stories that enliven the present.

The world is always more than meets the senses. What one experiences is a world which is connected: a harmony of the inner world of one's dreams and visions and the outer world of one's senses. The vision quest of the young teen seeks not so much a spirit as a harmony between the inner self and the surrounding world marked by taking a new name which reflects that harmony. When one is sick, harmony has been destroyed, either because some object has entered into the sick person or because one's inner world has been stolen. The task of the "medicine" man or woman is to bring into balance the inner and outer worlds so that health or wholeness returns.

This same harmony is achieved through prayers, offerings, and ritual actions. Prayers may be short or long but are always seen as creative. In a literate culture the "pen is mightier than the sword"; in an oral culture the spoken word is the creative and ordering word. Offerings are found in many forms, but the pipe ceremony was, and is, one of the most common.

Center of the Circle. Space, time, and inner and outer worlds are all connected in the circle. Circles are sacred for Indians because they reflect and imitate shapes in nature. To be in harmony means to live as part of the circle. When a person stands and thinks of the six directions at equal points around him or her, the person is at the center of a three-dimensional circle.

It is in this knowledge of one's place in the circle that one realizes one's home. The horizon one sees from one's place in the circle reflects that landscape which is home. Land itself is important and central because it is coextensive with one's sense of harmony and thus identity. "Here" includes the waters, the earth, the shape of the horizon, the variations in the weather. That is why so many Indian tribes designate the four points of the compass as important. Directions enable one to know where one lives. In ways of life that focus on the land, on telling the story, and on the harmony between the inner world of dreams and visions and the outer world of hunting or planting, anything can be religious. In the world of today's—

and tomorrow's—American Indians, awareness of one's place within the harmony and interdependence of life will lead to new questions and new answers about Indian religion and life.

—*Nathan R. Kollar*

See also Dances and dancing; Death and mortuary customs; Ethnophilosophy and worldview; Longhouse religion; Maru Cult; Midewiwin; Native American Church; Peyote and peyote religion; Puberty and initiation rites; Religious specialists; Sacred, the; Sacred narratives; Symbolism in art; Totems; Tricksters; Visions and vision quests.

BIBLIOGRAPHY

Deloria, Vine, Jr. *God Is Red*. New York: Grosset & Dunlap, 1973. A plea by an American Indian for recognition of the uniqueness and pervasiveness of Indian life and religion.

Fogelson, Raymond D. "North American Religion: History of Study." In *The Encyclopedia of Religion*, edited by Mircea Eliade. New York: Macmillan, 1986. A summary review of the foundational materials necessary to describe Indian religion.

Gill, Sam D. *Native American Traditions: Sources and Interpretations*. Belmont, Calif.: Wadsworth, 1983. Advocates recognizing the tribal diversity of American Indian religion while striving to discover what is unique to those tribes.

Hultkrantz, Ake. *Belief and Worship in Native North America*. Edited by Christopher Vecsey. Syracuse, N.Y.: Syracuse University Press, 1981. Describes American Indian religion through discussion of supernatural spirits, sacred events, and hunter-agricultural lifestyle influences.

Paper, Jordan. "Methodological Controversies in the Study of Native American Religions." *Studies in Religion/Sciences Religieuses* 22, no. 3 (1993): 365-377. Reviews the state of contemporary studies of Indian religion with an argument for what is pantribal.

Silko, Leslie Marmon. *Ceremony*. New York: Viking Press, 1977. A popular and easy-to-read description of important Indian rituals.

Vecsey, Christopher. *Imagine Ourselves Richly: Mythic Narratives of North American Indians*. New York: Crossroads, 1988. A review and thoughtful commentary on stories that exemplify the oral traditions of American Indians.

Religious specialists

TRIBES AFFECTED: Pantribal

SIGNIFICANCE: Religious specialists such as shamans, priests, elders, and, at times of cultural upheaval, prophets, have all been crucial in guiding and maintaining tribal cultures

Observers of American Indian religions from Western traditions have often focused on aspects of supernaturalism in Indian religions, but that is only one way of approaching it. Another viewpoint emphasizes religion as maintaining harmony and reflecting the interdependence of all life. Both views can provide insights into the roles of religious specialists in Indian cultures.

Specialists and Otherworldly Religions. The supernatural is the realm beyond the natural world of the senses. The natural and supernatural worlds are linked by spirits that move back and forth between the two worlds. These spirits have power to change things in the natural world, and their presence may be sensed through the power inherent in special (sacred) things, people, times, places, words, and actions.

Religious specialists can interact with the spirit world through the use of sacred symbols in a manner that respects both the natural and supernatural worlds. The religious specialist's title differs from tribe to tribe. The following discussion will use terms (such as shaman and priest) devised by academic theorists to describe American Indian religions as they existed before contact with European Christian religions and, in the case of prophets, as they changed after contact.

Shamans. Mircea Eliade's 1964 description of the shaman has left its imprint on all descriptions of religious specialization. He described religious specialists who, through the use of trances, leave their bodies to go to a supernatural world to bring back techniques for dealing with the problems of the everyday world. Shamans may be selected a number of ways. Their own ecstatic experience may mark them as shamans; they may inherit the role from a parent or other ancestry. They may also be chosen by the people themselves. Once they are chosen, they are taught how to interact with the spirit world through dreams, visions, or trances and through traditional techniques learned from other shamans.

In general, a shaman undergoes an ecstatic experience in order to gain a spiritual status so as to practice divination and healing. In North America, however, ecstatic techniques are seldom used outside the Subarctic and Pacific Northwest as a consistent technique for dealing with the spirit world. Nevertheless, a set of common traits can be offered which more or less are found in certain people in each tribe. It should be noted that shaman is not a word often used by American Indians to describe these people.

Certain individuals profess to have a supernatural power that they use in this natural world. Sometimes this power is obtained in an initiatory vision. Such initiatory visions are especially found among the Inuit, where the shamans describe themselves as going to a supernatural world and, through great trial, gaining certain knowledge and techniques which are beneficial to their people. Part of this knowledge and technique is reflected in the use of esoteric language and rituals that are used to manipulate the spirit world and its powers. This power, as expressed in esoteric formulas, charms, songs, and certain objects, is often translated into English as "medicine." "Medicine" therefore is the power of the supernatural world as found in these words, chants, rituals, and objects. Many of these objects are beautiful and could be considered works of art; others are rather common looking. The Crow medicine bundle might contain feathers, bird and animal skins, animal and human bones, teeth, herbs, pigments, and minerals. Outside the tribal religious context, these things appear valueless. Yet within its religious context, such a bundle contains the history, power, and authority of an ancient people.

This power and knowledge are used by the shaman to predict the future and decide a course of action for individuals or the entire tribe. A shaman is thought to be able to control the weather, game animals, the course of war, and the search for lost objects. Among the Inuit, for example, Sedna, who lives under the sea, is the mistress of animals. The shaman helps control the hunt by going to Sedna and caring for her. The shaman many times has to clean her hair, which has become filthy because of the people's breaking of taboos, so that she will allow the animals to be captured.

The ability to tell the future is demonstrated by Plains shamans in the Shaking Tent Ceremony. In this ceremony the shaman enters a tent and reads the messages communicated by the spirits through the shaking of the tent. Among the Algonquian peoples, divination many times occurs by scorching an animal's shoulder blade and reading the resultant cracks and spots to determine the future.

There are other individuals who use supernatural powers to deal with sickness and wounds. Within a supernaturalist perspective, sickness results either from some object entering the body or from one's spirit leaving the body. The shaman has techniques to deal with either of these causes of illness. The object in one's body may be there either because a person put it there or because an illness, with a spirit life of its own, enters the body. The common ritual for withdrawing the evil object is to suck it out, with a tube, a horn, or one's mouth. Sometimes the extracted object is shown to everyone; sometimes it is not. Contending with the spirit life that somehow is not in the body is a more complex affair. The shaman many times must go into a trance, enter the spirit world, and fight for the person's life spirit to deal with this type of illness. These trances involve dramatic rituals that usually fill spectators and patient alike with a sense of awe and mystery.

Shamans are essential to all tribes; some are recognized and honored for their role, while others are feared and avoided for the power they possess. The *ichta* among the Tlingit (in British Columbia and the Yukon) is an example of a shaman who lives at the edge of society. He is dirty, his hair is unkempt, and his dress is rags. He has a number of masks, however, each of which represents and attracts a particular spirit. His power depends upon his ability to control these spirits. By going into a trance and dancing like an animal, he achieves his objectives.

A shaman's power can be used for good or for evil; it is beyond the ordinary or natural means of control. In many traditional North American cultures, the shamanic role is usually open to men and women. Males generally predominate except in California, where there are more female shamans. While the shamanic roles are, for the most part, played by individuals, there are some shamanic societies. The midewiwin of the central Algonquian is an example of a shamanic society. Depending on the tribe, these societies act as carriers of knowledge, as sharers of power, and as necessary helpers in achieving certain ceremonial objectives.

A quick survey of the various American Indian cultural areas reveals that among the Inuit the shaman is closest to the now-classic model of Eliade (Eliade based his model on the study of Siberian tribes). They work individually or in groups through the use of ecstasy and dramatic performances to cure, control the weather, and procure game. Among the Northwest Coast Indians, techniques of ecstasy are less common. There is a shamanic festival during the winter months among some Northwest Coast Indians in which dramatic canoe journeys are taken into the spirit world to struggle with the spirits to win back the souls of the sufferers gathered at the ceremony.

The Basin, Plateau, and Northern California areas find the sucking techniques of great importance to the shaman. The costumes assume more importance there than in other shamanic areas. Although visions and trances are expected of many individuals among the Plains and Prairie Indians, shamans stand out in how their spiritual power shows itself in their celebration of public ritual, tipi decoration, and the medicine bundles. The Southwest has a complex culture with a mix of various spiritual specialists, including priests.

Priests. Another type of religious specialist is the priest. The priest stands as a constant intermediary between the natural and supernatural worlds. In societies that emphasize hunting as a means of subsistence, there is a sense in which every hunter may be considered a priest. Through ritual action, the hunter balances the needs of both worlds so that the natural world sustains its ability to provide the tribe with food and security. Hunting is a sacred responsibility wherein killing animals is a religious act that makes the hunter into a priest. The hunter must be careful of taboos and must show proper respect for the spirits. The Blackfoot hunter, for example, gained his role in the tribe through a vision quest. In his vision or dream he found his role as hunter and his connection with the spirit world; the weapons became part of the spirit world revealed to him in the dream.

In an agricultural society priests play a unique role. The Pueblo Indians of the American Southwest, for example, are an agricultural society with a significant priestly class of religious specialists. Pueblo life is one of rich ceremony which is woven into every part of the day and is manifested in all tribal members' relationships with others. Each Pueblo town has an independent society of priests in charge of the rituals.

A general rule, with many exceptions, is that shamans dominate hunter societies and priests dominate agricultural societies. There is another type of religious specialist who has helped American Indians to respond to the challenge of change in their way of life—the prophet.

Prophets. In 1925, sociologist Max Weber provided a topology used by many in discussing religious specialization. He wrote of three types of religious leaders: magicians, prophets, and priests. The description of the shaman used here includes many of the characteristics of what Weber would call the magician. Priests influence the spirit world by worship and petition; shamans influence it by the power of their spells and personal skills; priests are supported by the entire tribe and exercise their functions regularly; shamans work on an individual basis and do what is needed when it is needed; priests are powerful because of the class to which they belong and the

techniques they learn; shamans' power comes from their personal experience. Both priest and shaman are part of the everyday life of the tribe. In times of crisis there arises another specialist whom Weber calls the prophet.

Prophets are agents of change who take personal responsibility for breaking with the established way of doing things. Prophets claim to know what to do because of their visions. Much like shamans, prophets find their role in life through their visions; unlike shamans they receive no remuneration for what they do. The fulfillment of the prophet's vision is its own reward.

There have been many prophets since first contact: San Juan Tewa of the Pueblo people (1680), Neolin of the Delaware (1750's), Handsome Lake of the Seneca (1799), Tenskwatawa of the Shawnee (1811), Smohalla of the Wanapum (1855), Wodziwob of the Northern Paiute (1860's), John Slocum of the Puget Sound Salish (1880's). From these prophets and many more there came a common message: The ways of white culture were evil, a return to the ancient ways as described by the prophet was necessary for the salvation of the tribe, and strict codes of morality must be enforced. The message was ritualized in many different ways. The prophets and the religions which flowed from them have been a significant force in revitalizing the religions of American Indians.

Beyond the Supernatural: Harmony. A description of Indian religions from a supernaturalist perspective, while valuable and founded on large amounts of written material gathered by non-Indian researchers, is dualistic. It has a bias in that it tends to focus on what is, or was, important to the European Christian: God, spirits, the other world, the power to change things, and a deeply felt conversion experience. The supernaturalist description many times leaves one with the impression that Indian religions are dualistic, with the spirits "out there" in the supernatural world and the shaman, prophet, priest here in the natural world. This is a religious model very much dependent upon European Christianity. Indian religion can be better described not in a dualistic sense but by using a holistic model of harmony and interdependence. An essential characteristic of Indian religions has been their oral character. Any non-Indian religion had to adapt itself to this orality to make any deep and significant headway into the Indian way of life. An oral culture recognizes the need of interdependence and harmony among the generations for its continuance; the need to live in the circle of life for the continuance of life itself. This is best shown in the central role of the elders.

Elders and Other Specialists. One's age is very important in Indian culture. Most tribes have some form of initiation of the young, for example, which often corresponds to the beginning of religious awareness and the acceptance of religious responsibilities. There are many rites of passage which give social form to the necessity of bringing the young more deeply into what is required for community survival.

Many tribes have formal religious societies into which individuals are initiated. These societies are sources of religious authority in the tribe. Members of the Crow Tobacco Society, the Winnebago Midewiwin, and the Tewa "Made People" bear enormous responsibility for religious actions.

Elders are especially important because with them resides religious wisdom, religious memory, and religious experience. In an oral culture the elders bring the "how, what, and why" of the past into the present in order to forge the future. Without the elders there is no religion and no purpose and direction to life; in a sense, without their guidance there can be no tribe.

An oral culture also places great emphasis on storytellers. These religious specialists tell the stories which provide explanations for the why and how of present living. There are the stories told by the elders, but in many tribes there are also individuals who specialize in storytelling. Among the Zuni an individual is appointed as Kyaklo, responsible for telling the creation story cycle. Once every four or eight years Kyaklo comes to a Zuni village to tell the story. No Zuni ever hears the entire story in one telling, yet the story is told. In an oral culture telling the story or stories is essential to religious life. Although these stories may deal with everyday life and the reasons for its existence, they are religious since they provide a purposeful direction and unity to individual and social living.

The same is true of the Indian sense of place and home. Land itself is important and central because it is coextensive with one's sense of harmony and thus identity. "Here" includes the waters, the earth, the shape of the horizon, and the variations in the weather. That is why so many Indian tribes give a religious meaning to the four points of the compass. Directions enable one to know where one lives. The stories reinforce the sense of place. Those who tell the stories, build the homes, and provide for "home" are religious specialists. In the Tlingit religion, for example, the house is a ceremonial and spatial representation of the special landscape. The house is a holy place dwelt in by the most recent expression of the ancestor, the *yitsati*. The house is the male domain. The wife does not know the meanings of the carvings inside the house. Childbirth happens outside the house. The keeper of the house (yitsati) is a priest whose only task is to perform the rituals associated with the house. —*Nathan R. Kollar*

See also Dances and dancing; Death and mortuary customs; Ethnophilosophy and worldview; Longhouse religion; Maru Cult; Medicine and modes of curing, pre-contact; Midewiwin; Native American Church; Peyote and peyote religion; Puberty and initiation rites; Religion; Sacred, the; Sacred narratives; Symbolism in art; Totems; Tricksters; Visions and vision quests.

BIBLIOGRAPHY

Eliade, Mircea. *Shamanism: Archaic Techniques of Ecstasy.* Rev. ed. Princeton, N.J.: Princeton University Press, 1964. This is the classic work on shamanism.

Gill, Sam D. *Native American Religions: An Introduction.* Belmont, Calif.: Wadsworth, 1982. Gill is an exponent of how investigators have read into the written materials their own desires about Indian religion. He should be read to balance the exaggerated romantic claims for a historical pan-Indian religion.

Hultkrantz, Ake. "Spirit Lodge: A North American Shamanistic Seance." In *Studies in Shamanism*, edited by Carl-Martin Edsman. Stockholm: Almquist & Wiksell, 1962. Various definitions of shamanism are reviewed which lead one to conclude, if one uses ecstasy as a normative, that the term "shaman" can be used only in a broad sense when dealing with North America.

Paper, Jordan. "Methodological Controversies in the Study of Native American Religions." *Studies in Religion/Sciences Religieuses* 22, no. 3 (1993): 365-377. Argues that because of the dynamic character of Indian religion the individual religions adapted and shared what was necessary for survival. Thus there are common religious elements today among the various tribal religions.

Weber, Max. *Economy and Society: An Outline of Interpretative Sociology.* Translated by Ephraim Fischoff et al., edited by Günther Roth and Claus Wittich. Berkeley: University of California Press, 1978. Weber provided religious studies with practical categories for discerning religious leadership.

Relocation

TRIBES AFFECTED: Pantribal

SIGNIFICANCE: Though the relocation program launched by the U.S. government in the 1950's did not achieve its goal of assimilation, it did contribute to the rapid urbanization of Native Americans

The 1930's saw a departure in federal Indian policy from the usual goal of assimilating Indians into the mainstream of American society; instead, the "Indian New Deal" stressed the idea of tribal self-determination. After World War II, however, Congress and the Bureau of Indian Affairs (BIA) began to press for a return to assimilation. In the early 1950's several assimilationist policies emerged: termination, which sought to "free" Native Americans by dissolving their tribes; the assumption by the states of more legal jurisdiction over Indian communities; and relocation, which sought to move Indians to large cities. Although at the time termination gained the most attention, relocation proved more persistent and had the more lasting effect.

Planning and Implementation. The BIA began its relocation efforts on a small scale in 1948, with efforts to place Navajos, whose reservation was believed to be overcrowded, in western cities. In 1952 the program was expanded into the national Voluntary Relocation Program. Offices were established on most reservations and in Oklahoma. BIA agents working on a quota system employed a hard-sell approach as they pressured Indians to relocate. Los Angeles, Chicago, and Denver were first designated to receive the new urban dwellers; seven other western and midwestern cities were later added to the list. Indians were sometimes sent to more distant cities on purpose in the hope that distance would lessen tribal ties.

Indians volunteering for the program were given a month to prepare for the transition. When the time came, they were given one-way bus or train tickets, fifty dollars each to cover

COME TO DENVER

THE CHANCE OF YOUR LIFETIME !

Good Jobs

Retail Trade

Manufacturing

Government-Federal, State, Local

Wholesale Trade

Construction of Buildings, Etc.

Happy Homes

Beautiful Houses

Many Churches

Exciting Community Life.

Over Half of Homes Owned by Residents

Convenient Stores-Shopping Centers

Training

Vocational Training
Auto Mech., Beauty Shop, Drafting,
Nursing, Office Work, Watchmaking
Adult Education
Evening High School, Arts and Crafts
Job Improvement, Home-making

Beautiful Colorado

"Tallest" State, 48 Mt. Peaks Over 14,000 Ft.

350 Days Sunshine, Mild Winters

Zoos, Museums, Mountain Parks, Drives

Picnic Areas, Lakes, Amusement Parks

Big Game Hunting, Trout Fishing, Camping

A Bureau of Indian Affairs relocation poster promising good jobs and happy homes. (National Archives) moving expenses, and modest sums for subsistence. Once arrived in their new home cities, they received help from the local relocation office in finding housing and employment and a month's financial assistance (forty dollars a week for an individual or couple).

Urban Problems. The experience of many participants in the program often ended in frustration. Most reservation Indians were poorly prepared for life in urban America. Coming from cultures that were communal and cooperative, many found it hard to adjust to the impersonal and competitive character of metropolitan life. The BIA often provided little job training and inadequate counseling. Many Indians found that they could obtain only menial or temporary jobs. Too often, those relocating found themselves becoming slum dwellers cut off from family and friends. Alcoholism became a particular problem. The death in 1955 of war hero Ira Hayes, a Pima whose life was shattered by despair and alcoholism after he was relocated to Chicago, brought attention to the problems often faced by the new urban Indians. By 1959, a third of those participating in the program had returned to the reservation.

The BIA attempted to respond to mounting criticism of the program. Relocation officials began to moderate their sales pitches in the later 1950's, and more attention was given to preparing participants prior to departure. The program continued to attract criticism, however, and many Native Americans closely associated it with the widely hated policy of termination. After the latter policy was ended in 1962, relocation continued. During the John F. Kennedy Administration, the program's name and focus was changed to one of employment assistance. More attention was paid to job training, and more of an effort was made to place Indians in cities closer to their reservations.

Impact of Relocation. As a program to foster the assimilation of Indians into American society, relocation largely failed to achieve its aim. Yet, in other ways, some of them paradoxical, the program had important influences on Native American life.

The most evident effect of the program was to foster one of the most important Indian demographic trends of the second half of the twentieth century: urbanization. Despite the difficulties they encountered, Indians continued to move to urban areas. In 1940 only about 7 percent of Indians lived in cities; by 1980 almost half did, and by 1990 a majority lived in metropolitan areas. There is some irony in the fact that the majority of Indians who moved to cities did so on their own and not as program participants, largely because of suspicion of the BIA and the tendency to associate relocation with termination. The relocation program, however, did contribute to this informal migration. More than thirty-five thousand Indians relocated under the program, and the cities to which they moved (the ones with relocation offices) became the main centers of Native American urbanization.

Regardless of whether they were program participants, urban Indians continued to have more than their share of social problems. They also tended to be less tolerant of substandard conditions and more critical of government policies than reservation Indians. It is not surprising that many of the leaders of the more radical Indian movements of the 1960's and 1970's had urban backgrounds. Moreover, urbanization contributed to the growth of pan-Indianism. By bringing together Indians of many different tribal backgrounds, the relocation program encouraged interaction among them and the discovery that they shared many problems. It may be the greatest irony of relocation that this assimilationist program fostered instead a greater sense of Indian separateness and encouraged a more activist and confrontational attitude toward the federal government.

—William C. Lowe

See also Alcoholism; Bureau of Indian Affairs (BIA); Demography; Employment and unemployment; Hayes, Ira Hamilton; Termination policy; Urban Indians.

BIBLIOGRAPHY

Burt, Larry W. *Tribalism in Crisis: Federal Indian Policy, 1953-61*. Albuquerque: University of New Mexico Press, 1982.

Fixico, Donald L. *Termination and Relocation: Federal Policy, 1945-1966*. Albuquerque: University of New Mexico Press, 1986.

Olson, James S., and Raymond Wilson. *Native Americans in the Twentieth Century*. Provo, Utah: Brigham Young University Press, 1984.

Prucha, Francis Paul. *The Great Father: The United States Government and the American Indians*. 2 vols. Lincoln: University of Nebraska Press, 1984.

Sorkin, Alan L. *The Urban American Indian*. Lexington, Mass.: D.C. Heath, 1978.

Weddell, Jack O., and O. Michael Watson, eds. *The Indian in Urban Society*. Boston: Little, Brown, 1971.

Removal

TRIBES AFFECTED: Tribes located east of the Mississippi River

SIGNIFICANCE: Removal of the eastern Indian tribes marked the culmination of two centuries of dispossession of American Indians east of the Mississippi River

First suggested by President Thomas Jefferson in 1803, Indian removal, or the exchange of land by tribes east of the Mississippi for western lands, was originally intended by some as a means of protecting Indians from corruption and demoralization resulting from white encroachment. Among its proponents were several prominent humanitarians seeking to protect Indian culture. Removal was made policy, however, by President Andrew Jackson in 1830 as a direct response to pressures mounted by individual states to acquire Indian lands within their borders.

Removal Act. The impetus for removal legislation came principally from Georgia, which in 1802 had ceded its western land claims in exchange for a federal promise to extinguish Cherokee claims within its borders. The spread of cotton agriculture, facilitated by the invention of the cotton gin in 1796, and the discovery of gold on Cherokee land in 1829 exacerbated Georgia's impatience. After passing legislation which extended Georgia law to the Cherokee Nation, Georgia's bid to gain Cherokee land was sanctioned by Jackson. He was unsympathetic to the Cherokees, who had lodged their objections in Congress. The Indian Removal Act, signed into law on May 28, 1830, provided for the removal of all Indian tribes east of the Mississippi, thus culminating a process of dispossession begun with the earliest English settlement of North America. Disease, wars, demoralization, land speculation, and treaty violations had already severely depopulated Indians in the east by the end of the eighteenth century. Dense settlements of Indians still remained in the nineteenth century, however, including the Five Civilized Tribes of the southeast.

Cherokee Land Cases. The most strenuous resistance to the Indian Removal Act sprang from the most thoroughly "civilized" of the eastern Indian tribes, the Cherokee. In 1819, acquiescing to missionary lobbying, Congress passed an act which provided for "civilizing" the Indians. Mission schools were founded to teach Indians the purported benefits of sedentary agriculture, private property, and American social customs. The Cherokee Nation, in an effort to retain its ancestral lands, successfully embraced white traditions. Through the aid of a self-educated Cherokee, Sequoyah, who invented a syllabary, the Cherokees published a newspaper, adopted a representative government, and drafted a constitution patterned after that of the United States. When Georgia extended its state laws to the Cherokee Nation and seized Cherokee land, the Cherokees first protested to Congress and subsequently appealed to the United States Supreme Court. While previously the federal government had made treaties with Indian tribes as if they were sovereign nations, the constitutional status of Indians was nebulous. In two Supreme Court cases, *Cherokee Nation v. Georgia* (1831) and *Worcester v. Georgia* (1832), Chief Justice John Marshall defined Indian tribes as distinct political nations whose land was to be federally protected. Jackson, however, refused to exercise his executive authority in enforcing the Court's decision, and the Cherokees ultimately were forced to abandon their lands.

Impact. Ostensibly, removal was designed to protect Indian culture by providing tribes with land which they would forever retain that was far enough removed from white settlement to ensure non-interference. In practice, however, Indians ceded their ancestral lands for land in the west which was often of marginal quality or was in many cases already populated. Some tribes were forced to negotiate repeatedly, often moving several times after their initial relocation. Furthermore, Indians were virtually powerless to protect their treaty rights, and the American government was unwilling to uphold treaties in the face of white land hunger. Not all Indians were forced to move. Individuals could accept land allotments and remain east as American citizens; however, the fate of those choosing to remain was often precarious, as land speculators and squatters frequently cheated Indians of their land.

While the Indian Removal Act applied to all eastern Indian tribes, the Cherokee ordeal illustrates the brutality of Jackson's policy and his determination to enforce removal against Indian

resistance. In 1832, celebrating an apparent victory in Marshall's decision in *Worcester v. Georgia*, the majority of Cherokees refused to negotiate for removal. Jackson nevertheless authorized a treaty with an Indian minority party that favored swift removal. Thus in 1835 the Treaty Party, led by Elias Boudinot, Stand Watie, and Major Ridge signed a removal treaty which was clearly illegal but was enforced by Jackson. The subsequent forced marches of the Cherokees to Indian Territory became known as the Trail of Tears as a consequence of deprivation and brutality resulting in several thousand deaths.

While nineteenth century controversies surrounding removal focused on the Five Civilized Tribes, the small but numerous bands of Indians living in the north were also subject to removal. With the exception of some who migrated to Canada, their fate differed little materially from that of the southern tribes, and many also were forced to relocate several times before reaching their final destinations.

The impact of removal on Indian culture was demoralization and destruction. Shifts in geographical locations often eroded their culture and rendered subsistence patterns obsolete. In addition, Indians often faced hostile welcomes from western tribes. Ultimately, treaties were broken by the United States government as the whites' inexorable population growth and westward movement stimulated their interest in even the most marginal Indian lands. —*Mary E. Virginia*

See also Cherokee; Chickasaw; Choctaw; Creek; Indian Removal Act; Indian Territory; Indian-white relations—U.S., 1775-1830; Indian-white relations—U.S., 1831-1870; Seminole; Trail of Tears.

BIBLIOGRAPHY

Anderson, William L., ed. *Cherokee Removal: Before and After*. Athens: University of Georgia Press, 1991.

Burke, Joseph C. "The Cherokee Cases: A Study in Law, Politics, and Morality." *Stanford Law Review* 21 (1969): 500-531.

McLoughlin, William G. *After the Trail of Tears: The Cherokees Struggle for Sovereignty, 1839-1880*. Chapel Hill: University of North Carolina Press, 1993.

Prucha, Francis Paul. *The Great Father: The United States Government and the American Indians*. Vol 1. Lincoln: University of Nebraska Press, 1984.

_____. *Indian Policy in the United States: Historical Essays*. Lincoln: University of Nebraska Press, 1981.

Satz, Ronald N. *American Indian Policy in the Jacksonian Era*. Lincoln: University of Nebraska Press, 1975.

Renville, Joseph (c. 1779, near present-day St. Paul, Minn.—c. 1846, Lac Qui Parle, Minn.): Interpreter, guide, trader

TRIBAL AFFILIATION: Sioux

SIGNIFICANCE: Renville was an influential white sympathizer among the Minnesota Sioux

Born and reared until age ten in an Indian village south of present-day St. Paul, Minnesota, Renville was the son of a

French trader and a Sioux woman. After being sent to Montreal at age ten to receive a Catholic education, he returned to Minnesota a few years later to become a trader. At age nineteen he was employed by the Hudson's Bay Company.

During his young adulthood, Renville was a guide and interpreter for Zebulon Pike, traveling with him as he sought the headwaters of the Mississippi River and aiding him in establishing peace treaties with the Sioux.

Renville served as a captain for the British army during the War of 1812. While living in Canada, both during and after the war, he was an interpreter for the British government.

After returning to Minnesota shortly after the war, he helped found the Columbia Fur Company. At his trading post at Lac Qui Parle, Renville trained an armed company of Sioux to guard against attacks by the hostile Ojibwas. In 1834, he helped found a Presbyterian mission at Lac Qui Parle, and in 1837 he aided missionaries in translating the Bible into Sioux. Many of Renville's descendants, including his nephew, Gabriel Renville, continued his tradition of support for whites.

See also Missions and missionaries; Sioux; Trade; Trading posts.

Reservation system of the United States

TRIBES AFFECTED: Pantribal

SIGNIFICANCE: As the United States expanded and increasing numbers of white Americans moved westward, the confinement of American Indians to reservations was deemed the most efficient way to separate Indians and whites while allowing whites access to the greatest amount of land

In colonial times and the earliest years of the United States, there was little thought given to the need for a permanent answer to the competition for land between Europeans and Native Americans. Because there were vast uncharted areas of wilderness to the west, it was generally thought that the Indian population could be pushed westward—eventually, across the Mississippi—whenever problems arose. This was the main policy of the pre-Civil war era, as eastern tribes were "removed" westward, many to land in present-day Oklahoma.

The movement to place all Indians on reservations began in earnest after the Civil War during the presidency of Ulysses S. Grant. The policy came about because of the failure of previous programs and the desire of white Americans to open more western land for white settlement. From the end of the American Revolution to 1830, Indian tribes had been treated as if they were foreign nations within the United States. The federal government sent ambassadors to negotiate treaties with the tribes, and many groups such as the Cherokees in northern Georgia, had established their own governments and states within the United States. Others had traded territory in the East for land farther west. Trouble began in Georgia after the discovery of gold on Indian land. Eventually, Congress passed a law, supported by Andrew Jackson, offering territory west of the Mississippi River to tribes willing to relinquish their lands in the East. All Indians would have to accept this trade or face forced removal. Several wars and the infamous Trail of Tears,

which saw the deaths of thousands of Native Americans, followed the imposition of this removal policy.

Early Reservation Policy. Most of the new Indian lands were in the Plains region—or the "Great American Desert," as whites, who at first believed that it was too hot and dry for farming, called it. In the 1840's, thousands of white settlers began crossing this "desert" on their way to California and Oregon. Travel through Indian Territory could be dangerous and difficult because of Indian attacks, so travelers and settlers called for a safe corridor to be maintained by the army. From this proposal a concentration policy developed, under which Indians would be driven into southern and northern colonies with a wide, safe passageway to the Pacific in the middle. These Indian enclaves, it was said, would be safe from white settlement. In the early 1860's, these Indian lands were closed to all whites except those on official business. In 1869 Congress created a Board of Indian Affairs within the Department of the Interior to control the reservations, and two years later ended the policy of treating Indians as residents of foreign states within the United States. On March 3, 1871, the Indian Appropriation Act declared that tribal affairs would be managed by the U.S. government without consent of the tribes.

Indians were supposed to have enough land on their reservations so that they could continue to hunt, but this idea lasted only briefly as land hunger among white farmers and ranchers after the Civil War led to demands for greatly reducing the size of Indian Territory. If Indians learned to farm rather than hunt, Indian affairs commissioners and congressmen (and most whites) believed, more land could be put to productive use, and the natives would give up their "wild" ways and enjoy the fruits of civilization. Indians were given a choice: Either they could relocate, or volunteer armies would be recruited to force them to move. On the reservations, Indians were to get education for their children, rations from the government until they knew how to grow their own crops, and certain other benefits. By 1877 more than 100,000 Indians had received rations on reservations.

Reservation education programs did not work quickly enough to satisfy many in Congress; additionally, some claimed, they cost too much money. Maintaining a large army in the West to keep Indians within their boundaries also proved expensive. The notion that Indians would become farmers proved false. Congress reacted to these problems by reducing rations, which caused terrible suffering and malnutrition among Indians, and by reducing the number of reservations as more tribes were moved into Indian Territory (Oklahoma). The federal government mandated that all Indian males receiving rations would have to work, but since few jobs existed on Indian lands this policy proved a miserable failure. To improve education and help Indians become more like whites, Congress commanded that all instruction take place in English and that the teaching of Indian religions be banned.

General Allotment Act. In 1887 Congress changed Indian policy by passing the General Allotment Act (Dawes Severalty Act). Designed by Senator Henry Dawes of Massachusetts,

Crow Indians gathered to be paid annuities in exchange for agreeing to live on a reservation. (National Archives)

who considered himself a friend of the Indians, the new policy provided for an eventual end to the reservation system and the abolition of tribal organizations. In the future, Indians would be treated as individuals, not as members of tribes. Each head of a family would be allotted 160 acres of reservation land, and each adult single person would get 80 acres. The government would keep this land in trust for twenty-five years, and at the end of that period Indians would get title to the land and full citizenship rights. Land on reservations not distributed to Indians would be declared surplus land and could be sold to the highest bidder.

When the bill was passed, there were about 138 million acres of land on reservations. Between 1887 and 1900, Indians had been allotted only 3,285,000 of those acres, while almost 30 million acres were declared surplus and ceded to whites. In addition, of the 32,800 Indian families and individuals getting allotments, fewer than one-third managed to remain on their land for the required twenty-five years to attain full ownership. The program was never applied among the Indians of the Southwest, and these were the tribes most successful in retain-

ing their traditional cultures. In 1891 Indians received the right to lease their lands for agriculture, grazing cattle, and mining. The pressure for leases from cattle ranchers and mining companies was enormous, and hundreds of thousands of acres found their way to white control through leasing provisions that took advantage of Indian poverty. Many reformers and politicians denounced leasing, but only because it made Indians who lived off their leases idle—not because it took advantage of them and made them poor.

Between 1900 and 1921 Congress made it easier for Indians to dispose of their allotments. A 1907 law, for example, gave Indians considered too old, sick, or "incompetent" to work on their land permission to sell their land to whomever they wished. White reservation agents decided questions of competency. Under this program millions more acres were lost as impoverished Indians sold their property at very low prices just to survive. This policy was speeded up in 1917 under the "New Policy" of Indian Commissioner Cato Sells, who declared that all adults one-half or less Indian were "competent," as were all graduates of Indian schools once they reached

RESERVATIONS WITH HIGHEST AMERICAN INDIAN POPULATIONS, 1990

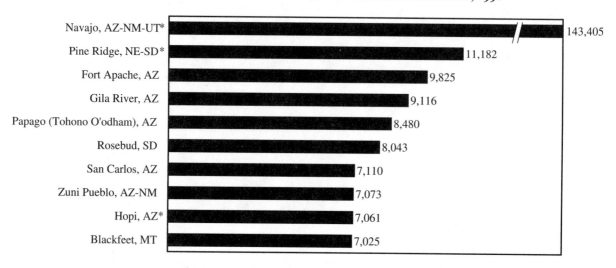

Navajo, AZ-NM-UT*	143,405
Pine Ridge, NE-SD*	11,182
Fort Apache, AZ	9,825
Gila River, AZ	9,116
Papago (Tohono O'odham), AZ	8,480
Rosebud, SD	8,043
San Carlos, AZ	7,110
Zuni Pueblo, AZ-NM	7,073
Hopi, AZ*	7,061
Blackfeet, MT	7,025

Source: U.S. Bureau of the Census, *We, the First Americans.* Washington, D.C.: U.S. Government Printing Office, 1993.
*Includes trust lands.

twenty-one years of age. Under this policy more than twenty-one thousand Indians gained control of their lands but then quickly lost them because they could not afford to pay state property taxes or went bankrupt. This policy was reversed in 1921, but Indians faced new problems as the federal government in the 1920's moved to end all responsibility over Indians.

In 1923, John Collier, a white reformer, became executive secretary of the Indian Defense Association, the major lobby defending Native American interests before Congress. Collier believed Indian civilization, especially Pueblo culture, to be superior in many ways to the materialistic, violent society found in the United States and Europe. For the first time, under Collier's leadership, Indians presented a program to Congress aimed at preserving their traditional values and way of life. Reservations, it was argued, had to be retained to save these old ways but needed economic assistance to survive. Collier's program called for civil liberties for Indians, including religious freedom and tribal self-government.

The "Indian New Deal." In 1928 the Bureau of Indian Affairs (BIA) issued an influential report by Lewis Meriam, a student of Indian culture. In *The Problem of Indian Administration*, Meriam criticized American policy, condemned the General Allotment Act, and concluded that the BIA showed little interest in retaining Indian culture. The report advocated spending more money for economic assistance and suggested that the aid go directly to local tribal councils. The councils, rather than BIA officials, should decide how to spend the funds. Meriam called for a policy of cultural pluralism: Native Americans should be allowed to live by their old customs and values if they chose.

The Great Depression hit Indian reservations, particularly the poorest in South Dakota, Oklahoma, Arizona, and New Mexico, very hard. By 1933 thousands of Indians faced starvation, according to reports from the Emergency Relief Administration. President Franklin D. Roosevelt appointed John Collier to lead the Bureau of Indian Affairs and deal with the crisis. Collier, with the president's help, pushed the Indian Reorganization Act through Congress in 1934. This law radically changed Indian-white relations and gave Native Americans control of their lands; it was nicknamed the Indian New Deal. The law ended the allotment system, gave local councils authority to spend relief money, and allowed Indians to practice traditional religions and customs. Congress increased appropriations for reservations from twelve million dollars to an average of forty-eight million dollars while Collier held his post. The commissioner had his critics, mainly advocates of assimilation and western senators and congressmen fearful of Indian self-rule. In 1944 the House Indian Affairs Committee criticized Collier's policy and called for a return to the old idea of making Indians into Americans. The next year Collier resigned, and many of his programs ended.

Policy Since World War II. Creation of the Indian Claims Commission in 1946, which was empowered by Congress to settle all Indian land claims against the government, resulted in victories for some tribes. Between 1946 and 1960 the commission awarded more than 300 million dollars to Indian tribes wrongfully deprived of their lands, but Congress saw this as an excuse to end other assistance to reservations. Some BIA officials foresaw the abolition of the reservation system. In the 1950's relocation became a popular idea. More than sixty thousand Indians were moved to cities such as Denver, Chicago, and Houston. To save money and hasten the end of separate development for Native Americans, Commissioner Dillon S. Meyer took away powers of tribal councils and returned decisions concerning spending to BIA headquarters.

In 1953 Congress terminated federal control over Indians living on reservations in California, Florida, Iowa, New York, and Texas. The states now had criminal and legal jurisdiction over the tribes. Results proved disastrous, especially after removal of federal liquor control laws. Unemployment and poverty increased under the termination program. The BIA tried to resolve the unemployment problem by expanding the relocation program, hoping that jobless Indians would find work in cities, but by 1958 more than half of the relocated workers had returned to the reservations.

In the 1960's Congress reversed direction yet again and revoked the termination policy. During the federal government's War on Poverty, it increased tribal funds for education, health care, and job training. Expanded federal aid greatly improved living conditions for Indians, and reservation population increased from 367,000 in 1962 to 452,000 in 1968. Life expectancy improved from a dismal 51 years (1940) to 63.5 (1968), not yet up to white American levels but a great improvement nevertheless. In 1975 the Indian Self-Determination and Education Assistance Act gave tribes control over school funds and returned most important economic decision-making powers to locally elected councils. Three years later Congress established a community college system

on reservations in which native languages, religions, and cultures were taught.

The American Indian Religious Freedom Act (1978) protected traditional practices, and the Supreme Court advanced Indian self-determination by authorizing tribal courts to try and punish even non-Indians for violations of the law committed on Indian territory. In a key ruling in 1978 the Court said that tribes could be governed by traditional laws even if they conflicted with state and federal laws. In the 1980's such ideas of separate development continued to dominate reservation policy, and the Reagan Administration followed a policy of "government-to-government relationships" among the states, the federal government, and the tribes. In many ways this "new" policy greatly resembled ideas first enunciated by George Washington in 1794, when Americans also doubted the possibility of assimilation and opted for a policy of pluralism and cultural separation. Although a few reservations have become quite rich because of the lease or sale of mineral rights, most remain very poor. When a Bureau of the Census study of poverty in the United States in the 1980's listed the ten poorest counties in the union, eight of them were on reservations. Cultural self-determination, improved education, and increased financial assistance had not yet improved economic conditions for many Native Americans. Reservations in South Dakota and New Mexico were the poorest; they also had the highest levels of alcoholism, divorce, and drug addiction found anywhere in the United States.

—*Leslie V. Tischauser*

See also Allotment system; American Indian Policy Review Commission; Councils, tribal; Courts, tribal; Employment and unemployment; General Allotment Act; Indian police and judges; Indian Reorganization Act; Indian Rights Association; Indian Self-Determination and Education Assistance Act; Relocation; Reserve system of Canada; Termination policy; Urban Indians.

BIBLIOGRAPHY

Brandon, William. *The Indian in American Culture.* New York: Harper & Row, 1974. A massive volume covering Indian-white relations since the beginning; includes an interesting discussion of reservation policy. Includes a good index.

Fritz, Henry E. *The Movement for Indian Assimilation, 1860-1890.* Philadelphia: University of Pennsylvania Press, 1963. A comprehensive analysis of government policy in the critical period when assimilation policy was the order of the day.

Priest, Benson. *Uncle Sam's Stepchildren: The Reformation of United States Indian Policy, 1885-1887.* New Brunswick, N.J.: Rutgers University Press, 1942. An old but still useful discussion of the origins of the General Allotment Act (Dawes Act).

Washburn, Wilcomb E., ed. *History of Indian-White Relations.* Vol. 4 in *Handbook of North American Indians.* Washington, D.C.: Smithsonian Institution Press, 1988. Contains several useful essays on past and current reservation policy, including William T. Hagan's "United States Indian Policies,

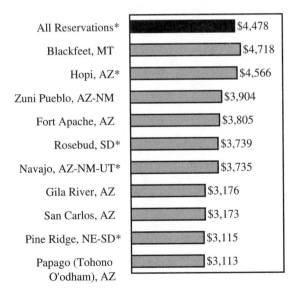

PER CAPITA INCOME ON LARGEST RESERVATIONS, 1990

Reservation	Per Capita Income
All Reservations*	$4,478
Blackfeet, MT	$4,718
Hopi, AZ*	$4,566
Zuni Pueblo, AZ-NM	$3,904
Fort Apache, AZ	$3,805
Rosebud, SD*	$3,739
Navajo, AZ-NM-UT*	$3,735
Gila River, AZ	$3,176
San Carlos, AZ	$3,173
Pine Ridge, NE-SD*	$3,115
Papago (Tohono O'odham), AZ	$3,113

Source: U.S. Bureau of the Census, *We, the First Americans.* Washington, D.C.: U.S. Government Printing Office, 1993.
*Includes trust lands.

1860-1900" and Lawrence C. Kelly's "United States Indian Policies, 1900-1988." Excellent index, detailed bibliography.

_____. *The Indian in America*. New York: Harper & Row, 1975. Arguably the best one-volume survey of the Indian experience in North America, with many useful insights and comments concerning the reservation system. Contains an extensive bibliography and comprehensive index.

Reserve system of Canada

TRIBES AFFECTED: Tribes residing in Canada

SIGNIFICANCE: Until well into the twentieth century, Canada's Indian reserve system assumed that lands not specifically defined "surrendered" to white settlement were for traditional Indian use; reactions to abuses in "surrender" arrangements brought more protective self-government and ownership provisions in the 1990's

By the early 1990's the percentage of land reserved by law for the specific use of Canadian Indian tribes varied considerably from province to province. In eastern provinces such as Newfoundland, reserves were largely symbolic, amounting to about .06 percent of all land. To the west, percentages were somewhat higher (2 percent in Alberta, for example), while in the Northwest Territories and the Yukon, a full third of what Canada calls the "traditional lands" remain reserved for the aboriginal tribes, referred to in Canadian law as "bands."

The situation of Indian self-government on reserve lands is a relatively recent development that must be viewed in the light of key legislation passed between 1930 and 1990. One can say, however, that the Canadian federal government has tried, since the 1930's, to ease strains created by unfortunate reversals of what long appeared to be a relatively enlightened history of protecting the lands (if not tribal governing autonomy) of Canadian Indians.

Ideal and Reality of Traditional Reserve Policy. The history of Indian reserves in Canada began at the end of the French and Indian War (1754-1763), when French claims on Canada were abandoned to British imperial control. A British royal proclamation in 1763 forbade governors of both the Canadian and the American colonies from issuing any land grants to colonists unless it was clear that the land in question was not "traditionally occupied" by Indians. This act began the so-called policy of protection, which stipulated that only the Crown held ultimate responsibility for protecting or acquiring traditional Indian lands. Such acquisition, or "surrendering over," was to be with the consent of tribes; what was not "surrendered" to the Crown was presumed to remain Indian property.

When the American Revolution ended in 1783, the influx of Loyalists into Canada caused pressures for colonial land grants to rise. In response, the Crown initiated a series of treaties and purchase agreements, particularly with tribes in Ontario. What was not turned over by sale or treaty agreement would from that date be called Indian "reserves." What appeared to be benevolent recognition of the Indians' traditional lands, however, was not always that generous. In a few extreme cases, such as the Chippewa (Ojibwa) agreement to surrender their Chenail Ecarte and St. Clair lands, only a very small portion was left for exclusive tribal use (in this case, some 23,000 acres out of a total of 2.7 million acres).

For a number of years there was no specific definition of what responsibilities the British might accept with respect to Indian rights within their reserves. This changed by the 1830's, when it became obvious that Indians even farther west were going to be affected by expanding white settlements and that, as their traditional way of life would no longer be possible in areas left as reserves, government assistance would have to be part of the land surrender process. Thus, an agreement concerning the Manitoulin Islands near the north shore of Lake Huron became, in 1836, part of a "new" attitude toward reserves: Indians there were to receive, free from "the encroachments of the whites . . . proper houses . . . and assistance . . . to become civilized and to cultivate land."

At the same time, it became increasingly apparent that the "traditional" reserve system would have to involve higher degrees of Indian dependence on Crown authorities to intercede between them and aggressive settler communities anxious to gain access to the natural resources on Indian land. In 1850, a decade and a half before Canada's federal/provincial arrangement (the Constitutional Act) placed the authority of the Crown across the entire width of the Atlantic, troubles broke out over settler access to minerals in the Lake Superior area. William Robinson was appointed treaty commissioner in order to define how Indian hunting and fishing rights could be preserved while sale and development of mining rights on the same land passed to outside bidders.

With the coming of Canada's independent status after 1867, it became apparent that a specific Indian act would be necessary and somehow should be binding on all provinces of the federal system. Neither the first Canadian Indian Act of 1876

ACREAGE OF CANADIAN INDIAN RESERVES, 1985		
Province or Territory	Number of Reserves	Total Acres
Ontario	182	1,727,989
Alberta	91	1,631,400
Saskatchewan	142	1,514,319
British Columbia	1,630	842,892
Manitoba	108	537,950
Quebec	33	192,030
New Brunswick	25	43,466
Northwest Territories	2	33,512
Nova Scotia	38	28,322
Prince Edward Island	4	1,667
Yukon	6	1,235
Newfoundland	—	—

Source: Department of Indian and Northern Affairs, Canada, *Number and Acreage of Indian Reserves, by Band*, 1985.

nor later acts, however, provided for the establishment of new reserves. The object of all Canadian Indian acts (into and through the twentieth century) was supposed to be to improve the management and developmental prospects of reserves that already existed. Nevertheless, the traditional but in many ways manipulated concept of what constituted a reserve in Canada continued, for nearly a century, to allow for "surrender" of lands considered to be in excess of tribal needs. Thus, in Quebec Province, some 45,000 choice acres considered Indian reserves in 1851 would be given over to white settlement between 1867 and 1904. The most spectacular case of additional surrenders occurred in Saskatchewan, the source for nearly half of the nearly 785,000 acres of Indian lands taken in the early twentieth century. In addition to formal acts of surrender, amendments in 1895 and 1918 to the Indian Act allowed the superintendent-general of Indian affairs to recognize private leases of reserve land that was not being exploited economically by the tribes.

Perhaps the most striking example of consequences that could come from application of these and other amendments occurred in the 1924 Canada-Ontario Indian Reserve Lands Agreement which would stand, despite challenges, into the 1990's. The 1924 agreement essentially acknowledged Indian rights to exploit *non*-precious minerals on their land, but provided for separate conditions to govern (external) exploitation of, and revenues from, precious mineral mines in Ontario (and by extension, elsewhere in Canada).

Post-1930 Trends Toward Self-Government on Reserves. The year 1930 was a watershed, for after that year, federal, or Dominion, approval for surrenders would become the exception rather than the rule. In the same year, the Dominion transferred public land control rights in the Prairie provinces to the provincial governments of Saskatchewan, Alberta, and Manitoba, with the express condition that existing Indian reserves would be maintained unchanged under federal control. The 1930 agreements nevertheless recognized the applicability of the 1924 precious metals "exception" (the Canada-Ontario Reserve Agreement noted previously) to any Indian reserves in the Plains provinces.

Rising governmental and public attention to Indian affairs came in the early 1960's, partially in the wake of the government's *Report on Reserve Allotments* (published in 1959), and partly following publication of a major study by Jean Lagasse on native populations in Manitoba. Lagasse's findings brought the beginnings of community development programs on Indian reserve lands, but they remained limited mainly to Manitoba itself. By 1975, a specific scheme for self-management and community government was legislated in the James Bay Agreement for northeastern Quebec, but this again had limited geographical scope.

Substantial change in conditions affecting life on reserve lands across Canada would not come until the late 1980's, and then specifically with passage of the 1989 Indian Act. A good portion of the local legislative precedents that formed the bases for the 1989 Indian Act can be seen to have been drawn from key decisions ranging from the James Bay Agreement

through the Municipal Grants Act of 1980 and the much broader 1986 Sechelt Indian Band Self-Government Act. When legislators extended such precedents to define the status of the totality of Canada's Indian population, the government in Ottawa granted for the first time several essential principles of self-government to tribes throughout the country. They now included the right to hold full title to property formerly considered their "reserves" (but ultimately controlled by Dominion authorities) and to dispose of that property legally as they might see fit (through sales, leases or rentals), through procedures they would determine via the autonomous channels of their own councils. —*Byron D. Cannon*

See also Fifteen Principles; Indian Act of 1876 (Canada); Indian Act of 1951 (Canada); Indian Act of 1989 (Canada); Indian-white relations—Canadian; Reservation system of the United States.

BIBLIOGRAPHY

Bartlett, Richard H. *Indian Reserves and Aboriginal Lands in Canada.* Saskatoon, Canada: University of Saskatchewan, Native Law Center, 1990.

Frideres, James. *Canada's Indians: Contemporary Conflicts.* Scarborough, Ontario: Prentice Hall of Canada, 1974.

Hawley, Donna L. *The Annotated 1990 Indian Act.* 3d ed. Toronto: Carswell, 1990.

Indian-Eskimo Association of Canada. *Native Rights in Canada.* Calgary: Author, 1970.

Nagler, Mark. *Natives Without a Home.* Don Mills, Ontario, Canada: Longman, 1975.

Resource use, pre-contact

TRIBES AFFECTED: Pantribal

SIGNIFICANCE: Native Americans traded food and other utilitarian resources along established routes

All Native Americans utilized surface and subsurface resources, which, in raw or finished form, were often traded with contiguous groups or to more distant areas along established trade routes. The natural differential occurrence of resources (and related manipulative skills) was the primary basis for some exogamous marriage patterns, the maintenance of complex group trading relationships, the development of inherited trading partners, and the existence of trade languages. Trade was conducted directly or by stages between groups from different culture areas, in some instances covering distances of many hundreds of miles. Trading by maritime groups and peoples inhabiting major riverine systems was facilitated by watercraft, and it was frequently a way for individuals to achieve socioeconomic status.

The control, esoteric knowledge, and skill of manipulating certain resources was sometimes based on a person's particular supernatural power, which was often maintained within a family by inheritance. Great respect for natural resources tended to characterize the worldview of Native Americans. Individual or collective ritual was observed before collecting and utilizing many food resources, and one's activities were controlled by behavioral and dietary taboos.

The primary concerns of all Native Americans, when exploiting and gathering natural resources, particularly foods, were the logistical strategies of converging at sites of productive occurrence when the resource was available, and of transporting such needed resources to inhabitation and storage areas. Consequently, hunters and gatherers subscribed to an annual subsistence round, one which required a high degree of mobility and knowledge of the terrain and its so-called carrying capacity, particularly of animal protein. Hunting and gathering cultures stored approximately three times the amount of food resources normally needed in case of prolonged winters or the destruction of stored foods by weather or animals. It was not unusual, during times of starvation, for people to partially exploit the stored nuts, seeds, and certain tubers of rodents and muskrats.

Dried high-protein foods, such as bison, salmon, and even pemmican, were traded to peoples devoid of such resources. The various highly prized by-products of land mammals and birds were traded in raw form or after skillful conversion by artisans. An example is laminated bows made of mountain sheep horn traded on the Plains. Traded food products became a necessary part of the utilitarian predation technology, but there was also a vast inventory of non-utilitarian trade resources, particularly various mollusk and dentalium shell beads.

Lithic (stone) materials, such as obsidian, slate, and chert for making projectile points and knives, were traded usually as "blanks"—the user would finish the tool as desired. Clays and orchers, and even native copper, were valuable natural resources, traveling considerable distances. In such cases, the item became more valuable the farther it was traded from the place of exploitation or mining. Resource areas, whether clamming beaches, hunting areas, nut or cambium groves, lithic sites, root fields, berry patches, or animal jumps, were the property of a particular group, but permission for exploitation (right of usufruct) was usually extended to non-kin members if requested.

The incursion of European American peoples and the early introduction of their trade items had, in some instances, a devastating effect upon the indigenous utilization and distribution of traditional resources, particularly the socioeconomic behaviors that had maintained land-use patterns. Tribalization and the insidious development of restricted reservations, invariably on nonproductive lands, essentially destroyed Native American access to and preservation of natural resources and effectively terminated a traditional way of life and sociopolitical and economic autonomy. For example, the destruction of bison and the reduction of salmon runs forced a drastic change in many people's subsistence base, bringing a rapid deterioration of health and creating a sense of relative deprivation.

As time passed, various governmental legislation further reduced the Native American land base and subsequent control of resources. In 1955, with the U.S. government's need for uranium, coal, oil, and certain metal ores facing off against pending native lawsuits for loss of traditional lands and resources, government legislation was passed to terminate reservations and Indian status. It is only relatively recently that some Native American tribes have been able to gain partial control of some of their resources, particularly in the development of tourism by those tribes situated on navigable bodies of water. Some Native American tribes receive annual per capita payments from resources, such as oil, gas, and timber, extracted from aboriginal areas. —*John Alan Ross*

See also Metalwork; Resources; Subsistence; Technology; Tools.

Resources

Tribes affected: Tribes possessing natural resources
Significance: Reservations and tribal governments confront a difficult task in deciding on the most effective ways to develop a reservation's natural resources

Natural resources such as coal, timber, natural gas, uranium, and oil have important places in many tribes' economic development plans. Reservations comprise some of the poorest regions in the United States, so the type of development and the extent of tribal control over these assets is crucial.

General History. Tribal economic dependence on the sale of natural resources gained importance in the late nineteenth century as tribal leaders and individuals began to sell reservation land and individual allotted lands. Though tribes retained possessory rights to timber and subsurface minerals, the absence of market demand and of legislation that granted tribes authority to sell timber or minerals apart from the land hindered development. Resources were simply ceded during land sales of this era, depriving tribes of benefits from these commodities.

In 1891, Congress enacted leasing legislation that provided a mechanism for tribes to lease land, coal, oil, and natural gas without selling their real estate. Tribes could control outside access to energy minerals by approving or disapproving of leases. At the time, few leases were made because of low demand for tribal resources.

Congress revised reservation leasing in the 1938 Omnibus Tribal Leasing Act, which required competitive bidding and the posting of bonds by successful bidders. The legislation favored outside developers, not the tribal landowners, because it emphasized quick monetary returns for the tribe in the leasing process rather than ensuring technical expertise on a tribe's behalf.

These reservation leasing guidelines were quickly outdated, but they remained operative for the next four decades. During that time, outsiders leased tribal minerals at less than market value and continued to enjoy the privilege thanks to continuous production clauses. Some outside interests even built power plants on reservations.

Energy Minerals. As a result of the 1970's energy crisis, tribal leaders demanded greater roles in making energy mineral decisions and in writing regulations governing reservation mineral development. Reservations possessed 3 percent of the nation's oil and natural gas reserves and 13 percent of the coal reserves.

RENTS AND ROYALTIES FROM LEASES ON INDIAN LANDS, 1986-1990					
Lease	1986	1987	1988	1989	1990
Oil royalties	$42,420,370	$45,813,797	$36,046,679	$40,835,885	$52,207,285
Gas royalties	$27,263,985	$22,240,298	$22,492,041	$24,632,980	$29,750,975
Coal royalties	$29,476,973	$30,481,374	$46,691,767	$47,677,927	$60,791,496
Other royalties	$5,867,330	$6,252,114	$7,052,181	$9,283,010	$9,243,132
Rents	$3,018,833	$1,206,406	$1,255,603	$1,454,523	$438,483
Totals	$108,047,491	$105,993,989	$113,538,271	$123,884,325	$152,431,371

Source: U.S. Department of the Interior, Minerals Management Service, *Mineral Revenues 1990, Report on Receipts from Federal and Indian Leases.* Washington, D.C.: U.S. Government Printing Office, 1991.

Note: Most Indian resource leases include provisions for rental payments once the lease is producing, but the standard lease does not provide for the payment of a royalty.

Rising demand for reservation energy resources created a false impression that tribes possessing coal, oil, and natural gas were wealthy. In 1976, the comptroller general reported that tribal resources were underdeveloped and that information on the extent of tribal energy resources was lacking, depriving tribes of revenue. At the same time, the United States failed to monitor lessor reclamation compliance, production figures, and royalty collection from reservation energy contracts. As a result, some tribes were reluctant to enter into energy development simply because too many questions remained unanswered. The Council of Energy Resource Tribes was created, its primary task to provide tribal leaders with energy mineral information. Tribal leaders became increasingly convinced of the need for local tribal control over energy mineral resources.

As a result of Native American assertions regarding control over resource development on tribal land, the Bureau of Indian Affairs in 1977 began requiring reservation energy mineral leasing contractors to comply with the provisions of the 1977 Surface Mining Control and Reclamation Act. In 1982, as a result of tribal initiative, Congress passed the Indian Minerals Development Act, allowing tribes to become energy producers.

Greater tribal control did not end energy mineral development problems. Monitoring and compliance issues continued to hinder tribal efforts to secure fair market value for their resources and to assure that tribal lands were not ruined in the process of mineral extraction.

Timber. In 1910, Congress passed legislation authorizing the logging of reservation forests. To fund a professional forestry program, administrative charges were deducted from tribal timber contracts. In 1972, the administrative fee program was modified and passage of the 1975 Indian Self-Determination and Education Assistance Act gave tribal leaders increased tribal control over reservation timber.

Reservation leaders began planning to increase timber revenues by developing value-added wood product industries. The creation of the Intertribal Timber Council in 1979 provided tribes with technical assistance to develop wood product industries. In 1990, Congress passed the National Indian Forest Resources Management Act, which increased tribal decision-making powers over reservation timber and provided the potential for greater monetary support for tribal conservation efforts.

Despite positive directions in reservation natural resource development, tribes do not possess adequate energy minerals and forested lands to control markets. As a result, tribes remain market dependent. At best, natural resource revenues provided sporadic, small per-capita payments to tribal members during the duration of a timber cutting contract or an energy mineral lease. Natural resources have not provided long-term reservation employment opportunities because of the vagaries of the energy and lumber markets. —*Richmond Clow*

See also Council of Energy Resource Tribes (CERT); Reservation system of the United States; Reserve system of Canada; Resource use, pre-contact.

BIBLIOGRAPHY

Ambler, Marjane. *Breaking the Iron Bonds: Indian Control of Energy Development.* Lawrence: University Press of Kansas, 1990.

Reno, Philip. *Mother Earth, Father Sky, and Economic Development: Navajo Resources and Their Use.* Albuquerque: University of New Mexico Press, 1981.

U.S. Congress. Senate. Select Committee on Indian Affairs. Special Committee on Investigations. *Final Report and Legislative Recommendations: A Report of the Special Committee on Investigations of the Select Committee on Indian Affairs.* Washington, D.C.: U.S. Government Printing Office, 1989.

Ridge, John Rollin (c. 1827, present-day Rome, Ga.— Oct. 5, 1867, Grass Valley, Calif.): Author, journalist

ALSO KNOWN AS: Nunna Hidihi (Yellow Bird)

TRIBAL AFFILIATION: Cherokee

SIGNIFICANCE: Ridge became a leading journalist, a noted poet, and a spokesperson for the plight of Indians in the late nineteenth century

Ridge was the son of a white woman and the Cherokee John Ridge, who, like his father, Major Ridge, was initially a strong opponent of the removal of the Cherokee to the west, but later became an active supporter of the relocation of his tribe to the Indian Territory.

The younger Ridge endured a controversial and often violent childhood. Both his father and his grandfather became involved in a bitter conflict over the removal of the Cherokee with the faction of their tribe led by John Ross, and they were murdered in 1839, together with a third man, in Indian Territory in retaliation for their support of the move west.

Lured by the prospect of quick riches in the gold fields of California, Ridge moved to that state in 1850. There he was not successful as a prospector, so he became involved in journalism. His pen name was Yellow Bird, a translation of his Indian name; essays written by him on the Indians in the nineteenth century and printed in newspapers and magazines have been compiled and published as *A Trumpet of Our Own* (1991).

During his lifetime, his most notable literary achievement was *The Life and Adventures of Joaquin Murieta, the Celebrated California Bandit* (1854), a fictionalized account of a Robin Hood-style character. Ridge was also a noted poet, and a compilation of his poetry was published in 1868, a year after his death.

See also Journalism; Ridge, Major; Ross, John.

Ridge, Major (c. 1770, Hiwassee, present-day Tenn.—June 20, 1839, Indian Territory, present-day Ark.): Tribal leader and orator

ALSO KNOWN AS: The Ridge

TRIBAL AFFILIATION: Cherokee

SIGNIFICANCE: Major Ridge, an influential Cherokee orator, fought against the Creeks and was a leading figure during the removal era

Ridge was born in eastern Tennessee in 1770. His paternal grandfather was a Highland Scot, but Ridge was brought up as a Cherokee. As a young man, called The Ridge after the Blue Ridge mountains, he became prominent as a hunter and warrior, sometimes raiding against white settlers. Ridge became an outstanding orator among his people, who made him a member of their central council. The Cherokees had a "blood law" decreeing death for anyone who sold Cherokee lands without the full consent of the nation. When Chief Doublehead violated this law, Ridge and Alexander Saunders assassinated him in 1807.

Observing the comparative prosperity of whites, Ridge concluded that Indian prosperity lay in becoming civilized and competing with whites in farming and trade, rather than in war. Ridge did so with such success that he soon became a wealthy planter in western Georgia. Without any formal education, he learned to understand English and could speak it brokenly, but he preferred to use Cherokee and translators.

During the War of 1812, when combat broke out between the Creeks and both the American government and rival tribes, Ridge led a Cherokee force against the hostile Red Stick Creeks, defeated them in several battles, then joined the army of Andrew Jackson, who made him a major. Ridge played a prominent role in Jackson's victory at Horseshoe Bend.

For the rest of his life, Ridge was known as Major Ridge; he used Ridge as his family name, so that his son became John Ridge. John was one of the most articulate and best-educated Cherokees; with his cousin Buck Watie (who changed his name to Elias Boudinot), he attended the Foreign Mission School at Cornwall, Connecticut, where he fell in love and became engaged to Sally Northrup, daughter of a prominent citizen. The townspeople objected to a mixed marriage, but when Major Ridge, dressed in an imposing uniform, came to town in a coach with liveried servants, they were impressed. After their marriage, John and Sally returned to Georgia, where John became prominent in Cherokee politics. Major Ridge was made speaker of the Cherokee Council.

In the late 1820's, Georgia began an ever-intensifying effort to drive the Cherokees out of the state and take over their property. The Ridges resisted removal for years, but it was a losing fight, as Georgia began confiscating Cherokee lands and selling them at lottery. Finally, despite his own prosperity, Ridge became convinced, like his son and nephew, that remaining in Georgia would only bring more persecution of the Cherokees and inevitable confiscation of their lands. He believed that the best solution would be to accept the best treaty they could get and make a fresh start west of the Mississippi. In 1835, he signed the treaty of New Echota, though doing so without the full consent of the Cherokee Nation made him liable to the "blood law" under which he had helped kill Chief Doublehead. The Ridges and Boudinot moved west without incident in 1836, but the Cherokees who followed Principal Chief John Ross in resisting removal were rounded up in 1838 by troops sent by President Van Buren, held in concentration camps, and finally sent west under armed guard on a death march known as the "Trail of Tears." About one third of them died on the way. Blaming the Ridge party, militant followers of Ross, without Ross's knowledge, condemned them to death and on June 22, 1839, murdered Major Ridge and his son and nephew.

See also Boudinot, Elias; Cherokee; Removal; Ross, John; Trail of Tears.

Riel, Louis, Jr. (Oct. 23, 1844, Red River Colony, Northwest Territories, Canada—Nov. 16, 1885, Regina, Northwest Territories, Canada): Revolutionary leader

ETHNIC AFFILIATION: Metis

SIGNIFICANCE: Riel organized the Metis during two rebellions: one in 1870, which successfully created the province of Manitoba, and the other in 1885, which ended in tragedy and transformed Riel into a heroic symbol of the oppressed

Louis Riel, Jr., was born the son of Louis Riel and Julie Lagimodiére in the Red River Settlement, south of Lake Winnipeg. It was an area with a large Metis population (Metis people are of mixed Indian and French parentage). Riel was one-eighth Metis through descent from his paternal grandmother. His mother was French, as was his father, a farmer and miller who had been brought up in Quebec. The thousands of Metis, Indians, and French and English settlers along the Red River were isolated and forgotten peoples at the time of Riel's childhood. Many worked for the Hudson's Bay Company (a fur trading monopoly), engaged in the traditional Metis buffalo hunt, or eked out a living as fur trappers and traders and as farmers.

Young Riel was sent to complete his education at the College of Montreal in preparation for the priesthood (his parents hoped he would become the first Metis missionary priest). The college dismissed him for lack of effort, however, and Riel took a position in the office of a radical anticlerical and anticonfederation attorney. In 1868, he returned to Red River. The Metis community was experiencing harsh economic times; crops had failed for two successive years. The Riel family was fortunate in that, with some livestock, they were able to hold together.

Canadian prime minister John A. Macdonald was pushing to expand the country and to tie it together with a continental railroad. The Northwest Territories were a key part of his plans, and when the Hudson's Bay Company offered to sell its lands to the new nation, he jumped at the opportunity. Macdonald sent survey teams to the territory. This surveying was done without informing or consulting the ten thousand Metis, Indians, English, and French living in the area. In addition, the surveying procedures did not respect the irregular farms and plots of settled land that existed along the river. Riel, literate, bilingual, and articulate, joined with other Metis to form a national committee. He helped draw up a petition to seek redress, which included recognition of existing landholdings, civil and political rights, and guarantees of consultation and participation.

At the beginning of what would become known as the First Riel Rebellion, the Metis rejected the territorial governor, took over Fort Garry, and declared a provisional government on December 9, 1869. Riel soon became president, and he pressed the Macdonald government to address the group's concerns. The willingness of the Metis to use force chastened the government, which did not want to harm its tenuous political ties with Quebec by waging war against Catholic, French-speaking Metis. The eagerness of Ontario's anti-Catholic Orange Order to fight the Metis heightened a sensitive situation. Riel exacerbated the climate of anxiety by ordering the execution of the Catholic-baiting Thomas Scott. This action enraged English-speaking Canadians, who put a price on Riel's head.

Macdonald prudently sought to settle the matter as quickly as possible. The result was the Manitoba Act of 1870, which granted virtually everything that was petitioned and incorporated the eastern portion of Metis lands into the small new province of Manitoba. Riel himself was forced to flee to escape revenge for the Scott execution. He headed eastward through the United States. At times he furtively entered Canada, sustaining his ties to the Metis.

Riel also sought to sustain his ties to French-speaking Catholicism. Priests regularly took him in and encouraged him. He traveled to New York and to Washington, D.C., hoping to form an alliance with the United States to encourage the annexation of the Northwest Territories. He became increasingly distraught at his lack of success, though he never wavered from the idea that he was a man of destiny. In 1876, he was overcome by a revelation that he interpreted as being a calling for him to revitalize the Catholic faith. His friends became disturbed at the design of this call, which spoke of changing the Sabbath to Saturday, polygamy, a married clergy, circumcision of males, and even brother-sister incest. Later he assumed the title of prophet and called for the transference of the papacy, first to Montreal and later to the Northwest. Friends committed him to psychiatric hospitals in Montreal and Quebec.

In 1875 the Canadian government finally granted him a pardon but insisted that he spend five years more in exile. He returned to the United States to seek work. Eventually he moved to a Metis and Indian community in Montana, involving himself in local politics and even taking American citizenship. By 1883, he had married Marguerite Monet, daughter of a Metis hunter. He became a schoolteacher. In 1884, he was approached by a delegation of settlers from Saskatchewan—whites, "half-breeds" (people with mixed Indian and English ancestry), and Metis—with grievances concerning land rights. Riel viewed the call as part of a divine plan for which he had suffered since 1870. The events that became known as the Second Riel Rebellion began to unfold.

Riel not only agreed to help formulate a petition of grievances but also assumed a leadership role. He insisted that the Northwest lands belonged to the half-breeds and the Metis and that the lands should be held in trust for future generations. He also demanded compensation for the years of privation and exile he had suffered. The Macdonald government considered his request blatant extortion. A force of Canadian regulars led by British officers marched on the Riel forces, which had mobilized on March 18, 1885. The government's anxiety and anger was stimulated by Indian attacks on white settlements. Riel, who had urged armed resistance, presumed that the government would attempt to negotiate, as it had in Manitoba. His Metis revolutionary army, however, attacked the Mounted Police at Duck Lake on March 26, an act which put negotiations out of the question. Beginning May 9, the government army assaulted the Metis forces for four days. Riel avoided confrontation and prayed for divine intervention. He was captured and held for trial along with eighty-five others.

The government planned to make an example of Riel. He was taken for trial to Regina, in the territory of Saskatchewan, a setting in which conviction was guaranteed (he would have a six-person jury, all of whom would be Protestant Anglo-Saxons). The jury took only half an hour to register a guilty verdict. The jury foreman asked for mercy, because the jury believed the government bore responsibility in that it had not dealt responsibly or fairly with the Metis, half-breeds, and Indians in the territory. The court had no recourse under the law, however, but to sentence Riel to death by hanging.

The Catholic church visited Riel and finally got him to renounce his personal theories on religion. His execution on November 16, 1885, made Riel a martyr. Louis Riel stands as a singular hero of Metis and native peoples in Canada.

—Jack J. Cardoso

See also Indian-white relations—Canadian; Metis; Pound-maker; Riel Rebellions.

BIBLIOGRAPHY

Bowsfield, Hartwell, comp. *Louis Riel: The Rebel and the Hero.* Toronto: Oxford University Press, 1971.

Davidson, William McCartney. *Louis Riel, 1844-1885: A Biography.* Calgary: Alberton, 1955.

Flanagan, Thomas. *Louis "David" Riel: Prophet of the New World.* Toronto: University of Toronto Press, 1979.

Howard, Joseph Kinsey. *Strange Empire: Louis Riel and the Métis People.* Toronto: J. Lewis and Samuel, 1974.

Howard, Richard. *Riel.* Toronto: Clarke, Irwin, 1967.

Osler, Edmund Boyd. *The Man Who Had to Hang: Louis Riel.* Toronto: Longman, Green, 1961.

Riel, Louis. *Diaries of Louis Riel.* Edited by Thomas Flanagan. Edmonton: Hurtig, 1976.

Stanley, George F. G. *The Birth of Western Canada.* 1936. Reprint. Toronto: University of Toronto Press, 1960.

_____. *Louis Riel.* Toronto: Ryerson Press, 1968.

Riel Rebellions

DATE: 1869-1870, 1885

PLACE: Manitoba and Saskatchewan, Canada

TRIBES AFFECTED: Assiniboine, Cree, Metis

SIGNIFICANCE: Two separate revolts against the government of Canada led to the dispersal and marginalization of the once thriving Metis

Canadian policies that threatened both the Metis and Indian ways of life were at the heart of two separate revolts in Canada's newly acquired prairie region. (Metis people are of mixed Indian and European descent.) In 1869 the Hudson's Bay Company relinquished its claim over Rupert's Land and the Northwest to the recently confederated nation of Canada. Prime Minister John A. Macdonald set out to build a great nation joined from the Atlantic to the Pacific by a rail line. Although the government negotiated treaties that established Indian reserves, it offered the Metis, whom it did not regard as legally Indian, no such consideration. This contributed significantly to the erosion of the Metis economic and social life.

Red River Rebellion, 1869-1870. Preparing to take over the new territories in the fall of 1869, Canada sent survey parties into the Red River region. The Metis of the region had for many years occupied long, narrow farmsteads along the riverbank. Contrary to this practice, the surveyors delineated square township lots. Both fearing the imminent arrival of large numbers of English-speaking Protestants and fearing that their long-established land tenure would be ignored once Canada asserted control over the area, the Metis and a few of the original white settlers declared a provisional government in early November, 1869. Prairie-born but Montreal-educated, Louis Riel, Jr., was elected secretary and, within a few weeks, president of the government of Assiniboia.

The Red River Rebellion actually involved very few military skirmishes. On November 2, 1869, the Metis seized Upper Fort Garry and arrested fifty Canadians including a mili-tant Orangeman named Thomas Scott. Scott escaped from custody twice but was recaptured each time. He was tried, convicted of treason against the Metis government, and executed in March, 1870. Scott's execution became a rallying point in English Canada against the mainly French Catholic Metis. Riel, who was president of Assiniboia at the time, was held responsible. He was forced into exile for much of the next fifteen years.

The Metis of Assiniboia had no intention of remaining independent of Canada and issued a declaration of their desire to join the Confederation of Canada as a new province with full representation in Parliament. According to their declaration, the new province would have both English and French as its official languages, control of public lands would remain with the local legislature, and the citizens would retain the property rights they held prior to entering confederation.

In May, 1870, after several months of negotiation between Ottawa and the Metis, the Canadian Parliament passed the Manitoba Act. While the establishment of the new province should have met many of the Metis demands, in practice it did not. The province was limited to 100,000 square miles, Parliament rather than the Manitoba Legislature retained control of the public lands, and the conveyance of the Metis' land titles was delayed so long that many Metis sold their rights to land speculators and moved farther west.

Northwest Uprising, 1885. Many of the same economic concerns that caused the 1869-1870 Red River Rebellion fueled the Northwest Uprising of 1885. This second revolt, however, included Cree and Assiniboine Indians as well as the Metis. Ottawa, fearing a general Indian uprising on the prairies, responded with swift military action rather than negotiation.

Faced with the near extinction of the buffalo and once again with the fear of being uprooted by new settlers, the Metis around Batoche on the Saskatchewan River invited Riel to return from exile to argue their claims with Ottawa. Riel, however, had changed greatly in the intervening decade and a half. He had spent several years in insane asylums in Montreal before settling on a farm in Montana. He was obsessed with the idea that it was his divine mission to establish a French Catholic state in the northwest. He viewed the arrival of four Metis emissaries on June 4, 1884, as divine intervention and returned to Canada to fulfill his mission.

Riel spent much of his time drafting petitions to Ottawa outlining the Metis' grievances. Finally, reminiscent of events in 1869, the Metis, led by Riel and Gabriel Dumont, seized the parish church at Batoche and declared a provisional government. The army and the Northwest Mounted Police responded promptly, and the entire revolt was crushed within two months. The Metis and the Indians, however, did inflict casualties. The first skirmish occurred near Duck Lake when the Mounted Police arrived to assert Canadian authority. The Metis, joined by a few Indians, killed ten of the police and forced the remainder to retreat.

The Indians, starving as a result of the loss of the buffalo and then Ottawa's withholding of treaty rations, were encouraged by the Metis victory at Duck Lake. The Cree and Assiniboine were easily persuaded to join the revolt. Several hundred hungry Indians under the leadership of Poundmaker attacked the fort at Battleford, burning the homes and looting the stores. Other Cree, led by Big Bear, killed nine people, including the Indian agent and two priests in what became known as the Frog Lake Massacre. Three others were spared by Big Bear.

The Canadian military response was swift. Eight thousand well-armed troops were dispatched to the region, and the revolt was summarily crushed. Among the leaders of the revolt, Dumont escaped to the United States, where he performed for a time with Buffalo Bill Cody's Wild West Show. Big Bear and Poundmaker each received three years in prison. Riel, who used his trial as a forum for his cause, was found guilty of treason and hanged on November 16, 1885. Many of the Metis and Cree fled to Montana. Others dispersed to the north. Fearing additional Indian uprisings, the Canadian government rushed to complete the Canadian Pacific Railroad and promptly began to settle the West.

—*Richard G. Condon and Pamela R. Stern*

See also Big Bear; Indian-white relations—Canadian; Metis; Poundmaker; Riel, Louis, Jr.

BIBLIOGRAPHY
Dempsey, Hugh A. *Big Bear: The End of Freedom.* Vancouver: Douglas & McIntyre, 1984.

Flanagan, Thomas. *Riel and the Rebellion: 1885 Reconsidered.* Saskatoon: Western Producer Prairie Books, 1983.

Miller, J. R. "The Northwest Rebellion of 1885." In *Skyscrapers Hide the Heavens: A History of Indian-White Relations in Canada.* Toronto: University of Toronto Press, 1989.

Purich, Donald. *The Metis.* Toronto: James Lorimer, 1988.

Stanley, George F. G. *The Birth of Western Canada: A History of the Riel Rebellions.* 2d ed. Toronto: University of Toronto Press, 1960.

Riggs, Lynn (Aug. 31, 1899, near Claremore, Indian Territory—June 30, 1954, New York City): Dramatist, poet
TRIBAL AFFILIATION: Cherokee
SIGNIFICANCE: Lynn Riggs is the best known of Native American playwrights

Lynn Riggs was born into an Oklahoma Cherokee family. His father was a cowboy, and young Lynn was at home with the open range. As a youth he drove a grocery wagon to make money and entertained himself with what he would later describe as "trashy lurid fiction." In his late teens, Riggs traveled on both coasts earning money as an office and factory worker, book salesman, and singer in motion picture houses. Following these experiences, he attended the University of Oklahoma and, as a sophomore, taught freshman English classes.

Riggs's first play was a farce, *Cuckoo*, written in 1921. Growing up, he was deeply influenced by the speech, music, and folklore of his neighbors. This play and subsequent works are deeply colored by Cherokee community observations. In 1923 he toured the west, singing tenor in a Chautauqua quartet, and ended up joining a Santa Fe artists' colony. He published some poetry, and the colony produced his play *Knives from Syria*.

Riggs left the artists' colony and settled in New York to write. He was given a Guggenheim fellowship in 1929 and spent a year in Paris writing the plays *Roadside* (later reworked as *Borned in Texas*) and *Green Grow the Lilacs*. Upon returning to New York, he experienced his first commercial success with a 1933 production of *Green Grow the Lilacs*. Later, Rodgers and Hammerstein acquired the play and transformed it into the Broadway production *Oklahoma!*

In later years, Riggs wrote several plays, but none achieved the artistic or commercial success of *Green Grow the Lilacs*. He lived for a time in Chapel Hill, North Carolina, and associated with playwright Paul Green, another American playwright who used folklore provocatively in drama.

Rite of Consolation
TRIBES AFFECTED: Iroquois Confederacy: Cayuga, Mohawk, Onondaga, Oneida, Seneca
SIGNIFICANCE: This religious, social, and political funeral ceremony functions to ease grief and restore leadership

The Rite of Consolation is a ceremonial event that takes place on the death of one of the principal chiefs of the Iroquois Confederacy. The members of the confederacy, in the persons of the assigned leaders, assemble. The bereaved nation is host and is visited by those called the "clearminded," who come to offer consolation, advice, and support. The rite consists of a prescribed series of songs and orations. Taken together, these compose a long elegy; the songs and speeches—traditionally keyed to belts of wampum—offer spiritual insight into the meaning of life and rationalize death within a philosophical system.

The rite offers more, however, than comfort for the loss of an individual. It reminds the participants of the founders and history of the league, in particular the heroic Hiawatha and his antagonist, Atotarho, making it an educational and patriotic event. Furthermore, the rite provides for the choice and installation of a successor to the late chief. The new leader is given the name of his predecessor, and in this way the names of the original leaders are preserved. The rite thus offers a symbolic death and rebirth, both of the individual leader and of the healed and restored community.

See also Hiawatha; Iroquois Confederacy; Political organization and leadership; Wampum.

Rites of passage
TRIBES AFFECTED: Pantribal
SIGNIFICANCE: Rite of passage ceremonies mark important, status-changing events in the life cycle, such as birth, naming, puberty, initiation, marriage, and death

Rites of passage are ceremonies associated with the transformation from one stage of life to another. The four primary events of birth, naming, puberty, and death are celebrated as spiritual occasions. The secondary events of marriage and initiation into societies are considered social by some tribes and spiritual by others.

Three stages can be identified in any rite of passage. In the separation phase one loses the old status; in the marginal phase one has essentially no identity; and in the re-entry phase one takes on a new identity within the community, gaining new rights and obligations. An element of danger exists in the transition. The time between two states has a mysterious quality, during which the individual requires protection from potential harm. This marginal phase is a symbolic death of the old status.

Childbirth. Among traditional people, childbirth was a time of crisis for mother and child, since the mortality rate for both was highest then. Childbirth was also regarded as a time of danger for males in the community. The miraculous new life within the mother's body held the sacred power of the Creator. It could endanger those not as powerful. This belief, along with the practical concerns of comfort and privacy, plus the need for concentrated attention during birthing, led to the segregation of women in labor. The period of labor represented the "between" phase, requiring protection for both mother and infant through petitions to the spirits for guidance.

A woman in labor was usually assisted in the birthing hut by other women, but a Southwest Caddo woman went alone to a nearby river when labor began. She built her own shelter, delivered her baby, and, even in winter, bathed herself and the child in the river. She returned to the village right away. Among the Nez Perce of Idaho, mother and infant were secluded for as long as three months after delivery, and in the Great Basin tribes the father also stayed in bed and ate special foods.

Naming. Anyone without a name was considered powerless, because the spirits would not recognize them. Not all babies received names; some tribes waited until a particular trait suggested a name. A name could be revealed through a parent's dream, or given in a formal ceremony after months or years of waiting. A person could have several names throughout life: as an infant, a young child, at puberty, and upon a worthy achievement.

Omaha newborns were thought to be just other beings in nature. An infant was presented to the powers of nature with prayers for safety on its journey through life. With its first steps, the baby became a member of the tribe and was given a new pair of moccasins containing a little hole. In case the spirits called, the child could respond, "I can't travel now; my moccasins are worn out."

Marriage. Some tribes had no marriage ceremony. A couple would announce their plans, but the tribe might not consider them truly married until a child was born. In more formal marriages, the groom brought gifts for the bride's parents, such as horses in the Plains, and cedar blankets or carved boxes in the Northwest. Marriage was accomplished through an exchange of gifts between both families among the California Pomo.

A Cherokee bride and groom feasted separately with their relatives, then met later in the community ceremony. The groom's mother gave him a leg of venison and a blanket; the bride's mother gave her an ear of corn and a blanket. The couple exchanged the food and wrapped themselves in their blankets. A similar ritual completed an Ojibwa marriage; in addition, the couple had the hems of their coats sewed together.

Hopi marriage customs required the girl to grind corn for several days at home, then go to her groom's home and grind corn for three more days. The groom's aunts called her lazy and jokingly taunted her for stealing their favorite nephew. On the wedding day, the two were joined for life when the couple's mothers washed the bride and groom's heads in one basin and twisted their hair together. Later, they went to the edge of the mesa to pray to the rising sun. After the wedding breakfast, the groom went with townsmen into the kiva (ceremonial chamber) to weave the bride's wedding garments while she spent the long days grinding more corn. The two white robes and the long white belt would be used eventually to wrap her body for her journey into the spirit world.

Death, Burial, and Mourning. The greatest of mysteries surrounds this final rite of passage, and the most varied ceremonies mark the transition. Among the Apache and Navajo, where death is deeply feared, burial is simple and swift, and mourning is brief. The deceased is bathed, dressed in fine clothing and jewelry, and then placed in a crevice and covered with stones. If the person died at home, the house and possessions were burned and the family moved to a new house.

In the Great Basin, burial sites were caves, and on the Plains, scaffolds and trees were used. Cremation was common in California; wooden cabins, boxes, or canoes on posts were burial places in the Northwest. The Eastern Ojibwa wrapped their dead in birchbark and placed them in a grave lined with cedar boughs. A small house was built over the grave, a fire was lit, and food was left for the spirit's journey.

The Iroquois Rite of Consolation, a ceremony for a deceased sachem (chief), recounted deeds of ancestors, acknowledged the departed one's greatness, and comforted the bereaved, symbolically reinforcing the past, present, and future of the Iroquois League.

The Huron of the East held a Feast of the Dead every ten to twelve years. The souls were released in an extended mourning ceremony as relatives removed bodies from temporary burial sites, cleaned the bones and put them into bundles. Mourners carried their bundles to a communal burial site, and at dawn, with a great wailing, they deposited their bundles into the pit. This mingling of ancestral bones symbolized an obligation to tribal unity.

An extraordinary burial custom existed among the Natchez of the Southeast, where the highest class members were required to marry commoners. When the highborn one died, the commoner spouse and children were sacrificed to accompany the deceased on the journey.   *—Gale M. Thompson*

See also Children; Death and mortuary customs; Feast of the Dead; Marriage and divorce; Names and naming; Puberty and initiation rites; Rite of Consolation; Women.

BIBLIOGRAPHY

Allen, Paula Gunn. *The Sacred Hoop: Recovering the Feminine in American Indian Traditions.* Reprint. Boston: Beacon Press, 1992.

Garbarino, Merwyn S. *Native American Heritage.* Boston: Little, Brown, 1976.

Johnston, Basil. *Ojibwa Ceremonies.* Illustrated by David Beyer. Toronto: McClelland and Stewart, 1982.

Niethammer, Carolyn. *Daughters of the Earth: The Lives and Legends of American Indian Women.* New York: Collier Books, 1977.

Turner, Victor W. *The Ritual Process: Structure and Anti-Structure.* Chicago: Aldine, 1969.

Rocky Boy (c. 1860-1914): Nomad leader

ALSO KNOWN AS: Stone Child

TRIBAL AFFILIATION: Chippewa (Ojibwa)

SIGNIFICANCE: Rocky Boy was a leader of nomad Chippewas, securing for them a land grant although they had refused to live on a reservation

Rocky Boy was a leader of the "Chippewa nomads," who were left out of treaties in both the United States and Canada. During the nineteenth century, roughly 350 Chippewas had left the main group in Wisconsin and gone to hunt in Montana. They were not settled on a reservation, and thus they were excluded from all treaty negotiations. As more land was fenced, the nomads' life became untenable and they were often reduced to begging.

Stone Child, often called "Rocky Boy" by settlers, emerged as a leader as the nomads' situation became desperate. He lobbied the Bureau of Indian Affairs, and after a number of years of bureaucratic indecision, "Rocky Boy's Band" was granted a tract of land on the Fort Assiniboin military reserve in Montana. The land grant finally came in 1914, the year that Rocky Boy died.

See also Ojibwa.

Rogers, Will (Nov. 4, 1879, near Oologah, Okla.—Aug. 15, 1935, near Point Barrow, Alaska): Humorist

ALSO KNOWN AS: Rabbit

TRIBAL AFFILIATION: Cherokee

SIGNIFICANCE: Rogers used homespun humor and satiric philosophy to point up the shortcomings of American society, government, and politics

Will Rogers spent his early years on his father's Verdigris River ranch in the Indian Territory, proud of the Cherokee heritage that came through both parents.

Will had ten years of schooling before he ended his education in 1898. His skill with a rope led him into work as a cowhand and then as a performer. Between rope tricks, he shared publicly the humor and philosophy for which he became famous.

In 1908, Will married Betty Blake, and the family eventually included four children, although Will's work as performer, speaker, and writer prevented a routine home life.

Rogers could never resist a good cause or a needy friend, and his generosity cost much of his family's financial security.

Will Rogers died in a plane crash in 1935 and was buried on his ranch near Claremore, Oklahoma.

See also Cherokee; Humor.

Roman Nose (c. 1830—Sept. 17, 1868, Beecher's Island, Colo.): Warrior

ALSO KNOWN AS: Sauts (Bat), Wokini (Hook Nose)

TRIBAL AFFILIATION: Southern Cheyenne

SIGNIFICANCE: Roman Nose was a fearless leader, though not a chief, during battles with white settlers and Union Pacific Railroad workers in the 1860's

Though some accounts of the story may vary, it was generally believed that a protective war bonnet, made for Roman Nose by a medicine man named Ice, could protect him against bullets and arrows in battle. His six-foot, three-inch bonneted frame led his warriors into many battles against railroad gangs laying rails along the Kansas frontier between 1864 and 1868. In 1866, at a council in Fort Ellsworth, Kansas, Roman Nose distinguished himself in his protestations against the Union Pacific Railroad on Indian hunting grounds. He vowed to stop the railroad. As the attacks against the railroad heightened, the government sent Major George A. Forsyth and fifty special scouts against the Cheyenne. Forsyth's forces tracked the Cheyennes to the Arickaree Fork of the Republican River, where Beecher Island is located.

Legend recounts that the night before the battle, as a guest in the home of a Sioux family, Roman Nose was served food lifted with a metal fork. This violated one of the laws that dictated the power of the bonnet. A purification ceremony would have restored the "medicine" to his bonnet, but his warriors called for him and he responded. Roman Nose announced his own death upon riding into the battle, and moments later he was struck down by gunfire. The battle went on for eight days.

See also Cheyenne; Indian-white relations—U.S., 1831-1870; Railroads; Tall Bull.

Rosebud Creek, Battle of

DATE: June 17, 1876

PLACE: Montana

TRIBES AFFECTED: Arapaho, Cheyenne, Sioux

SIGNIFICANCE: This battle was preliminary to the Little Bighorn fight; it neutralized General George Crook's northbound column of the 1876 Sioux campaign, bolstered the Indians' confidence, and opened the door for the Custer defeat

On January 31, 1876, the U.S. government issued an ultimatum that all Indians must reside on reservations or be deemed "hostiles." This declaration ultimately led to the army's 1876 summer campaign against the northern Plains Indians.

The campaign was a three-pronged pincer tactic designed to surround, push, and engage the "hostile" bands in present northcentral Wyoming and south-central Montana, with Colonel John Gibbons coming from the west, General Alfred Terry

An 1876 rendition of the Battle of Rosebud Creek, in which Sioux and Cheyenne warriors forced George Crook's forces to retreat southward. (Library of Congress)

and Colonel George A. Custer from the east, and General George Crook from the south. Embarking from Fort Fetterman, Wyoming, on May 29, Crook marched up the Bozeman Trail with more than a thousand troopers and established a base camp at present-day Sheridan, Wyoming. He was joined by more than two hundred Crow and Shoshone allies on June 14.

Mid-June was also when the Hunkpapa Sioux held their Sun Dance in which Sitting Bull experienced his famous vision of many soldiers falling into camp. The Indians knew of Crook's forces and were eager to fulfill Sitting Bull's vision. By June 16, Crook's troops had moved on to the Rosebud River. The next morning, while his forces were relaxing, Crazy Horse's warriors struck.

After the Sioux's initial charge the soldiers were able to regroup enough to take command of the high ground on the valley's northern bluffs. From there, Crook orchestrated his troop's movements. The Rosebud Valley is long, however, and the terrain broken with hills, ravines, and ridges. These created a disjointed battle with scattered pockets of fierce action stretching three miles along the valley. During the fight, Crook mistakenly believed that Crazy Horse's village lay northward and ordered Captain Anson Mills's detachment to find and seize it. The battle intensified, and Crook's Crow and Shoshone allies proved their worth throughout. In one instance they rescued an officer from the Sioux in a hand-to-hand struggle. Meanwhile,

Mills, finding no village, returned to the fight, coming to the rear of the Sioux and Cheyenne. This eventually caused the Indians to disengage and abandon the battlefield.

The battle lasted six hours and was filled with intense fighting. Crook proclaimed victory on the notion that he possessed the battlefield in the end. In truth, Crook's troops were bested by Crazy Horse's warriors, and had it not been for the valiant efforts of his Crow and Shoshone allies, Crook would have suffered greater casualties than his twenty-eight dead and fifty-six wounded. The Sioux and Cheyenne suffered comparable casualties but in the end forced Crook to retreat south with his dead and wounded, thus neutralizing his forces at the most critical juncture in the campaign. In Crook's defense, he faced (on onerous terrain) an unexpectedly unified force whose tenacious fighting was unparalleled—a combination Custer would face a week later with more disastrous results.

See also Crazy Horse; Little Bighorn, Battle of the; Sitting Bull.

Ross, John (Oct. 3, 1790, Turkey Town, Ala.—Aug. 1, 1866, Washington, D.C.): Tribal chief
ALSO KNOWN AS: Coowescoowe
TRIBAL AFFILIATION: Eastern Cherokee
SIGNIFICANCE: Ross was principal chief of the Eastern Cherokee during their removal to the West in 1838-1839,

after which he was chief of the united Cherokee Nation until his death

Born in Turkey Town, Alabama, John Ross was only one-eighth Cherokee; the rest of his ancestry was Scottish. His part-Cherokee mother saw that he learned his Indian heritage, and he identified himself with the Cherokees. As a young man, Ross prospered in merchandising until he turned to agriculture and developed a prosperous plantation at Rossville, Georgia, where he held slaves. After the War of 1812, in which he served under Andrew Jackson against the Creeks, Ross became increasingly active in tribal politics, and in 1827 helped develop a constitution for the Cherokee nation. The next year, he was elected principal chief of the Eastern Cherokees. It was a difficult time, for with the connivance of President Jackson, Georgia exerted tremendous pressure to have all the Cherokees removed to the West and meanwhile began confiscating Cherokee lands, including Ross's plantation, and selling them in a state lottery. After his estate was stolen in this fashion, Ross took refuge in a log cabin just over the Tennessee border, where he and his guest John Howard Payne— actor, playwright, and composer of "Home, Sweet Home"—were arrested illegally by Georgia guardsmen who had violated the state border; they were imprisoned for a week.

Ross fought stubbornly to preserve the Cherokees' ancestral lands, but a rival faction led by Major Ridge, John Ridge, and Elias Boudinot had become persuaded that the only way for the Cherokees to end the persecution against them was to make the best treaty possible and start over in the West. Accordingly, in 1835 they signed the Treaty of New Echota, thus violating the "blood law" of the Cherokees, since Ross and most of the tribe were not present and did not approve the treaty. The Ridge group moved west the next year, but Ross and his followers continued to resist until 1838, when President Martin Van Buren ordered the removal of all the approximately seventeen thousand Cherokees and sent in seven thousand troops to collect them in concentration camps and then escort them to Indian Territory, now western Arkansas and eastern Oklahoma. The removal became a death march known as the Trail of Tears, on which nearly a third of the Cherokees died, including Ross's wife. After the removal, a militant group of Ross's followers, without his knowledge, murdered John Ridge, Major Ridge, and Elias Boudinot all on the same day: June 22, 1839. Despite the killings, Ross was elected chief of the united Cherokee Nation in 1839 and remained chief until his death. During the Civil War, he advocated neutrality, but the Cherokees joined the Confederacy, and Boudinot's brother, Stand Watie, now a general, got belated revenge by burning Ross's house. Ross spent much of the war in Washington and died there on August 1, 1866.

See also Cherokee; Indian Removal Act; Removal; Ridge, Major; Trail of Tears; Watie, Stand.

Sacagawea (c. 1788, Lemhi Valley, Idaho—Dec. 20, 1812, Fort Manuel, Dakota Territory, present-day S.Dak.): Guide, interpreter

ALSO KNOWN AS: Tsakaka gia (Bird Woman, Boat Pusher)

TRIBAL AFFILIATION: Northern Shoshone

SIGNIFICANCE: Sacagawea accompanied Meriwether Lewis and William Clark on their expedition into Northwest America, performing invaluable, perhaps critical services as a guide and interpreter

The Lewis and Clark expedition was directed by President Thomas Jefferson in 1803 to explore the vast continent northwest of the Mississippi River and to look for a route to the Pacific Ocean. It is from expedition diaries that historians have learned most of what is known about Sacagawea (also spelled Sakakawea or Sacajawea).

On October 27, 1804, the expedition reached the villages of the Mandan Indians in North Dakota, where it wintered. It is here that Meriwether Lewis and William Clark met Sacagawea and her French-Canadian husband, Toussaint Charbonneau. Sacagawea was about seventeen years old and pregnant. She had belonged previously to the Hidatsa Indians, who had stolen her from her Shoshone home in Idaho. Charbonneau probably obtained her by gambling or barter when she was ten or twelve years old. She was one of Charbonneau's two or three Indian wives.

Lewis and Clark hired Charbonneau as an interpreter and believed that Sacagawea would prove her usefulness if the expedition encountered the Shoshone later on. On February 11 or 12, 1805, Sacagawea gave birth to her first child, a boy christened Jean Baptiste.

The expedition set out again on April 7, 1805, following the Missouri River. Sacagawea apparently first proved her usefulness to the expedition on April 9, when she unearthed wild artichokes to eat. Sacagawea earned Lewis' respect on May 14, when the supply boat capsized and began to sink. Sacagawea was on board. As the boat was righted she calmly and deliberately pulled on board any of the invaluable records and supplies that were near her—all the while holding her baby and balancing herself. Clark wrote glowingly of her that she had as much fortitude and resolution as any man on the boat. On May 20, they named a river after her.

On July 22, Sacagawea first recognized her home country near present-day Helena, Montana. Sacagawea assured Lewis and Clark that they were on the correct route to get to the Three Forks of the Missouri River. On July 28, she reaffirmed that the expedition was in Shoshone territory, having in fact reached the exact spot where she had lived five years earlier when the Hidatsa abducted her.

Lewis and Clark decided to follow the central tributary of the three rivers. On August 8, Sacagawea recognized the area as the Shoshones' summer home and assured the expedition that her people would be found on this river. Contact was made on August 15, and Sacagawea was reunited with her tribe. She acted as interpreter (her brother was now chief). Her presence likely helped to maintain the cordial relations between Indians and whites and facilitated Lewis and Clark's successful bargaining with the Shoshone to obtain twenty-nine horses, which were essential if the expedition were to continue. Although Sacagawea probably could have remained with the Shoshone, she stayed instead with the expedition and accompanied it to the Pacific Ocean.

On the return trip, she performed additional services for the Expedition. On May 11, 1806, she aided communication with the Nez Perce as an interpreter. Sacagawea recognized several of the areas the expedition passed through and reassured Clark that they were taking the correct route. She recommended the Bozeman Pass through the Rocky Mountains. Although they could have taken any of three passes, the Bozeman Pass was the most direct route to the Yellowstone Valley. Clark acknowledged that she had been of great service to him as a guide through this part of the trip.

On August 17, 1806, the Expedition reached Fort Mandan in central North Dakota, where Lewis and Clark parted company with Charbonneau and Sacagawea.

The rest of her life is undocumented and uncertain, and widely varying accounts have been written. The interested reader can consult Harold P. Howard's *Sacajawea* (1971) for discussion of these various accounts. Howard concludes, on the basis of what documentary evidence there is, that Sacagawea died at Fort Manuel, South Dakota, on December 20, 1812, during an Indian raid. She was buried there in an unmarked grave. She would have been about in her mid-twenties. (Other accounts have her dying around 1884, at approximately age ninety-six, on the Wind River Shoshone Reservation in Wyoming.)

Both Lewis and Clark wrote of their admiration and respect for Sacagawea and of what great services she provided to the expedition. Current historians no longer believe that Sacagawea's presence was vital to the success of the expedition, as earlier historians claimed. Had the expedition been left to its own resources it would have found its way, communicated with the Indians, and bartered for the vitally needed horses, they unconvincingly contend.

At the very least, there is no question that Sacagawea's presence significantly eased the way for the expedition, and perhaps her presence was her greatest contribution. She was a vital young woman of courage, loyalty, energy, and endurance—a true heroine. As Elliot Coues comments in *A History of the Expedition Under the Command of Captains Lewis and Clark* (1893): "Clark very sensibly followed the advice of the remarkable woman, who never failed to rise to the occasion."

—*Laurence Miller*

See also Shoshone.

BIBLIOGRAPHY

Duncan, Dayton. *Out West: An American Journey.* New York: Viking, 1987.

Howard, Harold P. *Sacajawea.* Norman: University of Oklahoma Press, 1971.

Lewis, Meriwether, and William Clark. *A History of the Lewis and Clark Expedition.* Edited by Elliot Coues. 4 vols. 1893. Reprint. New York: Dover, 1965.

A statue of Sacagawea was commissioned for this Portland, Oregon, city park. (Library of Congress)

_____. *History of the Expedition of Captains Lewis and Clark, 1804-5-6.* 2d ed. 2 vols. Chicago: A. C. McClurg, 1903.

Moulton, Gary E., ed. *The Journals of the Lewis and Clark Expedition.* Lincoln: University of Nebraska Press, 1988.

Sachem

TRIBES AFFECTED: Massachusett, Mohegan, Narragansett, Nauset, Niantic, Nipmuck, Pawtucket, Pequot, Pocomtuck, Quinnipiac, Wampanoag

SIGNIFICANCE: The general term "sachem" was used to designate band leaders and tribal chiefs among the Algonquian-speaking peoples of southern New England

Along the coastal region of southern New England in the early contact period, the word *sachem* was used for political leaders. In northern New England, the corresponding term was *sagamore*. The sachem was most commonly the head or leader of a single village (or band). Some sachems, however, had a more extensive but ill-defined influence over an entire tribe or alliance of villages. Examples of sachems with this wider influence were Massasoit and his son Metacomet (King Philip) of the Wampanoag, and Miantonomo of the Narragansett. Whether a sachem's authority was confined to a single village or was much wider, his power was limited by tribal traditions and exercised through persuasion. Important decisions were made in consultation with a council of important men (called *pneises* among the Massachusett and Wampanoag). Sachems were chosen from among men born into a chiefly lineage or family, the office descending most commonly from father to son. Occasionally women served as sachems (called "squaw sachems" by the English). Weetamoo of the Pocasset was an example. The sachem assigned agricultural fields, sentenced criminals, and was responsible for diplomacy and external trade. A sachem dwelt in an unusually large wigwam and was supported by the work of his wives, by the yield from special fields cultivated for him, and by gifts or tribute. This food and other goods were given back through feasts and reciprocal gifts.

See also Algonquian language family; Massasoit; Metacomet; Northeast; Political organization and leadership; Wampanoag; Weetamoo.

Sacred, the

TRIBES AFFECTED: Pantribal

SIGNIFICANCE: Every American Indian tribe holds a concept of the sacred at the core of its belief system; although known by different names, this concept is related to spiritual power

In American Indian tribal languages, there is no word for "religion." Religion is not a separate category with specific times and places for expression. Rather, the spiritual is embedded in everything that exists and is therefore part of every activity. Sacred ways were, and are, the technology of tribal peoples. Through a system of shared beliefs, symbols, and practices, this technology of the sacred provides the structure which determines the customs and guides the daily life of a people.

Aside from formal ceremony, everyday tasks such as hunting, gathering, preparing food, making art and music, and fashioning tools and clothing are performed within the context of sacred knowledge and often involve ritual action. When these common activities are combined with the use of symbols, colors, or numbers and various songs, chants, or prayers, the invisible is brought into visibility and is to some degree a manifestation of the sacred.

The sacred is equivalent to spiritual power, and according to tribal peoples, it can be manifested in seemingly inanimate objects such as a star, a lake, or a stone. These things are not worshiped for themselves but are honored because they express the intangible, yet very real power of the sacred. In this way, they become something else, while paradoxically remaining in their original forms. They are held in awe and respect by all, but only people who have power, or "medicine," can perceive their sacred quality and appropriately use sacred objects.

The acquisition of power is arduous and sometimes dangerous. Technicians of the sacred have gained their wisdom by experimenting with the forces of nature. After extensive guidance from an elder, and then ritual "purification" in preparation to receive it, they must undertake the solitary journey to seek their power. Once received, the power must be honored and rightly used. Spiritual power is respected, even feared, by the untrained. For example, some tribal people express concern about repercussions if they do not act correctly in the presence of a medicine bundle.

Spiritual leaders carry responsibility for sacred ways, not for themselves, but on behalf of the people. Humility and integrity are desirable characteristics for those granted power, because the use of sacred power for personal gain has serious consequences. Power can turn against the one who misuses it, and the result can be illness, loss of power, or even death. To keep the sacred ways alive, they must be shared by the people. In the context of sacred ceremony, both the people and the traditions are revitalized.

Names of the Sacred. The source of sacred power is known by various names such as *Manitou (Manido, Manito)* to the Ojibwa, *Wakan (Wakanda)* to the Sioux, and *Orenda* to the Iroquois, with each tribe having its own way of interpreting, contacting, and making use of this power. Manifestations of power can be found most often in nature, and these spiritual forces can be addressed through offerings, prayer, and a sacrifice, a term which means "to make sacred" or to empower with ritual. After the time of European contact, comparisons made to Christianity led to misinterpretations of some of the original meanings of the terms wakan, manitou, and orenda. For example, Kitchi Manitou, Great Spirit, became commonly accepted as the equivalent of God. Many tribes also use the term Creator when referring to this source of sacred power.

Manitou. As chief of the manitous, Kitchi (also spelled "Gitche" and "Gitshe") Manitou is not a personality but the expression of all good. Beneficent, yet invisible and nonmaterial, Kitchi Manitou is the Uncreated God, the source of all. Other manitous, eternal spirits brought into being at the creation, are prototypes of rocks, plants, animals, birds, and elemental forces. Sun, moon, winds, thunder, lightning, and even the seasons are manitous.

In Ojibwa belief, everything was animate, and manitous had power to cause great problems. Fortunately, in such a potentially hostile environment, the help of compassionate spirits could be obtained though humble petition. For the Ojibwa, the seeking of a vision was the preferred method for finding one's manitou or guardian spirit. The seeker went out in solitude, prayed, offered tobacco, and sacrificed by fasting for several days until contact had been made, often in a dream. It was believed that the more humble or pitiable the seeker, the more likely the spirits were to grant a vision.

Once a relationship was made, it was usually kept secret so that the sacred power received would not be diminished. The person could call upon the guardian spirit for help in many circumstances. Among the manitous were cedar and birch trees, deer, bear, moose, otter, sturgeon, hummingbird, and eagle. Spirit helpers responded to prescribed rules within the tradition, and members of the Midewiwin, the Grand Medicine Society, could assist in making contact with the appropriate manitous for any situation.

Wakan. As a general term, "wakan" means sacred or holy, imbued with the life-giving force of spiritual power. A thing or person is wakan to the extent that the principles of that sacred quality are expressed. Although originally wakan had many meanings and several manifestations, perhaps the order of spiritual powers of the Sioux would be most comparable to the hierarchy of Christian deities, with Wakan (Great Mystery) akin to the Godhead and Wakan-Tanka (Great Spirit) similar to God. Wanbli Galeshka (Spotted Eagle), who carries prayers to Great Spirit, could be compared to Jesus Christ.

A holy person, wichasha wakan, has the power to make others wakan. Their powers have been acquired through dreams and vision experiences, often over many years, and they are qualified to lead others in seeking spiritual vision. Holy people are sometimes incorrectly called "medicine people." In some traditions the terms "medicine" and "spiritual power" are synonymous; however, among the Sioux, a medicine person is one who has knowledge of curative herbs. When using herbs, a medicine person is said to be "doctoring." It is possible for a holy person to be a medicine person as well.

A wakan woman brought the calf pipe to the Sioux. White Buffalo-Calf Maiden, known also as Calf Pipe Woman, presented the pipe bundle to the people, calling it lela wakan, very sacred, and telling them, "When you pray with this pipe, you pray for and with everything." The sacred pipe, sometimes incorrectly called peace pipe, was given so the people might have knowledge. This wakan woman also taught that the wingeds, the two-leggeds, and the four-leggeds, and those born to them, were all wakan. As gifts from Wakan-Tanka (Father or Grandfather) they deserved respect. She explained that the earth (Mother or Grandmother) was wakan and that every step taken upon her should be a prayer. Through the sacred pipe, the people were connected to all that is sacred and

told to walk the path of life—the sacred red road—and to honor everything and everyone as wakan.

Orenda. The Iroquois term "orenda" identifies a power that can be likened to electricity in that it is invisible, flowing energy. As limitless power orenda is not a spirit or entity but is present in earth, sky, nature—all that exists. Inherent in this power, and derived from it, are the dualisms of visible and invisible, material and spiritual, life and beyond life. The Master of Life, who willed the world into being, had an evil brother who constantly battled against him. Although the Iroquois had no hierarchy of spirit beings to direct orenda, all supernatural power came from this impersonal energy, which was accessed through dreams. A deep reverence was held for one's own orenda. Beyond this power the Iroquois believed in animal spirits, such as eagle and bear, and many unranked supernaturals, including the Earth Mother, Sun, and the Master of Life.

Adults and young people sought to communicate with the supernatural individually through vision experiences or collectively through tribal ceremonies. The Iroquois had no category of spiritual guides to the people; such duties were performed as needed by those designated to maintain the traditions. These males and females were called Keepers of the Faith. Others had acquired the ability to cure illnesses. Members of the False Face Society, a well-known Iroquois curing society, would arrive at a patient's house wearing wooden masks carved to represent spiritual beings. Amid grunts, shouts, and scraping of their turtle-shell rattles, they entered the house and scattered ashes on the patient to drive away the illness. They were given gifts and special food in exchange for the curing ritual.

A practical application of the concept of the sacred exists within the Iroquois' agricultural tradition in the special designation given to the main foods of the Iroquois—corn, beans, and squash. They were known as "the three sisters," and the people called them "our life" or "our supporters." It was believed that each kind of food was originally brought about by supernatural causes, and it was the custom to offer the first harvest obtained to the particular spirit who controlled it. Festivals were held to honor strawberries, maple sap, green corn, and ripe corn.

Feminine Aspects of the Sacred. For many Pueblo tribes, the source of the sacred, the spirit within everything, is seen as predominantly female. Many tribal people consider the power to make life to be the source of all power. Old Spider Woman, Corn Woman, Earth Woman, and Thought Woman—all are aspects of this female Creator, for out of thought all things are born. In her various aspects, woman makes all things sacred. Creative power, made visible in the mystery of birth, gives predominance in many tribes to the role of mother. Nor is woman's power only life-giving; she also destroys. Born of Earth Mother, all life returns to her in death to complete the sacred cycle.

—Gale M. Thompson

See also Bundles, sacred; Calumets and pipe bags; Ethnophilosophy and worldview; False Face Ceremony; Kivas; Midewiwin; Religion; Religous specialists; Sacred narratives.

Bibliography

Allen, Paula Gunn. *The Sacred Hoop*. Boston: Beacon Press, 1986. Reprint. Boston: Beacon Press, 1992. Essays written from the perspective of a Laguna-Sioux Indian woman. Shows importance of Native American female deities to creation myths. Poetry, chants, and stories emphasize the significance of oral tradition. Detailed notes, extensive categorized bibliography, index.

Beck, Peggy V., Anna Lee Walters, and Nia Francisco. *The Sacred: Ways of Knowledge, Sources of Life*. Redesigned ed. Tsaile, Ariz.: Navajo Community College Press, 1992. A comprehensive study of sacred ways. Incorporates numerous quotations from well-known texts and from interviews with members of various tribes. Includes definitions within text. Suggests additional readings for each chapter. Photographs, illustrations, drawings, maps, and charts. Extensive bibliography, listing of films and filmstrips, index.

Black Elk. *The Sacred Pipe*. Edited by Joseph Epes Brown. Norman: University of Oklahoma Press, 1953. Narrative of teachings from Black Elk, holy man of the Oglala Sioux, from 1947 to 1950. Features story of the sacred pipe. ˥˙tails the seven rites of the Sioux, including sweatlodge, ˌon quest, and Sun Dance. Photographs, illustrations, index.

Brown, Joseph Epes. *The Spiritual Legacy of the American Indian*. New York: Crossroad, 1982. A collection of essays on the diversity of Native American spiritual heritages within the context of world religious traditions. Quotations, songs, chants, and myths. Chapter notes; map of North American culture areas.

Eliade, Mircea. The Sacred and the Profane. Translated by Willard R. Trask. New York: Harcourt, Brace, 1959. Defines the opposition between two modalities of experience: sacred and profane, or real and unreal. Discusses sacred space and time; examines concept of nature as sacred. Compares Christianity, Buddhism, Hinduism, and Native American religions. Bibliography, index.

Highwater, Jamake. The Primal Mind. New York: Harper & Row, 1981. A contrast of lifestyles and worldviews of American Indians with ideas and values of Western culture. Highwater redefines "primitive" mind and suggests the possibility of a potent blending of primal and Western thought. Bibliography, name and source index, subject index.

Landes, Ruth. *Ojibwa Religion and the Midéwiwin*. Madison: University of Wisconsin Press, 1968. An anthropological account of Ojibwa life in the 1930's. Enhanced by narratives from two Ojibwa informants, a shaman and a visionary. Rituals, songs, and prayers of the Midewiwin. Photographs and illustrations. Glossary, bibliography, index. Appendices include dreams, birchbark, scrolls, rock paintings.

Sacred narratives

Tribes affected: Pantribal

Significance: Sacred narratives, important to tribal identity and reflecting tribal philosophy, tell of such things as the origin of the world, of the people themselves, and of certain ceremonies

The most ancient and sacred narratives are those that recount the origins of the earth and the development of its life forms. Many of these events also incorporate understanding of historical events such as migrations, establishment of clans, or the transition from hunting-gathering to an agricultural economy. Two major creation story themes are the earth-diver story and the emergence myth; these stories explain how the present world of human beings and society came into being, and both are widely distributed over North America.

Earth-Diver Stories. Earth-diver stories tell of the creation or re-creation of the world. An Ojibwa (Chippewa) story provides an example. The great trickster/hero Wenebojo (or Manibozho) has, by failing to curb his instincts, caused a flood to cover the world; it has left him standing on top of a tree. Wenebojo sends down small animals to bring up a bit of earth, but the first ones fail. Finally, Muskrat floats up dead but with a grain of sand in each paw and in his mouth; Wenebojo breathes life back into Muskrat and then, flinging the grains of sand over the water, creates an island that will become the present world. The previous world was considered to be a different place, one which is now inaccessible to ordinary people. The story has been interpreted on various levels: a psychological/moral interpretation sees Wenebojo as Everyman, who must dive within himself to form his character; a symbolical/historical exegesis notes that the story offers a symbolic union between Wenebojo and the earth, establishing the people belonging to Wenebojo as the appropriate dwellers in this particular place.

Emergence Stories. Also distributed throughout the continent but most concentrated in the Southwest are emergence narratives of creation. These stories recount the travels of the people as they begin in lower worlds under the earth and move upward through succeeding levels until finally, with the help of powerful beings such as Hummingbird, they are able to squeeze through a narrow passageway such as a reed or hollow log into the present world. The number of underground worlds varies from story to story, as do the identities of the sacred helpers and the natures of the underground worlds.

These are stories of evolution and progression, modeled on the processes of fetal development and birth, which also depict moral and social evolution. Typically, the people begin in a sorry state, sometimes blind or maimed, copulating and killing indiscriminately, and they learn human and humane behavior as part of their progress to the present world. Emergence stories establish the relationship of the people to their territory through the metaphor of being born from the earth; they also include migration stories and establish the origins of clans and tribal laws. Choctaw origin stories show many of these features: the Choctaw origin story tells of a migration from the southwest, from the great cultures of central Mexico, and of an emergence from a sacred burial mound at the center of their homeland along the Mississippi.

Other Creation Stories. Emergence and earth-diver stories are well known and have been published in many versions and texts. Many other stories, equally profound, are less noted. For example, the creation myth of the Achumawi, a small nation living near Mount Shasta in northern California, is a story rich in insight, humor, and mystical understanding. The world emerges from a haze of mist and hills through the thinking and acting of mysterious beings Annikadel, Aether Man, Sun Woman and Moon Man, Coyote, Frog Woman and others. In many stories the first creator is a mysterious or remarkable being such as Annikadel, but in other cases the creator is a familiar creature, such as Grandmother Spider, who, in the Southwest, spins the world from her body and creates things by thinking of them and naming them.

Trickster Stories. The figure of Coyote the Trickster has entered the folklore of the mainstream culture. Originally, Coyote, like the other trickster figures, was a being of supernatural power who determined through his various adventures the shape and function of the present world. Paul Radin's publication of *The Trickster* (1956) and subsequent commentary by scholars such as Karl Kerenyi and Carl Gustav Jung made this figure one of the most familiar to non-Indians. The Winnebago trickster story is an extended meditation on the relationship between nature and society as it examines the possibilities and consequences of the behavior of purely "natural" man unmediated by any social structures. It has also been read as an allegory of development from immaturity and infantilism to something approaching adulthood, and it includes an account of trickster's part in creating the world. The Winnebago trickster is a warrior; other beings that play the part of trickster in different tribes include, besides Coyote, Blue Jay, Raven, and Hare.

Origins of Ceremonies. A great many sacred stories relate the origins of a religious ceremony. These stories often follow a pattern of infraction/punishment-exile/test/guidance/return. The protagonist breaks some rule or law, is punished by exile or even death, receives the guidance of supernatural beings in passing various tests, and eventually returns to the community with a ceremony or song that was learned on the journey and that will help the community heal and sustain itself. A highly elaborated example of one of these ceremonial origin myths is the story of the stricken brothers that underlies the Nightway, the most complex of the Navajo chantways. The journey theme of ceremonial origin myths has inspired contemporary writers such as Leslie Marmon Silko, whose novel *Ceremony* (1977) is structured as such a story.   —*Helen Jaskoski*

See also Ethnophilosophy and worldview; Manibozho; Oral literatures; Religion; Religious specialists; Tricksters; Twins.

BIBLIOGRAPHY

Bierhorst, John, ed. *The Red Swan: Myths and Tales of the American Indians.* New York: Farrar, Straus & Giroux, 1976.

Bright, William. *Coyote Stories.* Chicago: University of Chicago Press, 1978.

Diné bahane: The Navajo Creation Story. Translated by Paul G. Zolbrod. Albuquerque: University of New Mexico Press, 1984.

Hale, Horatio, ed. *The Iroquois Book of Rites.* 1883. Reprint. Edited by William N. Fenton. Toronto: University of Toronto Press, 1963.

Jones, William, ed. *Ojibwa Texts.* Edited by Truman Michelson. Publications of the American Ethnological Society 7, no. 2 (1919).

Matthews, Washington, ed. *The Night Chant.* 1902. Reprint. New York: AMS Press, 1978.

Radin, Paul, ed. *The Trickster: A Study in American Indian Mythology.* London: Routledge & Kegan Paul, 1956. Reprint. New York: Schocken Books, 1972.

Thompson, Stith, ed. *Tales of the North American Indians.* 1929. Reprint. Bloomington: Indiana University Press, 1968.

Salinan: Tribe

CULTURE AREA: California
LANGUAGE GROUP: Salinan
PRIMARY LOCATION: Monterey and San Luis Obispo counties, California
POPULATION SIZE: 301 (1990 U.S. Census)

Like many other California Indians, the Salinan are not distinguished by political or social organization but rather by language. The term Salinan has been adopted by modern scholars from the Salinas (Spanish for "salty") River, although others claim that the people's own name was Ennesen. Three subdivisions have been identified: Antoniaño, after Mission San Antonio (founded 1771), or Kahtritram; Migueleño, after Mission San Miguel (founded 1797), or Tepotrahl; and Playano, after the *playa* (Spanish for beach), or Lahmkahtrahm.

Europeans first encountered the Salinan, who numbered about three thousand, when Gaspar de Portolá led a Spanish expedition from San Diego in search of Monterey Bay. Based on several records of that expedition that described the Salinan as "docile," "friendly," and otherwise amenable, Franciscan missionaries established San Antonio and began the work of replacing native culture with Christianity and other aspects of Spanish culture. The effort was not wholly successful, as a report by the padres in 1814 indicated that many features of Salinan culture (language, diet, even religion) still persisted.

Despite the evidence of cultural survival, the numbers of Salinan at San Antonio and later at San Miguel underwent a steady downward progression. By the time of secularization, around 1834, the approximate population at San Antonio was less than 550 and at San Miguel around 600. Subsequent numbers are difficult to define because enumerators did not always identify Salinans clearly, but they almost certainly show a continued decline. A special survey in 1904 showed only 105 Salinans living in Monterey County and another ten in San Luis Obispo County. The federal roll of 1928 located eleven full Salinans of the San Antonio branch and four from San Miguel, as well as other combinations for a total of thirty-five people with varying degrees of Salinan ancestry. According to an informant in 1987, all pure Salinans had since died. Although some three hundred individuals who claimed to trace partial Salinan origin resided in the area at the time of the 1990 census, no recognized tribal organization has ever existed.

Even in the early twentieth century, when some pure Salinans were still alive to impart sketches of their language to linguists and recollections of their culture to anthropologists, most scholars conceded that Salinan culture was essentially extinct. Available evidence indicates that the Salinans differed little from other Indians of California. As hunter-gatherers, they consumed a wide variety of animals and plants, especially acorns. While some religious mythology has been recorded—shamans clearly played an important role in Salinan society—their religion seems to have regarded no animal as sacred and thus immune to hunting. The fur of some animals was used for winter blankets, but normal dress was nonexistent for men; women wore a simple apron. Pottery, metallurgy, masonry, and complex religious or political organizations were all unknown. The simplicity of Salinan culture made it highly vulnerable to white cultural conquest and contributed to its early elimination.

See also California.

Salish: Tribe

CULTURE AREA: Northwest Coast
LANGUAGE GROUP: Salishan
PRIMARY LOCATION: Northwest Washington State, southwest British Columbia
POPULATION SIZE: 4,455 in U.S. (1990 U.S. Census); 1,900 in Canada ("Straits Salish," Statistics Canada, based on 1991 census)

The term "Salish" refers to a category of Native American languages that are spoken by native peoples based largely in northwestern Washington and southwestern British Columbia, although extending into northern Idaho and Montana with the Flathead (or Inland Salish) tribes, who also speak a Salishan language, and as far north on the Canadian coast as the Bella Coola villages around Dean and Burke channels. The Salish-speaking peoples (whose various dialects have been extensively mapped and studied by Wayne Suttles of Portland State University) extend as far south as the Chinook at the mouth of the Columbia River in Oregon and Washington. There is a major dialect division between the Coastal Salish and the Inland Salish. It is presumed that Salish-speaking people first traveled from inland, down the Fraser River before spreading out along the coast, where their traditional lands now overlap major urban areas such as the Seattle-Tacoma area of Washington State and Vancouver in British Columbia.

While it is difficult to generalize about a large number of unique groups who share a general linguistic family, it is possible to say that the Coastal Salish developed a strong maritime culture, based on the extensive supplies of salmon, halibut, cod, and sea mammals, all of which they harpooned or netted in a variety of ingenious ways. The vast forests of the Pacific Northwest also allowed the Salish (as well as other coastal peoples of the Northwest such as the Tlingit and Haida) to develop artwork in wood and to build large plank-house dwellings. Cedar bark was even developed into a kind of textile, used for clothing. Canoes were another specialty, although the Northwest Coast peoples generally were not seafarers as were the Polynesians or the Scandinavian peoples.

Salish society was typically highly stratified, divided into elite, common, and slavery classes—classes that were maintained by elaborate social rituals and observance of a strict etiquette of behavior, such as marrying within one's level of society. Salish religious traditions were elaborate, placing particular emphasis on the importance of dreams.

See also Bella Coola; Chinook; Flathead; Quinault; Salishan language family.

BIBLIOGRAPHY

Barnet, Homer. "The Coast Salish of Canada." In The North American Indians: A Sourcebook, edited by Roger Owen, James Deetz, and Anthony Fisher. New York: Macmillan, 1967.

Drucker, Philip. "Indians of the Northwest Coast." In The North American Indians: A Sourcebook, edited by Roger Owen, James Deetz, and Anthony Fisher. New York: Macmillan, 1967.

Hill-Tout, Charles. The Salish People. Edited by Ralph Maud, 1978. Reprint. Seattle: University of Washington Press, 1987.

Suttles, Wayne, and Ralph Maud, eds. Coast Salish Essays. Seattle: University of Washington Press, 1987.

Salishan language family

CULTURE AREAS: Northwest Coast, Plateau
TRIBES AFFECTED: Bella Coola, Chehalis, Clallam, Coeur d'Alene, Columbia, Colville, Comox, Cowichan, Cowlitz, Duwamish, Flathead, Lake, Lillooet, Lummi, Methow, Muckleshoot, Nisqually, Nooksack, Okanagan, Puyallup, Quinault, Samish, Sanpoil, Seechelt, Semiahmoo, Shuswap, Siletz, Skagit, Snohomish, Snoqualmie, Songish, Spokane, Squamish, Suquamish, Thompson, Tillamook, Twana, Wenatchi

Salishan is a family of languages spoken in the Northwest Coast and Plateau culture areas. It comprises twenty-three languages; sixteen were spoken in the coastal area, and seven were spoken in the Plateau area (the Interior Salish languages). Some experts denote three large branches of Salishan: Coast, Tsamosan (formerly Olympic), and Interior. Others consider Coastal and Inland Salish to be the main distinctions and divide Coastal Salish into four groups: Bella Coola, Tillamook (including Siletz), Central, and Tsamosan.

The Coast branch contains Clallam, Comox, Halkomelem (including Cowichan), Nooksack, Pentlatch, Seechelt, Squamish, Northern Straits (Lummi, Samish, Semiahmoo, and Songish), Puget Sound Salish (Duwamish, Lushootseed, Muckleshoot, Nisqually, Puyallup, Skagit, Snohomish, Snoqualmie, and Suquamish), and Twana. Tsamosan contains Lower Chehalis, Upper Chehalis, Cowlitz, and Quinault. Interior Salish is subdivided into Northern Interior Salish, including Thompson, Shuswap, and Lillooet, and Southern Interior Salish, including Coeur d'Alene, Columbian (Columbia and Wenatchi), Okanagan (Okanagan, Colville, Lake, Sanpoil), and Kalispel, including Flathead and Spokane.

Salish was first documented in the latter part of the eighteenth century. In 1793, Europeans first recorded a Salishan language—twenty-five words of Bella Coola were recorded by the Alexander Mackenzie expedition. Systematic collection of Salishan terms and grammars did not begin until the early to mid-nineteenth century, when missionaries and ethnographers began to visit the area. Serious linguistic collection, under the direction of the Bureau of American Ethnology, began in 1884 and still continues.

Most Salishan languages are threatened with extinction; others are already extinct. There are probably slightly more than three thousand speakers of Salishan languages today, most speaking Interior Salish languages. The Interior groups were less affected by epidemic disease and forced schooling. Most important, they were less subject to forcible relocation to homogeneous reservations, where native languages could continue to exist with less interference from other languages and dialects. Numerous attempts have been made by universities and cultural committees to revitalize Salishan languages, but they have met with limited success.

See also Language families; Northwest Coast; Salish.

Salmon

TRIBES AFFECTED: Northwest Coast tribes
SIGNIFICANCE: The abundance of salmon in predictable spawning runs made them a critical food resource on the Northwest Coast

Salmon frequent the oceans off both coasts of North America, but Pacific salmon have had the greatest significance to American Indians. Pacific salmon (*Oncorhyncus*) are of five species: pink, chum, coho, sockeye, and chinook. All are anadromous, living primarily in the ocean and returning to fresh water to spawn. During those spawning runs, huge numbers of salmon surge upstream and can be caught with ease, usually with nets, weirs, or traps, but sometimes with spears, clubs, or even the hands.

Salmon transformed the Northwest Coast Indian way of life. All salmon spawn primarily in the fall, though chinook spawn almost year-round. Indians began coming to falls and rapids to capture salmon at least by 4000 B.C.E. By 1000 B.C.E. huge quantities of salmon were being caught, then dried and smoked for use throughout the year. Carrying the store of salmon through seasonal movements was no longer practical. Villages became fixed at or near good fishing spots, sometimes with a single year-round village, sometimes with separate winter and summer villages. Prosperity derived from salmon translated into great wealth, impressive arts, and material comfort. Chiefs controlled rights to particular salmon-fishing areas, consolidating their political power.

Traditionally, all aspects of salmon usage were surrounded with rituals and taboos. Overfishing and obstruction of waterways by dams have jeopardized the future of both commercial and traditional salmon fishing by Indians.

See also Fish and fishing; Northwest Coast; Water and water rights; Weirs and traps.

Salt

TRIBES AFFECTED: All agricultural tribes
SIGNIFICANCE: Salt, a necessary nutrient, was used as a condiment by agriculturalists; the salt trade was particularly significant in eastern North America

Human beings require salt in their diets, and hunting-gathering people usually consume adequate amounts of salt through the meat they eat. Agriculturalists, however, typically consume less meat and are forced to use salt as a condiment.

Salt was produced and traded extensively in prehistoric eastern North America after about 800 C.E. At Avery Island, Louisiana, for example, a salt dome was mined more or less constantly from around 800 to the mid-1600's. The salt removed was placed in pottery jars and traded to agriculturalist tribes around the South and perhaps as far north as Illinois. Certain tribes, such as the Tunica, became prosperous through the salt trade.

Salt also was produced by evaporation of briny water. This was particularly important in the Ohio Valley after about 1000 C.E. There, salty water was placed in distinctive broad, shallow ceramic vessels. After the water had evaporated completely, the salt crystals left behind were scraped from the bottom of these "salt pans." Salt for the tribes of the Southwest mostly was produced by evaporation on the coast and traded inland.

Wherever salt was used in native North America, there were taboos associated with it. Among the Pueblo peoples, for example, men had to abstain from consuming salt before participating in religious ceremonies in the kivas. Salt also typically was forbidden during rites of passage among many tribes.

See also Agriculture; Food preparation and cooking; Subsistence.

Samish

CULTURE AREA: Northwest Coast
LANGUAGE GROUP: Salishan
PRIMARY LOCATION: Puget Sound, Washington
POPULATION SIZE: 173 (1990 U.S. Census)

The Samish tribe is linguistically and culturally grouped with the Straits Salish, speaking the Straits dialect of the Coastal Salishan language. They are respected for their skillful carving of canoes, construction of longhouses, gift-giving potlatches, and strong spirituality based on the teachings of the Winter Spirit Dance Ceremony, having preserved their customs and implements during the years of repression by the federal government.

The Samish historically occupied land and maritime sites adjacent to Haro and Rosario Straits, with a sphere of influence extending from the crest of the Cascades down Puget Sound and out to the Pacific Ocean. There are about five hundred tribally enrolled Samish living mainly in the Puget Sound area. Tribal headquarters are located in Anacortes, Washington.

Although documentation shows that more than a hundred Samish men, women, and children were at the Point Elliott treaty grounds in 1854 and that they were included in the initial draft of the treaty, the Samish (and Lummis) were omitted from the final draft. They were therefore denied the land promised in pretreaty talks. Since 1859, the Samish have struggled to correct this injustice and to obtain federal recogni-

An 1857 engraving of Samoset with the Pilgrims. (Library of Congress)

tion. In 1979 the Bureau of Indian Affairs declared the tribe extinct; however, in 1992, federal judge Thomas Zilly reversed the Bureau's findings and remanded the issue to an administrative law judge on grounds of denial of Fifth Amendment due process rights.

See also Salish; Salishan language family.

Samoset (c. 1590—c. 1653): Chief
TRIBAL AFFILIATION: Pemaquid (Abenaki)
SIGNIFICANCE: Samoset was the first Indian to greet the Plymouth Pilgrims

On March 16, 1621, clothed only in a breechcloth despite the bitter weather, Samoset astounded the Plymouth colonists when he walked into their settlement and called, "Welcome, Englishmen." A sagamore of the Pemaquid band of Abenaki Indians of Monhegan Island off the Maine coast, Samoset had apparently learned English from coastal fishermen. He and the Wampanoag chief, Massasoit, had been clandestinely observing the Pilgrims since their arrival on Wampanoag land three months before.

The settlers clothed and fed Samoset, and he departed the next day with assurances that he would arrange a meeting with Massasoit. Several days later he returned with Squanto, a Patuxet Indian who had been enslaved and taken to England but, with the aid of a sympathetic Englishman, had returned to Massachusetts in 1619. Speaking fluent English, Squanto helped to negotiate an agreement between Massasoit and the Plymouth colony, thus launching friendly relations between the whites and the Indians.

In 1625, Samoset and another Pemaquid Indian, Unongoit, signed the first deed between the British and the Indians for the sale of Pemaquid lands, thereby initiating the Plymouth practice of purchasing Indian lands. In 1653, Samoset sold another thousand acres. He died shortly thereafter.

See also Abenaki; Indian-white relations—English colonial; Massasoit; Squanto.

San Lorenzo: Archaeological site
DATE: 1500-400 B.C.E.
LOCATION: Veracruz, Mexico
CULTURE AFFECTED: Olmec

The site of San Lorenzo, situated in the hot, swampy lowlands of the Coatzacoalcos River drainage in southern Veracruz, Mexico, represents one of the earliest and largest centers of Olmec culture. Massive earthmoving projects, monumental stone heads, an extensive stone drainage system, and a wide variety of fine stone sculptures and elaborate pottery vessels signal this center's central role in the flourishing of Olmec society during the Early Preclassic (1800 to 1000 B.C.E.) and early Middle Preclassic (1000 to 500 B.C.E.) periods.

San Lorenzo first came to the attention of archaeologists through the work of Matthew Stirling, of the National Geographic Society, in the 1930's and 1940's. He reported the existence of colossal stone heads carved of basalt. Detailed mapping and excavations at the site were undertaken between 1966 and 1968 under the direction of Michael Coe, from Yale University.

The earliest occupations of the site date to approximately 1500 B.C.E., at which time it was inhabited by village agriculturalists who cultivated maize, beans, and squash and produced gourd-shaped tecomate vessels similar to those being used on the Pacific Coast of southern Mexico at the time. As population density increased, the residents of San Lorenzo undertook large-scale construction activities motivated by ceremonial practices and presumably directed by centralized leadership. These included the erection of a massive platform built of different colors and textures of clay, the surface of which was covered with mounds arranged around courtyards and studded with numerous lagunas, artificial reservoirs that were waterproofed by lining them with stone blocks. A complex system of drains made of U-shaped basalt troughs capped with flat slabs carried water away from these lagunas.

The chief phase of activity is known as San Lorenzo (1150 to 900 B.C.E.), during which time a wide variety of carved ceramic vessels with esoteric motifs were produced. Their designs, hallmarks of the Olmec style, have been found at sites throughout the Mesoamerican region and signal a period during which there was a widespread participation in belief systems that appear to have had their most elaborate expression in the Gulf Coast region. Other characteristic artifacts included polished convex mirrors made of iron ore and thousands of obsidian blades imported from sources in the volcanic highlands of central Mexico and Guatemala.

Among the most impressive objects at San Lorenzo are a series of at least eight monumental stone heads, carved from basalt whose sources lay in the Tuxtla Mountains, some 50 miles distant. Each represents a distinct individual wearing unique caplike headgear and a stern expression. Other sculptures included flat-topped "altars," some weighing up to 40 tons, decorated with representations of elite individuals seated in niches and holding infants that are part human, part jaguar. One hypothesis is that the colossal heads were portraits of a succession of rulers or lineage heads and that both they and the altars were utilized as thrones by powerful members of the site's elite.

Around 900 B.C.E., San Lorenzo suffered a severe setback. Most of the stone heads were intentionally defaced, and a large number of monuments were thrown into a ditch and buried. Changes in pottery suggest the site's occupation by a different cultural group. One interpretation is that the residents of San Lorenzo suffered a military defeat, perhaps connected with the rise of competing ceremonial centers such as La Venta.

See also La Venta; Olmec; Veracruz.

Sand Creek Massacre
DATE: November 29, 1864
PLACE: Colorado
TRIBES AFFECTED: Arapaho, Cheyenne
SIGNIFICANCE: This attack on an almost defenseless Indian camp galvanized the Cheyenne and their allies into a war that lasted until 1869

The Treaty of Fort Laramie (1851) gave the Cheyenne and Arapaho a tract bounded by the North Platte and Arkansas rivers on the north and south and by the continental divide and a line from Dodge City, Kansas, to North Platte, Nebraska, on the west and east. The discovery of gold in 1858 brought many white settlers into this region, however, precipitating a conflict.

Background. Some Cheyenne and Arapaho leaders signed the Treaty of Fort Wise (1861), ceding all lands except a triangle bounded by Sand Creek and the Arkansas River. Efforts to live there were a failure, and many Cheyenne and Arapaho repudiated the treaty.

Governor John Evans tried to negotiate in the fall of 1863, but the Cheyenne and Arapaho refused his overtures. Clashes in the spring of 1864 between the Cheyenne and the First Colorado Cavalry alarmed settlers, who were already uneasy at the transfer of troops east to fight in the Civil War and deeply divided over the question of statehood. Cheyenne and Arapaho raids continued through the summer, prompting the War Department to approve the muster of a regiment of hundred-day volunteers. By the end of August, 1864, more than a thousand ill-equipped settlers eager for action had joined the new Third Colorado Cavalry.

Preparations. Command of the new troops, as well as those in the First Colorado Cavalry, fell to Colonel John M. Chivington, the commander of the Military District of Colorado. A Methodist minister from Ohio, Chivington had come to Denver in 1860 after preaching across the Midwest. When the Civil War began, he declined a commission as chaplain for the First Colorado Cavalry and became a major instead. After leading two successful cavalry charges during the Union victory at Glorieta Pass, New Mexico, in March 1862, he was promoted to colonel of the regiment.

Chivington apparently thought that quick and decisive action was necessary by the late summer of 1864. His veterans were ready for a fight, as were his new recruits. He also knew that the latter's enlistments would expire before the end of the year and that his other troops might be sent elsewhere if he did not win a dramatic victory. Finally, Chivington was politically ambitious—those who were pushing for statehood had already elected him to a seat in the United States House of Representatives (and Evans to the Senate) if Colorado were to be admitted.

Concerned with the situation, seven Cheyenne and Arapaho chiefs met with Evans and Chivington in late September, 1864. The pair refused to sign a treaty with the Indian leaders because the latter admitted that they had little control over many warriors. Upon the advice of Evans and Chivington, however, some of the Indians settled on Sand Creek, near Fort Lyon, about nine miles northeast of present-day Chivington. These Cheyenne and Arapaho, led by peace-minded chiefs such as Black Kettle, believed that they would be protected by the federal garrison.

Event. Chivington arrived at Fort Lyon in late November. He could have attacked a Cheyenne and Arapaho camp on Smoky Hill 50 miles beyond Sand Creek, but that concentration, which was definitely hostile, was much larger and could easily have eluded his troops. Instead he prepared for an attack on the smaller camp at Sand Creek, despite the protests of some of his officers and others in the federal garrison who insisted that the Indians had been promised safety. The force that Chivington led from Fort Lyon toward Sand Creek included about 250 members of the First Colorado Cavalry, approximately 500 members of the Third Colorado Cavalry, and more than 100 of the federal garrison.

At dawn on November 29, 1864, Chivington's force attacked. There were no more than 500 Indians, most of whom were women and children, sleeping in about 100 Cheyenne lodges and a few lodges of their allies, the Arapahos. Black Kettle raised a United States and a white flag over his lodge when the assault began, then fled when it had no effect. Other Indian leaders were killed after trying to persuade the troopers to stop. A few braves tried to establish a defensive position, but their simple weapons were no match for the modern rifles and howitzers of the attackers. Many Indians, including women and children, were shot as they dug shallow pits in the sand for protection.

Nine troopers were killed and thirty-eight were wounded in the attack, many of them by their own comrades. Reports on the number of Cheyenne and Arapaho casualties vary, but most agree that several hundred were killed. A large proportion, probably a majority, were women and children. The troopers systematically looted the camp after the assault, and many of them mutilated the Indian bodies that they found. Scalps, fingers, and other body parts were taken to Denver as trophies.

Aftermath. The Third Colorado Cavalry volunteers were greeted as heroes by their neighbors when they left the service in December, 1864, but officials in Washington were more critical. Benjamin F. Wade, chairman of the Senate Committee on the Conduct of the War, ordered an investigation, as did Army Chief of Staff Henry W. Halleck, who first demanded a court-martial but settled for a military investigation after Chivington resigned from the military during January, 1865. These inquiries were disrupted twice by the death of officers who testified against Chivington, and a distinctly hostile reception in Colorado soured congressional investigators, who condemned Chivington.

The scandal interrupted the political careers of some of those involved. Evans was forced to resign. Chivington lost at least one election to an opponent who raised the specter of Sand Creek, and he held only minor offices for the remainder of his life. The affair was also used as a political club by those who blocked Colorado statehood for another decade.

The massacre led to a general uprising among the Plains Indians, including the Cheyenne and Arapaho, and white settlers endured several years of attacks. Cheyenne raids in Colorado continued until the summer of 1869, when the Battle of Summit Springs ended their operations in that area. By that time, many Cheyennes had died, including Black Kettle. He was mistakenly reported as killed at Sand Creek but was shot in 1868 by federal troops on the Washita River in the Indian Territory, where he had led his followers in a vain attempt to save them.   —*Richard B. McCaslin*

See also Arapaho; Black Kettle; Cheyenne; Washita River, Battle of the.

BIBLIOGRAPHY

Craig, Reginald S. *The Fighting Parson: The Biography of Colonel John M. Chivington.* Los Angeles: Westernlore Press, 1959.

Dunn, William R. *"I Stand by Sand Creek": A Defense of Colonel John M. Chivington and the Third Colorado Cavalry.* Fort Collins, Colo.: Old Army Press, 1985.

Hoig, Stan. *The Sand Creek Massacre.* Norman: University of Oklahoma Press, 1961.

Schultz, Duane. *Month of the Freezing Moon: The Sand Creek Massacre, November 1864.* New York: St. Martin's Press, 1990.

Sievers, Michael A. "Sands of Sand Creek Historiography." *Colorado Magazine* 49 (Spring, 1972): 116-142.

Svaldi, David. *Sand Creek and the Rhetoric of Extermination: A Case Study in Indian-White Relations.* Lanham, Md.: University Press of America, 1989.

Sand Painting

TRIBES AFFECTED: Apache, Arapaho, Blackfoot, Cheyenne, Gabrielino, Luiseño, Navajo, Pueblo, Tohono O'odham

SIGNIFICANCE: Sand paintings are pictures made of finely ground sand derived from stone or other colored material; such paintings are at the center of the Navajo ceremonial system

Traditionally an impermanent art form between painting and mosaic, sand painting (or dry painting, as it is also known) has been used by American Indians of the Southwest and Plains for ceremonial and religious purposes. Little is known about sand painting done by tribes other than the Navajo, either because they did not do sand painting to a great extent, the paintings vanished from use, or they were never recorded. Navajo sand painting was borrowed from the Pueblos and altered to conform to the Navajo worldview. There are possi-

Two Navajos creating a sand painting in Ganado, Arizona. (Museum of New Mexico)

bly as many as six hundred different sand paintings referring to different aspects or events in Navajo mythology, with every chant or ceremony having its own paintings.

The paintings, representing the Navajo cosmological myths and events, are circular, semicircular, or rectangular in shape and are made in three major patterns composed with either a linear or radial emphasis or a dominant center motif. The design is surrounded on three sides by a guardian spirit, with the opening to the east. Designs are symmetrical overall but contain asymmetrical details. Motifs include plants, animals, astral bodies, and supernatural entities called "Yei." Abstracted figures are shown frontally or in profile with full face. Traditional sand paintings are softly colored in tones of brown, red, blue, black, and gold on a tan background.

In sand painting, the act of creating the painting is an essential element in the ritual use of the painting. The paintings are made by singers, also called chanters, with the help of many apprentice assistants, and are made from memory in a prescribed order. Left unfinished or incomplete, the paintings remain secular in nature. The paintings must be made completely and accurately in order to attract supernatural beings called "Holy People" to the paintings, making them sacred and efficacious to the ritual purpose. The final step occurs when the singer sprinkles the complete painting with sacred corn pollen. Immediately after ritual use, the paintings are destroyed to guard against misuse of the sacred power.

Because of the highly sacred nature of sand painting, the Navajo long did not allow them to be observed or made by laymen or unbelievers. When the Navajo began to allow them to be reproduced in permanent form around 1900, it was only because there was a growing concern for preserving this aspect of Navajo life. By leaving them incomplete or inaccurate, they believed the sacred content would be protected because the Holy People would be prevented from infusing them with their power.

Today, sand paintings are made and marketed by both Indians and non-Indians. The Indian Arts and Crafts Board has established criteria for authentic Navajo sand paintings in an attempt to designate as authentic only those sand paintings made by American Indians.

See also Arts and crafts—Southwest; Chantways; Indian Arts and Crafts Board (IACB); Navajo; Symbolism in Art.

Sanpoil-Nespelem: Tribes

CULTURE AREA: Plateau
LANGUAGE GROUP: Salishan
PRIMARY LOCATION: Northeastern Washington

The term Sanpoil is a French corruption of the native name *snpui' lux*, a riverine people who lived at the confluence of the Columbia and Sanpoil rivers and who have been ethnographically included with the Nespelem. They maintained close social and economic ties with the contiguous Nespelem and Lower Spokane peoples and spoke an Interior Salish dialect that was shared with the Colville, Okanagan, Lake, Nespelem, and Sinkaietk.

Traditional Lifeways. The dominant culture features were an annual subsistence round with an emphasis on fishing and root gathering that regulated socioeconomic life and certain religious behaviors. The Sanpoil had specialized fishing technology, mutual exploitation of root grounds and fishing stations, extended trade, leadership through inherited chieftainship and consensus of opinion, a sweathouse complex, vision quest for power and a tutelary (guardian) spirit, animism, shamanism, a midwinter rite of intensification ceremony and world renewal rites, bilateral descent, polygyny, and politically decentralized neolocal residence.

Though the Sanpoil used clay for medicines, cleaning buckskin, and making toys, they had no pottery, using bark and woven fiber burden and storage baskets. Food was cooked in earth ovens, by spit-broiling, or by stone-boiling. Status was gained by oratory abilities, generosity, hunting and utilitarian skills, storytelling, and curing. Social control was achieved through peer pressure, gossip, sorcery, and a well-defined supernatural hierarchy.

Historic Period. The estimated aboriginal Sanpoil population of 1,650 (including the Nespelem) was reduced by half in the smallpox epidemic of 1782-1783. Numbers were further reduced in 1846 and again in 1852-1853, from direct contact with European Americans. Major changes to Sanpoil culture were wrought by the introduction of Christianity, European American trade, settler conflict, and the Yakima War of 1855-1858. The Sanpoil, under the spiritual leader Kolaskin, adopted the Dreamer Religion or Prophet Dance, a syncretic nativistic movement that taught a distrust of white teachings and religion. A minority of the Sanpoil remained Catholic, following the devout Chief Barnaby, thereby causing further factionalism.

The Sanpoil population was estimated at 538 with the establishment of the Colville Indian Reservation by executive order of July 2, 1872, when they and twelve other ethnic groups were forced onto the reservation in an area that encompassed some of their aboriginal land. With intrusion by white settlers and gold miners, the northern half of the reservation was reduced by one-half (1,500,000 acres) in 1891.

Contemporary Period. The construction of Grand Coulee Dam in 1935 destroyed salmon fishing and its value as a trade item, thereby destroying the last of their traditional subsistence economy. There are today no full-blooded Sanpoil, and those few of diminished blood degree are members of the Confederated Colville Tribe, with tribal headquarters and a Bureau of Indian Affairs agency south of Nespelem. Main sources of income include tourism, logging, cattle raising, government and tribal employment, and to a lesser extent annual per capita payments and litigation settlements for the loss of aboriginal resource areas and water rights.

See also Colville.

BIBLIOGRAPHY

Cox, Ross. *Adventures on the Columbia, Including the Narrative of a Residence of Six Years on the Western Side of the Rocky Mountains*. 2 vols. London: Henry Colburn and Richard Bentley, 1831.

Lewis, Albert Buell. *Tribes of the Columbia Valley and the Coast of Washington and Oregon*. Reprint. Millwood, N.Y.: Kraus Reprint, 1983.

Ray, Verne F. *The Sanpoil and Nespelem: Salishan Peoples of Northeastern Washington*. Seattle: University of Washington Press, 1933.

Ross, John Alan. "Political Factionalism on the Colville Reservation." *Northwest Anthropological Research Notes* 2, no. 1 (1968).

Santa Fe Trail

TRIBES AFFECTED: Apache, Comanche, Osage, Pawnee
SIGNIFICANCE: The Santa Fe Trail was a westward route of commerce and migration for traders and settlers, stretching from Independence, Missouri, to Santa Fe in the present state of New Mexico

Although Spain had restricted trade between Santa Fe and American settlers to the north, in the 1820's the Mexican government opened the Santa Fe Trail. Beginning in 1822 and continuing for more than two decades, an annual armed caravan of American traders gathered each spring, first in Franklin, then in Independence, Missouri. The group finally started from Council Grove, Kansas, and proceeded south and west to Santa Fe on what was usually a forty-day to sixty-day trip. Council Grove was simply a strip of woodland on the Neosho River (a tributary of the Arkansas River) where representatives of the U.S. government met with the Osage tribe. About 150 miles west of Independence, Council Grove in the 1830's superseded the former town as a preferred outfitting and "jumping off" point for traders headed to Santa Fe. Unlike the Oregon Trail to the north, the Santa Fe Trail was initially, and remained primarily, a route for traders rather than for migrating settlers.

Leaving Council Grove, the Santa Fe Trail tracked west to Pawnee Rock (also called Painted Rock or Rock Point) at the Great Bend of the Arkansas River. The trail then followed the left or southern bank of the Arkansas past Dodge City, where the trail split: the mountain division took a northerly route through Bent's Fort (actually not a fort but simply a trading post with some settlement), then went south over steep Raton Pass, between Trinidad, Colorado, and Raton, New Mexico. It then went south and west to Santa Fe. The Cimarron division or cutoff was more direct, with no steep grades, but it had very little fresh water for people and animals. The Cimarron cutoff route sliced diagonally through the southwest corner of Kansas, crossed what is now the Cimarron Strip of Oklahoma (Oklahoma was called Indian Territory from 1830 to 1906), and went southwest to Santa Fe. The Cimarron cutoff route followed the Cimarron River for part of its length, but there was also a stretch of 70 miles without drinkable water and with poor grass even in summer. Therefore, each alternative route possessed limitations as well as advantages. The physical toil of traveling on either route, combined with the danger of encountering Apache, or to a lesser extent, Osage or Comanche, warriors, drove up freight prices on the route to ten cents per pound by the early 1840's.

In 1844, Mexican leader Antonio López de Santa Anna closed Santa Fe to American traders. Santa Anna's decision, following restrictive Mexican tariffs in 1842 and 1843, effectively halted the Santa Fe trade and marked the demise of the Santa Fe Trail. Still, more than twenty years of trade through an unforgiving country with some hostile tribes proved that heavily laden pack wagons, whether pulled by mule or oxen, could cross the Plains if sufficiently organized and protected.

Recent historians have suggested that Francisco Vasquez de Coronado's 1541 Spanish expedition approximated the route of the Santa Fe Trail some three hundred years before the fact, moving southward across the Oklahoma panhandle.

See also Apache; Comanche; Indian-white relations—Spanish colonial; Oregon Trail; Osage.

Sarsi: Tribe

CULTURE AREA: Plains
LANGUAGE GROUP: Athapaskan
PRIMARY LOCATION: Alberta
POPULATION SIZE: 810 (Statistics Canada, based on 1991 census)

The Sarsi (or Sarcee), a branch of the Athapaskan family, lived along the upper Saskatchewan and Athabaska rivers. Their name is from the Blackfoot *sa arsi*, meaning "not good." At one time, they lived farther north as part of the Beaver tribe, migrating southward by the early eighteenth century. They lived in bands of related families who traveled and hunted together. There was no tribal government; each loosely connected band was headed by a man whose counsel was respected but not necessarily heeded.

They obtained most of their food by hunting, especially for buffalo, which were typically driven over a cliff or into corrals by large groups of men gathered together for that purpose. The buffalo were used for food, clothing, skin tipis, bow strings, bone tools, and other necessities of life. Women were responsible for making and erecting the buffalo-skin tipis. Most medical care was provided by women, who lacked the knowledge of healing herbs that some other tribes had. Instead, they relied on cauterization for most treatments. Sarsi families consisted of a man and two to four wives, plus several children. Girls were members of their mother's band, while boys joined their father's band. Bands came together for ritual events, including Sun Dances.

The Sarsis' first contact with whites came in the late eighteenth century, when the Hudson's Bay Company set up trading posts nearby. Contact brought firearms and horses to the Indians, which in turn escalated their fighting. By the nineteenth century, the Blackfoot and the Sarsi had formed an alliance to defend themselves against the Cree and Assiniboine. The Sarsi suffered great losses from these attacks, and their population was diminished further by smallpox in 1836 and 1870 and by scarlet fever in 1856. In 1877, they signed a treaty with the Canadian government, giving up their lands. They were placed on a reservation near Calgary, Alberta, along with other members of their alliance. In the second half of the twentieth century, they made their living by farming, stock raising, and logging.

See also Athapaskan language family; Blackfoot and Blackfeet Confederacy; Buffalo; Diseases, post-contact; Plains; Sun Dance.

Sassacus (c. 1560, near Groton, Conn.—c. July, 1637, N.Y.): Tribal chief

TRIBAL AFFILIATION: Pequot

SIGNIFICANCE: Sassacus was the principal Pequot sachem when the tribe was virtually destroyed in war with the English during 1636-1637

A famous warrior, Sassacus was chosen "great sachem" of the Pequots of southern Connecticut when his father Tatobem was killed in 1633. His residence was a fortified village called Weinshaunks (now Groton, Connecticut) on the east bank of the Thames River. His short period as sachem was marked by continuing conflict with the Narragansetts to the east, a war with the English, and the secession of many dissatisfied Pequots. The largest seceding group established themselves as the Mohegans under the leadership of Uncas, a former Pequot angry because he had been passed over for the sachemship. The clash with the colonists grew out of the murders of several English fur traders, attributed to the Pequots. War began in 1636 when Pequot efforts at compensation failed and an English army entered Pequot country. In May, 1637, a joint English-Mohegan-Narragansett force struck a Pequot village by surprise and burned it, killing four hundred to seven hundred people. This event, and the superiority of English guns to bows and arrows, so demoralized the Pequots that they surrendered or fled by the hundreds, ignoring Sassacus' pleas to fight on. With forty loyal warriors and fifty pounds of wampum as a gift, Sassacus journeyed west to the Mohawk country in a desperate attempt to win military support from the Mohawks, the Pequots' traditional enemies. Instead, the Mohawks killed Sassacus and his men and sent Sassacus's scalp to the English. The Pequots' status as an independent tribe temporarily ended.

See also Mohegan; Mohawk; Narragansett; Pequot War; Sachem; Uncas; Wampum.

Satanta (c. 1830—Oct. 11, 1878, Huntsville, Tex.): Tribal chief

ALSO KNOWN AS: Guaton-bain (Big Ribs)

TRIBAL AFFILIATION: Kiowa

SIGNIFICANCE: Satanta was one of the major Kiowa leaders to sign the Medicine Lodge Treaty of 1867; later, he led raids against whites

Chief Satanta was the son of To-quodle-kaip-tau (Red Tipi). He spent his youth on the southern Plains south of the Arkansas River. One of his closest friends was Satank. He was also close to his half-brother, Black Bonnet, and his cousin, Stumbling Bear.

Satanta was distinguished by his red headdress; his red tipi, with red streamers; his *zebat*, or medicine arrow-lance; and his buffalo-hide shield, which was the last of the "sun shields."

The shield was carried into more than a hundred fights. When Satanta went to war, he wore a buckskin shirt painted red on one side and yellow on the other. He was known well enough as a warrior to speak at length at the Medicine Lodge Treaty meeting in 1867, a treaty he signed. In this treaty, the Kiowa agreed to cede their lands and move to a reservation.

In 1871, Satanta, along with Satank and Big Tree, led the Kiowa against the whites in the Red River valley. The leaders were arrested and sent to Fort Richardson for trial. Satank was killed trying to escape. The other two leaders were tried and sent to the Texas State Penitentiary at Huntsville. In 1873, the two were paroled and returned to Fort Sill.

In 1874, the Kiowa, joined by the Comanche, Cheyenne, and Arapaho, went to war against the whites to protect the remaining buffalo herds from slaughter. In this first ecological war, the United States Army prevailed tactically, but the buffalo were saved from extinction. Satanta was sent back to the prison in Huntsville, while the other tribal leaders were sent to Fort Marion in Florida. Satanta died in prison in Huntsville. It never has been decided with certainty whether he died trying to escape or committed suicide. He was buried in the prison cemetery.

Satanta left eight children. His descendants numbered more than 150 in 1993, the year that Satanta was elected to the National Hall of Fame for Famous American Indians in Anadarko, Oklahoma.

See also Kiowa; Medicine Lodge, Treaties of; Stumbling Bear.

Sauk: Tribe

CULTURE AREA: Northeast

LANGUAGE GROUP: Algonquian

PRIMARY LOCATION: Kansas, Oklahoma

POPULATION SIZE: 4,517 ("Sac and Fox," 1990 U.S. Census)

At the time they first encountered Europeans, the Sauk (also spelled "Sac") lived in present-day Wisconsin. By the late 1700's, they were settled in the Mississippi and Rock River valleys of modern Illinois. They are closely related by culture and language to the Kickapoo and Mesquakie (Fox); a formal alliance with the latter lasted from 1733 to 1850 and led the United States government to regard the two as a single "Sac and Fox" tribe.

In the early nineteenth century, the Sauk became divided over attitudes toward the United States. One group, led by Black Hawk, supported the British in the War of 1812 while another party, led by Keokuk, cultivated the Americans. An 1804 treaty sold Sauk lands in Illinois to the United States and led to the tribe's movement west of the Mississippi. An attempt by some to return to their old lands led to the disastrous Black Hawk War (1832).

After the war, the Sauk moved increasingly southward. Iowa lands were ceded, and the tribe settled in Kansas. Pressured there by settlers, in 1867 the tribe accepted a reservation in Indian Territory (present-day Oklahoma). In 1891, tribal lands were allotted to individual members and tribal govern-

Kiowa leader Satanta led Kiowas in battles with the U.S. Army in the 1870's. (National Archives)

ment was effectively dissolved. In the 1930's, the tribe reorganized as the Sac and Fox tribe of Oklahoma, with an elected chief.

See also Black Hawk; Black Hawk War; Fox; Keokuk; Kickapoo.

Saybrook, Battle of

Date: September, 1636-May, 1637
Place: Saybrook, Connecticut
Tribe affected: Pequot
Significance: Defeat in this battle, actually a nine-month siege of Fort Saybrook, led to the destruction of the Pequots as a power in the Northeast

The roots of the Battle of Saybrook are found in the 1634 treaty between the Pequots and Massachusetts Bay. The treaty granted the Pequots trade with Massachusetts and peace with the Narragansetts. In exchange the Pequots were required to deliver a specified amount of wampum to Massachusetts. When the Pequot wampum delivery did not meet expectations, Massachusetts officials viewed the wampum delivery as proof of the Pequots' subordinate status. John Winthrop, Sr., former and future governor of Massachusetts, said that the Pequots relinquished their right to Connecticut to Massachusetts in 1635. This claim provided the justification necessary for Massachusetts to involve itself in the settlement of the Connecticut Valley, a region beyond the boundary of the Massachusetts royal charter. Working in conjunction with the Saybrook Company, Massachusetts officials built Fort Saybrook at the mouth of the Connecticut River.

In July, 1636, John Winthrop, Jr., nominal governor of Fort Saybrook, met with the Pequots and issued an ultimatum. Winthrop demanded that the Pequots meet English expectations regarding wampum demands and hand over the killers of Captain John Stone. Winthrop knew that Western Niantics had killed Stone a few years earlier; his demands were not meant to be accepted. To avoid trouble, the Pequot sachem Sassacus placed the Pequot territory under Massachusetts' domain. Shortly thereafter, events occurred that produced the First Pequot War. Block Island Narragansetts killed Captain John Oldham in July, 1636. In August, 1636, colonial militiamen sailed to Block Island and looted and burned empty villages. Colonists then turned their attention to the Pequots. They wanted the Pequots' land, and they used Oldham's murder to justify an expedition against the Pequots. The expedition failed to subdue the Pequots, and the Indians saw the expedition as an injustice.

In September the Pequots took up arms, and by November, 1636, they had isolated Fort Saybrook. The Pequots chose not to attack more northerly communities such as Hartford. The militiamen stationed at Saybrook spent the next nine months cut off from the rest of the colonies, begging for help; none was forthcoming. The Pequots could isolate the fort for that long because the sponsor of the post, the Massachusetts Bay Colony, was distracted by an internal matter concerning the antinomian crisis.

Then in April, 1637, everything changed. In that month colonists drove the Connecticut Valley sachem Sequin and his followers off their land. This ran contrary to the agreements Sequin and the colonists had reached concerning the land. Sequin then appealed to the Pequots, to whom he paid tribute, to aid him. The Pequots did and on April 23, 1637, the Pequots attacked Wethersfield. Connecticut then used the Pequot attack on Wethersfield to justify an offensive war against the Pequots on May 1, 1637. The Pequots hoped their rivals the Narragansetts would support them in their war against Connecticut Valley settlers. The Narragansetts almost did, but Roger Williams secured a Narragansett-Massachusetts alliance that isolated the Pequots. This alliance allowed Connecticut soldiers to attack the Pequots at Mystic in late May, 1637. The predawn attack killed between three hundred and seven hundred Pequots and destroyed the remaining Pequots' will to continue the war. The peace treaty that followed, the Treaty of Hartford (1638), declared the Pequot Nation dissolved.

See also Pequot; Pequot War.

Scalps and scalping

Tribes affected: Tribes in most culture areas of Canada, United States, South America
Significance: Scalping appears to have been a widespread custom of warfare that antedated European contact; it is often connected with spirit-keeping traditions

Scalping was a widely diffused warfare custom among many Indian tribes in the United States, Canada, and South America. Strong evidence suggests that scalping was an aboriginal custom predating the arrival of Europeans, although Europeans, particularly the French and English, did eventually encourage scalp taking and paid bounties to Indian allies for enemy scalps. Scalping seems to have become more widespread after the arrival of Europeans.

The earliest European records carry accounts of scalping from widely different areas of the Americas. These European accounts express surprise at the practice of scalping, and they attempt to document and explain the ritualized customs connected with scalping. Indian languages from many culture areas also contain extensive and precise language referring to the scalp, the act of scalping, and the victim of scalping. Also widely diffused among tribes is the common hairdressing practice of wearing a small braid or lock of hair on the crown of the head. This scalplock was often adorned with paint or ornaments which marked achievements or honors. Hair, because it continues to grow throughout a person's lifetime, was commonly believed to be visual evidence that an individual's soul or spirit was a living thing. It was a commonly held belief among many tribes that the scalplock was synonymous with a person's identity or soul and so represented the metaphysical part of the individual's being. Therefore, it was a grave insult to touch the scalplock casually.

The physical act of scalping consisted of grabbing the braid of the scalplock with one hand and cutting a circle about two to three inches in diameter around the base of it with a knife; a

An eighteenth century English engraving of an "Indian warrior" carrying a scalp. (Library of Congress)

quick jerk tore the scalp from the skull. Scalps were taken from dead and wounded enemies, but the act of scalping was not fatal. If a living person was scalped, the skin grew over the wound but hair did not. Among many tribes those who survived a scalping were feared, because the physical emanation of the soul had been taken.

There were many elaborate customs connected with the taking and care of scalps, and these extended broadly across culture groups. A common practice was to stretch the scalp on a small hoop and then attach this to a long pole or to a bridle or an item of clothing. Most tribes who practiced scalping had a victory dance (often referred to as a "scalp dance") in which the scalps were displayed and the scalp takers were honored for their bravery. Many tribes considered the scalp a living spirit of the enemy and therefore practiced spirit-keeping rituals. The spirit-keeping rituals varied from tribe to tribe, but essentially the scalplock was cared for because it represented the soul of the individual, a respected enemy. The scalplock was sometimes painted, washed, wrapped in a bundle, or buried on the battlefield. There is also evidence that among some tribes scalps were taken to desecrate a hated enemy because

they would forever wander on this earth if they died an unwhole person.

See also Indian-white relations—Dutch colonial; Indian-white relations—English colonial; Indian-white relations—French colonial; Tomahawks; Warfare and conflict.

Scarface Charlie (c. 1837, near the Rogue River, Calif.—Dec. 3, 1896, Seneca Station, Indian Territory): Warrior

ALSO KNOWN AS: Chichikam Lupalkuelatko (Wagon Scarface)

TRIBAL AFFILIATION: Modoc

SIGNIFICANCE: Scarface Charlie was the chief adviser, interpreter, and battlefield tactician to Modoc chief Captain Jack; he performed honorably and brilliantly during the Modoc War of 1872-1873

Scarface Charlie acquired his name when, as a child, he hitched a ride on the back of a stagecoach and fell off. He received a deep and prominent scar on his right cheek either from hitting a sharp rock or from the rim of a wheel of the stagecoach. His involvement in the Modoc conflict with white settlers and the army began around 1851, when as about a sixteen-year-old youth he witnessed the murder by Modoc warriors of an emigrant party that had gotten lost.

Scarface Charlie is most known for his participation in the Modoc War of 1872-1873. He was involved in all the major battles of that war, serving as the most trusted friend, field commander, tactician, and interpreter for the Modoc leader, Captain Jack. Scarface Charlie was a man of peace and conciliation who opposed shedding blood at every meeting with his people. He was also a loyal warrior, brilliant field commander, and tactician who was forced into a tragic war by the depredations of the whites. These two sides of him manifested themselves in many instances but are perhaps best seen in his performance during the Battle of Hardin Butte (Thomas-Wright Massacre) in 1873. Scarface Charlie fought what Richard Dillon referred to in *Burnt-Out Fires* (1973) as "perhaps the classic, most perfect battle in Indian war history." With only twenty-two warriors, he ambushed eighty military men. After killing twenty-seven and wounding seventeen, unable to annihilate the rest, he abruptly called a halt to further killing, telling the survivors that "all you fellows that ain't dead had better go home. We don't want to kill you all in one day." Under his command, the Modocs never lost a battle. The only battle the Modocs lost, which caused their defeat and surrender, occurred when Captain Jack displaced Scarface Charlie as commander.

Several Modocs, including Captain Jack, were executed for their role in the war, but Scarface Charlie was spared, according to one observer because he was "the Bismarck of the band . . . a warrior in arms against our troops and today there are no regrets that he should be pardoned and at large."

Scarface Charlie was appointed Modoc chief after Captain Jack's execution, and he and the remaining Modocs were sent to the Quapaw reservation in Indian Territory. Scarface Charlie refused to interfere with the customs of the Modocs, and he was removed as chief. From 1874 to 1876, he appeared in a tour organized by one of the white principals in the Modoc War to familiarize people of the Midwest and East with the war. Scarface Charlie converted to Christianity and died on the reservation (of tuberculosis) in 1896.

See also Captain Jack; Modoc; Modoc War.

Scholder, Fritz (b. Oct. 6, 1937, Brekenridge, Minn.): Painter, sculptor

TRIBAL AFFILIATION: Luiseño
SIGNIFICANCE: Scholder broke the bounds of traditionalist Indian painting with his brightly colored portraits of contemporary Indians

Fritz Scholder began painting at age thirteen. He was graduated with a Bachelor of Arts degree from Sacramento State University in 1960, and he earned a Masters of Fine Arts degree from the University of Arizona in 1964. He was encouraged to pursue painting by Sioux artist Oscar Howe and by pop art painter Wayer Thiebaud and has been strongly influenced by European artists and styles, particularly Francis Bacon and Edvard Munch, as well as by American artist Georgia O'Keeffe.

Scholder was hired to teach at the Institute of American Indian Art, Santa Fe, in 1964, which he did until 1969. In 1967, he launched his famous "Indian series," with groups of pictures of monster Indians, Indians and horses, Dartmouth portraits, American portraits, contemporary Indians in Gallup, and Indian postcards. With these paintings, he began what one critic called the postmodern interrogation of the historically circumscribed image of the Indian, using Postimpressionist, expressionist, and pop art styles. The series was concluded in 1980, whereupon he vowed never to paint another Indian. In the 1990's, his figurative paintings became shamanistic, often featuring animals and female nudes. A prolific painter and

excellent colorist, Scholder has sought acceptance as an artist who happens to be Indian rather than as an "Indian artist." His work has been shown in numerous countries and has been the subject of three documentary films.

See also Art and artists, contemporary; Arts and crafts—Southwest; Howe, Oscar; Institute of American Indian Arts (IAIA); Paints and painting.

Sculpture

TRIBES AFFECTED: Pantribal
SIGNIFICANCE: Sculpture, whether in wood, pottery, stone, or—in more recent times—various metals, has been an important part of American Indian cultural expression

Native American sculpture represents a deep belief in rhythm, balance, and symmetry. For example, arrow and tool points from some twelve thousand years ago demonstrate admirable craftsmanship and a blending of form and function. Modern Native American sculptors embrace tradition, spiritual legends, and naturalistic symbols, combining these ideas with their own emotion to join feeling and design.

In the Hohokam culture (dating between 700 and 900 C.E.), carved bone objects were used for body ornamentations such as hairpins and armbands; designs included geometrics, birds, and animals. Clay figures decorated jars, and petroglyphs were distributed throughout the Southwest. The subject matter of the petroglyphs is fairly consistent: curvilinear patterns, geometric designs, and numerous life forms. Humans often appear sitting or standing, playing the flute, throwing a spear, or dancing in groups.

Skills in sculpture were passed down through the generations. As new materials became available and new techniques developed, each generation contributed interpretations and innovations. Regardless of their background, most contemporary Indian sculptors take pride in their ancestry and turn to tradi-

A frog effigy pipe from the ancient Hopewell culture, found in Ross County, Ohio. (National Museum of the American Indian, Smithsonian Institution)

tional culture for inspiration. One problem that arises from this approach is the issue of using sacred objects in designs. Sculptors must decide where to draw the line between artistic freedom and the violation of their tribe's spiritual essence.

A variety of sculpture exists in contemporary Native American art. Designs in alabaster, brass, bronze castings, porcelain, clay, black soapstone, limestone, and cottonwood (often used for kachinas and Shalakos) are only some of the materials being used. Subject matter is equally varied. Native American cultures share the idea that humans should live in harmony with nature. Motifs of almost every natural element—the sun, plants, animals—appear from ancient times to the present, and depictions of everyday life as well as more ceremonial matters are common.

See also Art and artists, contemporary; Arts and crafts—Arctic; Arts and crafts—Southwest; Effigy mounds; Gold and goldworking; Metalwork; Petroglyphs; Pottery; Sand painting; Symbolism in art; Totem poles.

Seattle (c. 1788, near Seattle, Wash.—June 7, 1866, Port Madison Reservation, Wash.): Tribal chief
ALSO KNOWN AS: Noah Sealth, Seathl
TRIBAL AFFILIATION: Suquamish, Duwamish
SIGNIFICANCE: As chief of the Suquamish, Duwamish, and other allied Puget Sound tribes, Seattle urged peaceful coexistence with U.S. settlers

Seattle (or Seathl), chief of the Duwamish, Suquamish, and other allied Puget Sound tribes, was the child of Scholitza (daughter of a Duwamish chief), and Schweabe, a chief of the Suquamish. It was not uncommon for upper class Duwamishes to intermarry with other tribes; such matrimonial ties were of political import. Born near the present-day city of Seattle (which bears his name) in 1788, Seattle won credibility among the tribes by providing leadership in time of war. The Duwamish (the "inside [the bay] people"), located at the outlet of Lake Washington along the Duwamish River, experienced extensive contact with white settlers by the 1840's. Seattle urged his people to befriend the immigrants, to allow them to settle on Indian land, and to seek employment among them. Seattle won the support of the tribes for the Point Elliott Treaty, which he signed on January 22, 1855. This provided for the creation of a reservation, submission to agency authorities, and land cessions.

The city of Seattle's "Pioneer Square" rose on the site of a Duwamish winter village. Within a year some Duwamish, Suquamish, Puyallup, Nisqually, and Taitnapam warriors attacked the infant city of Seattle, but the chief withheld his support from their actions. During the two-year conflict (1856-1858), Seattle assisted the Americans. A grateful citizenry named their new settlement in the chief's honor. Initially, Seattle was unwilling to accept this honor, because traditional belief held that after death a spirit would be troubled each time his name was spoken. To allay these fears, Seattle residents paid "a kind of tax" annually to compensate for his "broken sleep of eternity."

The Duwamish were not entirely happy with reservation life. It permitted only a subsistence economy and, because of close proximity to the Suquamishes, caused considerable tension. Starting in the summer of 1856, many Duwamishes resettled near their old home sites, some still living at Foster, Washington, near the city of Seattle, as late as 1910. Chief Seattle consistently urged peaceful coexistence during this time of potential antagonism.

Because of the influence of French Roman Catholic missionaries, Seattle was baptized (possibly taking the biblical name "Noah"). As a practicing Christian, Seattle instituted daily morning and evening prayers for his people, a practice continued after his death.

Chief Seattle, much beloved and admired by white settlers, was described as having "unimpaired sincerity," "an irenic spirit," and a "dignified" and "venerable carriage." He was often compared in character and appearance to Senator Thomas Benton. Following his death on June 7, 1866, at the Fort Madison Reservation, the chief was mourned by all. The city of Seattle erected a monument over his gravesite in 1890.

See also Duwamish; Suquamish.

Secotan: Village
DATE: Sixteenth century
LOCATION: Probably North Carolina
CULTURE AFFECTED: Algonquian

Secotan is perhaps the most familiar of all American Indian villages. The village of Secotan (or Secoton) was immortalized by the English watercolorist and first governor of the English colony on the island of Roanoke, John White, who visited this Indian town on July 15 and 16, 1585, as part of Grenville's exploration of the Pamlico Sound. Many of White's now famous watercolors of native life in the region of Roanoke Island are depictions of scenes from Secotan. Through the years, his painting of the village probably has been the most frequently reproduced depiction of any native subject.

The painting indicates that this Algonquian village consisted of eleven houses, several fields, charnel house, dance ground, paths, and communal fires and cooking areas. It was an open village, not enclosed by a stockade wall. Corn, tobacco, and sunflower were growing unmolested by wildlife, as the fields were watched over by a person on a stand. Secotan was the westernmost town of the Wingandacoa, or Secotan, whose leader was Wingina and whose territory was bounded by the Pamlico River and Albermarle Sound. The Secotan had been at war with their southern neighbors, the Pomouike of the Neuse River, just prior to the visitation by the Grenville party.

Unfortunately, more is known about the spatial arrangement of activities inside the village, because of White's painting, than is known about where the village was located. Several Englishmen mention the village during the era of the Roanoke voyages, giving a fairly good idea of its general position south of Roanoke Island and saying that it was the most southerly of their explorations.

The town itself was situated on the Pamlico River. A sketch map executed by an unknown artist in White's party placed

Secotan on the north shore. The White map of Raleigh's Virginia shows Secotan to be on the south side of the first large river south of Lake Mattamuskeet. David Quinn's exhaustive study of the documents pertinent to the Roanoke voyages of 1584-1590 reconstructs Grenville's journey to have taken the group up the Pamlico River past the Pungo River then right up Bath Creek, where they visited Cotan, back across the Pamlico and up Durham Creek to Secotan, which he would place at present-day Bonnerton, North Carolina. The possibility of "Cotan" and "Secotan" being the same village has been advanced in the past and should not be dismissed.

Several archaeological projects have attempted to locate the famous village along either shore of the Pamlico River, with almost every new researcher proposing a new location. Attempts were made in 1954, 1955, 1965, 1968, and 1980, although only in the latter two projects was the area targeted by Quinn searched. As a result of these projects, all candidates for the historic village have been eliminated with the exception of one on the north shore of the Pamlico River.

See also Algonquian language family; Pamlico; Prehistory—Southeast.

Secret societies

TRIBES AFFECTED: Widespread but not pantribal
SIGNIFICANCE: Secret societies performed important political and religious functions within a tribe

No secret societies existed in the Plateau or Great Basin. They seem to be associated with cultures with true political organization and relatively complex socioeconomic institutions. Though kinship was on occasion a reason for one's membership, acceptance was based on invitation, apprenticeship, and initiation rites. During initiation, the novitiate might be abducted by men disguised as spirit monsters and taken to a secluded area, where hopefully he would undergo a metamorphosis and acquire a tutelary spirit. Rarely did an individual belong to more than one secret society.

Membership was usually voluntary, and sometimes a fee would be paid, as with the Ojibwa. Members instructed the neophyte in the religious meanings of their rituals, and membership was believed to ensure a long and successful life for members. Recruitment in some societies was based on replacing a deceased member. Among some Plains secret societies, membership was achieved by exceptional acts of bravery or military accomplishments.

Some groups, like the Kwakiutl, would wear elaborate costumes with concealed animal bladders filled with blood, which was released at the appropriate time during initiations. Members used masks representing various spirits or animals, some elaborately carved, painted, and even articulated—the outer mask would open to reveal an inside mask, indicating the individual's spiritual transformation. With many secret society members, once they assumed the garb of a particular animal or bird, they were then empowered with that animal's unique characteristics of sound and motion.

Secret society rituals were invariably staged within sacred dwellings or chambers, which sometimes served as dormitories, where members kept their religious paraphernalia. Performances were heightened through the use of hidden speaking tubes in the wall, or through the use of tunnels with trap doors for a sudden appearance of an actor, or by the presence of suspended articulated animals or birds worked by hidden cords. The most dramatic ceremony was when a person would be possessed by a cannibal spirit and commit mock anthropophagy by eating a small, smoked bear corpse representing a human. Hallucinogens were sometimes used for spirit flight and prophetic predictions.

Secret societies were internally graded or ranked, and served specific functions for the group, such as influencing central political control, training shamans, curing disease, particularly in ceremonies, and instructing in mythology and religion. Matters of weather and the occurrence of economically important animals were the ritual concern of certain secret societies. Affiliation further served to integrate members and afford them status with their peers.

Some secret societies originated after European American incursion, probably as a response to deculturative effects, but they were not true nativitistic movements.

See also Military societies; Social control, traditional; Societies, non-kin-based.

Sekani: Tribe

CULTURE AREA: Subarctic
LANGUAGE GROUP: Athapaskan
PRIMARY LOCATION: Mackenzie (Arctic) drainage, British Columbia
POPULATION SIZE: 630 (Statistics Canada, based on 1991 census)

The four bands of Sekani were primarily hunters of caribou, moose, mountain sheep, and goats and trappers of all fur-bearing animals. Sekani waters were devoid of salmon, but whitefish, trout, and sucker were caught. Winter shelters were conical lodges covered with spruce bark. Summer structures were conical moosehide tents, or windbreaks of hide, bark, or firboughs. Transportation was primarily by foot, but spruce bark canoes were used for spring and summer hunting and—after the Sekani had established contact with whites—for transporting trade furs.

In 1793, Alexander Mackenzie became the first white to contact the Sekani. Fort Connelly was built in 1826 for trading of furs and other items with the Sekani and other more westerly groups. The Iroquois and other Indians helped the spread of Christianity, which later developed into messianic cults. In 1870, Catholicism was introduced; by 1924, most Sekani were Roman Catholic. The 1861 Omineca gold rush nearly destroyed the Sekani, reducing their population through disease and conflict. The construction of the W. A. C. Bennett Dam in the 1960's flooded great tracts of Sekani land and necessitated the removal of several intact Sekani groups.

See also Subarctic.

Semiahmoo: Tribe

CULTURE AREA: Northwest Coast
LANGUAGE GROUP: Salishan
PRIMARY LOCATION: Washington, British Columbia

The sea-oriented Semiahmoo lived in permanent winter dwellings. They maintained close socioeconomic relations with the contiguous Nooksack, Downriver Halkomelem, and other Central Coast Salish tribes. Fish were the main provider of subsistence, especially salmon, which stored well for winter. All methods of fishing were employed. Sea mammals, including the whale, were also taken, usually by harpooning. Land hunting and gathering provided a wide variety of foods and by-products. The Semiahmoo, like all Central Coast Salish, were noted weavers, using down, dog wool, and mountain-goat wool.

The Strait of Juan de Fuca was first discovered in 1787 by the fur trader Charles Barkley, and by 1827 the Hudson's Bay Company established Fort Langley on the Fraser River, which became a major trade center for the region. The Lummi Reservation was established on Semiahmoo territory in 1855 with the signing of the Treaty of Point Elliott. Many thousands of miners and gold-seekers entered the area when gold was discovered in 1858, creating further deculturation and conflict for the indigenous peoples.

See also Lummi.

Seminole: Tribe

CULTURE AREA: Southeast
LANGUAGE GROUP: Muskogean
PRIMARY LOCATION: Florida, Oklahoma
POPULATION SIZE: 13,797 (1990 U.S. Census)

The Seminoles were the last of the major southeastern tribes to evolve. During the eighteenth century, Oconees, Sawoklis and other groups from the Lower Creek (Muskogee) towns in modern Georgia and Alabama moved into northern Florida. The name Seminole, in fact, derived from the Muskogee word *seminola* (which in turn was borrowed from the Spanish *cimarron*), meaning "wild," and carried the sense of one going

Seminoles in the Everglades in the late 1940's; their ancestors took refuge in the Everglades in the 1830's to avoid removal to Indian Territory. (AP/Wide World Photos)

to live in an untamed area. The Creeks themselves were a diverse group, and many of those whose descendants became Seminoles sought to escape control by the dominant Muskogees and spoke Hitchiti and other non-Muskogee languages. Others hoped to distance themselves from the growing presence of English colonists in Georgia. The Seminoles also absorbed the remnants of earlier Florida tribes such as the Apalachees and Tocobogas. Lacking a central tribal government, the Seminoles did generally acknowledge a principal chief from the line established by Cowkeeper. Only gradually did the Seminoles acquire a sense of separate identity from their Creek relatives.

Nineteenth Century. After the American Revolution, friction developed between the Seminoles and the United States. Many Seminoles continued to look to Britain for protection, and American settlers complained that Seminoles raided their lands and provided a refuge for runaway slaves. There was some truth in the latter charge, for there came to be a substantial black presence among the Seminoles. Some black Seminoles were slaves, while others lived in their own communities. Many Seminoles supported the Red Stick faction of Creeks in the Creek War (1813-1814). After their defeat by General Andrew Jackson, many Red Sticks joined the Seminoles in Florida. In 1818 Jackson launched an invasion of Florida (the First Seminole War). The Seminoles were defeated and saw their towns in northern Florida destroyed.

After Florida was ceded to the United States in 1819, the Seminoles found themselves on land claimed by their old enemies. In 1823, they agreed to give up their claim to northern Florida. Soon the government began to pressure the tribe to leave Florida altogether. Using dubious methods, federal commissioners obtained the agreement of a few Seminoles to the Treaty of Payne's Landing in 1832, in which the tribe agreed to remove to Indian Territory (present-day Oklahoma). Seminole leaders regarded the treaty as a fraud. When attempts were made to begin removal in 1835, the Second Seminole War erupted. A protracted guerrilla struggle, the government declared it concluded in 1842, though about five hundred Seminoles evaded removal by taking refuge in the Everglades. Their numbers were halved by the Third Seminole War (1855-1858), which marked the last government attempt at forced removal.

Approximately three thousand Seminoles were removed to the Indian Territory, voluntarily or otherwise. Originally assigned to Creek lands, the Seminoles were reluctant to acknowledge Creek authority. Tension between the two groups also arose over black Seminoles (whom the Creeks regarded as escaped slaves). Eventually, in 1855, the Seminoles were given their own lands farther west. During the Civil War, most of the Oklahoma Seminoles desired to remain neutral. A minority signed an alliance with the Confederacy, however, and at the end of the war, the tribe was forced to give up all of its former land and was given a smaller area purchased from the Creeks (now Seminole County). Seminole slaves were freed and incorporated into the tribe. A new tribal government was organized, with its capital at Wewoka.

Twentieth Century. In 1906 the Seminole government was ended, along with those of other tribes in Indian Territory, and the tribe's land was allotted among its members, each one receiving 120 acres. A few Seminoles became wealthy when oil was discovered in Seminole County in the 1920's. Tribal government was reorganized in 1969.

Two hundred or so Seminoles had remained behind in Florida, surviving in small groups and adapting their lifestyle to the Everglades. In the 1890's, the federal government began to acquire reservation land for them, though it was not until the 1930's that a majority of Florida Seminoles lived on reservations. In 1957 the tribe organized as the Seminole Tribe of Florida, uniting both Muskogee and Hitchiti speakers. Some of the more traditionalist Hitchiti speakers, however, decided to preserve a separate identity, and in 1961 organized as the Miccosukee Tribe of Indians of Florida.   —*William C. Lowe*

See also African American-American Indian relations; Bowlegs, Billy; Chickee; Creek;, Creek War; Hitchiti; Micanopy; Osceola; Seminole Wars; Tiger, Jerome R.

BIBLIOGRAPHY

Howard, James H., with Willie Lena. *Oklahoma Seminoles.* Norman: University of Oklahoma Press, 1984.

Littlefield, Daniel F. *Africans and Seminoles: From Removal to Emancipation.* Westport, Conn.: Greenwood Press, 1977.

McReynolds, Edwin C. *The Seminoles.* Norman: University of Oklahoma Press, 1957.

Paredes, J. Anthony, ed. *Indians of the Southeastern United States in the Late Twentieth Century.* Tuscaloosa: University of Alabama Press, 1992.

Wright, James Leitch, Jr. *Creeks and Seminoles: The Destruction and Regeneration of the Muscogulge People.* Lincoln: University of Nebraska Press, 1986.

Seminole Wars

DATES: 1817-1818, 1835-1842, 1855-1858
PLACE: Florida
TRIBES AFFECTED: Creek, Seminole
SIGNIFICANCE: The Seminole Wars were among the fiercest Indian responses to the U.S. removal policy

The Seminole Wars were the most costly wars waged by the United States government against Native Americans. The death of more than fifteen hundred soldiers and an expenditure of more than thirty million dollars failed to achieve the government's policy objectives of Indian removal. The Seminoles were largely Indians who had separated themselves from the Georgia Creeks to live in Spanish Florida. There they were joined by refugees from other tribes as well as by escaped slaves from the Southeast. The wars were a result of American attempts to bring the area on its southern border, and its inhabitants, under the control of the United States government.

The First War, 1817-1818. In the 1810's, the U.S. Congress was dominated by "hawkish" politicians from the South and the West who wanted to annex territory on the southern

This engraving, portraying the Second Seminole War from the white perspective of the time, appeared in 1836. (Library of Congress)

border. The first area to be attacked was part of West Florida, where runaway slaves inhabited an abandoned British fort. A group of volunteers from Tennessee, Louisiana, and Mississippi were led by General Andrew Jackson to the fort on a river at a place called Prospect Bluff. The fort on Prospect Bluff was surrounded by free black farmers who numbered about a thousand. The garrison of the fort itself consisted of about three hundred blacks, various renegade Indians, and some Seminole warriors under the leadership of a former slave named Garcon. The U.S. government wanted to destroy this community because of its proximity to Southern plantations and its attraction to runaway slaves. Jackson and his volunteers made an illegal attack on the fort in the summer of 1816, killing almost all of its inhabitants and destroying all the farms in the vicinity. Garcon and some of the Indian chiefs survived the destruction of the fort but were later executed. Most of the farmers lost their property but not their lives.

The First Seminole War began in late 1817 as an effort to regain runaway slaves but quickly became a war of annexation. Soon after the founding of the country, the United States sought to expand its borders. Expansion on the southern border brought the country into conflict with Spain. Slaves had continually sought their freedom in Spanish Florida after escaping from plantations in Georgia and the Carolinas. After many decades of infuriating plantation owners, the runaway slaves were attacked; many were returned by military invasions led by Jackson. Eventually, Florida was annexed to the United States by a treaty ratified in 1821.

The capture of runaways brought the government into conflict not only with the Spanish, who sought to protect the slaves, but also with the Seminoles, who had befriended them. The blacks and Indians fought three American invasion forces in which they lost their dwellings and most of their posses-

sions. They regrouped, however, forming new villages to which runaways continued to be welcome.

The Second War, 1835-1842. In the aftermath of the first war and the annexation of Florida, General Jackson was sent there to form a territorial government. When this government was created by Congress in 1822, there were four thousand Indians and eight hundred blacks in Florida. Both groups posed problems for the new region. Florida citizens desired Indian lands, and Georgia slaveowners wanted their runaways returned. After a decade of broken treaties, cash-settlement negotiations, and general friction, another period of fighting ensued.

The second war occurred when the federal government tried to remove the Seminole Indians in Florida to the Indian Territory west of the Mississippi River. At the outbreak of the war in 1835, the Seminoles relied on African Americans as interpreters and consultants regarding American culture. Black leaders were active politically and militarily. Neither the Indians nor the blacks, however, could withstand the military power of the United States. Most Indians were moved into the Arkansas Territory, and many blacks were returned to slavery.

The Third War, 1855-1858. This final war resulted because the Second Seminole War had not fully succeeded. Billy Bowlegs, a Seminole leader, continued to attack whites from his headquarters in the Florida Everglades. Government bribes and harassment were of no avail. The black allies of the Seminoles were no longer available, and soon most of the war chiefs were gone; Bowlegs was the last to leave. In a few years another war would occupy the Union. The army was ultimately unable to remove all Seminoles from Florida.

—*William H. Green*

See also African American-American Indian relations; Bowlegs, Billy; Creek War; Indian Removal Act; Osceola; Seminole; Wildcat.

BIBLIOGRAPHY

Giddings, Joshua R. *The Exiles of Florida: Or The Crimes Committed by Our Government Against the Maroons Who Fled from South Carolina and Other Slave States, Seeking Protection Under Spanish Laws.* 1858. Reprint. Gainesville: University of Florida Press, 1964.

Littlefield, Daniel F., Jr. *Africans and Seminoles: From Removal to Emancipation.* Westport, Conn.: Greenwood Press, 1977.

McReynolds, Edwin C. *The Seminoles.* Norman: University of Oklahoma Press, 1957.

Mahon, John K. *History of the Second Seminole War, 1835-1842.* Gainesville: University of Florida Press, 1967.

Peters, Virginia Bergman. *The Florida Wars.* Hamden, Conn.: Archon Books, 1979.

Porter, Kenneth Wiggins. "Negroes and the Seminole War." *Journal of Southern History* 30 (1964): 427-450.

Wright, James Leitch, Jr. *Creeks and Seminoles: The Destruction and Regeneration of the Muscogulge People.* Lincoln: University of Nebraska Press, 1986.

Seneca: Tribe

CULTURE AREA: Northeast

LANGUAGE GROUP: Iroquoian

PRIMARY LOCATION: New York State

POPULATION SIZE: 9,167 in U.S. (1990 U.S. Census); estimated 1,000 in Canada; 6,469 enrolled members of Seneca Nation

The Senecas, members of the Iroquois Confederacy, have resided in western New York from at least the sixteenth century. Traditionally they lived in bark longhouses and traced descent through women. The women owned land, appointed chiefs, and raised maize, beans, and squash. Men were hunters, warriors, traders, and diplomats.

The fur trade and dependence on European goods resulted in competition with the French and other Indians. In 1687 the French destroyed Seneca fields and villages in retaliation for attacks. Afterward, one group of Senecas remained along the Genesee River and another moved west to the Allegany. The Senecas joined the British in the American Revolution, and at war's end found themselves abandoned. Some fled to Canada with other pro-British Iroquois, but most remained in New York. The Fort Stanwix Treaty (1784) imposed conquest conditions, and the Pickering Treaty (1794) defined Seneca boundaries. By 1797 the Senecas retained only 310 square miles in New York.

Demoralized by land speculators and whiskey, the tribe was revitalized in 1799 by the teachings of Handsome Lake, to whom representatives of the Creator had revealed a new way of life combining retention of traditional rituals with a new social structure based on nuclear households and male agriculture. Alcohol and witchcraft were forbidden. Reports of the movement's success came from Quakers residing with the Senecas.

Fraudulent land deals culminated in the 1838 sale of all remaining Seneca land in New York. With Quaker aid, a compromise treaty was adopted in 1842 by which the Senecas surrendered the reservations at Buffalo Creek and Tonawanda but retained those at Allegany and Cattaraugus. Disputes over annuity distributions led to the abolition of government by chiefs and withdrawal from the confederacy by Allegany and Cattaraugus. They jointly created the Seneca Nation of Indians (SNI) in 1848, adopting a written constitution which established an elected council and executive. The Tonawanda Senecas were able to repurchase part of their reservation in 1857, retaining government by hereditary chiefs and becoming the Tonawanda Band of Senecas.

Railroads crossed Seneca territory, and white villages developed within reservation boundaries, particularly at Allegany. The illegal villages were given congressional sanction in 1875 and reauthorized in 1892 for another century. Extremely low rents caused long-standing resentment among Senecas until the leases were renegotiated in 1992 at fair rates. The construction of Kinzua Dam in the 1960's flooded an additional 10,000 acres at Allegany, leaving only 10,000 for the Senecas and forcing the removal of nearly eight hundred people to two new communities of tract houses. Congressional compensation was used to provide college scholarships and to build government offices, medical clinics, and libraries on each SNI reservation as well as a museum, bowling alley, and sports complex.

By the end of the century many Senecas were Christian, but the Longhouse religion of Handsome Lake remained a strong force. Successful SNI enterprises such as gas stations, minimarts and Bingo provided employment for many, but conditions at Tonawanda were less favorable. Debates over the advisability of casino gambling polarized the reservations as leaders attempted to address unemployment and financial security issues.

See also Beaver Wars; Cayuga; Cornplanter; Fort Stanwix, Treaty of; Handsome Lake; Iroquoian language family; Iroquois Confederacy; Red Jacket.

Sequoyah (c. 1770, eastern Tenn. at Tuskegee—c. 1843, near San Fernando, Tamaulipas, Mexico): Scholar

ALSO KNOWN AS: George Guess (or Gist)

TRIBAL AFFILIATION: Cherokee

SIGNIFICANCE: Sequoyah's syllabary enabled Cherokees to become literate in their own language

Sequoyah, a mixed-blood Cherokee, was born near Fort Loudon, about 5 miles from the sacred Cherokee capital of Echota. He was a member of the "over the hill" Cherokees, so named because they lived west of the Appalachian Mountains, probably the son of trapper and trader Nathaniel Gist (or Guess), who abandoned Sequoyah's mother while she was still pregnant. Growing up west of the mountains, the young man became a prosperous hunter and fur trapper-trader. On a hunting trip while still quite young, he damaged one of his legs in an accident and was disabled for life. His hunting career over, he became a craftsman; his silver ornaments became widely sought by various Native American tribes and white traders, as well. While still a young man, Sequoyah moved from the over-the-hill region of Tennessee to Willstown, in present-day Alabama. He had little contact with the white people to the east until the 1790's, when he increasingly encountered white tradesmen. His knowledge of the white world was expanded during the War of 1812, during which he served as one of General Andrew Jackson's volunteers. With Jackson, he fought against the Red Sticks, a Creek faction that had allied itself with the British. In 1813, he participated in such battles as the attack on Tallaschatche, a Red Stick town. In 1814, he fought at the Battle of Horseshoe Bend, where Jackson and his forces decisively defeated the Red Sticks and effectively broke up their resistance to Anglo penetration of their region.

After the United States and his tribe signed the Cherokee Treaty of 1817, Sequoyah joined Chief John Jolly who led a group of the Native Americans into Arkansas country, as provided by the treaty. With his new wife, Sally, Sequoyah took land in present Pope County, Arkansas, and began farming. In his new home, Sequoyah continued to work on a syllabary he started during the War of 1812.

This Cherokee intellectual became fascinated when he observed white soldiers using "talking leaves" (writings on paper) to communicate with family and friends over vast distances. Sequoyah then set about to develop a system of writing for his people. In 1821, he completed the syllabary and "went public" with it. The table of characters included eighty-six syllables in the Cherokee language. Aside from a few characters he borrowed, he had little to do with English, a language he had never learned to speak or write. Once he had polished his work, he taught it to his young daughter and several of her

A portrait of Sequoyah with the syllabary he developed to write the Cherokee language. (Smithsonian Institution)

friends. Then he took the children before the Cherokee National Council at Echota, where they demonstrated what they had so easily learned. Impressed, the Council sanctioned it for the whole nation. Because of the syllabary's simplicity, it could be mastered in a few days at most. Soon, hundreds and then thousands of Eastern Cherokees had become literate in their own tongue. In 1822, Sequoyah took his "talking leaves" back to the Western Cherokees still living in Arkansas, who were soon to migrate into present-day Texas and Oklahoma. His western tribesmen easily mastered the syllabary, just as their eastern kinsmen had.

Subsequently, the syllabary contributed much to expand Cherokee culture and improve the quality of their lives. Education took on added meaning once the writing system was in place. Soon, books were being translated into—or written in—the Cherokee language. The famed missionary Samuel Worcester founded a press and quickly translated the Bible for his flock.

While still promoting his syllabary, Sequoyah developed other interests. The 1820's found him with the Western Cherokee delegation to Washington, D.C., where, with his companions, he lobbied for the interests of his nation. Meanwhile, just as he had earlier developed a system of writing for his people, he also developed a numbering system that his people could understand. Before his work with arithmetic, Cherokees had "mental" numbers up to one hundred but could not add, subtract, multiply, or divide. With Sequoyah's new system, tribal members could easily do so.

Even as he worked on his writing and numbering systems, Sequoyah also developed as an artist. With his paintings he became a natural realist. He took nature—everything he saw around him—and reproduced it.

By 1830, his band had moved into what is now present-day eastern Oklahoma, and Sequoyah himself settled near present-day Sallisaw. There, he developed another small farm and also raised cattle and horses. On his new farmstead he found a salt lick, and soon was able to add saltmaking to his list of practical accomplishments. The rugged Sequoyah also chopped enough wood to have a surplus, which he sold or bartered for other goods.

In the late 1830's, survivors of the Cherokee Trail of Tears reached Oklahoma. Sequoyah was one of the established leaders who helped them to reestablish their civilized way of life. Concurrently, he became a diplomat and helped bring peace—and stop a wave of violent assassinations—among three political factions: the old settlers (Western Cherokees); the Treaty Party, who had "given away" eastern lands to the whites; and the Ross Party, whose members had sworn to take vengeance on the Treaty Party.

Next, Sequoyah aided the Texas Cherokees, whom the whites had forced out of the Republic of Texas in 1839. He convinced those who had earlier promised retaliation to settle peaceably in Indian country and redevelop their way of life. His advice probably saved hundreds of lives, for the military might of Texas was too strong to be overcome. Had the Texas

Cherokees trekked back into the republic, massacre would have been the result.

In 1842, Sequoyah became interested in a new project. He traveled westward, looking for a Cherokee band that traditions said had moved well west of the Mississippi River before the time of the American Revolution. While searching for the missing band, Sequoyah became ill and died near the settlement of San Fernando, Tamaulipas, Mexico. Although the exact date of his death is disputed, it is agreed by most researchers that he died between 1843 and 1845.

Considered one of the ablest intellectuals ever produced by Native American societies, the man of the "talking leaves" was honored by the state of Oklahoma. Officials also placed his statue in Statuary Hall in Washington, D.C.

—*James Smallwood*

See also Cherokee; Education, post-contact; Indian Territory; Journalism; Missions and missionaries; Syllabaries; Trail of Tears.

BIBLIOGRAPHY

Foreman, Grant. *Sequoyah.* Norman: University of Oklahoma Press, 1938.

Foster, George E. *Se-quo-yah: The American Cadmus and Modern Moses.* New York: AMS Press, 1979.

Kilpatrick, Jack F. *Sequoyah: Of Earth and Intellect.* Austin, Tex.: Encino Press, 1965.

Mails, Thomas E. *The Cherokee People: The Story of the Cherokees from Earliest Origins to Contemporary Times.* Tulsa, Okla.: Council Oaks Books, 1992.

Smith, William Robert Lee. *The Story of the Cherokees.* Cleveland, Tenn.: Church of God, 1928.

Seri: Tribe

CULTURE AREA: Mesoamerica
LANGUAGE GROUP: Sonoran
PRIMARY LOCATION: Sonora, Mexico

The Seris are one of the smallest Indian groups in Mexico, numbering about five hundred people, a 90 percent drop from a 1600 estimate of the population. Their homeland was the southern part of the Arizona-Sonora desert along the Gulf of California and on Tiburón Island, where they hunted and fished. They call themselves the Kunkaahac ("Our Great Mother Race"), and six bands constitute the ethnic group.

The Spanish encountered the Seris in the seventeenth century and established missions for them. Given their nomadic lifestyle, however, most refused to join the Jesuit and Franciscan missions and continued raiding Spanish settlements. The seizure of Seri lands after 1748 saw raids continue intermittently through the century.

After Mexican independence, the government sought to resettle the Seris outside of Hermosillo, but trouble continued. In the 1920's the Seris remained on the margins of society, and the 1930's saw an economic revival when there was a demand for shark livers. When American sport fishermen discovered the area in the 1950's, many Seris found jobs as guides for fishermen and anthropologists. Protestant missionaries worked with them. Although the Seris resisted, they are an example of a largely non-Hispanized group that was finally incorporated into Mexican society.

Serpent mounds: Archaeological sites

DATE: 1000 B.C.E.-700 C.E.
LOCATION: From western New York State through the Great Lakes region and southeast to the Ohio and Mississippi river valleys
CULTURES AFFECTED: Adena, Hopewell

Earthen mounds, whether effigy mounds, burial mounds, or temple mounds, are especially prevalent in North America from western New York State through the Great Lakes region and down the Ohio and Mississippi river valleys to the Southeast. It was estimated early in the twentieth century that there were ten thousand mounds in the Ohio Valley alone, but many have been lost to farming, construction, fortune hunters, and even a few archaeologists. The mounds appear in a number of different configurations: Some are conical or sectioned triangles; others are effigies of birds, reptiles, beasts, and people. Perhaps the most well-known and certainly the largest effigy mound in North America is the Great Serpent Mound on Brush Creek in Adams County, Ohio.

Scholarly conjecture about the identity of the mound builders of ancient America has held since early in the twentieth century that the Great Serpent Mound was produced during the Adena cultural tradition, roughly between 1000 B.C.E. and 700 C.E. (The name "Adena" comes from the name of the estate of Thomas Worthington where, in 1901, William Mills excavated a mound and found many significant artifacts.) The Great Serpent is 1,254 feet long, 20 feet in average width, and 4 to 5 feet in average height. The earthen serpent has a writhing, circuitous shape with seven coils in its long body and a triple-coiled tail. Its jaws are wide open, holding an oval figure that might be a frog, an egg, or a moon or sun symbol.

A serpent symbol is prevalent in many cultures, but since there is no oral or written tradition to describe either the mound builders or their purposes in fabricating the mounds, it remains problematic to establish with any certainty the cultural use of the serpent mounds. The enlarged head creates a natural oval embankment that could be variously used as a fireplace or altar or as a place of community meeting, ritual, or worship.

The Great Serpent Mound has been preserved for posterity. In 1883, F. W. Putnam of the Peabody Museum, Boston, viewed the Great Serpent Mound when it still belonged to John Lovett, a farmer. When Lovett decided to sell his land in 1886, Putnam started a campaign to raise money to buy the land in order to preserve the mound. In 1887, on behalf of many (mostly Boston-area) contributors, the Peabody Museum purchased the Lovett farm, including the Great Serpent Mound. In 1888, complete with a turnstile and horse trough, the area opened as Serpent Mound Park. In 1900, the Peabody Museum deeded the land to the Ohio Archaeological and Historical Society; it remains today as a state park.

The Great Serpent Mound in Adams County, Ohio, is 1,254 feet long. (D. M. Reeves, American Museum of Natural History)

See also Adena; Effigy mounds; Hopewell; Mounds and mound builders; Prehistory—Southeast.

Serrano: Tribe

CULTURE AREA: California
LANGUAGE GROUP: Takic
PRIMARY LOCATION: Southern California
POPULATION SIZE: 265 (1990 U.S. Census)

The Serrano tribe occupied a portion of California east of Los Angeles. Serrano is Spanish for "mountaineer" or "highlander." The Serrano were hunters and gatherers who occasionally fished for subsistence. Women gathered acorns, piñon nuts, roots, bulbs, berries, and cacti fruit in baskets. Surplus materials were sun-dried. Periodically, gathering districts were burned over to increase plant yields. Men were in charge of hunting large animals, including deer, antelope, and sheep. Large game were trapped and/or shot with the bow and arrow. Smaller animals such as rabbits, rodents, and birds were captured in deadfalls, nets, and snares. Excess meat was dried in the sun for winter use.

Extended families lived in circular-shaped homes covered with tule thatches; village locations were determined by the proximity of water. Clothing was made of deerskin; rabbitskin blankets provided winter warmth. Ceremonial costumes were decorated with feathers.

Shamans were believed to have special psychic powers acquired through dreams. Dreams were enhanced by the use of the datura plant, which was dried and mixed with water to make a tea producing hallucinogenic effects. Serrano shamans were healers. They used herbal medicines or sucked out foreign objects that were believed to cause illness or pain. The Serrano believed in twin gods who created the world as well as various other supernatural beings.

First Indian-white contact probably occurred in the 1770's when the San Gabriel Mission was established or when Pedro Fage made an expeditionary trip through Serrano territory. These meetings had little effect on the tribe until 1819, when a small mission was built near Redlands. Between 1819 and 1834, many Serranos were forcibly taken into the missions. Not enough Serranos remained behind to retain a native way of life. In the region northeast of San Gorgonio Pass, a small group survived and preserved what little was left of Serrano culture. Throughout the remainder of the twentieth century, most Serranos lived on the Morongo and San Manuel reservations in Southern California. The Serrano continued to participate in native ceremonies and political organizations with other Indian groups.

See also Baskets and basketry; California; Missions and missionaries.

Shábona (c. 1775, Ohio or Ill.—c. July 17, 1859, Morris, Ill.): Tribal chief

ALSO KNOWN AS: Chambly

TRIBAL AFFILIATION: Potawatomi

SIGNIFICANCE: Initially a loyal follower of Tecumseh, Shábona advocated peace and accommodation with whites following the War of 1812

Shábona's mother was a Seneca and his father an Ottawa who may have been Pontiac's nephew. Traveling throughout Illinois in 1807, Shábona recruited tribes for Tecumseh's pantribal rebellion. During the War of 1812, Shábona supported the British, fighting with Tecumseh at the Battle of the Thames, 1813. In 1812, he rescued some white families at the Fort Dearborn Massacre.

Succeeding his wife's father as principal Potawatomi chief, Shábona thereafter advocated peace, becoming a federal ally. In 1827, he persuaded most Winnebagos to remain neutral during Red Bird's Winnebago Uprising. Accused of spying for the federal government, he was taken prisoner. During the Black Hawk War of 1832, Shábona warned Chicago settlers of an impending attack. In retaliation, he was captured by Sauks and Foxes who killed his son and nephew.

Granted land in Illinois following the rebellions, his people were nevertheless forced to relocate west of the Mississippi River. His land was sold at auction. Some grateful settlers bought Shábona a farm near Seneca, Illinois, where he lived for the rest of his life.

See also Potawatomi.

Shaker Church

DATE: Established 1882

TRIBES AFFECTED: Originally Skokomish; later, most Northwest Coast tribes

SIGNIFICANCE: The Shaker Church of the Northwest Coast area, originating in the late nineteenth century, stresses healing and refraining from behaviors such as gambling and alcohol use

The Shaker Church is a native religious movement of the Pacific Northwest and western Canada that originated among the various tribes of the area surrounding Puget Sound in Washington State. This movement should be carefully differentiated from the more widely known historical movement, the "Shakers," founded under the leadership of former Quaker Mother Ann Lee. This latter Shaker movement has very few adherents today (it tends to be associated with furniture styles

and American folklore), while the Indian Shaker Church is still widespread among native tribes of the Pacific Northwest. The two movements have no historic or ideological connection, and the "shaking" itself is a different phenomenon in each group.

The movement began as a result of the visions of John Slocum but was supplemented by the activities of his wife, Mary Slocum, who contributed the ritual movements that gave the church its "shaker" name.

Research by H. G. Barnett recorded a number of versions of the events leading to the founding of the Shaker Church, but a general description can be made. In 1881, John Slocum, a Skokomish (Coast Salish) Indian living at Mud Bay, Washington, appeared to die after spending many years involved in gambling and alcoholism. Many descriptions report that he said that he ascended into heaven, spoke with God, and was instructed to begin a new renewal movement to save the Indian people. The message appeared to involve a preparation for the second coming of Jesus Christ and demanded of his listeners that they stop gambling and give up alcohol. It was also suggested that the dead relatives of the Indian people would soon be restored. He was sent back to his body, where he began to awaken in the presence of family and friends who had gathered to mourn his death. His resurrection amazed his family and was the initial motivation for the starting of the movement. It is often said that Slocum immediately asked for a church building to be constructed, where he began to preach and teach the message that he believed he had been given.

After a period of time, Slocum himself returned to his previous lifestyle and went through another episode of near-death. During his long illness (or, in some versions, a second death), his wife Mary went to a riverbank to get some water; while there she was overcome by bodily shaking. When she returned to John's side, it was seen that her shaking was associated with John's recovery, and the shaking became a part of the movement at that time. This shaking was associated with healing power, and healing became one of the central activities of the adherents of the Shaker movement.

The movement spread rapidly among Northwest tribes, and adherents faced opposition and harassment by missionaries from other Christian denominations. There were also internal difficulties. The movement has experienced some divisions, based on both personalities and doctrine. In 1946, for example, a branch that asserted belief in the Bible broke away and called themselves "Full Gospel" to differentiate themselves from the Shaker Church, known among believers as the "1910 Shakers." The latter group maintains that the Bible is not central to its religious practice.

The movement asserts itself as a uniquely Indian movement, and whites are typically not invited to participate. Clearly part of Slocum's original vision was the restoration of Indian rights in the face of increasing white control of land. In 1855, tribes in the Puget Sound area had ceded all claims to their traditional lands and accepted reservations in return. The slow decline of many of the Northwest tribes resulted.

Today, the central tenets of the Shaker Church are the importance of the events of John Slocum's life and the significance of his message, and God's gift to the Shaker people of the shaking and its healing powers. The latter is particularly important, as Shaker Church members value healing as historically one of the most important activities of the movement. The movement can be considered a Christian sect and may be seen as related to other native renewal movements such as the Ghost Dance religion and the Longhouse religion. As with those other movements, modern practitioners are chary of open discussions of the exact nature of the rites, rituals, and beliefs of the movement, particularly with non-Indians.

See also Longhouse; Native American Church; Religion; Slocum, John.

BIBLIOGRAPHY

Barnett, Homer G. *Indian Shakers: A Messianic Cult of the Pacific Northwest.* Carbondale: Southern Illinois University Press, 1957.

Shaking Tent Ceremony

TRIBES AFFECTED: Cree, Menominee, Montagnais, Ojibwa, other northeastern Canadian tribes

SIGNIFICANCE: The Shaking Tent Ceremony, a shamanistic tradition, was particularly important in Cree culture

The Shaking Tent Ceremony is practiced mainly by the Cree Nation in Canada. Although Cree religious life today is dominated by the influence of Christian missionaries, some aspects of traditional belief remain. Cree religion includes varying forms of belief in a central "great spirit" (Kitchi Manitu) and varying versions of a belief in a malevolent, evil spirit (Matci Manitu) who must occasionally be placated in order to prevent illness and other problems of social life. There are shamans who are practiced in various forms of witchcraft. One of the most prevalent features of Cree religious/social life is the "Shaking Tent."

The actual tent is a structure reserved for this ceremony and storytelling. The ceremony is dependent on the context of shamanism as a major religious expression of the Cree Nation. A shaman figure would sit within a special tent erected solely for the ceremony, and the presence of various spirits would be perceived in the shaking of the poles and sides of the tent. Those who sought the help of the shaman in the shaking tent would typically be involved in an attempt to communicate with spirits, cure illness, or find the whereabouts of missing persons. A number of preparations were necessary to the ceremony, including fasting, praying, and a sweatlodge ceremony. Sometimes the shaman would participate in spectacular feats, such as escaping from fetters while hung upside down within the tent—attributed to the power of the spirits and the power of the shaman himself. The ceremony would involve hearing voices and discerning the spirits from the movement of the tent. The shaman would typically chant songs, sometimes revealed to him in dreams for his use in the ceremonies. The ceremonies were generally performed alone.

Although mainly a Cree phenomenon, the Shaking Tent ceremony spread among the Cree, Menominee, Montagnais, Ojibwa, Ottawa, and Saulteaux nations of northeastern Canada.

In European tradition, certain of the shamans gained fame or notoriety. Etienne Pigarouich, for example, was a seventeenth-century Montagnais who converted to Catholicism in 1639 but often reconverted—to the considerable consternation of the local Jesuits, who recorded many stories about him. There are many recorded instances of Jesuit challenges to the reality of the Shaking Tent powers.

Today, the Shaking Tent is still a feature of larger Cree social gatherings but often as a source of amusement rather than an occasion for awe at the power of spirits.

See also Cree; Religious specialists.

Shalako

TRIBE AFFECTED: Zuni Pueblo

SIGNIFICANCE: Shalako was a winter ceremony to mark the return of the supernaturals to the village, symbolizing the close relationship between the Zuni and the spirit world

In the Pueblo ceremonial calendar, summer ceremonies stress agricultural abundance and rain, while in the winter, curing, warfare, and hunting ceremonies occur. The shalako ceremony takes place at the end of the ritual year, in late November or early December, before the winter solstice ceremonies. Shalako marks the annual return of supernatural beings to the village and reinforces the harmony of the Zuni people with the spirit world. During Shalako, Zunis have the opportunity to bargain with the supernaturals, calling upon them to cure illness or remove evil.

During the ceremony, the Shalakos (six masked kachina figures) enter the village in a procession symbolizing the migration of the Zuni to "The Middle Place," or the world in which the people live. The Shalakos visit homes, where they are fed and spend the night, and where they hold a dialogue with the house owner, recounting the stories of creation and the migration of the Zuni people. In the morning, the Shalakos return to their home in the west.

See also Kachinas; Pueblo tribes, Western.

Shasta: Tribe

CULTURE AREA: California

LANGUAGE GROUP: Shastan

PRIMARY LOCATION: Base of Mt. Shasta, northern California, southern Oregon's Rogue River valley

POPULATION SIZE: 584 (1990 U.S. Census)

The Shasta people lived around the area of what is today Mt. Shasta in Siskiyou County, Northern California. The Shasta people recognize four groupings: the Klamath River people (Wiruwhitsu), the Scott Valley people (Irvaitsu), the Shasta Valley people (Ahotireitsu), and the Rogue River people (from Southern Oregon, Ikirukatsu). There are headmen of each of the four groups, but the head of the Oregon group is recognized as the leader overall, and he is often sent for in matters of great urgency. The Shasta are closely related to other Northern California tribal groupings, such as the Karok, Yurok, and Hupa.

The Shasta people were noted for the use of obsidian in the making of knives and arrow points as well as in wood work. They traditionally hunted deer, and, as with many California groups, the acorn provided the main staple for their diet. Acorns were ground to a kind of flour from which various breadlike products were produced. The Shasta also gathered berries. In these cultural traits the Shasta were traditionally very similar to other Klamath River groups.

While mostly a peaceful people, the Shasta would organize war raids on occasions of great tribal importance. Of equal importance, and practiced far more frequently, were elaborate peace negotiations and rituals. The Shasta practiced a form of shamanism to drive away the evil powers of spirits. Women could be shamans as well as men in the Shasta tradition. Other than a great fear of the power of spirits, the Shasta do not have an elaborate religious ideology.

See also Hupa; Karok; Yurok.

BIBLIOGRAPHY

Kroeber, Alfred L. "The Indians of California." In *The North American Indians: A Sourcebook*, edited by Roger Owen, James Deetz, and Anthony Fisher. New York: Macmillan, 1967.

Shawnee: Tribe

CULTURE AREA: Northeast
LANGUAGE GROUP: Algonquian
PRIMARY LOCATION: Oklahoma
POPULATION SIZE: 6,179 (1990 U.S. Census)

The Shawnee were a prominent Algonquian-speaking tribe of the Northeast. Their name means "Southerner," but the tribe moved so much in historic times that the original tribal homeland is somewhat obscure. Most scholars, however, believe that they originally hailed from the Cumberland River area of Tennessee. Through much of the eighteenth century, the Shawnee homeland was the Muskingum and Scioto River valleys in the Ohio country.

The tribe was divided into five main divisions: Chillikothe, Kispokotha, Piqua, Hathawekela, and Spitotha. There were as many as twelve clans in each division and descent was traced through the patrilineal family line. Authority was vested in hereditary clan and division chiefs; war chiefs were also important, usually warriors of proven ability.

The basic Shawnee dwelling was the *wegiwa* (wigwam), basically a framework of bent poles covered with elm or birch bark. Women tended corn and other crops, while the men supplemented the diet by hunting and fishing.

The tribe allied themselves with the British during the American Revolution, in part because land-hungry former colonists seemed the greater threat. After the war, American westward settlement increased, and the Shawnee took up the hatchet to protect their lands. They joined a coalition of tribes that managed to inflict two stinging defeats on United States

army forces, most notably when General Arthur St. Clair was crushed in 1791. The Indians were defeated at the Battle of Fallen Timbers in 1794, however, and the next year signed the Treaty of Greenville with the United States. Under the provisions of this pact, the Indians were forced to relinquish Ohio and part of Indiana to the victors.

The Shawnee chief Tecumseh led a resurgence of the tribe in the first decade of the nineteenth century. Tecumseh is generally acknowledged as one of the greatest Indians of all time. He condemned the sale of Indian lands to whites, urged abstinence from alcohol, and promoted intertribal unity. Tecumseh's forces clashed with an American army under General William Henry Harrison at Tippecanoe in 1811. The battle was a draw but was still a check on Tecumseh's prestige. He joined the British forces during the War of 1812; his death in battle was a great loss for all Shawnee and all Indians.

The Shawnee dispersed during the course of the nineteenth century. One group of Shawnee moved to Missouri and from there to a Kansas reservation. About 1845, scattered Shawnee from Kansas, Louisiana, Arkansas, and Texas migrated to Oklahoma, where they were collectively known as the Absentee Shawnee. Yet another group settled in Ottawa County, Oklahoma, where they were called the Eastern Shawnee. The main body of Shawnee incorporated with the Cherokee tribe in 1869.

Not all Shawnee made the trek south to Oklahoma. Small groups of Shawnee filtered back and settled in Ohio and Indiana. Their descendants make up the midwest's Shawnee Nation United Remnant Band. A milestone was reached when the Shawnee Nation United Remnant Band purchased a 28-acre tract for a sacred ceremonial ground. For the first time, the Shawnee reclaimed a piece of original territory.

See also Algonquian language family; Fallen Timbers, Battle of; Tecumseh; Tenskwatawa; Tippecanoe, Battle of; Wabash, Battle of the.

Shells and shellwork

TRIBES AFFECTED: Pantribal
SIGNIFICANCE: Shells have a long history of use for ornamentation by native peoples of the Americas; the presence of marine shells inland implies social interaction between groups

The oldest shell objects in North America may be the local freshwater gastropod shell beads recovered at the Ervin site in Tennessee, which are approximately seven thousand years old. Marine shells were modified as beads, cups, pendants, earspools, gorgets, hoes, and axes all across the eastern United States, where they largely appear as grave goods. Thirty-five species of marine shells (mostly gastropods) were utilized as beads during the Archaic period in western New York, for example. Most noteworthy are the gorgets and engraved shell cups of the Mississippian period, particularly those from the site of Spiro, and wampum used by Northeast tribes in historic times.

In the western United States, shell beads appeared about four thousand years ago. Shell button blankets were important ceremonial items in the Northwest. Shell jewelry and inlaid shell in the Southwest commonly consisted of the species *Oliva*, *Olivella*, *Glycymeris*, and *Conus*. Bracelets were the most popular jewelry form, followed by necklaces. Techniques for shellworking included incising, carving, abrading, mosaic, inlay, drilling, and etching. Etching was performed with a brew made from fruit of the saguaro cactus. The shell was covered with pitch to preserve a final shape, then acid was applied to the exposed shell. Etched shell was often painted.

Among the Maya, shell symbolized death, south, zero, completion, and fertility. In North American beliefs, gastropod shells served as hiding places for the soul and deities. Shell could hold the soul and help purify decaying flesh. In some regions shell bead usage resembled the usage of money, and in many regions below the Arctic, shell beads were among the most valuable items a person could own. *Dentalium* among the Northwest Coast tribes was so central to the social organization that young men were instructed to dream of *Dentalium* and to think of it when walking.

In some cases the species of a shell is sufficient to indicate its origin. Shells excavated in southwestern sites came from the Gulf of California or the Pacific coast. Those from the Gulf of California were brought up the Gila River into Hohokam territory, then traded northward. West Coast shell followed several routes into the northern and southern Southwest. The route of the few shells which came from the Gulf of Mexico is not clear. There are *Dentalium* shells from the West Indies present in Archaic sites in Alabama, and fossil *Dentalium* shells were quarried and used in South Dakota. Pacific *Dentalium* comes from local habitats. For the eastern United States, however, there are few species with limited habitats. There has been some success with chemically sourcing the Atlantic whelks of the *Busycon* genus, which has indicated origins for shells found in Kentucky, Missouri, and South Dakota as including both temperate and tropical waters. Other evidence suggests Tampa Bay and the coast of Veracruz as shell sources.

See also Dress and adornment; Hohokam; Middens; Mississippian; Money; Ornaments; Wampum.

Shikellamy (?—Dec. 6, 1748, Shamokin, present-day Sunbury, Pa.): Tribal leader

ALSO KNOWN AS: Ongwaterohiathe, Takashwangarous
TRIBAL AFFILIATION: Oneida
SIGNIFICANCE: As representative for the Pennsylvania Iroquois, Shikellamy helped negotiate their admittance into the Iroquois Confederacy

Shikellamy was born either French or Cayuga, or possibly a mixture of the two. He was kidnapped by the Oneidas when he was two years old, and later adopted by them. He lived with them along the Schuylkill River in Pennsylvania. James Logan, a leader of the Ohio Oneidas who became known as Mingos, was Shikellamy's son.

He rose to prominence among the Oneidas, and was assigned by the Iroquois council to represent Iroquois holdings along the Susquehanna Valley in Pennsylvania. At his post at Shamokin, he negotiated with leaders of tributary tribes, Pennsylvania officials, missionaries, and members of the Susquehanna Land company. Encouraging abstinence among his people, Shikellamy helped curb white distribution of alcohol.

Shikellamy helped engineer the agreement in 1736 by which Pennsylvania Indians were incorporated into the Iroquois confederacy. When he sold Delaware lands to the colony of Pennsylvania, Shikellamy initiated a period of unrest.

See also Iroquois Confederacy; Logan, James; Oneida.

Shinnecock: Tribe

CULTURE AREA: Northeast
LANGUAGE GROUP: Eastern Algonquian
PRIMARY LOCATION: Long Island
POPULATION SIZE: 1,522 (1990 U.S. Census)

The Shinnecock, Corchaug, and Montauk formed the Montauk Confederacy, living as horticulturalists in permanent villages of circular, domed, mat-covered houses. They supplemented their main diet of corn, beans, and squash by hunting moose, deer, and other animals in addition to fishing. The Shinnecock traded extensively and used wampum as a badge of office, adornment, and form of wealth.

The 400-acre Shinnecock Reservation, established in 1666, was effectively diminished by the Indians' renting land to white farmers. Disease reduced the Shinnecock population, and acculturation was enforced by a growing number of non-Indians and increased loss of land, forcing many Shinnecock into a cash economy. Most whaling crews were Indian, and Shinnecock lifeboat crews were well known for saving many lives.

The 1934 Indian Reorganization Act stimulated tribal incorporation and the establishment of various self-help organizations. Many Shinnecocks have now left the reservation for urban centers and university study.

See also Montauk Confederacy.

Short Bull (c. 1845, Niobrara River, northern Nebr.— c. 1915, Pine Ridge Reservation, S.Dak.): Tribal chief

TRIBAL AFFILIATION: Brule Sioux
SIGNIFICANCE: Short Bull introduced the Ghost Dance to the Sioux and preached a holy war against whites

According to Chief He Dog, Short Bull grew up with the future Oglala Sioux chief Crazy Horse, played with him as a boy, and later fought in wars with him. They were made chiefs at about the same time.

By 1880, the Sioux had been effectively confined to reservations and reduced to a sorry condition. Their crops and cattle died. A miserly Congress skimped and dawdled in sending clothing and food rations. Epidemics of measles, influenza, and whooping cough combined with hunger to ravage the reservation and cause many deaths. The Sioux were unable to hunt their own food and were forbidden to practice the traditional Sun Dance, an important source of spiritual help.

Into this atmosphere of despair and anger came news of a Paiute prophet or messiah, Wovoka. He preached the peaceful coming of a new world of hope and life for the Indian. By 1891, this new world would push the whites back across the ocean. The buffalo would return, and all Indians, past and present, would live happily for eternity. In order for this millennium to occur, Indians had to pray, sing, and dance the Ghost Dance.

In winter, 1889, Short Bull and ten other Sioux, as part of a chosen delegation, journeyed to Utah to see Wovoka. They returned in spring, 1890, full of enthusiasm and hope. Short Bull and Kicking Bear rose to prominence as the high priests of this new religion, representing themselves as the special vicars of Wovoka. They reinterpreted Wovoka's peaceful prophecies as a call to arms, however; they preached that the destruction of whites in a holy war was necessary to prepare for the new world. They wore ceremonial Ghost Shirts that would protect their wearers from the whites' weapons.

The new religion found many converts, especially on the Rosebud and Pine Ridge reservations. Major Sioux chiefs, among them Hump, Big Foot, and Sitting Bull, were attracted. Oglala and Brule Sioux spoke a fiery rhetoric and danced themselves into a trancelike condition. White settlers and the Pine Ridge agent began to panic and called for troops to restore order. Three thousand troops arrived.

Short Bull was arrested and imprisoned, and Hump was pacified. Sitting Bull was ordered arrested but was killed in the attempt. Big Foot surrendered at Wounded Knee, but tempers got out of hand. A skirmish broke out, and before it was over nearly three hundred Sioux and twenty-five soldiers had been killed. The Ghost Dance excitement faded away, and Short Bull fell into disrepute. Upon his release, Short Bull spent the rest of his days on the Pine Ridge Reservation and affiliated himself with the Congregationalists.

See also Ghost Dance; Sioux; Wounded Knee Massacre; Wovoka.

Shoshone: Tribe

CULTURE AREA: Great Basin
LANGUAGE GROUP: Uto-Aztecan
PRIMARY LOCATION: California, Idaho, Nevada, Utah, Wyoming
POPULATION SIZE: 9,215 (1990 U.S. Census)

At first European American contact, the Shoshone occupied the area around Death Valley in California, much of Nevada and northwestern Utah (Western Shoshone, including the Panamint), southern Idaho (Northern Shoshone), and western Wyoming (Eastern Shoshone). Culturally and linguistically the three groups form a single unit. The Shoshone were generally at peace with their Uto-Aztecan neighbors—the Utes, Paiutes, and Bannocks—but the Northern and Eastern Shoshone often fought the Blackfoot, Sioux, and Cheyenne when they moved onto the Plain to hunt buffalo. They resisted the invasion of their homeland by European Americans but were eventually settled on reservations and in tribal groupings scattered around their original territory.

Early History and Traditional Lifestyle. The origin of the Shoshone and their entry into the Great Basin is not well documented. Prehistoric Indians in the Basin had a lifestyle much like that of the Western Shoshone, but many students of the region believe that the Shoshone did not develop directly from Great Basin ancestors. Instead, they think the Shoshone moved into the Basin from its southwest corner between one thousand and two thousand years ago. They spread north and east, eventually reaching the Great Plains, into which they expanded north into Canada and east beyond the Black Hills. When the Blackfoot, Sioux, Cheyenne, and other tribes moved west from the eastern woodlands, the Shoshone retreated into the region they occupied at the time of contact.

The Shoshone present an excellent example of a people's versatile and efficient response to their environment. The groups occupying the Great Basin, where no single resource is available in abundance, made use of the many resources that were present in small amounts or were abundant for a time at a particular location. They used plant seeds (grasses, pines), and vegetative parts of plants (especially camas—a type of lily with edible bulbs). They hunted and trapped whatever large (bighorn sheep, deer) and small (rabbits, ground squirrels) game was available, and they fished when they had the opportunity (migrating salmon). Because the environment could not support large populations, they migrated around the Great Basin in small bands using resources as they became available. Because available forage was insufficient to support large horse herds, they traveled on foot, using dogs as beasts of burden. In winter, several bands gathered near caves from which food, collected and stored there during the summer, could be retrieved.

In contrast, the Northern and Eastern Shoshone who moved into the Plains responded to the availability of an abundant and versatile resource: the buffalo. Because an efficient buffalo hunt required large numbers of people, the buffalo hunters lived in large groups from the spring to the fall. They too used dogs to carry their belongings until the 1720's, when they obtained horses. The horse made both moving and buffalo hunting more efficient, and may have made it possible for some Eastern and Northern Shoshone to continue buffalo hunts in the Plains despite the opposition of Blackfoot, Sioux, and Cheyenne. Smaller extended family groups moved to sheltered valleys in the Rocky Mountain foothills for winter, where enough forage could be found for the horses of a small group, but not for larger herds.

The spiritual and social lives of the plains and Great Basin groups also differed, reflecting different group sizes and environments. Both groups were deeply spiritual, but the Plains Shoshone adopted the complex of dances, warrior societies, and other social and ceremonial activities of Plains Indians. The smaller Great Basin groups had one major ceremonial dance—the round dance—and a less elaborate ceremonial and social structure.

Transition and Contemporary Life. Except for the Mormons, European Americans initially showed little interest in the barren lands the Shoshone occupied. The discovery of gold and other mineral deposits in the Great Basin eventually brought on the familiar scenario of broken treaties and displaced Indians as European Americans moved westward. As a result, today the Shoshone struggle with many problems—lack of education, poverty, lack of opportunity, and threats to their culture. They have sued the federal government over water rights, land ownership, improper compensation for past treaties, and storage of nuclear waste on Shoshone land. They have not always won—the deck is somewhat stacked against any tribe arguing for ownership of a large part of a state (Nevada)—but their ability to function well in such battles is further evidence of Shoshone versatility and bodes well for the future of the tribe. —*Carl W. Hoagstrom*

See also Bannock War; Gosiute; Great Basin; Tendoy; Uto-Aztecan language family; Washakie.

Shuswap: Tribe
CULTURE AREA: Plateau
LANGUAGE GROUP: Salishan
PRIMARY LOCATION: British Columbia
POPULATION SIZE: 4,920 (Statistics Canada, based on 1991 census)

The Shuswap, a branch of the Salishan family, lived along the Fraser, Thompson, and Columbia rivers in present-day British Columbia. They were the dominant Salishan tribe in the region, holding more land and power than their neighbors—the Lillooet, the Thompson and the Okanagon—with whom they often fought. They called themselves *Sequa'pmug* or *Suxwa'pmux*, whose meaning is not known.

The Shuswap were divided into about seven autonomous bands, with their own hereditary chiefs. They owned slaves, whom they acquired in battle or trade. Their staple food was fish, especially salmon, which they caught with spears, nets, and traps. They also hunted bear, beaver, rabbit, raccoon, squirrel, and mountain goat. They made good use of the animals they hunted, using the skins for clothing, quills for ornamentation, and wool and hair for weaving cloth. Their homes were often made of logs or wood planks, and they housed four to eight families. Other villages had rectangular earthlodges with warming earth berms for winter and circular mat houses for summer. Some bands traveled widely throughout the year to search for food. For travel they used bark canoes, snowshoes, and horses.

In the early nineteenth century, the Hudson's Bay Company established trading posts nearby. The Shuswap traded skins, furs, and food for woven goods, steel weapons and tools, and glass beads. By the middle of the century, intertribal warfare had faded, but epidemics of measles, smallpox, scarlet fever, and other diseases wiped out large numbers of Shuswap and other Interior Salish peoples. Weakened numbers led to weakened influence. In 1945, in an attempt to force the Canadian government to be more responsive to their needs, the Shuswap joined with the Chilcotin and others to form the British Columbia Interior Confederacy. In the end, the Shuswap managed to hold on to their traditional lands and ways longer than most tribes. In the late 1970's they were given about 146,000 acres of reserve land in British Columbia, where they continue to maintain some of the old ways.

See also Chilcotin; Diseases, post-contact; Salishan language family; Thompson.

Sign language
TRIBES AFFECTED: Pantribal
SIGNIFICANCE: In North America, sign language facilitated communication and economic transactions among groups which spoke different languages, and it served additional purposes in some cultural settings

Sign language is a nonverbal communication utilizing movements of the hands or body to convey meaning. In many areas of the world, such as Africa or Australia, sign languages were used by hunters to communicate hunting strategies silently to one another.

In northeastern Mexico, Texas, and western Louisiana, sign language almost certainly predated European contact, since there are several early historical accounts of its use. A late seventeenth century journal entry of explorer Pierre le Moyne, Sieur d'Iberville records the use of sign language among the Bayogoula and other unnamed groups along the lower Mississippi River. Additional accounts of communication by signs were written by early traders.

It seems likely that the sign language used in these areas diffused northward into the Plains. In the nineteenth and twentieth century, the use of sign language continued to spread through the Plains and across the northern Plateau, as described in articles in D. Jean Umiker-Sebeok and Thomas A. Sebeok's *Aboriginal Sign Languages of the Americas and Australia* (1978). Among the Plains peoples, the Kiowa generally were deemed to be early users of sign language. The Kiowa occupied different locations at different time periods, but in the nineteenth century they were hunting bison in the southwestern Plains. Therefore aboriginal accounts uphold the thesis that sign language diffused from south to north and may have originated in the Gulf Coast region.

The Plains sign language is better documented than that of other areas, and the meanings of many signs were recorded; in the Southeast, on the other hand, the signs were lost at an earlier date. In addition, for the Plains area, information concerning the social context of sign language was recorded. For example, many nineteenth century reports indicate that signs were used primarily by Plains Indian men, although some women also knew the signs. Many Plains groups used signs in a variety of social contexts, such as during storytelling or intimate conversation among family members, in addition to recognizing its value for conversing with outsiders who did not speak the same language.

See also Captivity and captivity narratives; Oratory; Trade.

Siletz: Tribe
CULTURE AREA: Northwest Coast
LANGUAGE GROUP: Salishan
PRIMARY LOCATION: Oregon coast
POPULATION SIZE: 1,554 (1990 U.S. Census)

The Siletz are the band of Salish-speaking Tillamook people who traditionally lived along the river of the same name in northwestern Oregon. This band is generally thought to be the southernmost branch of Salishan peoples in the Northwest Coast culture area.

Before contact with European American peoples, the Siletz existed, as did most of the peoples of the Oregon coast, in a quiet, relatively isolated autonomy. The Siletz lived in bands and villages around the mouth of, and inland along, the Siletz River and were related by close familial and cultural bonds. Their lifestyle was based on fishing, hunting, and gathering of the abundant local maritime, estuarine, riverine, and woodland resources. They are related to the Nehalem, Tillamook Bay, Nestucca, and Neaehesna (Salmon River) peoples.

After contact with colonizing Americans, most native coastal peoples in Oregon were removed to a reservation in upriver Siletz territory around 1855. The Siletz reservation became the home for a wide variety of previously unrelated peoples for many years, and much mixing of languages and cultures occurred. Among the language groups and cultures represented on the Siletz reservation were Athapaskan, Yakonan, Kusan, Takelman, Shastan, and Sahaptian people from all over the coastal northwest. The peoples now identified as the Confederated Tribes of Siletz Indians of Oregon comprise at least twenty-two bands living together in and around what was once the traditional territory of the Siletz peoples alone.

See also Salish; Salishan language family; Tillamook.

Silko, Leslie Marmon (b. Mar. 5, 1948, Albuquerque, N.Mex.): Writer

Tribal affiliation: Laguna

Significance: One of the most well-known American Indian writers, Silko's fiction, essays, and poetry transcend boundaries between oral and written language

Although Indian people have often felt estranged from written literature, Indian communities have long recognized the importance of storytelling and the power of language. Leslie Marmon Silko's writing attempts to close the gap between oral and written stories and between Indians and literature.

Silko's poems and fiction often draw on stories she grew up hearing at Laguna Pueblo in northern New Mexico. Of Indian and European ancestry, like many other Indian writers, Silko has used her position of being both insider and outsider to give her largely non-Indian readership an appreciation for contemporary Indian lives.

After graduating with honors from the University of New Mexico, Silko began publishing poems and short stories. Her first book-length publication was *Laguna Woman* (1974), a volume of poems. Her first novel, *Ceremony* (1977), which was greeted with wide acclaim, concerned the spiritual healing of an Indian veteran of World War II. In *Storyteller* (1981), Silko juxtaposed family photographs with poetry, short stories, and stories told among Laguna people. In 1991, Silko published her second novel, *Almanac of the Dead*.

Leslie Marmon Silko has taught at a number of institutions, including Navajo Community College in Tsaile, Arizona, and the University of Arizona. Her many distinguished grants and awards include a John D. and Catherine T. MacArthur Foundation grant awarded in 1983.

See also American Indian studies programs and archives; Oral literatures; Pueblo tribes, Western.

Sinagua: Prehistoric tradition
Date: 500-1400
Location: Northern Arizona
Cultures affected: Anasazi, Hohokam, Mogollon

The Sinagua culture is known from sites in central Arizona around the Sunset Crater volcano near Flagstaff, Arizona, and in the upper Verde Valley. Its interpretation is complex, and Sinagua has been variously identified as a branch of the Mogollon, Patayan, or Hakataya traditions. In general, Sinagua is representative of a blending of cultural traits either through population movements or the adoption of features from neighboring peoples. This blending is a combination of earlier local traditions with those of neighboring Anasazi, Mogollon, and Hohokam peoples.

Three phases of Sinagua culture have been identified as dating to before major eruptions of Sunset Crater in 1064. These are Cinder Park (500-700), Sunset (700-900), and Río de Flag (900-1064). Sinagua culture shows a strong continuity of styles in ceramics, architecture, settlement patterns, and subsistence strategies through these early phases. Post-eruptive phases are the contemporaneous Padre, Angell, and Winona phases (1070-1120), followed by the Elden (1130-1200), Turkey Hill (1200-1300), and Clear Creek (1300-1400) foci. These are marked by increased variation in material culture, including occasional Hohokam elements. After 1400, the Sinagua population declined.

Sinagua Lifeways. Information on Sinagua culture comes from several sites, including Tuzigoot and Montezuma Castle. House types of the early phases of Sinagua culture include pit houses with circular to rectangular foundations. The earliest tend to be shallow and round, while later examples were deeper, more rectangular, and lined with timbered walls. Especially large circular pit houses may have had a ceremonial function similar to that of kivas at later sites in the Southwest. Stone-lined pit houses and aboveground masonry constructions appear in the later phases. During the pre-eruption phases of the site, dead were disposed of by cremation. In post-eruption phases, burials were made in pole-covered or recessed graves, with occasional flexed burials beneath the floors of pueblo rooms. Sinagua subsistence was based on maize farming, with evidence for cultivation using both rainfall and irrigation. This was supplemented with hunting and gathering.

The characteristic ceramic ware throughout the Sinagua culture sequence is Alameda Brown, made with crushed stone temper and finished with a paddle-and-anvil technique. Earlier phases have yielded evidence for occasional Hohokam and Kayenta Anasazi vessels that were probably obtained through trade. Circular ball courts of stone masonry have been identified at a number of later Sinagua sites, and the playing of a ritual ball game is often interpreted as evidence of influence from northern Mesoamerica.

Volcanic Eruptions and Migrations. Major eruptions of the Sunset Crater volcano have been documented for the years 1064-1065 and 1066-1067, with evidence for continued episodes of volcanic eruptions for two centuries afterward. Archaeologists had initially argued that the weathering of tephra from these eruptions provided a moisture-conserving mineral mulch and added nutrients to the soil, resulting in a local area of high agricultural fertility. Rainfall farmers who recognized the benefits of rich soils were believed to have colonized the region, resulting in a multicultural occupation that combined of Sinagua, Hohokam, Mogollon, and Anasazi peoples. The abandonment of the region after 1400 was attributed to the erosion of volcanic soils, resulting in a decrease in agricultural productivity.

This interpretation has been modified by more recent research that finds little support for either a substantial population increase or significant numbers of non-Sinagua migrants to the area. Hohokam presence in the Sinagua region is limited to a single pit house and associated trash midden at Winona Village that has been interpreted as the residence of a Hohokam trader. While thirteen ball courts in the Sinagua area may represent Hohokam influence, it is possible that these were erected without direct participation by Hohokam peoples. Although the introduction of stone masonry to the Sinagua has been attributed to the Kayenta Anasazi, there is evidence that this was present prior to the period of supposed migrations. Later Sinagua prehistory is now interpreted as a predominantly local process, affected by more extensive contacts with the Hohokam and Anasazi cultures.

Spanish explorers who arrived in the Verde Valley in the sixteenth century encountered the Yuman-speaking Yavapai tribe. Their specific relationship with earlier Sinagua culture remains poorly understood. —*John Hoopes*

See also Anasazi, Hohokam; Mogollon; Patayan; Prehistory—Southwest.

BIBLIOGRAPHY

Breternitz, David A. "Excavations at Three Sites in the Verde Valley, Arizona." *Museum of Northern Arizona Bulletin* 34 (1960).

————. "The Eruption(s) of Sunset Crater: Dating and Effects." *Plateau* 40, no. 2 (1967): 72-76.

Colton, Harold S. "Prehistoric Culture Units and Their Relationships in Northern Arizona." *Museum of Northern Arizona Bulletin* 17 (1939).

————. "The Sinagua: A Summary of the Archaeology of the Region of Flagstaff, Arizona." *Museum of Northern Arizona Bulletin* 22 (1946).

McGregor, John C. "Winona Village." *Museum of Northern Arizona Bulletin* 12 (1937).

————. "Winona and Ridge Ruin. Part 1, Architecture and Material Culture." *Museum of Northern Arizona Bulletin* 18 (1941).

Pilles, Peter J., Jr. "Sunset Crater and the Sinagua: A New Interpretation." In *Volcanic Activity and Human Ecology*, edited by Payson D. Sheets and Donald K. Grayson. New York: Academic Press, 1979.

Siouan language family

CULTURE AREAS: Plains, Southeast

TRIBES AFFECTED: Assiniboine, Biloxi, Catawba, Crow, Hidatsa, Iowa, Kansa, Mandan, Missouri, Ofo, Omaha, Osage, Oto, Ponca, Quapaw, Sioux, Tutelo, Winnebago

The tribes speaking Siouan languages once occupied areas as far north as Alberta, Saskatchewan, and Manitoba in Canada and lived in the United States as far south as Mississippi and Louisiana and, in isolated groups, as far east as the Appalachian Mountains in Virginia and the Carolinas. The arrival of European settlers and subsequent displacement of coastal Indians, however, led to intertribal wars that eliminated the Sioux in the Carolinas and pushed others relentlessly west. Since the nineteenth century, Sioux tribes have lived predominantly in the Great Plains and Mississippi and Missouri river valleys.

About one-third of all prehistoric Siouan languages died unrecorded except for their names; others, especially those in the Southeast, left few records before disappearing. The survival of the rest is in doubt. Even the largest of the known Siouan languages has had steadily shrinking numbers of speakers. The 1970 census reported that about twenty thousand people spoke Siouan languages in South Dakota, Nebraska, Montana, and Minnesota; the 1980 census found nearly sixteen thousand, the majority of whom were elderly; a 1986 survey placed the number at fewer than fourteen thousand.

Member Languages. Proto-Siouan began splitting into branches about three thousand years ago, and perhaps earlier if Catawba (a language once spoken in South Carolina) is included in the family. Siouan proper comprises four branches: Missouri River, Mandan (a language that constitutes a branch of its own), Mississippi Valley, and Southeastern. The Southeastern branch includes Tutelo, Biloxi, and Ofo, all extinct, although an Ofo speaker was alive as recently as 1908. The Mississippi Valley branch is the largest, both in the number of languages and surviving speakers: Dakota, with its dialects Santee, Teton (Lakota), Yankton, and Assiniboine (Stoney); Dhegihan, including the languages Omaha-Poncan, Kansa-Osage, and Quapaw; Chiwere, including the languages Iowa, Otoe, and Missouri; and Winnebago (Hochangara). The Missouri River branch consists of Crow and Hidatsa.

Linguists have partially reconstructed Proto-Siouan using cognates, shared sound structures, and shared grammatical features; its affiliation to other families is probable but not proved. In *Language in the Americas* (1987), Joseph H. Greenberg places the Siouan languages, together with Yuchi, in "Keresiouan" (containing Caddoan and Iroquoian as well), a grouping of families accepted by some scholars. Greenberg goes further, however: He assigns Keresiouan, along with Almosan, to Northern Amerind, one of the six large families of Amerind, a language phylum that includes most of the languages in

North America and all those in Central and South America. This phylum, conceived by Greenberg, is controversial.

Language Characteristics. Proto-Siouan was a polysynthetic, or incorporative, language. Like nearly all American Indian languages, it combined major sentence elements into single words. Its offspring languages retain this characteristic, although not as thoroughly as other Indian languages, and similarities in pronunciation, vocabulary, and grammar are still fairly common within branches, especially in the Mississippi River branch. In fact, in *Grammar and Dictionary of the Language of the Hidatsa* (1873), Washington Matthews claimed that Indians who spoke as many as five Siouan languages were common.

Proto-Siouan appears to have had fifteen consonants, five vowels, and three nasalized vowels. Some consonants could form clusters of two, and a distinction existed between aspirated (pronunciation accompanied by a rasp of breath) and unaspirated versions of the same consonant sound. Among surviving languages, Crow and Hidatsa have lost nasalization, and most languages have simplified the consonant clusters; Crow, Hidatsa, and the Southeastern languages have added vowels to the beginning of some syllables; and Dakota, among others, has developed voiced versions of unvoiced consonants. Consequently, the sound systems of offspring languages are more extensive than was that of Proto-Siouan. Lakota, for example, has twenty-nine consonants and Dakota twenty-three.

Vocabulary is based on roots, compounds, and combinations of roots and affixes, much as in English except that Siouan languages use affixes more extensively to turn verbs and adjectives into nouns or to indicate instrumentality in verbs. Compounds are usually descriptive and self-explanatory. For examples, the Dakota word for a steamship is *watapeta*, literally "fire boat," and the word for train is *hemani*, literally "walks on land." Siouan tongues also possess rich and diverse vocabularies for family relationships, reflecting tribal organizations based on the extended family.

The verb is the most complex unit of Siouan grammar. Prefixes, infixes, and suffixes are added to the verb to show plurality, aspect (duration and completeness), the object of the verb (if it is a pronoun), and instrumentality (how an action is performed). Auxiliary words indicate negation and whether the verb expresses emphasis, a statement, or a question. Nouns do not change form from the singular to the plural or for different grammatical functions, such as subject and object. Prefixes or separate pronouns signal possession, although the possessive pronoun may be incorporated into the verb. Subject and object pronouns usually merge with the verb, except that the third-person singular subject pronoun is never expressed. Yet another set of personal pronouns, demonstrative pronouns, interrogative pronouns, and relative pronouns are separated from the verb. Besides singular and plural pronouns, some Siouan languages have dual pronouns for referring to a speaker and the person being addressed.

Siouan word order in sentences follows a basic subject-object-verb pattern, which need not vary from statements to questions. Time expressions come first in a sentence. Adjectives, articles, and prepositions follow the nouns to which they refer. Linking verbs generally are omitted. Men and women may use different forms to express commands. —*Roger Smith*

See also Assiniboine; Language families; Plains; Sioux; Winnebago.

BIBLIOGRAPHY

Chafe, Wallace L. *The Caddoan, Iroquoian, and Siouan Languages*. The Hague: Mouton, 1976.

Greenberg, Joseph H. *Language in the Americas*. Stanford, Calif.: Stanford University Press, 1987.

Karol, Joseph S., and Stephen L. Rozman, eds. *Everyday Lakota: An English-Sioux Dictionary for Beginners*. Rev. ed. St. Francis, S.Dak.: Rosebud Educational Society, 1974.

Matthews, Washington. *Grammar and Dictionary of the Language of the Hidatsa*. New York: Cramoisy Press, 1873-1874. Reprint. New York: AMS Press, 1983.

Rood, David S. "Siouan." In *The Languages of Native America: Historical and Comparative Assessment*, edited by Lyle Campbell and Marianne Mithun. Austin: University of Texas Press, 1979.

Wolff, Hans. "Comparative Siouan." *International Journal of American Linguistics* 16 (1950): 61ff; 17 (1951): 197-204.

Working Indians Civil Association. *An English-Dakota Dictionary*. Fort Pierre, S.Dak.: Author, 1969.

Sioux: Tribal group

CULTURE AREA: Plains

LANGUAGE GROUP: Siouan

PRIMARY LOCATION: Montana, South Dakota, North Dakota, Minnesota, Nebraska, Manitoba, Saskatchewan

POPULATION SIZE: 103,255 in U.S. (1990 U.S. Census); 10,040 in Canada ("Dakota," Statistics Canada, based on 1991 census)

Sioux is the term popularly used to refer to a northern Plains Indian group most often considered in relation to their material culture—tipis, war bonnets, buffalo hunting, and an equestrian lifestyle. Among the Sioux the people call themselves Dakota or Lakota, terms which mean "friends" or "allies." Use of the term "Sioux" dates to the seventeenth century, when the Dakota were living in the Great Lakes area. Fur traders, explorers, and Jesuit missionaries heard from the Ojibwa (Chippewa) and Huron of the Nadouwesou tribe, which was much feared. Nadouwesou comes from the Ojibwa term meaning "adders." This term, shortened and corrupted by French traders, resulted in retention of the last syllable as Sioux. There are three major subgroups of Sioux—the Santee, Yankton, and Teton.

Origins and Westward Migrations. The term "Sioux" did not designate a single tribe or national entity, but a complex web of bands or tribes that were spread across forested regions of the upper Mississippi, across the prairies of Minnesota and Dakota Territory, and beyond the Missouri River on the high plains of Nebraska, North and South Dakota, Wyoming, Montana, Manitoba, and Saskatchewan. A common language was important in defining the Sioux as a nation. Those who spoke a dialect of Dakota considered themselves allies, while all who spoke any other language were considered enemies unless a peace was negotiated. The Sioux did not form a political unit that acted in concert to control tribal areas or enforce tribal laws, but they did share a common language and common philosophy that molded their national culture and shaped their political and social life. By the 1700's, while still located in the Great Lakes or Woodlands area, the Sioux formed a relatively loose alliance known as the Seven Fireplaces or Oceti Sakowin, consisting of the Mdewakanton (Spirit Lake Village), Wahpekute (Leaf Shooters), Wahpetunwan (Leaf Village), Sisituwan (meaning unknown), Ihanktunwan (End Village), Ihanktunwanna (Little End Village), and Tintatuwan (Prairie Village). These subdivisions were not culturally distinct from one another in their Woodlands home but became more distinct as the people moved westward.

The first four were collectively called Isanti (knife), because these people once lived near a large body of water known to them as Knife Lake. The French later changed "Isanti" to "Santee." The Santee are the easternmost Sioux and were the last to leave the lake region. They speak the Dakota dialect in which there are no *l*'s and the *d* is used.

The Ihanktunwan and Ihanktunwanna have come to be called Yankton and Yanktonais in English, and as a group they are sometimes called the Wiciyela, or "middle people," because they lived between the Santee and Teton. The Yankton were originally one tribe, but economic factors forced them to divide into two groups as they became more populous. They originally spoke the Nakota dialect, which uses the *n* in place of the *d*, although they most commonly speak the Dakota dialect today.

The Tintatuwan, or Teton, were the first to move westward onto the prairie. After the move the Teton became so numerous that by the late eighteenth century they in turn divided into seven tribes. This subdivision is also referred to as the Seven

Fireplaces, because the Teton's social and political order replicated the national alliance. By the 1860's the Teton were most commonly known by the seven tribal names: Sicangu (Burnt Thigh), also known by the French name Brule; Oglala (Scatters Their Own); Sihasapa (Blackfeet, not to be confused with the Algonquian-speaking Blackfeet Indians of Montana and Alberta); Oohenunpa (Two Kettle); Itazipco (Without Bows), also known by the French name Sans Arc; Minneconjou (Planters by the Water); and Hunkpapa (Campers at the End of the Horn). These people collectively refer to themselves as the Lakota, using the *l* in place of the *d*.

In the Great Lakes setting the Sioux were semisedentary and had a Woodlands economy based on fishing, hunting and gathering, and some cultivation of corn. By the mid-seventeenth century the Sioux had been pushed westward by enemy tribes, principally the Ojibwa, who obtained guns through the French fur trade. The Teton and middle divisions moved westward to the Great Plains, where they acquired horses and a dependence on the buffalo for food and many material needs such as housing, clothing, and implements. The Middle Sioux settled along the Missouri River, while the Tetons pushed farther west into the Black Hills and beyond to the present-day states and provinces of Nebraska, Wyoming, Montana, North and South Dakota, Manitoba, and Saskatchewan. Although they too were pushed westward, the Eastern or Santee Sioux remained essentially Woodland people in territory and culture, settling in the area of southwestern Minnesota and eastern North and South Dakota. By the early nineteenth century, political and cultural differences among the Sioux groups became pronounced, and true Eastern, Middle, and Teton (Western) divisions emerged.

Political and Social Organization. The core of traditional Sioux society was the smallest unit, the extended family, which was a group of relatives living together cooperatively. The next level of organization was the tiyospaye, or "lodge groups." These were social units often referred to as bands, collections of lodges of related people who were usually guided by a respected elder known as itancan or headman. The itancan was recognized as a leader by fully living a spiritual existence and demonstrating the values of his people—bravery, fortitude, generosity, and wisdom. The itancan's was not a permanent position; he served at the will of the people and could be replaced. Groups composed of several tiyospaye, and usually interrelated, were called oyate, meaning "people"; this is commonly understood today as a "tribe." The oyate corresponded to the "fireplaces" of the Seven Fireplaces.

The model of tiyospaye provided the mechanism for maintaining social and political order when the various oyate came together in the large summer encampments during the time of the Sun Dance and buffalo hunts. Councils of adult men represented the will of the people and met to deliberate on all matters pertaining to group welfare. The headmen acted as symbolic fathers to their various tiyospaye and helped provide direction and guidance to the council, composed of younger men. All decision making was by consensus, ensuring that all

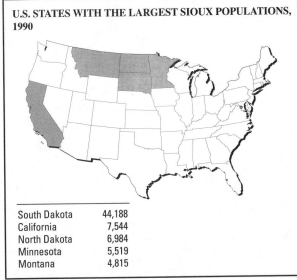

U.S. STATES WITH THE LARGEST SIOUX POPULATIONS, 1990

South Dakota	44,188
California	7,544
North Dakota	6,984
Minnesota	5,519
Montana	4,815

Source: 1990 U.S. Census.

A Sioux man photographed in ceremonial dance dress in 1899. (Library of Congress)

the people had a voice. No formal voting took place, and those who disagreed with council decisions were free to move and begin their own tiyospaye. Council decisions and social order were enforced by the akicita, or "soldiers lodge," which saw to it that all people cooperated for the common good. Membership in the akicita changed with each new encampment, so responsibility and authority for the people's well-being eventually fell to each male.

This sociopolitical structure of headman, council, and soldier lodge was replicated in every Sioux camp and served to create and maintain social order and cohesion as a people. In this system, group well-being was dominant over individual needs, and at all levels, group harmony was ensured by a government run by consensus.

When European nations, and later the United States, needed to conduct business with Indians, they looked for a single individual or a centralized government rather than dealing with the whole tribal group. Traditional tribal governments that operated by consensus incorporated guards against concentration of power to preserve values of freedom, respect, and harmony. Consensus building is a slow process and simply did not fit the European Americans' needs or ways of conducting business. Since the time of initial contact, Europeans sought out or appointed one individual with whom to deal—a "chief." As relations with the tribes changed over the years, both the United States and Canadian governments continued to look for ways to centralize Indian governments, and this tension between centralizing and maintaining tribalism still exists in relations between tribal groups and federal governments.

When Indian people were forced onto reservations in Canada and the United States, the federal governments of both countries attempted to dissolve the traditional governments and to extinguish the languages and spiritual beliefs and practices of the people. It was expected that the people would become Christian, farm, and eventually assimilate into the general population. Still, many of the people continued conducting their business according to more traditional patterns.

Early in the reservation era the various Sioux tribes banded together in councils to work on issues related to illegal seizure of lands and treaty violations. These councils followed traditional patterns; however, they had little success in dealing with the government agents who enforced assimilation policies. These early councils met to discuss matters of importance among the people, to plan social events, and to represent the concerns of their reservation to the federally appointed Indian agents. At all levels council meetings were open, and input from the people was solicited.

Wars, Treaties, and Reservations. The Sioux in both Canada and the United States negotiated treaties and later agreements with the governments beginning in the early 1800's. Constant broken promises, unresolved issues, and encroachment on tribal lands brought various Sioux divisions into direct conflict with the United States between 1862 and 1877. These encounters, famous in American history, are known collectively as the Sioux Wars and include such events as the Minne-

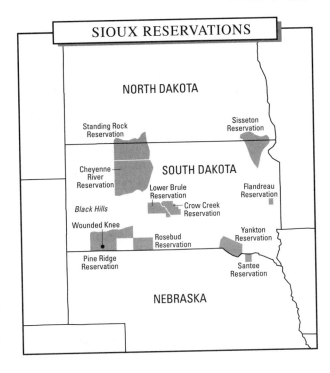

SIOUX RESERVATIONS

sota Uprising (1862), the war for the Bozeman Trail (1866-1868), the Wagon Box Fight (1867), and the Battle of the Little Bighorn (1876). The Sioux, especially the Teton, who placed greater emphasis on warfare than other Sioux, were the most active in opposing American expansion into their lands. Eventually the depletion of the buffalo herds, relentless attacks by the United States military, and growing numbers of settlers on their land caused many of the Sioux to seek refuge in Canada or settle on reservations in the Dakotas and Nebraska.

Most Sioux in the United States were settled on reservations by 1877, and life was miserable for the people. Prior to the 1870's, the Sioux had been living well on the basis of a buffalo hunting and trade economy, were rich in horses, had kept numerous tribal enemies in check, and lived in a vast territory. After confinement to the reservation, the Sioux were destitute, stripped of power, and forced to bend to the will of reservation authorities. Government policies were strict and sought to force assimilation by allotment of lands, encouragement in farming, Christianization, and establishment of educational institutions which sought to replace traditional values with mainstream American values; schools for Indian children often removed children from their homes. In order to hasten assimilation, laws were passed restricting practice of traditional religious and social practices. By 1889 the Sioux as a whole were in poor health, starving, and embittered over the loss of millions of acres of the Great Sioux Reservation. In this atmosphere, word of a revitalization movement known as the Ghost Dance passed among the people. Some Sioux participated in the movement. Although many did not, much government and military attention focused on Sioux involvement with the Ghost Dance. The resulting atmosphere of fear and mistrust culminated in the massacre at Wounded Knee (1890), where more than three hundred Sioux men, women, and children were killed by the Seventh Cavalry.

After Wounded Knee, government policies aimed at assimilation pressed relentlessly forward, and Sioux relations with the federal governments in both Canada and the United States have been marked by tensions involving efforts to end the reservation system and terminate the special legal status of Indians. The Sioux have struggled to maintain their cultural identity, define their reservations as homelands, exercise their sovereignty, and regain illegally seized land, particularly the Black Hills.

Politics in the Twentieth Century. In 1920 the Canadian government passed legislation intended to end the reserve system as a way to force assimilation and bow to public demands to acquire Indian lands. Tribal governments were weakened, but some patterns of traditional governance remained and councils were active in opposing government policy.

In 1934, with the passage of the Indian Reorganization Act (IRA), the U.S. government sought to shift its relationship with tribes throughout the country. By 1934 the Bureau of Indian Affairs was directing much of the day-to-day business on the reservations as well as influencing national policy in Indian affairs. The federal government sought to get out of micromanagement of reservation affairs by proposing that tribes establish constitutional forms of government and elect officials who would then govern their reservation and make some of the decisions that affected reservation residents on a local level. In actuality, the Bureau of Indian Affairs maintained a strong presence on the reservations. The IRA gave the tribes greater voice in stating opinions, but it did not give them much real power because the Bureau of Indian Affairs reserved the right to approve most tribal decisions, to certify elections, and so on.

The Sioux people living in both Canada and the United States seek to preserve their inherent tribal sovereignty and to preserve the Dakota/Lakota/Nakota heritage, doing things in the best interests of all the people and representing the people's wishes in conducting business and making decisions. The tribes exert sovereignty by pursuing legislation in Congress and Parliament on behalf of tribal members, manage a variety of programs formerly run by the federal governments, establish laws and rules of conduct on the reservation, and invest tribal capital in business ventures. In their governing system, the Sioux tribal nations seek to maintain continuity with the past as they work to preserve and protect the best interests of all the people.

The Sioux population continues to increase, with the largest concentration living in six reservations in South Dakota. Large off-reservation populations of Sioux exist in Rapid City (South Dakota), Denver, Los Angeles, and the San Francisco Bay area. The Sioux are leaders in implementing social and educational reforms and are particularly prominent in their Indian community colleges. Sioux reservations in Canada and the United States actively promote expressions of traditional Sioux culture and values through a wide range of events, arts, and ceremonies. —*Carole A. Barrett*

See also Black Hills; Bozeman Trail wars; Buffalo; Fort Laramie Treaty of 1851; Fort Laramie Treaty of 1868; Ghost Dance; Little Bighorn, Battle of the; Military societies; Minnesota Uprising; Pine Ridge shootout; Reservation system of the United States; Rosebud Creek, Battle of; Siouan language family; Sioux uprisings; Sitting Bull; Sun Dance; Wagon Box Battle; Wounded Knee Massacre; Wounded Knee occupation.

BIBLIOGRAPHY

Biolsi, Thomas. *Organizing the Lakota: The Political Economy of the New Deal on the Pine Ridge and Rosebud Reservations*. Tucson: University of Arizona Press, 1992. An insightful case study of the impact of the Indian Reorganization Act on two Lakota reservations. It focuses on the ways tribal organization ultimately failed to transfer power from the federal government to the newly organized tribal governments.

Brown, Joseph Epes, ed. *The Sacred Pipe: Black Elk's Account of the Seven Rites of the Oglala Sioux*. Norman: University of Oklahoma Press, 1953. A seminal work in understanding the spiritual teachings as well as rituals of the Sioux people as told by a sometime practitioner.

Densmore, Frances. *Teton Sioux Music and Culture*. Lincoln: University of Nebraska Press, 1992. Songs and ethnohistorical data gathered in 1918 provide important information on the social and religious beliefs of the Lakota. Most information was gathered on the Standing Rock Reservation in North and South Dakota.

Hassrick, Royal B. *The Sioux: Life and Customs of a Warrior Society*. Norman: University of Oklahoma Press, 1964. This book is often regarded as a standard resource in study of Sioux society in the period between 1830 and 1870. Focus is on the male role, structure of society, and psychological aspects of the culture.

Hyde, George E. *Red Cloud's Folk: A History of the Oglala Sioux Indians*. Norman: University of Oklahoma Press, 1937. A tribal history of the Oglala Sioux. The book recounts in detail all the major episodes in the Sioux tribe's relationship with the United States through treaties, battles, and negotiations. It explores reasons for divisions within the tribe and sheds light on certain contemporary reservation situations.

————. *A Sioux Chronicle*. Norman: University of Oklahoma Press, 1956. A compilation of historical information from intertribal warfare, battles with the United States, and an exploration of the vagaries of federal Indian policy in the early reservation era.

————. *Spotted Tail's Folk: A History of the Brule Sioux*. Norman: University of Oklahoma Press, 1961. Focuses on the history of the Rosebud Reservation in South Dakota, explores internal divisions within the tribe, aspects of the Sioux Wars, and tribal history. Somewhat cynical in tone but a solid reference.

Meyer, Roy. *History of the Santee Sioux*. Lincoln: University of Nebraska Press, 1967. A good exploration of the eastern or Santee Sioux. The book is thorough and contains an extensive bibliography.

Mooney, James. *The Ghost Dance Religion and the Sioux Outbreak of 1890*. Annual Report of the Bureau of American

Ethnology 14. Washington, D.C.: Government Printing Office, 1896. The seminal work in exploring the Ghost Dance and its aftermath. First published by the Bureau of American Ethnology in 1896, this book remains the key source for understanding the Ghost Dance.

Black Elk, with John Neihardt. *Black Elk Speaks*. Lincoln: University of Nebraska Press, 1979. An important as-told-to narrative of a Lakota holy man who, though a convert to Christianity, remained committed to his enduring vision of the traditional Sioux way. This narrative also contains interesting eyewitness accounts of the Fetterman Fight, the Battle of the Little Bighorn, and the Wounded Knee Massacre.

Robinson, Doane. *History of Dakota or Sioux Indians*. 1904. Reprint. Minneapolis: Ross and Haines, 1956. Originally published in 1904. Although now dated, Robinson's work contains many interesting details not found elsewhere and is regarded as an important contribution to the literature on the Sioux.

Walker, James R. *Lakota Belief and Ritual*. Edited by Raymond J. DeMallie and Elaine Jahner. Lincoln: University of Nebraska Press, 1983. This volume explores the theological underpinnings of Lakota spiritual belief and provides explanation of some rituals, particularly the rites connected with the Sun Dance. Walker gathered this information from Lakota informants between 1896 and 1914.

_____. *Lakota Society*. Edited by Raymond J. DeMallie. Lincoln: University of Nebraska Press, 1982. This book contributes important information to the understanding of Lakota social structure. Walker, a physician on the Pine Ridge Reservation from 1896 to 1914, gathered and recorded the material from informants.

Sioux uprisings

DATE: 1854-1864
PLACE: Northern Plains
TRIBES AFFECTED: Sioux and affiliated bands
SIGNIFICANCE: These conflicts led to the Sioux Wars of 1866

The Sioux, a large tribal group of the Northern Plains, were a formidable force by the middle of the nineteenth century. Through superior horsemanship and military and hunting skills, they dominated the area of Minnesota, the Dakotas, Nebraska, Iowa, and eastern Montana and Wyoming. Unfortu-

An 1863 engraving of the mass execution at Mankato of participants in the Minnesota Sioux uprising of 1862. (Library of Congress)

nately, this last golden era of the Sioux Nation met a wave of white settlers who swept across the Plains in the 1840's and 1850's. The Sioux responded to this onslaught with defiance and hostility. After the Treaty of Fort Laramie between the United States and the Northern Plains tribes was signed in 1851, the Sioux showed reluctance to allow safe passage for the emigrants and responded with hostilities that would last for more than three decades.

The violence came to a head in 1854 near Fort Laramie, where an impetuous young army officer attacked a band of Sioux for butchering an emigrant's stray cow. The resulting massacre left the officer and his entire command dead and brought on a war between the Sioux and the United States military in 1855. Violence escalated throughout the 1850's, as Indian forces attacked wagon trains and harassed passing emigrants. A few isolated military skirmishes intensified the growing antagonism. In 1855, a group of Teton Sioux battled General William Harney's unit at Ash Hollow, Nebraska, and in 1857, other Teton forces attacked settlements around Spirit Lake, Iowa, and Jackson, Minnesota.

The Minnesota theater of the uprisings saw the most vicious and terrifying warfare. By 1860, whites had poured into Minnesota and tried to pressure their Sioux neighbors into farming. Troubled by these inducements and other grievances, the Minnesota Sioux united under Chief Little Crow in 1862 and slaughtered eight hundred settlers. From 1862 to 1864, skirmishes continued in both the eastern and western theaters of Sioux hostility, later escalating into the Sioux Wars of 1866.

See also Fort Laramie Treaty of 1851; Fort Laramie Treaty of 1868; Indian-white relations—U.S., 1831-1870; Little Crow; Oregon Trail; Sioux.

Sitting Bull (c. 1831, Many Caches, S.Dak.—Dec. 15, 1890, near Bullhead, S.Dak.): Tribal leader

ALSO KNOWN AS: Tatanka Iyotanka
TRIBAL AFFILIATION: Hunkpapa Lakota (Sioux)
SIGNIFICANCE: Sitting Bull was a prominent leader in resisting military and civilian encroachment on traditional Lakota territory

Sitting Bull (Tatanka Iyotanka) was born in the early 1830's along the Grand River near the present-day western South Dakota town of Bullhead, at a site called Many Caches. As a young boy he was called Hunkesni (Slow) because of his deliberate demeanor, a lifelong characteristic. Sitting Bull distinguished himself as a hunter at the age of ten by killing a buffalo and at the age of fourteen by "counting coup"—a deed in which the warrior strikes an enemy with a stick. After these deeds the youth was publicly praised for his courage, and his father gave him the name Sitting Bull in a special ceremony.

Sitting Bull continued to earn many honors in battle against enemy tribes, principally the Crow, Hidatsa, Gros Ventre, and Assiniboine. At about the age of twenty, he was made a member of the prestigious Strong Hearts warrior society, and he became a sash wearer. Only the bravest men wore sashes, strips of scarlet wool cloth that passed over the shoulder and

dragged on the ground. In a battle, sash-wearers would stake themselves to the ground by a lance or picket and could not leave their post until a fellow Strong Heart released them. In one battle against the Crow, Sitting Bull was wounded in the foot; he walked with a pronounced limp for the rest of his life. By 1856, Sitting Bull had so distinguished himself as a warrior that he was made a member of the Midnight Strong Heart society, an honor reserved for only the most elite. Sitting Bull achieved high status among the Hunkpapa people as a leader in this society as well as for his kindness and generosity toward his people.

At about the time he began his career in the Strong Hearts, non-Indian encroachments began in the northern Great Plains. Initially, these incursions occurred along the southern edge of Lakota territory. Sitting Bull's people, who lived farther to the north, did not become involved until United States troops led expeditions in 1863 along the edge of Hunkpapa territory in search of the eastern Sioux who were involved in the Minnesota Uprising. Sitting Bull directed attention to United States military activity in this region and gained national recognition as a military leader in 1866 for his attacks on soldiers and settlers at the site of Fort Buford, where the Yellowstone and Missouri rivers come together.

Sitting Bull was quickly recognized as a force to be dealt with. In an effort to negotiate a truce and encourage Sitting Bull to move closer to the Indian agencies, Catholic missionary Pierre Jean DeSmet traveled to Sitting Bull's camp in 1867 and 1868. Sitting Bull received DeSmet cordially but reaffirmed his determination to protect his people's homeland and their lifeways, a message he was to repeat often in subsequent years.

Sitting Bull was a principal military leader and strategist, with a large following of Lakota from many bands committed to preserving their traditional existence. Sitting Bull's position was unique in Lakota history, in that he had an alliance of numerous Lakota bands; war leaders were usually recognized only within their own bands. Sitting Bull kept his distance from non-Indians, and tensions abated somewhat with the withdrawal of troops along the Bozeman Trail as part of the 1868 treaty. By 1872, however, gold prospectors were beginning to explore the Black Hills area—and their numbers increased after the government-sponsored 1874 Black Hills expedition confirmed large amounts of gold in the area. Gold seekers poured into the Black Hills. The federal government failed to enforce the 1868 treaty or to negotiate purchase of the Black Hills from the Sioux. As fortune hunters continued pouring into their lands, the Sioux became angry, and thousands left their agencies and assembled under Sitting Bull to defend their right to their lands. In response, by the spring of 1876, the U.S. Army was sent to round up the "hostiles."

In the middle of June of 1876, during the annual Sun Dance, Sitting Bull had a vision of soldiers falling into camp. And on June 25, 1876, Sitting Bull's prophecy came true with the defeat of Custer's command at Little Bighorn. Sitting Bull, as was customary for an older warrior, apparently did not fight

Sitting Bull in his later years, probably during the time of his participation in wild west shows. (Library of Congress)

but directed strategy. After this battle the Sioux broke into smaller bands and were relentlessly hunted down by soldiers for the rest of the summer. By the fall of 1876, Sitting Bull was one of the few leaders still resisting surrender and living outside his agency. In May, 1877, Sitting Bull and about one thousand of the most determined traditionalists sought refuge in Canada.

Life proved difficult in Canada; many people on the edge of starvation gradually returned to the United States. By July of 1881, after considerable discussion with Canadian and American officials, Sitting Bull and two hundred followers crossed into the United States and surrendered their horses and weapons. Despite government assurances that he would be immediately repatriated with the Hunkpapa at the Standing Rock Agency, Sitting Bull and most of his followers were held in detention for two years at Fort Randall in South Dakota.

In May, 1883, Sitting Bull was permitted to join his people at Standing Rock. There he came under the jurisdiction of Indian agent James McLaughlin. McLaughlin and Sitting Bull clashed. Sitting Bull was struggling to maintain the sense of nationhood and preserve the traditional values of the Lakota; the agent, backed by government policy, was systematically working to destroy the old ways and organizations and compel the Sioux to accept a new way of life and new values.

McLaughlin permitted Sitting Bull to leave the reservation and participate in wild west shows in 1884 and 1885, possibly to get this outspoken critic of government policies off the reservation. Sitting Bull remained at home thereafter; the United States government was seeking to divest the Sioux of 9 million acres of their lands, and he was in opposition to forfeiting any land. The land was finally lost in 1889.

Sitting Bull continued to clash with McLaughlin and continued to be the leading opponent of the government's assimilation policies. Against this backdrop, word of the Ghost Dance spread among the Sioux. People at Sitting Bull's camp participated in the Ghost Dance, and McLaughlin quickly implicated Sitting Bull and began to petition the government for permission to arrest him. By McLaughlin's own accounts, the Ghost Dance was a convenient excuse to remove his most formidable rival in order to control the Sioux at Standing Rock. On December 12, 1890, arrest orders for Sitting Bull were sent from Washington, and by daybreak on December 15, 1890, Sitting Bull, eight of his people, and six Indian police lay dead or dying.

Sitting Bull, famous for his role in the Sioux Wars, is remembered most by Indian people for his belief in the strength of the traditional values and lifeways.   —*Carole A. Barrett*

See also Black Hills; Bozeman Trail wars; Fort Laramie Treaty of 1868; Gall; Ghost Dance; Grass, John; Little Bighorn, Battle of the; Wounded Knee Massacre.

BIBLIOGRAPHY

Burdick, Usher. *The Last Days of Sitting Bull, Sioux Medicine Chief.* Baltimore: Wirth Brothers, 1941.

McLaughlin, James. *My Friend the Indian.* 1910. Reprint. Lincoln: University of Nebraska Press, 1989.

Manzione, Joseph. *"I Am Looking to the North for My Life": Sitting Bull, 1876-1881.* Salt Lake City: University of Utah Press, 1991.

Utley, Robert M. *The Lance and the Shield: The Life and Times of Sitting Bull.* New York: Henry Holt, 1993.

Vestal, Stanley. *Sitting Bull: Champion of the Sioux.* Boston: Houghton Mifflin, 1932.

Siuslaw: Tribe

CULTURE AREA: Northwest Coast
LANGUAGE GROUP: Yakonan
PRIMARY LOCATION: Southwestern Oregon
POPULATION SIZE: 44 (1990 U.S. Census)

The Siuslaw people live in the creek and river bottoms draining into the Siuslaw River along the southern Oregon coast. The temperate maritime rain forest is mild in climate and rich in resources. They are classified as Penutian speakers of Yakonan genetic stock, though such classifications are disputed by some tribal members.

Prior to white contact the Siuslaw lived a relatively isolated lifestyle focused on hunting, gathering, and fishing. Salmon was a primary food source. Large and small game, migratory waterfowl, many kinds of fish, shellfish, and marine mammals, as well as an abundance of plant life, provided them with many other foods. There was no need for farming. Life was relatively simple.

After contact the Siuslaw were rapidly forced to the margins of their environment as white settlers poured into the coastal river valleys in the middle and late 1800's in search of gold and farmland. They entered into a political confederation with their neighbors to the south, the Lower Umpqua and the Coos, in 1855. In spite of this the Siuslaw were forced to move onto a reservation on the Siletz River.

Their numbers declined, and they became federal wards. They attempted to make treaties in good faith, but their lands were taken over by settlers and their property looted or burned. They lost their property, their way of life, and much of their unique tribal cultural heritage and political legacy. They endure today, though there are only a few families left.

See also Coos; Umpqua; Yakonan language family.

Skagit: Tribe

CULTURE AREA: Northwest Coast
LANGUAGE GROUP: Salishan
PRIMARY LOCATION: Washington State
POPULATION SIZE: 1,362 (Skagit, Stillaguamish, Swinomish, 1990 U.S. Census)

The Skagit tribe has always lived along the Skagit River in northwestern Washington State, traditionally in a marine-oriented culture. The tribe was divided into two groups, the Upper and Lower Skagit. The Upper Skagit lived further east, toward the Cascade Mountains, and were more heavily influenced by the culture of Plateau Indians to their east. The Lower Skagit lived near the mouth of the Skagit River at Puget Sound.

The Swinomish people were often grouped together with the Lower Skagit since they lived nearby and spoke very similar dialects of the Southern Coast Salish language. They are, however, a separate group. The Kikiallus people are a subdivision of the Lower Skagits and once inhabited two villages south of present-day Mount Vernon, Washington, and adjacent Camano Island. (The Skagit River was formerly named the Kikiallus; the meaning of the word "Skagit" is unknown.) The Stillaguamish people, a related tribe, centuries ago lived in twenty-nine villages along the Stillaguamish, slightly south of the Skagit River. The Stillaguamish had close ties with the Kikiallus people.

All these groups based their economies on salmon and cedar. Living in permanent villages of large cedar plank long-houses and highly organized according to clans, they moved seasonally to follow sources of seafood, living in temporary shelters made of cattail mats. Cedar was used to make canoes, clothing, and baskets as well as tools and ceremonial items. Weaving, berry gathering, clam digging, camas root digging, and (after European contact) potato cultivation were women's activities. Men hunted for game.

Contact with the English and Spanish changed life for these groups, especially after the establishment of a Hudson's Bay Company trading post north of Skagit territory in 1827. American settlers started disrupting Skagit lands and lifestyle in the 1850's and 1860's, and the Treaty of Point Elliott (signed by the Puget Sound tribes and the U.S. government in 1855) meant the end of tribal recognition for some groups and the loss of much land. Several tribal groups were forced to live on reservations dominated by larger tribes, and as of 1990, the federal government still had not recognized the Kikiallus as a tribe. In 1976, the federal government did recognize the Stillaguamish as a tribe but did not provide for trust land or a land base. The Swinomish reservation is home to the Swinomish proper, along with some Lower Skagits (others of whom live on the Lummi reservation) and Samishes. The Samish tribe is closely related to the Skagit.

See also Lummi; Northwest Coast; Salishan language family; Samish.

Slave: Tribe

CULTURE AREA: Subarctic
LANGUAGE GROUP: Athapaskan
PRIMARY LOCATION: Alberta, British Columbia, Yukon Territory
POPULATION SIZE: 5,120 (Statistics Canada, based on 1991 census)

Related to other Athapaskan tribes, the Etchaottine (possibly meaning "people dwelling in the shelter") were given the name Awokanak, or "Slave," by their Cree neighbors, and this designation was adopted by explorers and traders. (The spelling "Slavey" is also used.) Their location may once have extended as far south as Lake Athabasca, but in more recent times they have been located in reserves in the Yukon Territory, British Columbia, and Alberta in Canada.

Tribal governance was informal, with effective organization in independent bands. War leaders were chosen when necessary, and a council of hunters provided direction at other times. The Etchaottine diet consisted primarily of fish and game. Fish were caught with hooks and nets, while snares were used to catch beaver and other game animals. Their food was cooked in vessels of spruce bark or woven spruce roots. Clothing for men and women included shirts, leggings, and moccasins made of skins. Spruce roots were woven into caps for women, and babies were transported in bags made of rabbit fur. Canoes of birch or spruce bark (and, less frequently, of moose hide) enabled the Etchaottine to travel over water; snowshoes and toboggans facilitated overland travel.

Two families might share a fireplace in their summer lodges, although winter cabins were usually large enough only for one family. Etchaottine men were known for showing respect to women and for taking especially good care of the elderly and ill. Burial customs were typical of Subarctic Athapaskans; bodies of the dead were either placed on scaffolds or covered with leaves and snow. The unusually contemptuous name "Slave" derives from the relationship of the Etchaottine with the powerful Cree, who early received weapons from Europeans and used them to encroach on Etchaottine land, dominate the tribe, and turn many of them into captives, either for labor or for sale to other tribes. The name, also used by Europeans, reflects the subservient position of the tribe in their locality. Eventually the Etchaottine found refuge on the islands of the Great Slave Lake. Contact with traders, explorers, and others began in 1789 with the visit of Alexander Mackenzie.

See also Athapaskan language family; Cree; Subarctic.

Slavery

TRIBES AFFECTED: Widespread but not pantribal
SIGNIFICANCE: Before European settlement, slavery helped determine status within many Indian societies; after European settlement, Indian slavery became an important economic institution and significantly influenced Indian-white relations

Slavery, a social institution which existed in most human societies before the twentieth century, was practiced by many native North American cultures.

Aboriginal Slavery. All forms of slavery exist to bring honor and power to the master. Before contact with Europeans, American Indian societies did not envision status and power in economic terms, and slavery was not primarily a system of labor. Aboriginal Indian bondage brought power and honor to the master through his absolute domination of a living being.

Most Indian slaves were acquired as war captives, and their enslavement was viewed as a substitute for death in battle. As a replacement for actual death, Indian slavery became a living "social death." The war captive forever lost his status as an independent person and became an appendage of his master's will. The loss of status was marked by rituals of dishonor. The heads of slaves were often shorn as a symbol of dishonor.

Among the Tlingit of the Northwest Coast, female slaves were not allowed to adorn themselves with facial decorations. Slaves were often renamed to dishonor them and to sever connections with their lineage and past. The Nootka gave their female slaves insulting names. The Cherokee and Iroquois word for "slave" was also used to refer to dogs, cats, or other nonhuman living things that were owned. The master's absolute power reached its highest level in the Pacific Northwest, where Indians often killed their slaves while mourning dead family members or celebrating important ceremonial occasions.

Slave Trade. European settlement changed Indian slavery into an economic institution. The Europeans needed laborers to develop their colonies and often purchased Indian slaves. An elaborate Indian slave trade system eventually spanned the North American continent.

Each of the European nations which colonized North America participated in this system. In the 1640's, the Dutch colonists of present-day New York purchased slaves from the Indians and sold them to European colonies in the West Indies. Beginning in the late seventeenth century, French traders from Canada purchased slaves through Illinois middlemen. By the 1720's, French traders from Louisiana were conducting a thriving trade for Indian slaves with the Pawnee and Osage. Some slaves worked on French plantations in Louisiana; others were resold to the French West Indies. Russian settlers in Alaska began using Aleut and Eskimo slaves in the 1790's. Slavery caused a rapid decline in the native population, prompting the Russians to purchase slaves from the Fraser Valley and the region surrounding Puget Sound.

The Spanish and English conducted the largest trade in Indian slaves. In the 1530's, Spanish traders from Mexico began purchasing Indian slaves in the American Southwest. Although the Spanish government outlawed Indian slavery in the sixteenth century, the laws were often violated. By the mid-seventeenth century, the Spanish trade had expanded to the American Great Plains. During the eighteenth century, Taos in present-day New Mexico became an important trading center for Indian slaves. As late as the 1850's, the Taos-based slave trade remained active as the Utes sold their captives to Mexico. The Apaches, Comanches, and Pueblos were most often the victims of the Spanish slave trade.

The first Indians enslaved by the English were war captives, seized by Virginians in battle in 1622. Subsequently, every English colony used Indian slaves. By the 1670's, the English slave trade reached far into the interior of North America through Indian intermediaries. At a time when English settlement extended only 100 miles beyond the Atlantic Coast, the English slave trade reached beyond the Mississippi River. English colonists purchased slaves originally captured in Illinois, Missouri, and Oklahoma. Most of the English slave trade funneled through the Carolina colony. From Charleston, Indian slaves were sold to New England, New York, and the West Indies. Some slaves were kept in the Carolina colony, and in 1708 Indian slaves constituted nearly 15 percent of the Carolina population.

The trade in Indian slaves significantly influenced diplomatic relations among Indian nations. Because most Indian societies obtained their slaves from war captives, the economic demand for Indian slaves caused some tribes to wage war solely for the purpose of acquiring slaves. European colonies and Indian nations formed several military alliances to obtain slaves through warfare. English, Spanish, and French colonists often sold their own Indian war captives to the West Indies.

Decline of Indian Slavery. During the eighteenth century, Indian slavery declined as whites came to prefer African slaves. Indian slaves were increasingly hard to obtain because of the rapid decline of the native population from new diseases borne by white settlers. Whites also found it difficult to prevent Indian slaves from escaping in their own native land, and Africans provided more efficient labor because of their familiarity with large farms in Africa. The enslavement of Indians often created tension with nearby Indian societies and led to diplomatic difficulties for European colonies. Nevertheless, the use of Indian slaves by whites was surprisingly long-lived. There were still some Indian slaves in Louisiana and Rhode Island during the 1770's, in Massachusetts during the 1790's, and in the American Southwest during the 1850's.

Black Slavery Among the Indians. During the early nineteenth century, the international market for cotton caused the rapid expansion of white settlement into lands inhabited by southeastern Indian nations. Responding to this development, the Cherokee, Chickasaw, Choctaw, and Creek nations also turned to commercial farming and began to use black slave labor. Even after their forced migration to the Indian Territory in present-day Oklahoma during the 1830's, these Indian nations continued to use black slaves. By 1860, black slaves made up 14 percent of the population in the Indian Territory. During the Civil War, many Indian slaveholders supported the Confederacy against the Union. After the Union victory, the U.S. government required the abolition of slavery among the southeastern Indians, which was accomplished by treaty in 1866.   —Harold D. Tallant

See also Adoption; African American-American Indian relations; Captivity and captivity narratives; Keetoowah Society; Northwest Coast; Southeast.

BIBLIOGRAPHY

Bailey, L. R. *Indian Slave Trade in the Southwest*. Los Angeles: Westernlore Press, 1966.

Patterson, Orlando. *Slavery and Social Death: A Comparative Study*. Cambridge, Mass.: Harvard University Press, 1982.

Perdue, Theda. *Slavery and the Evolution of Cherokee Society, 1540-1866*. Knoxville: University of Tennessee Press, 1979.

Starna, William A., and Ralph Watkins. "Northern Iroquoian Slavery." *Ethnohistory* 38, no. 1 (Winter, 1991): 34-57.

Washburn, Wilcomb E., ed. *History of Indian-White Relations*. Vol. 4 in *Handbook of North American Indians*, edited by William Sturtevant. Washington, D.C.: Smithsonian Institution Press, 1988.

Wiegers, Robert P. "A Proposal for Indian Slave Trading in the Mississippi Valley and Its Impact on the Osage." *Plains Anthropologist* 33 (May, 1988): 187-202.

Slocum, John (1830's-c. 1896): Religious leader

TRIBAL AFFILIATION: Northwest Salish

SIGNIFICANCE: John Slocum founded the Indian Shaker Church

John Slocum, a Skokomish (Coast Salish) man, was the founder of the Indian Shaker Church in the early 1880's. Previously, he had spent his adult years in gambling and drinking. Oral tradition, as recorded by many scholars who have studied the Shaker Church, recounts that in 1881 Slocum appeared to die. Then, in the presence of family and friends who had gathered to mourn his death, he awoke. He said that he had ascended to heaven and spoken to God. Slocum was told to return to earth and start a movement that would save his people. Among other things, they were all to abstain from gambling and drinking.

Eventually Slocum himself resumed his old ways, however, and in a few years experienced another bout of sickness and (in some accounts) another near-death. It was during this illness that his wife, Mary, underwent the shaking that was believed to have helped heal her husband. A belief in this type of healing then became an important element in the Shaker Church.

See also Shaker Church.

BIBLIOGRAPHY

Amoss, Pamela T. "The Indian Shaker Church." In *Northwest Coast*, edited by Wayne Suttles. Vol. 7 in *Handbook of North American Indians*, edited by William C. Sturtevant. Washington, D.C.: Smithsonian Institution Press, 1990. Features a photograph of John Slocum as well as a summary of important research since Barnett's classic study.

Barnett, Homer G. *Indian Shakers: A Messianic Cult of the Pacific Northwest*. Carbondale: Southern Illinois University Press, 1957.

Smohalla (c. 1815, Wallula, Wash.—c. 1907): Religious leader

ALSO KNOWN AS: Smóqula (the Preacher), Smokeller, Waipshwa (Rock Carrier)

TRIBAL AFFILIATION: Wanapam

SIGNIFICANCE: Smohalla's teachings formed the basis of the Dreamer religion, which flourished among the tribes of the Pacific Northwest well into the twentieth century

Smohalla (or Smóqula, "the Preacher") was one of a core of leaders among the Wanapam who resisted the United States' attempts to place them on reservations. This resistance culminated in the 1,500-mile Long March in 1877. He also was a spiritual leader who fused aspects of Christianity and native traditions into the Dreamer religion, which swept the Northwest United States before the better-known Ghost Dance of the Plains.

Early in his adult life Smohalla distinguished himself in battle, despite being a hunchback. He incurred the personal enmity of Moses, leader of the neighboring Sinkiuses. The two men met in hand-to-hand combat, after which Moses left Smohalla for dead. Smohalla was not dead, however; he made his way to a nearby river, and floated downstream in a boat, beginning a journey that eventually took him down the Pacific Coast to Mexico, then back to Wanapam country through Arizona and other inland points.

Smohalla's reappearance among his people caused a degree of awe that was impressive for a spiritual leader. Smohalla came bearing teachings said to have been acquired on a visit to the Spirit World: that all native peoples should reject the whites' beliefs and artifices. He counseled native peoples to stay away from reservations and to restore traditional ways of life. The Dreamer religion included dances done in hypnotic rhythm to bells, drums, and other musical instruments.

Smohalla survived the Long March and lived until 1907. He was buried at the Satus graveyard in Washington State, and his nephew Puckhyahtoot ("the Last Prophet") carried on his Dreamer religion.

See also Moses; Wanapam.

Snake Dance

TRIBE AFFECTED: Hopi

SIGNIFICANCE: The Snake Dance promotes harmony between the Hopis and the universe and facilitates a bountiful supply of food, rain, and good hunting

The Hopi tribe believes itself to be an integral and interrelated part of nature and the universe. All parts must be kept in harmony, balance, and equilibrium. If the tribe upsets this balance, then it will suffer catastrophe. The Snake Dance is one of several Hopi ceremonial dances that facilitate this harmony and balance. It also enhances correct succession of the four seasons, an abundant supply of food and rain, and a profitable season of hunting.

The Snake Dance is performed in late August each year. A solar observance that begins about four in the afternoon, it is held in different villages during odd- and even-numbered years. The dance is an open ceremonial; visitors may attend and observe.

The dance is preceded by extensive preparation. Males of the snake and antelope fraternities leave their kivas in paint and costume. They go into the desert in each of the four directions for four days to gather snakes. The snakes are placed in a cottonwood tower, or *kisi*, in the center of the village plaza. A wooden plank covering a hole in the ground sits in front of the kisi and symbolizes the entrance to the underworld, or *sipapu*. Antelope priests line one side of the plaza to await the arrival of the snake priests. Upon arriving, the snake priests jump on the sipapu and so announce to the underworld gods the commencement of the snake dance.

Dance rattles made from gourds are vibrated to imitate the rattlesnake, and a chorus sings. At the end of the song the snake priests, who have lined up along the side of the plaza opposite the antelope priests, break up and regroup in threes. As they pass by the kisi, one is handed a snake by a priest hidden in it and places the snake in his mouth. The second member places his arm over the shoulder of the snake bearer and controls the snake if necessary. The third member walks behind.

Each snake priest dances a circle four times. He then drops the snake to the ground, and the third member picks it up. Depending on how many snakes have been caught and how many priests participate in the dance, a priest may repeat the dance several times with different snakes. When all the snakes have been danced with, they are dropped onto a circular design made of corn meal drawn on the ground. The snake priests then grab several snakes and run from the village into the desert to release them. The antelope priests jump on the plank so that the underworld knows the ceremony has ended, and the village then celebrates for four days.

See also Dances and dancing; Pow-wows and contemporary celebrations; Pueblo tribes, Western.

Snake War

DATE: 1866-July, 1868
PLACE: Southeastern Oregon, southwestern Idaho
TRIBES AFFECTED: Northern Paiute (especially the Yahuskin and Walpapi bands), Shoshone
SIGNIFICANCE: After two years of guerrilla warfare, peace talks between Brevet Major General George Crook and Snake leader Old Weawea effectively pacified most Snake bands

The Snakes (named Gens du Serpent by early French explorers) were ancient inhabitants of the Great Basin along upper reaches of the Missouri River southward to the Sweetwater River. From the seventeenth century onward, they invariably had been described as a very poor, largely itinerant people whose chief preoccupation was scrounging food from hard country.

After the failure of Oregon and Nevada volunteers to end Snake attacks on miners during Civil War years, the U.S. Army's First Cavalry and Fourteenth Infantry under General George Crook assumed responsibility for operations in 1866. Thereafter, in a remorseless campaign of forty-eight battles, resulting in five hundred Indian casualties and the death of Chief Pauline, Crook suppressed the Snakes' guerrilla war by exhausting them. Eight hundred Snakes were led to Fort Harney, Oregon, in July, 1868, by Old Weawea, signaling peace. Most Snake survivors retired to the Klamath and Malheur River reservations.

See also Bannock War; Comanche; Paiute, Northern; Shoshone.

Snaketown: Archaeological site

DATE: 300-1150
LOCATION: Southern Arizona
CULTURES AFFECTED: Hohokam, Pima

The site of Snaketown, near the city of Phoenix in southern Arizona, was the largest of the early pit house villages. With occupations dating from between 300 and 1150, it remains the best-known center of Hohokam culture. It is situated on an upper river terrace in the Phoenix Basin, near the confluence of the Salt and the Gila rivers. The site was excavated by archaeologist Emil Haury in 1934-1935 and again in 1964-1965. This research provided detailed information on the Southwest's first irrigation farmers.

The earliest village at Snaketown is estimated to have had a population of approximately one hundred people. Dwellings were constructed by excavating a round foundation with a sloping ramp entryway and erecting a wooden superstructure supported by four main posts. Over time, pit houses became smaller and more rectangular; they eventually developed an elongated oval floor plan, shortest from the entrance to the back wall.

Around 600, there was a marked increase in the size and density of Snaketown and other Hohokam settlements. Ball courts, suggestive of contacts with Mesoamerican cultures, were constructed for contests played with imported rubber balls. Low platform mounds made of adobe covered with plaster that were probably used to support ceremonial structures have also been traced to influence from Mexico.

After 900, Snaketown grew to its maximum size of approximately 125 pit houses covering an area of almost half a square mile, with a population estimated at between five hundred and a thousand inhabitants. Dwellings and mounds were arranged around a central plaza that probably served as the center for dances and other communal activities.

Hohokam subsistence was based on the cultivation of maize as a staple crop, although wild foods such as saguaro cactus, mesquite pods, and cholla remained important components of the diet. Planting strategies included single or dual croppings of maize, beans, cotton, and amaranth. The most significant Hohokam innovation was an extensive system of canal irrigation, constructed along the lower Salt Valley. Fourteen principal irrigation canals, the longest measuring more than 12 miles, carried water to a vast network of smaller canals. Their construction and use implies the existence of sophisticated systems of labor management, as well as a certain degree of social differentiation as a result of varied access to water for agricultural production.

Craft activities at Snaketown included the manufacture of fine red-on-buff ceramics decorated with motifs that included snakes and lizards and artifacts for individual ornamentation. Long-distance trade is indicated by the presence of shell from the Gulf of California. It was worked into beads, bracelets, rings, and pendants, some of which bore designs etched into the shell with acid. Other exotic items recovered at the site include copper bells and slate mirrors with pyrite mosaic inlays that were probably manufactured in Mexico.

Snaketown appears to have been abandoned shortly after 1150, when Hohokam settlements shifted to the lower Salt River Valley. As occurred elsewhere in the Southwest, pit house villages evolved into communities living in above-ground pueblos. It has been suggested that the modern Pima and Tohono O'odham (Papago) Indians are the descendants of the ancient Hohokam.

See also Architecture—Southwest; Ball game and courts; Hohokam; Irrigation; Pit house; Prehistory—Southwest.

Snohomish: Tribe

CULTURE AREA: Northwest Coast
LANGUAGE GROUP: Salishan
PRIMARY LOCATION: Lower Snohomish River and south end of Whidbey Island, Washington
POPULATION SIZE: 402 (1990 U.S. Census)

The socioeconomically stratified Snohomish were dependent upon the sea for much of their food. The basic residential group was the permanent winter village. Though warfare was essentially defensive, one could gain status as a warrior. Numerous intergroup socioeconomic ties were sustained by intermarriage.

The first European American contact was in 1792 with George Vancouver, who explored Hood Canal and Puget Sound. Sustained contact commenced in 1827 when Hudson's Bay Company established Fort Langley on the Fraser River. Introduced ideas and technology brought major changes to the traditional cultures of the area, which had already experienced numerous devastating epidemics. Christian missionary work began in 1839 when Jesuit priests used Chinook jargon to deliver prayers and teach doctrine. During the 1950's, termination of Indian land and status was successfully opposed by the Inter-Tribal Council of Western Washington.

See also Salishan language family.

Snoqualmie: Tribe

CULTURE AREA: Northwest Coast
LANGUAGE GROUP: Salishan
PRIMARY LOCATION: Snoqualmie River, Washington
POPULATION SIZE: 345 (1990 U.S. Census)

The inland Snoqualmie (including the Skykomish) depended to a large extent upon hunting and gathering, despite their access to saltwater and freshwater fish. Cattails, tules, and shredded cedarbark were used by women to make a variety of utilitarian products. The Snoqualmie lived in permanent winter gable-roofed and shed-roof dwellings, and in temporary structures at other times. The politically autonomous villages had permanent membership. Young men practiced vision quests to acquire a tutelary spirit.

After the arrival of European Americans, little ethnographic information about the Snoqualmie was systematically gathered, and what was documented was done long after depopulation by disease and conflict with settlers. The Treaty of Point Elliott of 1855 called for the cession of land annuity provisions, antislavery, fishing rights, and the eventual removal of Indians living west of the Cascade Mountains.

The nonreservation and unrecognized Snoqualmie, along with the Duwamish, Samish, Snohomish, and Steilacoom, petitioned to be recognized in the 1974 fishery treaty, but Judge George Boldt denied their motion in 1979. Boldt's decision maintains that the traditional fisheries are protected by the 1854 and 1855 negotiated treaties.

See also Duwamish; Samish; Snohomish.

Social control, traditional

TRIBES AFFECTED: Pantribal
SIGNIFICANCE: Social control among Indian tribes was maintained by mock battles, ridicule, gossip, public beatings, and execution, among a variety of other means

All Native American tribes had definite rules of behavior and strict concepts of what constituted permissible and antisocial behavior, as defined by the group's established norms. These norms, or mores, were traditionally accepted rules based on a peoples' religion and were long established through oral history as a "given way" for individual and group behavior, if the group was to successfully survive. Admittedly, as in warfare and certain types of intergroup theft, in-group behavior could differ from how one interacted with nontribal or non-aligned people. In fact, one could acquire certain status by violating the property of an antagonistic individual of an enemy group, or even taking the life of an enemy.

As with most unicentric political and legal systems, social control resided within the kin group and in daily face-to-face association with other village or band members. It was generally assumed that an extended family would resolve its conflicts privately. For example, among the Illinois, a man could punish his wife's adultery with mutilation or death. Once a conflict escalated and became public, however, the village or a council would intercede in an effort to restore harmony by resolving the family's problem. Social stability was favored; in-group antisocial behavior was deemed dysfunctional, interrupting basic survival tasks or leading to ongoing conflict.

Despite the usual involvement of the group with adjudication, there existed what is termed "self-help," or right of direct reprisal, often in the cases of murder, wife-stealing, or theft. For example, among the Inuit, when an individual was found guilty of a serious crime, a man was publicly executed by stabbing; a woman was publicly strangled.

Certain crimes of a public nature, ones detrimental to a group's welfare and tribal authority, often were reviewed by a council, chiefs, or, in some instances, by elders who gave advice and assistance in resolving moral transgressions and secular crimes. These leaders and advisers seldom had absolute power or the force to implement any decisions, but relied upon their office and prestige for settling transgressions and grievances, serving as mediators without coercive prerogatives. Consequently, legal decisions usually reflected the group's consensus of opinion. Among most Plains tribes, however, particularly during communal bison hunting, military societies were a real force who possessed undisputed authority to maintain uniform communal action, disciplining men whose individual actions jeopardized the hunt. The guilty man's weapons, property, and horse could be confiscated.

Witchcraft was a major crime, resulting usually in the accused's death. Accused sorcerers likewise could be assassinated without repercussions by the accused person's kin group. One accused of murder may provide the family of the deceased with wampum, or be expiated by other forms of traditional wealth, depending upon the tribe. The bereaved family may refuse compensation, however, and could retaliate in kind without condemnation. An incorrigible thief could be killed with no fear of retaliation, for vengeance was rare and usually the offended family accepted compensation.

Among some Northwest Coast tribes, local feuds or accusations were settled by payment of traditional forms of wealth or by staging mock battles to resolve conflicts, sometimes "capturing" and holding as hostage high-ranking individuals. Many bands and tribes feared actions and retaliations that could lead to feuds, which usually meant counteraction and breaches, and could lead to excommunication or segmentation of a kin group if an equitable settlement was not reached.

The methods of social control differed cross-culturally, but the most effective means were through threat of sorcery or witchcraft, ridicule, consensus of opinion, mock battles between groups, gossip, excommunication, execution, public beatings or whippings, and even threats of serious illness or spiritual death. The Inuit employed song duels to ridicule their adversaries and engaged in public fistfights and wrestling, but withdrawal also remained an effective means of conflict resolution. Delinquent adolescent Native American children could be ostracized, mocked, or simply ignored.

Traditional native legal systems began to disintegrate in many northerly groups with the advent of the fur trade. Throughout North America, traditional native legal systems changed drastically through tribes' confinement to a reservation system, European American-induced religious and sociopolitical factionalism and the accompanying breakdown of clan and general kinship structure, replacement of traditional leaders by the Bureau of Indian Affairs, and general dominance by a multicentric European legal system.

—*John Alan Ross*

See also Clans; Incest taboo; Joking relations; Political organization and leadership.

Societies, non-kin-based

TRIBES AFFECTED: Pantribal

SIGNIFICANCE: Non-kin-based societies provided American Indians with a sense of prestige, position, identity, and fraternity; ceremonies presented and supervised by the societies renewed tribal unity and traditions

Traditional American Indian societies had a wide variety of societies whose memberships were not limited to relatives or fellow clansmen. Non-kin-based societies served many functions for their membership and the tribe as a whole. These social organizations provided members with friendship, prestige and a sense of identity outside the family unit. Many societies supervised and/or performed public ceremonies that entertained, recounted tribal legends, celebrated traditions, and increased tribal unity.

Many societies existed for more than one purpose and did not fit into a single category. The lines defining different societal classifications, membership qualifications, and responsibilities were often intertwined. Membership qualifications were as varied as the number of societies. Memberships

were based on personal achievement or ability, common beliefs, age, occupation, inheritance, or even a physical feature. Though a few societies accepted women, most memberships were restricted to adult males.

Medicine Societies. Medicine societies were the most widespread of Indians societies. Medicine society membership included shamans and curers considered to have special curative powers and/or contacts with the spiritual world. These societies usually met secretly and exchanged information regarding the curative powers of various rituals and plants. These clandestine meetings ensured that an element of secrecy and mysticism would cling to the society's curative powers. Each society possessed its own songs, dances, rites, and medicines particular to its area of expertise. Many medicine societies were formed to cure specific illnesses. Others contained experts in a particular treatment. The northeastern Little Water Society used water to cure the sick. The Plains Blood Doctors practiced bloodletting.

Membership requirements differed. Some candidates applied to a shaman for instruction. Others were recruited. Several societies accepted members who had been afflicted by and cured of a malady the society treated. Other members joined as a result of a dream directing them to become a member. Members sometimes belonged to more than one medicine society. Most members of the northeastern Shake the Pumpkin Society belonged to other medicine societies. This practice increased the expertise and prestige of the principal society.

As a group, medicine societies presented ceremonies believed to strengthen their medicine and cure the ill. During these celebrations, society members often demonstrated their remarkable powers. Members of the powerful Hopi Bear Shamans appeared to eat a human liver without harming the victim. Members of the Iruska Fire in Me Society, which treated burns, displayed their powers by walking on hot coals.

Medicine societies sometimes existed for reasons other than curing ill members of the tribe. Many medicine societies were in charge of annual celebrations and religious rituals. Curer societies of the Pueblo Indians were also responsible for the general welfare of the tribe. Pueblo curers were in charge of providing sufficient rainfall and ensuring fruitful harvests and healthy domestic animals. The Hopi Powamu Society possessed powers to make maize and beans grow. The headmen of the three Cochita Pueblo Indian medicine societies, the Flint, Giant and Shikami, chose important officials for the tribe, including the War Captains. The prestigious Kwakiutl Cannibal Society and the Hopi Agaves Society were in charge of initiating young males into the tribe.

Warrior Societies. Warrior and hunting societies were most prevalent in the western half of the United States. In many tribes, a man was not considered an adult until he was initiated into one of these societies. Most tribes had more than one warrior society. A single warrior society usually boasted the bravest fighters, and rivalry among the societies was common.

Membership requirements varied from tribe to tribe and society to society. Warrior society membership was usually voluntary. Every adult male in the Southwestern Hopi tribe became a member of the Hopi Warrior Society. Some societies had to be applied to; others required an invitation. Some societies required the accomplishment of a special feat or act of bravery for membership. Laguna Pueblo warriors had to return with an enemy scalp to become a member of the Scalp-Takers. Two Cheyenne warrior societies allowed women to participate in feasts and dances.

Among the Cheyenne, boys between the ages of thirteen and sixteen, with some exceptions, could choose which society they wished to join. Most chose to enter their father's warrior society. Candidates were rigorously trained for membership and then initiated in an elaborate celebration that often lasted several days. Feasts were given by the new warrior or his parents to celebrate. Warrior society members gathered prestige through courageous actions in raids and warfare. They were expected to be brave in battle and not allowed to leave the battlefield alone. Members of the Sioux Sacred Bow Society were expected to fight to the death.

Age sometimes placed conditions on the society a candidate could join or affected their rank within the society. Teen members might still be considered in training. Older warriors could retire from the society or become inactive members. Some societies were formed specifically for older members, like the Sioux Chief's Society or the Crow Muddy Hands. The Mandan Dog Society had three strata to accommodate different age groups—the Little Dogs, Dogs, and Old Dogs.

Some warrior and hunting societies were temporary, formed for a specific purpose. When the Pawnee decided to conduct a raid, a Wolf Society was formed. The wolf was the spiritual patron of warfare and members of the society modeled themselves after their spiritual guide by covering themselves in wolfskin when going into battle. A Wolf Society raid was led by any man who presented himself as leader, usually an outstanding warrior. The leader could call off the raid at any time and was expected to be bravest in battle. Anyone wishing to follow the party smoked from a sacred pipe. Priests blessed the group through special prayers and ceremonies. Sacred bundles and special foods were carried to secure their power. Successful or not, the society disbanded when the party returned.

Warrior societies also performed ceremonies that demonstrated their power and recounted stories of the warriors' successes and failures. The dances and rituals purified society members and renewed the power of warriors and their weaponry. Each society had its own songs, dances, body paint, and regalia. The Horse Dance of the Great Basin not only honored the society's guiding spirit, but rallied support and increased tribal unity.

Some warrior societies provided other services to the tribe. The Blackfoot Prairie Dogs acted as an internal camp police force. At times, the Cheyenne Dog Soldiers, which contained up to half of the Cheyenne warriors, controlled tribal politics. Older members of the Warrior or Scalp Society guarded Pueblo Indian medicine society meetings.

Ceremonial and Secret Societies. Ceremonial and secret societies were the keepers of tribal history, legend, and customs. The rites and celebrations performed by these societies entertained and renewed tribal identity, heritage, and pride. Some ceremonial societies developed into religious movements.

Many of the secret societies of the Northwest coastal culture region were formed as prestigious, ritual dance fraternities. Members performed an elaborate series of dances at feasts, potlaches, and ceremonies. These dances were inspired by powerful spiritual beings encountered by the society's ancestors. Dancers dramatized the spiritual encounter, its possession of and exorcism from the societal elder. Dancers of the Northwest coast utilized elaborate masks, rattles, costumes, and body paint and performed amazing physical feats during ceremonies. The Kwakiutl Cannibal Society appeared to eat human flesh. Members of the Fire-Throwing Society swallowed or walked on hot coals.

Northwestern secret societies usually had strict membership qualifications and were often stratified. Nobles were allowed to join higher grade societies. The Wakashan and Bella Coola secret societies required individuals to inherit or marry into the right to be initiated. The Bella Coola Sisaok Society was restricted to relatives of certain chiefs. Women were allowed to participate in the lower dances, but there were no secret societies exclusively for women. Tribesmen could join as many societies as desired and societal memberships were proudly displayed at feasts and public ceremonies.

Ceremonial presentations performed by the Bella Coola Kusiut included demonstrations of their supernatural powers. Young male candidates for the Kusiut, or Black Face, Society were forcibly recruited. Masked Society members grabbed potential candidates, painted their faces black and took them to a secret hut outside the village for instruction on the methods used to deceive audiences. Any nonmember who discovered the society's secrets was either initiated or killed. Any member who divulged society secrets was killed.

The Midewiwin, or Medicine Lodge, Society of the Northeast was one of the most influential in the region. The Midewiwin Society began as a nativistic medicine society and later controlled many aspects of tribal life. The Midewiwin Society officiated at many feasts and celebrations. Members of the Mide priesthood were the keepers of tribal traditions, history, mythology, and legends. They possessed knowledge of curative plants, medicine bundles, and other objects that hurt or healed.

Midewiwin Society practices varied among the different tribes. Among the Chippewa, Midewiwin membership began when a person became ill or dreamed he should join the society. The candidate then sought advice from a Midewiwin priest who agreed to instruct him. Substantial fees were required and were sometimes paid in the form of blankets and pails. Candidates were expected to host a number of feasts. During a period of training, candidates learned the society's curative secrets, stories, and songs. At initiation, new members received birchbark scrolls with pictographic representations of

Mide songs and Mide bags containing healing herbs. The Ottawa and a few other tribes allowed women to join their Midewiwin Society.

Spiritual Societies. Spiritual societies protected their tribe from evil spirits and delivered the gifts of kind spirits. Dances and rituals performed by the society worshiped and glorified the spirit world and warded off wicked spells. Members were often considered shamans because they had the ability to keep evil spirits at bay.

The Plains Bundle Societies existed to honor sacred bundles that had been given to the tribe or society as ancient gifts from the stars. Members of the society were not only responsible for the physical sacred bundle but the legends and ceremonies surrounding it. Sacred bundles ensured successful raids, hunting, warfare, and the well-being of the tribe. Separate societies were formed around each bundle.

Candidates for membership in a Pawnee bundle society, such as the Horse, Brave Raven, or Those Coming Behind societies, had to undergo tests specific to the bundle society before initiation. If the candidate failed the test, he was forever barred from that bundle society, but he could apply to others. Those who could not pass any test might form their own society.

Some societies were formed by members who shared similar spiritual guides, such as the Iroquois Bear, Buffalo, and Otter societies. Society rituals glorified and gave thanks to the society's spiritual mentor, who provided food and materials for the tribe. Society members often took on characteristics of their spiritual animal and imitated its traits at ceremonial dances.

Male or female members of the California Kuksu secret societies were held in high regard by other members of the tribe. Kuksu ceremonies recreated gods, ghosts, spirits, and sacred times prior to the creation of man in order to renew the spirit of the tribe. Candidates were invited to join based on birthright or personal achievements. Candidates underwent strenuous rites of passage and instruction before initiation into the society.

The southwestern Kachina Societies honored the ancient spirits of the various kachinas believed to live in the mountains and lakes surrounding the tribes. Kachinas were kind, benevolent, fun-loving, and sometimes comical creatures who provided the tribe with many of their needs. Society members impersonated kachina characters in their dances and retold stories of their lives, adventures, and kindnesses in order to cure the ill and ensure a good harvest.

The Iroquois False Face Society, so named for their use of masks, existed to counteract witch societies believed to be in league with the Evil Spirit. Members were people who dreamed they should join and left when they dreamed they should. The society was proficient at curing nosebleeds, toothaches, swellings, and eye inflammations, as well as at protecting the tribe from evil spirits.

Miscellaneous Societies. Additional societies included the Contraries of the Plains, Great Basin, and Southwest tribes. If a Sioux Indian dreamed of clowns, it was a sign he should join the Heyoka or Thunder Dreamers Society. Members talked and walked backward. They ate scalding hot food and complained that it was too cold. The Crow Contraries, or Crazy Dogs Wishing to Die, was a more serious, and usually very temporary, society. Members were motivated to join by feelings of desperation resulting from the loss of a relative or personal embarrassment. Crazy Dogs also did ordinary things backward. Members painted themselves in black war paint during peacetime or ignored an enemy attack on their camp. Crazy Dogs also performed "courageous" deeds in battle, however, coming closest to the enemy and usually dying first.

A few tribes had Berdache societies. Society members were men who dreamed or decided they should take on the role of a woman. After a ceremony in which they were initiated by the other sex, they dressed and acted as women. Among some tribes, berdache were considered powerful shamans. Others took a berdache with them into battle because they were considered good luck.

Several tribes had women's societies or allowed women to join men's societies. Female members usually did not acquire the same status or privileges as male members. Women were allowed to become active members of the Californian Kuksu secret societies. Plains Indians had Shield Bearer Societies for the mothers and wives of great warriors. Normally, women were not allowed to touch weaponry, but Shield Bearers were allowed to carry weapons during special ceremonies. Other women's societies acknowledged skill in artistry. The Plains Indian Quill Workers were women adept at weaving with porcupine quills.

Non-kin-based societies suffered as a result of population declines, acculturation, and dispersion of tribes. Memberships dwindled, and many societies dissolved. Other societies have witnessed a resurgence in popularity as a result of interest in renewing tribal heritage and tradition. Midewiwin ceremonies are still practiced in the Northeast when tribes gather. A number of Native Americans consult medicine society members to cure illnesses, and many of the kachina and warrior society dances are still performed. *—Leslie Stricker*

See also False Face Ceremony; Hamatsa; Husk Face Society; Kachinas; Kuksu rituals and society; Masks; Midewiwin; Military societies; Potlatch; Secret societies.

BIBLIOGRAPHY

Laubin, Reginald, and Gladys Laubin. *Indian Dances of North America: Their Importance to Indian Life.* Norman: University of Oklahoma Press, 1977. Describes ceremonial rituals performed by North American Indians. Details dances, costumes, and ceremonial objects used and the meanings behind their use.

Murie, James R. *Pawnee Indian Societies.* New York: The Trustees, 1914. Vol. 11, part 7, in the series Anthropological Papers of the American Museum of Natural History, published by the museum's trustees. This work details Pawnee societies as well as other aspects of Pawnee life.

Oswalt, Wendell H. *This Land Was Theirs: A Study of North American Indians.* 4th ed. Mountain View, Calif.: Mayfield, 1988. This work takes representative tribes from each culture area and describes their spiritual life, social relations, subsistence activities, technology, and history.

Sturtevant, William C., gen. ed. *Handbook of North American Indians*. Washington, D.C.: Smithsonian Institution Press, 1978. This multivolume set is an excellent reference for every aspect of North American Indian tribal life. It also includes maps, charts, and photographs.

Underhill, Ruth M. *Red Man's Religion: Beliefs and Practices of the Indians North of Mexico*. Chicago: University of Chicago Press, 1965. Details the origins and beliefs of many North American tribes from each culture area. Describes songs, dances, prayers, and rituals practiced and the societies in which they were practiced.

Wissler, Clark. *Societies and Ceremonial Associations in the Oglala Division of the Teton-Dakota*. New York: The Trustees, 1912. Vol. 11, part 1, in the series Anthropological Papers of the American Museum of Natural History, published by the museum's trustees. Gives insight into Plains warrior societies by concentrating on the Oglala Sioux.

Society of American Indians (SAI)

DATE: 1911-1924

TRIBES AFFECTED: Pantribal

SIGNIFICANCE: Headed by educated Native American professionals, the SAI advocated native educational and social advancement, true historical representation, native franchise, and legal assistance

On October 12, 1911, more than fifty Native American delegates met in Columbus, Ohio, at the Society of American Indians' (SAI) founding conference. The date, Columbus Day, was significant: This gathering marked a reclaiming of indigenous voices, a rediscovering of native pride.

The "father" of this organization was a non-Native American sociologist from Ohio State University, Fayette A. McKenzie. Six months prior to the October conference, McKenzie had met with Dr. Charles A. Eastman (Sioux), Dr. Carlos Montezuma (Apache), attorney Thomas L. Sloan (Omaha), Laura Cornelius (Oneida), and Henry Standing Bear (Sioux). Coming from different backgrounds, these educated professionals united to form a native-run association. Already assimilated into the dominant society, they sought to retain their Native American identity. Calling themselves the American Indian Association, the group rallied around pan-Indian reforms, especially in the educational arena.

At the October convention, the historical, legal, and cultural bonds connecting all natives were emphasized. The delegates drafted a constitution that advocated native advancement, true historical presentation, native citizenship, and legal assistance. To assert that this was a native movement and not a "white-run" organization, delegates changed the name to the Society of American Indians. National meetings were to be held annually, and Washington, D.C., was designated as the society's headquarters.

The SAI's publication, the *Quarterly Journal*, was first issued on April 15, 1913. The masthead was framed with the society's emblem, the American eagle, on one side and a lighted torch on the other. Below this was the SAI's motto: "The honor of the race and the good of the country shall be paramount."

The journal's editor, Arthur C. Parker (Seneca), was the SAI's most intellectual influence. With his anthropological background, Parker sought to design the SAI after Tecumseh's historical visions. Parker ardently fought for educational reforms, for an American Indian Day, and for visible Native American role models.

As a peacekeeper, Parker often tempered the rising factionalism in the SAI. In 1913 the SAI was at its membership height with more than two hundred active (native) members and more than four hundred associate (non-native) members. Friction in the following years sharply eroded membership numbers, however; lacking resources for assisting tribes with legal aid and for affecting the structure of the Bureau of Indian Affairs (BIA), members began to air their frustrations internally. Conflicts involved arguments over the abolition of the BIA, the denouncement of peyote religion, and the responsibility of individual tribal complaints. The SAI officially rejected peyote religion, but no consensus was reached on the BIA question, an issue that eventually splintered the SAI.

A change in focus was attempted by renaming the society's publication *The American Indian Magazine*. One of its editors, Zitkala-Sa (Gertrude Bonnin), a Yankton Sioux, became involved in the SAI by opening an educational center among the Utes. Even with Zitkala-Sa's strong contributions, however, the SAI's status remained precarious.

In the early 1920's, a sense of despair clouded the SAI's visions. Pan-Indian unification attempts had failed, BIA abolition was hopeless, political clout was slight (many members were not franchised), and individual interests were detracting from pantribal ones. On June 2, 1924, the Indian Citizenship Bill was signed, marking the success of one of the SAI's hardest fought battles. By this time, however, the group was almost completely defunct, and symbolically, this date marks the end of the SAI.

See also Activism; Bonnin, Gertrude Simmons; Eastman, Charles Alexander; Montezuma, Carlos; Pan-Indianism; Peyote and peyote religion.

Sooke: Tribe

CULTURE AREA: Northwest Coast

LANGUAGE GROUP: Salishan

PRIMARY LOCATION: Washington

The Central Coast Salish Sooke (or Sunghees) were a maritime people with bilateral kinship. They lived in large, rectangular split, hand-hewn cedar dwellings in permanent winter villages that cooperated in defense. The Sooke intermarried with adjacent people, particularly the Nitinaht. Their principal food source was the sea; they fished and harpooned sea mammals. During the summer and fall they hunted and gathered numerous types of animals and plants for food and utilitarian products. The major ceremonies were the Spirit Dances, the Secret Society, First Salmon Ceremony, and the Cleansing

Ceremonies. Potlatching was staged for certain rites of passage, house erection, canoe launching, and change of status. Young men trained for a vision quest to become shamans and to attain a tutelary spirit. Little is recorded of these people; after 1850 their population was greatly reduced by the influx of gold miners and settlers, who brought disease.

See also Salishan language family.

Southeast: Culture area

LANGUAGE GROUPS: Algonquian, Atakapa, Caddoan, Chitimacha, Iroquoian, Muskogean, Natchez, Siouan, Timucuan, Tunican, Yuchi

TRIBES: Ais, Alabama, Anadarko (Hasinai Confederacy), Apalachee, Apalachicola, Atakapa, Bayogoula, Biloxi, Calusa, Cape Fear, Catawba, Cheraw, Cherokee, Chiaha, Chickasaw, Chitimacha, Choctaw, Coushatta, Creek, Guale, Guasco (Hasinai Confederacy), Hitchiti, Houma, Jeaga, Manahoac (Mahock), Mobile, Nabedache (Hasinai Confederacy), Natchez, Ocaneechi, Ofo, Pamlico, Pawokti, Powhatan Confederacy, Seminole, Texas (Hasinai Confederacy), Timucua, Tiou, Tohome, Tunica, Tuscarora, Tuskegee, Tutelo, Waccamaw, Yamasee, Yazoo, Yuchi

The Southeast culture area is located in the southeastern United States and is one of ten Native American culture areas found in the United States and Canada. The various Southeast Indian groups generally shared the following culture traits: a material culture that included dugout canoes, rafts, blowguns, shields, pipes, bird feather cloaks, basketry, mats, houses made of pole, thatch, or bark, and stockaded towns, and a nonmaterial culture based on hunting, gathering, and agriculture, dual leadership, socially powerful women, clans, social stratification with a sharply defined class system, sun symbolism, the Green Corn Ceremony, elaborate mortuary rituals, the Chunkey game, warfare, and war captive torture-sacrifice.

Culture Areas. The culture area concept was developed by Otis T. Mason (1838-1908), Clark Wissler (1870-1947), and Alfred L. Kroeber (1876-1960), among others. These scholars grouped North American aboriginal cultures into geographic regions, defined by cultures in each area which shared numerous similarities. These shared culture traits are considered to have regional significance, representing either common adaptations to the environment or diffusion among the aboriginal groups in the region. Culture areas provide synthetic overviews of human achievements within the different regions of North America. The areal typology organizes the cultural data into regional units which can then be further studied and analyzed. Culture areas allow anthropologists and geographers to move beyond the minutiae of local events to search for broad regional trends and to develop theories of culture contact, diffusion, and change. Taken to the extreme, however, the culture area concept can neglect the influences and histories of tribes and individuals within regions, since it emphasizes broad regional events rather than local occurrences. While the culture area typology was an important theoretical concern to early- to mid-twentieth-century anthropologists—

and is still generally employed as a useful organizing principle for discussing Native American groups—anthropological theory has moved beyond the issues of innovation and diffusion that were so important in the early 1900's.

Southeast Geography. The Southeast culture area covers the southeastern United States and generally includes Louisiana, Mississippi, Alabama, Florida, Georgia, southwestern South Carolina, western North Carolina, Tennessee, and southern Arkansas. The boundaries fluctuated, sometimes expanding to include portions of eastern Texas, eastern Arkansas, the Carolinas, Virginia, West Virginia, and Kentucky.

Generally, the Southeast climate is characterized by year-round warm temperatures and seasonally abundant precipitation, with local variation depending on the latitude or altitude. Physically, the Southeast consists of coastal plains and lowlands, interior fertile river valleys, including the lower reaches of the Mississippi River, and interior low plateaus, with occasional higher peaks, such as the Blue Ridge Mountains, the Appalachians, the Ozarks, and the Ouachita Mountains. The majority of the region is low-lying (elevations of less than 500 feet above sea level), and prehistoric and historic human settlement was concentrated in the coastal and riverine ecozones.

Language, Social Organization, and Subsistence. The Southeast was home to a large number of different Indian groups speaking diverse languages but sharing cultural traits. Speakers of the Muskogean languages dominated in terms of numbers, but there were also speakers of Algonquian, Caddoan, Iroquoian, and Siouan languages, as well as of Atakapa, Chitimacha, Natchez, Timucua, Tunica, and Yuchi.

Beginning in the late prehistoric or early historic period, some southeastern peoples also used a pidgin language for trading purposes, called Mobilian Jargon (also termed Mobilian Trade Jargon, or the Chickasaw-Choctaw Trade Language). The lexical sources are mostly from Muskogean languages, Chickasaw and Choctaw in particular.

Among the Indians of the Southeast, social complexity ranged from loosely structured small hunting and gathering groups to more complexly organized sedentary towns. Generally the settled agricultural peoples are emphasized in regional syntheses, since these groups, with their larger populations, had a greater impact on historical events in the Southeast. In addition, these cultures were featured in colonial documents and histories, since Europeans were better able to understand the lifeways of settled farming peoples than those of the less settled hunting and gathering groups.

Generally, regardless of the degree of social complexity, there was separation by gender in the daily activities of southeastern communities. Women often gathered or cultivated the plants, prepared the food, manufactured the pottery, made baskets, prepared animal skins, made clothing, and manufactured tools for these activities. Male tasks often included hunting, making tools, constructing buildings, clearing land, and waging warfare. The men's lives often revolved around the winter hunting season, whereas the women participated most actively in the planting cycle and household routines. The

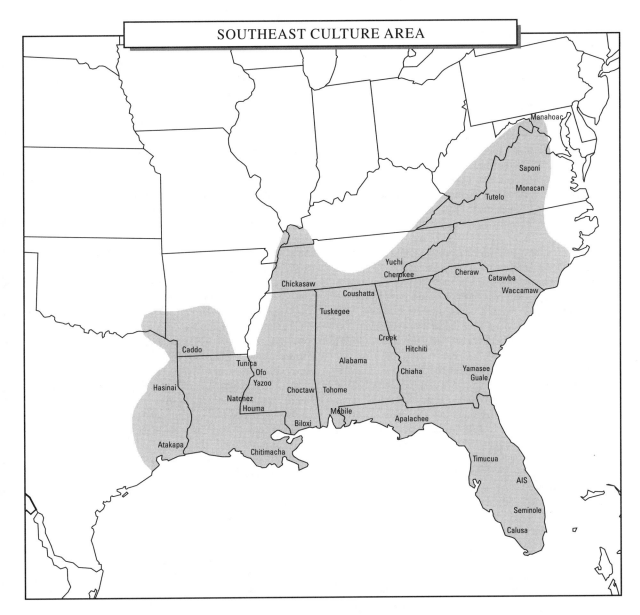

SOUTHEAST CULTURE AREA

Manahoac
Saponi
Monacan
Tutelo
Yuchi
Cherokee
Cheraw
Catawba
Waccamaw
Chickasaw
Coushatta
Tuskegee
Creek
Hitchiti
Caddo
Alabama
Chiaha
Tunica
Ofo
Yamasee
Yazoo
Guale
Hasinai
Choctaw
Tohome
Natchez
Houma
Mobile
Biloxi
Apalachee
Atakapa
Chitimacha
Timucua
AIS
Seminole
Calusa

sexes were often physically separated in ceremonies, in the case of the women during menstruation or birth, and in the case of the men during raiding events.

Occasionally, men or women did not wish to participate in these culturally sanctioned gender roles. In these cases, among many of these groups, it was permissible for a male to behave as a woman or for a female to behave as a man. Transvestism might include a sexual relationship, although not necessarily, and generally such behavior was not censored. This gender-role switching was typically accepted in many North American Indian cultures.

Subsistence-related activities were aided by the manufacture of various tools. Fish were caught using the hook and line, spears, nets, traps, and weirs. Hunters used the bow and arrow

and the blowgun, killing deer, turkeys, and buffalo, and often utilized fires or decoys to aid in capturing the animals.

Localized resources, such as salt or flint, were often traded among different groups. The Southeast was noted for the extensive trails and trading arrangements which connected communities to a vast regional system. With European contact, the newcomers contributed their goods and political power to this existing network, which resulted in further changes to a dynamic regional economy. For example, upon the adoption of European arms and trading strategies, aboriginal hunting was often conducted to obtain deer skins for trade rather than only for deer meat and hides for local use.

Farming groups grew domesticated corn, beans, and squash, plus many plants native to the Southeast, such as bottle gourds, sunflowers, sumpweed, chenopodium, pigweed, and knotweed. With the arrival of the Europeans, foreign crops and animals were rapidly adopted: figs, peaches, and watermelon, and chickens, pigs, horses, and cows. Corn served as the subsistence staple and appeared (either boiled, baked, or fried) at almost every meal. Food was preserved through drying, either over the fire or on the ground under the sun. Harvested crops were stored in the houses or sometimes in special granaries.

Farming groups generally lived in large established towns with a central plaza and meeting house. Villages in warmer locations often consisted of wall-less shelters. Some communities built summer and winter houses to cope with varying climatic conditions. Similar climatic adaptations determined the type of clothing, which ranged from minimalist skirts and breechcloths in summer to warmer garments in winter. People often tattooed their faces and bodies and wore various decorative adornments, such as armbands, bracelets, and other items made from copper, shell, or other raw materials.

Southeastern social organization was typically based upon matrilineal kinship—kin relationships traced through the female line of descent. Women could own land, houses, and other possessions and were often honored members of the community, as signified by the Creek and Cherokee "Beloved Women" titles.

Matrilineal kinship ties created a strong bond between the mother's brother and her children, since they were members of the same kinship unit. There was a different sort of bond between the father and his offspring, since they were members of different kinship groups. This fundamental difference in social relationships was not understood by the European colonists who were more accustomed to the father-son relationship typical of a patrilineal society (descent traced through the male ancestors). Europeans were accustomed to dealing with male power and authority, and they often insisted on conducting transactions with men. With colonialism, the traditional authority of women in some cultures was gradually eroded. In addition, colonial economics altered the marriage arrangements among many Southeast groups. The growth of the deerskin trade increased the value of women's work (hide preparation), for individual men could hunt vastly more animals than they could process. It seems likely that the economic incentives to increase deerskin production resulted in increased numbers of polygynous unions, since one man with several wives was a more viable economic unit.

Many of the groups in the Southeast had stratified social classes, often with some sort of dual organization. Many had two leaders, the peace chief and the war chief. In other cases, the villages might be divided into two types; among some Creek, for example, certain communities promoted peace and other communities were devoted to warfare.

Beliefs and Ceremonies. Many of the peoples of the Southeast had similar beliefs concerning the origins of the world and its structure. Often it was envisaged as possessing many levels, each with its own creatures, and special significance was generally attached to the four cardinal directions. For example, many cultures associated the west with the realm of the dead.

There were strong beliefs concerning purity and pollution. For many people, bathing in a stream was an appropriate way to begin the day, providing a sense of purity. Southeastern peoples consumed a ritual beverage, known as the Black Drink, prepared from the leaves of a species of holly (*Ilex vomitoria*), which served to purge their bodies both physically and spiritually.

Various individual rites of passage marked the significant steps from birth through puberty, marriage, and death. The mortuary ceremonies were much commented upon by the European colonists, since they were often spectacular, shocking, and public, in contrast to other more private rituals. For this reason, there is much information available concerning funerals and post-death treatment of the body. For example, the 1715 funeral of Tattooed Serpent, a Natchez war chief, is well documented. His death initiated a months-long chain of events which included public viewing of the body, the provision of food, human sacrifices, the burning of his house, and special treatment of the corpse. Such complex mortuary arrangements were typical for the southeastern elite.

Another ceremony which had importance among the southeastern farming groups was the Green Corn or Busk Ceremony. It was scheduled after the harvest, and therefore its exact occurrence varied from year to year and from south to north, ranging from May to September. This was an event celebrating the bounty of nature and often fertility in general. It typically involved fasting, sexual abstinence, and other forms of purification. The climax of the multiday ritual was the kindling of a new fire and the consumption of the new corn, accompanied by dancing, drumming, playing of the ball game, and other events.

Southeast History. European history of the Southeast commenced with the sixteenth century explorers. By midcentury, Spanish missions were established in Florida and Georgia, and by 1607, the English had founded Jamestown, Virginia. By the late seventeenth century, the English were heavily involved in Indian slavery and deer-hide trading in South Carolina, while the French were exploiting the Mississippi River territories. Southeast Native American life was forever altered by the impact of Europeans in the area, but it nevertheless continued. Over the centuries, various wars, treaties, and legal maneuvers resulted in native peoples losing much territory; probably the most infamous of these events began with the 1830 Indian Removal Act signed by President Andrew Jackson. This act was designed to allow European settlers to establish farms on lands previously occupied by farming Native Americans. Ironically, it penalized those Indians who had assimilated most successfully into European American society, namely the "Five Civilized Tribes": the Cherokee, Chickasaw, Choctaw, Creek, and Seminole. From 1830-1839, these peoples were systematically marched from their southeastern homes to land in present-day Oklahoma. The routes they took became known as the "Trails of Tears," and they were marked by innumerable shallow graves and abandoned possessions. Despite these ordeals, once in Oklahoma, these refugee groups organized themselves as nations. In 1980, the Five Civilized Tribes in Oklahoma numbered approximately 60,000 Cherokee, 24,000 Choctaw, 15,500 Creek, 6,000 Chickasaw, and 5,000 Seminole.

Twentieth Century. As in Oklahoma, Native Americans in the Southeast have a variety of economic strategies for survival in today's world. These range from individual money-making endeavors based on traditional crafts (such as basket-making) or activities (fishing) to community financial undertakings such as bingo and other gambling and various industries. Contemporary Indian communities must decide on the balance that they wish to maintain between, on the one hand, a traditional Native American lifestyle and, on the other, the dominant American worldview. For many Indian groups, this decision-making process is marked by internal dissention and disagreement concerning the tribal future.

According to the 1980 census, the three largest Southeast Indian groups still in the Southeast are the Cherokee, the Choctaw, and the Seminole. The Eastern Band of Cherokee, located on the Qualla Reservation in North Carolina, had a census-reported population of 5,482; however, Eastern Band tribal rolls included approximately 9,000 members. These people maintain the Southeast's largest federal reservation, founded in 1889.

The Mississippi and Louisiana Choctaw number fewer then 5,000 (although there are 50,000 Choctaw in the United States). The Florida Seminole include approximately 10,000 people, of whom few live on reservations.

Current estimates of southeastern Native American numbers are imprecise measures, since there are many definitions of who is to be considered Indian; numbers vary depending on whether one is enumerating federally recognized Indians, state-recognized groups, or individuals who declare that they are "Indian." (Other ethnic groups in the United States and Canada generally are self-ascribed and do not have to demonstrate their ethnicity.)

In the United States, recognition by the federal government is based on Indian documentation and demonstration that the Native American community has possessed separate and distinct tribal government processes since European contact. The group must be able to prove descent from a historic tribe, and it must be identified in the available records as a distinct cultural entity. Because of these stringent federal criteria, most Native Americans in the Southeast are not federally recognized. Federally recognized groups in the Southeast include the Louisiana Chitimacha (520 members in 1985), the Louisiana Coushatta (350 members in 1985), the Louisiana Tunica-Biloxi (250 members in 1985), the Mississippi Band of Choctaw (8,080 enrolled members in 1990), the Alabama and Florida Poarch Band of Creeks (1,850 enrolled members in 1986), the Florida Seminole (approximately 1,600 enrolled members in 1990), the Florida Miccosukee (approximately 400 members in 1990), and the North Carolina Eastern Band of Cherokee (with a 1980 census population of 5,482 people, while tribal rolls list about 4,000 more members).

The Southeast also is home to a number of triracial groups, descendants of Native Americans, Europeans, and Africans. Generally, such groups have been cut off from federal benefits available to "Indians," although in some cases they have managed to obtain state recognition for their Indian ancestry. In the Southeast, the presence of these triracial groups and the racial divisions within twentieth century American society meant that many Native American peoples were denied educational opportunities. For example, the Houma Indians of southeastern Louisiana were classified as black and thus were not permitted to attend white schools. As a result, many southeastern Native Americans abandoned their Indian heritage in order that their children might have increased opportunities in a segregated society. The 1964 Civil Rights Act worked to desegregate the schools, expanding the educational options of these Native Americans and permitting many Indian descendants to rediscover their heritage.   —*Susan J. Wurtzburg*

See also Alabama; Architecture—Southeast; Arts and crafts—Southeast; Black Drink; Catawba; Cherokee; Chickee; Choctaw; Creek; Green Corn Dance; Hitchiti; Mississippian; Powhatan Confederacy; Prehistory—Southeast; Seminole; Southern Cult; Trail of Tears.

BIBLIOGRAPHY

Barker, Alex W., and Timothy R. Pauketat, eds. *Lords of the Southeast: Social Inequality and the Native Elites of Southeastern North America.* Archaeological Papers 3. Washington, D.C.: American Anthropological Association, 1992. Anthology of articles concerning late prehistoric and early historic Native Americans. No comprehensive index.

Boxberger, Daniel L., ed. *Native North Americans: An Ethnohistorical Approach.* Dubuque, Iowa: Kendall/Hunt, 1990. Useful chapter on the Southeast. Charts, maps, illustrations, and photographs. No index.

DePratter, Chester B., ed. *The Late Prehistoric Southeast: A Source Book.* New York: Garland, 1986. An anthology of historically important articles dating from 1788 to 1974. Useful introduction and additional references, but no index.

Hudson, Charles. *The Southeastern Indians.* Knoxville: University of Tennessee Press, 1976. Coverage of prehistory and history, beliefs, social organization, subsistence, ceremonies, arts, and games. Good index, illustrations, and maps.

Kehoe, Alice B. *North American Indians: A Comprehensive Account.* 2d ed. Englewood Cliffs, N.J.: Prentice Hall, 1992. Contains a useful chapter on the Southeast and recent Native American history. Index, charts, maps, illustrations, and photographs.

Paredes, J. Anthony, ed. *Indians of the Southeastern United States in the Late Twentieth Century.* Tuscaloosa: University of Alabama Press, 1992. Anthology of articles concerning contemporary Native Americans. Comprehensive index, maps, and photographs.

Swanton, John R. *The Indians of the Southeastern United States.* 1946. Reprint. Washington, D.C.: Smithsonian Institution Press, 1979. Overview of Southeast Native American culture and a description of the individual groups. Index, charts, maps, drawings, and photographs.

Usner, Daniel H., Jr. *Indians, Settlers, and Slaves in a Frontier Exchange Economy: The Lower Mississippi Valley Before 1783*. Chapel Hill: University of North Carolina Press, 1992. Detailed reconstruction of the period 1699-1783. Index, charts, maps, and illustrations.

Williams, Walter L., ed. *Southeastern Indians Since the Removal Era*. Athens: University of Georgia Press, 1979. Anthology of articles concerning historic Native Americans. Comprehensive index, photographs.

Wood, Peter H., et al., eds. *Powhatan's Mantle: Indians in the Colonial Southeast*. Lincoln: University of Nebraska Press, 1989. Anthology of articles concerning historic Native Americans. Comprehensive index, maps.

Southern Cult: Archaeological complex

DATE: 1100-1300
LOCATION: Southeastern North America
CULTURES AFFECTED: Mississippian

The Southern Cult, also known as the "Southeastern Ceremonial Complex," refers to beliefs, rituals, and symbols associated with specific artifacts and motifs of the Mississippian tradition in the southeastern United States. There is no evidence that this cultural complex was actually a "cult." Instead, it represents a complicated network or series of networks of social interaction and exchange over a wide geographical area. Its principal features are ritual objects decorated with esoteric motifs alluding to or depicting human sacrifice. These are found as far north as Minnesota and as far west as Oklahoma, and they extend eastward and southward to the Atlantic Coast and Gulf of Mexico.

The largest concentrations of Southern Cult artifacts come from burials at Moundville, Etowah, and Spiro. These materials were rare at Cahokia, the largest site of the Mississippian tradition. Traits of the Southern Cult identified by archaeologists A. J. Waring, Jr., and Preston Holder include polished stone axes in which the blade and handle are carved from a single piece of stone, polished stone batons or clubs, shell pendants with crosses created by cut-out sections, engraved shell disks or gorgets, ceramics with specific motifs, and representations of warriors executed in hammered copper sheets. Southern Cult artifacts often bear esoteric motifs and designs, including crosses, hands with eyes, skulls, spiders, woodpeckers, vultures, rattlesnakes, flying or feathered serpents, men in bird costumes, warriors with axes or batons, and trophy heads. Among the most striking of these objects are ceramic vessels in the forms of severed heads with closed eyes and mouths. The predominance of individuals with weapons and severed heads suggests that the Southern Cult was associated with warfare and human sacrifice.

The enormous quantities of these objects found at Spiro Mound, Oklahoma, and general similarities to traits of Postclassic Mesoamerican cultures such as the Toltecs have suggested that the cult originated in the eastern portion of the Mississippian world. Scholarship has also hinted that cross motifs of the Southern Cult may be related to ancient traditions of warfare and sacrifice connected with observations of the planet Venus. What is known for certain about the Southern Cult is the fact that it indicates the existence of far-flung trade networks. Decorated shell gorgets from eastern Oklahoma were made from species that were probably collected on the Atlantic Coast. Hammered copper axes and decorated sheets from sites in the southeastern United States were made from native copper imported from the Great Lakes region. The effort and skill that went into the production and distribution of these items, as well as the existence of the rich burials that contained them, indicate the existence of a highly ranked social organization. Why the Southern Cult appeared and disappeared remains unknown, but its existence is testimony to a period of rich and complex ceremonial life.

See also Etowah; Mississippian; Mounds and mound builders; Moundville; Spiro; Toltec.

Southwest: Culture area

LANGUAGE GROUPS: Athapaskan, Keres, Kiowa-Tanoan, Uto-Aztecan, Yuman, Zuni
TRIBES: Acoma, Apache (including Chiricahua, Jicarilla, and Mescalero), Cochiti, Havasupai, Hopi, Isleta, Jemez, Karankawa, Laguna, Nambe, Navajo, Picuris, Pima, Pojoaque, San Felipe, San Ildefonso, San Juan, Sandia, Santa Ana, Santa Clara, Santo Domingo, Taos, Tesuque, Tohono O'odham, Walapai, Yaqui, Yavapai, Zia, Zuni

The United States Southwest includes Arizona, New Mexico, and southern Utah and Colorado. The area features rugged terrain and an arid landscape in which agriculture provided an unlikely but solid foothold for the growth of settled populations among the deep canyons and dun-colored mesas. It remains home to many of the most culturally conservative tribes, notably the Navajos and the Pueblo Indians. Southwestern archaeological remains—carefully planned masonry or adobe communities—are major tourist attractions in the region.

Paleo-Indian/Archaic Era. The earliest commonly accepted evidence for humans in the Southwest is from people archaeologists call Paleo-Indians. It dates from the last thirteen thousand years. Widespread habitation probably began about 9000 B.C.E., when highly mobile bands hunted large game animals, gathered wild plants, and killed smaller game as opportunities arose.

By 6000 B.C.E., many of the largest game animals were extinct, and early southwesterners shifted to more generalized hunting and gathering. Archaic period Indians probably operated from central base camps in defined territories by 1800 B.C.E. Archaic culture ended with the adoption of maize horticulture, probably around 1500-1000 B.C.E., but the people were cautious about depending on these new ways, continuing to hunt and gather along with caring for the crops.

Hohokam and Mogollon Cultures. The cultures of the Hohokam and Mogollon, known from their archaeological remains, had developed from Archaic populations in southwestern New Mexico and southern Arizona by 200 B.C.E., the Hohokam in the valleys of the Gila and Salt rivers, the Mogollon in the uplands of those drainages. The Hohokam had irrigation technology by 700 C.E. There were 500 kilometers (slightly over 300 miles) of main canals in the Salt Valley alone, watering fields of corn, beans, squash, and cotton.

Raw or woven cotton was probably an important export in trade, as were elaborate shell ornaments, pottery, turquoise, jet, and obsidian. Copper bells, parrots, and macaws suggest trade ties to ancient Mexico, as do Hohokam ballcourts and platform mounds. Local exchange of goods and services, however, was probably the main cement that bound the culture together; they probably never shared a single government.

The Mogollon are known for making the earliest pottery yet found in the Southwest, about 300 B.C.E. They lived in small, egalitarian pithouse villages with specialized ceremonial rooms, depending on a combination of agriculture and hunted and gathered resources. By 700 C.E. they were trading regularly with the Hohokam, and the cultures mixed at the Mogollon western edge. The Mogollon began irrigation and water run-off control about that time and, particularly in their eastern and northern areas, began to build aboveground architecture, sometimes with large ceremonial structures. The Mimbres Mogollon variant produced finely painted figurative pottery, ceremonially "killed" for interment with the dead.

Both Hohokam and Mogollon cultures disappeared around 1350-1400. The people of southern Arizona reduced the scale of their agriculture, probably because of depleted desert soils and climate change. The Mogollon population split, some withdrawing into northern Mexico while others faded into their Anasazi neighbors to the north.

Anasazi Culture. Most Pueblo Indians today are descended from the Anasazi, a Navajo term meaning "ancient others." Anasazi territory included the Little Colorado, San Juan, and northern Rio Grande drainages in New Mexico, Arizona, Colorado, and Utah.

The Anasazi relied on horticulture, hunting, and gathering wild foods. The earliest Anasazi, the Basketmakers, began about 100 B.C.E. as a semi-nomadic population, ranging out from pit house villages. By 400-700 C.E. they were building separate, large ceremonial structures (kivas) and grew beans, cotton, and maize.

The Anasazi began building their characteristic masonry apartment-house style pueblos about 700 C.E., along with irrigation and soil-control features. The bow and arrow replaced the spear, and the turkey was domesticated. Between 900 and 1100, the Anasazi built planned communities of up to eight hundred rooms throughout their territory. Probably the largest and best known are in Chaco Canyon, but outlying "great houses" of Chacoan style also dot the remainder of the San

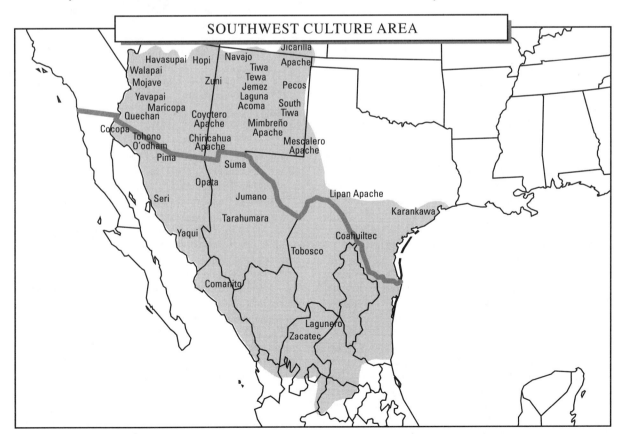

SOUTHWEST CULTURE AREA

Juan basin. Another Anasazi variant of this period is represented at Mesa Verde National Park, Colorado. Both areas were largely abandoned by 1300, when prehistoric Puebloan peoples began concentrating in the areas where modern Pueblo tribes live today.

The Pueblos. There are twenty different tribes of Pueblo Indians today, representing four major language families and six languages. Three Tanoan languages (Tewa, Tiwa, and Towa) join Keresan, Hopi, and Zuni as language groups still actively spoken in their pueblos. A fifth language group, Piro, is now extinct in the Southwest.

The Tanoans and Keresans, called the Eastern Pueblos, live mainly along the northern Rio Grande and its tributaries in northern New Mexico. They include the Tanoan pueblos of Jemez, Taos, Picuris, Isleta, Sandia, San Juan, Santa Clara, San Ildefonso, Nambe, Pojoaque, and Tesuque, as well as the Keresan towns of Zia, Santa Ana, San Felipe, Santo Domingo, and Cochiti. Two other Keresan groups, Acoma and Laguna, are farther west. Zuni and Hopi are the Western Pueblos.

Despite linguistic diversity, the Pueblos share similar architecture and organization of their apartment-house-style villages; horticulture of corn, beans, squash, and sometimes cotton; finely made painted pottery; the beliefs of their ancestor-based kachina religion; and philosophy in which personal aggrandizement is discouraged and group harmony is of paramount importance.

Eastern Pueblo men, women, and children participate in kiva ceremonies. Societies are usually organized by division into moieties (halves), each associated with one kiva. Each moiety has a chief, and power is rotated between moieties semiannually. Moieties also organize community labor for such tasks as caring for the irrigation systems that bring Rio Grande water to the fields. Although many Eastern Pueblo people practice Christianity, indigenous religion also survives in belief and practice, closely guarded and distinct from introduced practices. Many Eastern Pueblo villages are famous for their fine pottery; Keresans are skilled workers in turquoise and shell beads.

The two largest Western Pueblo groups, Hopi and Zuni, are organized into matrilineal clans and into kiva societies in the kachina religion. Usually only men participate in kachina ceremonies, dancing for rain and fertility. Both Hopi and Zuni are noted for fine jewelry and pottery.

Navajos. The Navajos, or Diné, as they call themselves, are the largest traditional Indian tribe in the United States and have the largest land holdings.

Navajo oral and religious history accords with archaeological evidence that they came to their present area between six hundred and eight hundred years ago, probably from Canada. They and the Apaches, also Athapaskan speakers, were probably one group then. In 1598 early Spanish colonists in northern New Mexico encountered Apachean raiders and soon began to differentiate between corn-growing "Apaches de Navaju," probably ancestors of the modern Navajo, and those who were mainly hunters and gatherers, still called Apaches today.

Differences between these two Athapaskan groups strengthened after the Pueblo Revolt of 1680, in which Pueblo Indians, aided by some Athpaskans, drove the Spanish colonists out of New Mexico for nearly twenty years. Fearing reprisal, many Rio Grande Puebloans fled to live with the Navajos. Pueblo traits, such as masked dancers, painted pottery, masonry construction, and probably weaving, along with Spanish livestock, entered Navajo culture. In the mid-eighteenth century, after the Puebloans had returned home, most characteristics now considered a part of traditional Navajo life crystallized, including sheep and goat pastoralism, extended family household units based on the mother-child bond, and the Blessing Way (Chantways) ceremony.

The old raiding pattern remained also, and Navajos often came into conflict with their Pueblo, Spanish, and later American neighbors. This situation led eventually to the capture of more than nine thousand Navajos by Kit Carson in 1863; they were then marched 300 miles to internment at Fort Sumner, or Bosque Redondo, on the brutal "Long Walk." After five years of sickness and starvation, they were allowed to return to about 10 percent of their former range. Reservation lands have been increased many times since 1868. Navajos are known for their fine weaving and silversmithing.

Apaches. For the other southern Athapaskans, the Apaches, raiding as an economic strategy became increasingly important in the eighteenth and nineteenth centuries. Although some Apache women planted corn, beans, and squash, the products of the hunt—whether wild or domestic animals—were far more integral to Apache life. Conflict between settlers and Apaches led to warfare, and then to the establishment of seven reservations, the Jicarilla and Mescalero in New Mexico and five Western Apache reservations in Arizona. Some of the Chiricahua and Lipan moved onto Mescalero lands; other Chiricahuas, those who had rebelled under Geronimo, were removed to Oklahoma. Most Apaches were settled by 1872.

O'odham. The modern descendants of the Hohokam people are the Akimel O'odham, or River Pima, and the Tohono O'odham, the Desert Pima or Papago, of southern Arizona. In the historic period, they have traditionally lived in rancherias (communities of family homesteads) near streams, irrigation canals, or wells. Homesteads usually consist of an elderly couple and the families of their married sons, who grow maize, beans, and pumpkins.

The O'odham had sporadic contact with the Spanish from 1540 on and adopted cattle, wheat, and fruit trees from them in the late seventeenth century. Contacts became increasingly negative, however, through the nineteenth century as ranchers and miners encroached on O'odham land, driving a few to become nomadic, living entirely on wild resources. Two main reservations were established in the late nineteenth and early twentieth centuries.

About four thousand Yaqui, a mainly northwestern Mexico tribe, also live in southern Arizona, having moved into the United States as a result of an early twentieth century sovereignty dispute with the Mexican government. Their traditional way of life was similar to that of the O'odham, though each rancheria belonged to one of eight towns. When Mexico wished to assert dominion over the eight towns in 1825, a rebellion began which has continued sporadically since.

Pai. The Yuman-speaking Pai, including modern groupings called the Walapai (or Hualapai) and the Havasupai, live along the most lowland drainage of the Colorado River and a tributary, the Gila. They are related to the Yuma, Mojave, and Maricopa and were once divided into numerous local groups of up to sixty persons who lived by hunting, gathering, and gardening. These small groups joined into larger units only at certain times of the year around particular resources—good gardening areas in summer or large stands of edible wild plants at ripening. At those times, marriages and friendship renewed connections between the groups. They were informally and flexibly organized, each local group coalescing around a respected leader who, though influential, was never in a position of command.

European and American contact with the Pai was sporadic and limited until the establishment of a gold field in their area in 1865 led to war from 1866 to 1869. They were ultimately placed on two reservations, the western and southern Pai together on the Walapai Reservation, and the northeastern band on designated Havasupai lands.   *—Linda B. Eaton*

See also Anasazi; Apache; Architecture—Southwest; Arts and crafts—Southwest; Hohokam; Mogollon; Navajo; Pima; Pottery; Prehistory—Southwest; Pueblo tribes, Eastern; Pueblo tribes, Western; Tohono O'odham; Walapai; Yuman language family.

BIBLIOGRAPHY

Crown, Patricia L., and W. James Judge. *Chaco and Hohokam: Prehistoric Regional Systems in the American Southwest*. Santa Fe, N.Mex.: School of American Research, 1991. A collection of articles on the complex archaeological societies of the Southwest.

John, Elizabeth A. H. *Storms Brewed in Other Men's Worlds: The Confrontation of the Indians, Spanish, and French in the Southwest, 1540-1795*. College Station: Texas A&M University Press, 1975. Outlines the early confrontations between Indians of the Southwest and the Spanish and French.

Kehoe, Alice B. *North American Indians: A Comprehensive Account*. 2d ed. Englewood Cliffs, N.J.: Prentice Hall, 1992. Kehoe includes an informative overview of Southwest cultures.

Ortiz, Alfonso, ed. *Southwest*. Vol. 9 in *Handbook of North American Indians*. Washington, D.C.: Smithsonian Institution Press, 1983. Articles by the currently recognized authorities on aspects of the Navajos, Apaches, Pimas and Papagos, Pais and other non-Puebloan peoples of the Southwest. Well illustrated, excellent bibliography.

Sovereignty

TRIBES AFFECTED: Pantribal

SIGNIFICANCE: The rights and obligations of American Indians according to U.S. law have been shaped by the concept of domestic sovereignty, which differs radically from traditional European conceptions of sovereignty

The European concept of sovereignty, evolving over many centuries, found a unique expression in American constitutional law. This American system of sovereignty came to intermesh in a novel way with the special status of domestic sovereignty which was recognized as adhering in American Indian nations.

European Concept. In the Middle Ages, the concept of sovereignty was attenuated and confused by the intricacies of feudalism and the independent claims of papal legislative authority. With the end of the High Middle Ages and the coming of the Renaissance, European legal and political philosophers such as Niccolò Machiavelli, Marsilius of Padua, and Thomas Hobbes rediscovered the ancient concept that sovereignty is at once illimitable and indivisible. Sovereignty can place limits upon itself, but only so long as it wishes to enforce those limits upon itself.

In the English system, for example, the King-/Queen-in-Parliament is legally omnipotent, and no rights granted in the English Bill of Rights, in the Magna Carta, or in any other document can stand against an act passed by Parliament and signed by the monarch. In addition to the illimitability and indivisibility of sovereignty, the European notion of sovereignty necessitated a monopoly of authority by one sovereignty over a given territory.

By the eighteenth century, the European conception of sovereignty had become dogma. British Tories "refuted" the demands of the American colonies for greater self-government under Parliament with the maxim that one cannot have an *imperium in imperio*—a sovereignty within a sovereignty.

In the aftermath of the American Revolution, the framers of the U.S. Constitution elaborated an intricate system of checks and balances within the national government and a scheme of federalism with reserved powers to states and reserved rights to individual citizens. Although this constitutional order preserved an unlimited and undivided extraordinary sovereignty in the amendment process, its ordinary sovereignty was both limited and divided. Within this system, the problem which Indian nationhood presented was addressed by crafting a unique type of sovereignty—a domestic, dependent sovereignty—for the tribal nations.

Indian Domestic Sovereignty. In the American constitutional order, the domestic sovereignty of the Indian nations bears certain similarities and certain dissimilarities to the sovereignty of the states within the Union. The Constitution specifically recognized the existence of the Indian nations, permitting the courts to view Indian sovereignty as a residual sovereignty which the Constitution was recognizing rather than creating.

In *Johnson and Graham's Lessee v. William McIntosh* (1823), the Supreme Court under Chief Justice John Marshall recognized the residual Indian sovereignty: "[D]iscovery gave an exclusive right to extinguish the Indian title of occupancy, either by purchase or by conquest; and gave also a right to such a degree of sovereignty, as the circumstances of the people would allow them to exercise." The inherent limits of this sovereignty were made clear, however: "[T]he Indian inhabitants are to be considered merely as occupants, to be protected, indeed, while in peace, in possession of their lands, but to be deemed incapable of transferring the absolute title to others." Furthermore, in his famous opinion in *Cherokee Nation v. Georgia* (1831), Marshall rejected utterly the notion that the Indian nations constitute foreign nations, holding rather that they were "domestic dependent nations."

Until 1871, agreements with the Indians took the forms of treaties. Treaties, however, provided little security to the Indian nations, for a later act of Congress can invalidate part or all of any treaty, as was made clear in the *Cherokee Tobacco* case (*Boudinot v. United States*, 1870). The lands over which Indian tribes exercise a domestic sovereignty, furthermore, remain under the superseding sovereignty of the United States.

After the 1870's. From the 1880's onward, a seesaw effect was produced by, on the one hand, court decisions that recognized serious and far-ranging implications inherent in Indian sovereignty, and by, on the other hand, legislative enactments and subsequent court decisions restricting those implications and even moving toward eliminating such sovereignty totally.

In *Ex parte Crow Dog* (1883), the Supreme Court freed the Brule Sioux Chief Crow Dog, who had been sentenced to death by a federal district court for the murder of Spotted Tail on Indian territory. Federal law, the Court held, does not automatically apply to Indian lands unless so extended by Congress. Two years later the Major Crimes Act (1885), upheld by the Court in *United States v. Kagama* (1886), sought to overcome the problem posed by *Ex parte Crow Dog* by placing several categories of serious crimes on Indian land under the jurisdiction of the federal courts.

In the General Allotment Act (or Dawes Act, 1887), Congress moved to eliminate all Indian sovereignty eventually by transforming Indian tribal land into land held individually as ordinary, privately owned U.S. land; Indians were to receive U.S. citizenship. The Curtis Act (1898) went on to attempt to impose that which Congress had attempted to achieve by negotiation under the auspices of the Dawes Act, and in *Stephens v. Cherokee Nation* (1899), the court upheld the Curtis Act. In *Lone Wolf v. Hitchcock* (1903), furthermore, the court recognized a plenary power to reside in Congress concerning Indian relations.

Eventually, after much destructive interference with Indian sovereignty, Congress relented and attempted to reverse direction with the Indian Reorganization Act (Wheeler-Howard Act, 1934), which undid much of the Dawes Act and actively encouraged tribal organizations.

In a further shift of position by the federal government in the 1950's, Indian sovereignty again came under assault. By Public Law 280 (1953), Congress extended state criminal jurisdiction to Indian territory, and in 1954, under the so-called termination policy, Congress provided for the withdrawal of federal jurisdiction from the Menominee Indian tribe and for their holding of land as an ordinary association or corporation. (Nearly twenty years later, in a full swing of policy, the termi-

nation of the Menominee tribe was reversed by the Menominee Restoration Act.)

In *Native American Church v. Navajo Tribal Council* (1959), the U.S. Court of Appeals held that the First Amendment did not bind tribal councils, although in *Colliflower v. Garland* (1965), the U.S. Court of Appeals held that a federal court had the authority to issue a writ of habeas corpus to determine the validity of the detention of a person by a tribal court.

The American Indian Civil Rights Act of 1968 applied the Bill of Rights to the relations of Indians to their tribal governments and required the consent of tribes to the imposition of state jurisdiction over Indian territory. That law represented an elaborate compromise regarding Indian sovereignty. Extending the Bill of Rights to individual Indians in their relations with Indian tribal authorities involves a serious interference with Indian sovereignty, although one that is arguably to the benefit of individual Indians. This interference was balanced by undoing the interference of Public Law 280 through making any application of state law the free choice of the tribal government.

In *Oliphant v. Suquamish Indian Tribe* (1978), the Supreme Court upheld the claim of Mark Oliphant, a non-Indian residing on a reservation who was charged with a crime, not to be subject to the tribal courts. Indians protested what they saw as a reduction of their sovereignty, but the decision was in line with prior precedent and practice.

The inherent sovereignty of Indian nations was upheld in *United States v. Wheeler* (1978), in which a claim of double jeopardy was rejected because one of the trials involved had been under the separate sovereignty of an Indian nation. Again, in *Santa Clara Pueblo v. Martinez* (1978), the federal courts held that in the Civil Rights Act of 1968, Congress had provided habeas corpus petitions as the sole remedy, with all other suits against the tribe prevented by its sovereign immunity.

The concept of domestic sovereignty has served as the basis for the legal relations of tribal nations with the U.S. government since the adoption of the Constitution, but the plenary power of Congress over that sovereignty has led to a history of shifts swinging alternatingly from attempts to maintain conditions suitable for the preservation of the unique Indian cultures to periods of forced assimilation with a concomitant attempt to destroy domestic sovereignty and its implications.

—*Patrick M. O'Neil*

See also *Cherokee Tobacco* case; Civil rights and citizenship; Crow Dog; Ethnophilosophy and worldview; General Allotment Act; Land claims; *Lone Wolf v. Hitchcock*; Public Law 280.

BIBLIOGRAPHY

Prucha, Francis Paul, ed. *Documents of United States Indian Policy*. 2d ed. Lincoln: University of Nebraska Press, 1990.

Shattuck, Petra T., and Jill Norgren. *Partial Justice: Federal Indian Law in a Liberal Constitutional System*. New York: Berg, 1991.

Tyler, Lyman S. *A History of Indian Policy*. Washington, D.C.: Government Printing Office, 1973.

Wilkinson, Charles F. *American Indians, Time, and the Law: Native Societies in a Modern Constitutional Democracy*. New Haven, Conn.: Yale University Press, 1987.

Williams, Robert A., Jr. *The American Indian in Western Legal Thought: The Discourses of Conquest*. New York: Oxford University Press, 1990.

Spirit dancing

TRIBE AFFECTED: Salish

SIGNIFICANCE: Male members of the Salish tribe danced the Spirit Dance to communicate with their personal spirits

Spirit dancing was practiced by male members of the Salish tribe, a group of Indians living along the Northwest Coast. The reason for this dancing was to welcome the visitation of a participant's spirit. Since the Salish people believed that the spirits were on the other side of the earth during the summer, the visitations were always in the winter, when the tribal members had more time for leisure.

Whenever a spirit paid a visit to a person, that person would begin to sing his spirit song, while others would join in as they learned his particular song. In addition to this singing, the person undergoing the visitation would have his face painted. He would then sing and dance wildly around a fire within the confines of his house. As he danced, he uttered low moans and glanced about as though he were in a trance. Spectators helped to ensure that the dancer, in his frenzy, did not hurt himself by running into the posts of the house or jumping into the fire.

See also Salish.

Spiro: Archaeological site

DATE: 1000-1350

LOCATION: Eastern Oklahoma

CULTURE AFFECTED: Caddo

Spiro, in eastern Oklahoma, was the most important western center of Caddoan culture in the Late Prehistoric period (1200-1350). It is situated within an area of escarpments along the Arkansas River, in a location that was strategic for contacts between the southern Plains and the lowlands of the Mississippi Valley. The site covers an area of 80 acres, although not all of this area was occupied simultaneously. It is best known for its elaborate burials and thousands of art objects of shell and copper. The site was first occupied during the Late Archaic period (circa 2500 to 500 B.C.E.), but its most spectacular features date between 900 and 1350 C.E.

Prior to the site's disturbance, it included nine prominent mounds. Of these, six were low, dome-shaped mounds that covered the foundations of structures, and two were platform mounds, designed to elevate perishable structures. The dome-shaped mounds, ranging from 2.5 to 3.5 feet high and 30 to 75 feet in diameter, were built over dismantled structures. The platform mounds, shaped like truncated pyramids with earthen ramps, had rectangular ground plans. The largest, Brown Mound, measured 18 feet high and 200 by 175 feet at the base.

It is believed to have at one time contained burials, but these were subsequently destroyed by looting. Craig Mound, the largest feature at the site, was constructed of four conical mounds joined to form a continuous feature. It measured 300 feet long, with a maximum width of about 100 feet. The main cone was 33 feet high, while the smaller ones were about 15 feet high.

Craig Mound covered a series of ground-level mortuaries, some of which may predate the mound's construction. The largest, known as the Great Mortuary, contained the most elaborate collection of grave goods ever reported in the continental United States. These were the object of intense pillaging and looting, however, resulting in the destruction of burials and structures. The central chamber of the Great Mortuary held spectacular burials of the site's highest-ranking elite in the form of cedar pole litters that contained skeletal remains and precious objects such as decorated shell cups and gorgets, shell and pearl beads, and fine textiles. One burial was accompanied by at least three large copper plates with embossed representations of warriors. The Great Mortuary dates to circa 1200-1350, at which time Spiro was clearly a major center for ritual activity.

The destruction of mound burials at Spiro is one of the most tragic chapters in American archaeology. In the 1930's, "mining rights" were sold to local treasure hunters, who tunneled into the site's major structures. Attempts to prevent the site's destruction through legislation only exacerbated the looting, and the main cone of Craig Mound was gutted in the summer of 1935. An archaeologist who visited the site found sections of cedar poles scattered on the ground and an area littered with thousands of fragments of feather and fur textiles, broken pottery, engraved shells, and beads of shell, stone, and bone. As an expression of their annoyance, the looters dynamited the mound. Subsequent archaeological excavations suggested the existence of a large, open chamber at the center of the mound framed by cedar poles and filled with piles of textiles, beads, and other objects. This chamber and others were the source of thousands of artifacts purchased by dealers and private collectors.

The artifacts from Spiro include a wide variety of ornaments, including earspools, shell gorgets, and copper headdress plates. There were a large number of weapons, among them stone axes, warclubs, and chipped stone blades. Masks, staffs, figurines, and pipes were among the ritual objects. Textile items included multicolored mantles, skirts, headbands, and caps. Some burials were placed in large, boxlike baskets. The engraved shells from Spiro, mostly cups and gorgets, provide a larger corpus of iconography and images of prehistoric Southeastern culture than any other source. They are decorated with representations of warriors, human sacrifice, and a wide variety of esoteric symbols associated with the "Southern Cult."

The objects at Spiro indicate the existence of a strongly ranked society with a powerful and wealthy elite. Objects of native copper from Lake Superior or the southern Appalachians and quantities of marine shell from eastern Florida testify to the existence of networks for long-distance exchange. The site appears to have been an important ceremonial and political center with strong ties to Mississippian cultures of the Southeast. Its decline is probably linked to a widespread dissolution of "temple town" societies that also affected centers in the Mississippi Valley prior to the arrival of Europeans.

See also Caddo; Mississippian; Mounds and mound builders; Prehistory—Southeast; Southern Cult; Woodland.

Spokane: Tribe
CULTURE AREA: Plateau
LANGUAGE GROUP: Salishan
PRIMARY LOCATION: Northeastern Washington State
POPULATION SIZE: 2,118 (1990 U.S. Census)

The Spokane of northeastern Washington spoke a Salishan language shared, in different dialects, with the Coeur d'Alene, Flathead, and Kalispel. They called themselves *Spoqe'ind* ("round head"). The subsistence orientation of the three bands of Spokane was culturally reflected by permanent winter villages, specialized fishing technology, a sweathouse complex, shamanism, vision quest, tutelary spirits, the Blue Jay and Midwinter Ceremonies, leadership through consensus of opinion, modified bilateral descent, and extensive utilization of fish and vegetal products gathered during spring, summer, and fall for winter consumption.

Exploitation of resource areas was further facilitated by intergroup marriage through exogamy, polyglottalism, and established trade relations. Even prior to the introduction of the horse, in the early 1800's, the Spokane ventured annually onto the Plains to trade and hunt for bison.

First mention of the Spokane by white travelers was by Captains Meriwether Lewis and William Clark in 1805 and David Thompson of the Northwest Fur Company, who surveyed the area from 1808 to 1811. Cultural change, however, had already commenced in the early 1700's with diffusion of European American trade items. The devastating epidemics of 1846 and 1852-1853 created severe population decline. Consequently, the rise of religious nativistic revitalization movements, particularly the Dreamer Cult, modified traditional belief systems. Protestant missionization commenced in 1839 with the establishment of the Tshimakin Mission.

Uncontrolled encroachment by white miners and other settlers ultimately led to warfare with the U.S. Army and to the 1858 military defeat of the Spokane at the battle of Four Lakes by Colonel George Wright, who destroyed Spokane livestock, horses, farms, and crops. As a consequence, a January 18, 1881, executive order set aside 154,898 acres of public land for the establishment of the Spokane Indian Reservation. The Spokane experienced severe deculturation as a result of tribalization, confinement to a reservation, government schooling, a dramatic shift to non-indigenous foods, and the introduction of religious and political factionalism.

A major event that disrupted Spokane access to fish as a primary food source was the 1911 construction of Little Falls Dam. The later construction of Grand Coulee Dam, under the August 30, 1935, New Deal authorization, effectively stopped the annual migration of all salmon to their spawning areas.

The Spokane reservation is organized around an elected tribal council with headquarters, museum, community center, and tribal store located at Wellpinit. Both Protestant and Catholic churches are on the reservation, but not the Indian Shaker or Pentacostal churches. Factions are based on religious affiliation and geographical areas. Dominant contemporary concerns are issues of legalizing gaming, high unemployment, and ongoing litigation over loss of fishing sites and resource areas. Small per capita payments are generated by land leases and timber sales. In 1989 the Spokane tribe established a successful fish hatchery staffed by enrolled members. Approximately 50 percent of the 2100 enrolled Spokane live on the reservation.

See also Plateau; Salishan language family.

BIBLIOGRAPHY

Chalfant, Stuart A. *Ethnohistorical Reports on Aboriginal Land Use and Occupancy.* Vol. 4 in *Interior Salish and Eastern Washington Indians.* New York: Garland, 1972.

Ross, John Alan. *An Ethnoarchaeological Survey of the Spokane Indian Reservation.* 17 vols. Wellpinit, Wash.: U.S. Bureau of Indian Affairs and U.S. Department of Forestry, Spokane Tribal Council, 1993.

_____. "The Spokan." In *Indians of the Plateau,* edited by Deward E. Walker, Jr. Vol. 12 in *Handbook of North American Indians,* edited by William Sturtevant. Washington, D.C.: Smithsonian Institution Press, 1994.

Spotted Tail (c. 1823 or 1824, near present-day Pine Ridge, S.Dak.—Aug. 5, 1881, Rosebud, S.Dak.): Tribal chief
ALSO KNOWN AS: Sinte Gleska
TRIBAL AFFILIATION: Brule Sioux
SIGNIFICANCE: After a youth spent fighting whites, Spotted Tail came to advocate peace; he is widely considered one of the greatest Sioux leaders

The name Spotted Tail is a result of a raccoon tail given to him while a young man by a white trapper. He wore this as a sacred object in his first battles, and after surviving, he took the name Spotted Tail.

Spotted Tail grew to be a warrior during wars with the Pawnee. In 1841, he selected a Brule girl for a wife who was also being courted by Running Bear (Mato Wakuwa), a Brule chief. They quarreled; Spotted Tail killed the chief and took the girl as his first wife. She bore him thirteen children.

At the September, 1855, battle of Bluewater Creek near modern Oshkosh, Nebraska, a severely wounded Spotted Tail fought a delaying action against advancing cavalry to allow the escape of women and children. Soon after, Spotted Tail was branded a murderer and his surrender demanded as a precondition to peace. On October 18, 1855, Spotted Tail surrendered to General W. S. Harney at Fort Laramie, Wyoming. While a prisoner of war at Fort Leavenworth, Kansas,

Brule Sioux chief Spotted Tail was a primary Sioux leader of the 1870's. (National Archives)

Spotted Tail came to realize that the number and power of whites was indeed frightening.

In 1870, Spotted Tail and Red Cloud were invited to Washington to confer with President Ulysses S. Grant and other officials. While there, Spotted Tail did not lose the opportunity to scold the president over his failure to comply with the Laramie Treaty of 1868.

Throughout the plains war of 1876-1877, Spotted Tail remained the most popular spokesman of the Sioux people. In 1877, he was responsible for negotiating the final surrender of hostile Sioux bands at Fort Robinson, Nebraska. It was to Spotted Tail's camp at Rosebud, South Dakota, that his nephew Crazy Horse fled to avoid confrontation and arrest by General Crook.

Spotted Tail's last years were spent in advocating Brule social and economic needs. In June, 1880, he raided the Carlisle, Pennsylvania, Indian school and removed several Brule children, returning them to their parents in South Dakota. On August 5, 1881, Spotted Tail was shot and killed by Crow Dog, a political opponent. The Little Missouri Sioux winter count (record) for that year said, "This year that brave and wonderful chief was killed by Crow Dog." The Dakota court sentenced Crow Dog to hang. The case was appealed to the Supreme Court, however (*Ex parte Crow Dog* 1883), and the Court concluded that state courts have no jurisdiction on Indian reservations. Crow Dog was released.

See also Crow Dog; Red Cloud.

Spybuck, Ernest (1883, on the Potawatomi and Shawnee Reservation, Oklahoma Territory—1949, near Shawnee, Okla.): Artist
ALSO KNOWN AS: Mahthela
TRIBAL AFFILIATION: Shawnee
SIGNIFICANCE: Spybuck was one of the first Native American artists of the twentieth century to create a narrative style of painting depicting tribal culture

Spybuck began drawing and painting as a small child; he never received formal art training. His most frequent subjects were horses, cowboys, ranch scenes, round-ups, Native American ceremonies, traditional dancers, and peyote scenes. His experience was limited to his hometown, and he was more than fifty years old before he traveled outside Pottawatomie County, where he was born.

Spybuck met M. R. Harrington of the Museum of the American Indian (Heye Foundation) in 1910 in Shawnee. The museum commissioned him to paint several works as an ethnographic series. He later did commissions for the Creek Council House and Museum in Okmulgee, Oklahoma, and the Oklahoma Historical Society Museum in Oklahoma City. In 1937, he participated in the American Indian Exposition and Congress in Tulsa.

Spybuck is known for genre painting that is illustrative of cultural life in the early twentieth century. He depicted clothing, housing, and activities in detail, portraying the acculturation between the Native American and white worlds. For indoor scenes he used a window technique to show what was happening inside a building or tipi. This also permitted him to show details such as the time of day and the season of the year to give a context to the ceremony or event represented.

See also Art and artists, contemporary; Auchiah, James; Paints and painting; Sweezy, Carl.

Squamish: Tribe

CULTURE AREA: Northwest Coast
LANGUAGE GROUP: Salishan
PRIMARY LOCATION: British Columbia
POPULATION SIZE: 2,030 (Statistics Canada, based on 1991 census)

The Squamish were both maritime and river-oriented, living in politically autonomous permanent winter villages with rectangular dwellings of split and hewn cedar. Hunting of land animals and gathering of food plants supplemented a diet of many different fish and sea mammals. Kinship was bilateral with patripotestal authority. Intervillage socioeconomic relations were maintained by trade and marriage. Life was regulated by an annual round of moving to areas, in search of food, according to the season. Concurrently, there were ceremonies of redistribution of resources, known as potlaches.

Charles Barkley probably established contact with the Squamish in 1787; he was followed by land-based fur-traders. Fort Langley on the Fraser River was established as a trading post in 1827. Consequently, the drastic effects of introduced disease and forced deculturation demoralized and greatly reduced indigenous populations. By the 1880's the Indian Shaker Church helped, and continues to help in some cases, to ameliorate cultural deprivation and aid in the curing of some diseases. Today Squamish work as fishermen, loggers, and in various skilled labor positions. There have been numerous efforts to revitalize traditional language, myth, and crafts.

See also Suquamish.

Squanto (c. 1580-1622): Diplomat, interpreter

Also known as: Tisquantum
Tribal affiliation: Patuxet, Wampanoag
Significance: Squanto helped the first English settlers survive in America

Many a schoolchild has heard around Thanksgiving each year the saga of Squanto, the New England Indian who, according to the traditional account, helped the forlorn Pilgrims stave off starvation by teaching them how to grow corn by fertilizing it with dead fish. For many indigenous activists, Squanto's magnanimous gesture represents one more example of the uncredited or thankless role indigenous peoples played in furthering European American civilization in the Americas. Recently, however, historians have cast doubt on the origin of Squanto's agricultural knowledge. (One argues rather convincingly that such fertilization techniques were unknown to indigenous people in New England, that Squanto learned the custom from the English in Newfoundland and in effect was demonstrating to one group of English settlers a technique that was common in areas of England other than those from which they came.)

That irony aside, Squanto did play an important role in the first few years of English settlement in Plymouth. A member of the Patuxet tribe in eastern Massachusetts, Squanto was among twenty individuals that Thomas Hunt, a member of John Smith's 1614 expedition, captured for sale as slaves. Hunt took Squanto to Spain but was unable to sell his slave candidates. Somehow Squanto made his way to London, where he lived at the home of John Slany, treasurer of the Newfoundland Company, and endeared himself to English entrepreneurs, who saw Squanto as a valuable tool for establishing friendships back in Massachusetts. With his fluency in English and knowledge of European and indigenous customs alike, Squanto would make the ideal ambassador.

In 1619, he returned to New England and proceeded to help the English win the trust of the Nemasket and Pokanoket tribes. In an attack on Martha's Vineyard, Squanto was captured again, but he apparently returned to the Pokanoket around present-day Narragansett Bay. In March, 1621, Squanto was instrumental in helping the Pokanoket and Plymouth English set up a treaty. Squanto then lived among the Pilgrims and acted as a diplomat and interpreter. He also helped in obtaining seed corn and teaching planting techniques. Behind the scenes, however, Squanto tried to put the epidemic-ravaged remnants of his Patuxet tribe back together, incurring some English wrath. The Pilgrims still protected him, because they could play him off against the Pokanoket

chief, Massasoit. The next summer, 1622, Squanto died, and the English found themselves without the services of this capable man.

See also Indian-white relations—English colonial; Massasoit; Wampanoag.

Squash

Tribes affected: All agricultural tribes
Significance: One of the earliest domesticated foods in North America, squash was widely eaten and used for implements

"Squash" covers a variety of related plants, divided into the hard squashes (including pumpkins and many gourds) and soft squashes (such as zucchini). Hard squashes can be stored for several months and have high sugar content; they were domesticated in Mesoamerica and diffused to North America at least by 4500 B.C.E. The soft squashes are bountiful but somewhat less nutritious and impossible to store simply. Recent research suggests that soft squashes were domesticated in Arkansas around 1000 C.E.

Hard squashes were eaten baked or boiled, and their seeds usually also were eaten, either raw as snacks or ground into flour. Soft squashes usually were eaten boiled, often as part of stews.

While squashes were used primarily for food, they also were important for the making of tools. Hard gourds provided ready-made bottles; a hole was drilled, the seeds were removed, and a stopper was added. Slightly more ambitious cutting created spoons, ladles, cups, and other implements. Left completely intact, a gourd will dry, and its seeds will separate from the shell, creating a natural rattle. The early spread of squashes may have been hastened by the exchange of rattles, since the dried seeds remain viable for many years.

See also Agriculture; Beans; Corn; Food preparation and cooking; Subsistence.

Standing Bear (c. 1829—Sept., 1908): Chief

Also known as: Mochunozhin
Tribal affiliation: Ponca
Significance: The civil rights case *Standing Bear v. Crook* rendered the decision that an Indian was a person within the meaning of U.S. law

An 1858 treaty guaranteed the Ponca people a permanent home on the land of their ancestral Niobrara River in Nebraska. An 1868 treaty, however, established boundaries for the Sioux people that included the Ponca land. In 1875, the government agreed to rectify the error, but instead of returning the land, they appropriated money to compensate for the Sioux attacks and removed the Ponca to Indian Territory (Oklahoma). In 1879, Standing Bear and some thirty followers walked forty days to traverse the five hundred miles to the Omaha (Nebraska) Reservation. General George Crook's garrison returned the Ponca people to Oklahoma. The return journey of fifty days and the following year on the Quapaw Reservation claimed the lives of nearly a fourth of the five hundred Poncas. Among the dead were Standing Bear's children. In January of 1879, desiring to bury his son on traditional Ponca land, Standing Bear and sixty-six followers set out for the Niobrara. When Standing Bear reached the Omaha Reservation, he was placed under guard by Crook, who was to return the Ponca to Indian Territory. Several attorneys, members of the public, and newspaper correspondent Thomas H. Tibbles protested the treatment of the Ponca people.

Attorneys A. J. Poppleton and John L. Webster served Crook with a writ of *habeas corpus* to determine by what authority he was holding the group. The U.S. attorney countered that the Indian peoples had no right to *habeas corpus* because they were not "persons within the meaning of the law." On April 18, 1879, Judge E. S. Dundy rendered the famous decision in the *Standing Bear v. Crook* case: An Indian was a person within the meaning of the law of the United States, and no authority existed for removing any of the prisoners to Indian Territory during time of peace. Standing Bear's speech climaxed the trial: "My hand is not the same color as yours, but if you pierce it, I shall feel the pain. The blood will be the same color. We are men, the same God made us. . . . All I ask is what is mine—my land, my freedom, my dignity as a man." To prevent other tribal peoples from using the decision as precedent to leave other reservations, the commissioner of Indian affairs ruled that Dundy's decision applied only to Standing Bear and his people.

In the winter of 1879-1880, Standing Bear toured the East with correspondent Tibbles and interpreters Francis and Susette La Flesche. His message was one of nonviolent resistance and justice. Although the government finally appropriated funds to the Ponca people, those in Indian Territory were never allowed to return to the Niobrara.

See also Indian Territory; La Flesche, Francis; La Flesche, Susette or Josette; Ponca.

Standing Bear, Luther (c. 1868, Pine Ridge, S.Dak.—
Feb. 20, 1939, Huntington Park, Calif.): Writer
ALSO KNOWN AS: Plenty Kill
TRIBAL AFFILIATION: Oglala Sioux
SIGNIFICANCE: Author of four books, Luther Standing Bear was one of the few early twentieth century Indians to provide accounts of the transition from the old ways to reservation life and to offer a first-hand account of Sioux history and traditions

Born to a man who was probably a Brule band leader, Luther Standing Bear described himself nonetheless as an Oglala Sioux. According to his own account, Plenty Kill—as he was named as a child—grew up in the traditional Sioux manner at a time when the old life was being threatened and destroyed by white settlers and the U.S. cavalry. In 1879 he entered the Carlisle Indian School in Pennsylvania, where he was given his name and where he got his only formal education. In 1902 Standing Bear traveled with Buffalo Bill's Wild West Show, performing in the United States and England. He later moved to California, where he lectured and acted.

Sioux writer Luther Standing Bear, author of Land of the Spotted Eagle. *(Library of Congress)*

In 1928, Standing Bear published his first book, *My People, the Sioux*, primarily an autobiography highlighting his youth, Carlisle years, the Ghost Dance, and Wild West Show experiences. *My Indian Boyhood* (1931), written for an adolescent audience, is also autobiographical. *Land of the Spotted Eagle* (1933), perhaps his most important book, is an ethnographic description of traditional Sioux life and customs, criticizing whites' efforts to "make over" the Indian into the likeness of the white race. Standing Bear also collected versions of his tribe's tales and legends, publishing them in *Stories of the Sioux* (1934). In an essay written for the *American Mercury*, Standing Bear argues that loss of faith has left a void in Indian life and that the white man would do well to grasp some of the Indian's spiritual strength.

See also Sioux.

BIBLIOGRAPHY
Standing Bear, Luther. *Land of the Spotted Eagle*. Reprint. Lincoln: University of Nebraska Press, 1978.

Stereotypes
TRIBES AFFECTED: Pantribal
SIGNIFICANCE: Outmoded stereotypes of Native Americans have long dominated various media; these stereotypes may affect public policy as well as individual perceptions

Stereotypes are generalizations concerning groups of people. Because they are commonly based on false or incomplete information, they are frequently inaccurate. A central problem with stereotypes is that behavior toward individuals may be based on stereotypical assumptions concerning a group to which they belong, which means that people may be penalized (or occasionally rewarded) for traits which they as individuals may not in fact possess. Such behavior is manifestly unfair, and for this reason it is important to understand stereotypes concerning Native Americans and to correct these misconceptions.

Stereotyping of American Indian groups is not a recent phenomenon, and it is not confined to non-Indian stereotyping of Indians. Many Indian groups' names for themselves simply mean "the people" in their native tongues. Outsiders, however (including other Native Americans), often used names for them which were considered derogatory, such as Eskimo (said to mean "eaters of raw flesh") or Atakapa ("eaters of people"). Traditionally, many Indians considered those who did not speak their languages or share their cultural norms to be less than human. In anthropological terms, such behavior is called "ethnocentric," a reference to people's tendency to esteem their own culture and denigrate those of others, describing others' behavior as deviant or inappropriate.

Early European Stereotyping. With the arrival of Europeans in the Americas, additional stereotypes emerged and were soon recorded in various media. The first stereotypes appeared in the print media, such as literature, journalism, and government archives, and visual media, such as drawings, paintings, and photographs. Later came film and video images and aural recordings of music and spoken dialogue. Since the Europeans and their descendants in the Americas maintained extensive written and visual records, most studies concerning stereotyping of Native Americans concern the historic period.

The earliest historic descriptions of "New World" cultures were written by the Spanish about peoples of the Caribbean and Central and South America. They did not describe the Aztec and Maya as possessing different but worthwhile cultural traits; rather, Spanish narratives characterized them as lacking Christianity and "civilization." These distinctions allowed the Spanish to place native populations in a category apart from Europeans and to justify their own horrific treatment of aboriginal peoples.

The later colonization of North America by the English and French (among others) incorporated the assimilated Spanish preconceptions. The terms "Indian," "savage," "infidel," "barbarian," and "heathen" were widely used by the seventeenth century English to identify a large number of different Native American cultures and to treat them all as members of the same group. The French used the term *sauvage* for the same purpose. This collapsing of individual and cultural differences into broad generalizations was typical of the colonial period in North America. Such mental templates occasionally justified illogical policies, such as plans to relocate different cultural groups onto the same tract of land. The planners did not seem

An eighteenth century engraving that captures well the early stereotype of the "merciless Savage." (Library of Congress)

to recognize, or did not care, that such policies often resulted in severe cultural conflicts.

It was common (and, given the mindset of Europeans at the time, probably unavoidable) to describe Indians not simply as they were but in terms of their differences from Europeans; the differences were generally regarded as deficiencies. Europeans often evaluated Native Americans according to their own Christian moral code, dismissing as immoral behavior that which was perfectly appropriate and sensible within the distinctive cultures they were so judging.

"Good" and "Bad" Indians. Colonialism gave rise to two general categories of Native American stereotypes that, with variations and refinements, continued for centuries: the "good" Indian and the "bad" Indian. These categorizations had far more to do with intellectual currents among Europeans than with Indian cultures themselves. If Europeans wished to criticize their own society, they often turned to accounts of American Indians, supposedly unspoiled by the artificiality and constraints of civilization, to demonstrate the deplorable state of European culture. These conventions are most apparent in eighteenth century French literature and philosophy, as in the works of Jean-Jacques Rousseau and his notion of the "noble savage." Conversely, when Europeans wished to uphold the worth of their own social mores, they often called upon the stereotype of the Indian as dirty, wretched, and bloodthirsty to enhance, by comparison, the value of European society.

Among early English colonists, Puritan publications such as captivity narratives had didactic and social motives, namely to trumpet the virtues of Christianity, to support Christian conversion of Native Americans, and to justify colonial settlements on Indian lands. The "good" Indian motif was not prevalent in America until independence from England. At that time, American literature with indigenous themes came to seem patriotic. American literary nationalism discovered the "proud and noble" Indian, and this theme was later incorporated into the works of painters and photographers. By the mid-1880's, authors had turned their frontier obsession to cowboys. "Wild west" shows became a popular form of public entertainment, combining stereotypical images of cowboys, soldiers ("Indian fighters"), and Indians.

Twentieth Century. With the arrival of the twentieth century, radio, films, and television continued to popularize various outdated views of Native Americans. A general misconception, still prevalent, is that Indian culture was timeless and unchanging until contact with the Europeans, at which time it was destroyed. This denial of both Native American history and survival suggests that the only true Indians existed before European contact and that their descendants somehow do not exhibit real "Indianness." This type of misconception underlies accounts of North American history which describe white settlement as progress advancing across a huge expanse of seemingly unoccupied vacant land and pushing the frontier west. Such accounts ignore native peoples as prime movers in their own right, and they deny the ethnicity and cultural diversity of a significant proportion of the North and Central American populations. Since the 1970's, American Indians themselves, in addition to non-Indian scholars, have confronted these and other stereotypes. Through publication and educational reform, they work to break the pattern of ongoing stereotyping.   —*Susan J. Wurtzburg*

See also Captivity and captivity narratives; Gender relations and roles; Journalism; Wild west shows; Women.

BIBLIOGRAPHY

Allen, Paula Gunn, ed. *Studies in American Indian Literature: Critical Essays and Course Designs*. New York: Modern Language Association of America, 1983.

Barnett, Louise K. *The Ignoble Savage: American Literary Racism, 1790-1890*. Westport, Conn.: Greenwood Press, 1975.

Bataille, Gretchen M., and Charles L. P. Silet, eds. The Pretend Indians: Images of Native Americans in the Movies. Ames: Iowa State University Press, 1980.

Berkhofer, Robert F., Jr. *The White Man's Indian: Images of the American Indian from Columbus to the Present*. New York: Vintage Books, 1979.

Hilger, Michael. *The American Indian in Film*. Metuchen, N.J.: Scarecrow Press, 1986.

Howard, Helen Addison. *American Indian Poetry*. Boston: Twayne, 1979.

Larson, Charles R. *American Indian Fiction*. Albuquerque: University of New Mexico Press, 1978.

Muñoz, Braulio. *Sons of the Wind: The Search for Identity in Spanish American Indian Literature*. New Brunswick, N.J.: Rutgers University Press, 1982.

Nichols, Roger L., ed. *The American Indian: Past and Present*. 4th ed. New York: McGraw-Hill, 1992.

Washburn, Wilcomb, E., ed. *History of Indian-White Relations*. Vol. 4 in *Handbook of North American Indians*, edited by William C. Sturtevant. Washington, D.C.: Smithsonian Institution Press, 1988.

Stomp Dance

TRIBES AFFECTED: Creek, Seminole

SIGNIFICANCE: Marking the beginning of the Creek and Seminole yearly ceremonial cycle, the Stomp Dance is an all-night dance first performed in the early spring, then repeated several times between spring and fall

Referring both to the nighttime dances held at the Square Ground (the physical center of religious and political life) and to a specific form, the Stomp Dance is a principal feature of Creek and Seminole ceremonial life.

After purifying themselves by washing and drinking *Hoyvniji*, an emetic, men begin the Stomp Dance at the Square Ground, where a sacred fire is burning. Like most Creek and all Seminole ceremonial dances, the fire is a focal point for the dancing ritual.

The Stomp Dance consists of a leader who begins dancing in a clockwise circle around the fire, inviting other experienced male dancers to join him. The dancers are accompanied by "shell-shaker girls" wearing leg rattles who provide the rhythmic background for the dance. After all the male dancers are participating, women are permitted to join them. A principal ceremonial feature of the dance is the sacrifice of meat, which is fed to the sacred fire.

Stomp dances are performed in early spring, in May and June as preliminaries to the Green Corn Ceremony (the major ceremonial observance of the year), and also in August and September.

See also Creek; Dances and dancing; Green Corn Dance; Seminole.

Stumbling Bear (c. 1832—1903, Fort Sill, Indian Territory, present-day Okla.): Tribal chief

ALSO KNOWN AS: Setimkia (Charging Bear)

TRIBAL AFFILIATION: Kiowa

SIGNIFICANCE: Initially a fierce warrior, Stumbling Bear embraced peace after signing the Treaty of Medicine Lodge in 1867

As a young man, Stumbling Bear was an important war chief. Along with his cousin Kicking Bird, Satanta, and Satank, Stumbling Bear participated in Kiowa raids against Pawnees, Navajos, Sauks, and Foxes as well as whites. Against Colonel Christopher "Kit" Carson at the first Battle of Adobe Walls in 1864, Stumbling Bear was principal war chief.

During negotiations for the Treaty of Medicine Lodge in 1867, establishing reservations in Kansas, Stumbling Bear was the primary Kiowa spokesman. Upon signing the treaty, he abandoned hostilities and thereafter advocated accommodation with whites. During the Kiowa, Comanche, and Cheyenne uprising known as the Red River War, from 1874 to 1875, he called for peace—opposing the Kiowa war leader Lone Wolf. In 1872, Stumbling Bear and Kicking Bird were the major Kiowa representatives during negotiations in Washington, D.C. In appreciation of his services, the U.S. government, in 1878, built a home for him in Indian Territory.

See also Adobe Walls, Battles of; Kicking Bird; Kiowa; Lone Wolf; Medicine Lodge, Treaties of; Satanta.

Subarctic: Culture area

LANGUAGE GROUPS: Algonquian, Athapaskan, Eskimo-Aleut
TRIBES: Ahtna, Beaver, Carrier, Chilcotin, Chipewyan, Cree, Dogrib, Haida, Han, Hare, Ingalik, Inland Tlingit, Koyukon, Kutchin, Montagnais, Mountain, Naskapi, Saulteaux, Slave, Tagish, Tanaina, Tanana, Tsetsaut, Yellowknife

The Subarctic culture area covers a huge region, spanning three continents and the coasts of three oceans. For the purposes of a study of North American native cultures, the area can be considered to cover Alaska, the Yukon, the Northwest Territories, Labrador, and the northern portions of British Columbia, Alberta, and Manitoba. There is, however, no clear break between the cultures of North America and those of Greenland, Siberia, and Northern Scandinavia, as these cultures spread long before current boundaries between nations were established, and the cultures remain very similar.

Generally, the native population of the area can be divided into three groupings: Eskimos and Aleuts, Athapaskan Indians (sometimes spelled Athabaskan—the actual sound is an aspirated *p*, which cannot be rendered in the English alphabet), and the Northwest Coast Indians. These are three distinct cultures and will be discussed separately below. It should be noted that the term "Eskimo" has engendered some controversy (with many Canadian Arctic and Subarctic natives, for example, preferring "Inuit"), but it is used here because it incorporates a large number of groups that cannot easily be united under any other term and because it has a long scientific tradition of usage.

Prehistory. The people of the Subarctic did not have a written language before the arrival of European explorers and missionaries, and physical evidence is in short supply owing to the harsh climate and sparse population. Most modern archaeologists, however, have agreed that the North American continent was first settled by immigrants from Asia during the last Ice Age, over a land bridge across the Bering Strait, which now separates Alaska from Siberia. During the Ice Age, sea

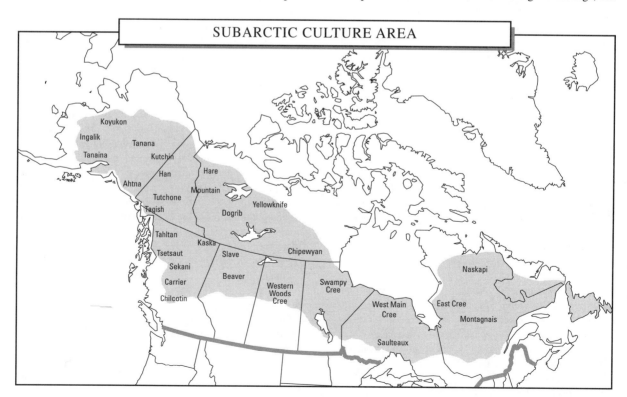

SUBARCTIC CULTURE AREA

level was considerably lower, and the islands that now exist in the Bering Strait were once almost certainly mountain peaks on that land bridge.

At least two, and probably three, separate migrations occurred, according to linguistic evidence. It is impossible to date these migrations accurately, but the land bridge probably existed from about twenty-five thousand to ten thousand years ago, so the migrations must have taken place during those time spans. It is likely that the people we call Athapaskans were the first to arrive, because they later made much farther inroads south. Surprisingly, the Athapaskan languages of Alaska are closely related to the Apache and Navajo but are not apparently related to the language groups that exist in the huge area between Alaska and the Southwest United States. The area in between is populated by people who speak a completely different family of languages, including Tlingit, Haida, and Tsimshian in Alaska and a great number of languages in Washington, Oregon, and Northern California. The gap in cultures remains a mystery, but these groups may represent a second migration.

The third group involved were the Eskimos and Aleuts. Modern linguists generally believe that the two groups split about three thousand years ago. Between eight hundred and eighteen hundred years ago, the Eskimo language split into a number of dialects, but the dialects are not nearly as different as one might expect, considering the huge distances involved. The language and culture of Eskimos in northern Alaska and in Greenland are similar enough so that the people can communicate more easily than can most people in bordering countries in Europe.

The Natural Environment. Before considering the conditions of modern-day Subarctic cultures, it is important to dispel some stereotypes that many people unfamiliar with the territory have formed. There is a stereotypical tendency to picture Eskimos in igloos, living in a frozen wasteland that is dark six months out of the year. While this environment certainly exists, it is limited to areas near the North Pole and at high elevations. Several other climatic situations exist in the Subarctic.

Along the west coast of Alaska, British Columbia, and Washington State, there is a warm ocean current (the Japanese Current), similar in nature to the Gulf Stream that warms the western coast of Europe, and the temperatures are warmer than one might expect. Temperatures in Anchorage, Alaska, are actually warmer, on the average, than in many parts of New York and New England. In the interior, temperatures can reach 70 degrees (Fahrenheit) below zero during the long winter nights, but summer days can be as warm as 80 above.

The Eskimos. The old Eskimo culture is a rapidly dying one. While there are still people living in igloos and wearing seal skins, and while Eskimo languages are still spoken, most modern Eskimos have taken advantage of Western civilization and removed themselves from the harsh life of their ancestors. By and large, it is only in the most remote places that Eskimo civilization as it once existed can still be found.

These areas are remote indeed. In Alaska, for example, only one road runs north of Fairbanks; beyond the Yukon River it is a private road built by the Alaskan Pipeline companies that is still inaccessible to the general public. The Alaskan Highway is built of gravel and is unsuitable for travel by car for about half the year. There are still villages largely untouched by Western civilization. These villages are reached by plane or by dogsled, and they are hardly tourist attractions.

According to archaeological evidence, Eskimos once occupied considerable inland territory that is now mostly inhabited by Athapaskans and people of European ancestry, but it is impossible to determine when they abandoned these lands to others. At present, Eskimos are largely confined to the coasts of the Arctic, Atlantic, and Pacific Oceans and probably number about thirty to forty thousand, an extremely sparse population considering the area involved.

The Aleuts. There are only a few thousand people in the present day who consider themselves Aleuts. They primarily inhabit the Aleutian Islands, an archipelago stretching southwest from the Alaskan mainland. They are apparently related closely to the Eskimos, at least linguistically, but they may also be related to the Athapaskans farther inland. They also may have a tie to the natives of Siberia, though this is much harder to determine.

The Athapaskans. The Athapaskans presently comprise a great number of tribes over a wide range of territory. For some undetermined reason, as mentioned above, they appear to be closely related to some of the tribes in the southwestern United States, but there is a large group of tribes in between. Currently, they inhabit most of interior Alaska as well as the Yukon and the Northwest Territories.

The Athapaskans encompass what is in some ways a strange mixture of cultures. They were among the last American Indians to be "discovered" by people of European descent and were largely unknown before the Alaskan gold rush of the late nineteenth century. When gold was discovered along the Yukon River, the Athapaskans were found to be already in control of the land; they were not especially upset by the arrival of whites. There was an attempt by Christian missionaries to convert the native people they found in Alaska and the Yukon. This effort was successful to some extent, but only on a superficial level. Until the 1970's, most of the territory the Athapaskans controlled in Alaska was still Indian Territory, never ceded to the United States by treaty. During that time, much of the land became national park or national monument land, but this has had little effect on the lifestyles of the people who live there.

The largest numbers of Athapaskans in the Subarctic live along the Yukon and Tanana Rivers in Alaska and the Yukon. Most speak English, although the native dialects are still used for religious ceremonies. Generally speaking, Christianity is common but has not replaced older customs. Like many American Indian groups, the Athapaskans believed in many gods and had no objection to accepting Jesus Christ into the pantheon. At important times such as births, deaths, and marriages, two ceremonies often take place: a Christian ceremony conducted in English and a native one conducted in the native language. —*Marc Goldstein*

See also Architecture—Subarctic; Arts and crafts—Subarctic; Athapaskan language family; Eskimo-Aleut language family; Plank house; Prehistory—Subarctic; Totem poles.

BIBLIOGRAPHY

Bancroft-Hunt, Norman. *People of the Totem.* New York: G. P. Putnam's Sons, 1979. A description of the Northwest American Indian culture, including a study of their history, ceremonies, and contemporary conditions.

Bandi, Hans Georg. *Eskimo Prehistory.* Translated by Ann E. Keep. College: University of Alaska Press, 1969. An archaeological study of early Eskimos, including illustrations, diagrams, and maps, and discussing their history from their arrival on the American continent until the 1960's.

Bone, Robert W. *Fielding's Guide to Alaska and the Yukon.* New York: Fielding Travel Books, 1990. A traveler's guide, mostly involving areas that can be reached by car. Includes some useful information about where to find artifacts and living examples of the native cultures of the area.

Hamilton, Charles. *Cry of the Thunderbird: The American Indian's Own Story.* Norman: University of Oklahoma Press, 1972. A compilation of articles by American Indians about their culture, including memories of childhood, historical beginnings, and contemporary conditions.

Spencer, Robert F., Jesse D. Jennings, et al. *The Native Americans.* 2d ed. New York: Harper & Row, 1977. An encyclopedic discussion of American Indian culture, from prehistory to contemporary times.

Subsistence

TRIBES AFFECTED: Pantribal

SIGNIFICANCE: In their thousands of years of residence in the Americas, Native Americans have obtained their food by various strategies

The Asians who crossed the Bering land bridge and became the first American Indians were hunter-gatherers, relying entirely on the plants and animals provided by nature for their food supplies. Over the millennia, their descendants developed a great variety of ways of gaining their livelihood, some continuing to exploit nature exclusively, some domesticating and cultivating crops, some herding domestic animals, and some combining these subsistence modes. Choices regarding what modes of subsistence to follow were neither capricious nor dictated by ignorance of other options: rather, they were rational decisions based on the advantages and disadvantages of each. The option that was chosen carried strong implications for the way of life, often leading a people down a path from which later departure was difficult.

Hunting-Gathering. The hunting-gathering way of life was based on utilizing food sources as they occurred naturally. Berries were picked from the berry patches, but no berry seeds were planted to create new berry patches; deer were stalked and killed, but they were neither herded nor bred to intensify characteristics preferred by the hunter. Fish were netted, but they were not impounded in ponds for breeding and harvest.

This simplified view of hunting-gathering overlooks some purposeful human modification of the environment. Indians in both the Northeast and California, for example, selectively burned areas, encouraging the growth of certain plants that colonize disturbed areas. Many of the weeds that first grow in burned areas were excellent eaten as greens and often bore starchy seeds that could be made into flour. Berry bushes also entered such areas soon after burning, and hunter-gatherers could take advantage of their fruits. Most important, deer (the most common meat source for North American hunter-gatherers) would find more browsing fodder in recently burned areas, and their numbers would increase. Burning, then, provided a measure of control over the foods that nature produced, encouraging the types desired by people; nevertheless, hunter-gatherers remained basically dependent on what nature offered.

Dependence on nature did not limit the ingenuity of American Indian hunter-gatherers in designing and using technology to aid hunting and fishing. Clever traps and weirs captured game and fish while the hunter or fisher was doing something else; spearthrowing aids effectively lengthened the hunter's arm in throwing a spear, increasing the power generated; plant poisons that stunned fish but did not render their flesh toxic to human beings were used widely in quiet stretches of rivers. In contrast, the gathering of plants remained labor-intensive, with few devices to improve its efficiency.

Hunting-gathering provided a generally good life. Except in marginal environments such as deserts, hunter-gatherers typically could obtain a day's food for their families with only a few hours' work, leaving much time for other activities. The wide variety of foods eaten by most hunter-gatherers provided sufficient nutritional diversity to maintain good health. Hunter-gatherers found it desirable to move with the seasons, taking advantage of the seasonal abundance of one or another food source and settling near it for the period it was available; this movement ensured hunter-gatherers of clean, new quarters on a regular basis, again helping preserve good health.

The requirements of hunting-gathering, however, placed some restrictions on American Indians following this mode of subsistence. Seasonal movements were necessary to take advantage of natural distributions of food sources over time and space; therefore, hunter-gatherers were limited in the amount of material items they could accumulate or transport. Duplicate tools could be made and stored at the different settlements in anticipation of next year's return, but it was difficult or impossible to stockpile large quantities of food. This was a limitation in seasonal environments, such as northern regions where several months of winter saw limited food supplies and sometimes starvation. The limitation of available food for the lean season meant that populations could attain only moder-

A Diegueño woman, Susana Beresford, demonstrates pounding acorns the way her hunter-gatherer ancestors once did. (National Museum of the American Indian, Smithsonian Institution)

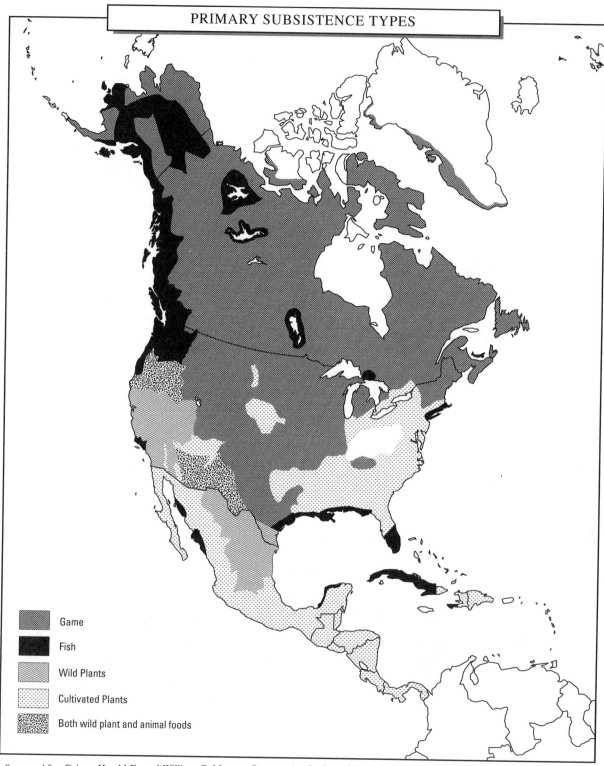

PRIMARY SUBSISTENCE TYPES

Game

Fish

Wild Plants

Cultivated Plants

Both wild plant and animal foods

Source: After Driver, Harold E., and William C. Massey, *Comparative Studies of North American Indians*, 1957.

ate densities in most environments. The same problem meant that the number of people in a settlement could not be too large, since the surrounding locale could provide only so much food.

Hunter-gatherers usually had relatively uncomplicated ways of governing themselves. Their leaders typically served at the pleasure of the community, and leaders rarely could do more than encourage people to follow the course of action they deemed appropriate. Hunter-gatherers usually had religions that stressed individual relations to spirits, and shamans often were the primary religious functionaries. Kinship relationships usually were patrilineal (traced through the male lines).

Transition to Agriculture. While hunting-gathering was a basically desirable way of life, the limitation on the amount of food available during the lean season was a serious one. Hunter-gatherers searched for ways to increase the amount of food they provided their families, but the limitations remained. Food scarcity in the lean season resulted in higher child mortality. Rarely did children starve, and parents usually tried to protect them from the worst shortages, but undernourishment resulted in lowered resistance to disease, and children probably bore the brunt of lean-season deaths.

All peoples have realized the connection between seeds and plant growth. Hunter-gatherers doubtless turned to cultivating plants in an attempt to limit the problems of the lean season. Some of the earliest plant cultivation in the Americas is known from the Tehuacán Valley of central Mexico around 6000 B.C.E. Avocados and chili peppers were grown there by American Indians as an adjunct to hunting-gathering. These same Indians began growing corn by 5000 B.C.E. and beans and squash within the next few centuries. Not until 3500 B.C.E. or later, however, did these cultivators establish year-round settlements. Instead, they continued their seasonal movements and emphasis on hunting and gathering nature's bounty. Eventually, however, they became dependent on agriculture and placed their primary efforts in that field, utilizing wild plants and animals only as adjuncts to their agricultural produce. At this point, their ties to fields and storage facilities became greater than the benefits of seasonal movement, and they became sedentary.

The same process that took place in the Tehuacán Valley occurred in many other places in the Americas, though at different times. Between 3500 and 500 B.C.E. in the Southwest, the same process of using a few cultivated crops as an adjunct to hunting-gathering evolved into agricultural dependence; between perhaps 1200 B.C.E. and 800 C.E. in the Illinois Valley, a parallel process occurred.

As people became dependent on agricultural crops, they no longer were satisfied to continue growing wild plants. Instead, they modified them, choosing those with the fastest growing season, the largest fruits or seeds, or the greatest resistance to drought. By selecting the seeds or cuttings of these individual plants, the next generation would have a higher frequency of the desired trait, and gradually the plant

was modified. This is the selective breeding process used in modern agronomy to establish new varieties of crops, and it achieved tremendous success in pre-Columbian America. Over thousands of years, tiny cobs of corn no larger than a little finger were converted to the sausage-sized cobs of historic times; beans became larger and more drought-resistant; squash became larger and sweeter. The process of domestication was so successful that some crops, corn included, lost their ability to reproduce themselves without human intervention.

Agriculturalists domesticated and cultivated a large inventory of crops in the Americas, including chili peppers, avocados, corn, squash, beans, sunflowers, tomatoes, potatoes, sweet potatoes, manioc, pineapples, and amaranth, a tiny seed crop eaten extensively in various places. The most important crops always were ones that could be stored effectively. In this way, agriculture helped reduce the problem of the lean season, and regional populations always grew at the onset of agricultural dependence. After a few generations, the ability to return to hunting-gathering probably was lost, since the higher population levels required the greater amounts of food that came with agriculture, especially during the lean season.

At some point as agriculture became more important, people had to settle down. Moving from one place to another with the seasons became impractical, since carrying their supply of stored foods would require unreasonable amounts of labor. With this sedentism, people could begin accumulating larger amounts of material goods, and they could live in larger communities. These communities often found it desirable to have a leader who had greater authority than any individual did under the hunter-gatherer system. In some places, populations were large enough so that the people submitted to leaders who wielded coercive power, permitting these chiefs to enforce their decisions. The ultimate in this development was the Aztec Empire of Mexico, with its divine emperor who had life-and-death power over every member of the empire.

The relations between the sexes also changed under agriculture. Most hunter-gatherers assigned men the more dangerous task of hunting and women the more time-consuming chores of gathering plants, which typically formed the greatest part of the hunter-gatherer diet. Fishing might be assigned to either sex. As hunter-gatherers invested more in agriculture, women transferred their control of wild plants to domesticated crops. Fields often were controlled or even owned by women, who passed them on to their daughters. In this manner, the emphasis shifted in many cases to reckoning kinship primarily through women: matrilineality. A concern with the success of agriculture also began a greater focus on group-oriented religious ceremonies.

Pastoralism. For reasons that are unclear, American Indians never domesticated many animals. In South America, llamas and other camelids were domesticated for food and transportation, but in North America and Mexico, only turkeys and muscovy ducks were important domestications.

(Dogs probably had been domesticated by the time they crossed over the Bering land bridge with the first American Indians.) When Europeans came into the Americas after 1492, they brought a variety of domesticated animals with them, especially horses, cattle, and sheep. These provided North American Indians with the first opportunity to begin pastoralism, the raising of domestic animals as a primary mode of subsistence.

The death and dislocations that accompanied the European conquest of the Americas kept most Indian groups from adopting pastoralism, but a few groups in the Southwest have done so successfully, notably the Navajo, some Apache groups, and the Tohono O'odham.

The Navajo serve as the prime example of pastoralists, since they typically move with their flocks. They focus on sheepherding, and most rural Navajo family groups have at least a few sheep. The demands of these livestock mean that the family must maintain considerable flexibility. If the grass runs out, the sheep have to be shifted to new pasturage, and bad years mean many shifts. If circumstances are particularly bad, relatives must be called upon for assistance, and flexibility in reckoning kinship ties is important. The size of the household must reflect the size and viability of the herd, and a bad year may mean that the family splits up for a time.

Pastoralists rarely can produce all their needs, and they usually have strong trading ties with settled agriculturalists. Because of this trade, some pastoralists may be able to accumulate a fair amount of wealth, at least enough to permit them to settle in a town and live off their profits. These individuals,

called "ricos" among the Navajo, often abandon their former pastoralist ways.

Culture Areas and Subsistence. In traditional times, North American Indians in certain portions of the continent shared similar lifestyles and patterns of culture. In part, these similarities were engendered by living as neighbors, interacting and communicating with one another. Other similarities, however, probably were more the result of similar modes of subsistence.

In eastern North America, for example, Indian tribes shared considerable similarity. All tribes south of the latitude of central Maine were agriculturalists, relying heavily on corn, beans, and squash. All of these plants had been domesticated in tropical Mexico, and it had taken centuries for them to be transported this far and to be adapted to the rigors of the colder climate in eastern North America. These same plants had been adopted earlier in the Southeast, and population levels had risen, achieving higher levels there than in the Northeast. The largest towns in the Southeast before European contact were probably two or three times as large as their counterparts in the Northeast.

As a result, many of the Southeast tribes had developed the chiefdom form of government, with a coercive leader. The Natchez, for example, had a single ruler called "the Sun," who had total control over his subjects, though he could be removed from office for lack of bravery or other offenses. In the Northeast, government was less strong and intrusive, and leaders were more likely to lead by example than decree. The leadership of the Iroquois tribes, while more coercive than that of their Algonquian neighbors, was far less able to en-

Buffalo meat drying in the sun; Plains subsistence was transformed when horses were brought by Europeans. (National Archives)

force an unpopular decree than were most leaders in the Southeast.

Before the advent of Europeans in North America, the Plains tribes were mostly similar to Eastern Woodlands tribes. They were agriculturalists, carving farms out of the tough sod of the prairies and living in villages of rarely more than a dozen families. Their leaders led by example, and religious ceremonies largely were conducted by kin groups and voluntary societies. Kinship was primarily matrilineal.

The coming of the Europeans, however, brought the horse, and it changed Plains life massively. Tribes formerly had hunted bison on foot seasonally, but the inefficiency of the process meant that this could not be relied upon as the primary means of subsistence. The horse, however, made bison hunting efficient, and most Plains tribes abandoned farming in favor of a new lifestyle based first on bison hunting and later augmented with raiding on neighbors and Europeans. As the tribes converted from agriculturalists to hunter-gatherers, they returned to reckoning kinship through the male line, and many group-oriented ceremonies became less central to the community.

The Indian tribes of the Southwest before the coming of the Europeans fell into two groups: settled agriculturalists (the Pueblo peoples and the Pima and Tohono O'odham) and the mobile hunter-gatherers (the Apache, including those that later would become the Navajo) that lived in the areas between their settlements. The matrilineal agriculturalists lived in quite sizeable settlements, practicing group-oriented religious ceremonies and recognizing leaders who ruled by example. The hunter-gatherers exploited the foods of nature, traded with the settled peoples for corn and other goods, and occasionally took advantage of their mobility to raid the settled villages for goods.

The Northwest Coast of North America is a great exception to the generalizations presented about the relationship between subsistence and way of life. Tribes of this culture area never adopted agriculture, but the Northwest Coast possessed great natural bounty, especially in terms of salmon and other fish. As a result, dense populations developed and settled into sedentary villages along prime fishing rivers. The control of fishing areas was largely in the hands of the chiefs, and they often developed considerable power over others, in part through their personal wealth, in part through the coercive power given them by the people. This is one of the few cases known around the world where coercive leadership has developed among a hunting-gathering society.

In the far northern parts of North America, the growing season was too short to permit agriculture of any kind, and hunter-gatherers were the exclusive residents of these areas. The environment dictated small group sizes, great seasonal mobility, and the uncluttered government that is desirable under these characteristics. While hunter-gatherers typically gain most of their food from plants, far northern Indian tribes and the Inuit are exceptional. In this area, plants are few and the growing season is short, so people must resort to a diet dominated by animal flesh. Such a diet is likely to be short of vitamins, but the eating of internal organs, a major source of vitamins, helps offset that deficiency.   —*Russell J. Barber*

See also Agriculture; Buffalo; Fish and fishing; Hunting and gathering; Ranching.

BIBLIOGRAPHY

Byers, Douglas S., ed. *Prehistory of the Tehuacán Valley*. Austin: University of Texas Press, 1967. This multivolume work provides great detail on all aspects of the archaeology of the Tehuacán Valley. Articles by Richard S. MacNeish summarize changes in subsistence, plant domestication, and associated adjustments in settlement size and seasonal movement.

Flannery, Kent V. "The Origins of Agriculture." In *Annual Reviews in Anthropology 2*. Palo Alto, Calif.: Annual Reviews, 1973. An excellent review of thinking on why agriculture developed and the adjustments it required from the hunting-gathering lifestyle. Emphasis is on agriculture in the Americas.

Kupferer, Harriet J. *Ancient Drums, Other Moccasins: Native American Cultural Adaptations*. Englewood Cliffs, N.J.: Prentice Hall, 1988. An overview of ten Indian tribes, approached from the viewpoint of the relationship between subsistence and culture. Accessible and nontechnical, but not very detailed.

Lee, Richard B., and Irven DeVore, eds. *Man, the Hunter*. Chicago: Aldine, 1968. A classic collection of essays on hunter-gatherers around the world. They explode many myths—that hunter-gatherers work long hours, that they do not understand seed growth, and so forth. The articles by Suttles and Sahlins on the Northwest Coast are particularly relevant.

Steward, Julian. *Basin-Plateau Aboriginal Sociopolitical Groups*. Bulletin 120. Washington, D.C.: Bureau of American Ethnology, 1938. A truly classic discussion of how ecological constraints and hunting-gathering shaped the social and political structures of tribes in western North America's desert.

Suicide

TRIBES AFFECTED: Pantribal
SIGNIFICANCE: The destruction of traditional culture and the corresponding economic deprivation of much reservation life has made suicide epidemic in the Indian population

Traditionally, Native Americans recognized the sanctity of life and stressed family and community responsibility. Suicide was thus uncommon, though it was permitted in some cultures under exceptional circumstances. Throughout North America, the aged and infirm often asked to be left to die rather than impose a burden. Among Plains Indians, suicide was sometimes regarded as preferable to social disgrace or severe physical deformity. Some saw suicide as permissible to avoid pain if all responsibilities had been fulfilled. Others, such as the Navajo, discouraged suicide, believing that it left behind a dangerous ghost.

Studies begun in the 1940's, however, uncovered a disturbing trend. With the breakdown of cultural traditions, family instability, poverty, and lack of opportunity, Indian suicide has

SELF-REPORTS OF SUICIDE ATTEMPTS BY RURAL AMERICAN INDIAN ADOLESCENTS

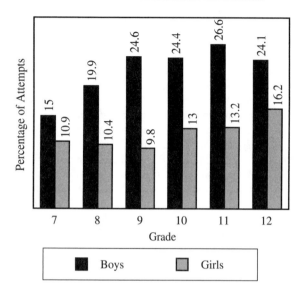

Source: Indian Health Service and Robert Wood Johnson Foundation, *The State of Native American Youth Health,* 1992.

Note: Based on a survey of 13,923 rural American Indian and Alaska Native adolescents; the survey sample was not a true random sample.

become commonplace, especially among young males. The overall suicide rate for Indians is 30 percent higher than for the general population, and for young males (ages twelve to twenty-four), the rate is double. After age forty-five, the comparative rate begins to decline, and for the elderly it is significantly below the national average.

See also Alcoholism; Employment and unemployment; Reservation system of the United States.

Sun Dance

TRIBES AFFECTED: Arapaho, Arikara, Assiniboine, Blackfoot, Crow, Dakota, Gros Ventre, Hidatsa, Kiowa, Lakota, Ojibwa, Plains Cree, Sarsi, Shoshone, Siseton, Ute

SIGNIFICANCE: Conducted primarily to ask the Spirit to bring the tribe a successful bison hunt, the Sun Dance also celebrates the creation of the world, re-creating the interaction of time, space, mass, and energy as mythologically perceived by various tribes, all of whom added their own sequences of steps to signal syncretic features unique to their own perceptions

"Ceremony is a picture of one's relationship to that which is being honored," said Nicholas Black Elk. Ritual is a ceremony repeated at specific times for specific purposes. To gaze at the sun while dancing and be gazed at by the sun while dancing was the only calendrical ritual of the Plains tribes done by a group, band, or tribe. It was (and is) held annually either

during the full moon when the berries ripen (June-July) or during the moon when the cherries blacken (July-August). Various bands gathered for the great "making of meat"—the hunting, cutting, spreading, drying, preserving, and storing of buffalo meat. The bison were central to the economy of the Plains tribes, and the bison is "of the earth." It occupied a central place in the mythology of many tribes.

History. The Sun Dance goes by different names—"dance without drinking" (Cree), "ceremony of the life renewal" (Cheyenne), "the sacred or mysterious dance" (Ponca), and "the sun gazes at the dance" (Dakota). Sun Dancing was most elaborate among the Arapaho, Cheyenne, Crow, and Sioux. The Pawnee, Comanche, Kiowa, and Ute copied it as late as 1890, the time when the wave of Ghost Dances was sweeping many Indian nations. When the horse was introduced to Indian cultures, it changed the syncretic sequences of various dances, and since that time immediate histories of various tribes have been inscribed onto the Sun Dance.

Following the years 1890-1891 and the massacre at Wounded Knee, and under reservation strictures, the pattern of the dance was curbed and changed drastically. From 1881 to 1920 the Sun Dance involving piercing of the flesh went underground. Semisecret Sun Dances without piercing were held in the 1920's. Following the Indian Reorganization Act of 1934, Sun Dances without piercing were held openly. In the late 1950's, enthusiasm revived, and Sun Dances including piercing became common on Plains reservations. The Pine Ridge Tribal Council even promoted them as a tourist attraction, "a re-enactment of the old ways," and presented a dance in conjunction with the Fourth of July Fair. A number of descriptions of Sun Dances have been published, dating from as early as 1882. No two Sun Dances even in the same tribe are conducted the same; perhaps they never were.

Honoring and Giving Back. The Sun Dance is a picture of the tribe's "relationship to that which is being honored," and that relationship changes with time and with the various Sun Dance intercessors' (holy men's) interpretations. In the old times, the "Tree of Life," the Sun, the Buffalo, the "Center of the Universe," and warrior societies were honored. These icons were honored with thanksgiving prayers for their very existence. In the long underground years from 1881 to 1934, many of the original instructions were reinterpreted. Much Christian, especially Catholic, influence came to bear. The Sun Dance, originally a thanksgiving rite, changed to a rite of repentance and selfmortification. In the old days there were flesh offerings, dragging of skulls, and suspension from skewers in the skin attached by rope to scaffolds or the center tree of life, but such acts were considered "giving back." In the beginning, according to Albert White Hat, Jr., a tribal archivist at Sinte Gleska College on the Rosebud Reservation, the very first power created all there is by "opening a vein" and letting energy flow. Thus, returning some of one's own flesh and blood to the Creator was considered a thanksgiving, a giving back; it was not considered immolation, mortification, or torture.

Originally those who vowed to dance for personal reasons usually did so because their life or a loved one's life had been spared or because a medicine was given and instruction for its use granted. Personal vows often took months, sometimes a year of preparation. Proper preparation for a Sun Dance requires months of constructing and readying the instruments used in the ceremony. Abstinence from sexual activity is recommended, varying with tribes from four days to four months before the ceremony.

Sun Dances were powerful and deeply emotional rituals lasting four days from opening to close and involving much personal sacrifice. Dancers abstained from food or water during the dance. They suffered from the heat and from hyperventilation caused by blowing continually on an eagle bone whistle. Some dancers also used the ritual to make giveaways of personal possessions. In giving thanks by making a blood sacrifice in one of several ways at this communal annual ritual, people prayed for the welfare of the entire tribe.

To paraphrase Frances Densmore's *Teton Sioux Music* (1918), a vow to dance was usually made at sunrise and was made to the daybreak star of understanding. A proper offering of bison fat was held in the left hand, and the right hand was raised as the vow was spoken. The spoken vow was only that the man would participate in a Sun Dance, but in his heart was the secret vow of the form of that participation. The man would vow either to dance, to be suspended from poles, or to drag buffalo skulls.

In mid-June of 1876, many bands gathered along Rosebud Creek in southeastern Montana. It was known that the U.S. Army was coming at them from three sides. Sioux, Cheyenne, and some Arapaho decided to hold the Sun Dance rather than run. Sitting Bull, among all the great men who were there, was chosen leader. Surrounded by the army, the Plains tribes held to their ancient beliefs and sought the power and a successful bison hunt. Sitting Bull knew that the army was close, but he also knew that the Indians would be safe during the Sun Dance. On June 17, two days after the dance, the bands were attacked by General Crook. One thousand Indian warriors forced seven hundred army troops into retreat. The Indians then moved to a river called the Little Bighorn, where they were attacked again by General George Custer. It was their last great victory.

The Sun Dance Today. Today the dance seems to be primarily a celebration of personal renewal. There is a special relationship between the dancer and the spiritual world, and the Sun Dance is an event of a highly religious nature. The revival of this ritual in our times is more than a visual representation. This ritual takes place on both mythological and real planes of existence and is the source of symbolic and expressionistic power. Because the mythological element is still so evident, many Indians do not understand why nontribal members would want to Sun Dance. They believe that non-Indians who dance without any clear understanding of the mythology being re-enacted are probably dancing for personal gratification or egotistical need. Purists also complain about the crass commercialism and religious degeneration of these dances.

The most visible Sun Dances held in the United States in modern times are on the Pine Ridge and Rosebud reservations in South Dakota and on the Crow Reservation in Montana. Many modern Sun Dances have become arenas where traditionalists and those who wish to capitalize on the ritual vent their anger toward one another. Yet modern Sun Dances satisfy the social needs of the tribes, whether members are traditionalists or modernists. Thousands of tribal people attend the Sun Dances, setting up old-style nomadic camps and catching up with friends and relatives from other reservations. Regardless of whether the contemporary Sun Dance is a syncretic version of old and new, it exists as a powerful mediating force between factions on reservations and allows all in attendance to assert their religious beliefs.

Among all tribes there are certain similarities and consistencies in the Sun Dances. There is always the establishment of a sacred center, symbolizing the center of the universe. This helps any of the various tribes experience their place of emergence, as nearly all American Indians have myth stories describing their "emergence" into this plane of existence. At the finding of the center, prayers, songs, drums, and rattles are used to drive away evil. Members of the scout society who conduct their lives in an exemplary way are sent to find the tree which will be placed in the center. Every action pertinent to the ritual is supported by prayers and songs. Sweatlodges and purification by smoke from sage, sweetgrass, and cedar are central to the ritual. Sacred icons or instruments such as pipes, arrows, or sacred bundles are also central to the rituals. There is always a recitation of the mythology of the people. There are often naming ceremonies for children. At Sun Dances each year, tribal identities are upheld and sustained. There is always a feast at the conclusion of the dance.

The Sun Dance is conducted by holy men (interpreters), who talk with spirit forces. If the camp circle is very large and several holy men are present, they will decide among themselves who will conduct the dance. It is generally known who will be the intercessor, and often the same man will serve in this capacity for a number of years. Bearing this responsibility requires long and special preparation. The duties traditionally included offering prayers for all the people, singing certain ancient songs at exactly the right time, painting sacred objects, handling the most sacred instruments of the nation, and preparing the sacred place. A Teton Sioux man named Red Bird once told Frances Densmore that "the tribe would never appoint an unworthy man to the office of intercessor. In his prayers and offerings he represented the people, and if he were not a good man he might even send disaster upon the tribe."

There is much confusion surrounding Sun Dances today. Traditionalists say that one should dance to see and that there are too many now who are dancing to be seen. Many dance unprepared; others dance with little or no knowledge of the mythology of the people whose ceremony they are enacting. A proper Sun Dance may be likened to a carefully orchestrated symphony of the entire religion of the people. Power is called and set in motion for another year, "that the people may live."

—*Glenn J. Schiffman*

See also Dances and dancing; Ghost Dance; Little Bighorn, Battle of the; Okeepa; Plains; Religion.

BIBLIOGRAPHY

Bonnefoy, Yves. *Mythologies.* Translated by Wendy Donniger. Vol. 2. Chicago: University of Chicago Press, 1991.

Brown, Joseph Epes, ed. *The Sacred Pipe: Black Elk's Account of the Seven Rites of the Oglala Sioux.* Norman: University of Oklahoma Press, 1989.

Dorsey, George A. *The Cheyenne Indians: The Sun Dance.* Glorietta, N.Mex.: Rio Grande Press, 1971.

Mails, Thomas E. *Sundancing at Rosebud and Pine Ridge.* Sioux Falls, S.Dak.: Center for Western Studies, Augustana College, 1978.

Neihardt, John. *Black Elk Speaks.* Lincoln: University of Nebraska Press, 1979.

Schiffman, Glenn, ed. *Black Elk Speaks.* Illuminated Books and Manuscripts: An Interactive Program. Los Angeles: IBM, 1990.

_____. *Relationship with Fire.* Los Angeles: Word of Mouth Press, 1988.

Suquamish: Tribe

CULTURE AREA: Northwest Coast
LANGUAGE GROUP: Salishan
PRIMARY LOCATION: West side of Puget Sound, Washington
POPULATION SIZE: 726 (1990 U.S. Census)

The Suquamish were typical of Northwest Coast peoples, relying mostly upon marine resources, occupying permanent winter villages, practicing extensive trade and intermarriage, and performing elaborate ceremonies.

The first European American contact was probably in 1792 when George Vancouver explored the region. In 1824 John Work of the Hudson's Bay Company traversed the area, and in 1827 he established Fort Langley on the Fraser River, which commenced sustained trade within the region. Roman Catholics were the first missionaries, teaching their doctrine in Chinook jargon. The 1846 Treaty of Washington gave the area to the United States, and the 1850 Donation Land Act of Oregon opened the region to settlers. Eventually, most Suquamish settled on the Suquamish Reservation.

The Suquamish Museum was established in 1985; it depicts their history and houses a museum store for selling traditional crafts, mostly cedar boxes, Salish weaving, and basketry. There has been a revival of winter spirit dancing, bone games, and other traditional activities. Tourism and other economic ventures are a significant means of income for the tribe.

See also Squamish.

Susquehannock: Tribe

CULTURE AREA: Northeast
LANGUAGE GROUP: Iroquoian
PRIMARY LOCATION: Pennsylvania
POPULATION SIZE: 125 (1990 U.S. Census)

The Susquehannocks, a member of the Iroquoian language group, are known primarily from seventeenth century historical records and twentieth century archaeological excavations. First mentioned by Captain John Smith in 1608, the Susquehannocks at the time of European contact lived in the lower Susquehanna River valley in southeastern Pennsylvania and northern Maryland. Archaeological evidence suggests that their original homeland was on the North Branch of the Susquehanna River, in an area north of the Wyoming Valley and south of Binghamton, New York.

Throughout the historical period, the Susquehannocks were in conflict with the Iroquois over questions of trade and hunting rights. In the early seventeenth century the Susquehannocks served as middlemen between European traders and other Indian groups to the north and west, including the Iroquois; when the Iroquois, particularly the Senecas, wanted more direct access to European trade goods, they waged war on the Susquehannocks, forcing them out of their homeland and into the lower Susquehanna River valley. The Susquehannocks were militarily defeated by the Iroquois in 1676 and were forced to resettle near the Oneidas in New York. Later, allowed to return to southeastern Pennsylvania, they settled near Lancaster, where they became known as the Conestogas. Throughout the historic period, the Susquehannocks' numbers diminished from warfare and disease introduced by Europeans. An estimated population of five thousand in 1600 had been reduced to only twenty persons in 1763 when the last full-blood Susquehannocks were massacred by whites angered by the failure of the Pennsylvania Assembly to make reprisals for attacks by Indians on the western Pennsylvania frontier.

Very little is known about the Susquehannocks other than their role as traders. During the historic period, they lived in palisaded towns along the Susquehanna River, but these towns were probably a response to warfare. Archaeological research suggests that originally the Susquehannocks lived in widely scattered hamlets comprising only a few families. They practiced a mixed economy based on hunting wild animals, gathering wild plants, and shifting cultivation of corn and a few other agricultural products. Thought to be closely related to the Cayugas, the Susquehannocks are believed to have been quite similar socially to the Iroquois, with a similar division of labor; women did the farming, and men hunted and engaged in war. The Susquehannocks apparently practiced matrilineal kinship, as did other Iroquoian cultures; descent and inheritance were passed through the mother's line, and women were socially influential. Archaeologically, the Susquehannocks are best known from their burials and their distinctive pottery. In the prehistoric period, the Susquehannocks buried their dead without grave goods in a flexed position in previously dug cache pits. In the seventeenth century, town-dwelling Susquehannocks buried their dead in cemeteries outside the town in specially dug graves; the dead were accompanied by pottery vessels and personal belongings. Susquehannock pottery was made using a paddle-and-anvil (rather than coiled) method; starting with a circular lump of clay, the potter shaped the bowl against the fist with a cord-wrapped paddle. The resulting pottery was incised with patterns around the lip; occasionally human faces were modeled into the lip.

Throughout the historic period, the Susquehannocks were known by a variety of names, including the Conestoga, the Andaste, the Meherrin, and the Minquaas. This variety has led some researchers to speculate that the Susquehannocks were not a distinct tribe but a confederacy of tribes formed in opposition to the Iroquois. There is no evidence to support the confederacy theory, however. It is more likely that the various names arose out of European confusion and the similarities between the Susquehannocks and their Iroquoian neighbors.

See also Iroquoian language family; Northeast; Pottery.

Swallah: Tribe

CULTURE AREA: Northwest Coast
LANGUAGE GROUP: Salishan
PRIMARY LOCATION: Washington

The maritime Swallah had bilateral kinship and lived in permanent winter villages located near water. Some villages were palisaded for protection, as conflict was common between villages. Different types of dugout canoes were used for travel, fishing, and warfare. Major rites were the Spirit Dance, First Salmon Ceremony, Secret Society, and Cleansing Ceremonies. The Swallah potlatch served to recognize status change, redistribution of wealth, house-raising or canoe launching, and hereditary naming. The Swallah had a complex mythology in which Raven and Mink were tricksters. The Swallah maintained considerable social and economic ties with other Central Coast Salish tribes.

The Strait of Juan de Fuca was discovered by Europeans in 1787 by Charles Barkley. British and Spanish explorers visited the area, and by 1811 fur traders had established themselves at the mouth of the Columbia. The 1846 Treaty of Washington divided the Central Coast Salish into British and American regions. Because of disease, indigenous populations had greatly declined since the late 1700's.

See also Salishan language family.

Sweatlodges and sweatbaths

TRIBES AFFECTED: Pantribal
SIGNIFICANCE: Sweatlodges and sweatbaths are widely used for ceremonial, social, and medicinal purposes

The sweatlodge is a traditional ceremonial enclosure, usually circular in design. It is generally framed with saplings,

The entrance to a Yurok sweatlodge; the Yuroks are a Northern California tribe. (Library of Congress)

wooden poles in a conical arrangement, or cedar planks. The enclosure can be from 4 to 8 feet across and 4 to 6 feet in height. It was traditionally covered with animal skins, bark, or earth. Today blankets or other coverings are often used. Lodge design is varied according to tribe and available building materials.

A shallow pit, approximately a foot across, is dug in the center of the sweatlodge floor. This pit is the receptacle for the seven to twenty-eight stones used to heat the enclosure. They are brought in, in one to four rounds of approximately fifteen to twenty minutes duration. Volcanic stones hold heat the best. Temperatures in the sweatlodge can exceed 200 degrees Fahrenheit.

Participants disrobe, either completely or partially, and walk clockwise around the lodge. They enter the lodge from the east side and sit on the earthen floor. It is covered with cedar or other evergreen boughs. The entry is closed, and the interior is dark except for the glowing stones.

Water is scooped from a gourd or other container and poured on the stones to make steam. A sacred pipe is sometimes passed. It is filled with tobacco, sage, and other medicinal plants which can also be sprinkled on the stones, making the steam fragrant and healing. Prayers are made and songs are sung. This continues until the stones cool. The specifics of the structure of the sweatlodge and ceremony used vary from one community to another.

See also Ethnophilosophy and worldview; Medicine and modes of curing, pre-contact; Religion.

Sweezy, Carl (c. 1879, near Darlington, Okla. Territory—May 28, 1953, Lawton, Okla.): Artist

ALSO KNOWN AS: Wattan (Black)
TRIBAL AFFILIATION: Arapaho
SIGNIFICANCE: Sweezy was one of the earliest to use the Native American narrative genre style of painting, and he developed it beyond ledger-book-style drawings

Sweezy began drawing as a child and learned to do watercoloring in school. At age twenty, he became an informant for James Mooney, anthropologist of the Smithsonian Institution, when the latter did a study of the Cheyenne and Arapaho. Mooney needed an artist to restore paint on old shields and to copy designs, and Sweezy did that for him. Mooney liked his work and encouraged him to continue his "Indian" style of painting. Although Sweezy's most prolific period was while he worked with Mooney, he continued painting the remainder of his life and retired in 1920 to dedicate himself completely to painting.

Sweezy's paintings are important ethnographically and represent important values. He portrayed such themes as hunting buffalo, riding horseback, the defeat of Custer, ceremonies, and portraits, including details of costumes. His paintings of the Sun Dance are some of the best early visual documentation of that ceremony, and his portraits give details of dress and ritual paraphernalia. His work has been included in many exhibitions, and it is included in the collections of the National Museum of the American Indian, University of Oklahoma Museum of Art, and the Oklahoma Historical Society Museum, among others.

See also Art and artists, contemporary; Paints and painting; Spybuck, Ernest.

Syllabaries

TRIBES AFFECTED: Pantribal
SIGNIFICANCE: Syllabic writing systems first made it possible to record American Indian languages; Sequoyah, a Cherokee, produced the first syllabary for an Indian language

A syllabary is a phonetic transcription of a spoken language. It is distinct from pictographs, which are symbols of objects and actions. Technically, it may also be distinguished from an alphabet; in a syllabary, symbols represent syllables, whereas in an alphabet, they represent shorter units of sound (consonants and vowels).

It is generally accepted that the first knowledge the Indians had of alphabets was when they were contacted by European explorers starting in the late fifteenth century. Among the explorers were Christian missionaries, who were very much interested in converting the natives and therefore tried both to teach them European languages and to transliterate native languages into European alphabets. Considerable difficulties were involved, however, and early attempts were unsuccessful.

In 1821 a Cherokee leader named Sequoyah created the first syllabic writing system for an American Indian language. Sequoyah had been a volunteer under General Andrew Jackson, and he had been impressed with the white people's method of writing that enabled them to communicate over great distances. Sequoyah's syllabary had eighty-six characters for syllables in the Cherokee language. Although he used some English characters, the sounds they represented were distinct from those they represented in English. The Cherokee tribal council, impressed at its effectiveness, sanctioned its use.

The *Cherokee Phoenix*, begun in 1828 and called the first American Indian newspaper, printed articles in both English and the Cherokee syllabary. As use of the syllabary spread, books were translated into the Cherokee language; soon books were being written using the syllabary. The Bible was translated into the Cherokee syllabary by missionary Samuel Worcester. Soon other missionaries and tribal leaders alike began to use the syllabic approach. Missionary John Fleming developed a syllabary for the Creek language; Cyrus Bovington created one for the Choctaw language that could also be used by the Chickasaws. Farther north, a syllabary came into use among the Cree people of Canada and was adapted by some Inuit groups.

Eventually the alphabet used by the European settlers and their descendants won out over syllabic systems in most areas. One reason is simply that most books were available in European languages and were not available in the syllabaries. There has always been difficulty in translating native languages into the Roman alphabet because the phonetic systems are extremely different; scholars and linguists have grappled with these problems for many years with varying degrees of success.

See also Boudinot, Elias; Journalism; Sequoyah.

Symbolism in art

Tribes affected: Pantribal

Significance: The seemingly abstract designs that appear on American Indian structures, baskets, and pottery represent various aspects of Indian cosmology

Art historians distinguish between abstract and representational Native American art, but in the sense that all design elements are significant, all can be said to be representational. A ubiquitous element is the circle. Oglala mystic Black Elk explained the importance of circularity as imitating an important principle of the universe; hence tipi design, the whole tipi village, and designs on clothing and houses signify the circular wholeness of the earth and the circle of the seasons. Circularity also represents the sun, the central divinity and astronomi-

cal anchor of the nomadic Plains people, and a circle or concentric circles with branches or rays appears in beadwork, painted on hides, and worked into other artifacts.

Circularity is significant in house design in many tribes, whether grass houses in California or the Southwest, Navajo hogans, Eskimo winter dwellings or Apache wickiups; the house is a symbolic microcosm of the earth, and some groups place the opening to the east to receive the day's first light, symbolizing the creative mating of earth and sky. On a smaller scale, circularity is inherent in such artifacts as coiled baskets and pottery, where applied or inlaid design often reflects natural forms such as spider webs or coiled snakes. Tiny pottery seed pots from the southwestern pueblos symbolize the earth, with a minute hole representing the maternal opening through which the first people emerged in the process of creation.

The complementary abstract figure is the cross or x-shaped figure. This design element most often signifies the four directions; when placed within a circle, it represents a centering of the individual within the community and of the community

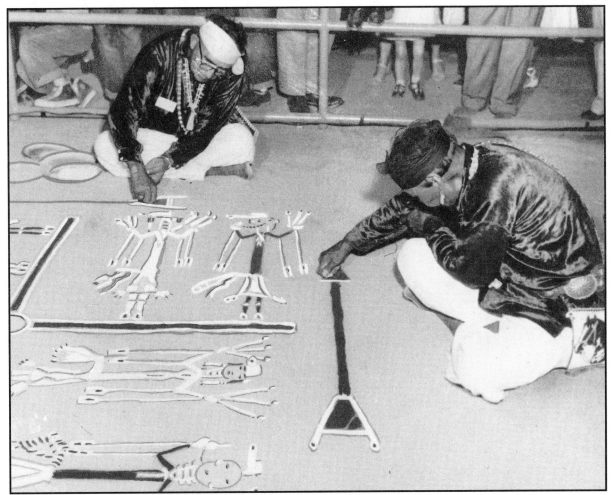

Sand paintings representing Navajo myths and events are central to the Navajo ceremonial system and contain numerous symbolic motifs. (AP/Wide World Photos)

within the universe. Black Elk alludes to such a figure in describing his great vision, and the figure of the quartered circle appears in such creations as Navajo sand paintings. The quartered circle is also part of the general patterning of four that recurs in many Plains and Southwest cultures: Sets of pairs and multiples of four recur in all aspects of art, including numbers of repetitions of songs during ceremonies, figures in sand paintings and on woven blankets, jewelry, household implements, and other artifacts. A major significance of such quarternary patterning is the idea of balance: matched pairs of opposites represent the balance between male and female, light and dark, hard and soft, life and death, and good and evil that must be maintained in the universe. Not all groups have four as their significant number; five and seven are also significant, as are other numbers.

Color symbolism is highly elaborated in many traditions, though different meanings may be associated with colors. Hence, black may signify the north in one context, while white is the color for the north in another; in body painting, black may signify mourning for one people, whereas it is part of a warrior's outfit for another. The idea of balance is also expressed through color symbolism, as in the alternating black and white stripes of Hopi clowns.

The distinction between art and non-art is not central to native traditions, and symbolic significance permeates the creation of almost every object, whether for practical use or aesthetic contemplation.

See also Art and artists, contemporary; Arts and crafts—Arctic; Arts and crafts—California; Arts and crafts—Great Basin; Arts and crafts—Northeast; Arts and crafts—Northwest Coast; Arts and crafts—Plains; Arts and crafts—Plateau; Arts and crafts—Southeast; Arts and crafts—Southwest; Arts and crafts—Subarctic; Ethnophilosophy and worldview; Paints and painting; Sculpture.

Tahltan: Tribe
CULTURE AREA: Subarctic
LANGUAGE GROUP: Athapaskan
PRIMARY LOCATION: Subarctic Cordillera, British Columbia
POPULATION SIZE: 1,330 (Statistics Canada, based on 1991 census)

The Tahltan had four named matrilineal clans based on moiety structure. Their society was stratified, with rankings indicated by titles and economic privileges. Winter dwellings were rectangular, roofed with vertical stripped saplings. Subsistence was based on hunting caribou, black and grizzly bear, moose, mountain sheep and goat, wood buffalo, and on trapping fur-bearing animals. Both men and women joined in fishing. They traded cured hides, leather goods, and babiche for coastal dentalia, copper plates, eulachon oil, slaves, and blankets. Divorce and polygyny were equally rare.

First European American contact with the Tahltan was in 1799 by fur traders, and later gold miners, who introduced numerous changes in land-use patterns, trade relations, and goods. Approximately three-fourths of the Tahltan population died from disease during the nineteenth century. By 1874, white traders had effectively disrupted the previous Tlingit-Tahltan trade relationship, forcing many people to adopt a wage economy. During World War II, many Tahltan men worked on the Alaskan Highway. Currently, the main sources of income are guiding, packing for outfitters and sportsmen, and government employment.

See also Tlingit.

Tall Bull (c. 1830—July 11, 1869): Tribal leader
ALSO KNOWN AS: Hotóakhihoois, Hotúaeka'ash Tait, Otóahhastis
TRIBAL AFFILIATION: Central Cheyenne
SIGNIFICANCE: Tall Bull, the most noted Dog Soldier chief and leader, featured prominently in the Plains Wars of the late 1860's

When the famous treaty council met at Medicine Lodge Creek (southern Kansas) in October, 1867, Tall Bull played a major role. He was one of the first Cheyenne leaders to visit the commission camp. Tall Bull declared at the council that the Cheyenne did not want war and had never done the whites harm.

In September of 1868, Tall Bull was with Roman Nose in the fateful Beecher Island battle. He is reportedly the one who warned Roman Nose of the need for a purification ritual. Roman Nose was killed in the battle.

When General George Armstong Custer's troops destroyed Black Kettle's village of so-called friendly Cheyennes on the Washita River the following year, Tall Bull led 165 lodges of Dog Soldiers and their families to establish a village on the Republican River. The village was attacked in the spring of 1869 by Major Eugene Carr, in which twenty-five of Tall Bull's five hundred warriors were killed. During the retaliation that ensued, Tall Bull was killed by the commander of Carr's Pawnee scouts, Major Frank North, near Summit Springs in northeastern Colorado. Tall Bull's wife and six-year-old daughter were taken prisoner. The Battle of Summit Springs marked the end of the Dog Soldiers' power on the Great Plains.

See also Bull Bear; Medicine Lodge, Treaties of; Roman Nose; Sand Creek Massacre; Washita River, Battle of the.

Tallchief, Maria (b. Jan. 24, 1925, Fairfax, Okla.): Ballerina
ALSO KNOWN AS: Ki-he-kah-stah (the Tall Chiefs)
TRIBAL AFFILIATION: Osage (Wazhazhe)
SIGNIFICANCE: Maria Tallchief was a renowned prima ballerina, dancing with the Ballet Russe and the New York City Ballet

Maria Tallchief was born to a full-blood Osage father and a Scottish-Irish mother on an Osage reservation in the southwestern United States. As a child, she enjoyed playing the piano as well as watching the dancers of the Osage tribe. Her enthusiasm for music and ballet launched her into local stage performances by age five. She and her sister Marjorie, also a ballerina, often performed together when they were young.

When Tallchief finished high school she moved to New York City. There she performed with the Ballet Russe de Monte Carlo between 1942 and 1947. During this time she studied with the well-known choreographer and ballet director George Balanchine, whom she later married.

From 1947 to 1965 she performed with the New York City Ballet as its prima ballerina. She led many noted performances, including the ballet *The Firebird*, for which she was renowned. In 1980, Tallchief founded the Chicago City Ballet, and she served as its director until 1987.

See also Dances and dancing; Osage; Women.

Tammany (c. 1625—c. 1701): Tribal chief
ALSO KNOWN AS: Tamanend (the Affable)
TRIBAL AFFILIATION: Lenni Lenape
SIGNIFICANCE: Tammany sold the Delawares' homeland to William Penn, who dubbed the land "Pennsylvania"

Tammany was a seventeenth century Unami Delaware (Lenni Lenape) leader. Little is known for certain about his life; fact and legend are probably inextricably linked. It is said that he greeted William Penn when Penn arrived in Pennsylvania. Tammany's name appears on two 1683 treaties (one of which sold to William Penn the land between Neshaminy and Pennypack creeks), and on another signed in 1697. Tammany was apparently friendly toward whites throughout his life, and the white settlers respected him. Well after his death, a number of societies during the American Revolution (and after) were named for Tammany (nicknamed "Saint Tammany"), who came to symbolize resistance to British colonial rule. The Society of St. Tammany, founded in New York in 1789, eventually evolved into the Democratic Party organization in New York.

See also Lenni Lenape.

Tanaina: Tribe

Culture area: Subarctic
Language group: Athapaskan
Primary location: Southwestern Alaska
Population size: 490 (1990 U.S. Census)

Tanaina Indians occupied the south-central region of Alaska. Five species of salmon, which made up the basis of Tanaina subsistence, inhabited local lakes. In summer, men used nets, spears, and basket traps to catch fish, which the women split and dried. In autumn, hunters used bows and arrows as well as harpoons to hunt harbor seals. Arrows tipped with copper, antler, or stone were used to kill caribou, sheep, moose, or goats. After entering the fur trade, the Tanaina trapped during the spring and fall.

The Tanaina traveled extensively on lakes and rivers, using birchbark canoes and mooseskin boats. Snowshoes aided winter travel. Tanaina Indians lived in large, multifamily dwellings that housed ten or more families. Both men and women wore long caribou-skin tunics with animal-skin shirts on top. Clothing was decorated with porcupine quills, shells, and ermine tails.

The Tanainan Indians placed great importance on the accumulation and display of wealth. The richest tribesman acted as headman, in charge of the health and welfare of others. He accumulated animal skins, manufactured items, wives, and slaves. Rich men were noted for their generosity. They gave lavish parties, called potlatches, which included large gift-giving ceremonies.

Tanainan religion revolved around shamans, men or women who acted as doctors and priests for the tribe. They were believed to receive their powers—sometimes unwillingly—through dreams and could cast spells both good and bad. The Tanaina also believed in spirits and animals with supernatural powers.

Russian fur traders searching for otter first entered Tanaina territory after 1741. Though they traded with Russian posts, Tanainans were very opposed to the establishment of any permanent settlements. During the first half of the nineteenth century, the Tanaina were struck by a number of epidemics. Smallpox, tuberculosis, and syphillis killed more than four thousand.

In 1845, Russian Orthodox missionaries arrived and slowly converted the Tanainans. Fur prices fell at the turn of the century, and salmon canneries prevented the Indians from fishing in the most productive streams. Fish and fur-bearing animal populations dwindled. Some natives found jobs in the canneries, and gradually tribesmen became involved in commercial fishing.

See also Athapaskan language family; Indian-white relations—Russian colonial; Subarctic.

Tanana: Tribe

Culture area: Subarctic
Language group: Athapaskan
Primary location: Alaska
Population size: 349 (1990 U.S. Census)

The Tanana inhabited the southeastern portion of Alaska around the Tanana River, hunting and fishing for their subsistence. The Tananas' most important food source was caribou—in the fall, tribesmen trapped them against fences, then killed them with lances and arrows. Surplus meat was dried for winter use. In the spring, the Tanana hunted moose, muskrat, and beaver. Beginning in June, whitefish and salmon were caught in nets and cylindrical fishtraps. Women gathered berries and roots and snared marmots and squirrels.

Tanana shelters varied with the seasonal activity. Dome-shaped lodges covered with skins were used in winter camps. Log lean-tos which held two families were used in more temporary camps. Bark-covered huts were constructed in fishing camps. Tanana Indians used birchbark or skin canoes for water transportation. Snowshoes and toboggans pulled by women were used for land travel. Tanana made clothing of tanned caribou decorated with shells and porcupine quills.

Each band had a chief and a "second chief" who, together, owned the caribou fences. The Tanana believed that shamans possessed supernatural powers. Illnesses were attributed to evil spirits which entered the body, and shamans possessed the power to remove them.

The first documented Tanana-white contact occurred around 1875 and was with trader-prospector A. C. Harper. Although non-Indian trade goods had already found their way into the area through Russian trading posts, Tanana Indians primarily traded through intermediaries. Participation in the fur trade changed annual migration patterns for the Tanana. When this occurred, economic importance shifted from the entire group to the family.

In 1886, the discovery of gold brought thousands of non-Indians into Tanana territory. Roads transformed little villages into large towns. Many natives hunted food for miners. The tribe suffered epidemics of measles, influenza, and tuberculosis, which devastated a number of villages. In the 1880's, Anglican ministers established missions and mission schools, which brought Tanana Indians into more permanent settlements. In 1958, when Alaska became a state, fish and game laws had the net effect of essentially ending old patterns of life and forcing the Tanana into wage-labor jobs.

See also Athapaskan language family; Indian-white relations—Russian colonial; Subarctic.

Tanning

Tribes affected: Pantribal
Significance: Tanning enabled animal hides to be preserved and used

The tanning of deer, elk, bison, and small animal hides was accomplished by women, using the brains of the animals or human urine. Most hides were tanned on both sides, but sometimes the hide was tanned only on the underside (if the hair was left in place). In the Arctic, the Inuit tanned only with urine, which was often stored during the winter in ice troughs. Plains and Plateau peoples would mash animal brains with moss into small cakes for later use in tanning. A woman's status was determined by her ability to do hide work, which included preparing the hide, tanning, and sewing.

To remove the hair, a woman could bury the hide in ashes for several days, or she could use a sharpened hand stone or one hafted to a leg bone as a scraper. The hide was next beamed with an animal rib to break the grain, then pegged to the ground or placed on a vertical rack to facilitate rubbing the brains or urine into the hide. After tanning, the hide could be smoked with "punk" wood in a small tipi structure in order to prevent it from cracking when it was dried after being wet.

See also Buffalo; Hides and hidework.

Tarhe (1742, near Detroit, Mich.—Nov., 1818, Crane Town, near Upper Sandusky, Ohio): Military leader
ALSO KNOWN AS: Crane, Le Chef Grue, Monsieur Grue
TRIBAL AFFILIATION: Wyandot (Huron)
SIGNIFICANCE: Although initially resisting westward white settlement, Tarhe became an ally of the Americans during the War of 1812

Tarhe was a shaman and chief of the Ohio Hurons known as the Wyandot. In his youth, he vigorously resisted American encroachment on western lands, fighting beside Shawnee leader Cornstalk against the whites during Lord Dunmore's War in 1744. At the Battle of Fallen Timbers, during Little Turtle's War (1790-1794), he was one of thirteen chiefs who fought against the American General "Mad" Anthony Wayne. After being abandoned by their British allies, the Indians suffered devastating losses. Subsequently Tarhe acknowledged white military superiority and was a principal supporter of the Treaty of Greenville (1795), as a result of which Indians were forced from their lands. He was thereafter an ally of the Americans.

Tarhe, along with his close friend, Shawnee Leader Catahecassa, refused to join Tecumseh in his attempts to organize a pan-Indian resistance to whites. During the war of 1812, Tarhe led his warriors in several battles against the British and earned the admiration of William Henry Harrison. Although he counseled accommodation, Tarhe was respected by most Indians in the Northwest Territory. His funeral was attended by many notable Indian leaders including the Seneca Red Jacket.

See also Catahecassa; Fallen Timbers, Battle of; Fort Greenville, Treaty of; Huron; Little Turtle; Tecumseh's Rebellion.

Tattoos and tattooing
TRIBES AFFECTED: Widespread but not pantribal
SIGNIFICANCE: Tattooing was one of the most widespread native practices in pre-contact North America and later

Tattooing was one of the most widespread native practices in the Americas. Techniques ranged from cutting with blades to pricking with needles or other sharp instruments. Among the Aleut and Northwest Coast peoples, a common technique was to "sew" the design into the flesh with a needle. The most common pigment was charcoal, and all parts of the face and body were tattooed.

Tattooing was used to enhance physical beauty, indicate social status, and commemorate rites of passage. High-ranking

Bella Coola men were tattooed with their parents' totemic animals. Among the Mandan, chiefs were usually the only men with tattoos, often on one arm and breast. Natchez nobility wore tattoos on their faces, arms, legs, chests and backs. Osage shamans tattooed their chests with symbols associated with their heritage of knowledge. The Tlingit often made tattoos during the final potlatch of the mortuary cycle, and they used hand tattoos as a sign of nobility.

Tattooing was often undertaken as medicine. Ojibwa healers used tattooing to treat arthritis, toothaches, broken bones, sprains, dislocated joints, and backaches. Instruments included three or four fish spines, bone splinters, or needles inserted and fastened into a split stick handle. Charred birchbark, gunpowder, or other medicines were applied either to the affected area or to the pricking instruments. Tattoos were made in the form of circular spots above the source of pain. When the affected area was large, marks were made in rows or lines.

Tattoos appear to have been most frequently worn by women. Women in the Great Plains tattooed their faces between the mouth and the chin. Tattoos were considered among the most attractive features of Netsilik Eskimo women, for whom there were separate afterlives for women with tattoos (who joined skillful hunters) and without them (who sat through eternity with bowed heads).

See also Dress and adornment.

Tavibo (c. 1810, Mason Valley, Nev.—c. 1870): Religious leader
ALSO KNOWN AS: the Paiute Prophet
TRIBAL AFFILIATION: Paiute
SIGNIFICANCE: Tavibo's prophecies about the destruction of whites helped lead to the founding of the Ghost Dance religion in the 1890's

Tavibo was a shaman who may have participated in several Indian wars, including the Pyramid Lake War (1860), the Owens Valley War (1863), and the Bannock War (1875).

Tavibo received a series of visions prophesying the destruction of whites. The first of these visions proclaimed a natural catastrophe which would destroy all whites but spare the Indians. A second vision modified the first: An earthquake would kill all people, but Indians would be resurrected. In a third vision, only his followers would be resurrected. Tavibo's influence spread to neighboring Bannocks, Shoshones, and Utes. His prophecies formed the basis for the Ghost Dance religion of the 1890's, created by Tavibo's son, Wovoka. In 1889, during an eclipse of the sun, Wovoka received a vision of Indian renewal echoing and further refining Tavibo's visions.

See also Ghost Dance; Wovoka.

Tawaquaptewa (c. 1882, Oraibi, Third Mesa, Ariz.—April 30, 1960, Oraibi, Third Mesa, Ariz.): Village chief
TRIBAL AFFILIATION: Hopi (Bear Clan)
SIGNIFICANCE: Tawaquaptewa tried to lead his clan and the Progressives through major civil strife in the Hopi Nation;

he is blamed for the degradation of the ancient pueblo of Oraibi

Appointed chief of Oraibi, the oldest continuously occupied settlement in America, in 1901, Tawaquaptewa represented one of two factions of Hopis, the Friendlies, or Progressives, led by Lololma of the Bear Clan. The Hostiles, or Traditionals, were led by the dynamic and irascible Yukioma. The factions arose over a dispute about how much the Hopi should depend on the federal government for assistance. Lololma had earlier signed an agreement with the Bureau of Indian Affairs that pledged government support for the Hopi in their efforts to keep Navajo from trespassing on the Hopi reservation. The Hostiles believed that such agreements would lead to increased government intervention and further degradation of their spiritual and ceremonial roots; they wanted the policing of their land to be done without outside assistance. In 1891, a Navajo murdered Lololma's nephew on the Hopi reservation. The bureau reluctantly arrested a Navajo suspect, then allowed him to escape, adding to the tension between the two factions.

In September of 1906, Tawaquaptewa attempted to force Lololma's allies, led by Yukioma, from Oraibi. The skirmish would have led to civil war if not for the efforts of Reverend H. R. Voth, a Mennonite missionary. Tawaquaptewa and Yukioma agreed to a "push of war," a physical contest between the two chiefs, to settle the dispute. The contest, staged on September 6, eventually disintegrated into chaos as allies for each faction joined in, trying to push their respective leaders across the line. Yukioma eventually lost after what has been documented as "hours of bloodless struggle." He and his followers abandoned Oraibi that night, establishing a spiritual center at nearby Hotevilla.

In 1912, Yukioma, still chief of the now popular and powerful center of Hotevilla, was jailed by the Bureau of Indian Affairs for threatening the matron of a government Indian school. This left Tawaquaptewa as the undisputed leader of the Hopi, a role for which he was unqualified and unprepared. Having received a routine American education from 1906 to 1910 in California, he could not reconcile his newfound knowledge with Hopi spiritual traditions. Oraibians began to abandon traditional ceremonies and, by 1933, the pueblo numbered only 112 people. At his death in 1960 the Bear Clan disintegrated, and Oraibi was in ruins.

See also Navajo; Pueblo tribes, Western.

Technology

TRIBES AFFECTED: Pantribal

SIGNIFICANCE: Technology has had a powerful impact on Native Americans, resulting in both improvement and deterioration of their quality of life

There is an old story about a group of Quechan Indians who were being brought to Mexico City by train to be wined and dined by politicians who wanted to buy some of their land. As the locomotive left the station, one of the Quechan, Yellow Feather, pointed at a nearby bluff and said something calmly in his native tongue that the Mexicans who were with them did not understand. Soon passing an enormous cactus, again Yellow Feather pointed and spoke, though he spoke more quickly this time because the train was moving faster now. As the train picked up steam, now racing through his ancestral lands, Yellow Feather pointed here and there, every moment speaking more quickly and frantically. Then it was quiet. Startled by the sudden silence, one of the Mexican escorts looked over and noticed that Yellow Feather was now only looking out the window and weeping. "What's wrong with him?" the escort asked. "It is our custom," replied one of the other Quechan, "to recall who we are and where we come from as we travel through our lands. Landmarks, such as the Coyote's Blood Cliffs or the Cactus Giant, have stories attached to them, which we tell as we travel by them. This not only helps us to remember who we are, but it is also an honor to the spirits who inhabit each place. Yellow Feather cries because the locomotive travels so fast that it is impossible for him to remember himself."

Technology and Change. Technology has always been an agent of change. Typically, "technology" refers to the application of an idea to a particular problem. In other words, technology solves problems. When a weight needs to be lifted but is too heavy for a human to lift alone, perhaps a lever and fulcrum may be applied to the weight to shift it. The lever, as simple as it is, constitutes "technology" because it solves the problem of how to move a heavy weight. For the same reason, using a sharp rock to scrape the hair from a hide or tying a piece of leather to one's forearm to prevent chafing from a bowstring are also technologies. It is important to understand, however, that when a particular technology solves a particular problem, new problems frequently arise from the solution. In the story above, Yellow Feather solves the problem of taking weeks to travel to Mexico City for an important meeting by agreeing to go by train; but because the train moves so quickly, Yellow Feather must forgo the ancient tribal custom of geographic storytelling.

The application of technology accomplishes several things simultaneously. First, it makes living easier in some way— since it solves a problem—though it can make other aspects of life more difficult. Second, technology helps humans control their environment. By building huts with mud-covered stone, many Native Americans were able to keep cool in the heat and warm in the cold. By cutting channels from rivers to farm fields with specially made stone tools, agriculturally based Indians were able to irrigate land that would otherwise have been unusable. Third, technology changes people's relationship with the environment. An undesirable environment—dry soil, predators, clay that makes fragile pottery—can be changed with irrigation ditches, bows and arrows, and fiber-tempered clay. Finally, technology changes people's relationship with others. Perhaps a member of a tribe discovers that a harpoon point that rotates freely on the end of its shaft is a more effective weapon for hunting seals than a harpoon with a fixed point. That inventor may become greatly admired among the tribe, and on a more extended level, that tribe may come to be more respected, or despised, by other neighboring tribes. Thus, technology initiates change in both obvious and desirable ways, and in ways unexpected and sometimes disastrous. For both pre- and post-contact Native Americans, the most significant technological developments were made in five general areas: tools, hunting and gathering, agriculture, battle gear, and transportation.

Pre-contact Influences—Tools. Technology, by its nature, requires tools. For pre-contact Native Americans, tools were often as simple as specially shaped stones, bones, and wood. With these materials, hand axes, scrapers, hammers, chisels, files, grinders, and knives were made. As the tools were improved, so were the crafts that they helped make. A good tool can help a craftsperson make an even better tool, which, in turn, can help make the craftspeople develop better technology. For example, early North American spears were tipped with stones that were somewhat sharp, though their characteristics were not uniform because stone-shaping was difficult. To offset the weight of the stone points, hunters used long, heavy shafts; these ensured a more controlled flight. The drawback with these early spears was that because they were so cumbersome, they were difficult to carry and throw, especially in a forest or with heavy garments on. Eventually, hunters found that a dull-pointed piece of bone could flake off small pieces of a stone much more easily than a piece of rock, which had been their previous tool. Using the bone tool, they found that they could better control the shaping of a stone, which subsequently allowed them to make smaller, lighter, and sharper blades than before. This meant that spears and arrows could be lighter, and so could travel farther, and were more deadly.

Hunting and Gathering. North American natives originally drew their sustenance from hunting and gathering food that grew in the wild. Crudely made stone axes and knives were in use more than seventy thousand years ago for activities such as scraping and cutting hides, stripping the bark from branches, and chipping other stones into new tools. By the 1500's, Native Americans were using their tools to design and build complex equipment that helped to make their lives easier. They were perfecting stone arrow and spear points and shafts for maximum penetration; they were experimenting with improved nets and weirs, and were developing highly efficient traps and snares; they were inventing new ways to prepare foods, including stone ovens and nonmetallic containers that could contain and store hot liquids; they were developing airtight and waterproof baskets; and they were becoming increasingly aware of how best to protect themselves from the elements using a combination of natural fibers and leather. These improvements were changing the Native Americans.

Provided that the natural resources were available, hunting and gathering became more effective and efficient: With a bow and arrow, a hunter's stealth becomes less important than his or her accuracy with the weapon. Airtight containers meant food could be preserved longer, making wandering tribes less dependent on locating wild crops. Better garments meant fewer injuries, which meant more healthy workers to help support the tribe. All of these technological improvements created new problems, such as having too many healthy, hungry people for a given area to support and migration delays that resulted in the people arriving late to areas and finding that the region's food had rotted and that the game had already migrated or hibernated.

Agriculture. Many anthropologists attribute the waxing of Native American agriculture and the waning of hunter-gatherer societies to technological development. According to this theory, as tools, weapons, and pottery became more effective, it became less necessary for the people to wander from location to location looking for food. With their improved tools, it was now easier to stay in one place, harvesting the local crops and hunting the local animals, and storing the surplus for difficult times. By developing ways of planting and irrigating soil, that is, by controlling their environment, the agriculturally inclined Native Americans were better able to control their food supplies, and thus their lives. As their technology improved, they became less subject to the whims of nature.

Battle Gear. As in any other culture, desperation, envy, jealousy, and greed often compelled Native American neighbors to fight with each other, sometimes quite ruthlessly. The tools of war were developed along with hunting tools and weapons. Wooden and leather shields were constructed to protect against arrows and spears. Arrow tips were designed to pierce the new shields, as were more powerful bows. Stories abound as to the power of these weapons, one of the most telling being found in a nineteenth century diary that describes a man's skull suspended from a tree trunk and held in place by a single deeply embedded arrow piercing both sides of the bony cranium. Simple forms of body armor and helmets were developed by some tribes to protect them in battle from throwing knives, throwing sticks, and clubs. Like other technologies, the development of weapons was self-perpetuating. Curved arrow shafts gave way to artificially straightened arrow shafts that dramatically improved the arrow's flight and the archer's accuracy. Spears went from being heavy and short-ranged to being lighter and having more range. Even in these early times there was an arms race.

Transport. Because other developing technologies were encouraging the transformation of the hunter-gatherer into a farmer, the technologies involving transportation remained fairly undeveloped in pre-contact times. The primary means of getting around were by foot, raft, and canoe. Improved footwear in the form of sandals, moccasins, and boots made foot travel more comfortable. This comfort made the traversal of longer distances and difficult terrain more possible. Pre-contact rafts, usually fashioned from logs and branches lashed together with vine and water weeds, were more often grasped than ridden. More often than transporting people, rafts carried supplies. Canoes at this time were mainly hollowed-out tree trunks, sometimes with an outrigger for stability. In general, a tribe's transport by land or water increased its contact with other people, environments, and customs. This created situations that were sometimes complementary and sometimes hostile.

Post-contact Influences. After 1500 C.E., Native American technology changed more than it had in the previous fifty thousand years. Along with the technological changes, there were also tremendous social and cultural changes. The primary catalysts for these changes were the Europeans, who, having discovered the "new world," were now enduring danger and hardship to explore it and claim it as their own. As they encountered Native Americans, they sought to "civilize" them by encouraging them in more or less hostile ways to abandon their natural developmental process and to adopt a way of living, technologically speaking, that was hundreds of years in the Native American's future. After contact, Native American technological changes were not so much developmental as they were adoptive.

As trade began between the Europeans and the natives, stone knives and axes gave way to the metal knives and axes that were more easily handled and that could hold a sharper edge better. Iron and steel tools, such as chisels and plows, became highly desirable among the tribes, especially among those that were quickly adopting European ways of life.

While early European guns were inferior to bows and arrows both for hunting and warfare, their foreignness, complexity, and loudness impressed Native Americans. Oral and written accounts of how natives used guns suggest that, prior to the development of a reliable repeating rifle, natives used guns as symbols of their wealth, rather than as weapons; it required many supplies to trade for a single firearm, and more still to get the lead and black powder to fire it. Frontier journals indicate that a skilled archer could powerfully and accurately shoot at least ten arrows in the time it took an early rifler to shoot once, reload, and fire again.

The development of railroads and commercial waterways also changed the ways of Native Americans, especially since both of these transportational technologies helped bring in more invaders. Eventually, Native Americans learned to distrust the European Americans, who with increasing frequency broke treaties and invaded their lands with large machines.

In the nineteenth and twentieth centuries, the technologies that govern natural resources became particularly important for Native Americans. For more than a century, Native Americans have fought for the right to exploit the natural resources that exist on their lands but that are being stolen by European American technologies such as dams, artificially made canals, oil drilling, strip mining, and timbering. Using legal and political power, contemporary Native Americans are slowly regaining some of the rights over the oil under their land, the ores in their mountains, and the waters that flow through their land.

Technology allows people to solve problems and to dominate particular forces. When the Europeans came to North America with their more advanced technologies, Native Americans were often awed, impressed, and afraid. In the diaries and journals written on the early American frontier by Europeans making their way through "Indian country," one gets the sense that, for these invaders, the Native Americans were the problem to be solved. The old saying, "The pen is mightier than the sword" is particularly relevant to the issue of Native American technology, because with both of these technologies—the pen that wrote treaties never meant to be kept, that wrote bills of sale for millions of acres of land for a few supplies, that signed away the children of illiterate Native American parents to European mission schools; and the sword, which was brought to bear on natives who would not cooperate with the pen—the European invaders dominated all of North America, ultimately changing the oldest inhabitants on the continent into one of the most oppressed peoples in the Western Hemisphere.   —*Kenneth S. McAllister*

See also Agriculture; Baskets and basketry; Fish and fishing; Food preparation and cooking; Irrigation; Metalwork; Pottery; Subsistence; Tools; Transportation modes; Weapons; Weaving; Weirs and traps.

BIBLIOGRAPHY

Ambler, Marjane. *Breaking the Iron Bonds: Indian Control of Energy Development.* Lawrence: University Press of Kansas, 1990. A well-researched and developed book that introduces the history of federal Native American policies, particularly those that relate to reservation energy development. Includes numerous illustrations, maps, and tables, as well as an excellent bibliography and index.

Browman, David L., ed. *Early Native Americans: Prehistoric Demography, Economy, and Technology.* New York: Mouton, 1980. An anthology of articles with varying perspectives addressing the issues surrounding the entry and early technological development of human beings in North America. Many excellent photographs, charts, and time lines, along with an index of names and an index of subjects.

Johnson, Jay K., and Carol A. Morrow, eds. *The Organization of Core Technology.* Boulder, Colo.: Westview Press, 1987. A collection of essays that reexamine the way that tool manufacturing developed in North and Central America up to the contact period. Several dozen tables detail locations, materials, and types of early tools.

Laubin, Reginald, and Gladys Laubin. Photographs by Gladys Laubin. Drawings by Reginald Laubin. *American Indian Archery.* Norman: University of Oklahoma Press, 1980. An engagingly written book about bows, arrows, spears, and darts that combines scholarship and anecdote. Includes both black-and-white and color photographs along with numerous drawings, a bibliography, and an index.

Sassaman, Kenneth E. *Early Pottery in the Southeast: Tradition and Innovation in Cooking Technology.* Tuscaloosa: University of Alabama Press, 1993. A book that discusses the socio-economic and political importance of early pottery and cooking technology, refuting long-held interpretations about the significance of these technologies on the Native Americans' change from hunters and gatherers to farmers. A lengthy bibliography and an index.

Van Buren, G. E. *Arrowheads and Projectile Points: With a Classification Guide for Lithic Artifacts*. Garden Grove, Calif.: Arrowhead, 1974. Basically intended for field researchers, this book details a system by which stone tools can be correctly identified and archived. There are many excellent photographs and drawings of tools such as scrapers, arrow points, and spear heads, as well as historical and formative information about them. Contains a bibliography and index.

Tecumseh (1768, Old Piqua, a Shawnee village on the Mad River in western Ohio—Oct. 5, 1813, near Moraviantown in modern Ontario, Canada: Chief

TRIBAL AFFILIATION: Shawnee

SIGNIFICANCE: Tecumseh was one of the first Indian leaders to attempt (and, to a degree, succeed in) the forging of an alliance among all Indians to resist the westward expansion of white settlements in North America

During the autumn of 1768, a Creek woman named Methoataske (Turtle Laying Eggs) gave birth to her fifth child in a Shawnee village in western Ohio near modern Chillicothe. She named the boy Tecumseh, which means "shooting star" in the Shawnee language. Her husband, Puckeshinwa, a Shawnee war chief, had married her during the French and Indian War (1756-1763). Methoataske subsequently bore her husband four more children.

Puckeshinwa died in battle during Pontiac's Rebellion in 1774. Tecumseh's oldest brother, Chiksika, attempted to provide for the family, but Methoataske often had to rely on the charity of her husband's kinsmen to survive. When the American Revolution began in 1776, Shawnee warriors participated in raids on U.S. settlements in Kentucky, provoking a war between U.S. citizens and the Shawnee. Many Shawnee subsequently moved west to avoid the horrors of war. Methoataske and her youngest children joined an exodus of more than one thousand Shawnee to southeastern Missouri. Tecumseh and his older siblings remained in Ohio, where they were cared for by their older sister, Tecumpease, and her husband.

Tecumseh grew to manhood during a turbulent time in his tribe's history. In the period between 1780 and 1782, George Rogers Clark led two U.S. military expeditions against the Indian villages along the Mad and Great Miami rivers. In 1782, the Shawnee joined with other tribes to defeat a U.S. military attack led by Colonel William Crawford, with the Americans suffering large losses. In alliance with the British, the Shawnee also participated in an invasion of Kentucky in 1782. Growing to manhood during the turmoil of war profoundly influenced Tecumseh's subsequent development. The prolonged struggle magnified the importance of war chiefs and warriors among the Shawnee. Tecumseh, at the age of fourteen, took part in several of the battles against the Americans in 1782-1783.

After the revolutionary war, the U.S. government concluded a series of treaties (of questionable legality) with minor Indian chiefs which transferred much Shawnee land in Ohio to the U.S. government. Many Shawnee leaders refused to recognize

Tecumseh led a pantribal alliance that attempted to resist westward white expansion. (Library of Congress)

the legitimacy of the treaties and resisted white settlement in the region by force. Tecumseh took part in the numerous raids on white settlements, usually in war parties led by Chiksika. Chiksika died from wounds he received in one of those raids (this one in Tennessee) in 1787. Most of the Shawnee returned to Ohio after Chiksika's death, but Tecumseh and a small band of warriors stayed in Tennessee and continued to raid white settlements. Tecumseh led the band, and his reputation as a sagacious warrior and a war chief began to grow.

Returning to Ohio in 1790, Tecumseh found that although many tribes were threatened by American expansion, they could not form a united front against their foes. As a result, the U.S. army defeated the individual tribes piecemeal, and the white frontier continued to expand westward.

In 1805, Tecumseh's younger brother, Lalawethika, fell into a trance. When he awakened, he reported that the Master of Life had shown him how the Shawnee and the other Indian tribes could rid themselves of the white man and reclaim their cultural heritage, along with their hunting grounds. The way to salvation was to give up all vestiges of the white man's culture—muskets, clothes, especially whiskey—and return to the life their fathers had lived. If they did this, the Master of Life would expel the whites and give the Indians their knowledge, which had been intended for the Indians all along.

Lalawethika took the name Tenskwatawa ("Open Door," but he was often simply called the Prophet), and his message rapidly spread widely among not only the Shawnee but all the Indian tribes in the old Northwest Territory, and even beyond. By August, 1805, Tenskwatawa and several hundred Shawnee established a village near Greenville in western Ohio. He was joined by new converts from the Senecas, Wyandots, and Ottawas. The Prophet's message formed the basis for the first great American Indian revitalization movement, which eventually galvanized most of the major Indian tribes in the Ohio River valley, and many beyond.

Tecumseh at first played a role subordinate to the Prophet in the revitalization movement, content to allow his brother to unify the tribes under the aegis of the new religion. During the ensuing seven years, Tenskwatawa established a new center for his growing millennial movement at Prophetstown in western Ohio, where he was joined by converts from as far away as Iowa and Canada. Among the converts were many war chiefs and warriors who hoped the Prophet would lead them in a successful war against the Americans. Tenskwatawa was no warrior, however, and Tecumseh often spoke for him in strategy-planning sessions.

As the war of 1812 approached, Tecumseh began attempting to forge the growing Indian religious unity into political and military unity. Allying himself with the British, Tecumseh secured promises of military support from all the surrounding tribes and more distant tribes, including the Creeks. Alarmed at Tecumseh's activities, the U.S. government dispatched William Henry Harrison with a large force of regular and militia troops to Prophetstown to disperse the leadership of the Indian movement. Tecumseh was absent in 1812 when Harrison's men defeated the Indians at the Battle of Tippecanoe. Tenskwatawa's ineffective leadership in the battle led to his permanent decline in influence among the Indians. Tecumseh became the unquestioned leader of the Indian movement.

Despite some initial successes against the Americans, the Indians and the British ultimately found themselves pushed out of the United States by the Americans. Many of Tecumseh's Indian allies deserted him as the war wore on, and the promised aid from the British was always inadequate and slow in coming. Attempting to resist Harrison's invasion of Canada during the autumn of 1813, the British and Indians suffered an overwhelming defeat at the Battle of Thames, northeast of Detroit. After the British fled the battlefield, Tecumseh suffered a mortal wound. Without him, the Indian movement withered away and disappeared. *—Paul Madden*

See also Fallen Timbers, Battle of; Fort Greenville, Treaty of; Fort Mims, Battle of; Northwest Ordinance; Shawnee; Tecumseh's Rebellion; Tenskwatawa; Thames, Battle of the; Tippecanoe, Battle of.

BIBLIOGRAPHY

Edmunds, R. David. *Tecumseh and the Quest for Indian Leadership*. Boston: Little, Brown, 1984.

Gilpin, Alec. *The War of 1812 in the Old Northwest*. East Lansing: Michigan State University Press, 1958.

Klinck, Carl F., ed. *Tecumseh: Fact and Fiction in Early Records*. Englewood Cliffs, N.J.: Doubleday, 1961.

Oskison, John. *Tecumseh and His Times*. New York: W. W. Norton, 1938.

Tucker, Glenn. *Tecumseh: Vision of Glory*. Indianapolis: Bobbs-Merrill, 1956.

Tecumseh's Rebellion

DATE: 1809-1811

PLACE: Old Northwest (Great Lakes region)

TRIBES AFFECTED: Tribes of the Old Northwest

SIGNIFICANCE: Tecumseh, a powerful advocate of united Indian resistance to American encroachments onto Indian lands east of the Mississippi River, led what many believe was the last great hope for effective Indian opposition to the advance of the European American frontier in the eastern portion of the United States

Soon after the conclusion of the Treaty of Fort Greenville in 1795, frontiersmen, land speculators, and settlers surged into the newly opened lands and beyond into Indian country, thereby exacerbating tensions with the tribes. As pressure mounted for further expansion beyond the line delimited under the terms of the Treaty of Fort Greenville, the governor of the new Indiana Territory, William Henry Harrison, inaugurated a policy designed to acquire additional territory from the Indians incrementally. Hence, between 1802 and 1809, Harrison and Governor William Hull of the Michigan Territory concluded a series of treaties under the terms of which a significant portion of the area between the Great Lakes, the Ohio River, and the Mississippi River were opened for settlement. As the white settlers pressed against the Indians from the south and east, the tribes north of the Ohio Valley were simultaneously pressed from the west by the expansive Chippewa and Sioux in the upper Mississippi region. Hence, under vicelike pressure from several directions, the tribes increasingly concluded that they would have to coordinate their policies and be prepared to fight or perish.

Indian Resistance. Tecumseh and his brother, the Shawnee Prophet (Tenskwatawa), emerged determined to preserve the identity and territorial integrity of the tribes and their lands in the region between the Great Lakes and the Ohio River Valley. Tecumseh maintained that the Americans had been successful in depriving the Indians of their lands because the tribes had consistently failed to stand unified against external encroachments. Hence, he argued that the tribes must create a meaningful confederation and agree not to cede additional lands to the United States without the concurrence of all the tribes in the union. Only in this way could the tribes negotiate with the Americans from a position of strength. Moreover, Tecumseh and his brother called upon the Indians to purge themselves of corrupting influences, such as alcohol, and return to traditional ways. Finally, notwithstanding the Indian disillusionment with the British as a result of Britain's abandonment of the Indians in 1794, Tecumseh again looked to Great Britain for political and material support in his effort to coalesce effective resistance to the Americans. Indeed, because of escalating Anglo-American tensions as a result of the Chesapeake Affair of 1807, the British were more willing to extend the support sought by Tecumseh. Consequently, Tecumseh and his brother made considerable progress toward the establishment of an Indian Confederation and the renewal of Indian society.

In 1808, as momentum gathered behind Tecumseh and his new confederation, he and his brother founded Prophetstown, located near the confluence of Tippecanoe Creek and the Wabash River. The Indian leaders hoped that Prophetstown would serve as a center of the confederation movement and that from it Tecumseh and his brother could influence the policies of the tribes throughout the region bounded by the Great Lakes, the Mississippi River, and the Ohio Valley. In addition, in 1808 Tecumseh visited the British at Fort Malden, across the U.S.-Canadian border near Detroit. On this occasion, the British assured Tecumseh of their full support of the tribes' combined efforts to form a confederation and to resist further American encroachments upon their lands. The British authorities, however, urged the Indian leaders not to be the ones to initiate hostilities along the frontier.

As a result of continued efforts by American authorities to detach additional Indian lands (culminating in the Treaty of Fort Wayne in 1809), American intransigence concerning the implementation of the various treaties negotiated since the Treaty of Fort Greenville, and, finally, continued encroachment by American frontiersmen into Indian territory, hostilities again erupted along the frontier in 1810. Both Tecumseh and the British attempted to ameliorate the crisis, but radical elements among the tribes pressed for more aggressive military action against the Americans.

During the summer of 1811, Tecumseh traveled south of the Ohio River in an effort to enlist the support of the Creek, Cherokee, and Choctaw tribes. The Creeks expressed support for Tecumseh, but Cherokee and Choctaw leaders were reluctant to take actions that might provoke open warfare with the United States government.

Tippecanoe. With Tecumseh absent from his center of power north of the Ohio, Harrison decided to avail himself of the opportunity and attack the geographic heart of the confederation movement—Prophetstown. By November 6, 1811, Harrison's force had moved to a position less than a mile from Prophetstown. The following day, on November 7, as Harrison had hoped, the Indians, unrestrained because of Tecumseh's absence, attacked the American force and were severely defeated amid heavy fighting. Following this costly victory at the Battle of Tippecanoe, Harrison's force destroyed Prophetstown before returning to their base of operations at Vincennes.

Following the Tippecanoe Campaign, the frontier war continued; eventually it was submerged in the context of the greater struggle between the United States and Great Britain in the War of 1812. Tecumseh was killed at the Battle of the Thames on October 5, 1813. In many respects, the death of this great Indian leader marked the end of the last real hope of effective Indian resistance to American settlement east of the Mississippi and the extinction of the traditional Indian culture in the eastern portion of the United States.   —Howard M. Hensel

See also Fallen Timbers, Battle of; Fort Greenville, Treaty of; Fort Mims, Battle of; Fort Wayne, Treaty of; Northwest Ordinance; Shawnee; Tecumseh; Tenskwatawa; Thames, Battle of the; Tippecanoe, Battle of.

BIBLIOGRAPHY
Billington, Ray Allen. *Westward Expansion*. New York: Macmillan, 1949.
Philbrick, Francis S. *The Rise of the West, 1754-1830*. New York: Harper & Row, 1965.
Prucha, Francis Paul. *The Sword of the Republic*. New York: Macmillan, 1969.
Tucker, Glenn. *Tecumseh: Vision of Glory*. Indianapolis: Bobbs-Merrill, 1956.

Teedyuscung (c. 1705, near present-day Trenton, N.J.— 1763, Wajomick, Pa.): Tribal leader, orator
TRIBAL AFFILIATION: Lenni Lenape (Delaware)
SIGNIFICANCE: Teedyuscung was an eloquent defender of Indian land rights
Teedyuscung's career was one of opposition to white English encroachment on Indian lands. He was born in New Jersey, where he lived in a small Lenni Lenape community. Encroaching English settlement led the group, in about 1730, to move to the Delaware River valley in eastern Pennsylvania. Along with other Indians, Teedyuscung protested the unfairness of the Walking Purchase of 1737 under which Pennsylvania seized land from the Indians. Complicating the Lenni Lenape claims to the land were land grants made by the Iroquois, who claimed the smaller tribe as their subjects.

Teedyuscung was converted to Christianity by Moravian missionaries, but he later gave up his involvement in the church to take up duties as war chief against the Iroquois. In 1754 the Lenni Lenape were expelled, with Iroquois cooperation, to Wyoming, near Wilkes-Barre. During the Seven Years' War (1755-1763), Teedyuscung was a leader of a group of warriors from several tribes living in Wyoming. Teedyuscung appeared at a number of important meetings, including the Albany Conference of 1754. He became a symbol of the unfairness of proprietary policy toward Indian land rights, and his speeches were published by Benjamin Franklin. While opposing settlement of the northeast Pennsylvania frontier, Teedyuscung was burned to death at home in Wyoming, likely a victim of arson/murder by land speculators.

See also Lenni Lenape.

Tekakwitha, Kateri (c. 1656, near present-day Auriesville, N.Y.—Apr. 17, 1680, near Montreal, Canada): Indian nun
ALSO KNOWN AS: Catherine Tagaskouita, Tegakwith (She Pushes with Her Hands)
TRIBAL AFFILIATION: Mohawk
SIGNIFICANCE: Tekakwitha, the first Indian nun, was beatified by the Vatican in 1980
Born of a Mohawk man and a Christian woman of the Erie tribe who had been taken captive by Mohawks, Tekakwitha was orphaned at the age of four as a result of a smallpox epidemic. The epidemic almost claimed her as well, and the disease left her with a scarred face and failing eyesight. She was reared by extended family members in a Mohawk village

in present-day upstate New York. Some family members were opposed to Christianity, while others espoused it. Tekakwitha became entangled in this conflict because she had desired to practice Christianity, but family members arranged a marriage for her with an anti-Christian young man.

She rebelled by escaping from her village and traveling north to the budding Catholic Mohawk community of Kahnawake, along the St. Lawrence River. Once there, she was baptized and became known for her extreme devotion to Christianity, excessive self-mortification, fasting, and other forms of penance. Tekakwitha also ministered to the needs of the sick and elderly at Kahnawake, and, along with several other young women, desired to form a convent. The Jesuit missionaries did not allow them to do this, but they did permit Tekakwitha to take a "vow of perpetual chastity." Her health failing, the young woman died prematurely on April 17, 1680 according to Jesuit legend, while uttering the names of Jesus and Mary. It is also said that shortly after her death, her pock-marked faced became beautiful and miracles were performed in her name. There soon developed a devotion to her not only among Catholic Mohawks but also among French colonists in the adjacent communities.

Her birth and death places became pilgrimage sites, and by the end of the twentieth century, she had achieved the status of "Blessed Kateri Tekakwitha" within the Catholic Church. She is a source of empowerment for many Indians who adhere to Catholicism. More than fifty biographies of her have been written, in at least ten languages, along with several plays, operas, films, and countless devotional tracts. The Kateri Conference is an annual meeting of Catholic Native Americans that draws thousands from all over North America.

See also Indian-white relations—French colonial; Missions and missionaries; Mohawk.

Ten Bears (1792, southern Great Plains—Nov. 23, 1872, near Fort Sill, Okla.): Tribal chief

ALSO KNOWN AS: Parra-Wa-Samen
TRIBAL AFFILIATION: Comanche
SIGNIFICANCE: Ten Bears led efforts to preserve peace between the Comanche and white settlers moving into Comanche territory

A member of the Yamparika Comanche, Ten Bears was born south of the Arkansas River on the wide southern Plains. By 1860, when conflicts were beginning between the Comanche and white settlers, Ten Bears was a chief and spokesman for his people. His peacemaking twice took him to Washington, D.C.

Ten Bears' most famous speech, a masterpiece of oratory, was delivered in 1867 at the Council of Medicine Lodge Creek in Barber County, Kansas. He forcefully defended the Comanche, declaring that most conflicts were initiated by U.S. soldiers. The most emotional part of the address was Ten Bears' appeal that the Comanche be allowed to live as their ancestors had lived—on the open plains, unrestricted by walls or fences. The treaty signed at the conclusion of the council,

however, the last treaty ever made with the Comanche, restricted them to a reservation.

In 1872, Ten Bears made his second visit to Washington, D.C. He attended a reception given by President Ulysses S. Grant. The conclusion of the visit again brought sorrow to the Comanche and disgrace to their aged spokesman. The order was given, and agreed to by Ten Bears, that all Comanche temporarily move to within ten miles of Fort Sill, Oklahoma.

Soon after his return, Ten Bears died at the age of eighty at the reservation near Fort Sill. After a life of service to the Comanche, he had been abandoned by all except his son.

See also Comanche; Indian-white relations—U.S., 1831-1870; Isatai; Medicine Lodge, Treaties of; Oratory.

Tendoy (c. 1834, Boise River area in Idaho—1907, Fort Hall, Idaho): Chief, trader, negotiator

TRIBAL AFFILIATION: Bannock
SIGNIFICANCE: Tendoy influenced his people to work peaceably with the white settlers of Wyoming

When his father, Kontakayak, a Bannock war chief, died in combat with the Blackfoot, Tendoy (The Climber) became war chief of the Lemhi Bannock band. An ally of Washakie, to whom he was related, on his mother's side, Tendoy believed in accommodating white settlement in the highlands of what would become Wyoming.

Unlike many Bannocks, who became destitute with the demise of their hunting economy, Tendoy and his band prospered by maintaining a trading relationship with white settlers, miners, and others. Even during the Nez Perce War, he maintained that his people would prosper by seeking accommodation. In February, 1875, President Grant issued an order allowing the Lemhi Bannocks to remain on their ancestral lands. In 1892, however, they were removed to Fort Hall, Idaho. After Tendoy died there, local residents built a monument in his honor.

See also Bannock; Nez Perce War.

Tenino: Tribe

CULTURE AREA: Plateau
LANGUAGE GROUP: Sahaptian
PRIMARY LOCATION: Oregon

The Tenino (also known as the Warm Springs tribe), a branch of the Sahaptian family, originally occupied the valley of the Des Chutes River in Oregon. As is generally true for the Sahaptian tribes, there is no ethnographic evidence or traditional lore to show where the Tenino lived earlier than their first encounter with white explorers and traders in the early 1800's. Sahaptian tribes lived in village communities of varying size. Because they relied on hunting and fishing—salmon was a chief staple of their diet—as well as on gathering roots and berries, they were forced to move throughout the year to find food in different seasons. This necessity prevented the villages from growing and developing as political or social centers over time. Sahaptian tribes do not seem to have relied on agriculture. They were skilled with horses and used them in their travels seeking food. For the most part, Sahaptian tribes dealt peacefully with their neighbors and with white settlers—largely because of the refusal of the Sahaptian to engage in violent retaliation for ill treatment. There is no record of any major battles between the Tenino and whites. Under the terms of the Wasco Treaty of 1855, the Tenino were placed on the Warm Springs Reservation in Oregon, along with the Tyigh and other tribes. Their population as a separate group has not been counted since.

See also Plateau; Tyigh.

Tenochtitlán: City

DATE: c. 1300-1521
LOCATION: Present-day Mexico City
CULTURE AFFECTED: Aztec

Tenochtitlán was the capital city of the ancient Aztec empire, which extended from the Valley of Mexico to the shores of the Gulf of Mexico on the east, the Pacific on the west, and northern Guatemala on the south. Tenochtitlán so impressed the Spanish soldier Bernál Díaz de Castillo, who entered the city with Hernán Cortés, that he claimed it was larger than any European city of the sixteenth century.

With a population of about 150,000 by 1519, Tenochtitlán was indeed larger than Venice or London. The city grew from modest beginnings, however; it began as a lump of mud in the shallow lake that filled much of the Valley of Mexico. The Aztecs, or Mexica as they called themselves, were latecomers

to the valley, and they were driven to this sanctuary by the already established tribes which lived along the shores of the lake. Later, Aztec mythology would claim that the wandering tribe found this site through a prophecy. They were told that their wanderings would cease when they beheld an eagle sitting on a cactus, eating a snake. The city's name, Tenochtitlán, means "place of the cactus" in Nahuatl, the Aztec language. This symbol, now depicted on the flag of Mexico, reflects the greatness that the Aztecs would obtain.

Tenochtitlán was located on an island; it was a water city, divided by hundreds of canals and waterways. As the city grew and more dry land emerged, these canals provided a means of transportation to the lake shore for trade as well as into the lake for fishing. Later, causeways were built and bridges constructed. The neighboring district of Tlatelolco, another island emerging from the lake, was joined to Tenochtitlán, and the two grew together, eventually forming a square with each side about two miles long. The central avenue connected Tenochtitlán with the lake shore, and two aqueducts brought drinking water down from the hills at Chapultepec.

In the center of the city were the main temples and the house of the emperor. The greatest temple was that of the Aztec war god, Huitzilopochtli, at which human sacrifices were offered regularly. There were also temples to the gods Quetzalcóatl and Tezcatlipoca as well as a school for the nobility's sons. The palace of the emperor served both as his residence and as the administrative center of the empire. The palace had two

The Great Temple of the Aztecs' capital city, Tenochtitlán, as reconstructed by Ignacio Marquina. (American Museum of Natural History)

stories. On the upper level were the rooms of the ruler's family. The ground floor contained administrative offices, along with the treasury, storehouses, and rooms for servants.

The Aztec capital held many urban amenities. There were zoos and aviaries, and markets where numerous items could be purchased. Corn, fruit, beans, and peppers were sold in one location; elsewhere, there were skins and cloth. Prepared foods were available, and there was a place for craftsmen who worked with bricks, wood, precious stones, and feathers. Although now buried beneath modern Mexico City, Tenochtitlán was the greatest metropolis of the Americas until it was largely destroyed by the Spanish in 1521.

See also Aztec; Pochteca; Teotihuacán.

Tenskwatawa (Mar. 1768, Piqua, Ohio—Nov., 1837, Argentine, Kans.): Prophet
ALSO KNOWN AS: Lalawethika (the Rattle), the Shawnee Prophet
TRIBAL AFFILIATION: Shawnee
SIGNIFICANCE: Tenskwatawa led a spiritual and cultural revival among the tribes of the Old Northwest during the first decade of the nineteenth century

Tenskwatawa was one of two surviving triplets born to Methoataske several months after his father Puckeshinwa was killed at the battle of Point Pleasant (October, 1774). Puckeshinwa was a great war chief of the Kispokotha Shawnee. In his youth, Tenskwatawa was known as Lalawethika ("the Rattle") because of his excessive boasting. He was blind in one eye because of a childhood accident. As a young man, Lalawethika was given to drunken sloth.

He accompanied his brother Tecumseh to Fallen Timbers (1794) to fight against the American army of Anthony Wayne. In the years after the Indian defeat at Fallen Timbers, Lalawethika was trained in magic and medicine by Penagasha. In April, 1805, Lalawethika fainted in his lodge. When he recovered, he began to preach a new gospel given to him by the Master of Life.

Taking the name Tenskwatawa ("the Open Door"), he urged all Indians to renounce whiskey, sexual promiscuity, and the technology of European Americans. He advocated a return to the communal life of his Shawnee ancestors. Tenskwatawa's reputation was greatly enhanced when he successfully predicted a solar eclipse on June 16, 1806.

From 1804 until 1811, agents of the U.S. government negotiated numerous treaties with various tribes of the Old Northwest, under which the government purchased millions of acres of Indian land. Tenskwatawa and his brother Tecumseh challenged the validity of the treaties.

Indiana Governor William Henry Harrison became increasingly concerned about the growing strength of the intertribal cultural revival being led by Tenskwatawa. The Shawnee Prophet attracted followers from many Indian nations to his village Prophetstown, on the banks of the Wabash River. Convinced that Tenskwatawa and Tecumseh posed a real threat to European American interests on the frontier, Harrison raised an army and marched to Prophetstown. Harrison arrived near the Indian village while Tecumseh was on a southern journey. Tenskwa-

tawa encouraged his multitribal army to strike first. He promised them that the power of his magic would lead to victory.

The Indians struck the American army in the predawn hours of November 7, 1811. After hours of fierce fighting, they were defeated in what came to be known as the Battle of Tippecanoe. Following the battle, Prophetstown was burned, and Tenskwatawa was discredited as a religious leader.

During the first year of the War of 1812, Tenskwatawa attempted to continue to live with a small band of followers in the Wabash River Valley. American pressure forced him to flee to Canada. The defeat of the British and the death of Tecumseh shattered any hope of revitalizing Tenskwatawa's cultural movement.

Tenskwatawa lived in Canada until 1825, when he returned to live among the Ohio Shawnee. He aided Governor Lewis Cass of the Michigan Territory in his efforts to convince the Ohio Shawnee to move west across the Mississippi. In 1827, he established his home on the Shawnee Reservation in Kansas, where he lived out the remainder of his life.

See also Fort Wayne, Treaty of; Tecumseh; Tecumseh's Rebellion; Thames, Battle of the; Tippecanoe, Battle of.

Teotihuacán: City, civilization
DATE: 200 B.C.E.-750 C.E.
LOCATION: Highland Mexico north of Mexico City
CULTURES AFFECTED: Teotihuacán, Toltec

From beginnings at 200 B.C.E., Teotihuacán expanded between 1 and 600 C.E. to become the largest urban center in North America, with a population between 125,000 and 200,000. Located in the central Mexican highlands north of Mexico City, Teotihuacán was the focus of a major archaeological project directed by René Millon in the 1960's. Teotihuacán includes 20 square kilometers (nearly 8 square miles) of buildings laid out on a grid, dominated by the Street of the Dead. The Pyramid of the Moon at the north end, the larger Pyramid of the Sun nearby on the east side, and the Great Ciudadela (Citadel) and Great Compound at the city core dominate the Street of the Dead, which is lined by some seventy-five temples for 2 kilometers.

Teotihuacán rose to prominence by control of an irrigation system and control of production and distribution of obsidian artifacts from Pachuca, Mesoamerica's only source of green obsidian, 50 kilometers (31 miles) to the north. Most Teotihuacanos lived in about two thousand apartment compounds associated with more than six hundred specialized craft workshops, mainly for production of obsidian artifacts for local use, regional exchange, and long-distance trade. Teotihuacán had declined by 750 with the rise of other civilizations and its loss of control of obsidian production and distribution.

See also Monte Albán; Toltec.

Termination policy
DATE: 1953-1962
TRIBES AFFECTED: 109 tribes and bands in eight states
SIGNIFICANCE: The attempt by the United States government to dissolve Indian tribes and end its trust relationship with

Indians ended in failure and increased Indian suspicion of federal policy

After World War II, federal Indian policy moved away from the support of tribal self-determination that had characterized the Indian New Deal and returned to assimilation as a goal. Supporters of the change in course argued that Indians should be "freed" from the federal government's control and treated like other citizens. In addition, the Hoover Commission on government efficiency recommended in 1947 that the United States get out of the business of providing special services to Native Americans. Tribes were seen as barriers to assimilation, while their communal focus made them seem communistic in the context of the early Cold War.

During the early 1950's the Bureau of Indian Affairs (BIA) began to draft policies that would dissolve tribes as legal entities and merge Indians into American society. Two members of Congress provided leadership in moving termination forward: Senator Arthur Watkins of Utah and Representative E.Y. Berry of South Dakota. At their urging, Congress passed House Concurrent Resolution 108 on August 15, 1953. The resolution stated that it was the policy of Congress to end the trust relationship that had existed between the government and tribal Indians and make Native Americans subject to the same laws as other citizens.

Between 1954 and September, 1962, Congress passed twelve termination acts affecting 109 tribes and bands in eight states. Under these laws, tribal governments were scheduled for dissolution, reservation land and other assets were either divided among tribal members or put under the control of a corporation, and a date was set for the withdrawal of federal services. Tribes selected were often pressured to go along, sometimes by Congress making payment of past claims against the government contingent on termination.

In practice, termination did not succeed in mainstreaming former tribal members into American society. Instead, the policy proved bitterly unpopular with the majority of Native Americans, while the government found that increased unemployment and welfare costs offset any savings from the withdrawal of BIA services.

In addition to the economic difficulties associated with termination, many Native Americans opposed it as a threat to Indian identity. As rocky as it often was, the special relationship between the federal government and Indian tribes was an important part of Indian identity. However acculturated Indians might be, the majority viewed themselves as distinct from the general population and wanted to keep things that way.

The last termination act was passed in 1962, but by this time public opinion was turning against termination. The Menominees' well-publicized campaign to have their termination reversed succeeded in 1973 and sparked efforts by other groups. By 1991, all but a handful of tribes and bands had been restored. For most Indians, even those not affected by the policy, termination left a legacy of distrust toward the federal government that contributed to the Indian activism of the 1960's.

See also Civil rights and citizenship; Indian Claims Commission (ICC); Indian-white relations—U.S., 1934-1995; Land claims; Menominee; Public Law 280; Relocation; Urban Indians.

Texas

The term "Texas" was originally used to designate the Hasinai tribes of East Texas. It was extended from the Indians to the adjacent country and finally to the territory which became the state of Texas. The word (pronounced "techas") meant "friends" or, more technically, "allies." The name was used generically to identify the Hasinai ("our own people"), Caddo, and others who were enemies of the Apache.

The Hasinai did not use the term for themselves; it was used as a greeting. The term was apparently first written in a 1683 Spanish report which talks of the "Gran Reyno de los Texas," first identified by West Texas Indians. The Spanish misunderstood the everyday use of the term and applied it to the Hasinai, who were the largest politically organized allies that they encountered and the people identified in the early report. In the 1690's Father Francisco de Jesus María, who had lived among the Hasinai, said that the correct name of the Indians living in the upper Neches and Angelina valleys, "which in New Spain they called Texias," is "Aseney" or "Asenay." There is ample evidence from other Spanish and French sources to this effect as well, but the error persisted.

See also Caddo.

Texas Rangers

DATE: November 24, 1835 to the 1880's
TRIBES AFFECTED: Apache, Biloxi, Caddo, Cherokee, Comanche, Creek, Quapaw, Seminole, Shawnee, Tonkawa, Waco, Wichita
SIGNIFICANCE: Formed to maintain peace along the Texas border, the Texas Rangers battled with more than fifteen Indian peoples in Texas

Officially established on November 24, 1835, by the Republic of Texas, the Texas Rangers were an irregular, mounted, armed, informally disciplined body of men whose mission was to preserve the peace along a thousand miles of Texas boundary and frontier. In Texas three distinctive cultures—Mexican, Indian, and American—interacted, intertwined, and frequently clashed. This situation called for a regional force that could combat a wide range of enemies. The early Texas Rangers were plagued by drunkenness, poor discipline, and inexperience, but eventually leadership and discipline improved. Between 1835 and 1880, beginning with raids, battles, and massacres such as those at Linville, Victoria, and Plum Creek in 1840 and at the Llano in 1841, the Texas Rangers served as a major force in defeating Comanches, Apaches, and their allies as well as expelling Cherokees, Creeks, Seminoles, and other "unpacified" Indians from Texas.

See also Apache; Caddo; Comanche; Quapaw; Shawnee; Tonkawa; Victorio; Waco.

Thames, Battle of the

DATE: October 5, 1813

PLACE: Kent County, Ontario

TRIBES AFFECTED: Fox, Huron, Iroquois Confederacy, Kickapoo, Lenni Lenape, Miami, Ojibwa, Ottawa, Potawatomi, Sauk, Shawnee, Sioux, Winnebago

SIGNIFICANCE: This battle of the War of 1812 destroyed the last serious Indian resistance to American settlement in the Old Northwest and ended British influence among the Great Lakes tribes residing within U.S. territory

Never during the War of 1812 did the American Indians of the Old Northwest achieve the degree of unanimity they had in the Indian wars of the 1790's. Nevertheless, the confederacy that Tecumseh and his brother Tenskwatawa (the Prophet) forged between 1807 and 1812 constituted a formidable force when combined with the British forces operating in the Detroit River region. Inflicting a series of defeats on the Americans, especially at Mackinac Island, Chicago, and Detroit during the summer and fall of 1812, the Indian-British operations drove the Americans from the Upper Great Lakes. Indian efforts to drive the Americans across the Ohio River failed, however, when expeditions against Fort Wayne and Fort Harrison, Indiana, were repulsed. Under the leadership of Major General William Henry Harrison, the United States began a counterattack in the fall and winter of 1812-1813.

Although an advanced guard of Harrison's force met bitter defeat at the River Raisin (modern Monroe, Michigan) on January 22, 1813, the American general established an outpost known as Fort Meigs at the Maumee River rapids (modern Perrysburg, Ohio) and repelled two British-Indian assaults. More significant for Tecumseh's confederacy was the assembling at Presque Isle Bay (modern Erie, Pennsylvania) of a U.S. Navy squadron commanded by Oliver Hazard Perry. Commodore Perry's defeat and capture of a Royal Navy squadron at the battle of Lake Erie (September 10, 1813) destroyed the logistical lifeline by which the British troops and Indians in the Detroit region sustained themselves. Over the protests of Tecumseh, British Major General Henry Procter began a retreat up the Thames River in late September, with Harrison in fast pursuit. As the British withdrew from their homelands, most of Tecumseh's Indian allies deserted him.

With Harrison's army nipping at his heels, Procter decided to make a stand outside Moraviantown (modern Thamesville, Ontario) on October 5. Possibly only five hundred Indian warriors and only slightly more British soldiers were available to stop Harrison's onslaught of more than three thousand soldiers, mostly Kentucky volunteers bent on revenge for what they termed the "River Raisin massacre." Colonel (and future Vice President) Richard M. Johnson's cavalrymen broke the British line and, with Harrison's infantry, drove the redcoats and their Indian allies from the field. The British suffered twenty-eight officers and 606 men killed and captured; the Indians suffered heavily in deaths with the remainder fleeing into the woods.

Most important, Tecumseh was dead, and with him died the last attempt in the Midwest at pan-Indian unity to oppose the American settlers. At the same time the British desire to establish a neutral Indian barrier between the United States and Canada collapsed. On the other hand, the sacrifice of Tecumseh and his allies during the 1812-1813 was a critical factor in preserving Upper Canada (modern Ontario) as part of British North America.

See also Tecumseh; Tecumseh's Rebellion; Tenskwatawa; Tippecanoe, Battle of.

BIBLIOGRAPHY

Allen, Robert S. *His Majesty's Indian Allies: British Indian Policy in the Defence of Canada, 1774-1815*. Toronto: Dundurn, 1993.

Dowd, Gregory Evans. *A Spirited Resistance: The North American Indian Struggle for Unity, 1745-1815*. Baltimore: Johns Hopkins University Press, 1992.

Stanley, George F. G. *The War of 1812: Land Operations*. Canadian War Museum Historical Publication No. 18. Ottawa: National Museum of Man, 1983.

Thompson: Tribe

CULTURE AREA: Plateau

LANGUAGE GROUP: Salishan

PRIMARY LOCATION: Southwestern British Columbia

POPULATION SIZE: 3,925 ("Ntlakapamux," Statistics Canada, based on 1991 census)

The Thompson, a large branch of the Salishan, lived along the Fraser, Thompson and Nicola rivers in southwestern British Columbia. They called themselves Ntlakyapamuk, whose meaning is unknown. They lived in scattered villages along the rivers. The Lower Thompson, who lived at the lower end of the Fraser, were divided into several small bands. The Upper Thompson were divided into four bands, the largest of which was the Nicola. These bands, made up of related families, lived mostly independently. Each had a hereditary chief, who had little authority. A central council of older men made decisions for the tribe. The Thompsons' primary food was fish, especially salmon, which they caught with spears, nets, and traps. Men hunted bear, deer, elk, beaver, and caribou, while women worked to preserve the meat and to gather berries and roots. The Thompson were skilled at making and using birchbark canoes and snowshoes. They also made beautiful juniper bows and birchbark and cedar root baskets. Their homes in winter were circular pole frame lodges. These were half-buried in the ground for warmth and were entered through the roof. In summer, the Thompson lived in circular mat houses. They also had sweathouses for ritual use.

Their first contact with whites was probably with Simon Fraser in 1809. Within a decade, the Hudson's Bay Company established trading posts in the area. The contact and trading was at first beneficial to both sides. When gold miners arrived in 1858, however, tension led to fighting and death. In 1863, the Thompsons lost many people to a smallpox epidemic. These pressures caused a decline in population from about five thousand in 1780 to about eighteen hundred in 1906. During the twentieth century, conditions improved, and numbers increased. In the late twentieth century, many were still living in their traditional territory on several reserves. They continued to hunt, fish, and trap but added to their income with new pursuits: farming, the sale of crafts, and wage labor.

See also Diseases, post-contact; Plateau; Salishan language family; Sweatlodges and sweatbaths.

Thorpe, Jim (May 22, 1888, near Prague, Okla.—Mar. 28, 1953, Lomita, Calif.): Athlete
ALSO KNOWN AS: Wa-tho-huck (Bright Path)
TRIBAL AFFILIATION: Sauk, Fox
SIGNIFICANCE: Thorpe was one of the greatest and most versatile athletes in American history

James Francis Thorpe was born near Prague, Oklahoma. His Indian ancestry included Sauk and Potawatomi, and he was the great-grandson of Black Hawk, the great war chief of the Chippewa (Ojibwa). Thorpe was proud of his heritage.

Jim Thorpe, shown here playing football circa 1911, is considered the greatest all-around American athlete of the early twentieth century. (AP/Wide World Photos)

Jim Thorpe's athletic career began in 1908 at the Carlisle Institute in Pennsylvania under football coach Glenn "Pop" Warner. On Thorpe's second play on the varsity team, he ran 75 yards for a touchdown. Following two years of professional baseball, Thorpe returned to Carlisle for the 1911 and 1912 football season, in both of which he was a first-team All-American.

The versatility of Jim Thorpe was revealed at the 1912 Summer Olympics in Stockholm, Sweden, where he won both the pentathlon and the decathlon. Although his gold medals were taken away because of his earlier professional baseball career, they were eventually returned to his family in 1982.

After many years of professional baseball and football, Thorpe retired from athletics in 1929. He died at his home in Lomita, California, in 1953.

See also Black Hawk; Fox; Sauk.

Thule: Prehistoric tradition
DATE: c. 900-1450
LOCATION: Bering Sea, northwestern Alaska, northern Canada, islands of the Beaufort Sea, Labrador, Greenland
CULTURES AFFECTED: Aleut (Atka, Aleut, Unalaska Aleut), Inuit (Eskimo)

Archaeological evidence on the Thule tradition was assembled initially by Therkel Mathiassen, Knud Rasmussen, Henry Collins, Diamond Jenness, and James Ford between 1900 and the mid-1950's. Their studies, along with later contributions by James L. Giddings, Jr., among others, identified the principal cultural characteristics of the pre-Eskimo Thule tradition and provided it with an accurate historical context. These same archaeologists loosely borrowed the name Thule from the ancient Greek's designation of the world's northernmost lands to depict the climactic phase of late prehistoric Inuit development in the subarctic.

Excavations of sites along the Bering Strait have made possible the construction of an eight-stage chronology beginning before 2000 B.C.E. with Okvik and Old Bering Sea cultures—the Arctic small tool tradition—which were superseded by the Birnik, Punuk, and then Thule cultures. From these, in turn, arose both the Prehistoric Recent and Modern Eskimo cultures. Certainly by 900 C.E. a Thule tradition had emerged from Birnik culture in northern Alaska. Composed of an Inuit people originally living along the Bering Strait, the Thule culture was marked by a sophisticated adaptation to Arctic whaling (particularly of the bowhead whale), fishing, and seal, walrus, and caribou hunting.

Artifacts yielded by the excavation of Thule sites across thousands of miles of the subarctic include skillfully crafted, often elegant, harpoon heads, umiaks (skin boats), cutting tools, snow goggles, eating utensils, fishhooks, throwing sticks, bow drills, saws, female fetishes, and the remains of elaborate pit houses, sustaining Robert McGhee's conclusion that the Thule enjoyed an abundant, secure economy and a quality of life as rich as any other in the nonagricultural and nonindustrial world.

An extended period of climatic warming from the tenth through the fifteenth century presumably allowed Thule culture to spread rapidly eastward (during the same centuries when sustained warming allowed the Norse to move westward into Iceland and then Greenland), doubtless following whales and seals among the relatively ice-free islands and straits of the Beaufort Sea. By the eleventh century, the Thule tradition had extended itself 2,600 miles east from its origins in northern Alaska and the Bering Sea islands across subarctic Canada and into Labrador and northwestern Greenland, perhaps overlapping or displacing the indigenous Dorset culture, but more likely filling in areas vacated by the earlier collapse of the Dorset tradition. There is ample archaeological evidence that by the fifteenth century, the Thule had firmly established their culture throughout these eastern coastal regions, where some evidence indicates they encountered the Norse. There, in the east, Thule culture subsequently underwent regional adaptations or tribal specializations, from which sprang the Inuit or Eskimo culture known to historic times.

See also Architecture—Arctic; Arts and crafts—Arctic; Dorset; Prehistory—Arctic; Whales and whaling.

Tiger, Jerome R. (July 8, 1941, Tahlequah, Okla.—Aug. 13, 1967, Eufaula, Okla.): Painter
ALSO KNOWN AS: Kacha (Tiger)
TRIBAL AFFILIATION: Creek, Seminole
SIGNIFICANCE: Tiger added emotion, subtle colors, and delicate strokes to traditional Indian painting

Jerome Tiger spent his first ten years in communal living with the numerous visitors to West Eufaula Indian Baptist Church Camp. Even after moving to Muskogee, Oklahoma, his family returned often to the camp and the Creek stomp dances. At fifteen, he became head of the art department at a local business, then left school to spend two years in the Navy. From 1962 until 1967, Tiger produced hundreds of paintings and sketches of the Creek stomp dance in all its phases (ribbon dance, stomp dance, taking medicine, stickball, meals), of Seminole individuals, of windswept Indians on the Trail of Tears, and of contemporary Indians in everyday activities. He learned about Indian art from his older brother, then attended Cooper School of Art in Cleveland (with funds from the Indian Relocation Act), where he developed his technical expertise. By 1966, his distinctive style—a delicate line on blue or brown posterboard using one or two tempera colors—was established. Tiger was also a boxer, and in 1966 he won the Golden Gloves middleweight title. His life was ended by a self-inflicted accidental gunshot wound days before he would have finished his first clay sculpture for casting. Before his untimely death, he won dozens of prizes at leading Indian art competitions. He rarely interacted with other Indian artists and never traveled outside Oklahoma. His brother Johnny and daughter Dana are artists.

See also Art and artists, contemporary; Creek; Seminole; Stomp Dance.

Tikal: Archaeological site
DATE: 900 B.C.E.-900 C.E.
LOCATION: Petén jungle, western Guatemala
CULTURE AFFECTED: Maya

The ancient city of Tikal, located in the jungles of Petén in western Guatemala, was one of the largest cities and ceremonial centers of Maya Classic culture. Although the central area measures only one square mile, the total extent of the site is approximately 222 square miles. More than 13,440 structures have been discovered in this area since 1848, when it was officially examined by the government of Guatemala.

Like many Maya centers, Tikal was populated from about 900 B.C.E. to 900 C.E. First occupied as a small village, it had grown to be an important ceremonial center by 300 B.C.E. with the construction of large pyramids and temples. During the Classic period (300-900 C.E.), great plazas and palaces were built. Hieroglyphic writing appeared, and a complex system for counting time (the long count calendar) began to appear on inscribed stelae. Maya art in the form of sculptures and painted vases also flourished. The height of this civilization occurred around 700, when the population in the main city reached approximately ten thousand inhabitants, with at least fifty thousand people living in the outlying areas.

In the Early Classic period, Tikal was an important post in the great trading network established by the metropolis of Teotihuacán. The people bartered for such materials as obsidian, pyrite, and jade. After the decline of Teotihuacán, Tikal extended its control over a large portion of the southern lowlands in the Late Classic period.

It is difficult to study the architecture of the earliest inhabitants of Tikal. It was common for the Maya to build new structures over old ones or to destroy earlier constructions and put the materials to secondary use. Preclassic temples involved a series of superimposed platforms with one or more stairways ascending to the top platform. During the Early Classic period, the temple structure sat on top of a step pyramid and usually had three frontal doorways. By the end of the Classic period, the temples were taller, narrower, and had only one doorway. This was done consciously to give a strong impression of physical height and symbolic elevation. The largest pyramid-temple at Tikal is 229 feet high. Temple art depicted the gods of the heavens, the cycles of Venus, and the mysteries of the calendar. In contrast to the temples, palaces and other structures of the city were long and low, with little decoration.

The city center of Tikal contains eight huge pyramid-temples and more than eighty lesser buildings. These buildings are arranged in clusters, often around plazas. Although thousands of peasants flocked to this ceremonial center, only the upper classes were allowed to enter the temples. The great range of quality among housing structures indicates social and economic diversity.

Decline set in at Tikal around 800, and by 900 the area had been abandoned. The last dated stela at the site is placed at 889. It is unknown why this important area was deserted. Some authorities believe the expanding population exhausted the agricultural productivity of the land; others claim that political strife and internal power struggles caused its demise.

See also Chichén Itzá; Copan; Maya; Palenque; Quetzalcóatl; Uxmal.

Tillamook: Tribe

CULTURE AREA: Northwest Coast
LANGUAGE GROUP: Salishan
PRIMARY LOCATION: Oregon coast
POPULATION SIZE: 65 (1990 U.S. Census)

Tillamook is a Chinook name which means "people of Nekelim." It was more often spelled and pronounced "Killamook." The Tillamook were the principal and probably most powerful tribe on the Oregon coast in the early nineteenth century. They lived along a long coastal strip extending from Tillamook Head (near Seaside) to the Siletz River in Lincoln County.

Their population in the early nineteenth century has been estimated at about twenty-two hundred. The Tillamook lived primarily in numerous small villages built near the mouths of the main rivers that flow into the Pacific. Their economy was one of hunting, fishing, and gathering. Salmon, a variety of plants, shellfish, and both land and water mammals were consumed.

The Tillamook apparently developed an extensive regional trading network. Hides, canoes, and baskets were taken to the Columbia River to trade for or purchase shells, buffalo hides, wapato roots, and other items. Transportation, as well as gathering of seafood, was accomplished primarily by rivergoing and seagoing canoes which could hold from twelve to thirty people.

In addition to traveling between villages and trading, the Tillamook ventured forth to capture slaves. They raided neighboring tribes to the south and sold captured slaves mainly to the northern Clatsop and Chehalis tribes in Washington.

Individual villages were presided over by a chief, a position based on wealth and possession of supernatural powers. Additionally, task leaders occupied an important role in planning and performing various tribal activities. These shaman, headmen, and warriors each had particular areas of expertise (medicine, accumulation of wealth, hunting, war, and slave raiding). These individuals, generally male (although some powerful and important shamans were women), were the high class and elite of the village. Unlike tribal members of lesser status, the elite were polygynous. Women's status was based on the status of their family, husband, or guardian. Each shaman sponsored a winter ceremonial dance in order to revitalize his or her powers. Singing, dancing, and the generous proffering of food and gifts over a five-to-ten-day period characterized the most elaborate of Tillamook ceremonies.

The Tillamook apparently did not worship any deities. The earth was viewed as all-powerful and judgmental of Tillamook behavior. Much of an individual's status and prestige was determined by that individual's ability to form a life-long relationship with a guardian spirit.

Primarily as a result of disease epidemics in the 1830's, the population declined precipitously, with populations of twenty-five and ten being reported in the 1910 and 1930 censuses, respectively.

See also Northwest Coast; Salishan language family.

Timucua: Tribe

CULTURE AREA: Southeast
LANGUAGE GROUP: Possibly Muskogean or Chibchen-Paezan
PRIMARY LOCATION: Northern Florida

The Timucua (or Utina, which means "earth") is a collective name for early tribes living in northern Florida. The Timucua may have been connected to the Muskogee group, which dominated the southeastern quarter of what would become the United States. First European contact with the Timucua tribes occurred about 1513, when the Spanish explorer Ponce de Leon entered the area, followed by Panfilo de Narvaez in 1528 and Hernando de Soto in 1539. At that time, the Timucua numbered between thirteen thousand and fifteen thousand and lived in large houses in permanent, well-fortified villages. They depended heavily on agriculture and surrounded their villages with extensive cornfields. De Soto was soon followed by French settlers, who gave way again to the Spanish. The Timucua were gradually conquered and converted, although a rebellion is documented in 1656. Disease and war reduced their numbers severely, so that by 1736 only a few Timucua remained in Volusia County. Those few were probably absorbed by the Seminoles, refugees from other tribes who entered north Florida in the late 1700's to escape the encroachment of white settlers. No Timucua Indians remain today.

The Timucuas were highly organized, building permanent homes and cultivating large tracts of land. They were most easily distinguished for their practice of tattooing their bodies—the men extensively, the women less so. Like most Southeastern Woodlands tribes, the Timucua women were responsible for planting, cultivating, and preserving the crops, primarily corn, beans, and squash. Although the men helped with major tasks such as clearing land and harvesting, they spent most of their time hunting, fishing, and warring.

Women were also important in the social structure of these tribes. Most southeastern Indians followed a clan system, a loose organization of family groups. Membership followed the mother's line, and status in a clan depended on the mother's connections. Women were responsible for the corn crop, important not only as a dietary staple, but as part of the religious symbolism of the tribe. The most significant and universally observed communal celebration, the Green Corn Dance, was a ceremony of forgiveness, purification, and thanksgiving that usually involved the entire tribe.

See also Seminole; Southeast; Timucua language.

Timucua language

CULTURE AREA: Southeast
TRIBE AFFECTED: Timucua

An extinct language, possibly of Chibchen-Paezan stock, the Timucua language was originally spoken along the Atlantic coast from central Florida to Georgia and inland, perhaps as far as the Tennessee-North Carolina-Georgia border. It was the primary native language in this area at the time of European contact in the 1500's. Evidence indicates that it had been the primary language in the area since 2000 B.C.E. By the mid-1700's, the remnant Timucua speakers had been moved to Cuba where they were resettled in San Augusta Nueva, also known by the Timucua name Ceibamocha, meaning "speaking place by the ceiba tree." There are no current speakers of Timucua.

The written records of the language come from catechisms prepared by two priests, Francisco Paneja and Gregorio de Movilla, in the early 1600's. They are written in the Mocama dialect of Timucua. Other dialects were Potano, Itafi, Yufera, Tucururu, Agui Fresca, Agua Salada, Acuera, Oconi, and Tawasa. There were apparently still speakers of Tawasa until the early 1800's; a 1797 vocabulary of Tawasa still exists. There are also two seventeenth century letters extant to the Spanish crown from Timucuan leaders in the Potano dialect.

The orthography used in these letters as well as in the other sources was designed by Pareja. It is based on Spanish but takes into account phonological discrepancies between Spanish and Timucua.

The derivation of the word "Timucua" is perhaps *ati-muca*, literally "servants attend upon him," or "ruler." The language was first recognized as a distinct language in scholarship in 1858. With the exception of Edward Sapir, most linguists considered Timucua an isolate. Joseph H. Greenberg in *Language in the Americas* (1987), however, places it in the Paezan and Chibchan family. This family is found in South and Central America, and it was thought to be limited to those areas. Greenberg's reclassification is doubly startling; he finds relations for Timucua which had previously been thought unrelated, and he erases the long-accepted boundaries for Chibchan-Paezan.

See also Seminole; Timucua.

Tiou: Tribe

Culture area: Southeast
Language group: Tunica
Primary location: Yazoo River, Mississippi

Nothing is known of the traditional culture of the Tiou except that they lived in several permanent villages and had established peaceful relations with neighboring groups. Being horticulturalists, they were largely dependent upon their maize, beans, squash, and other cultivated plants. These foods were supplemented by hunting and trapping. When not farming, women gathered roots, nuts, and a variety of seeds.

First mention of the Tiou was probably made in 1697. The Tiou were described as living in two large villages, one above the Tunica and one below. Their population was greatly reduced by introduced diseases, and by 1699 some of the survivors settled among the Natchez after having been driven from their homes by the Chickasaw. The Tiou became fragmented. Some remained on the Yazoo River, while later some were

absorbed by the Bayogoula and some by the Acolapissa. By 1731 they probably had been destroyed by the Quapaw.

See also Natchez; Tunica; Tunica language.

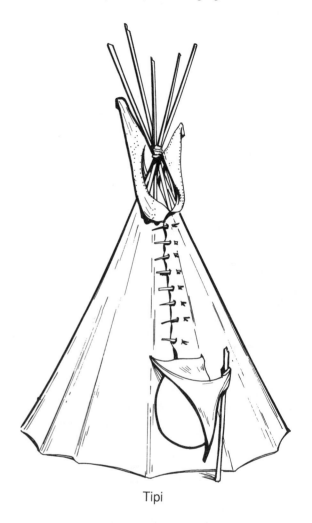

Tipi

Tipi

Tribes affected: Arapaho, Cheyenne, Crow, Dakota, Kiowa, Pawnee, others

Significance: Undoubtedly the most widely known of all American Indian structures, the tipi is a practical and comfortable form of shelter that was ideally suited to life on the Plains

The tipi (or tepee) is a cone-shaped dwelling made of wooden poles covered with skin or bark that was used primarily by the Plains peoples. The word is Dakota in origin and combines the words *ti*, meaning to dwell, and *pi*, which refers to the third-person plural, or "they." Thus the word in translation means "they dwell."

The tipi was made of three primary poles, usually of willow because of its smoothness and strength, 20 to 30 feet long tied together at the top. Fifteen to sixteen more poles, slightly shorter, were added, along with the lifting pole used to raise them. Two smoke flap holes were used to aid in the control of air flow. The conical structure was tilted slightly to keep rain out and assist air circulation. It was covered with animal hides, usually buffalo or deer, or with bark of various sorts, depending on locale. A flap was used for the door, which was secured with wooden pegs.

Before the introduction of the horse, these portable lodgings would be about 12 to 15 feet across at the base and could be readily and rapidly assembled and disassembled. They were dragged along behind large domesticated dogs, the main poles slung across their backs, with the secondary poles and skin covering carried between them. After the horse became an integral part of Plains life, the tipi increased in size and could be from 20 to 30 feet across at the base.

For winter use a secondary lining was made for the interior to increase the insulating properties of the outer covering. A fire pit was dug in the middle of the floor, and the ground was often cleared and packed hard, then covered with grasses, leaves, and hides. These dwellings were very warm and comfortable in the winter, and they could be made open and airy in the warmer seasons by removing the lining, opening the flap, and raising the outer covering a few inches above the ground to increase air flow.

Modern tipis are made using a variety of materials for the poles. They are often covered with canvas and can measure up to 40 feet across at the base.

See also Architecture—Plains; Hides and hidework; Horses; Plains.

Tippecanoe, Battle of

DATE: November 7, 1811
PLACE: Indiana
TRIBES AFFECTED: Huron (Wyandot), Kickapoo, Lenni Lenape, Miami, Potawatomi, Shawnee, Winnebago
SIGNIFICANCE: The destruction of Prophetstown by an American army broke the religious power of Tenskwatawa (the Shawnee Prophet) but failed to demoralize the Indian movement led by his brother Tecumseh

During the early nineteenth century Tenskwatawa began to preach a new religious message among the tribes of the Old Northwest. At the heart of his message was a rejection of

The Battle of Tippecanoe ended Tenskwatawa's spiritual influence but not his brother Tecumseh's resistance efforts. (Library of Congress)

European American influence. Aided by his brother Tecumseh, an intertribal Indian movement took hold which threatened the ability of U.S. Indian agents to force land cessions on the tribes of the Old Northwest.

In the spring of 1808, Tenskwatawa and Tecumseh led their followers to the banks of the Wabash River and began to construct a capital for their movement which came to be known as Prophetstown. Working from this base of operations, the two brothers proselytized among the Indian villages of the Great Lakes and the Ohio River Valley. Thousands of warriors from numerous tribes flocked to Prophetstown, causing alarm among American settlers in the region. Tensions increased after Indiana Governor William Henry Harrison concluded the Treaty of Fort Wayne (1809), which provided for a land cession of three million acres of Indian land.

Convinced that Tecumseh was plotting to kill him, Harrison raised an army of a thousand men and prepared a campaign to destroy Prophetstown. When Tecumseh journeyed to the south to bring his message to the Choctaw and the Creek, Harrison saw his opportunity. On November 6, 1811, the American army was on the west bank of the Wabash, within a mile of Prophetstown.

In the absence of his brother, Tenskwatawa had little control over the warriors in his village. The Shawnee Prophet sent a delegation to meet with Harrison on the afternoon of November 6, seeking to assure the governor that they did not have hostile intentions toward Americans. Unimpressed by these words, Harrison planned to attack the Indian village the following day. During the night, Tenskwatawa exhorted his Indian warriors to attack the enemy before dawn. He assured them that his magic would confuse the American soldiers. He also instructed them to kill Harrison.

The Indians struck Harrison's camp two hours before sunrise. Alert sentries fired warning shots in time to wake the Americans. A few warriors managed to penetrate the interior of the American camp, but Harrison managed to escape and rally his troops. Fierce fighting bent the American line on several occasions, but Harrison was able to shift troops skillfully in time.

At dawn, the Indian warriors began to retreat, and Harrison ordered his troops to charge. The American advance forced Tenskwatawa to abandon Prophetstown. During the fighting, Tenskwatawa prayed to the Master of Life for victory. Unfortunately, his spiritual powers failed. Tenskwatawa was discredited by the battle of Tippecanoe. Many angry warriors confronted the Prophet after the defeat. He blamed the failure of his magic on his wife's unclean state.

Harrison's victory was far from overwhelming. Of the estimated seven hundred warriors who attacked his camp, about fifty were killed and eighty were wounded. The larger American force sustained 188 casualties. Harrison burned Prophetstown, but he failed to end hostilities. The defeated warriors returned to their villages and led further attacks against frontier settlements throughout the Old Northwest.

See also Fort Wayne, Treaty of; Shawnee; Tecumseh; Tecumseh's Rebellion; Tenskwatawa.

Tlingit: Tribe

CULTURE AREA: Northwest Coast
LANGUAGE GROUP: Na-Dene
PRIMARY LOCATION: Northern California to southern Alaska coast
POPULATION SIZE: 13,925 in U.S. (1990 U.S. Census); 1,170 in Canada (Statistics Canada, based on 1991 census)

Tlingit literally means "the people." Among the Tlingit people themselves, there is a growing use of the spelling "Lingit" in order to avoid the use of the initial *t* sound, which is a European attempt to render a somewhat difficult initial sound in the Tlingit language (for the purpose of this article, the traditional spelling will be maintained).

It is probable that the Tlingit people began to occupy roughly their present southeastern coastal Alaska locale soon after the last Ice Age, or roughly 6000-5000 B.C.E. In this area, where the modern Alaskan city of Sitka also celebrates its Tlingit heritage, the weather is much more moderate than inland because of the prevailing currents from Asia which bring milder temperatures. Population estimates for 1740 were roughly 10,000 Tlingit. In 1992, population estimates for the Tlingit people, including those who live in urban areas throughout the Northwest ranged close to 18,900. This represents an impressive endurance, particularly given the devastation of smallpox in 1836, brought by (vaccinated) Russian settlers and tradespersons.

In 1741, Russian ships first made contact with the Tlingit peoples. The Russians were attracted by the mild temperatures and the presence of otter and seals. Quickly following the Russian tradesmen were Russian missionaries, and Russian Orthodoxy remains a widely professed form of Christianity among the Tlingit as well as among other Alaska and Northwest Coastal native peoples.

Kinship and Social Status. There are two important kinship divisions ("moieties") of the Tlingit, the Raven (sometimes called Crow), and the Eagle (sometimes called Wolf). Each of these divisions are divided into a number of clans or sibs. In Tlingit tradition, an Eagle should marry a Raven, although in modern practice, this is not always observed scrupulously. The political organization of the Tlingit people is based not on the larger moieties but rather on the clans. Sib identity is permanent, and there is a recognized sib/clan leader; there is no recognized leader for the two main groupings of Raven and Eagle. The clans, in turn, are divided into "house groups." Identity is passed through the mother rather than the father, so children must spend time with the mother's male relatives in order to learn about their identity.

Wealth and social status are singularly important in Tlingit society, but status is determined as much by distribution and generosity in distribution as it is by one's inherent wealth. The most widely known example of this is the ceremony of the potlatch (based on the Chinook/Salish term *patshatl*), forms of which are found among many Northwest Coastal Indians along the Alaskan, Washington, and Canadian coasts. The potlatch ceremony takes careful preparation and is not merely

The Tlingit village of Sase on Bering Bay, photographed in 1888. (American Museum of Natural History)

and crudely to be understood as a massive "giveaway." There are important spiritual and social elements to the ceremony in Tlingit life.

Tlingits, as did other Northwest Coast peoples, maintained slaves, who were normally prisoners of war or their descendants. It was possible for a slave to become a free person and even to marry into the lower levels of Tlingit society, but mixing too widely across the castelike status boundaries was not encouraged.

Religion and Expressive Culture. Tlingit spirituality is evident in an elaborate mythology of the powers of animal spirits in the maintenance of life. All animals have spirits that can communicate to humans, and there is an element of reincarnation to some Tlingit spirituality. Shamanism is an important practice among the Tlingit, as protection from "Kushtaka" (evil spirits) is an important consideration for families and individuals. While elaborate, Tlingit religion is largely non-ideological in content and is concerned primarily with the maintenance of order, nature, and life. One of the most important aspects of Tlingit spirituality is the great significance attached to the interpretation of dreams and the communication with animal spirits that takes place during dreams. In Tlingit mythology, there is an elaborate cycle of stories about Raven, the most important character in Tlingit mythology, who is also considered the progenitor of the people themselves.

Tlingit culture is perhaps most notable for its elaborate and strikingly beautiful artwork, which can be found both in the wood carvings that decorated boats and homes and in woven clothing such as the famous "Chilkat" blankets. Basketry is also a well-developed art form among the Tlingit. Elements of Tlingit art motifs can be found with variations in other coastal peoples such as the Haida.   —*Daniel L. Smith-Christopher*

See also Chilkat blankets; Na-Dene language family; Northwest Coast; Potlatch.

BIBLIOGRAPHY

Dauenhauer, Nora M., and Richard D. Dauenhauer, eds. *Haa shuka, Our Ancestors: Tlingit Oral Narratives*. Seattle: University of Washington Press, 1987.

_____, eds. *Haa Tuwunaagu yis, for Healing Our Spirit: Tlingit Oratory*. Seattle: University of Washington Press, 1990.

Krause, Aurel. *The Tlingit Indians*. Translated by Erna Gunther. Seattle: University of Washington Press, 1956.

Pelton, Mary Helen, and Jacqueline DiGennaro. *Images of a People: Tlingit Myths and Legends*. Englewood, Colo.: Libraries Unlimited, 1992.

Tobacco

TRIBES AFFECTED: Pantribal, but especially Southeast and Southwest tribes

SIGNIFICANCE: Tobacco was an important recreational and ceremonial substance for many Indian tribes

As early as 1500 B.C.E., the Tamaulipas farmers of Mesoamerica (Central America) cultivated tobacco. In the Southwest, tobacco was grown as early as 630 C.E., though the tobacco grown by eastern Indians was not introduced until after the Spanish conquest. The Southwest Pima tribe approached tobacco farming scientifically, cultivating seed crops and rotating planting sites. Their neighbors, the Tohono O'odham, simply planted all the seed from a previous year. Only old men and some women smoked, as both the Pima and Tohono O'odham believed that tobacco inflicted a cough and made one lethargic and less resistant to cold. Southwest Indians did not chew tobacco. They still grow a small amount of tobacco today.

Exploring Florida in 1539, John Hawkins reported that the Indians were smoking a dried herb. This tobacco was apparently introduced to the Florida Indians by Spanish explorers. In the piedmont and the Cumberland Plateau, Algonquin farmers raised tobacco plants three feet high, dried the leaves over a fire, and ground them to smoke in pipes. They eventually adopted a milder tobacco from the West Indies, introduced into Virginia by John Rolfe. In the north, the explorer Jacques Cartier reported that the Indians around present-day Montreal were growing and using tobacco. By the eighteenth century, tobacco cultivation had become a major enterprise among the Cherokee, Choctaw, Chickasaw, Creek, and Huron Indians. Much of the agricultural process of growing tobacco was ultimately learned from the Indians by white agricultural interests.

See also Calumets and pipe bags; *Cherokee Tobacco* case; Pipestone Quarries; Tobacco Society and Dance.

Tobacco Society and Dance

TRIBES AFFECTED: Widespread; highly developed among the Crow

SIGNIFICANCE: Tobacco societies controlled the complex rituals surrounding planting, caring for, and harvesting tobacco

Of all North American tribes, the Plains Crow developed the most elaborate Tobacco Society. The tobacco species *Nicotiana multivalvis* was considered holy, a supernatural gift having its own ceremony and mystically associated taboos. After the earth was formed, the Creator saw a human, transformed a star into a tobacco plant, and decreed that the Crow should honor tobacco with ceremony. Consequently, tobacco was their mainstay of living.

From this founder or ceremonial "father" came adopted novices, newcomers who had independent visions that revealed unique revelations for adopting further novices. Approximately thirty groups, under the leadership of a Mixer, possessed their own distinctive songs and emblems. These groups formed independent military societies, each with its own bird and animal symbols.

The main function of the Tobacco Society was to perpetuate the welfare of society and integrate society with the supernatural and natural worlds by controlling the complex ritual required to plant, care for, and harvest this sacred plant. Tobacco was believed to be capable of conferring special benefits to its votaries. A main element of the tobacco complex was dreaming and visions, ones prophetic of future deeds. Tobacco vi-

sions helped decide who should become a member. A man or woman was adopted by a "father," and usually a husband and wife were initiated together. The candidate was instructed in songs and rituals during the winter, and in the spring was formally initiated, after the tobacco planting. Installed members encouraged nonmembers with gift-giving.

The four-day spring Tobacco Dance was staged in a specially built conical lodge of ten large pine trunks, with an altar strewn with juniper to represent the Tobacco Garden. Drummers participated, but the distinctive instrument was the rattle to imitate thunder. The specially painted participants laid their bundles of sacred tobacco seed in a row. Participants sang individual songs, danced, and then sweated in a willow sweatlodge and were washed with wild carrot root infusion or scrubbed with sagebrush to purify them and help them resist disease for one year.

See also Crow; Plains; Tobacco.

Tohome: Tribe

CULTURE AREA: Southeast
LANGUAGE GROUP: Muskogean
PRIMARY LOCATION: West bank of Tombigbee River

There may have been two major divisions of the Tohome: the Big and the Little Tohome. The Tohome were, like their neighbors, horticulturalists, dependent on cultivated maize, squash, beans, and other field plants. Men supplemented the diet with the hunting of bison, deer, and other animals. Women gathered food and medicinal plants. Prior to European American incursion, the Tohome maintained socioeconomic liaisons with other groups, particularly the Mobile.

The Tohome were probably first visited by the Spanish in 1559, and later by Pierre le Moyne Iberville in 1702. The pressures created by European American settlers and introduced disease greatly reduced their population. It is believed the Tohome and Mobile eventually united with the Choctaw.

See also Choctaw; Mobile.

Tohono O'odham: Tribe

CULTURE AREA: Southwest
LANGUAGE GROUP: Piman (Uto-Aztecan)
PRIMARY LOCATION: South-central Arizona
POPULATION SIZE: 16,041 (1990 U.S. Census); 17,704 (1990, Arizona Commission of Indian Affairs)

The Tohono O'odham, as this tribe has always called itself, means "desert people." They are also known as the Papago, but the tribe prefers their own ancient name of Tohono O'odham. A cave called Ventana Cave has produced evidence of eleven thousand years of human existence. Some have considered the Tohono O'odham to be descendants of the ancient Hohokam, an extinct agricultural people who had learned to irrigate the desert by a series of canals.

The Spanish conquistadors and padres, in their contacts with the Tohono O'odham in the late seventeenth, eighteenth, and early nineteenth centuries, considered them peaceful farmers who were quick to accept the ways of the newcomers.

By 1762 Spanish missions had started the process of breaking down the culture of the desert people. The United States continued the process when in 1848 it acquired from Mexico the territory in which the Tohono O'odham lived. In the 1870's the United States introduced the reservation system to the Tohono O'odham. They began to live on the reservations of Sells, San Xavier, Ak-Chin, and Gila Bend. Sells is their largest reservation.

The Indian Reorganization Act of 1934 set the terms for the Tohono O'odham organization of their reservation into eleven political districts. Each district has its own council from which two members are elected to represent it on the Tohono O'odham Tribal Council. In addition to the twenty-two council members, there are elected at large by the tribe a chair, vice-chair, secretary, and treasurer.

Many Tohono O'odham live and work outside the reservations in towns and cities. The majority choose to live on the reservations and continue to farm, work in the mines, or work at schools, stores, or other facilities.

See also Hohokam; Pima; Southwest.

Tolowa: Tribe
CULTURE AREA: California
LANGUAGE GROUP: Athapaskan
PRIMARY LOCATION: Northwest California
POPULATION SIZE: 504 (1990 U.S. Census)

Though the patrilineal Tolowa acquired wealth in order to gain prestige, their society lacked social stratification. They lived in eight permanent river villages with houses of square horizontal-set split redwood planks with sloping roofs. They exploited sea mammals, fish, land mammals, and numerous plant foods, particularly acorns. Each village controlled clamming beaches, sea stacks, berry patches, and adjacent wooded areas.

The first documented European American contact with the Tolowa was in 1828 by Jedediah Smith, though disease had been introduced earlier. By 1850, white settlement had increased through gold mining, logging, and farming, resulting in a drastic reduction of the Indian population. In 1908, a tract of land on the mouth of the Klamath was acquired by the government for displaced California Indians; it became the Smith River Rancheria. The Tolowa were influenced by the Ghost Dance of 1870 and the Indian Shaker movement in 1929. Today some Tolowa pursue traditional woodworking skills. On a cash basis, many Tolowa work in local lumber businesses as well as in clerical and administrative jobs.

See also Acorns; California.

Toltec: Tribe
CULTURE AREA: Mesoamerica
LANGUAGE GROUP: Nahuatl
PRIMARY LOCATION: Northwestern Mexico

The Toltecs became a prominent tribe in central Mexico in the Post-Classic era after the fall of Teotihuacán. They were originally one of the Chichimec or barbarian tribes from the north of Mexico before moving toward the central valley and establishing themselves at Tula. The name "Tula" is a corruption by the Spanish of Tollan, or "place of rushes," and Toltec meant "one from Tollan." This site, located on a ridge overlooking the Tula River, is about thirty miles northwest of modern Mexico City, on the northern fringe of the heavily populated Valley of Mexico.

In the early tenth century, the Toltecs became the dominant tribe, and they ruled a wide area of central Mexico for about two hundred years. While not as artistic or original as the inhabitants of the nearby, but deserted and destroyed, Teotihuacán, the Toltecs were the first of the indigenous tribes to have a recorded history. This history, a mixture of epic tales and facts, is significant for two reasons. First, it describes a cleavage in society that may explain the growth of a militaristic state. Second, it presents one of the most complete depictions of the flight of the god-king Quetzalcóatl. Toltec history begins with a king, Mixcóatl (Cloud Snake), who was assassinated by his brother. The dead king's pregnant wife fled and gave birth to a son, called Tolpiltzin, who became a priest to the god Quetzalcóatl, the Feathered Serpent, most often identified as an agricultural deity. Tolpiltzin returned to Tula and avenged the death of his father by killing his uncle and taking the throne. He ruled as a priest-king, becoming so identified with the god that he became Tolpiltzin-Quetzalcóatl. One day, the story goes, Tezcatlipoca, a jealous rival god of war, tricked Tolpiltzin-Quetzalcóatl and made him drunk. When he awoke, Tolpiltzin found himself with his sister and, in shame, fled his city. The legend said he traveled over the water to the east and that he would one day return to regain his throne. This tale would haunt the Aztecs hundreds of years later when the Spaniard Hernán Cortés was believed to be this god returned.

The story may have described a challenge to the agricultural ruling class by a warrior group bent on conquest; the society did become more aggressive. Heavily armed warriors, along with fierce jaguars and eagles, were carved on stone reliefs to mark the increased importance of warfare among the Toltecs. The *chacmool*, a stone carving of a reclining figure with contorted features, held a vessel in which human hearts may have been placed. This thoroughly militaristic society dominated a wide area for nearly two hundred years, only to fall before continued onslaughts of new tribes coming from the north in the middle of the twelfth century. Among these tribes were the Mexica, who would become known as the Aztecs.

See also Aztec; Olmec; Quetzalcóatl; Teotihuacán.

Tomah (c. 1752, near present-day Green Bay, Wis.—c. 1817, Mackinaw, Wis.): Tribal chief
ALSO KNOWN AS: Thomas Carron
TRIBAL AFFILIATION: Menominee
SIGNIFICANCE: Although he initially resisted Tecumseh's call for armed resistance, Tomah joined the British as they fought the Americans in the War of 1812

Tomah, the son of an Indian man who was part French and a woman who was probably Abenaki, was widely respected by the Menominee for his intelligence and leadership. When the hereditary chief, Chakaucho Kama, was judged incompetent, the Tribal Council appointed Tomah acting head chief.

In 1805, Tomah became a guide for United States Army Lieutenant Zebulon Pike, who was searching for the headwaters of the Mississippi River. Pike was impressed with Tomah's apparent loyalty to whites. Indeed, when the Shawnee chief Tecumseh visited the Menominee to solicit their support in the rebellion he was fomenting, Tomah refused to join. He was apprehensive that his small tribe would fare poorly in a pan-Indian alliance. Tomah also feared white encroachment, however, and when it appeared that the Americans might be defeated in the War of 1812, he aided the British. Along with his protégé, Oshkosh, Tomah and approximately one hundred braves helped defeat the Americans at Fort Mackinaw, Michigan, and Fort Stephenson, Ohio.

With Tomah's death in 1817, Menominee resistance to white encroachment collapsed. Later, under Oshkosh's leadership, the Menominee fell victim to Indian removal.

See also Menominee; Oshkosh; Tecumseh.

Tomahawks

TRIBES AFFECTED: Pantribal
SIGNIFICANCE: Tomahawks were both weapons and tools that aided North American Indians in fundamental survival

"Tomahawk" comes from the Algonquian word *otomahuk*, meaning "to knock down." Tomahawks are small axes that were used by North American Indians as tools, weapons, and hunting devices.

Originally, tomahawks consisted of a head made of stone or bone mounted on a wooden handle. These tomahawks generally measured eighteen inches in length or less and were light in weight. Following the arrival of the Europeans, hatchets with metal heads were being made by white artisans. These tomahawks became a valuable trading item between whites and Indians.

Indians used tomahawks as throwing hatchets against their enemies in battle. They were also used to chop wood, to drive stakes into the ground, and to hunt food. Some tomahawks were used simply for ceremonial purposes. One example of this type of tomahawk is a "pipe tomahawk," which had a pipe bowl attached to its head and a hollow handle. These tomahawks were smoked during ceremonies. It is widely believed that the expression "bury the hatchet" came from the Indian custom of burying a tomahawk as part of a peace ceremony at the end of hostilities among Indians.

See also Bows, arrows, and quivers; Scalps and scalping; Warfare and conflict; Weapons.

Tomochichi (c. 1650, Apalachukla, Ala.—Oct. 15, 1739, Yamacraw, Ga.): Headman

TRIBAL AFFILIATION: Creek
SIGNIFICANCE: Tomochichi went to England to plead the cause of American Indians; he inspired much public sympathy for Indian issues

Possibly the son of a Creek father and Yamasee mother, originally from the Chattahoochee River area, Tomochichi was banished by the Creeks and established the village of Yamacraw, near Savannah, Georgia, along with a number of followers. Tomochichi's importance grew with the arrival of the English in the colony of Georgia in 1733.

James Oglethorpe desired the cooperation of the Creeks in his settlement. Along with Mary Musgrove, Tomochichi forwarded Oglethorpe's invitation for a meeting to the Upper and Lower Creeks, and with their affirmative response, Tomochichi was regarded by the newly-arrived English as an important connection with their powerful neighbors.

So great was Tomochichi's importance in the eyes of English and Creek leaders that he was chosen with English and Indian approval to head a diplomatic party of Creeks to England. The visit lasted from June 19 to October 31, 1734. Tomochichi, his wife Senauki, and seven others were welcomed and their visit was a social success. The visiting Indians met King George II at Kensington Palace and made a speech of friendship and peace. Perhaps reflecting the Creeks' matrilineal society, Tomochichi particularly addressed the Queen as the "common mother and protectress of us and all our children." To the last, Tomochichi favored a Creek-English alliance.

See also Creek; Indian-white relations—English colonial.

Tonkawa: Tribe

CULTURE AREA: Plains
LANGUAGE GROUP: Tonkawan
PRIMARY LOCATION: Oklahoma
POPULATION SIZE: 261 (1990 U.S. Census)

The Tonkawa lived a nomadic life over vast stretches of eastern and central Texas. "Tonkawa" comes from the Waco language and means "they all stay together," although they lived in twenty or so independently wandering bands. Their name for themselves was *Titska watitch* ("the most human of people"). The Tonkawa hunted for most of their food, eating bear, deer, and buffalo as well as smaller game, including rattlesnake. When they were near the coast, they ate fish and shellfish. Their religious beliefs kept them from eating coyote and wolf. They also ate nuts, berries, and herbs that they gathered in their wanderings. The early Tonkawa practiced a form of peyote religion, eating the mescal "bean" from a shrub that grew in their territory. This ingestion caused a blinding red vision and vomiting. For the Tonkawa, the red symbolized success in battle and hunting; the vomiting purged the body of evil. By the 1890's they had substituted the milder and less dangerous peyote.

Judging by the traditional stories of neighboring tribes, the Tonkawa were disliked by their neighbors, who thought them warlike and dishonest. They were said to be good with bows, whether aiming at game or at enemies. They were almost always at war with the Apache and the Comanche. In 1782, some four thousand Tonkawa and Apache met to trade horses and to discuss the possibility of forming an alliance against the

Spanish, who were proving an even greater threat. They could not reach an agreement, however, and hostilities soon broke out again. In 1855, they were removed with other Texas tribes to two small reservations on the Brazos River. Three hundred strong, they were moved again four years later to the Washita River in Oklahoma. In 1862 they were attacked by a large group of enemy tribes, and all but a hundred or so were massacred. After more wandering, they were finally settled on a small reservation near the Ponca River in Oklahoma.

See also Apache; Peyote and peyote religion; Plains; Tonkawa language.

Tonkawa language

CULTURE AREA: Plains
TRIBE AFFECTED: Tonkawa

The Tonkawa language is considered by some experts to be an independent linguistic stock, unrelated to any other Native American language. Smaller tribes such as the Sana, situated between the Tonkawa and the Coahuiltecan-speaking tribes, may have spoken a language related to the Tonkawa, but there is no evidence to prove so. A relationship between Tonkawa and the Coahuiltecan languages has been postulated, but the difficulty of proving this relationship is profound because of the scarcity of material. Therefore it is necessary to consider Tonkawa as an independent language.

According to Tonkawa tradition, the tribe centered their early modern activities on the Edwards Plateau west of the Colorado River in what is now central Texas. They were forced to the southeast by the advancing Lipan Apache and Comanche peoples. On Stephen F. Austin's map of the region, the Tonkawa were placed between the San Antonio and the Colorado rivers. By the late nineteenth century, the Tonkawa had been forced to relocate into Indian Territory and then again at Fort Griffin, Texas. In 1884 the Tonkawa were removed to reserved land in Indian Territory. They have remained there around their principal settlement, Fort Robinson, Oklahoma, where they live today.

Knowledge of the Tonkawa language stems largely from the informant John Rush Buffalo, a Tonkawa, Albert S. Gatschet, who collected Tonkawa material in 1884, and the systematic work of Harry Hoijer in the twentieth century.

The theme carries the concrete significance of the word or phrase. The affixes serve either to amplify or to restrict this meaning or to relate the word to the rest of the sentence. Grammatical variations in Tonkawa words are accomplished chiefly by affixation. The predominant form is through affixation (for example, the definite article, case, number, tense, mode, and aspect). Prefixes are used much more sparingly. They are more concrete in meaning than the suffixes, adding significance to the word rather than serving to relate it to other concepts in the sentence. The technique of combination ranges from a very loose semi-independent type of affix to a firm combination of theme and affix.

There are two parts of speech in Tonkawa: independent themes and themes plus affixes. The former indicate terms which may be nominal, act as an adjective, pronominal, or act as an adverb. The latter terms have verbal significance. The Tonkawa sentence is dominated by the verb complex. It includes the subject and object pronouns and defines the tense, mode, and aspect of the action. The verb is the most complex part in structure. It is generally synthetic, attributing to a subject something determined by observation rather than by analysis, with a tendency toward polysynthetic structure. Prefixes are all mixed relational in character. They serve to add both significance to the term and to relate it to other concepts in the sentence. They are all verbal prefixes. For example, *da'* is used in combination with pronominal prefixes to indicate the indirect object of an intransitive verb: *He'malew-o'c*, "I dance"; *da'-he'malew-o'c*, "I dance with him." Word order is only important in distinguishing function.

See also Tonkawa.

Tools

TRIBES AFFECTED: Pantribal
SIGNIFICANCE: The many tools that were manufactured by American Indians enabled them to hunt, fish, farm, make clothing, build their homes, and protect themselves from both wild animals and hostile strangers

Before European traders and settlers emigrated to North America, American Indians were limited in the materials available to them for the preparation of their tools. Inland Indian tribes utilized stone, wood, and animal bone almost exclusively. Indians living near the oceans also used seashells. In most tribes each man or woman made his or her own tools, and considerable time was spent in searching for the right piece of a useful mineral or for a type of wooden branch to make into the desired tool. Effort was spent in the conceptualization of how to prepare a desired tool most appropriately from the few materials available and how to make it most attractive. Tool preparation was arduous in most cases, and the tools that Indians used—axes, arrowheads, arrows, bows, clubs, hammers, harpoons, knives, farm and home implements, nets, scrapers, spear heads, tomahawks, traps, and so on—combined ingenuity and aesthetic sensibility.

Hammers, Axes, and Adzes. Preparation of these tools first required the choice of an appropriate stone. Hammers, very common Indian tools, were prepared in several stages. First the chosen stone was chipped roughly with another stone and a bone chisel to produce the general shape of the desired hammer. Then more careful chipping yielded a more exact hammer shape. Finally, grinding with wet sand or sandstone completed the process. The stone most often chosen for hammers was granite, because the repeated pounding that is involved in hammering does not easily split or shatter this exceptionally tough stone.

Good stone axes were rare because minerals that could yield a sharp enough point to shape logs were scarce. Even the best axes Indians could make (prior to their contact with Europeans, who provided metal tools) were poor shaping tools. Only in the American Northwest did Indians do extensive wood-

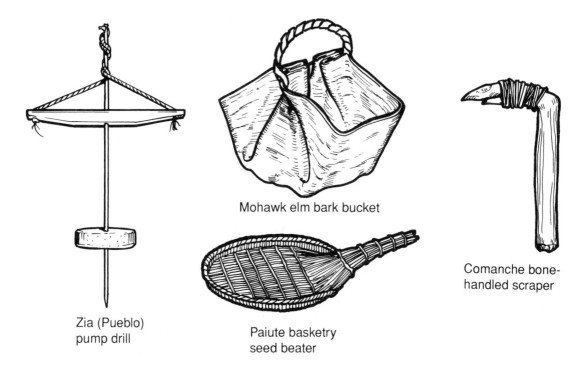

Zia (Pueblo)
pump drill

Mohawk elm bark bucket

Paiute basketry
seed beater

Comanche bone-
handled scraper

working. There, available minerals such as serpentine could be used to make adzes (cutting tools with thin, arched blades).

Clubs and Tomahawks. Two other very common Indian tools were clubs and tomahawks, although these Indian artifacts were most commonly used as weapons in warfare. Clubs were often made by shaping a heavy piece of wood with a knot at one end. The eastern Indian tribes, especially the Algonquian groups, are credited with the invention of the tomahawk. The first tomahawks were clubs with a pointed stone inset into the knot in the club. Tomahawks were heavier, sharper, and deadlier than were clubs and spread slowly through the Indian tribes. They reached the height of deadliness and wide use only after European traders introduced the axlike metal tomahawks that many tribes came to favor.

Arrowheads, Harpoons, Knives, Scrapers, and Spearheads. These ubiquitous Indian implements were very often made of flint, chert, or black obsidian (volcanic glass), all stones that can be chipped to produce very sharp cutting edges. In order to make them (an arrowhead, or projectile point, for example), the Indian artisan positioned a bone chisel against a chosen place at the edge of the stone to be used. Then the chisel was struck repeatedly with a hammer, until a stone chip was knocked off by the percussion. After chipping away at the entire edge of the chosen stone, a sharp, serrated edge was produced. Then, carrying out the same overall procedure on the other edge of the stone produced a typical arrowhead. Longer stones of various sizes, edged on one side only, became knives or scrapers. The blades of harpoons and spears were made in a similar fashion, but they were much larger.

In a great many instances, these implements were attached to short handles (such as knife hafts) or long handles (spear or arrow shafts). Stone implements were thus necessarily engineered so that the haft or the shaft could be attached by the use of rawhide or sinew straps. Harpoons were designed so that a long rope was firmly attached to the harpoon head. This was necessary for efficient recovery of the fish or other aquatic creatures hunted with these tools.

Bow and Arrow Design. The bow-and-arrow combination derived from efforts of Indians to cast spears for longer distances than was possible when they were simply thrown by hand. The wooden or reed shafts of arrows were chosen for straightness, strength, and lightness. The arrow's back end was notched to fit a bow string and fletched with two or three bird feather pieces. Fletching facilitated straight flight upon release from a bow. Arrows were considered to be quite valuable and were very time-consuming to make, so most Indians marked them so that they could be easily identified and reclaimed for reuse.

Bows were made of strong, springy wood (such as hickory, oak, or ash) that was reinforced for even greater strength by use of added bone and sinew. These tools of the hunt and of war varied according to whether the Indian using them traveled on foot or on horseback. Those who rode on horses used short, curved bows. Such bows were often double-curved compound bows of the shape sometimes called a Cupid's bow. Made mostly of wood or animal horn, they were strengthened in the middle by pieces of bone or sinew. Indians who traveled on foot often used very simple wooden bows usually as long as the bow wielder was tall; they were much less curved than the bows of horsemen. The bow strings utilized by various

Indians varied from twisted plant fiber cords to animal sinew, depending on the tensile strength that was required by the user.

Farm and Home Implements. The axes, hammers, knives, and scrapers previously described were everyday tools that were used both in the home and in the fields. In addition to stone tools, many bone implements were utilized because of their hardness, the plentiful occurrence of bone in game animals eaten, the varied shapes and sizes of animal bones, and the fact that bones could be broken into very sharp fragments when struck with hammers or even with unworked stones. Sharp bone slivers could be used as awls that drilled holes in skins to make into footwear and other clothing or as chisels utilized in toolmaking. The shoulder blades of large animals were also made into hoes by some tribes that farmed. Deer antlers were used as picks for the digging of the ores and gemstones (copper and turquoise, for example) used to make jewelry. Bone, stone, or wood hooks used to catch fish were also made by many tribes.

Sinew, Tools, Nets, and Traps. Animal sinews were highly valued items widely used in Indian toolmaking. Their use was based on their strength and on the fact that a wet sinew shrinks when it dries. It has already been mentioned that sinew was used for bowstrings wherever possible. In addition, sinew lashings were the preferred way to affix bladed tools to their handles. Where sinew was used, it was first wet thoroughly. Then it was used to tie the stone part of the tool to its handle tightly and allowed to dry. The shrunken, dried lashings held the parts of the tool together firmly and became quite hard.

Nets and other types of animal traps were also widely utilized by American Indians in their hunting and fishing activities. Nets were made of the fibrous inner bark of trees, of grasses woven into cordage, or of combinations of these materials and strips of animal hide or sinews. They were used to catch fish or smaller land animals. Sometimes they were also incorporated into traps into which aquatic animals or land animals were driven by large groups of Indians. Other traps for catching solitary, large game included wooden pens, spring traps, and deadfall traps. These last two types of traps caught animals by dropping heavy weights on them or by catching them by a foot after they were attracted by bait. It is now believed that many Indian tribes obtained more food animals with nets and traps than with archery, spear casting, and hook fishing.

Simple Wooden Tools. Many tools used by Indians were made of wood only. For example, many arrows used to hunt birds and other small game were merely sharpened sticks. Such arrows were more expendable, and stone points were not necessary to kill such animals. Planting sticks used by Indians who farmed were usually long branches, forked near the bottom. One fork end was sharpened to be used in the actual planting; the other end was a foot rest. In addition, many hoes and clubs were made of wood only.   —*Sanford S. Singer*

See also Agriculture; Bows, arrows, and quivers; Fish and fishing; Lances and spears; Technology; Tomahawks; Weapons; Weirs and traps.

BIBLIOGRAPHY

Adair, James. *Adair's History of the American Indians*. Edited by Samuel Cole Williams. 1930. Reprint. New York: Promontory Press, 1974. This book, first published in 1775 and edited by Williams, describes the lifestyle of many American Indians, therein illustrating the preparation and the use of many Indian tools.

Hothem, Lar. *Arrowheads and Projectile Points*. Paducah, Ky.: Collector Books, 1983. This well-illustrated book describes arrowheads and other projectile points, their preparation by various Indian tribes, the materials and techniques used, and ways to identify fakes of various types. It is interesting and contains very good illustrations.

_____. *Indian Flints of Ohio*. Lancaster, Ohio: Hothem House Books, 1986. Illustrates Indian tools and their provenance from 8000 B.C.E. to 1650 C.E. Engenders an understanding of the evolution of Indian toolmaking and of how the tools were mated with components that completed them.

Montgomery, David R. *Indian Crafts and Skills: An Illustrated Guide for Making Authentic Indian Clothing, Shelters, and Ornaments*. Bountiful, Utah: Horizon, 1985. Most interesting here are the illustrated descriptions of the preparation of common Indian tools and of several types of traps. Tools and traps are related to other aspects of Indian life.

Russell, Virgil Y. *Indian Artifacts*. Boulder, Colo.: Johnson, 1981. Describes and illustrates most types of Indian tools and other artifacts. Explains how many of the Indian artifacts were fabricated.

Torture

TRIBES AFFECTED: Pantribal
SIGNIFICANCE: Torture was widespread among indigenous tribal peoples for military, social, and religious reasons

Many, if not most, indigenous tribal peoples practiced one or more forms of physical torture of enemies, prisoners, captives, and miscreants within the tribe. Some tribal groups, such as the Puebloan cultures of New Mexico, may have committed very little or no torture. European Americans, themselves no strangers to torturous acts, commented regularly on what seemed to them purposeless or completely sadistic actions by "devilish savages." Numerous accounts of scalpings and bodily mutilations, such as the famous ones including Colonel Charles Crawford in northern Ohio in 1782 or the Hungate family near Denver in 1864, became standard conversation fare of the frontier and parlor alike. Certainly European Americans misunderstood the reasons behind such actions; falling into stereotyping and feeding readers what they wanted to read, European American writers also undoubtedly overstated the case. Yet actual torture occurred frequently, especially in the Eastern Woodlands and on the Plains.

Torture took place in several varieties. Often the captors tied enemies to a stake or other framework and burned them with bonfires, firebrands, or coals. Stabbing, beating, and cutting the victims often occurred along with the burnings, as did mutilation and dismemberment. Torturers often shot arrows or, after obtaining guns, bullets into the suffering captives. Some of the unlucky experienced the horrors of feeling themselves disemboweled, flayed, or scalped while they were still alive. On many occasions, however, the goal of torture was not death. With such customs as the gauntlet, in which victims had to run or stagger through rows of kicking, punching, and beating tribal members lined up in parallel or spiral formations, a tribe was often testing captives as potential adoptees or slaves. If a captive showed pluck or fortitude, he or she might even be rewarded with freedom.

To individual tribal groups, torture probably had many and different meanings. On one level it was surely an expression of simple revenge. Yet for most groups, torture also served military, social, and religious needs. Tribes could earn a terrifying and fearsome reputation through renowned torture. Members who had not participated in the actual battle or capture could join communally in a torture ceremony. Many indigenous peoples also believed that enemies would haunt them in an afterworld, and mutilation would distinctly disable those enemies. Sometimes torture was propitiation of certain spirits, manitous, or windigos. Whatever the case, torture was not, as many European Americans feared and believed, random, unthinking violence, but rather a custom integrated into the tribal worldview.

See also Adoption; Captivity and captivity narratives; Ethnophilosophy and worldview; Scalps and scalping.

Totem poles

TRIBES AFFECTED: Northwest Coast tribes

SIGNIFICANCE: The cultural hallmark of the native peoples of the Northwest Coast is the totem pole, a meticulously carved column representing family history, social rank, and ethnic identity

Totem poles are among the largest wooden sculptures ever created. Typically carved from the single trunk of a western red cedar, they reached up to 80 feet in height in the nineteenth century, with one twentieth century piece from Alert Bay in British Columbia being an astounding 173 feet high.

There are different types of carved poles that are usually collectively referred to as "totem poles." These include freestanding poles erected in front of houses or along village beaches, interior house posts that make up part of the framing,

Haida totem poles on Queen Charlotte Island, off the coast of British Columbia. (Thomas Lunt, American Museum of Natural History)

and frontal poles set alongside the main entrance. A dramatic variant of this latter type has an entrance right through the pole itself. A Haida pole at Ninstants, for example, depicts a grizzly bear devouring a human being, and the entrance passes right through the bear's stomach. Funeral customs are also reflected by the erection of memorial poles, grave markers, and mortuary poles which contain the ashes or support a box with the remains of the deceased chief. Not all tribes had all types of pole.

The images on the poles are not really "totems." They are best seen as valuable family crests which depict a mythic or historic event in their past. This might include the encounter of a clan ancestor in the origin times with a supernatural creature, who bestowed upon him the right to use his crest as well as entitlements to hunting and fishing territories, wealth, or other distinctions. Sometimes historic events were recounted, such as how one clan outsmarted another or how a rival chief had been humiliated. These stories helped to legitimize social standing for the chief, his clan, and his children and to lay claims to new rights. By socially manipulating crest images on totem poles and other works of art, chiefs energetically competed for rank, prerogative, and privilege.

Although abstracted and complex, crests could usually be identified by the inclusion of conventionalized features. Beaver always had a cross-hatched tail and two large incisors. A toothy "V"-shaped smile with spines over the eyes revealed Sculpin. Similar iconic devices disclosed Sea Grizzly, One-Horned Goat, Giant Rock Oyster, Fog Woman, Lightning Snake, Thunderbird, and a host of others.

The carving of totem poles flourished in the mid-1800's because of an influx of metal tools and commercial paints. Along with these aids, however, came acculturative forces that led to the virtual extinction of the art form by the early 1900's. The potlatch, a ceremonial feast central to the erection of totem poles and the telling of their stories, was outlawed by the Canadian government in 1884. Disease as well as missionary and other pressures undermined the social and ceremonial fabric that supported carving.

A resurgence of ethnic pride has reversed this trend. A revised Canadian Indian Act of 1951 dropped the ban on potlatching. Church-related groups such as the Alaska Native Brotherhood gave up resistance to traditional ceremonialism. Training schools for artists were established, and totem poles once again began to be raised. Carving began to be accepted as art rather than merely as an ethnic curiosity, and poles can now be found from museums to malls and internationally from Germany to Japan.

See also Architecture—Northwest Coast; Arts and crafts—Northwest Coast; Chilkat blankets; Hamatsa; Northwest Coast; Potlatch; Totems.

Totems

TRIBES AFFECTED: Pantribal

SIGNIFICANCE: Totems were animal spirit guardians who helped individuals and families survive

American Indians share the concept of the totem, or guardian spirit, with many aboriginal peoples, including those of Australia. Help with survival in a demanding environment was sought by individuals and families, and among some tribes, an individual might have a personal guardian spirit as well as a clan totem associated with his or her extended family.

Creation myths and other oral tales of American Indians refer to a time when animals talked and behaved much as people do, and the idea of a totem spirit that communicates to those seeking its assistance may be linked to those stories.

Many of the Pacific Northwest and Alaskan tribes carved elaborate wooden totem poles that served as illustrations of the lineage of the clan. The totem pole also served to trace the history and interrelationship of the clans, with important events recorded symbolically on the poles.

The acquisition of a personal guardian spirit was made through a visitation of the spirit, usually in animal form, in a dream or during a vision quest. The spirit might take the form of a bear, eagle, beaver, or other familiar animal. Less often, the spirit was associated with natural forces such as lightning, and an individual associated with such a totem would be regarded as powerfully protected. The spirit might teach the chosen individual certain songs to call forth its power, and different types and levels of power were associated with various totem spirits.

During its appearance, the spirit would also convey certain taboos or activities necessary to observe in order to keep the totem's favor. Entire families of the Bear Clan, for example, would refrain from killing or eating bears, for the spirit was believed to take the animal's form to appear, and they could not risk angering it.

While not all tribes believed that people were descended from animals, some tribes might consider the animal spirits to be their ancestors, and worthy of the highest respect.

One may be born into a family already possessing a certain totem, but the protection of any particular spirit was never actively sought. It was believed that the spirit chose whom it believed to be worthy. Not every seeker received a guardian, and the totem could withdraw its favor and protection if something was done to displease it.

See also Religion; Totem poles; Visions and vision quests.

Toys

TRIBES AFFECTED: Pantribal

SIGNIFICANCE: The toys with which American Indian children played were meant both to amuse and to prepare children for their roles as adults

In traditional American Indian societies, children played with toys, as children in every society do. Many traditional Indian toys were similar to the types of toys widely found in other cultures, such as dolls, spinning tops, noisemaking toys, items (such as balls and sticks) used in games, and miniature versions of tools used by adults. Toys were generally made of materials that could easily be found locally—wood, stone, bone, or clay.

Toys designed for infants were intended to be amusing and to hold attention. These types of toys included rattles and attractive objects hung on the bow of the cradleboard, such as strings of carved bones that would rattle when the baby moved them by hand.

Children often made crude clay figurines of sheep, goats, horses, dogs, cats, cradleboards, canoes, and humans. They utilized bits of stone, wood, and rags in their play, much as children do today when pretending. Dolls were common, and it was not unusual for dolls to have clothing, cradleboards and houses. Some dolls were actually hollow pottery with pebbles inside. Small play utensils and implements helped children learn the work that would be required of them as adults. Children of most tribes made cat's-cradles with string, jumped rope, spun tops, bowled hoops, and played with balls. The tops were made of wood, stone, or bone and spun with a long thong of buckskin. The handles for the tops were made of sticks, sometimes whittled into a spoonlike shape. As the children matured they played with checkers, dice cut from sticks, knucklebones, or shells and pitched quoits.

"Buzzer" or "hummer" toys operated by strings were common. Boys in some tribes had bull-roarers, which were made of a flat piece of wood, tapered at one end, with a stout cord that passed through a hole at the other end. When this toy was swung rapidly at arm's length, its blade rotated and produced a roaring noise that could be heard for some distance. Some tribes regarded this to be an important sound producer and used it in ceremonies, but most thought it a child's toy. Boys were given miniature bows and arrows and were taught to stalk game and hunt very early. During play, boys would imitate medicine men and had medicine bags made of squirrel or bird skins with small white shells or pebbles for charms. Boys of the Sioux tribe, and probably others, imitated white traders, using fur for a beard and birchbark for hats and shirts. They would smear their faces with light-colored dirt to imitate pale skin.

Hopi children received kachina dolls and toy weapons from adults during the kachina dances. Children also had drums and peashooters. Inuit children possessed sleds, boats, hunting outfits, bows and arrows, carved figures of ducks or seals, and dolls (often with fur clothing), which were carved from ivory, wood, or stone. The children of Plains Indians had dolls, sleds, clay blocks, balls, and tops. Ojibwa children had dolls and small animals made of cattails.

See also Children; Games and contests; Hand games.

Trade

Tribes affected: Pantribal

Significance: Before Europeans arrived in the Americas, American Indians had well-established systems and routes of trade; the European concept of trade soon altered the traditional ways

Pre-contact Indian tribes had philosophies about property that differed dramatically from those of most Europeans; their philosophies limited the notion of what was to be traded and

by whom. Most Indian property was personal, such as clothing, weapons, and subsistence items. This personal property did not usually include land. Indian tribes and kin groups, rather than individuals, had rights to land. There was no concept of real estate as being privately owned. Among agricultural groups of Indians, garden areas were tended by groups; produce from these areas was shared. When Indians gathered or fished, they had the right to do so at will anywhere within their group's or tribe's territory. The same was the case for hunting. In addition, Indians interpreted land rights as rights to use the land productively. Land was not to be destroyed or even left unused, and if land were left unused for some time, it was ordinarily allotted to other groups within the tribe. Since land could not be traded or sold in the ethic of most tribes, there was an inevitable conflict with Europeans who wanted to purchase tribal properties.

Traditional Trade Patterns. With a great range of climate, topography, and flora and fauna, Indian peoples conformed to their environments in diverse ways. East of the Mississippi, in heavily forested areas, tribes traded extensively with one another by traveling on established trails or on rivers. In the Southeast, among the Creeks, for example, corn was a product communally produced and offered to other tribes. Plains tribes subsisted largely on buffalo, and they traded buffalo meat and skins with other tribes that came west such as the Sioux, Cheyennes, and Arapahos. In the Southwest, the Navajos planted crops on the floors of canyons and arroyos, while the Indians of the Great Basin and California wandered in small family groups, gathering seeds and nuts and snaring small animals. Each of the above cultures considered itself a self-sufficient people with communal functions and responsibilities. None considered itself an owner of properties in a European sense. Trade entailed gift-giving and a mutual exchange of items of use. It was not commerce with the European idea of accumulating material toward wealth. It was also not commerce in the sense of acquiring material that would be considered personally owned indefinitely.

Trade with Europeans. Many Indian tribes, however, were increasingly fascinated by European goods. French and English, and later Dutch and Swedish, explorers viewed trade with Indians as a way of acquiring domination over them. After 1600, with colonies established on the eastern coast of North America, trade was not only a simple exchange of goods from which each side benefited; the process of post-contact interaction became a cultural conflict and a struggle over land rights and uses. Initially, some Indians converted European articles to functions other than those originally intended, such as wing tools and body ornaments. This changed, however, with European objects such as guns and farming tools. Indian cultures were being changed by trade with whites, while European settlers and adventurers were acquiring large tracts of Indian territories through trade. Commercial hunting began to overtake traditional Indian subsistence hunting, and it demanded far more time and effort. Indians were soon becoming more dependent on European markets for their raw materials and were affected by fluctuating European prices. Hunted species dwindled, hunters traveled to other tribes' territories, and intertribal conflicts ensued. A debtor dependency developed, with Indians often being forced to give up land in this new commercial process.

The forced transition to reservation life was the final blow to the hope that Indian groups could effectively participate in large-scale trade with the dominant culture as the United States became increasingly populated and industrialized. It was not until the second half of the twentieth century that tribes began to enter the mainstream economy in significant numbers, and success has varied widely among tribes. Types of participation in the modern economy included ranching, the production of resources (such as gas and oil), the tourist trade, the sale of Indian art and crafts (such as jewelry), and, most recently, running gambling casinos on Indian land. In the case of bingo halls and other gambling centers, the federal Indian Gaming Regulatory Act (1988) recognized the right of tribes to engage in this type of economic activity on their own land without having to follow the same restrictions that apply to non-Indians. A number of controversies and questions have arisen, however, over the possible participation of organized crime groups in some operations, over non-Indian management of some centers, and over whether this type of "trade" should be considered appropriate use of a group's environment. Nevertheless, gambling centers represent one Indian adaptation to the European American concept of trade that has resulted from the extremely limited possibilities that exist on the land to which most Indian groups were restricted.

—*Max Orezzoli and William T. Osborne*

See also Beaver Wars; Gambling; Gifts and gift giving; Hudson's Bay Company; Indian-white relations—English colonial; Indian-white relations—French colonial; Money; Resources; Trade and Intercourse Acts; Trading posts.

Trade and Intercourse Acts

DATE: 1790-1834

TRIBES AFFECTED: Pantribal

SIGNIFICANCE: These acts were efforts by the U.S. government to restrain private settlement and enterprise by European Americans in Indian territory; the restrictions eroded as a part of the market revolution of the nineteenth century

In the late eighteenth and early nineteenth centuries, the United States government feared that rapacious private traders and land-grabbing settlers were creating resentment among Indians that could lead to war on the frontier of white settlement. Therefore, the government sought to prevent the wholesale migration of white settlers westward to lands controlled by Indians, regulate the trade in furs between Indians and European Americans, and acculturate Indians to Euro-American norms. The government hoped that these efforts would preserve peace between Indians and European Americans. The vehicles for these goals were the successive Indian Trade and Intercourse Acts. The first Trade and Intercourse Act was passed in 1790 and was scheduled to expire at the end

of the congressional session of 1793. Before expiration, a new Trade and Intercourse Act was passed in 1793. Further laws were enacted in 1796, 1799, and 1802. The 1802 act was made permanent; it stood until 1834.

The Trade and Intercourse Acts built upon precedents established by the Continental Congress in an ordinance of August 7, 1786. The Ordinance of 1786 empowered the federal government to issue licenses to United States citizens allowing them to reside among or trade with Indians. Like the later Trade and Intercourse Acts, the ordinance was an assertion of federal over state power in the regulation of Indian affairs.

The Trade and Intercourse Act of 1790 provided for the licensing of private traders and outlined the penalties for trading without a license. The act of 1790 also detailed the punishments for crimes committed by whites against Indians. The act of 1793 reiterated the provisions of the 1790 act in stronger terms and further authorized the distribution of goods to Indians to promote acculturation to Euro-American mores. In response to the continuing influx of white settlers, the act of 1796 delineated the boundaries of territories belonging to Indians, the first such delineation by the federal government. The acts of 1799 and 1802 were substantially similar to the act of 1796.

In 1834, the federal government for the last time passed an Indian Trade and Intercourse Act. The 1834 act defined Indian territory as all lands west of the Mississippi River excluding the states of Missouri and Louisiana and the territory of Arkansas. The 1834 act banned liquor from the trade and outlawed white fur trappers from operating in Indian territory. Unlike any of the previous acts, however, the 1834 law empowered the federal government to use force to stop intertribal wars in order to protect the interests of fur trade companies. Ironically, a series of acts that began in 1790 by reining in white traders in order to preserve peace ended in 1834 by policing Indians in order to protect traders.

See also Indian-white relations—U.S., 1775-1830; Proclamation of 1763; Trade; Trading posts.

Trading posts

TRIBES AFFECTED: Pantribal

SIGNIFICANCE: Trading posts served as places of economic exchange in the period when the fur trade was significant

In 1670 the Hudson's Bay Company received the right to control all trade in lands drained by waters flowing into that great bay. In this huge territory, covering thousands of square miles, the company established its "factories," which became the first permanent trading posts in North America. Company agents exchanged firearms and metal tools, the items most preferred by Indians, for beaver pelts. These pelts, rather than money, became the standard exchange medium in the north country. This system was used until 1810.

In the United States from 1790 to 1876, furs were the most important economic trade goods exchanged between American Indians and whites. West of the Mississippi, Indian survival depended upon trade in beaver pelts and buffalo hides.

At the end of the Trail of Broken Treaties caravan, protestors occupied the Bureau of Indian Affairs building for six days after security guards tried to remove them. (Library of Congress)

Until 1822 most of this trade came through government-owned trading posts. Congress began to establish the posts in 1796 to guarantee fair treatment of Native Americans. Indians were to receive a just price for their goods. Some members of Congress hoped that by treating Indians fairly and by allowing them to acquire American-made products they would acquire new desires—for shoes and cotton cloth perhaps—that would gradually draw them away from their traditional cultures.

The government-owned system lasted until 1822, when John Jacob Astor, founder of the American Fur Company, persuaded Congress to open Indian trading posts to private companies. Between 1822 and 1840, Astor opened 140 posts in the West and became the dominant force in many American Indian economies. Wherever there were posts, Indians began to cluster, and they soon became exposed to epidemics, alcohol—which had been forbidden at government posts—and economic dependence on white trade. The impact of these posts was generally negative, as thousand of Indians began to die from white diseases such as smallpox and whooping cough. Astor's posts remained open until the mid-1870's; by that time the railroads and a number of related factors had killed most of the buffalo, and most beaver had been hunted out of existence. After those disasters, trading posts were gradually replaced by a reservation economy based at least partially on tourism.

See also Blankets; Diseases, post-contact; Hudson's Bay Company; Trade; Trade and Intercourse Acts.

Trail of Broken Treaties

DATE: 1972
PLACE: From across the United States to Washington, D.C.
TRIBES AFFECTED: Pantribal
SIGNIFICANCE: The Trail of Broken Treaties caravan protested past treaty violations and current treatment of American Indians by the U.S. government

During the summer of 1972, Hank Adams (a leader of "fish-ins" in the state of Washington) and Dennis Banks met with other Indian activists in Denver to plan a "Trail of Broken Treaties" caravan. Their hope was to marshal thousands of protesters across the nation to march on Washington, D.C., to dramatize the issue of American Indian self-determination. The group issued its Twenty Points, a document that sought to revive tribal sovereignty.

The Twenty Points advocated the repeal of the 1871 federal statute that ended the treaty-making era, the restoration of treaty-making status to tribes, the establishment of a commission to review past treaty violations, the resubmission of unratified treaties to the Senate, the governance of all Indians by treaty relations, the formal recognition of more reservations, and the elimination of state jurisdiction over American Indian affairs.

Armed with its demands, the Trail of Broken Treaties caravan moved on to Washington, D.C. Upon arriving on November 3, 1972, days before the presidential election, the protesters learned that there was not enough lodging, so they elected to stay in the Bureau of Indian Affairs (BIA) building for several hours until security guards tried to remove them forc-

ibly. At that point, events turned violent. The protesters seized the building for six days and asserted their demands that tribal sovereignty be restored and immunity be granted to all protesters. Files were seized, and damage was done to the BIA building. American Indian Movement (AIM) leaders claimed that federal agents had infiltrated the movement and had done most of the damage. On November 8, 1972, federal officials offered immunity and transportation home to the protesters. The offer was accepted, and the crisis was resolved for the moment. A few months later, the same issues arose at the occupation of Wounded Knee. In 1976, AIM and other native groups coordinated another nationwide caravan, the Trail of Self-Determination.

See also Activism; American Indian Movement (AIM); Banks, Dennis.

Trail of Tears

DATE: 1830-1839
PLACE: Southeastern United States
TRIBES AFFECTED: Choctaw, Creek, Chickasaw, Cherokee Seminole
SIGNIFICANCE: Conducted under the authority of the United States government, this event brought to a tragic end the traditional life of the five major tribes in the southeastern part of the nation

The Indian Removal Act, passed by Congress in 1830, set the stage for the eviction of the southeastern tribes from their ancestral lands and their removal to Indian Territory. These tribes had few defenders as they sought to resist removal. Their efforts were further complicated by their own failure to unite for their common defense.

Choctaws. Problems for the Choctaws of southeastern Mississippi began in 1805. By the Treaty of Mount Dexter, the Choctaws were forced to cede 4 million acres of land in exchange for the cancellation of debts at government trading posts. The debts had been encouraged by the government for that desired effect.

In 1820, the Treaty of Doak's Stand approved the exchange of 5 million more acres for 13 million acres in Arkansas and the Indian Territory (present-day Oklahoma). White settlers were already occupying parts of that land, however, and the Choctaws refused to move. In 1829, the state of Mississippi abolished the government of the Choctaws and extended Mississippi law over Choctaw territory. The Treaty of Dancing Rabbit Creek in 1830 gave all remaining Choctaw land to Mississippi. Although a provision of the treaty stipulated that any Choctaw who desired to stay in Mississippi could do so, only token compliance with that provision was allowed.

In December of 1830, the Choctaws began emigrating to the Indian Territory, many dying along the way. By 1832, only about six thousand of twenty-three thousand Choctaws were left in Mississippi, most of whom migrated over the next twenty years.

Creek. The Choctaw experience inspired the twenty-three thousand Creeks, in eastern Alabama, to resist removal bit-

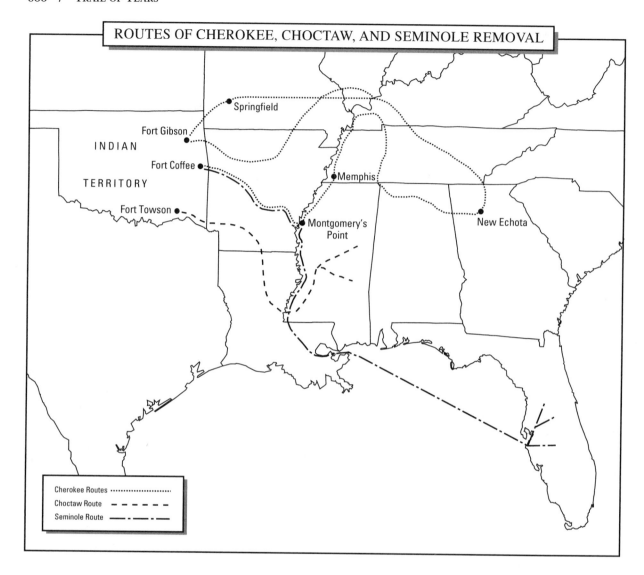

ROUTES OF CHEROKEE, CHOCTAW, AND SEMINOLE REMOVAL

Springfield

Fort Gibson

INDIAN

Fort Coffee

TERRITORY

Memphis

Fort Towson

Montgomery's
Point

New Echota

Cherokee Routes ·············
Choctaw Route — — — —
Seminole Route — · — · — ·

terly. After years of abuse, however, the Creeks finally signed the Treaty of Washington in March, 1832, ceding their land to the United States. Numerous promises made by the government in that treaty were soon ignored. Conditions eventually became intolerable for the Creeks, and they had no choice but to begin their trip to the west. In 1834 and 1835, small parties of Creeks made the journey.

In May of 1836, bands of Creeks launched reprisal raids against white settlements, resulting in an order for the army to remove them forcibly. By July, more than two thousand were on their way to the Indian Territory. Ironically, about the same time, several hundred Creek men were forced into service against their Seminole cousins in Florida. By May of 1837, the removal was in full operation. By 1838 it was complete.

Chickasaws. The most uneventful removal was that of the five thousand Chickasaws from northern Mississippi. The process was initiated by the Treaty of Pontotoc Creek in October,

1832, which ceded their land to the United States. Actual removal followed the Treaty of Doaksville in January, 1837, when suitable land was secured in the Indian Territory and travel arrangements were made. The majority of the Chickasaws moved west in 1837, but small groups emigrated as late as 1850.

Unlike most other tribes, the Chickasaws were able to take many possessions with them, and very few died en route. Their major difficulties were horse thieves and substandard food. After their relatively smooth removal, however, the Chickasaws faced great hardships in the Indian Territory. The most serious were attacks by hostile tribes, a smallpox epidemic, and the failure of the government to supply promised food.

Cherokees. The Cherokees, who fought the most determined legal battle to avoid removal, best illustrate the Trail of Tears. In 1830, almost sixteen thousand Cherokees remained on 7 million acres, mostly in north Georgia.

Events leading to Cherokee removal began with the Georgia Compact of 1802. In 1828, after gold was discovered on Cherokee land, Georgia incorporated a large portion of the Cherokee Nation and nullified Cherokee laws. As squatters invaded Cherokee territory, Principal Chief John Ross took the Cherokees' case to federal court. In 1832, a surprise decision by Chief Justice John Marshall favored the Cherokees, but President Andrew Jackson refused to enforce that decision.

In December of 1835, a minority of Cherokee leaders signed the New Echota Treaty, declaring that all Cherokees would move west within two years. Protesting this agreement, John Ross and the majority refused to emigrate.

The forced removal began with the roundup of Cherokee families in June, 1838. This was followed by "the trail where they cried" to the Indian Territory. The Cherokees were moved west partly by water, but mostly by land. The difficult journey left four thousand unmarked graves along the way. About a thousand Cherokees escaped the removal by fleeing into the southern Appalachian Mountains.

Seminoles. The Seminoles are descendants of the Creeks who had moved to Florida in the eighteenth century. By the nineteenth century, their population in the swamps of central Florida had increased to more than six thousand and included a large number of African Americans, both escaped slaves and free blacks. Soon after the United States acquired Florida from Spain in 1819, efforts to remove the Seminoles were initiated. The motives for the removal were to stop Seminole raids against white settlements and to cut off the escape route for runaway slaves from the southern states.

The Treaty of Payne's Landing, signed in 1832 by an unauthorized group of Seminoles, declared that all Seminoles would give up their land. Resistance, led by Osceola, resulted in the Second Seminole War in 1835. As Seminoles were captured, they were sent to the Indian Territory. The war had ended by 1842, and the remaining Seminoles slowly migrated west. By 1856, except for a large group in the inaccessible Everglades, the Seminoles had been forced out of Florida.

Forced removal exacted a heavy toll from the southeastern tribes. In addition to the incalculable lives lost on the journey, there were tremendous hardships faced as the survivors had to adapt to a new environment that could not support their traditional lifeways.

—*Glenn L. Swygart*

Artist Robert Lindneux's 1942 painting Trail of Tears*; the painting is somewhat misleading in that most Indians made the arduous journey on foot.* (Robert Lindneux, Wollaroc Museum, Bartlesville, Oklahoma)

See also Cherokee, Chickasaw; Choctaw; Creek; Dancing Rabbit Creek, Treaty of; Indian Removal Act; Indian Territory; Removal; Ridge, Major; Ross, John; Seminole; Seminole Wars.

BIBLIOGRAPHY

De Rosier, Arthur H. *The Removal of the Choctaw Indians*. Knoxville: University Press of Tennessee, 1970.

Ehle, John. *The Trail of Tears: The Rise and Fall of the Cherokee Nation*. New York: Doubleday, 1988.

Foreman, Grant. *Indian Removal*. Norman: University of Oklahoma Press, 1932.

Gibson, Arrell. *The Chickasaws*. Norman: University of Oklahoma Press, 1971.

Hudson, Charles. *The Southeastern Indians*. Knoxville: University of Tennessee Press, 1976.

Transportation modes

TRIBES AFFECTED: Pantribal

SIGNIFICANCE: Long before their contact with European civilization, American Indians had developed a number of unique modes of long-distance transportation, many of which, in their original or modified forms, are in use today

American Indians have traditionally used a wide variety of modes of travel, especially watercraft. Some of these modes are still in use today and have been adopted by the descendants of European settlers. In other cases, traditional ways of transport have been replaced by those made possible by European technology.

Transportation on Land. The North American Indians never developed the wheel, which was basic to European land travel. In South America, the wheel was developed but was used only in children's toys; apparently it was never considered a serious means of transportation. The probable reason for this is that wheeled vehicles require a flat, well-maintained road, and Indian cultures never built these to any great extent.

Traveling on foot was therefore the only means of land transportation practiced in the temperate climates of North America until Europeans brought horses to the Americas. A variety of containers, frequently of animal skin or of woven fibers, were developed for carrying necessary travel provisions or trade goods. The Plains tribes used a device called the travois, which consisted of two shafts that could be pulled by a dog (or a person); the shafts supported the load, hung or suspended between them. In snowy conditions, snowshoes were commonly worn for winter travel. They were often made of local wood, wetted and heated to make it pliable; the snowshoes were shaped, then webbed with hide. In other cases they were made entirely of woven hide.

Apart from walking, the major mode of land transportation in temperate climates was horseback riding. Although fossil evidence suggests that a small type of horse was once native to the Americas, they were extinct before European explorers arrived. The Europeans introduced modern horses at the end of the fifteenth century, and many American Indian tribes, especially in the Great Plains, quickly adopted this mode of transportation.

Sleds were a common mode of transportation, especially in the Arctic and Subarctic regions. Among some Inuit groups, dogs were originally considered sacred, and sleds were pulled by humans. At some point, dogs were used, possibly because of the influence of the Athapaskans, the other major group of Arctic and Subarctic natives, who had long been using dogs to pull sleds. Dogsleds were very often quite large, up to 14 feet in length, and could carry heavy loads.

Boats. As was the case in pretechnological European society, water travel was considered far more important than land

Nootka dugout canoe

Algonquian birchbark canoe

Inuit kayak

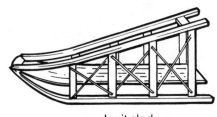

Inuit sled

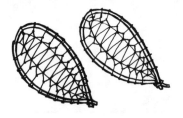

Apache snowshoes

The travois was used to carry anything from children to tipis. Originally small travois were pulled by dogs; when horses arrived on the Plains, travois became larger. (Library of Congress)

travel for several reasons. Lakes and rivers already existed—no trails needed to be blazed. Many Indian tribes lived by the shores of lakes, rivers, or oceans, as waterways provided an excellent source of food. Travel was faster and easier because waterways are generally unobstructed. Finally, once a route along a waterway was known, it would always be there, and previous travelers could easily explain the routes to others.

The type of boat most commonly used by Indians was the canoe, and there were a number of varieties. Dugout canoes were widely popular. These were formed by splitting large trees and hollowing out the middle of half the tree by fire or simply by scooping or chipping out the inside with stone or wooden implements. Also common were canoes made of bark or skin, sometimes caulked with the resin from trees or with animal fat.

Canoes varied widely in size. At one extreme, the Iroquois of New York and southeastern Canada made canoes up to 40 feet long. Many other tribes made canoes for one or two persons. The Tlingit of Alaska made dugout canoes of cedar, sometimes as long as 45 feet, which could hold up to sixty people; they also made much smaller canoes for one or two persons.

Canoes were paddled in a variety of ways. Usually there were a number of paddles used by people on both sides, with steering accomplished by means of one side paddling while the other side sat idle. Sometimes, however, especially in the longer canoes containing a larger number of people, there was a short paddle used in the back of the boat. The Inuits used kayaks, a variation on the canoe that was paddled with a single oar, swung from side to side.   —*Marc Goldstein*

See also Birchbark; Boats and watercraft; Dogs; Horses.

BIBLIOGRAPHY

Bancroft-Hunt, Norman. *People of the Totem.* New York: G. P. Putnam's Sons, 1979.

Hamilton, Charles, ed. *Cry of the Thunderbird: The American Indian's Own Story.* Norman: University of Oklahoma Press, 1972.

Oswalt, Wendell H. *This Land Was Theirs: A Study of North American Indians.* 4th ed. Mountain View, Calif.: Mayfield, 1988.

Spencer, Robert F., Jesse D. Jennings, et al. *The Native Americans.* 2d ed. New York: Harper & Row, 1977.

Viola, Herman J. *After Columbus: The Smithsonian Chronicles of the American Indians*. Washington, D.C.: Smithsonian Institution Press, 1990.

Treaties and agreements in Canada

TRIBES AFFECTED: Pantribal

SIGNIFICANCE: The character of treaties between the Canadian government and Canada's Indian peoples has varied as Indians have lost and partially regained power

The capture of Quebec from the French in the Seven Years' War in 1760 allowed Britain to consolidate its holdings in North America. In order to establish colonial governments in the newly obtained Quebec and Florida, King George III issued what has become known as the Royal Proclamation of 1763. A provision of the proclamation reserved for the Indians all lands to the west of Upper Canada and provided a mechanism for the Crown to purchase these and other lands from the Indians. Since the French had never recognized aboriginal title in their colonies, however, Quebec and those portions of the Maritimes captured from the French were exempted from this provision of the proclamation.

The early Indian treaties reflected the strong military position of the Indians, and the stated purpose of most treaties was simply peace and friendship. The Indians were important in military rivalries, first between the French and the British and later between the British and the Americans. There were relatively few Europeans compared with Indians, so land cessions were relatively small and were accomplished with one-time payments (usually in the form of trade goods).

After 1812, the Indians were no longer militarily significant, and the character of treaties changed. In recognition of their weaker position, Indians began to make greater demands for relinquishing their lands. European needs for agricultural lands increased at the same time as a result of increased emigration from Europe. In an effort to save money, the Europeans began the practice of issuing annuities rather than one-time payments. In 1817, a land cession treaty was signed with the Saulteaux and Cree to permit the establishment of the Red River Colony of Thomas Douglas, Earl of Selkirk. This was the first treaty which entirely ceded native title to lands west of Upper Canada.

In 1850, Special Commissioner W. B. Robinson concluded two treaties with the Ojibwa living along the northern shores of Lakes Huron and Superior. Known as the Robinson-Huron and Robinson-Superior treaties, they were signed after the Ojibwa requested that the Europeans purchase the land before mining it. These two treaties set the precedent of permitting Indians to continue hunting and fishing on their ceded territory.

The Situation at Confederation. Canada was created as a nation in 1867 with the confederation of Nova Scotia, New Brunswick, Quebec, and Ottawa into the Dominion of Canada. The British North America Act, which created Canada, charged the Dominion with discharging the Crown's duties toward the Indians. In 1870, much of the remainder of present-day Canada was transferred from the Hudson's Bay Company to the new nation. This transfer illustrates a paradox in the history of relations between natives and whites in Canada. While the Royal Proclamation of 1763 preserved native title to this transferred territory and established the Crown as the only legitimate purchaser of Indian lands, the sale of Rupert's Land by the Hudson's Bay Company indicated disregard of aboriginal title. Furthermore, in order to facilitate white settlement in the new territory and to connect, via railroad, the settlements in eastern Canada with the colony of British Columbia, the Crown moved to extinguish any remaining native title to that region. Seven treaties, covering much of present-day Canada, were concluded between 1871 and 1877. The provisions of the treaties varied only slightly and were similar to the two Robinson treaties.

The Numbered Treaties. Treaties 1 and 2, negotiated in 1871, were virtually identical and covered lands held by the Swampy Cree and Chippewa (Ojibwa) in southern Manitoba and southeastern Saskatchewan. In exchange for relinquishing title to 52,400 square miles, the Cree and Chippewa were promised 160 acres of reserved land for each family of five, a school, farm implements, a gift of three dollars for each person, and an annuity of three dollars per person. Chiefs and headmen were awarded additional payments. The area covered by Treaty 1 included the Red River farmsteads of the Metis.

With the signing of Treaty 3, known also as the North-West Angle Treaty, in 1873 by the Saulteaux, the initial payment was raised to twelve dollars and the annuity was increased to five dollars per person. Larger reserves (one square mile per family) were also granted, as well as the continued rights to hunt and fish on unoccupied lands. This provision to allow traditional subsistence activities on the ceded territories appears in the remainder of the numbered treaties. As the prairie provinces were established, however, most of the Crown's lands were transferred to the provinces. Increasingly, the courts have ruled that native Canadians are subject to provincial game laws.

Treaty 4, signed in 1874 by the Saulteaux and Cree, encompasses southern Saskatchewan and small portions of Alberta and Manitoba. Treaty 5 was made in 1875 with the Saulteaux and Cree of central Manitoba and extended to northern Manitoba in 1908. The Blackfeet, Blood, Piegan, Sarcee (Sarsi), and Assiniboine tribes of southern Alberta agreed to Treaty 7 in 1877.

Treaty 6 was made in 1876 with Poundmaker's and Crowfoot's Plains and Wood Cree bands in central Alberta and Saskatchewan; however, the bands led by Big Bear refused to sign until 1884 and succeeded in obtaining somewhat greater concessions. The failure of the government to meet the obligations to which it agreed in the treaty are among the factors that contributed to the Riel Rebellion of 1885. Treaty 6 is interesting also in that it is the only one of the numbered treaties that mentions medical care for Indians. It provides that the Indian agent on each reserve maintain a "medicine chest" for the benefit of the Indians. It is likely that medical care was verbally promised during negotiation for other treaties but was not written into the final documents.

Twenty-two years passed between the signing of Treaty 7 and the next set of treaty negotiations. The last four numbered treaties were made in order to make way for northern resource development rather than to permit white settlement. Treaty 8, signed in 1899 with the Beaver, Cree, and Chipewyan, covers portions of Saskatchewan, Alberta, the Northwest Territories, and British Columbia. It is the only treaty covering the Indians of British Columbia. Several small treaties had been negotiated between coastal tribes of British Columbia and the Hudson's Bay Company in the 1850's, but because the Hudson's Bay Company had no authority to negotiate for the Crown, these treaties were not considered valid. After British Columbia entered Confederation in 1871, an attempt was made to have that province negotiate treaties; other than granting several small reserves, the province refused to acknowledge aboriginal title.

Ontario joined with the federal government in the making of Treaty 9 with the Ojibwa and Cree of north central Ontario in 1905 and 1929. The Cree and other Indian groups ceded their remaining territory in northern Saskatchewan with Treaty 10 in 1906.

Treaty 11 was signed in 1922 with the Dene (Slave, Dogrib, Loucheux, and Hare) Indians who occupy the Mackenzie River region between the sixtieth parallel and the Arctic coast. The impetus for this treaty was the discovery of oil a year earlier at Norman Wells.

The numbered treaties presumably settled all land claims based on aboriginal title for Indians living in the prairie and western Subarctic regions, but several court cases have thrown that issue into question. In one of the most important of these cases, *Re Paulette et al. and the Registrar of Titles* (1974), the court held that the Indians covered by Treaties 8 and 11 had not, in fact, extinguished their aboriginal titles to the land.

Piegans arriving at Fort MacLeod, Alberta, to sign a treaty in 1882. (National Museum of the American Indian, Smithsonian Institution)

Modern Land Claims Agreements. The court decisions, coupled with the politicization of Native Canadians, led the federal government to rethink its position on the issue of aboriginal title. The government's desire to develop the natural and mineral resources in its northernmost territories created the conditions necessary for comprehensive land claims settlements. Between 1975 and 1992, five major land claims agreements were concluded. Varying levels of progress were made on several others.

The first of these modern land claims agreements, known as the James Bay and Northern Quebec Agreement, was signed in 1975 by Inuit and Cree of northern and northwestern Quebec, the federal government, and the Province of Quebec. The agreement cleared the way for Quebec to begin hydroelectric development in James Bay. The Northeastern Quebec Agreement, concluded in 1978 with the Naskapi, was for the same purpose.

The James Bay and Northern Quebec Agreement provided $225 million, divided proportionally between the Inuit and the Cree for the lands (excluding mineral rights) in the immediate vicinities of their communities. The natives were allowed to retain exclusive hunting and fishing rights over a much larger area; however, the flooding caused by the hydroelectric development has caused major disruptions of wildlife.

The Inuit chose to form public municipal-type village governments with powers over zoning, taxation, public health, housing, and education. The Cree made their communities into reserves. Representatives of both groups serve on environmental and economic development boards meant to monitor the development of the region.

National native organizations have been highly critical of the James Bay land claims agreements largely because of the clauses that extinguish aboriginal rights. Because the term "aboriginal rights" was not defined, future understandings of its scope have also been negotiated away. In addition, the vague language of the agreement has allowed both the Quebec and federal governments to shirk their obligations.

Far more generous than the James Bay Agreements are the two land claims settlements achieved by the Inuit of the Northwest Territories. The Inuvialuit Final Agreement, which was signed in June, 1984, settled the claim of the twenty-five hundred Inuit living between the Yukon border and central Victoria Island. Under the agreement, the Inuvialuit (or western Inuit) retained title to 91,000 square kilometers but mineral rights to only one-seventh of that land. The Inuvialuit surrendered land covering 344,000 square kilometers. In exchange for the land cessions the Inuvialuit received $152 million to be paid over a thirteen-year period. In an arrangement similar to that established by the Alaska Native Claims Settlement Act, the money has been paid to the Inuvialuit Regional Corporation, which was chartered to invest the proceeds and to manage the land retained by the Inuvialuit. In contrast to the provisions of the numbered treaties, all income earned by the Inuvialuit Regional Corporation from either its lands or investments is subject to taxation.

The Eastern Arctic Claim was negotiated between the federal government and the Tungavik Federation of Natives. Signed in 1992, it settled the claim of seventeen thousand Inuit living in the area of the Northwest Territories between Coppermine and Baffin Island. The claim established Inuit title to 352,000 square kilometers (9.9 percent of the total land and offshore area), making the Eastern Arctic Inuit the single largest landholder in Canada. Unlike other land claims agreements, the Eastern Arctic Agreement includes offshore areas, which continue to be vital food sources. In exchange for relinquishing claim to the remaining territory, the Inuit are to receive $580 million as well as resource royalties earned from their lands. Perhaps the most substantial concession made by the federal government was to allow the Inuit to govern themselves through the formation of a new territory to be known as Nunavut.

Negotiations between the governments of Newfoundland and Canada and the thirty-five hundred Inuit of Labrador have proceeded slowly since 1978. In 1988, agreements in principle were signed between the federal government and the Yukon Council of Indians and with the Dene-Metis Association of the Mackenzie River region. Neither agreement was concluded. At their annual meeting in July, 1990, the Dene Assembly failed to ratify the accord because of divisions within the organization over the "extinguishment" of the still undefined aboriginal rights. After the failure of the Dene-Metis Land Claims Agreement, the federal government agreed to settle the claim on a region-by-region basis. The communities situated along the lower Mackenzie River signed the Gwich'in Final Agreement a year later. The agreement provides resource royalties and $75 million cash in exchange for relinquishing aboriginal rights and title to most of the region. The Gwich'in (Delta area) natives retained title to slightly more than 21,000 square kilometers. They also retained the subsurface mineral rights to about one-fourth of that land. As with the Eastern Arctic Agreement, the Gwich'in Final Agreement established a framework for self-government.   —*Pamela R. Stern*

See also Alaska Native Claims Settlement Act; Big Bear; Fifteen Principles; Hudson's Bay Company; Indian-white relations—Canadian; Poundmaker; Proclamation of 1763; Reserve system of Canada; Riel Rebellions; Sovereignty; White Paper of Canada.

BIBLIOGRAPHY

Dickerson, Mark O. *Whose North? Political Change, Political Development, and Self-Government in the Northwest Territories*. Vancouver: U.B.C. Press, 1992. Discusses the contemporary political issues facing the Dene, Metis, Inuit, and non-native residents of northern Canada.

Getty, A. L., and Antoine S. Lussier, eds. *As Long as the Sun Shines and the Water Flows: A Reader in Canadian Native Studies*. Vancouver: University of British Columbia Press, 1983. A collection of articles covering relations between the Indians and the Canadian government from the time of the Royal Proclamation of 1763 to the constitutional crisis of the 1980's.

Morris, Alexander. *The Treaties of Canada with the Indians of Manitoba and the North-west Territories.* Toronto: Belfords, Clark & Co., 1880. Reprint. Toronto: Coles, 1971. An account by one of the negotiators of Treaties 3 through 6.

Morse, Bradford W., ed. *Aboriginal Peoples and the Law: Indian, Metis, and Inuit Rights in Canada.* Ottawa: Carleton University Press, 1985. A thorough discussion of all aspects of Canadian law (including treaties) as they apply to native peoples.

Purich, Donald J. *The Inuit and Their Land: The Story of Nunavut.* Toronto: James Lorimer, 1992. Contains a thorough discussion of each of the Inuit land claims agreements, paying special attention to the Eastern Arctic Agreement and the preparations for native self-government in the proposed New Nunavut Territory.

Tres Zapotes: Archaeological site

DATE: c. 1200-100 B.C.E.
LOCATION: Veracruz, Mexico
CULTURE AFFECTED: Olmec

In the southern part of the Mexican state of Veracruz, extending down the Gulf of Mexico coast, are a series of mountains known as the Tuxtlas; within them lies an ancient archaeological site known as Tres Zapotes. There, in 1862, a colossal stone head weighing twelve tons was discovered. Its features were male, with combined human and jaguar characteristics. Later, in 1939, when the first scientific exploration of the site occurred, two discoveries were made: male heads, like the 1862 one, and a fragmentary stone slab covered with inscriptions on one side and a man-jaguar mask on the other. The inscriptions on the slab were identical to Maya calendric symbols, but when calculations were made, the slab inscriptions predated the oldest Maya inscription by three centuries. Radiocarbon analysis of organic material at the site confirmed the calendric calculations. This slab is now known as Stela "C." Archaeologists interpreted the Stela "C" date as conclusive evidence of a very ancient and advanced civilization predating all other pre-Columbian Mesoamerican civilizations. Named Olmec by archaeologists, this civilization achieved very high intellectual and artistic levels, developed ceremonial centers, and invented the calendrical and mathematical systems used by later Mesoamerican civilizations.

See also Olmec; Veracruz.

Tribe

The word "tribe" has deep roots in Indo-European languages and cultures. In Indo-European the word *tre* refers to trees and the way they branch. This later became the word *tri*, meaning one-third, or division into three parts. The word *bus* refers to "bush," or branching plant. In Latin, *tribus* was used in reference to the three groups—Latin, Sabine, and Etruscan—who united to form Rome. The original term comes from the Etruscans. It has come into modern usage through French and Middle English derivations and was carried into North America by colonial peoples.

Definitions. This term describes various human social groups who share a common name, territory, ancestry, and feeling of community. Peoples with similar customs and cultural, linguistic, and religious homogeneity are thought by Western Europeans and European Americans to be tribes. In some areas populated by groups considered tribes, people traveled in nomadic groups loosely bound by family ties. In others they settled and established their tribes on a clan basis; in still other regions the power structure was based on a village or community system.

Some social scientists consider a tribe to be an organized band or group of bands who have shared means of resolving disputes and making communal decisions and possess a written language. A tribe is also thought to be a self-sufficient group of people living and working together but producing little or no surplus goods or services.

A tribe is larger than a family or a band yet smaller than a chiefdom, kingdom, or empire. Some scholars say the term refers to early stages in the development of human political systems and nation-states. This assumes that a tribe lacks a state apparatus, civil government, and the complex political organization commonly associated with the more easily recognized governmental forms of chiefdoms, kingdoms, and empires.

Unfortunately the word "tribe" is often used to refer to any group of people considered "primitive" by others—groups who live a "simple" life of traveling, hunting, migrating, marrying, and meeting for ceremonies and who share a common dialect, customs, culture, and worldview. Such peoples are generally lacking in advanced technology and are organized in ways considered "uncivilized" by citizens of nation-states.

Some of the things that bind any human community together include family and kinship ties; shared beliefs about self, group, and their origins; and the best ways to care for and relate to the environment. The variety of types of social, political, and religious organization regulated through ritualistic, governmental, and other institutional forms are numerous and diverse. Any people who share a language, social structure, worldview, and territory can be assumed to qualify as a tribe.

Tribes and the American Experience. Some indigenous American tribes were so loosely organized that no tribal unit is said to have existed. Their lives were thought to "border on anarchy." They were nomadic or migratory. They had no secret societies, tradition of hereditary nobility, complex clan structures, or settled places of constant habitation. They were small groups, often called "bands," who shared a common identity because of their common presence and activities.

Some assembled into duly constituted independent states when they gathered all their numbers together, while other groups entered into an even higher organic state by confederating with neighboring tribes, (a level of organization that could qualify them as nations). Others forced many smaller tribes to take part in the formation and maintenance of an empire, as among the Aztecs, Mayas, and Incas.

Tribe, in its European denotation, signifies only a political unit, whereas the actual diversity among American Indian peoples of organizational forms indicates a wide variety of complex social expressions of the communal uniting of personal and environmental conceptions. Social relations depended on the self-evident order of nature and a people's place in it.

American Indian peoples traditionally had no commonly agreed-upon concept of "tribe." They were generally animists, meaning that they believed everything to be alive and related; all things were defined by their relationship to all other things. They had many varieties of kinship groups, clans, lineage systems, and social structures. Each group had a name for itself in its own language, most often a word that meant "the people" or "human beings." For example, the Tsalagi (Cherokee) word *Junwiya*, the Navajo word *Diné*, and the Nez Perce word *Nimipuu* all mean "the people."

Colonial Europeans often thought of all peoples unlike themselves as primitives and therefore as "tribes." It was their tendency, because of the categorical and reductionist strains of their thinking and languages, to reduce the diversity of indigenous American peoples to a general category of "primitives" or "tribes." They did not recognize or understand the communities and peoples they encountered in their drive to colonize the Americas and to develop new sources of raw materials, generate income for the European monarchies, and procure converts to Christian churches. They generally looked upon native peoples in the Americas as savage, barbaric, uncivilized, primitive, and worthy only of extermination or exploitation.

As the United States developed into a nation, these abstract generalizations were projected onto all indigenous peoples who organized themselves in ways not recognizable to Anglo-Europeans. Indigenous tribal peoples in Hawaii and the Philippines, for example, were viewed as primitives who needed to be controlled or exterminated either by force of arms or by coercive cultural assimilation.

Each tribal community in the Americas is the product of distinctive conditions, circumstances, and experiences from which the community derives the shape of its culture and the form of its identity. There were originally thousands of unique peoples in the Americas before contact with Europeans. Only after contact with Europeans did it eventually become a legal necessity to define oneself in terms of tribal affiliation.

Modern, Legal and Political Considerations. Many indigenous peoples consider the term "tribe" to be offensive, seeing its use as a typical European attempt to justify "civilizing," forcibly assimilating, or exterminating them. Yet they also realize that they must struggle today to receive and maintain recognition as "federally recognized tribes" in order to receive protections under the law and fulfillment of treaty rights and benefits.

Alternative terms such as "ethnicity," "minority group," and "identity group" have been suggested, but any such redefinition involves political (and economic) issues. "Tribe" is a term with distinct political connotations in the United States. American Indian peoples have a constitutionally mandated relationship with the government as defined by treaties and other agreements between recognized Indian nations and their enrolled

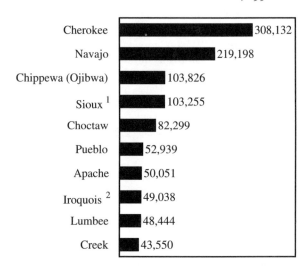

LARGEST AMERICAN INDIAN TRIBES, 1990

Tribe	Population
Cherokee	308,132
Navajo	219,198
Chippewa (Ojibwa)	103,826
Sioux [1]	103,255
Choctaw	82,299
Pueblo	52,939
Apache	50,051
Iroquois [2]	49,038
Lumbee	48,444
Creek	43,550

Source: U.S. Bureau of the Census, *We, the First Americans.* Washington, D.C.: U.S. Government Printing Office, 1993.

1. Any entry spelled "Siouan" was miscoded to Sioux in North Carolina.

2. Reporting/processing problems affected the Iroquois census data.

citizens. This is called the federal-Indian trust relationship and is carried out through various intra- and intergovernmental contacts and institutions. Tribes' inherent, although limited, sovereignty and inalienable right to self-determination is thereby supposed to be assured. At the same time, the federal government's duties and obligations to modern tribes are spelled out.

For these reasons federally recognized Indian tribes traditionally did not seek civil rights. They believed, and many still believe today, that the U.S. government and Indian peoples are best served through the fulfillment of treaties rather than the passage of laws in the interest of immigrant minority groups. There is considerable money and power at stake; thus, what tribe a person is enrolled in and what factors determine membership in an Indian tribal nation become matters of great political and social import. In the United States one cannot receive benefits as a beneficiary in the federal-Indian trust relationship unless one is "an enrolled member of a federally recognized tribe." In other words, an individual must be a citizen of a legally and politically defined "Indian nation" with rights under federal law.

Exactly what defines membership in a federally recognized tribe varies from one group to another. Ancestry, blood quantum, and acclamation are all legally sound bases used to support claims to tribal membership. These bases go against traditional methods of identification such as language, clan membership, and religion. The process of imposing Western political and legal standards tends to erode traditional forms of organization.

Legal definitions are of great import today. Tribes are not states but "dependent" nations with limited sovereignty and an inherent right to self-determination and self-government, even if the specific governmental forms are imposed from without. Many tribal groups maintain their traditional forms of governing themselves, while creating federally recognized nation-state frameworks that allow them to participate in nation-to-nation relationships. This is essential to the preservation of cultural integrity on the one hand and to the fulfillment of treaty obligations on the other.

The concept or term "tribe" is thus ambiguous and represents a superimposition of European modes of viewing and defining the cultural, social, and political organization of indigenous peoples. It is a term of convenience used to designate all North American Indian peoples even though only about half of them actually had any form of tribal organization. The indigenous peoples of North America lived in a wide spectrum of identity groups, including families, clans, bands, villages, tribes, chiefdoms, and empires. Their social and political systems were diverse and distinctive; they were expressions of each group's unique adaptations to the many geographical and environmental conditions evident in North America from prehistoric times to the present.

—*Michael W. Simpson*

See also American Indian; Bureau of Indian Affairs (BIA); Certificate of Degree of Indian Blood (CDIB); Civil rights and citizenship; Federally recognized tribes; Native American; Political organization and leadership; Sovereignty; Termination policy.

BIBLIOGRAPHY

Deloria, Vine, Jr., and Clifford M. Lytle. *The Nations Within: The Past and Future of American Indian Sovereignty.* New York: Pantheon Books, 1984. An excellent in-depth study of the development of tribal nationalism and of the political meaning of being an enrolled citizen of a federally recognized Indian tribe.

Drinnon, Richard. *Facing West: The Metaphysics of Indian-Hating and Empire-Building.* Minneapolis: University of Minnesota Press, 1980. The author explores the intellectual process which defines indigenous tribal groups as primitive and leads to violence between nations and tribes. Includes many helpful illustrations and an extensive bibliographic essay.

Fried, Morton H. *The Notion of Tribe.* Menlo Park, Calif.: Cummings, 1975. An exploration of the development and meaning of the concept of tribe.

Gluckman, Max. *Politics, Law, and Ritual in Tribal Society.* 1966. Reprint. New York: Blackwell, 1977. This book studies tribal organization and the ways tribal groups develop and maintain their integrity. Though not focused specifically on American Indian tribes, it provides a comprehensive conceptual basis for investigation of the concept. Illustrated in the original.

Sahlins, Marshall D. *Tribesmen.* Englewood Cliffs, N.J.: Prentice Hall, 1968. This book has illustrations which represent tribal life in all its diversity.

Tricksters

TRIBES AFFECTED: Widespread, but not pantribal

SIGNIFICANCE: Tricksters are ambiguous supernatural figures common to North American Indian mythology who are said to have helped in creating human culture

Tricksters were common features of North American Indian mythology. Supernatural in origin, tricksters played an important mythological role in giving significant technologies or cultural traits, such as fire or food plants, to a particular cultural group, though often unintentionally. Tricksters were not thought to be basically concerned with human welfare; rather, their gifts to humanity were usually the result of a joke or an accident. Tricksters were often seen as good-natured buffoons, and trickster tales were a source of entertainment as well as morality tales for children.

Ambiguous Natures. The fundamental characteristic of a trickster figure was its ambiguity. Tricksters were seen as being supernatural in their origins, but they were definitely not godlike: They laughed, played jokes, and reveled in bawdy or scandalous behavior. They most often took the form of an animal, especially a coyote, raven, or hare, but an animal that could talk and act like a human; alternatively a trickster could be portrayed as an old or ageless man. Whatever their form, tricksters could usually transform themselves, as from male to female or from animal into human form. Never the biggest, strongest, or best-looking of supernatural characters, tricksters lived by their wits. Nevertheless, they were usually too clever for their own good, with their schemes or jokes rebounding on them to get them into trouble. In fact, the sly trickster was also a numbskull, fooled by his own guile into fighting with his own reflection or eating his own body parts. Even successful tricks seldom paid off for the trickster; after securing a meal through a trick, for example, the meal would be lost through the trickster's foolishness. Many of a trickster's actions might seem heroic, such as fighting with a monster or giving humanity some key skill such as flint-knapping, but the heroic behavior was usually unintentional. Moreover, the hero trickster often turned around and next did something disrespectful or disreputable. Tricksters wandered the earth, with their enormous appetites for food and for sex getting them into one tight fix after another. Tricksters were ageless. They could die, and often did as a result of their exploits; however, the trickster was able to survive death and would rebound in another form or be caught in another predicament.

Creators of Humankind. Tricksters were often seen as the creators of a particular culture. For example, among the Nez Perce, the trickster was Coyote. In the Nez Perce origin myth, a monster exists that eats all the animals except Coyote, who ties himself to a high mountain to escape. Finding he cannot reach Coyote, the monster befriends him instead. Using his friendship, Coyote asks if he can go into the monster's stomach and visit his animal friends who were eaten, and to this the monster agrees. Once inside the monster's stomach, Coyote builds a fire and then cuts out the monster's heart with a knife; all the animals are able to escape. Coyote dismembers the monster with his knife and throws the parts around the earth. Everywhere a piece lands, a tribe of Indians is created. When Coyote is finished, his friend Fox points out that there is no tribe on the spot where the monster died. So Coyote washes the monster's blood from his hands and lets the drops fall to the ground; the Nez Perce are created in this way. Coyote says, "Here on this ground I will make the Nez Perce. They will be few in number, but they will be strong and pure." The tale is typical of trickster myths in which the trickster acts as the creator of humankind.

In other tales humans already exist, but they lack the necessary skills or social behavior really to be human beings. Among the usual gifts the trickster bestows on humanity are fire, flint, tobacco, food animal, or cultivated plants, and the regulation of weather or the seasons. In the Northwest, Raven as trickster creates dry earth as well for humans to stand on. In addition, the trickster often brings mortality, portrayed as natural or necessary, to humanity. In the Winnebago trickster tale, Hare originally makes humans immortal but soon realizes that immortality will cause humanity to cover the earth, which would create great suffering from insufficient food supplies. He thus undoes his gift to create a natural balance between humanity and the ability of the earth to support life.

Telling the Tale. Trickster tales were usually narrated by highly respected specialists in the community. These specialists memorized the tales, which were maintained by an oral tradition, and presented them in creative and dramatic tellings. Most of the members of the community knew the outline of the tales, but the specialist's acting ability brought them alive. These specialists were permitted to expand or embellish on the tales as they saw fit; the fundamental plot and the primary actors were retained, but considerable liberty could be taken with the details. Trickster tales were among the most entertaining these specialists presented; the combination of buffoonery, scandalous behavior, and drama in the tales made them good listening. In addition, trickster tales were presented as morality tales for children. As the trickster found himself in trouble because of excessive pride, lust, or greed, children could be reminded of proper behavior. Some authorities believe that the trickster tales served as safety valves for adults as well by making fun of serious rituals or difficult social situations. When the trickster joked with his mother-in-law—ordinarily a very formal relationship among North American Indians—or flaunted the fasts which accompanied many rituals, he was doing something many would have liked to have done but could not because of social requirements. All in all, the trickster was—and is—a popular figure in North American mythology. Even if he was too vain, clever, or greedy for his own good, he was always amusing, and he accomplished much for humankind, even if by accident.

—*David J. Minderhout*

See also Humor; Manibozho; Religion; Sacred narratives.

BIBLIOGRAPHY

Boas, Franz. *Race, Language, and Culture*. New York: Macmillan, 1940.

de Waal Malefijt, Annemarie. *Religion and Culture: An Introduction to Anthropology of Religion*. 1968. Reprint. Prospect Heights, Ill.: Waveland Press, 1989.

Pandian, Jacob. *Culture, Religion, and the Sacred Self*. Englewood Cliffs, N.J.: Prentice Hall, 1991.

Radin, Paul. *The Trickster: A Study in American Indian Mythology*. London: Routledge & Kegan Paul, 1956.

Wilson, Samuel M. "Trickster Treats." *Natural History*, October, 1991, 4-8.

Tsatoke, Monroe (Sept. 29, 1904, near Saddle Mountain, Okla.—Feb. 3, 1937): Artist

TRIBAL AFFILIATION: Kiowa

SIGNIFICANCE: Tsatoke was a member of the Kiowa Five group of painters who contributed to the formation of the twentieth century Oklahoma styles of Native American painting

Tsatoke was one of the Kiowas in a Fine Arts Club organized in Anadarko, Oklahoma, by Susie C. Peters in early 1926. Students did drawing, painting, and beadwork. In the fall of that year, special classes were set up for them outside the regular academic curriculum at the University of Oklahoma, and they studied there the next two academic years. In addition to being an artist, Tsatoke was a good singer and served as chief singer at Kiowa dances for many years.

Although he painted standard images, such as warriors, he was best known for paintings of dance scenes, drummers, and peyote cult subjects. While seriously ill with tuberculosis, Tsatoke joined the Native American Church and became active in the peyote ceremony. He did a series of paintings that explored his religious experience, and he is known for exploring spiritual themes.

His work has been included in many exhibitions and has been collected by the National Museum of the American Indian, Oklahoma Historical Society Museum, University of Oklahoma Museum of Art, and the Museum of New Mexico, among others.

See also Art and artists, contemporary; Asah, Spencer; Auchiah, James; Hokeah, Jack; Mopope, Stephen; Paints and painting.

Tsetsaut: Tribe

CULTURE AREA: Subarctic

LANGUAGE GROUP: Athapaskan

PRIMARY LOCATION: British Columbia

The highly mobile Tsetsaut probably comprised five named composite bands, divided into two matrilineal clans, the Eagle and Wolf. They subsisted primarily on inland game hunting and trapping, descending only in the summer to the Portland Inlet to fish and dry salmon for winter storage. Their principal food was marmot, supplemented with porcupine, mountain goat, and bear. Winter travel was facilitated by snowshoes and the use of rare yellow cedar dugout canoes in spring and summer. The Tsetsaut had no permanent villages, only temporary camps and shelters of single or double lean-tos covered with bark.

The Tsetsaut were probably first contacted in 1862 by fur traders of the Hudson's Bay Company post at Port Simpson. In the same year, William Duncan established a new Christian village of Metlakatla and entered into competition for furs. Robert Tomlinson established a mission at Kincolith in 1867, and when Franz Boas visited the site in 1894 he found that the Tsetsaut population numbered only twelve, a reduction from five hundred only sixty years earlier.

See also Subarctic.

Tsimshian: Tribe

CULTURE AREA: Northwest Coast
LANGUAGE GROUP: Tsimshian
PRIMARY LOCATION: Northwestern British Columbia, southeastern Alaska
POPULATION SIZE: 4,550 in Canada (Statistics Canada, based on 1991 census); 2,432 in U.S. (1990 U.S. Census)

Archaeological evidence suggests a Tsimshian residency of some five thousand years in the area. There are three major divisions: Tsimshian proper (which have been separated into the Southern Coast and Tsimshian), Niska (Nishga), and Gitksan. Each speaks a different dialect. Tsimshian derives from *emsyan* ("inside the Skeena River").

The Tsimshian subsisted on a variety of land and sea animals as well as plants that were gathered seasonally. Salmon was the most important food source. Eulachon, or candlefish, were particularly important for their oil or grease. The Tsimshian had a virtual monopoly on candlefish and the grease trade and became very wealthy as a result. The Tsimshian transported themselves between areas primarily in canoes.

The Tsimshian lived in fishing villages and camps in the spring and summer and in large houses made from red cedar in the winter. A chief's house might measure 50 by 30 feet. The chief and his family lived in several cubicles at the rear of the house. Other families of lesser status occupied the side walls. The houses were also used for dances during the winter ceremonial season.

The Tsimshian were divided into four phratries (tribal subdivisions, comprising several clans): Eagle, Wolf, Raven, and Killer Whale. Membership in a phratry was matrilineal, and marriage outside the phratry was prohibited. Each phratry controlled a defined territory. Social order and customs were maintained through elaborate ceremonial feasts and potlatches.

The readily available and plentiful sources of sustenance allowed the Tsimshian time to devote to other activities. The Tsimshian became expert artisans and are especially well known for their intricate totem poles. Copper was the highest symbol of wealth, and the Tsimshian hammered native copper for their chief into beautiful ceremonial shields.

In the late eighteenth century the Tsimshian traded extensively with Europeans and Americans, and many moved to trading posts on the peninsula, where they built settlements. Contact with the outside world was intensified by the discovery of gold in 1867 and the building of a railroad. In 1871 the Canadian government assumed responsibility for the Tsimshian. Reserves were created at traditional sites, and allocations were unilaterally imposed by the government. The effects of missionization were also felt, and Tsimshian villages became a hybrid mixture of English and Indian custom and tradition. The Tsimshian have actively resisted government controls and usurpation of their aboriginal lands.

An entirely separate community of about thirteen hundred Tsimshians resides on Annette Island in Alaska in a community known as New Metlakatla. These are the descendants of the original fifty Tsimshian whom a missionary named William Duncan moved to Metlakatla in 1862. The colony moved to Alaska in 1887 after a disagreement with church authorities. It retains much of its traditional values even today.

See also Northwest Coast.

Tubatulabal: Tribe

CULTURE AREA: California
LANGUAGE GROUP: Tubatulabal
PRIMARY LOCATION: Southern Sierra foothills, California
POPULATION SIZE: 29 (1990 U.S. Census)

The highly mobile Tubatulabal comprised three discrete bands speaking mutually intelligible dialects, each with their own chief. They occupied either patrilineal or matrilineal exogamous, semipermanent hamlets of several extended families, but they had no strict rules of exogamy or endogamy above the hamlet level. Chiefs were even-tempered, enunciated sound judgment, possessed oratory skills, and were generous with advice and their time. Leaders had limited authority, but they negotiated arbitration and resolved conflict. Living structures were simple but effective, made of domed, bent willow covered with brush and mud, with tule mats for beds and floor coverings. Women made coiled and twined baskets of split willow, yucca roots, and deer grass in representative and geometric designs. The most important foods were acorn and piñon nuts, collectively gathered and stored for winter consumption. All land mammals were hunted, and great amounts of various insects were dried as winter stores. Individual and communal fishing made an important contribution to their diet. Jimson weed was used probably only in curing ceremonies.

The first European American contact was in 1776, when Francisco Garcés explored the lower Kern River. By 1850, white settlers and cattlemen had established homesteads and ranches; and in 1857, the Kern River gold rush brought miners, who eventually displaced most of the Tubatulabal. After considerable conflict, the Tubatulabal located themselves on the Tule River Reservation from 1900 to 1972.

Today, the major source of income for most Tubatulabal men is working as cowhands. Some tribal women are employed as secretaries. There are only a few elders who pursue certain types of traditional technology, particularly basketry and root digging. The low population and deculturation of the Tubatulabal reflects the historical 1863 massacre by whites and the devastating effects of disease and epidemics. Migration from the area and intermarriage with non-Indians have further decreased the tribe's numbers.

See also California.

Tula: Archaeological site

DATE: 900-1200
LOCATION: Hidalgo, Mexico
CULTURES AFFECTED: Aztec, Maya, Toltec

Tula is the name of a modern Mexican town 70 miles north of Mexico City where lie the ruins of Tollán—the ancient capital of the Toltec, who lived in what is now Hidalgo, Mexico, between about 900 and 1200 C.E. The Toltec were a composite group of Nahua, Otomi, and Nonoalca Indians led at one time by a semilegendary figure named Mixcoatl and his son Topiltzin. The latter adopted the name Quetzalcóatl ("Feathered Serpent"), a chief god of the Toltec. Under Topiltzin's direction, the Toltec formed an empire and made Tollán ("Place of Reeds"), now called Tula, the administrative center for an area spanning central Mexico from the Atlantic to the Pacific.

The Toltec, literally "the reed people," were highly skilled builders and craftsmen, trading services and products for food from the farmers of nearby villages. As the builders of Tollán or Tula, they created fine metalwork, monumental porticoes, serpent columns, gigantic atlantean warrior statues (four of which still surmount Pyramid B, the most impressive building at Tula), carved human and animal standard bearers, and *chacmools*—statues of reclining figures with hands grasping a plate held over the belly. So far as is known, chacmools are a purely Toltec invention, unique to Tula and Chichén Itzá (a place to where some Toltecs later migrated); they served as receptacles for the hearts of sacrificed human victims.

The religion and art of Tula all reflect a very militaristic theme. Deities worshiped at Tula required human sacrifices. Painted and sculptured friezes depicted marching felines and canines, birds of prey devouring human hearts, and human faces gaping from the jaws of serpents. Three military cults, represented by the coyote, the jaguar, and the eagle, worshiped the god Tezcatlipoca ("Smoking Mirror") rather than the more peaceful Quetzalcóatl. This caused internal conflict, and Topiltzin (Quetzalcóatl) was forced to leave Tula in 987. He went to the Gulf Coast, and tradition states that he got on a raft made of serpents and headed for Tlapallan ("Red Land"), some day to return to redeem his people. During the twelfth century, nomads invaded the Toltec empire. As they settled in the Valley of Mexico, Tula was overrun and destroyed by violence in 1156 or 1168, but its memory was forever glorious in the minds of later Mesoamericans. Nearly all subsequent ruling dynasties claimed their descent from the Toltec of Tula. The Aztec later honored the Toltec as the founders of urban civilization at Tula.

In its heyday, Tula was the largest city in Mesoamerica, with an estimated population of between thirty and forty thousand. The archaeological remains are concentrated in two clusters at opposite ends of a low ridge. The Grand Precinct at the south edge was the heart of the city. This area contains several open plazas surrounded by small, but highly decorated, temples (built atop large pyramids), ball courts, government administration buildings, and palaces. Thousands of single-story masonry houses with flat roofs surrounded this end of the city. Two-thirds of a mile north of the Grand Precinct was Tulachico, a group of mounds that formed a civic center. The El Salitre swamp at the bottom ridge provided reeds for the making of baskets and mats and was probably the inspiration for the name Tollán.

See also Aztec; Chichimec; Quetzalcóatl; Toltec.

Tule

TRIBES AFFECTED: Widespread
SIGNIFICANCE: Tule was widely used for food, mats, boats, hats, and dwellings

Tule (*Scirpus acutus, S. occidentalis,* and *S. validus*) is a strong, pithy, long, cylindrical stemmed, perennial plant with stout rootstalks that grows below mud in wetlands and on the edges of many lakes throughout much of North America. It was used extensively for food and utilitarian purposes by Native Americans. Immature roots yielded a sweet syrup when crushed and boiled. In late summer, the pollen was gathered and pressed into cakes that were baked. The starchy root was eaten raw, baked, or ground into a nutritious white flour after drying. Tule seeds gathered in the fall were used whole, parched, or ground into a nutritious mush.

After a killing frost, women gathered the tules into bundles, and during the winter the cylindrical stalks were made into mats for floors and for layering over dwellings. Using pointed stone awls to make holes in the tules, women sewed the tules together with hemp and bone needles. The tule was utilized by some groups for making bundle boats, hats, rain capes, storage hut roofs, dwelling covers, and floors. Tules were also interwoven into flat eating mats, trays, baskets, and even fishtrap liners.

See also Food preparation and cooking; Tools.

Tunica: Tribe

CULTURE AREA: Southeast
LANGUAGE GROUP: Tunica
PRIMARY LOCATION: Louisiana
POPULATION SIZE: 33 (1990 U.S. Census)

The Tunica traditionally lived in Mississippi and Arkansas, just north of the area where the Yazoo River joins the Mississippi. They farmed, fished, and hunted, and they lived in small villages of rectangular thatched-roof houses; villages often included a temple building. They made pottery, wove cloth of mulberry fibers, and mined salt to trade with other tribes. The culture involved a high level of material security, and chiefs enjoyed nearly kinglike status.

The Tunicas were friendly with the French and were allies with them in French struggles against other tribes, notably the Natchez. In 1731 a large party of Natchez and allies attacked the Tunica, leading to heavy casualties on both sides; the principal chief of the Tunica was killed in the fight. Around the 1730's, the population began to decline, primarily because of diseases brought by the Europeans. When only a few hundred remained, the remnants of the Tunica and other Tunica-speaking tribes started to band together. In the late 1700's, the combined group moved up the Red River and settled near what is now Marksville, Louisiana. Some also migrated to the Oklahoma area with their Choctaw neighbors around that time.

See also Choctaw; Natchez; Southeast; Tunica language.

Tunica language

CULTURE AREA: Southeast
TRIBE AFFECTED: Tunica
Long believed to be an isolate, Tunica was spoken by people in three locations: the lower Yazoo River, the eastern shore of the Mississippi River in Louisiana, and Avoyelles Parish, Louisiana. The language is extinct and there is no extant Tunica writing system.

A controversial 1987 grouping (Joseph H. Greenberg, *Languages in the Americas*) places Tunica with Chitimacha in the Gulf Group of the Penutian family. Among the other members of this group are Natchez, Muskogean, and, most unexpectedly, the Yuki and Wappo languages of California. The suggestion is that Yuki and Wappo speakers migrated from homes in the Delta area to California, picking up some Pueblo lexical items during their migration.

Evidence exists that Hernando de Soto met the Tunica. The Yazoo town of the tribe was first encountered by three priests, one of whom, Father Davion, stayed with them beginning in 1699. The Tunica during this period were allies of the French, especially in regard to their war with the Natchez. The Tunica numbered about fifteen hundred during this period. The census of 1910 gave forty-three Tunica in all, including many mixed-bloods. By 1930 there was only one remaining Tunica who could speak the language. The language died out after that.

See also Chitimacha language; Penutian language family; Tunica.

Turquoise

TRIBES AFFECTED: Great Basin, Mesoamerican, Southwest tribes
SIGNIFICANCE: Turquoise was made into jewelry used in burial ceremonies and was an important trade item in Mexico and the Southwest
Turquoise is a carbonaceous mineral that was prized by many Native American groups primarily for its bright blue-green color. Major turquoise sources were located throughout the American Great Basin, the Southwest, and western Mexico, and turquoise was traded extensively throughout the western United States and Mexico.

As early as 300 B.C.E., the Anasazi Basketmaker culture as far north as Utah worked turquoise for jewelry, which was commonly interred in burials, and traded it as far south as central Mexico. Native American craftsmen from the Ameri-can Southwest traded turquoise for shell from the Gulf of California and the Pacific coast. Turquoise was frequently worked into thin tesserae used in mosaic inlays over shell ornaments. Similar mosaics covered burial masks from the central Mexican site of Teotihuacán during the fifth and sixth centuries, as well as later Aztec and Mixtec sculpture. By 1000 C.E., large-scale Anasazi sites such as Chaco Canyon in northwestern New Mexico contained specialized turquoise workshops and served as distribution centers for interregional turquoise trade networks. Twentieth century Navajo and Pueblo artisans, particularly Hopi and Zuni, maintained a strong tradition of turquoise jewelry and carved fetish figures during the nineteenth and twentieth centuries. In addition, ground turquoise frequently provided pigment for blue paint.

Turquoise held high symbolic import because of its distinctive bright color and relative scarcity. Turquoise stones or nuggets were believed to possess spiritual power and were common components of shaman's medicine bags as curing charms. The color blue commonly symbolized concepts of rain or water, freshness, fertility, and the western horizon, the direction of the setting sun. Mesoamerican cultures revered jade for similar reasons. In Pueblo mythology, turquoise was so revered that a specific divinity, called *Huruing Wuhti* in Hopi (loosely translated as "Hard Substances Old Woman"), was considered the patron deity of turquoise, shell, and coral.

See also Arts and crafts—Southwest; Dress and adornment; Metalwork; Mosaic and inlay; Shells and shellwork; Trade.

Tuscarora: Tribe

CULTURE AREAS: Northeast, Southeast
LANGUAGE GROUP: Iroquoian
PRIMARY LOCATION: New York, Ontario
POPULATION SIZE: 2,943 in U.S. (1990 U.S. Census); estimated 1,200 in Canada
The Tuscarora probably originated in New York and Pennsylvania and migrated southward to the coastal plain and the eastern piedmont of North Carolina after 500 B.C.E. The Tuscarora were principally farmers who produced corn, hemp, gourds, beans, peaches, and apples in great abundance. Despite their skills as farmers, the Tuscarora placed a greater reliance on hunting and gathering than neighboring Indian peoples.

The colonization of North Carolina by the English prompted the Tuscarora War of 1711-1713. The English encroached upon Tuscarora lands, enslaved the Tuscarora, and cheated them at trade. In the war, an alliance of the English and the Yamasee Indians defeated the Tuscarora. Nearly one thousand Tuscarora were killed and another seven hundred enslaved. In the peace treaty, the Tuscarora forfeited their rights to lands south of the Neuse River but received a small reservation in Bertie County, North Carolina.

Shortly after the war, about fifteen hundred Tuscarora moved to New York to seek shelter with the Iroquois Confederacy, which accepted the Tuscarora as members in 1722 or 1723. Over the next ninety years, the remaining Tuscarora moved northward, and in 1804, the North Carolina reservation closed.

During the American Revolution, most of the Tuscarora and many of the Oneida broke with other Iroquois and supported the Americans against the British. As a result, Tuscarora villages were attacked and destroyed by the British and other Iroquois, forcing the Tuscarora to find new lands to the west at Lewiston, New York. These lands became the site of the modern Tuscarora Reservation. The American Revolution also divided the Tuscarora. In the 1780's, a small pro-British faction of the Tuscarora moved to English Canada near the Grand River. These lands became the site of the modern Six Nations Reserve in Ontario.

Studies of the Tuscarora in the late twentieth century showed that they retained an unusually large portion of their traditional culture, social structure, and national identity. In the late 1950's, the Tuscarora challenged an effort by a utility company to build a reservoir on the Tuscarora Reservation. Although the U.S. Supreme Court ruled against the Tuscarora, their legal struggles helped inspire the emerging Indian rights movement of the 1960's.

See also Hancock; Hewitt, John N. B.; Iroquoian language family; Iroquois Confederacy; Yamasee.

Tuskegee: Tribe

CULTURE AREA: Southeast
LANGUAGE GROUP: Muskogean
PRIMARY LOCATION: Between the Coosa and Tallapoosa rivers, Alabama

Little ethnographic data exist for the Tuskegee, who were horticulturalists and warriors. They possessed stone tools, practiced extensive intertribal trade, and possessed specialized predation and war technology. As did many tribes with maize economies, they had complex ceremonies, including fertility cults and planting and harvesting rituals. They gathered salt from natural sources, and collected ash from burnt hickory, animal bones, and certain mosses. They exploited the bison for food and by-products.

It is known that Hernando de Soto visited these people in 1540. By the end of the seventeenth century they had probably divided into two bands, one settling on the Chattahoochee River near Columbus, the other on the upper Tennessee near Long Island. By 1717 French rule led to the removal of the Tuskegee (who had by that time been absorbed by the Creek); the Tuskegee formed a town in Oklahoma on the southwestern part of the Creek territories. Their greatly diminished population finally settled to the northwest near Beggs.

See also Creek.

Tutchone: Tribe

CULTURE AREA: Subarctic
LANGUAGE GROUP: Athapaskan
PRIMARY LOCATION: Yukon Territory
POPULATION SIZE: 1,610 (Statistics Canada, based on 1991 census)

The six bands of highly mobile matrilineal Tutchone were organized into two moieties, and lived in coastal-type rectangular dwellings of logs. Subsistence was gained primarily through hunting caribou, moose, and mountain goat, and the trapping of smaller land mammals. Migratory waterfowl were taken, in addition to freshwater fish and salmon. Some gathering of vegetable foods and berries supplemented the Tutchone diet.

The first European Canadian contact with the Tutchone was made by Robert Campbell of the Hudson's Bay Company in 1842; he established Fort Selkirk in 1848. In 1874, white traders reentered the area and established Fort Reliance for fur traders. Thousands of gold prospectors arrived in 1898, but by 1900 only a few continued to mine for gold, silver, and copper. With the collapse of the fur trade in the 1930's, woodcutting became a main source of income for many Tutchone families. Surface and subsurface mining attracted non-Indian populations, which was facilitated by the 1942 Alaskan Highway. Most Tutchone are involved in the wage economy, locally or through migration to urban centers. The Tutchone population was estimated to be about fifteen hundred in the mid-1970's.

See also Kutchin.

Tutelo: Tribe

CULTURE AREA: Northeast, Southeast
LANGUAGE GROUP: Siouan
PRIMARY LOCATION: Virginia, North Carolina

The Tutelo were a northern Siouan people who came into the present-day Virginia piedmont from the upper Ohio Valley. The meaning of the name is unknown; it was probably taken from a southern Indian language by the Iroquois. They were also known as Katteras or Shateras. In 1671, English explorers visited a Tutelo village, Shamokin, near present-day Salem, Virginia. By the beginning of the eighteenth century, the tribe had moved itself to an island in the Roanoke River, near the junction of the Stanton and Dan, and shortly thereafter to the headwaters of the Yadkin River in western North Carolina, where they were able to hunt elk and bison.

By 1709, the Tutelo and five other tribes (Saponi, Ocaneechi, Keyauwee, Shakiori, and Stuckanox) were estimated to total only 750 in population. For their own survival, this group of peoples gradually moved eastward, settling at Fort Christanna on the Meherrin River. Following the peace of 1722 between the Iroquois and Virginia tribes, the Tutelo, along with the Saponi, moved north, and by 1744 had settled in Pennsylvania under the protection of the Iroquois. By then the Manahoac, Monacan, and Saponi tribes had been mostly absorbed by the Tutelo. In 1753, they were admitted into full membership of the League of the Iroquois. In 1771, they settled on the east side of Cayuga Inlet and established a town, Coreorgonel, which was destroyed by General John Sullivan in 1779. Following this defeat, some of the tribe continued to live with the Cayuga and retained their own language. A remnant of the tribe located near Buffalo, New York. Others settled and intermarried with the Iroquois.

Little is known about the social organization of the Tutelo except that they gathered in clans. A tribal leader and council made political and social decisions. It is believed the leadership was not by lineage. During the nineteenth century, cultural and linguistic material was gathered on the Tutelo by the Smithsonian Institution. The last full-blooded Tutelo died in 1871, and the last person to speak the Tutelo language died in 1898.

See also Manahoac; Siouan language family.

Tututni: Tribe

CULTURE AREA: Northwest Coast
LANGUAGE GROUP: Athapaskan
PRIMARY LOCATION: Lower Rogue River and southwest Oregon coast

The Tututni language group includes Upper Coquille, Tututni, Chasta Costa, and Chetco. All these tribes were typical of the Northwest Coast with stratified societies, winter plank houses, extensive overland and water trade, and traditional forms of wealth. Only the Tututni were matrilineal. The Tututni comprised seven divisions: Kwatami, Yukichetunne, Khwaishtunnetunne, Chetleshin, Mikonotunne, Chemetunne, and Tututni. Though they were oriented toward the sea and rivers, they gained most of their food from land animals, small animals, roots, tubers, seeds, berries, nuts, and insects. Differential food and utilitarian resources encouraged trade and intermarriage.

Robert Gray first contacted and traded with these people in 1792. In 1826 the botanist David Douglas visited the Upper Umpqua. The population for these groups was greatly reduced by disease, gold seekers, and the Rogue River War of 1855-1856. Some people were settled on the Siletz and Grand Ronde Reservations and became adherents to the Ghost Dance movement after its 1871 introduction.

See also Athapaskan language family; Siletz.

Twana: Tribe

CULTURE AREA: Northwest Coast
LANGUAGE GROUP: Salishan (Twana)
PRIMARY LOCATION: Washington
POPULATION SIZE: 714 ("Skokomish," 1990 U.S. Census)

The patrilocal and patrilineal Twana (including the Skokomish and Toanho people), like their neighbors, lived in permanent winter villages. Both maritime and land hunting were specialized in technology and associated ritual. The socially stratified Twana maintained their positions through birth, redistribution of wealth, and certain physical and religious attributes.

George Vancouver explored Puget Sound and Hood Canal in 1792. In 1827 the Hudson's Bay Company established Fort Langley on the Fraser River, which became a major trading post. The Indian Shaker Church influenced the Twana and Skokomish (a tribe of the Twana) in the early 1830's. In 1910 there were only sixty-one Twana.

The Twana Reservation at Skokomish had a population of 1,029 in 1984, which did not include all off-reservation Twana or recognize those of varying blood degrees from other groups. The Southern Coast Salish tribes have experienced considerable socioeconomic, political, and cultural revitalization because of recent changes in federal legislation and policies, particularly in sovereignty and fishing rights.

See also Salish, Salishan language family.

Twins

TRIBES AFFECTED: Widespread, but especially Navajo, Pueblo tribes, Seneca, Sioux
SIGNIFICANCE: The concept of twins formed an important part of religious mythology, explaining the process and structure of creation and providing models for human behavior

Twins are common in Native American mythology, but their roles have tribal variants. For the Seneca, the twins Sprout and Flint represent the bipolar structure of existence, the tension between good and evil. Sprout makes deer, and Flint makes mountain lions to eat them. Sprout creates fruits and berries; Flint, thorns and poison ivy.

More common is the myth of the War Twins, who are sons of the Father Sun. In the Zuni tradition, they help with creation, leading the Zuni to the surface world and transforming them into humans. Like the Navajo twins, Monsterslayer and Born of Water, they receive weapons from Father Sun and rid the world of monsters, becoming protectors of the tribe. They also often have astronomical significance, creating constellations from the monsters they have slain. In Zuni myth, the twins are identified with the evening and morning stars.

In Navajo culture, the twins serve as models for boys as they develop into adulthood. Like the twins, male children receive toy weapons from their father. The twins are important figures in rites of passage. In Lakota Sioux culture, twins have a special sacredness, and many healers claim that their power comes from a previous existence as a twin.

See also Astronomy; Ethnophilosophy and worldview; Religion.

Two Leggings (c. 1844, along the Bighorn River, Mont.—April 23, 1923, Hardin, Mont.): Anthropological informant

ALSO KNOWN AS: Big Crane, His Eyes Are Dreamy
TRIBAL AFFILIATION: Crow
SIGNIFICANCE: Two Leggings provided invaluable insights regarding his life as a Crow warrior to anthropologist William Wildschut

Two Leggings, originally known as Big Crane, was born along the Bighorn River in Montana. He received the name His Eyes Are Dreamy following an unusually long and failed vision quest. As a young Crow warrior, he participated in raids for horses against the traditional Crow enemies, the Sioux. At that time, the Crow were peaceful toward white settlers.

Between 1919 and 1923, Two Leggings related his life story to a Montana businessman and anthropologist, William Wildschut. Under the sponsorship of the Heye Foundation of the Museum of the American Indian, Wildschut recorded Two Leggings' detailed observations regarding everyday Crow life

Two Leggings related his life story, filled with details of everyday Crow life, to anthropologist William Wildschut. (Library of Congress)

and the lifecycles of a Crow warrior. Wildschut's manuscript, entitled *Two Leggings: The Making of a Crow Warrior*, was edited by anthropologist Peter Nabokov and published in 1967. It is an invaluable source of anthropological data on the tribe. Two Leggings married Ties Up Her Bundle, and together they reared two adopted children, Red Clay Woman and Sings to the Sweat Lodge.

See also Crow; Horses; Plains.

Two Moon (c. 1847—c. 1917): Tribal chief
ALSO KNOWN AS: Ishi'eyo, Ishaynishus
TRIBAL AFFILIATION: Cheyenne
SIGNIFICANCE: An ally of Sitting Bull and Crazy Horse in the Sioux Wars of the 1870's and a leader in the war for the Black Hills of 1876-1877, Two Moon also distinguished himself as an informant to the writer Hamlin Garland

Sometimes confused with his uncle Two Moons, who was chief in the Bozeman Trail wars of 1866-1868 and an ally of Red Cloud's Sioux people, the younger Two Moon fought with Sitting Bull and Crazy Horse in the Sioux Wars of the 1870's. Two Moon fought troops on the Powder River in Montana in March of 1876 and fought at the Battle of the Little Bighorn in June of 1876.

Two Moon surrendered to Colonel Nelson Miles in 1877 and served under Miles as an army scout in the Nez Perce War of 1877. Two Moon was also one of six Cheyennes who met Little Wolf and his followers in March, 1879, following their exodus from Indian Territory. Hamlin Garland's article "General Custer's Last Fight as Seen by Two Moon" (*McClure's Magazine*, 1898) was based on Two Moon's information.

See also Bozeman Trail wars; Crazy Horse; Little Bighorn, Battle of the; Nez Perce War; Sitting Bull.

Two Strike (1832, southern Nebr.—c. 1915, Pine Ridge Reservation, S.Dak.): War chief
ALSO KNOWN AS: Two Strikes, Nomkahpa (Knocks Two Off)
TRIBAL AFFILIATION: Brule Sioux
SIGNIFICANCE: Two Strike was a prominent leader of the Sioux during the time before the closing of the frontier at Wounded Knee in 1890

Two Strike's Brule Sioux name, Nomkahpa, meant "Knocks Two Off." The name was earned in battle, after Two Strike knocked two Utes off their horses with a single blow of his war club. Two Strike figured prominently in the history of the Brules late in the nineteenth century, up to and including the "closing" of the frontier at Wounded Knee in 1890.

Born near the Republican River in what would become Nebraska, Two Strike played an important role in raids on the Union Pacific Railroad during Red Cloud's War (1866-1868). During the 1870's, Two Strike allied with Spotted Tail and tried to insulate his people from the European American invasion. In the 1880's, Two Strike became an advocate of the Ghost Dance. A month before the massacre at Wounded Knee, however, Two Strike heeded whites' advice to give up the dance and its promised delivery from white domination. After the slaughter of native people under Big Foot at Wounded Knee in late December of 1890, Two Strike led his people on an angry rampage with other Sioux. He desisted only after General Nelson Meils promised fair treatment for his people. Two Strike's people surrendered a second time on January 15, 1891. After the turn of the century, Two Strike lived quietly at Pine Ridge, where he was buried after his death in about 1915.

See also Ghost Dance; Railroads; Wounded Knee Massacre.

Tyigh: Tribe
CULTURE AREA: Plateau
LANGUAGE GROUP: Sahaptian
PRIMARY LOCATION: Oregon

The Tyigh (also spelled "Tygh"), a branch of the Sahaptian family, were so named by white explorers and traders because they lived near the Tyigh and White rivers in what is now Wasco County, Oregon. As is generally true for the Sahaptian tribes, there is no ethnographic evidence or traditional lore to show where the Tyigh lived earlier than their first encounter with whites in the early 1800's. Sahaptian tribes lived in village communities of varying size. Because they relied on hunting and fishing (salmon being a chief staple of their diet)

Two Strike was a major Brule Sioux leader from the 1860's to the 1890's; he was allied with Spotted Tail in the 1870's. (Library of Congress)

as well as on gathering roots and berries, they moved throughout the year to find food in different seasons. This prevented villages from growing and developing as political or social centers.

Sahaptian tribes do not seem to have relied on agriculture. They were skilled with horses and used them in their travels. Tyigh speak the Tenino language. Under the terms of the Wasco Treaty of 1855, the Tyigh were placed on the Warm Springs Reservation in Oregon, along with the Tenino and other tribes. Their population as a separate group has not been counted since.

See also Plateau; Tenino.

Umatilla: Tribe

CULTURE AREA: Plateau
LANGUAGE GROUP: Sahaptian
PRIMARY LOCATION: Oregon
POPULATION SIZE: 1,159 (1990 U.S. Census)

The Umatillas are recognized as Plateau Indians who traditionally inhabited the Mid-Columbia Plateau. They are a Sahaptian-speaking group, and their population was estimated at fifteen hundred in 1780. Today their descendants reside on the Umatilla Reservation, which is located in northeastern Oregon.

The Umatillas, part of the larger Mid-Columbia Plateau culture, existed for ten thousand years in the Columbia Basin before the coming of European Americans. During this period, their culture remained relatively stable, with seasonal moves to winter villages; there were rich salmon fishing resources on the Columbia River as well as roots and berries that were gathered. By the time of European American contact, the horse was part of Umatilla culture. Horses changed Umatilla subsistence patterns but not to the extent that the horse changed Nez Perce culture. Perhaps because of the plenitude of their resources, particularly salmon, the Umatillas' economy still consisted primarily of fishing and gathering, whereas some Plateau tribes began to hunt bison with the arrival of the horse.

Although there is evidence of epidemics, such as smallpox brought by trading ships, occurring in the Mid-Columbia Plateau as early as 1775, white settlement did not directly affect the Umatillas until the 1840's. Their villages were near the Emigrant Road, or Old Oregon Trail. When the Cayuse War broke out after the Whitman Massacre in 1848, some Umatillas took part. In 1855, the Walla Walla Council, led by Washington Territorial Governor Isaac Stevens, had an immediate impact on the Umatillas in that the Umatillas ceded lands in return for the Umatilla Reservation, an area originally established with 245,699 acres. Today the reservation comprises 85,322 acres. The Umatilla Reservation was to be home to the Umatillas, the Walla Wallas, and the Cayuse. It came to be known as the Confederated Tribes of the Umatilla Indian Reservation after the tribe organized in 1949 under the Indian Reorganization Act (1934).

The Umatillas, similar to many other Indian tribes, lost land after the General Allotment Act of 1887. Earlier, they had lost lands under the Donation Land Law, which allowed settlers to homestead lands in Oregon before the Indians rescinded their right to the land. Beginning in 1951, the Confederated Tribes of the Umatilla Reservation began filing claims with the Indian Claims Commission to recover lost lands or a financial settlement in lieu of land. Other lawsuits concerned lost fishing rights. In the case *Maison v. The Confederated Tribes of the Umatilla Reservation* (1958), Indian fishing rights were recognized. Other suits involved lost water rights on the Umatilla River as a result of dam construction. The Confederated Tribes of the Umatilla Reservation received several monetary compensations for these claims.

Today, the Confederated Tribes of the Umatilla Reservation rely on an economy of grazing and farming, particularly wheat, with limited industry. Some aspects of traditional life are still evident, as some members practice the Waashat religion and can speak the tribal language.

See also Cayuse; Cayuse War.

Umpqua: Tribe

CULTURE AREA: Northwest Coast
LANGUAGE GROUPS: Athapaskan, Penutian
PRIMARY LOCATION: Southwestern Oregon
POPULATION SIZE: 653 (1990 U.S. Census)

The Umpqua people traditionally lived along the Umpqua River of southwestern Oregon. The river flows from the Cascade Mountain Range in eastern Oregon to the Pacific Ocean in the west. The terrain through which it flows is mostly mountainous. The environments along its shores are varied, from cool, dry, upland coniferous forests in the east to lush, temperate-zone rain forests near the sea.

There are two fairly distinct Umpqua subgroups, the upper Umpqua and lower Umpqua. The people who live along the upper Umpqua River are most probably of Athapaskan origin, whereas the people of the lower river are apparently more closely related to other Penutian speakers of Yakonan stock. These assertions are disputed by some. Many Umpqua people believe they originated in their traditional homeland. The dividing point between upper and lower areas of the river is commonly considered to be at the town of Scottsburg.

Before white contact in the early nineteenth century, the Umpqua lived relatively solitary lives, hunting, gathering, and fishing. They would join with their neighbors, the Siuslaw to the north and the Coos to the south, for common defense and occasional potlatches.

After contact with white settlers, the Umpqua were pushed toward the margins of their homeland, then placed on the Siletz reservation in the 1850's. The lower Umpqua joined in political confederation and formed the Confederated Tribes of the Coos, lower Umpqua, and Siuslaw Indians. This confederation exists today as a federally recognized Indian nation.

The upper Umpqua fought for their land and sovereignty and are now recognized as the Cow Creek Band by the U.S. government.

See also Coos; Northwest Coast; Penutian language family; Siuslaw; Yakonan language family.

Uncas (c. 1606—c. 1682): Tribal chief

ALSO KNOWN AS: Wonkas (the Fox), Poquiam
TRIBAL AFFILIATION: Mohegan
SIGNIFICANCE: Uncas protected his people's interests in a period of conflict and change in seventeenth century New England by allying himself with the English

Uncas was sachem of the Mohegan branch of the closely related Pequot and Mohegan peoples of southern Connecticut. When Tatobem, great sachem of the Pequots (the dominant group), died in 1633, Uncas was passed over in a struggle to succeed him. Uncas and his supporters seceded, establishing themselves as a small, entirely separate tribe. With Uncas as sachem, the Mohegans were located west of the Thames River, while the majority Pequots held the territory east of it. During the Pequot War of 1636-1637, Uncas assisted the English, leading sixty warriors in a joint English-Mohegan-Narragansett attack that destroyed the Pequots as an independent people. As a reward, the Mohegan and the Narragansett were each allowed by treaty to incorporate captured Pequots as adoptees. The Mohegans adopted many more, and rivalry between the Mohegan and Narragansett for predominance then led to years of conflict. In these clashes Uncas skillfully cultivated English favor. In a battle in 1643 near Norwich, Connecticut, Uncas and four hundred Mohegans defeated a thousand Narragansetts and took prisoner their principal sachem, Miantonomo, executing him at English urging. During King Philip's War (1675-1676), Uncas again assisted the English against their Indian enemies. The English considered Uncas wily and unscrupulous, but he was so consistently loyal that their alliance endured for more than forty years.

See also Indian-white relations—English colonial; King Philip's War; Miantonomo; Narragansett; Pequot; Pequot War.

Urban Indians

Tribes affected: Pantribal

Significance: It is estimated that more than half of the United States' Native American population resides in a metropolitan area for most or all of the year; in many cities urban Indians go unnoticed by other ethnic groups

The term "urban Indians" is problematic for most non-Native Americans. Whether thinking of Native Americans brings forth positive, negative, or neutral images, most non-natives do not imagine natives as members of an urban, technological society, and this lack of urban image has led to a blindness regarding the presence and needs of Native Americans in the cities. Identification of the urban Native American has therefore been one of the central problems surrounding government policy-making regarding American Indians since the early 1960's.

Relocation and Migration. All members of a federally recognized tribe in the United States, according to the U.S. Constitution, are due certain benefits and services, by right of their heritage. This unique legal relationship with the U.S. government was never meant to end once an individual moved to a metropolitan area, but in effect that is what has happened. In the mid-1950's, the Bureau of Indian Affairs (BIA), in accord with Congress, began the Voluntary Relocation Program. BIA officers on each reservation were instructed to "sell" the idea of city living to likely candidates. Individuals, and sometimes families, were given a one-way ticket to the chosen city, where housing and employment awaited, all arranged by the BIA. Subsistence money was guaranteed for six weeks, after which these newest immigrants were on their own. It was informally known as a "sink-or-swim policy." As anthropologist Sol Tax noted twenty years after relocation, however, "Indians don't sink or swim, they float."

Most Indians who arrived in the city under the relocation program left as soon as they got a good look at their new way of life. Many of the jobs were unskilled, and Native Americans found they were able to afford only the worst housing available in the city. Under these conditions, transition to city dwelling was, for many, impossible. Yet the BIA did not recognize the shortcomings of its multimillion-dollar program and continued to relocate as many Native Americans as possible. Noticing that many of their clients were returning to their reservations, the BIA began relocating people as far away from their reservations as could be managed, to make it as difficult as possible to return. Part of the plan was to terminate the reservations eventually. Authors Watt Spade and Willard Walker illustrate one Indian view of this phase of the relocation program. They wrote of overhearing two Indian men humorously discussing the government's wanting to land a man on the moon. It could be done, one man said, but nobody knew how to get the man home again after he landed on the moon. All the government had to do, he said, was put an Indian in the rocket ship and tell him he was being relocated: "Then, after he got to the moon, that Indian would find his own way home again and the government wouldn't have to figure that part out at all." The Voluntary Relocation Program was a failure according to its own goals. This program was based on the prejudiced notion that Native American culture and lifeways will, and should, disappear. The BIA and the U.S. Congress of the 1950's counted on America's cities to speed that process.

Most Native Americans presently living in urban areas did not arrive through the relocation program but migrated independently, usually looking for employment, and settled near relatives or friends from their reservation or hometown. Many are permanent residents, but an approximately equal number are transient—relocating within the city, going from city to city, or spending part of the year in the city and part on the reservation. There is no known "typical" pattern of migration; tribal nations, families, and individuals differ according to their needs. A family may live in the city during the winter so the children can stay in school, then leave for the reservation in the summer. Construction workers are often busy in the cities during the warm months and leave in the winter. The pow-wow season and harvests also draw many urban Native Americans back to the reservations. Jeanne Guillemin points out in *Urban Renegades* (1975) that the young Micmac women of Boston often prefer to return to their kin in the Canadian Maritime Provinces when it is time to give birth. There they receive the physical, emotional, and spiritual support they need and avoid the frightening aspects of the city, such as its clinics and hospitals. The frequent moving to and from the reservation and within the city is one factor in the urban Native American's invisibility or elusiveness.

Urban Indian Identity. Another factor until recently has been their reluctance to identify themselves as Native Americans to non-Native Americans in the city. In 1976 the director of the American Indian Health Service in Chicago illustrated this problem with an anecdote. A young man had been playing baseball and had been hit hard by the bat. When he was taken

METROPOLITAN STATISTICAL AREAS WITH LARGEST NATIVE AMERICAN POPULATIONS, 1990	
Metropolitan Statistical Area	Population
*Los Angeles-Anaheim-Riverside, CA	85,004
Tulsa, OK	48,116
Oklahoma City, OK	45,623
*New York-Northern New Jersey-Long Island, NY-NJ-CT	44,437
*San Francisco-Oakland-San Jose, CA	39,255
Phoenix, AZ	37,708
*Seattle-Tacoma, WA	29,643
Minneapolis-St. Paul, MN-WI	23,621
Tucson, AZ	20,231
San Diego, CA	19,564
*Dallas-Fort Worth, TX	18,608
*Detroit-Ann Arbor, MI	17,731
Sacramento, CA	16,650
Albuquerque, NM	16,201
*Chicago-Gary-Lake County, IL-IN-WI	15,098
*Denver-Boulder, CO	13,600
*Portland-Vancouver, OR-WA	13,034
*Philadelphia-Wilmington-Trenton, PA-NJ-DE-MD	10,962
Washington, DC-MD-VA	10,685
*Houston-Galveston-Brazoria, TX	10,677

Source: U.S. Bureau of the Census, *Census of Population and Housing, 1990: Summary Tape on CD-ROM.* Washington, D.C.: U.S. Government Printing Office, 1991.

* Indicates a combined metropolitan statistical area (CMSA).

to the emergency room, he removed all his turquoise beads, giving them to a friend to keep for him, and stuffed his long braids inside his baseball cap; he said, "Now the receptionist will think I'm a Mexican." His friend said they frequently try to pass as Mexicans in order to be treated better. The urban Native Americans' attempts to remain unidentified, coupled with the tremendous mobility of individuals and families, has made it impossible in past years for the U.S. Census to come close to an accurate count in the cities. In the 1990 U.S. Census, however, there was a huge increase in people identifying themselves as Native Americans, Eskimos, and Aleuts. As the increase cannot be completely explained by actual population growth, there is much speculation regarding what has made so many more Native Americans willing to be identified. Some cynical observers insist that the motive must be monetary: to obtain funds and services that are due Native Americans under the law. One thing that scholars studying Native American culture have learned over the decades, however, is that Native Americans usually cannot be coaxed to take a particular course of action because of the promise of money. Most Native Americans living in cities do not receive federal funds or services of any kind, because of distrust of Indian or non-Indian agencies and a preference for finding survival strategies among one another.

In the past, most sociological studies have focused on the atypical urban Native American—the one most visible, "lying in the gutter," cut off from kin. It is important to learn how most urban Native Americans (neither the upper middle-class professionals nor the indigent) have found their way in this foreign environment, maintaining strong kin relationships and networks and not necessarily assimilating. Native Americans have arrived in cities all over the United States for many reasons; work opportunities and education are the most commonly cited. Guillemin states another very important reason in her chapter "The City as Adventure." For the Micmac of Canada, she points out, going to Boston is seen as extending one's tribal boundaries. While trying to survive in this environment, the young Micmac learn much about coping with conditions as they meet them in the South End, a settling ground for immigrants from all over the world. Their risk-taking and networking are important parts of a young urban Native American's education. Flexibility is seen as one key to their tribal nation's survival. While it is often assumed that cities temper and neutralize (if not actually melt) the unique cultures of their residents, in this case a native people is claiming the city as their own and using it for their own purposes—to strengthen themselves as members of an Indian nation as well as to survive and enjoy themselves. Some cities, such as Chicago, operate high-quality schools for Native American children as further insurance against their losing precious traditions and ways of thinking.

Gambling as Urban Legacy. One clear consequence of Native Americans' learning to deal with the bureaucratic state has been the success stories of Indian nations using the existing laws to repair damages done to their nations, such as bringing an economic base to their reservation. One example comes from the small Pequot Nation in Ledyard, Connecticut. In response to a 1988 ruling holding that federal law allows recognized Indian tribes to have gambling on reservations if the state in which they live allows some sort of gambling off the reservation, the Pequots set up a large gambling center, the Foxwoods Resort and Casino. The gambling question affects reservations all over the country; from California to New Jersey, Native Americans are debating the serious question of what effects the presence of casinos would have on their reservations. Many are now in operation. Although most reservation casinos are not located in large metropolitan areas, the situation clearly involves the bringing of some aspects of the city (in concentrated doses) to the reservation. Although various forms of gambling have existed traditionally among many Native American nations, the dangers and problems that seem to surround non-Native American casino centers worry many people. It has been predicted that the Pequots will become millionaires, for example; whether this will help the Pequots to strengthen their nation or will pull it apart at the seams is an unanswered question. Many of the same questions that have concerned native peoples for generations—about the quality of life left for their people—continue to worry them, whether they be on an impoverished reservation, in a large city, or on a reservation that has made casino gambling the economic base of its people's lives. Certainly the revenues are benefiting many people now, Indian and non-Indian alike.

It is impossible to predict accurately what the long-term effects of such changes will be, but it is likely that current and future generations of Native Americans will be able to draw upon the resilience typical of Indian peoples. They will remain strong and independent as a group while balancing the need to protect their traditions with the need to accept, even embrace, change. *—Roberta Fiske-Rusciano*

See also Activism; Alcoholism; Employment and unemployment; Gambling; Relocation; Termination policy.

BIBLIOGRAPHY

Fiske, Roberta. "Native American Artists in Chicago." In *A Report on the Chicago Ethnic Arts Project*. Washington, D.C.: Library of Congress, American Folklife Center, 1978.

Guillemin, Jeanne. *Urban Renegades*. New York: Columbia University Press, 1975.

Johnson, Kirk. "Seeking Lost Culture at a Powwow: Pequots Draw Ritual Dancers Across U.S. with Rich Prizes." *The New York Times*, September 19, 1993, 52.

Kaufman, Michael T. "A James Bond with $100 Tries out a Tribal Casino." *The New York Times*, March 18, 1994, C1.

Lurie, Nancy. "The Contemporary American Indian Scene." In *North American Indians in Historical Perspective*, edited by Eleanor Burke Leacock and Nancy Lurie. New York: Random House, 1971.

Spade, Watt, and Willard Walker. "Relocation." In *The Way: An Anthology of American Indian Life*, edited by Shirley Hill Witt and Stan Steiner. New York: Alfred A. Knopf, 1972.

Ute: Tribe

CULTURE AREA: Great Basin
LANGUAGE GROUP: Uto-Aztecan
PRIMARY LOCATION: Utah, Colorado
POPULATION SIZE: 7,273 (1990 U.S. Census)

The Utes (or Yutas) inhabited the eastern fringe of the Great Basin and the Colorado and northern New Mexican Rocky Mountains; some hunted buffalo as far east as the Great Plains. Utes called themselves *nutc* ("the people"). The state of Utah is named for the Utes.

Early History. Utes were nomadic hunters and gatherers, traveling in extended family groups in established nomadic circuits. They lived in either brush huts or, when large game was available, skin-covered tipis. With the acquisition of the horse in the seventeenth century larger bands congregated, the nomadic circuit extended, and larger game became more accessible. These bands were identified by their geographic locations and were led by chiefs whose authority lay in their hunting and raiding power. Utes were regarded as warlike, and raiding became a natural extension of hunting. Ute religion was not complex, and most religious observances were related to healing ceremonies or folkloric rituals and taboos.

European Contact. The Utes' first contact with Europeans was with the Spanish in New Mexico by the seventeenth century and was based on trade, both at New Mexican settlements and with traders who penetrated into Colorado and Utah. Ute-Spanish relations were generally friendly, although conflict was not unknown. From the Spanish the Utes obtained horses and arms in return for buckskins and Indian captives. The Utes became a major link in the spread of the horse to other Indians.

Although fur trappers had operated throughout the Ute territory, extensive white penetration began in 1847 with the Mormon arrival in Utah, and in 1848 when the Mexican-American War brought an influx of U.S. citizens to New Mexico. Although relations remained generally friendly in Utah, antagonism flared briefly in 1853 under Walkara and again from 1863 to the 1870's under the direction of Black Hawk. During the 1860's Utah Utes were consolidated on the Uintah Reservation. Once there they became known as Uintah Utes. A related tribe, part Ute and part Paiute, known as the Pahvant, remained friendly to the Mormons; they converted almost en masse to that religion and successfully resisted removal to the reservation.

A preliminary treaty between the United States and Utes in Colorado and New Mexico was signed as early as 1849. As precious minerals were discovered in the Colorado Rockies, however, additional treaties were negotiated, ceding increasingly larger tracts of land in 1863, 1868, and 1873. During these negotiations a central Colorado Ute chief, Ouray, rose to prominence because of his ability to communicate with whites and his ability to convince other chiefs to conciliate with, rather than fight, the United States. As a result Ouray was appointed the spokesman and head chief of the "consolidated" Ute Nation.

With the treaties came agencies that localized Ute bands and gave rise to modern identifications: The three major northern Colorado bands (the Yampa River, Grand River, and White River Utes) became the White River Utes, the central Colorado Tabeguaches became the Uncompahgre Utes, the Mouache and Capote became the Southern Utes, and the Weeminuche became the Ute Mountain Utes.

The Meeker Massacre. In 1879 Nathan C. Meeker, a new agent at the White River Agency, antagonized northern Utes by moving the agency to, and plowing up, their prized winter horse pasturage and race track. When Meeker called for troops to protect him, troops under the command of T. T. Thornburgh were dispatched to the reservation. The Utes feared that the troops were there to remove them forcibly to Indian Territory (Oklahoma). On September 29, more than three hundred Utes under the direction of Captain Jack, Antelope, and Colorow attacked and besieged the column as they entered the reservation. Upon hearing of the attack on Thornburgh, other Utes massacred the agency personnel and took the women there captive.

As punishment for the uprising, the White River bands were forced to cede their reservation to pay reparations and were removed to the Uintah reservation in Utah. Although the other

Southern Utes meeting with Bureau of Indian Affairs officials, probably in 1880. The Southern Utes managed to avoid being removed from their southern Colorado reservation. (National Archives)

Ute bands had refused to join in the uprising and Ouray had assisted the U.S. government in quelling the violence and retrieving the captives, the remainder of the Utes were forced to negotiate another treaty in 1880. Within a year, using a technicality in the treaty, the Uncompaghres were also expelled from Colorado and given a barren reservation (called the Ouray reservation) adjoining the Uintah reservation. The Southern Utes successfully resisted attempts to remove them from their narrow, southern Colorado reservation, though conflicts involving bloodshed were not infrequent. Some Utes affiliated with the Ute Mountain Tribe also obtained southeastern Utah lands through homesteading.

In 1887 the U.S. Congress passed the General Allotment Act, under which Indian lands were to be allotted as individual homesteads and the residual opened to white settlement. By the early twentieth century most Ute land had been allotted except on the Ute Mountain Ute Reservation. Unfortunately, many of the Indian allotments were subsequently lost through taxes, irrigation assessments, and entangled inheritance questions.

Modern Period. In 1934 the Indian Reorganization Act allowed the Utes to develop self-governing tribal entities, and three tribal organizations were formed: the Uintah-Ouray Ute Tribe, the Southern Ute Tribe, and the Ute Mountain Ute Tribe. Tribal organizations helped regain alienated lands and obtained legal counsel for court battles. Working together as the Confederated Ute Tribe, the three tribes were the first American Indians to combat the federal government successfully over reparation claims; as a result of their suit, the Indian Claims Commission was established in 1946 with the Confederated Utes as its first successful (and largest) claimant. During the 1980's and 1990's other legal battles were fought to regain jurisdictional rights over original reservation lands and water rights. Tribal governments have established tribal industries, judicial and policing services, and social services and activities.

Although many traditional Ute ways have given way to western technology, Ute values continue in modern religious manifestations such as the Ute Sun Dance, Bear Dance, and, for some, the Native American Church.

See also Captain Jack; Colorow; General Allotment Act; Indian Claims Commission (ICC); Indian Reorganization Act; Ouray; Uto-Aztecan language family.

BIBLIOGRAPHY

Delaney, Robert. *The Southern Ute People.* Phoenix: Indian Tribal Series, 1974.

_____. *The Ute Mountain Utes.* Albuquerque: University of New Mexico Press, 1989.

Denver, Norma, and June Lyman, comps. *Ute People: An Historical Study*, edited by Floyd A. O'Neil and John D. Sylvester. Salt Lake City: University of Utah Press, 1970.

Emmitt, Robert. *The Last War Trail: The Utes and the Settlement of Colorado.* Norman: University of Oklahoma Press, 1954.

Jorgensen, Joseph G. *The Sun Dance Religion: Power for the Powerless.* Chicago: University of Chicago Press, 1972.

Rockwell, Wilson. *The Utes: A Forgotten People.* Denver: Sage Books, 1956.

Uto-Aztecan language family

CULTURE AREAS: Great Basin, Southwest

TRIBES AFFECTED: Bannock, Comanche, Hopi, Kawaiisu, Mono, Nortern Paiute, Numaga, Pima, Shoshone, Southern Paiute, Ute, Yaqui

In historical times, speakers of Uto-Aztecan languages have lived in widely diverse western landscapes, from harsh desert to lush woodlands. Their territory lies as far north as central Idaho and as far south as northern Central America and covers large tracts of the Great Basin and Southwest. As diverse as the landscape are the types of cultures represented among Uto-Aztecan tribes—hunter-gatherers, nomads, agriculturalists, city dwellers, and empire builders. The family's surviving daughter languages are spoken not only by some of the most famous tribes in the West—Paiute, Shoshone, Hopi, Comanche, and Pima—but also by the architects of one of Mesoamerica's most sophisticated civilizations, the Aztecs.

Nahuatl, the Aztec language, first received formal study when Padre Fray Andres de Olmos, a Spaniard, wrote a grammar of it in 1547. Appearing only twenty-six years after Hernán Cortés conquered the Aztecs, the grammar was part of missionary efforts to convert the pagan Americans and stands as one of the earliest works of New World linguistics. Few of the other Uto-Aztecan languages, especially those in the United States, attracted scholarly attention until the late nineteenth and early twentieth centuries. By then some already had become extinct.

Member Languages. Scholars generally agree on the subdivisions of the Uto-Aztecan family and the member languages of each. There are eight branches: Numic, which includes Northern Paiute, Mono, Monoachi, Koso, Shoshone, Comanche, Ute, Kawaiisu, Southern Paiute, and Chemehuevi; Tubatulabal; Takic, which includes Gabrielino (extinct), Fernandeño, Kitanemuk (extinct), Serrano, Luiseño, Cahuilla, and Cupeño; Hopi; Pimic, which includes Pima, Pima Bajo, Tepecano (extinct), Northern Tepehuan, and Southern Tepe-

huan; Taracahitic, which includes Tubar (extinct), Tarahumara, Guarijío, Yaqui, Opata, and Cahita; Corachol, which includes Cora and Huichol; and Aztecan, which includes Pochutla (extinct), Pipil, and classical and modern Nahuatl. The first four branches and Pima from the Pimic branch are spoken in the United States, mostly in the Great Basin or areas near the southern Sierra Nevada and in southern Arizona and New Mexico. The number of speakers in these areas has declined steadily in the twentieth century. Pima is typical: It shrank by nearly two-thirds between 1970 and 1980, according to the U.S. Bureau of the Census. The languages in Mexico and Central America fared much better during the same period.

Origins. The origins of Uto-Aztecan are obscured in prehistory. Nevertheless, vocabulary among the member languages, especially common plant and animal names, provides some clues, as has evidence from archaeology and anthropology. Linguists have proposed that about five thousand years ago Uto-Aztecan tribes lived in a cohesive area covering part of southeastern California, the tip of Nevada, much of Arizona, the southwest corner of New Mexico, and a corridor extending as far south as Chihuahua in Mexico. Thereafter, the family split into a northern subfamily (Numic, Tubatulabal, Takic, and Hopi), which either stayed in place or drifted northward into the Great Basin, and a southern subfamily (Pimic, Taracahitic, Corachol, and Aztecan), which moved toward the Yucatán peninsula.

The relation of Uto-Aztecan to other American Indian language families is generally agreed upon, although it is far from having been worked out in detail. It clearly shares affinities, for example, to two other Central American language families, Tanoan and Oto-Manguean, but few linguists feel sure of further connections. In his controversial *Language in the Americas* (1987), Joseph H. Greenberg suggests that these three language families make up Central Amerind, one of six divisions of ancient Amerind, the primal language of the first migrants to the North American continent. Amerind, Greenberg suggests, may have split from northern Asian and European languages tens of thousands of years ago.

Characteristics. Like most other American Indian tongues, Uto-Aztecan languages are highly incorporative, or polysynthetic, and place verbs after subjects and objects in clauses. Verbs dominate sentences and can constitute sentences on their own. They do so because many grammatical functions that require separate words in, for example, European languages are blended into the Uto-Aztecan verb in the form of suffixes, prefixes, infixes, or vowel variation; these functions include subjective, objective, and reflexive pronouns and markers for tense, voice, mode, and direction. Thus, in classical Nahuatl, *onikpix* was a complete sentence meaning "I held it," *o-* (past tense marker), *ni-* ("I"), *k-* ("it"), *pix* ("to have," "to hold").

Although there is much variation among the languages, common and proper nouns stand independent of the verbs; however, often a redundant pronoun may be inserted into the verb even when a subject or object noun is present. Under some circumstances one noun alone, with pronominal affixes, can make up a sentence: for example, classical Nahuatl *tinopiltzin*, "You are my son," *ti-* ("you"), *no-* ("my"), *pil-* ("son"), *-tzin* ("reverential").

The original Uto-Aztecan language appears to have had thirteen consonants—*p, t, c, k, kw, s, h, m, n, l, w, y*, and a glottal stop (a check to the airflow made in the back of the throat)—and five vowels: *i*, "barred" *i, u, o*, and *a*, each of which could be long or short. This reconstruction is based on comparisons of modern members of the family, in whose systems some of the sounds have disappeared or mutated.

—*Roger Smith*

See also Aztec; Comanche; Great Basin; Language families; Ute.

BIBLIOGRAPHY

Andrews, J. Richard. *Introduction to Classical Nahuatl*. Austin: University of Texas Press, 1975.

Dayley, Jon P. *Tümpisa (Panamint) Shoshone Grammar*. Berkeley: University of California Press, 1989.

Fowler, Catherine S. "Some Lexical Clues to Uto-Aztecan Prehistory." *International Journal of American Linguistics* 49 (1983): 224-257.

Greenberg, Joseph H. *Language in the Americas*. Stanford, Calif.: Stanford University Press, 1987.

Karttunen, Frances, and James Lockhart, eds. *The Art of Nahuatl Speech: The Bancroft Dialogues*. Los Angeles: University of California at Los Angeles, Latin American, Center Publications, 1987.

Miller, Wick R. "The Classification of the Uto-Aztecan Languages Based on Lexical Evidence." *International Journal of American Linguistics* 50 (1984): 1-24.

_____. *Uto-Aztecan Cognate Sets*. Berkeley: University of California Press, 1967.

Sapir, Edward. *The Southern Paiute Language*. 1930. Reprint. New York: AMS Press, 1984.

Steele, Susan. "Uto-Aztecan: An Assessment for Historical and Comparative Linguistics." In *The Languages of Native America*, edited by Lyle Campbell and Marianne Mithun. Austin: University of Texas Press, 1979.

Uxmal: Archaeological site

DATE: 600-900

LOCATION: Yucatán, Mexico

CULTURES AFFECTED: Maya, Toltec

Uxmal is the name of the ruins of an ancient Maya city located 50 miles south of the modern city of Mérida in the state of Yucatán, Mexico. Although the main ruins cover approximately 160 acres, the remains of the residential districts oc-

Ruins of the Palace of the Nuns, part of the Nunnery Quadrangle, at Uxmal. (H. S. Rice, American Museum of Natural History)

cupy considerably more ground. Water for the population was furnished by wells (*cenotes*) within the city or by collecting pools located in the western part of the site.

Uxmal emerged as the capital of a large Late Classic period state (850 C.E.) centered in the eastern Puuc region and is the most important representative of the Puuc architectural style. It is by far the largest Puuc site and is one of the triumphs of Maya civilization. Unlike southern Maya construction, which was organized in clusters because of topography, the level, dry, grass savanna area of Uxmal allowed buildings to be constructed on large platforms that were widely spaced from one another. Rather than solid core walls, the walls of buildings had a rubble core that was faced with clean-cut building stone (usually limestone) so expertly fitted together that mortar is not discernible in many cases.

The Puuc style at Uxmal and the northern lowland culture associated with it seem to have continued for a century or so after the decline and abandonment of such southern Maya lowland sites as Palenque, Tikal, and Uaxactun. After about 1000 C.E., when Toltec (or Toltec-related) invaders arrived in Yucatán and established their capital at Chichén Itzá, major construction at Uxmal ceased. According to tradition, the site continued to be occupied and was a participant in the political League of Mayapán. With the demise of the league, Uxmal was abandoned (about 1450), as were other great cities of the north.

Uxmal is dominated by two great temple-pyramids, the Great Pyramid (with its large rain-god masks) and the House of the Magician. An old Maya legend states that an elderly witch hatched a child from an egg. After a year, the child had grown to the size of a dwarf and had supernatural powers. The Lord of Uxmal challenged the dwarf to build a temple in one night or suffer death. Having succeeded at this task, the dwarf eventually became the Lord of Uxmal. His temple, the House of the Magician, sits on top of a giant pyramid whose unique feature is the rounded or oval shape of its edges.

Below the Great Pyramid stands the largest building at Uxmal, the Governor's Palace, which sits on its own artificial terrace. It is thought to have housed the royal, ruling family. It is 300 feet long and decorated with sculptures and a geometric mosaic frieze that contains twenty thousand individual tiles. Another important structure is the Nunnery Quadrangle, a group of four buildings (constructed at different times) surrounding an open court that probably was used for ceremonial purposes. Other buildings at Uxmal include the House of Turtles (named after the carved stone turtles on the cornices), the House of Pigeons (another quadrangle, in which one of the buildings resembles a huge dovecote), and the Pyramid of the Old Woman (the home of the legendary elderly witch).

See also Chichén Itzá; Copan; Maya; Palenque; Tikal; Toltec.

Veracruz: Prehistoric tradition, archaeological site
DATE: 1200-400 B.C.E
LOCATION: Southern Mexican Gulf Coast
CULTURES AFFECTED: Aztec, Maya, Olmec

In the jungles of Mexico's Gulf Coast, now the modern states of Veracruz and Tabasco, a culture emerged which set the patterns for later civilization in Mesoamerica. Nothing is known of the origin or the ultimate fate of the people who established this ancient and elaborate civilization, but they produced the pre-Columbian art known as "Olmec." Father Bernardino de Sahagún, a Jesuit monk, wrote of the Olmec ("rubber people") from Tamoanchán, a Mayan name meaning "Land of Rain or Mist"; the Mayan name suggests a linguistic relationship. Many later civilizations in Mexico traced their ancestry to the Olmec.

Three basic cultural traits of Mesoamerican civilization are believed to have originated with the Olmec; worship of a fertility and rain god, monumental architecture, and extensive trade. Southern Veracruz, the Olmec "heartland," was dense tropical forest and swampy lowland with an annual rainfall of 120 inches. Extremes of the environment brought about a religion which involved ritual and ceremony for controlling rainfall and protecting people from jungle spirits.

The cult of the jaguar was Mesoamerica's first formal religion; it was based on the legendary union of a woman and a jaguar which produced the race of infantlike monsters called "were-jaguars"—men with sacred jaguar blood. These "jaguar babies," gods of rain and fertility, evolved into the Mesoamerican image of the rain god.

In the Formative Period, between 1200 and 400 B.C.E., this complex culture flourished, first at San Lorenzo, then by 900 B.C.E. at La Venta, its most important religious center. In both centers massive architecture and huge stone carvings were the focus of daily life organized and directed by the elite class. The level of Olmec civilization is judged by the presence of major public works, the first built in North America. These included ceremonial plazas, pyramids with temples, reservoirs, and well-developed water transport systems.

Monumental sculptures, another indicator of a complex civilization, were evident throughout Veracruz. La Venta was a site of the famous colossal heads carvings, some weighing more than 20 tons, each carved from a single stone. These helmeted images combined features of a human infant and a jaguar, likely the rain god, first of the Mesoamerican deities. The same distinctive art style was also expressed in small clay figurines and finely detailed jade pendants which carried images of the snarling infant-jaguar god.

Religious symbolism in Olmec art served as a visible common bond within the culture, linking peasants with political and royal leaders, who were intermediaries between gods and men. A balance was achieved as peasants farmed corn to provide food for royalty, while royalty organized public life in the spiritual, political, and economic realms via an intricate ritual and civic calendar.

Seasonal markets where vast amounts of food and goods were exchanged provided structure through the year. Artifacts found in locations far from Veracruz indicate that Olmec political and economic influence extended via trade routes to the central Mexican highlands and along the Pacific Coast to El Salvador. Some theories suggest that Preclassic Olmecs might have been Mayas who later moved into the Yucatán peninsula.

See also Aztec; La Venta; Maya; Olmec.

Victorio (c. 1825, present-day southwestern N.Mex.—Oct. 16, 1880, Tres Castillos, Mexico): Tribal chief
ALSO KNOWN AS: Bidu-ya, Beduiat, Lucero
TRIBAL AFFILIATION: Mimbreño Apache
SIGNIFICANCE: Victorio led his band in raids against U.S. and Mexican forces; his death and the destruction of his band marked the midpoint of the Apache Wars

Victorio was born a Mimbreño Apache in what is today southwestern New Mexico. Although some assert that he was a Mexican captive reared as an Apache, contemporary and Apache sources agree he was Apache by birth. In his formative years, Victorio experienced the encroachments of Mexican miners and then American prospectors and ranchers onto Apache lands. He also absorbed the legacy of hatred engendered by two hundred years of Apache-Mexican warfare.

Most of Victorio's life was spent in relative peace and accommodation with the United States. He signed an 1853 provisional compact with the U.S., and requested a reservation for his people in 1869. The Mimbreños settled first at Cañada Alamosa, were removed to Tularosa River, and then to Ojo Caliente in 1874. An 1877 attempt to consolidate Apaches on the San Carlos Reservation in southeastern Arizona brought the Mimbreños there under protest, where they suffered neglect and conflict with the Chiricahua Apaches.

In September, 1877, Victorio led more than two hundred Apaches off the reservation and asked to be returned to New Mexico. When the United States decided to return them to San Carlos, Victorio and fifty warriors fled. Though still willing to surrender, when he learned of a warrant for his arrest he dropped negotiations and began a year-long war of escape and raiding that terrorized southern New Mexico, southeast Arizona, and northern Mexico.

Meanwhile, U.S. troops either actively pursued, engaged, or searched for Victorio and his band. At first, Victorio experienced extraordinary successes against U.S. forces as a result of his intimate knowledge of the rough terrain; the addition of other renegade Apaches (including Geronimo for a time), who swelled his ranks to several hundred; and his acknowledged military genius in picking and fortifying strategic positions.

The turning point in the war came in May, 1880, when Apache scouts ambushed Victorio's band, wounding him and killing nearly fifty, many of them his most able warriors. Soundly defeated for the first time, Victorio fled back to Mexico, where he clashed with Mexican troops. Although he twice more attempted to reenter the United States through Texas, U.S. forces repulsed him both times.

An army of almost three hundred Mexicans was organized in August to operate against Victorio. Warning U.S. troops

Mimbreño Apache leader Victorio was a central figure in the Apache Wars. (National Archives)

away from Mexico, the Mexicans searched for Victorio until October 15, 1880, when they ambushed and trapped the Apaches on the barren upthrust known as Tres Castillos. By morning the battle was over, and Victorio lay dead by his own hand. His warriors were scalped, and their woman and children were captive.

Victorio fought against placing his people on a hostile reservation, but like other leaders in the Apache Wars, he was doomed by the attrition of his finite band and the overwhelming numbers and firepower of his enemies.

See also Apache; Apache Wars; Cochise; Geronimo; Mangas Coloradus; Nana.

Visions and vision quests

TRIBES AFFECTED: Pantribal

SIGNIFICANCE: In the vision quest, an individual fasts in a secluded place, seeking knowledge or help from the spiritual world

The vision quest is a ritual conducted traditionally by men, but occasionally by women, seeking spiritual help. The vision quest is a personal experience. In an isolated place—sometimes a secluded place away from the village, sometimes a confined space such as a pit—a man fasts, avoiding food and water, commonly for a period of four days. The man humbles himself before the Great Mystery and seeks health or help for himself or his family. For example, a man might seek the courage needed to undergo a Sun Dance, seek protection before going to war, or pray for the health of a sick relative. He might go on a vision quest in thanksgiving because a great gift has been bestowed, or he might simply seek help in providing

food and shelter for his family. Afterward, a holy man interprets the dream or spiritual instruction that has been received during the fast. Personal visions are kept in confidence.

"Vision question" is an American term for the process. Nicholas Black Elk called it "to go out lamenting," a translation of the Sioux word *hanbleceya*. *Hanbleceya* has also been translated as "crying for a dream," or "night journey."

To understand the purpose of a vision quest, the spiritual difference between "being called" and "having a calling" must first be understood. Among Indian nations it was not uncommon for young men, usually before they reached puberty, to have a profound religious experience in the form of a vision. The vision or dream involved one or more of the archetypal spirit masks of the tribe. A spiritual teacher would instruct a young man on how to use his visionary experience for the good of the people, since spiritual gifts were useless if not shared. The process of instruction about how to use the spiritual knowledge invariably involved fasting and sacrifice, the experience that in modern times has become known as the vision quest.

Whether men only or both men and women can seek visions is particular to each tribe. The fasting experience of the Arapaho involves teams of men and women chosen by elders, and it is sacred to that culture that sharing the experience with non-Arapahos is out of the question. Plains, Eastern Woodland, Southeast, Great Southwest, and Northwest Coast cultures trained their medicine people in very different ways, but in each case fasting and personal sacrifice were involved.

Traditionally, vision quests commonly resulted in instructions on how to use power from the spiritual world in the course of conducting tribal rituals and ceremonies, dreams of where to find curative herbs for the health of the people, or dreams of animals—these animals might help the seeker feed his family, help a warrior in battle, or help a scout in pursuit of the enemy. Animal visions often gave the seeker a song which would call that animal helper in the future.

Nearly all tribes shared the belief that anyone could have a personal, unique religious experience, one which was also sent for the good of all the people. Those with similar visions would form dream societies that might be dedicated to healing or to dancing—even sacred clown societies were formed. Spiritual gifts humble the gifted; in humility the power is enhanced. Thomas Mails's *Fools Crow: Wisdom and Power* (1989) discusses Fools Crow becoming a "hollow bone" through which spiritual power flowed.

Today, if a man or a woman chooses to undertake a night journey to discover his or her calling or purpose in life, the person will usually present a gift and a cultural instrument of prayer (Plains tribes use a stone pipe) to a respected holy person and ask for guidance and help in the undertaking. A purification rite is performed in a sweatlodge preceding the quest. The seeker is then taken to an isolated place by the holy man. The faster is told to stay in that place "no matter what happens" until the holy man returns. The vision circle in which the seekers stays is often a pit, but it does not have to be. When a pit is not used, prayer flags (colored cloth symbolizing the four directions, with tobacco offerings bundled into them and tobacco ties attached to a string) create a circle around the seeker. As described in *Black Elk Speaks* (1932): "Within the circle thus formed, two paths are created, one running north and south, the other east and west. The seeker walks these paths, praying and weeping."

Finally, it should be noted that in recent years the vision quest has become widely known (as well as widely misunderstood) and commercialized; commercialization of vision questing disregards the original purpose of the rite: the channeling of spiritual healing or instructional power through an individual (a humble servant) to then be shared for the good of the people. —*Glenn J. Schiffman*

See also Black Elk; Puberty and initiation rites; Religion; Rites of passage; Totems.

BIBLIOGRAPHY

Brown, Joseph Epes, ed. *The Sacred Pipe: Black Elk's Account of the Seven Rites of the Oglala Sioux.* Norman: University of Oklahoma Press, 1989.

Mails, Thomas E. *Fools Crow: Wisdom and Power.* Tulsa, Okla.: Live Oak Press, 1989.

Vizenor, Gerald R[obert] (b. Oct. 22, 1934, Minneapolis, Minn.): Writer, educator

TRIBAL AFFILIATION: White Earth Chippewa (Ojibwa)

SIGNIFICANCE: Gerald Vizenor is known for his provocative and theoretically sophisticated works of fiction, nonfiction, and poetry

Gerald Vizenor's success as a scholar and writer did not come easily or quickly. Before beginning his graduate studies at the University of Minnesota in 1962, Vizenor served in the National Guard and in the U.S. Army in Japan. In the early 1960's, Vizenor worked as a corrections agent in Minnesota, while also writing poetry. In the late 1960's, Vizenor worked as a journalist for the *Minneapolis Tribune*. Vizenor's teaching career began in Minnesota public schools; he went on to teach literature and American Indian studies at a number of colleges and universities, including the University of Minnesota, the University of California, Berkeley, and the University of California, Santa Cruz.

Vizenor's writing, often in the form of satire, has tended to focus on issues concerning contemporary native identities, relationships between oral and written native histories and literatures, trickster figures, and the ways in which native people have been represented in literature, social science, and photography. Vizenor has published numerous volumes of poetry; his novels include *Darkness in Saint Louis Bearheart* (1973) and *Griever: An American Monkey King in China* (1987). His many works of nonfiction include an edited volume of literary criticism, *Narrative Chance: Postmodern Discourse on American Indian Literatures* (1989), and *The People Named the Chippewa: Narrative Histories* (1984).

See also American Indian studies programs and archives; Ojibwa; Tricksters.

Voting Rights—Canada

TRIBES AFFECTED: Pantribal

SIGNIFICANCE: The special rights granted to Native Canadians by treaties and by the various Indian Acts of Parliament were long given as reasons to deny the ballot and other citizenship rights to Canada's native population

The history of native voting rights in Canada is linked to government attempts to use the Indian Acts and other forms of coercion to assimilate Native Canadians into white society. These attempts were unsuccessful; most Canadian natives remained disenfranchised until 1960. Prior to confederation in 1867, there had been some isolated instances in which Indians in Ontario, Quebec, and British Columbia voted, but because of restrictive voter qualifications, Indians were, by and large, barred from the polls. After confederation, Indians were prevented from voting both by statute and by requirements of residence or property ownership.

The Indian Acts, the British North America Act, and various treaties established clear distinctions between natives and non-natives, providing both benefits to and restrictions on natives. The treaties obligated the government to pay annuities to all Indians. One of the most valued benefits of the Indian Acts was exemption from taxation for any Indian living on a reserve. This exemption prevented the complete loss of Indian lands through forfeiture, but it also prevented Indians from obtaining full citizenship rights in Canada.

The Indian Acts provided a mechanism for Indians to become Canadian citizens: enfranchisement. Indians who were deemed to be of good moral character, who could read and write French or English, and who were free of debt could apply for enfranchisement. Choosing to become enfranchised, however, meant giving up all the benefits of Indian status, including the right to live on reserve land, annuity payments, and exemption from taxation. It was in the interest of the government to enfranchise as many Indians as possible, and enfranchisement was a stated goal of the Indian Acts. Few Indians, however, opted for enfranchisement. Between 1867 and 1920, only 102 individuals did so. A 1920 amendment to the Indian Act made it possible for the superintendent general for Indian affairs to enfranchise people involuntarily, and activists were sometimes threatened with the stripping of their Indian status. One noted example of this is the case of Frederick Ogilvie Loft, who founded the League of Indians of Canada in 1918. Loft lobbied for Indian civil rights, including Indian control of band funds and the right to vote. In an effort to silence him, the Department of Indian Affairs informed Loft that it was considering his enfranchisement. The League of Indians ultimately floundered, but not before the involuntary enfranchisement provisions of the Indian Act were repealed when the Liberals assumed control of Parliament in 1921.

The Elected Councils. At the same time that natives were barred from voting in provincial and federal elections, they were forced to elect band councils and chiefs. Claiming to provide Indians with modern institutions of local government, Parliament passed the Enfranchisement Act of 1869. The act forbade traditional methods of leadership selection and imposed municipal-type councils on Indian bands. As in non-native elections of this time, this limited franchise was extended only to men. For the members of the Six Nations, whose leaders were traditionally chosen by women, this was a supreme violation of their sovereign rights. Many bands resisted Ottawa's interference in local politics and continued to choose leaders by traditional methods or to elect the traditional leaders. The statute was relaxed in 1880 to make elected band councils voluntary, but passage of the Indian Advancement Act in 1884 made them mandatory once again. The 1884 act also permitted the superintendent general or his agent to depose any chief or council member deemed unfit to serve. Thus, although Indians were required to elect leaders, they were often denied the leaders that they had chosen.

The Franchise Act of 1885. For the first eighteen years after confederation there were no federal election laws in Canada. Voter eligibility was determined by provincial statutes, which barred Indians from the polls on either racial or class grounds. The Conservative government of Prime Minister John A. Macdonald introduced the Franchise Act in 1885, which established the first federal criteria for the franchise. Careful to preserve the rights of the wealthy, Macdonald's legislation established strict property ownership guidelines for voters. Looking for likely Conservative voters, Macdonald extended the franchise to Indian men living on reserves in Eastern Canada if they possessed and occupied a distinct tract of land valued in excess of $150. It appears that many eligible Indians feared that this was merely a scheme to deprive them of their exemption from taxation and thus dispossess them of their land. Macdonald responded that they need have no such fear. Voting privileges for Indians were short-lived, however; the Liberals, led by Wilfred Laurier, gained power in 1896 and repealed the Franchise Act. No separate federal franchise was reestablished until 1920. Indians living on reserves were barred from voting.

Since 1917. Large numbers of Indians enlisted in the Canadian armed forces during World War I. In recognition of their service, Indian veterans were granted the vote in 1917 along with all other members of the armed forces and non-Indian women who had male relatives in the armed forces. The franchise was extended to all white women the following year.

Then, in 1920, while specifically excluding Indians living on reserves, the federal government did grant the franchise to Metis. There were no major changes in native Canadian access to the polls until after World War II. The wives of Indian veterans were granted the vote in 1948. In 1950, Indians who waived their immunity from taxation were permitted to vote. That same year the Inuit were granted the franchise on the grounds that they were not deemed wards of the state, nor were they exempt from taxation. It was not until 1960 that all native Canadians, regardless of status or residence, were permitted to vote in federal elections.

The ten provinces and two territories of Canada varied considerably with regard to native voting rights. British Co-lumbia granted the franchise to native residents in 1949. Newfoundland permitted Indians and Inuit to vote when it entered the confederation that same year. Manitoba granted the vote to Indians in 1952, followed by Ontario in 1954. The franchise was extended to the Indians of Saskatchewan and the Northwest Territories in 1960 and to those in Prince Edward Island and in New Brunswick three years later. Quebec withheld voting privileges from Indians until 1969. Although there were never any specific proscriptions against Indian enfranchisement in Nova Scotia or the Yukon Territory, requirements of residency or property effectively kept Indians from the polls until the middle of the century. —*Pamela R. Stern*

See also Department of Indian Affairs and Northern Development (DIAND); Indian Act of 1876 (Canada); Indian Act of 1951 (Canada); Indian Act of 1989 (Canada); Indian-white relations—Canadian; Reserve system of Canada; Treaties and agreements in Canada.

BIBLIOGRAPHY

Bartlett, Richard H. "Taxation." In *Aboriginal Peoples and the Law: Indian, Metis, and Inuit Rights in Canada*. Edited by Bradford W. Morse. Ottawa: Carleton University Press, 1985.

Garner, John. *The Franchise and Politics in British North America, 1755-1867*. Ottawa: University of Toronto Press, 1969.

Satzewich, Vic, and Terry Wotherspoon. *First Nations: Race, Class, and Gender Relations*. Scarborough, Ontario: Nelson Canada, 1993.

Titley, E. Brian. *A Narrow Vision: Duncan Campbell Scott and the Administration of Indian Affairs in Canada*. Vancouver: University of British Columbia Press, 1986.

Ward, Norman. *The Canadian House of Commons, Representation*. Toronto: University of Toronto Press, 1950.

Voting Rights—United States

TRIBES AFFECTED: Pantribal

SIGNIFICANCE: The related issues of Indian citizenship and suffrage mirror the larger views of the U.S. government and the American public regarding the status of Indians in society

In the early years of the United States, Indians were viewed as sovereign or semi-sovereign peoples. The primary means of dealing with them was through treaties. This Indian "sovereignty" was a legal fiction whose result was that courts avoided treating Indian land claims like vested property rights. Such rights would have afforded the tribes, and possibly individual Indians, stronger legal claims. The first United States treaty with an Indian tribe was concluded in 1778, ten years before the Constitution came into operation. More than six hundred others were to follow.

Questions of Indian citizenship or voting rights did not arise in this early legal context, especially since the Constitution gives the power to decide who is eligible to vote to state governments. It is the states who decide who can vote, subject of course to any federal constitutional requirements. It was not until the passage of the Fourteenth and Fifteenth Amendments just after the Civil War that Indian suffrage could have been considered at all.

Amendments and Legislation. The Fourteenth Amendment, ratified in 1868, defines "[a]ll persons born or naturalized in the United States and subject to the jurisdiction thereof" as citizens of the United States and of the state in which they reside. The Fifteenth Amendment, ratified in 1870, forbids the states to deny any one the right to vote on account of race or color. At first glance, these amendments appear to settle the question of Indian citizenship and voting, but the continuing fiction of Indian sovereignty was used to disparage the citizenship of Indians who had not clearly left their tribes or reservations. It was argued that they were not "subject to the jurisdiction" of the United States and thus did not fall within the terms of the Fourteenth Amendment. The result was that Indians who remained in "Indian country" and who did not dissociate themselves from their tribes continued to be ineligible to vote. This disfranchisement continued throughout the years of the "allotment and assimilation" movement. Under the allotment plan, Indians could receive grants of land for their personal use, presumably for farming. Once the land had been worked for twenty-five years, title would vest in the individual owner and he or she then became a full citizen of the state and eligible to vote, at least in the formal sense. The plan failed, largely because the majority of Indians did not care to become farmers. Most Indians remained ineligible to vote.

By the beginning of the twentieth century, Congress began to look for other solutions to the continued poverty and disorganization of the Indian tribes. In 1919, Congress passed an act which conferred citizenship on those Indians who had served in the armed forces during World War I. In 1924, the Indian Citizenship Act granted full citizenship to all Indians who had been born in the United States, regardless of tribal affiliation or reservation treaty status.

Obstacles to Voting. Thus, in theory, all Indians were eligible to vote from 1924 on. In practice, however, many of the same barriers to voting that were used against potential black voters were raised for prospective Indian voters. Grandfather clauses, poll taxes, and discriminatory literacy tests were all used. Prospective Indian voters also had to meet state government standards about severance of tribal relations; Indians who adhered to their tribes were not viewed as "civilized" persons and were therefore ineligible to vote. Opponents of Indian suffrage also argued that because the state had no power over Indian conduct on the reservation, the Indians were not "true" residents of the state. In some states, Indians

had to meet the claim that as wards of the federal government they were in a state of guardianship and hence legally incompetent to vote. Indeed, Arizona's Supreme Court maintained this position beginning in 1928 and did not reverse itself until 1948. Since then, however, all legal barriers to Indian suffrage have either been repealed or struck down by the courts.

In areas of heavy Indian population, political establishments still occasionally attempt to devise new ways of perpetuating white political control. Contemporary strategies can be subtler than the old. Redistricting so as to "dilute" the Indian vote is one such strategy. Today the major problems that formerly frustrated the Indian desire to vote have been solved. Both the federal government and the states have come to respect the principle of nondiscrimination in voting.

Voting Rights Act, 1965. This act has been particularly effective in the expansion of voting rights for minorities. In this law, Congress provided for federal voting registrars who can be sent into states and regions where fewer than 50 percent of the eligible voting population is registered and where a voting device like a literacy test has been used. In 1975, the act was expanded to require states to provide bilingual ballots and voting information in twenty-four states where Spanish, Asian, Indian, and Alaskan dialects and languages are spoken by large numbers of voters. Thus, the language barrier that discouraged many non-English-speaking minority group members has been largely eradicated.   —*Robert Jacobs*

See also Allotment system; American Indian Civil Rights Act; Civil rights and citizenship; Indian Citizenship Act; Reservation system of the United States; Sovereignty; Voting rights—Canada.

BIBLIOGRAPHY

Cohen, Felix S. *Handbook of Federal Indian Law*. Washington, D.C.: Government Printing Office, 1942. The first and most important treatise on federal treaties and statutes dealing with Indians, written by a brilliant government lawyer. The standard reference for events up to the time of its publication.

Deloria, Vine, Jr., and Clifford M. Lytle. *American Indians, American Justice*. Austin: University of Texas Press, 1983. An excellent layperson's introduction to Indian law in historical perspective.

Price, Monroe E., and Robert N. Clinton. *Law and the American Indian: Readings, Notes, and Cases*. 2d ed. Charlottesville, Va.: Michie, 1983. Prepared as a complement to Cohen's monumental study, this edition discusses the far-reaching changes in Indian law, including the area of voting rights, of the 1960's and 1970's. The excerpted cases are particularly well chosen.

Waban (c. 1604, present-day Concord, Mass.—c. 1677, present-day Newton, Mass.): Tribal leader and town official

Tribal affiliation: Nipmuck

Significance: Waban adapted his tribal leadership capabilities to serve as town clerk and justice of the peace in the earliest of the Massachusetts "praying towns"

Waban, most likely of the Nipmuck tribe, was born around the beginning of the seventeenth century in or near the present-day site of Concord, Massachusetts. Nothing is known of the first half of his life, but by 1646, when he first encountered the missionary John Eliot, he had become a chief at Nonantum, a few miles west of Boston. There, on October 28, Eliot preached a sermon based on Ezekiel 37:9, beginning, "Then said he unto me, prophesy unto the wind." It happened that Waban means "the wind," a coincidence that impressed him favorably.

Even more impressive to the chief was Eliot's ability, cultivated over many years, to speak to the Indians in their own language. Eliot returned about every two weeks from his parish in Roxbury to teach Christianity to Waban and his people. By 1650, however, with white settlers encroaching on Nonantum, Waban asked the Massachusetts General Court for more space and received a tract on the Charles River in Natick; it became the first of Eliot's "praying towns." When Waban, who seems always to have been interested in the administration of justice, asked Eliot how the town should be governed, Eliot answered with a scheme he had learned from the Mosaic law: a judge for every ten people, a higher one for every fifty, another for every hundred. An older Indian was chosen the highest ruler, Waban one of the leaders of fifty.

The settlement soon established a church for whose aspiring members a public confession of faith was required, but Waban's confession struck the white ministers as inadequate, and, although a believer, he did not gain full membership for many years. He was named town clerk, however, and later justice of the peace, as Natick developed into an Indian town of several hundred citizens.

The outbreak of King Philip's War in 1675 caused serious problems for the Natick Indians. Though only a handful of them were sympathetic to Philip's goal of reestablishing Indian control of the region by warfare, two hundred Natick Indians, among them Waban, were seized as a precautionary measure by order of the General Court and confined on Deer Island in Boston Harbor throughout the severe winter of 1676. Eliot visited them periodically and did his best to encourage them. Some months after the death of Philip the following August, the Praying Indians were resettled, but Natick never prospered as an Indian village thereafter.

In his seventies, Waban seems to have gone with a small group back to Nonantum. Shortly before his death around 1677, Waban became a full-fledged Christian, expressing his desire "not to be troubled about matters of this world." Today, two adjacent stations of the Massachusetts Bay Transportation Authority Green Line through Newton to Boston bear the names of the missionary and his first important Native American convert: Eliot and Waban.

See also Indian-white relations—English colonial; King Philip's War; Nipmuck; Praying Indians.

Wabash, Battle of the

Date: November 4, 1791

Place: Mercer County, Ohio

Tribes affected: Huron, Iroquois Confederacy, Lenni Lenape, Miami, Ojibwa, Ottawa, Potawatomi, Shawnee

Significance: Usually known as St. Clair's defeat, this victory of the Maumee Valley tribes and their confederates from around the Great Lakes and Ohio Valley constitutes perhaps the most dramatic defeat of the U.S. Army at the hands of Native Americans in the history of the Indian wars of 1790-1890

During the 1780's and 1790's, Indian resistance to American encroachment north of the Ohio River rose to new heights. Led primarily by the Miami, Shawnee, and Lenni Lenape (Delaware), the western Algonquian-speaking peoples felt betrayed by the Treaty of Paris of 1783, which placed their homelands within the United States. They also assumed that the Treaty of Fort Stanwix (1768) was still valid, with its prohibition of white settlement in what became the Northwest Territory. The British encouraged them by stationing soldiers at Fort Detroit and through the blandishments of their Indian Department representatives, who raised Indian expectations.

Many of the militant Indians settled along the upper Wabash and Maumee River valleys. Under the nominal leadership of the Miami war chief Little Turtle (Michikinikwa), the tribes most associated with him were the Shawnee (led by Blue Jacket, or Wyeapiersenwah) and the Lenni Lenape (led by Buckongahelas). Little Turtle's warriors inflicted a critical defeat on the first United States military incursion into their territory. Brigadier General Josiah Harmar's expedition to the Maumee forks (Fort Wayne, Indiana) was badly mauled in two engagements by a pan-Indian force in October, 1791. This defeat caused President George Washington to name the Northwest Territory's governor, Arthur St. Clair, as a major general commanding a second expedition into the Maumee Valley.

Harmar's defeat raised Little Turtle's reputation and increased Indian Unity throughout the region. The Maumee Confederacy's contacts and support stretched from Lake Superior to the Lower Creek villages in modern Alabama. The coalitions of Pontiac and Tecumseh were never as broad or as unified as this one. Miami, Shawnee, and Lenni Lenape warriors would be joined by Ojibwa, Potawatomi, Huron (Wyandot), and Ottawa militants and there was some coordination with the Cherokees and Creeks to the south. With Little Turtle in nominal command, the Indians' consensual and tribal kinship approach to combat proved effective in this campaign.

St. Clair's ill-trained and poorly equipped regulars, plus even less effective and less disciplined militia volunteers, left Cincinnati at the end of September, 1791. St. Clair's regulars constituted almost all the combat troops in the U.S. Army. By

November 3 they had advanced only 89 miles, and discipline was so poor that entrenched encampments were no longer maintained. The American encampment near the Wabash River's source (now Fort Recovery, Ohio) was divided between regular and militia units, thereby diluting St. Clair's command authority even more.

The Indians advanced south from the Glaize (modern Defiance County, Ohio), keeping their presence and size hidden from St. Clair. Little Turtle struck at dawn on November 4, and his thousand warriors quickly overran the militia camp, pushing the survivors into an ever smaller killing zone among the regulars. With his forces encircled, St. Clair's attempts to rally his defense failed. Indian marksmanship directed at the officers contributed to the disorganization. Eventually a breakout to the south was successful for about a third of the fourteen hundred American soldiers. The remainder were killed, wounded, or taken prisoner. Never before or since has such a high proportion of the total United States military establishment been defeated. Approximately twenty-one Indians died, and forty were wounded.

It would be three years before Major General Anthony Wayne would lead a third expedition toward the Maumee Valley. In the meantime, Indian unity declined. Wayne's subsequent victory at the Battle of Fallen Timbers opened the Ohio country for American settlement.

See also Fallen Timbers, Battle of; Fort Greenville, Treaty of; Fort Stanwix, Treaty of; Indian-white relations—U.S., 1775-1830; Little Turtle.

BIBLIOGRAPHY

Dowd, Gregory Evans. *A Spirited Resistance: The North American Indian Struggle for Unity, 1745-1815.* Baltimore: Johns Hopkins University Press, 1992.

Eid, Leroy V. "American Indian Military Leadership: St. Clair's 1791 Defeat." *Journal of Military History* 57 (January, 1993): 71-88.

Tanner, Helen Hunt. "The Glaize in 1792: A Composite Indian Community." *Ethnohistory* 25 (Winter, 1978): 15-39.

Waccamaw: Tribe
CULTURE AREA: Southeast
LANGUAGE GROUP: Siouan
PRIMARY LOCATION: South Carolina
POPULATION SIZE: 1,023 (1990 U.S. Census)
The Waccamaw were a relatively small horticultural tribe, living in permanent villages. They relied mostly on maize, beans, squash, and other cultivated plants, and various roots, tubers, seeds, nuts, and fruit gathered by women. Little is known of their early encounters with European Americans, except that the Cheraw probably attempted to incite them to attack the British in 1715. A trading post was established in their territory in 1716, and in 1720 they staged a brief war with the colonists in which many of their people were killed. In 1775, while living in white settlements, they and some Pedee were killed by warring Natchez and Cherokee.

See also Cheraw; Cherokee; Natchez.

Waco: Tribe
CULTURE AREA: Plains
LANGUAGE GROUP: Caddoan
PRIMARY LOCATION: Oklahoma
The Waco, a small group, were a part of the Caddoan family, which had inhabited the southern Great Plains for thousands of years before their first contact with European Americans. "Caddo" is a shortened form of *Kadohadacho* ("real chiefs"). The Waco were either neighbors of another Caddoan group, the Tawakoni, or a division of that tribe. Both spoke a dialect similar to that of the Wichita, the dominant tribe in the area. Not much is known about the early history of the Waco. Tradition tells that they moved about with other Caddoans through Oklahoma and Texas.

The name "Waco" does not appear in records until after 1824, when white people encountered them living in a village where Waco, Texas, now stands. "Waco" may be a derivative of *Wehiko* ("Mexico"), given because they were continually fighting the Mexicans. The Waco lived in round thatched houses and in 1824 had some 200 fenced acres under cultivation. They were involved in no major skirmishes with whites, but they suffered greatly at the hands of northern Great Plains tribes. A smallpox epidemic in 1801 further decimated their numbers. They joined with the Wichita in treaties made with the United States and in 1872 were given a reservation in Oklahoma. In the 1990's the Waco were experiencing a renewed interest in tribal heritage. They made recordings of stories and songs and worked to pass traditions to their children.

See also Caddo; Plains; Wichita.

Wagon Box Battle
DATE: August 2, 1867
PLACE: Wyoming
TRIBE AFFECTED: Sioux
SIGNIFICANCE: This last major conflict of the Bozeman Trail wars marked the turning point in the U.S. Army's superiority over the Indian forces with the introduction of the breech-loading Springfield rifle
At the Fort Laramie Council of 1866, a delegation of Brule and Oglala Sioux headed by Red Cloud refused federal demands to allow the improvement and fortification of the Bozeman Trail. The Sioux's insistence that trespasses into their lands were unallowable led to numerous conflicts, including the Wagon Box Battle.

In late July, 1867, following the annual Sun Dance, a number of bands (mostly of Oglala Sioux and Northern Cheyenne) gathered at the Little Bighorn River, determined to destroy the army posts along the Bozeman Trail and push the white tide back. Their strategy was to send five hundred to eight hundred warriors, mostly Cheyenne, against Fort C. F. Smith, while another thousand to fifteen hundred accompanied Red Cloud to Fort Phil Kearny. On August 2, Red Cloud's warriors attacked a detachment of thirty troopers from Fort Phil Kearny, under Captain James N. Powell, who were detailed to guard wood choppers who were harvesting logs for building and fuel. The wagon boxes had been removed from their gears and corralled on a small open plain at the foot of the Bighorn Mountains near Big Piney Creek, a small tributary of the Powder River in Northern Wyoming. That morning, while the majority of troopers were lounging about, Red Cloud's Sioux attacked. The troopers, each with the new breech-loading Springfield and sufficient ammunition, secured themselves within the corralled wagons. The Sioux first seized the mule herd, then turned their attentions to the troopers. The warriors alternated sniper fire with massed charges that carried almost to the wagon corral before being rebuffed. The Indians' intent, believing the troopers were armed only with muzzle loaders, was to cause the soldiers to expel their rifles and then rush in before they could reload—a tactic which had worked well at the Fetterman Massacre. The Sioux were continually turned back, however, by the rapid firepower of the new breech loaders.

Their first advance came from the north, with the warriors on foot, as they were for all the other charges. (Some warriors on horseback circled the wagons and rained arrows onto the troopers.) Many arrows which dropped into the corral had burning pitch tied to them; the pitch ignited the loose hay and dried manure, creating flame and smudge which burned throughout the fight. The fires, mingled with the rifle smoke, hampered the troopers' vision and caused many to suffer intensely from thirst. In addition, the soldiers had little cover and no entrenchments from which to fight. The battle lasted roughly five hours before a relief force from Fort Phil Kearny reached them and sent the Sioux fleeing with howitzer fire. The army lost only six dead and six wounded. The Sioux's losses were much heavier, with estimates varying from four hundred to a thousand (about four hundred seems the most plausible figure). Sioux warriors traditionally removed fallen warriors from the field of battle. The fight had a debilitating effect on the Sioux and on Red Cloud himself, who witnessed the battle from a nearby hillside. He was said to have claimed that he lost the flower of his nation in the fight.

See also Bozeman Trail wars; Fort Laramie Treaty of 1868; Red Cloud; Sioux; Sun Dance.

Wakashan language family

CULTURE AREA: Northwest Coast
TRIBES AFFECTED: Bella Bella, Haihais, Kwakiutl, Makah, Nitinaht, Nootka, Oowekeeno

Wakashan is a language family found exclusively in the Northwest Coast culture area. It comprises two major linguistic divisions: Kwakiutl and Nootka. Kwakiutlan languages are located in regions of the northeast portion of Vancouver Island and the adjacent mainland to the east (Alert Bay and north toward Charlotte Sound) in the Canadian province of British Columbia. Nootkan-related languages extend down the western coast of Vancouver Island and can also be found along the coast in the state of Washington. The southern portion of Vancouver Island, however, is dominated by Salish-speaking groups whose languages are not related to Wakashan.

Comparative linguists have divided Kwakiutl into three subgroups: Haisla, Heiltsuk, and Kwakiutl proper (Kwakwala). Each of these subgroups is located in the general Kwakiutl area; however, these languages are not mutually intelligible, indicating a significant degree of linguistic divergence. Haisla and Heiltsuk are located on the mainland north of Alert Bay, extending to the Queen Charlotte Sound and Prince Royal Island regions. These subgroups include three tribal units: Bella Bella, Haihais, and Oowekeeno. Kwakiutl proper was located entirely on the Northeast coast of Vancouver Island. During the historic period, however, Kwakiutl speakers could be found in more frequent numbers on the mainland, especially in the area of Alert Bay.

Nootkan languages have also been divided into three linguistic subgroups: Nootkan, Nitinaht, and Makah. Nootkan and Nitinaht are situated along the western coast of Vancouver Island. The Makah language subgroup is found on the Olympic peninsula across the straits of Juan de Fuca in the state of Washington, and is the southernmost representative of the Wakashan family.

In 1929, Edward Sapir proposed that Wakashan be subsumed under a language phylum that he named Algonkin-Wakashan. Sapir believed that certain structural features of Wakashan, such as grammar, phonology, and lexicon, demonstrated a distant affinity with eastern Algonquian languages. Most comparative linguists, however, believe that this relationship cannot be substantiated; similarities which may exist between the two language families are generally considered coincidental.

See also Bella Bella; Kwakiutl; Nootka.

Walam Olum

TRIBE AFFECTED: Lenni Lenape
SIGNIFICANCE: The creation story and pre-contact history of the Lenni Lenape (Delaware) nation is told in this set of verses

The Walam Olum is a long set of verses keyed to mnemonic drawings and preserved as the creation myth and traditional history of the Delaware (Lenni Lenape) people, who formerly lived on the East Coast in the present state of Delaware. The poem begins with the creation of the world by the great creator, Manitou; it is a peaceful paradise in which men and animals live harmoniously. An evil snake threatens this paradise, but the world is saved through the efforts of Nanabush the trickster/creator, who shapes the present world on the back of a great turtle. Following these events is an account of migration from a land of wind and snow to a land with milder climate where technology emerges. The remaining verses recite clan origins and the list of chiefs up to the first encounter with Europeans.

The present text of the Walam Olum derives from a manuscript written down in the early part of the nineteenth century by an unknown scribe who was apparently not fluent in Delaware; it was first printed by Daniel Brinton in *The Lenape and Their Legends* (1885). Delaware is an Algonquian language, and themes and characters such as the earth-supporting turtle and the character of Nanabush are familiar from other Algonquian traditions.

See also Algonquian language family; Lenni Lenape; Tricksters.

Walapai: Tribe

CULTURE AREA: Southwest
LANGUAGE GROUP: Yuman
PRIMARY LOCATION: Colorado
POPULATION SIZE: 1,207 (1990 U.S. Census)

The Walapai (or Hualapai) were divided into seven autonomous divisions. Men hunted deer, elk, antelope, and bear, and women gathered seeds, nuts, berries, tubers, and roots. Acorns were an important food, storing well in winter granaries. A wide range of insects, particularly grasshoppers and locusts, were gathered in communal hunts. Their technology, partially specialized for leaching tannic acid from acorns, had other applications as well. A variety of types of baskets were used daily for stone-boiling, storage, burden, and other utilitarian purposes. The Walapai, had a high degree of mobility and were intimately aware of their territory and where to find plant resources within it.

The area inhabited by the Walapai was probably visited in 1540 by Spanish explorer Hernando de Alarcón, and later in 1598 by Marcos Farfan de los Godos. In 1776, Francisco Garcés made contact with the Walapai but recorded scant ethnographic data. Population decline is attributed mostly to introduced disease; from an estimated 700 in 1680, population fell to around 450 in 1937. The Walapai Reservation was established in northwest Arizona. Today, Walapai income is gained from wage labor, cattle raising, government employment, and urban jobs.

See also Southwest; Yuman language family.

Walla Walla: Tribe

CULTURE AREA: Plateau
LANGUAGE GROUP: Sahaptian
PRIMARY LOCATION: Umatilla Reservation, Oregon
POPULATION SIZE: 228 (1990 U.S. Census)

The Walla Walla, a branch of the Sahaptian family, lived along the lower Walla Walla, Columbia, and Snake rivers in Washington and Oregon. Their name means "little river." As is generally true for the Sahaptian tribes, there is little or no ethnographic evidence or traditional lore to show where the Walla Walla lived in prehistoric times. Their first encounter with white people occurred in 1805, when the explorers Meriwether Lewis and William Clark passed through their territory. Like other Sahaptian tribes, the Walla Walla lived in village communities of varying size.

Because they relied on hunting, fishing, and gathering roots and berries, they moved throughout the year to find food in different seasons. They were skilled with horses. For the most part, they dwelt peacefully with whites, largely because of their refusal to engage in violent retaliation for ill treatment.

The middle of the nineteenth century proved devastating for the Walla Walla. Epidemics of smallpox and measles, probably brought by traders, trappers, and miners, killed many of their people. When gold was discovered in the area in 1855, miners flooded onto Walla Walla lands. The fighting that eventually resulted ended with the shooting or hanging of several chiefs. Under the terms of an 1855 treaty signed at the Walla Walla Council, the Walla Walla, Cayuse, Nez Perce, and other tribes were forced to give up 60,000 square miles of their lands and were placed on the Umatilla Reservation in Oregon. They were given three cents per acre for their land, and they were assured the right to fish using traditional methods off reservation land. In actuality, these fishing rights were not protected, and this remained a source of strife for more than one hundred years afterward. By the end of the twentieth century, the Confederated Tribes of the Umatilla Reservation had lived and worked together for decades. They present an annual rodeo and pageant, the Pendleton Roundup, to demonstrate and pass on traditional culture and skills.

See also Diseases, post-contact; Plateau; Umatilla; Walla Walla Council.

Walla Walla Council

DATE: May 24-June 11, 1855
PLACE: Ancient Indian council grounds at modern Mill Creek, Walla Walla, Washington
TRIBES AFFECTED: Cayuse, Nez Perce, Umatilla, Walla Walla, Yakima (observers)
SIGNIFICANCE: The resulting treaty drastically reduced the area of Indian lands, marking the end of a centuries-old era and forcing Native Americans to make a radical adjustment to white civilization

The westward migration of settlers and immigrants reached the Northwest by the mid-1800's. In 1848 about five thousand immigrants and one thousand wagons arrived in Oregon, more than the combined population of the Nez Perce, Cayuse, and Walla Walla tribes.

In 1855 Isaac I. Stevens, governor and superintendent of Indian affairs of the Washington Territory, took steps to implement treaties with the Indians to acquire their land (to provide room for white settlers) and preclude hostilities with the increasingly anxious and angry Indians. He also sought to clear the way for a northern route for the Pacific Railroad. The resulting council was one of the largest tribal gatherings in the United States. Negotiations were carried on in an atmosphere of suspicion, fear, and mistrust of the white negotiators, acrimony between factions of Indians, and even an aborted plan by the Cayuse to massacre all the whites. It was not until between June 9 and 11 that three treaties were finally agreed upon and signed by the Indians, under considerable duress and pressure as well as recognition of the inevitable.

Under the treaties the Indians ceded about 30,000 square miles of land in eastern Oregon and east-central Washington. In return they were given two reservations and promised up to $200,000 per tribe. Emphasis was placed on "civilizing" the

Indians by having the government supply personnel and build mills, shops, schools, and hospitals.

The majority of the Nez Perce remained faithful to the treaty. Other tribes, however, felt coerced and betrayed; moreover, they were convinced that whites would never live up to the terms of the treaty. They refused to accept the end of their traditional way of life. Almost immediately turmoil and war began; strife was to continue for more than twenty years before some tribes were finally subdued.

See also Cayuse; Nez Perce; Nez Perce War; Walla Walla; Yakima; Yakima War.

Wampanoag: Tribe

CULTURE AREA: Northeast
LANGUAGE GROUP: Algonquian
PRIMARY LOCATION: Southeastern Massachusetts, eastern Rhode Island
POPULATION SIZE: 2,175 (1990 U.S. Census)

The Wampanoag, also known as the Pokanoket, spoke the Massachusetts language, one of the five Eastern Algonquian languages spoken in southern New England. The Wampanoag, like all southern New England groups, have deep historical roots. Archaeologists point to the evolution of prehistoric cultures from the Paleo-Indian cultural time period of some twelve thousand years ago up through the historic cultural time period of 1500 C.E. and the beginning of European exploration and trade along the Atlantic coast. The Wampanoag are best known for this latter contact period when Europeans began to document their visits to the native peoples via diaries, letters, and books. In 1620, the English colonists known as the Pilgrims landed in present-day Plymouth, Massachusetts. There began the now famous relationship between the Indians and colonists and there occurred the celebration of the first Thanksgiving.

The most important seventeenth century Wampanoag figures included the supreme sachem Massasoit and his sons and successors Wamsutta (Alexander) and Metacomet (King Philip). These sachems signed treaties, and they traded and bartered lands with the Pilgrims. Toward the end of the century, they were also fighting with the Pilgrims. The supreme sachems were supported by sachems of several territorial subdivisions. All sachems were skillful and generous leaders who governed their people not through absolute power but through consensus and charisma. Sachems worked with councils of "esteemed men," and together they maintained balance between the spirit world and the people.

The Wampanoag lived in various locations and in various family groups depending on the season. During the summer, they lived in farming hamlets near their cornfields. These hamlets consisted of a few wigwams (bark and mat-covered houses) which housed several related nuclear families or an extended family. These hamlets were also near the fishing resources of the coast. During winter, families moved to the warmer inland areas and set up larger "longhouses" to house up to fifty or more people. This settlement pattern alludes to the Wampanoags's rich and eclectic diet: From their fields they harvested northern flint corn along with a variety of beans and squashes, Jerusalem artichokes, gourds (for storage containers), and tobacco (for smoking). From the sea they harvested shellfish, a variety of ocean fish, and beached whales. From the inland areas they took deer, beaver, squirrel, fox, and other small game.

Wampanoag cosmology taught the people how to use these resources. Resources were never to be wasted but were to be used in their entirety. For example, from the deer came meat, the hide for clothing, the organs for pouches and sinew, and the brain for tanning agents. The pow-wow was the religious leader who oversaw resource use. He also conducted rites such as the Green Corn Ceremony, in which the Creator was thanked for the bounty of corn.

The relationship between the Pilgrims and the Indians came to a head in 1675 with the outbreak of King Philip's war. The Wampanoag sachem King Philip attempted to confederate Indian tribes throughout New England in the hope that Indians would be able to take back their lands from the colonists. His war failed, and Philip was killed.

During the eighteenth and nineteenth centuries, surviving Wampanoag lived in small Indian enclaves or in white communities throughout southeastern Massachusetts and on Cape Cod. Some of the best known of these Indian communities included Mashpee on Cape Cod and Gay Head on Martha's Vineyard.

See also Indian-white relations—English colonial; King Philip's War; Massasoit; Metacomet; Mohegan; Narragansett; Pequot.

BIBLIOGRAPHY

Campisi, Jack. *The Mashpee Indians: Tribe on Trial.* Syracuse: Syracuse University Press, 1991.

Peters, Russell M. *The Wampanoags of Mashpee.* Mashpee, Mass.: Indian Spiritual and Cultural Training Council, 1987.

Weinstein, Laurie. "We're Still Living on Our Traditional Homeland: The Wampanoag Legacy in New England." In *Strategies for Survival*, edited by Frank W. Porter III. New York: Greenwood Press, 1986.

Weinstein-Farson, Laurie. *The Wampanoag.* New York: Chelsea House, 1989.

Wampum

TRIBES AFFECTED: Widespread but not pantribal
SIGNIFICANCE: Native Americans used wampum to record the lives of significant people, tribal laws and events, and treaties or alliances

The historical literature points out that the term "wampum" is not an Indian one. Instead, wampum was coined from New England settlers who shortened an Algonquin term, *Wampumpeag*, meaning a string of white beads. In the Seneca language, it is called *Otekoa*, a name for a small freshwater spiral shell. Wampum has been described as finely embroidered belts or strings, many with glass beads that were typically cylindrically shaped, about one-fourth of an inch long and half that in diameter. The original bead, before glass ones were introduced, was purported to be a round clam shell (called *quahog*) that was traditionally drilled by hand, using stone or reed drills, before iron drill bits came from Europeans. Porcupine quills and animal whiskers were also traditionally used, and the Mohawks claim that even eagle feathers were earlier evident in wampum.

The first to use wampum were the coastal Indians along the Atlantic seaboard and the New England indigenous peoples. The Long Island Indians were especially noted for their skill in manufacturing wampum, which took a lot of labor and patience in a time-consuming process. The belts and strings could be of varying length and width, depending on their representative purpose. Five- to ten-foot lengths of wampum could be made in one day. Wampum strings were made from bark or leather, and later beaver skins and painted sticks were utilized.

The native nations primarily used wampum for commercial relations, often symbolizing a ritualization of reciprocity. It was only later that the belts were made for ornamentation or adornment to wear as jewelry, which eventually led them to be viewed as craft art showpieces for exhibition. A wampum myth is that the term is synonymous with "Indian money"—the traditional Indian societies never used it as currency. It was actually American colonialists who were the first to initiate its use as money. The Dutch, in 1627, were the first to produce counterfeit wampum.

Wampum was originally used for documentation and recordkeeping of significant events and agreements, such as treaties between two sociopolitical entities, as well as seals of friendship. They were also viewed as certificates of authority and credentials that guaranteed a message or promise. They were thought of as ritual ratification when accompanying treaties or alliances, which may have involved emigration, a prisoner's ransom, or the extradition of a criminal. The Iroquois used wampum for both official communication and religious purposes. According to their oral history, it was introduced to the Eastern Woodland nations by Hiawatha at the time of the founding of the League of the Five Nations.

The Iroquois Council meetings were recorded with wampum, and there were Wampum Keepers who kept the records among the Onondaga Nation. At special councils, these recordkeepers would recite the message or law that went with a particular wampum to a gathering of the people. It is also said that the Great Orator first introduced wampum to the Mohawks to bring binding peace among disagreeing parties, and to take the place of the shedding of blood.

Each people among the Iroquois traditionally had a unique design of wampum that was to represent their respective nation. It is also said that traditionally every chief of the confederacy and every clan mother had a designated wampum as a certificate of his or her esteemed office. Wampum could also be named for an individual important to the confederacy or a particular membership group among the people of the nations. Some of the most well-known wampum belts are named after significant events in tribal history.

Even though there are still a few native individuals who act as guardians of certain wampum belts and strings, most of those that have not been lost are found in glass-enclosed showcases in U.S. museums. A very few non-Indians may even have one or two in their own private possession as collector's items, but this is unusual. The traditional meaning and use of wampum has been denigrated by American law and policy. Its mnemonic significance is still a powerful one of unity and hope for the future among those native nations who still honor its sacred symbolism, if not its secular use in rituals of ratification and reciprocity.

See also Beads and beadwork; Money; Oral literatures; Shells and shellwork.   —*M. A. Jaimes*

BIBLIOGRAPHY

Beauchamp, W. M. "Wampum Used in Council and As Currency." *American Antiquarian* 20, no. 1 (January/February, 1931): 1-13.

Fenton, W. N. "The New York State Wampum Collection: The Case for the Integrity of Cultural Treasures." *Proceedings of the American Philosophical Society* 115, no. 6 (December, 1983): 437-461.

Tehanetorens. *Wampum Belts*. Reprint. Ohsweken, Ontario: Iroqrafts, 1983.

Wanapam: Tribe

CULTURE AREA: Plateau
LANGUAGE GROUP: Sahaptian
PRIMARY LOCATION: Washington State

The Wanapam, a branch of the Sahaptian family, lived in northwestern Oregon and southwestern Washington. The significance of their name is unknown. They were closely related to the Palouse. As is generally true for the Sahaptian tribes, there is no ethnographic evidence or traditional lore to show where the Wanapam lived earlier than their first encounter with whites in the early 1800's. At this time, their population numbered approximately eighteen hundred. Sahaptian tribes lived in village communities of varying size. Because they relied on hunting, fishing (salmon was a chief staple), and gathering roots and berries, they moved throughout the year to find food in different seasons. This prevented the villages from developing into political or social centers. Sahaptian tribes do not seem to have relied at all on agriculture. They were skilled with horses and used them in their search for food. There is no record of any major battles between the Wanapam and white settlers. No official enumerations of Wanapam have been made since the eighteenth century. The tribe was probably absorbed by the Palouse.

See also Palouse; Plateau.

Wapasha (c. 1718-1876): Line of chiefs

ALSO KNOWN AS: Red Leaf
TRIBAL AFFILIATION: Mdewakanton Sioux
SIGNIFICANCE: Several prominent Sioux chiefs in the eighteenth and nineteenth centuries were named Wapasha; they were members of the same family

"Wapasha" was the name of several important Mdewakanton Sioux chiefs between roughly 1750-1870. The eldest known to the historical record was born in about 1718 in present-day Minnesota. As a chief, he spent much of his time making war or negotiating peace with the Chippewas. Later in his life, he made contact with the English when they withdrew trading relations following the murder of a merchant. Wapasha captured the culprit and set off to deliver him to his accusers. When the prisoner escaped, Wapasha offered himself as a substitute. The English refused the offer but made an ally. Wapasha died near Hokah, Minnesota.

Wapasha ("Red Leaf"), son of the elder Wapasha, was born on the site of present-day Winona, Minnesota. He met Zebulon Pike's 1805 expedition in search of the Mississippi River's source. Though he was generally an ally of immigrating Americans, the British claimed his loyalty in the War of 1812 but regarded him as suspect to the point of court-martial. He died of smallpox and was followed as tribal leader by his brother (some accounts say nephew), Joseph Wapasha.

In 1862, Joseph Wapasha became the Mdewakanton Sioux's principal chief. He continued the accommodationist policies of his two forebears of the same name. By the 1840's, however, white immigration to Minnesota had reached unprecedented levels, and friendliness was becoming more difficult to maintain without abject surrender.

Reluctantly, Joseph Wapasha surrendered to pressure to join in the Great Sioux Uprising that began in 1862 under Little Crow. Wapasha and his people did their best to stay out of the hostilities, but after the war they were caught in the general colonists' fervor to rid Minnesota of all Indians. Vigilantes drove Wapasha and his people to a reservation on the upper Missouri. They later moved to the Santee Agency in Nebraska, where Joseph Wapasha died in 1876 at the age of fifty-one.

See also Little Crow; Sioux; Sioux uprisings.

Wappinger: Tribe

CULTURE AREA: Northeast
LANGUAGE GROUP: Algonquian
PRIMARY LOCATION: Connecticut, New York

The Wappinger are often considered to have comprised two main subgroups, the Western Wappinger (who lived in what is now New York State, along the lower Hudson River) and Eastern Wappinger (who lived eastward to the lower Connecticut River valley). It is estimated that at the first encounter with the Dutch, in the early 1600's, the Western Wappinger numbered about 3,000 and the Eastern Wappinger about 1,750.

The Wappinger were closely related in customs and organization to the Delaware (Lenni Lenape) and to Indians of southern New England. They hunted, fished, and grew crops, primarily corn. They were noted for their manufacture of wampum beads. Their totem was the wolf. The tribe was headed by a sachem (male or female) and a council of lesser chiefs.

With the arrival of Dutch settlers and traders, the Wappinger were thrown into close proximity with whites. Indians and whites managed to coexist relatively peacefully for a number of years, and the Western Wappinger became involved in fur trading. In 1640 a number of sources of friction led to a five-year war between whites and Indians, including the Western Wappinger. Destruction and casualties were inflicted by both sides, with the Indians losing half their population, the Western Wappinger bearing the brunt. Disease further reduced their population. Nevertheless, the tribe remained intact until 1756, when they joined the Nanticoke; both tribes were later absorbed into the Delaware. Their last public appearance was at the Easton Conference in 1758.

In contrast, the Eastern Wappinger never warred with whites. They gradually sold off their land to settlers and merged with other tribes, including the Scaticook and Stockbridge. At this point, the Wappinger tribe ceased to exist as a separate entity.

See also Algonquian language family; Algonquin; Lenni Lenape.

Wappo: Tribe

CULTURE AREA: California
LANGUAGE GROUP: Wappo
PRIMARY LOCATION: Napa River, Clear Lake, and Alexander Valley, California
POPULATION SIZE: 125 (1990 U.S. Census)

The Wappo, contiguous with the Southern Pomo, Central Pomo, Patwin, and Lake and Coast Miwok, were territorially divided into the Clear Lake and the Southern Wappo. They located their oval, grass houses in permanent villages on stream systems, acquiring subsistence by fishing, hunting, trapping, and gathering food plants including acorns, tubers, roots, and numerous grasses. They tended to be monogamous and discouraged divorce. The Wappo excelled in manufacturing baskets.

There are indications that the Wappo fought against the Spanish in the Napa Valley; some Wappo were apparently held at the Sonoma Mission. The reservation at Mendocino was established in 1856, closing in 1867. Disease, displacement of groups, degradation of the environment and its resources by European Americans, and ensuing conflict all served to reduce the Wappo population and traditional lifeways. By 1910, only twenty Wappo had any knowledge of their language and traditional ways. By 1960, only five Wappo speakers remained.

See also Miwok; Patwin; Pomo.

War bonnets

TRIBES AFFECTED: Apache of Oklahoma, Arapaho, Arikara, Assiniboine, Atsina, Blackfoot, Cheyenne, Comanche, Cree, Crow, Flathead, Fox, Hidatsa, Iowa, Jicarilla Apache, Kansa (Kaw), Kiowa, Lipan Apache, Mandan, Missouri, Nez Perce, Omaha, Osage, Oto, Pawnee, Ponca, Sarsi, Sauk, Shoshone, Sioux, Ute, Wichita
SIGNIFICANCE: In Plains societies, a war bonnet was one of the most valued articles that a warrior could own

Plains culture centered on the hunt and war, making conflict an integral part of western Indian society. The war bonnet was one way warriors recorded their achievements in battle. Two types of bonnets characterized those headdresses designed for battle: the golden eagle-feathered headdress and the split-horned bonnet.

The golden eagle-feathered bonnet was fashioned by placing twenty-eight to thirty-six eagle tail feathers into a circular skullcap base made of buffalo hide. The different cone shape formed by the arrangement of the feathers was often an indication of the tribe to which the owner belonged. The tail of the bonnet, also made from buffalo hide, hung from the cap to the ground and was decorated with approximately thirty eagle tail feathers. The feathers were attached by their quills with rawhide and flannel cloth. Fixed to these feathers with glue and white clay were horse hair and eagle feathers. The size of these war bonnets was considerable; however, they could be rolled and folded into a diameter of eight inches, then reopened to achieve their perfect shape.

Every part of the eagle-feathered headdress had special meaning that was understood by the tribe members, including the tubular form of the Cheyenne and Blackfoot war bonnets. The feathers standing straight up from the skullcap were radiating shafts of light that symbolized the universe and brought enlightenment to the wearer from the One Above. Red, the sacred color, was the most commonly used dye on feathers, used to indicate the owner's accomplishments in battle.

The second type of war bonnet, the split-horned headdress, held the highest position in the warrior society. Only a few of the highest-ranking leaders in each band were given the right to wear the split-horned bonnet. This headdress was constructed with a buffalo hide and a tail cut into two lengths. The short tail still had the buffalo fur on it and hung to the middle back of the warrior, while the long tail was decorated with eagle wing, hawk, or owl feathers placed at right angles. The bison horns, after being hollowed out to reduce their weight, were attached to the skullcap. Items placed on the skullcap often marked significant moments in the warrior's life. These items might include sea shells, clusters of split or whole feathers, braided and dyed horse tails, beaded headbands, white ermine skins, and felt fringe. All split-horned war bonnets also possessed a long plume, the Sun Dance plume, which extended twenty-four inches from the peak of the bonnet.

A man might make four to five bonnets in his lifetime, each one a little different from the others. The war bonnets, though not worn into battle until the outcome was assured, were always worn in religious gatherings. Periodically, the headdresses were blessed in ceremonial dances performed by honored women selected to wear the bonnet during the dance. A war bonnet, which might bring three horses if bartered, was one of the most valued articles that a warrior could own.

See also Dress and adornment; Feathers and featherwork; Headdresses; Plains; Warfare and conflict.

Ward, Nancy (c. 1738, Chota, Tenn.—c. 1824, Polk County, Tenn.): Tribal chief
ALSO KNOWN AS: Nanye-hi (One Who Goes About)
TRIBAL AFFILIATION: Cherokee

SIGNIFICANCE: Ward was a chief of the Cherokee Nation and a staunch advocate of peace between Indians and European settlers

Nancy Ward was born in the capital of the Cherokee Nation to an important Cherokee family. Nancy and her husband, King Fisher, fought against the Creeks in 1755 in the Taliwa battle. King Fisher was mortally wounded, and legend has it that Nancy fought so valiantly the Cherokee declared her "Most Honored Woman"—a powerful distinction. Shortly after being widowed, Nancy married Bryant Ward, an English trader who had come to Chota. Nancy Ward is described as a strikingly beautiful woman with rose-colored skin. Because of this attribute, she was given the nickname "Wild Rose." She had two children by each of her husbands.

In 1775, the Cherokee met with English agents at Sycamore Shoals in what is now eastern Tennessee. The issues were whether more land should be sold to the English and what role the Cherokee should play in the English-American conflict. There was disagreement among the Cherokee chiefs as to which side to favor, but they needed weapons and selling land to the English seemed to be the only way to obtain what they needed. Nancy Ward's voice was one of peace—in opposition to her cousin, Dragging Canoe, who desired weapons to drive the settlers east across the Appalachian Mountains. In 1776, it was decided to wage war against the white people. Nancy Ward prepared the ceremonial "black drink" that was purported to give the warriors success. She then informed the white settlers of the impending attack by releasing three white traders the Cherokees had held captive. Raids were carried out against settlements on the Holston River, and because of Nancy Ward, many lives were saved on both sides.

Nancy Ward was vocal in the 1781 peace talks between the Cherokee and white settlers at Long Island (near the present city of Kingsport, Tennessee). Though the consequences of the talks were short-lived, Nancy continued to speak for peace until her dying day. In her later years she moved to the Ocoee River area to be near her family. There she became a successful innkeeper. Nancy Ward died in 1822 and is buried near Benton, Tennessee.

See also Cherokee; Indian-white relations—English colonial; Indian-white relations—U.S., 1775-1830.

Warfare and conflict
TRIBES AFFECTED: Pantribal
SIGNIFICANCE: The causes and modes of Indian warfare before contact with Europeans reflected the social values and religious beliefs of the various Indian cultures; the arrival of Europeans modified and intensified Indian warfare

Warfare was endemic among the Indian peoples of North America before European contact. War was most emphasized and most frequent in the Northeast, Southeast, and Great Plains culture areas. It was much less emphasized in the Great Basin, Plateau, and California culture areas and among many of the peoples of the Southwest area. In many places there were traditional alliances, and individual tribes often had traditional enemies with whom war was more or less constant. The practices and motives discussed below applied—with specific cultural variations—throughout North America.

Economic Causes of War. Before the arrival of Europeans, there seem to have been few economic reasons for waging war. Traditional subsistence economies offered little incentive to attack neighbors and few effective means for occupying and exploiting a neighbor's lands. There were examples, however, of a tribe yielding part of its territory because of repeated raids by a neighbor. Another exception, found especially in the Northeast, occurred when a powerful tribe forced a weaker one to acknowledge its client status and pay an annual tribute. The two were then allies with reciprocal responsibilities, but one tribe was dominant. The Pequot, for example, forced a number of weaker tribes to become tributaries. In the Northeast in the early seventeenth century, tribute came to be paid in wampum. There were other exceptions to the weakness of economic motives in aboriginal warfare, such as the raids of Athapaskan-speaking hunter-gatherers on the settled Pueblo peoples of the Southwest after the Athapaskans arrived there about 1500 C.E.

Mourning War. In eastern North America and in the Great Plains, the most common form of warfare has been labeled "mourning war" by historians. Mourning war resulted from grief over the death of a family member. Usually, but not always, the lost loved one had been slain by an enemy. Among the Iroquois of the Northeast, such grief was expected to be extreme, even temporarily incapacitating, and it could only be assuaged by securing an enemy life in retaliation. Such revenge was also necessary to quiet the angry spirit of the slain. It was a moral duty, therefore, to join in such a raid. The family of the deceased, especially the women, would urge kinsmen to join a raiding party. To refuse would be to risk the charge of cowardice. A raiding party would be organized under the leadership of a recognized warrior or war chief; with the appropriate rituals performed, the party would set out for an enemy village. Typically, there were a number of nations with whom a tribe considered itself always at war. Such a war party might be very small (a half-dozen men or even fewer), or it might number a hundred or more. In either case, its aim was to kill a few of the enemy—or, even better, to take prisoners—and to return with no casualties of its own. Such raids had no purpose other than to inflict a few deaths and thereby relieve the grief of suffering kinsmen. These raids, the most common mode of aboriginal warfare, had no economic motive.

Adoption of captives. A captive brought in by a raiding party would belong to the warrior who had taken him (or her), typically by being first to lay hands on the victim. An adult male captive would be required to "run the gauntlet"—when blows would be rained on him by the assembled people, who in this way acted out their rage. The successful warrior would then make a grieving friend or relative a present of the prisoner. The recipient would decide the captive's fate: If adopted, the prisoner would become a member of the family, taking the place of a lost son, husband, daughter, or other family member. Raiding for prisoners was a widely practiced means of restor-ing families and of maintaining numbers in tribal groups experiencing population decline. In time, hundreds of white captives were adopted in this way, and the accounts that some of them wrote ("captivity narratives") are a fascinating historical source. Captives rejected as unsuitable for adoption were usually killed—often tortured to death by burning—thereby appeasing the spirits of the grieving. These torture rituals, probably most elaborate among the Iroquois and Huron, were religious ceremonies as well, with the prisoners being dedicated to the god of war.

Public War. The raiding parties that characterized mourning war were typically organized and carried out without reference to or permission from any village or tribal council or authority. There was sometimes a "higher" form of war, however, in which tribal chiefs in council, or sachems and their councils, made decisions for or against war that involved an entire people. Participation in such a larger war was left to individual decision, however. There was no compulsion, largely because participation in war was so bound up with religion and personal magic.

Warfare, Religion, and Magic. A prisoner burned by the Iroquois was dedicated to Aireskoi, their god of war, and great care was taken to keep the prisoner alive through the night-long burning with firebrands so that he might be taken outdoors at dawn and placed on a special raised platform. When the first sliver of the sun appeared, the charred but still living victim was killed by a blow. Then the body was butchered and boiled in a kettle, and the flesh was shared in a community-wide feast. If no human enemies had been sacrificed for a time, the Iroquois might sacrifice a bear to Aireskoi, with apologies.

Before joining a war party, a warrior would devote much care to purification rituals in order to strengthen his personal magic or "medicine." If the warrior felt doubts about his medicine, or if his preparation rituals were inadvertently spoiled, it was understood that he was to abandon the project. Village shamans would perform augury rituals to divine the raid's prospects, and unfavorable signs would produce its cancellation. Each warrior had a personal medicine pouch or bundle with sacred objects connected with his tutelary spirit. Among some peoples, such as the Cherokees, Chickasaws, and Creeks of the Southeast, the leader of a war party carried on his back a special wooden box, about a foot wide by a foot-and-a-half high, filled with sacred objects of proven power. Pre-raid and post-raid war rituals, in which the entire village participated, served to strengthen group solidarity.

War Honors and Personal Status. War was so important in the cultures of many American Indian societies that success in war was the principal means of attaining personal esteem and status. As a result, war trophies and war honors had a special significance in many cultures. The best-known example is the taking and displaying of scalps. Most historians agree that scalping—the removal of the skin and attached hair from the top of the head—was widely practiced in pre-contact North America. Jacques Cartier reported the custom along the St. Lawrence River in 1535, and members of the Hernando de

This Edward Curtis photograph of a Brule (Sioux) war party shows both the Plains war bonnets and the importance of horses in the nineteenth century. (American Museum of Natural History)

Soto expedition (1539-1543) reported it in the Southeast at almost the same time. While each tribal group had its own particular customs, the curing and preserving of enemy scalps for display on certain ceremonial occasions was a widely practiced custom. In such ceremonies, the warrior was permitted to recite his war exploits, while other warriors or elders affirmed them. Among many peoples of eastern North America, it was the practice for men to wear their own hair in a special "scalplock," with the rest of the head shaved.

In the Southeast culture area, the winning of war names and titles was of fundamental importance. Among the Creek, for example, a warrior winning recognition would be given a traditional war name owned by his clan ("Crazy Snake" was one) in an impressive ceremony. In the Chickasaw ceremony in which war names were conferred, the recipients wore red moccasins and other special adornments. Creek warriors were ranked in three grades: warriors, big warriors, and war chiefs. Promotion through these ranks depended on war exploits, especially the number of scalps taken. Before taking scalps (and being recognized as a warrior) a Creek continued to do the menial work required of boys.

Among the Plains tribes, although scalps were taken, they did not have the importance as war honors that scalps had in the Northeast and Southeast. Among Plains Indians, the "coup" (from the French for "a blow") was more important. A warrior "counted coup" by touching an enemy with his hand or with a "coup stick." Many Plains warriors carried a specially decorated coup stick to be used to "strike coup." This was a light wand, not a weapon. Among the Cheyenne, it was striped like a barber's pole. To touch the person of an enemy

during battle, as opposed to shooting him with a bow or gun, was to demonstrate one's fearlessness. Killing an enemy, therefore, unless it involved touching him, was less honored than counting coup. To be the second, third, or even the fourth to touch an enemy carried merit in a recognized scale of honors. The Cheyenne allowed three men to count coup on the same enemy, with the first to touch him accorded the greatest merit. The enemy need not even be alive; to be the first to touch the body of a fallen enemy also conferred honor. Other war honors were earned by taking something from the enemy in battle, such as a shield, a gun, or a horse. Capturing horses from an enemy camp by stealth, especially a horse picketed near its owner's tipi, was another feat conferring honor. These graded war honors both emphasized personal courage and encouraged military aggression in the form of raiding.

War honors were recognized and publicized in a number of ways. In war dances before and after a raid, the entire band or village celebrated such achievements. A warrior's exploits could be painted on his tipi cover. He recited his deeds on special occasions, and many Plains tribes used a special symbolism in the construction of feather headdresses or war bonnets. An Assiniboine wore an eagle feather for each slain enemy. As in eastern North America, the winning of war honors and the quieting of the grief of mourners were the principal motives of aboriginal warfare on the Plains.

European American Influences on Warfare. The arrival of European fur traders and colonists began to modify Indian warfare patterns in the early seventeenth century, because European guns were deadlier than aboriginal bows and warclubs. Even in the early seventeenth century, muskets had a much longer effective killing range than did bows, so that a group armed with muskets could inflict heavy losses on an enemy armed with bows. Indians quickly recognized the advantages of the new weapons (and the superiority of steel knives, hatchets, and arrowpoints) and exerted themselves to obtain them. This was imperative, because warriors armed with traditional weapons were vulnerable not only to European soldiers but also to Indian enemies equipped with European weapons. Almost the only way to obtain these weapons was through the fur trade.

The fur trade, and in the Southeast the deerskin trade, had ramifications that extended ever more deeply into eastern North America, intensifying warfare and providing new economic motives for it. Some of the most spectacular and best-documented effects occurred in the wars of the Iroquois, especially with their traditional enemies, the Huron.

By the 1620's the Iroquois were obtaining guns in significant numbers at the Dutch trading post of Fort Orange (Albany, New York), near the junction of the Hudson and Mohawk rivers. The beaver, which provided the bulk of the pelts in the trade, were trapped out by about 1640 in the home territories of the Iroquois nations. Their scarcity started the Beaver Wars. By the 1640's, to obtain furs, the Iroquois were raiding far to the north to intercept Algonquian and Montagnais hunters as they were carrying their catch to market, as well as raiding the villages of their neighbors—Hurons, Eries, Neutrals, Petuns, and Susquehannocks—to drive them out and win their hunting territories. Within a few years, the Iroquois were raiding into Ohio and as far west as Illinois. The scale of these attacks, especially the number of deaths produced, eclipsed that of traditional warfare. In these same years, a series of severe epidemics sharply reduced the populations of Iroquois villages, bringing an even greater need for captives to maintain numbers. This intensified warfare cost more lives, necessitating more raids for captives. The Huron Confederacy and the Erie, Neutral, and Petun nations were destroyed, and entire villages of the defeated were adopted as Iroquois. By the end of the seventeenth century the Iroquois themselves acknowledged defeat.

Although the eruption of the Iroquois was the most extreme example of the European American impact on Indian warfare, the effect was felt everywhere. On the Plains, the arrival of the horse (and later, the gun) had profound consequences. As Plains Indians became mounted, economic motives for warfare appeared. Capturing horses became the most common reason for raids. —Bert M. Mutersbaugh

See also Adobe Walls, Battles of; Adoption; Apache Wars; Beaver Wars; Cayuse War; Ethnophilosophy and worldview; French and Indian Wars; King Philip's War; Lord Dunmore's War; Navajo War; Peach Wars; Pequot War; Powhatan Wars; Scalps and scalping; Snake War; Weapons; Yamasee War.

BIBLIOGRAPHY

Axtell, James, and William C. Sturtevant. "The Unkindest Cut: Or, Who Invented Scalping?" *William and Mary Quarterly*, 3d ser., 37 (July, 1980): 451-472. An excellent scholarly inquiry into a tradition that has been seen as a stereotype of Indian culture.

Ewers, John C. "Intertribal Warfare as the Precursor of Indian-White Warfare on the Northern Great Plains." *Western Historical Quarterly* 6 (October, 1975): 397-410. A look at pre-contact war among various Indian nations.

Hudson, Charles. *The Southeastern Indians.* Knoxville: University of Tennessee Press, 1976. A thorough examination of the Southeast nations and warfare in social and political terms.

Richter, Daniel K. *The Ordeal of the Longhouse: The Peoples of the Iroquois League in the Era of European Colonization.* Chapel Hill: University of North Carolina Press, 1992. A study of traditional warfare and how it was influenced by the arrival of Europeans.

_____. "War and Culture: The Iroquois Experience." *William and Mary Quarterly*, 3d ser., 40 (October, 1983): 528-559. A brief treatment of the Iroquois reasons for and approach to warfare.

Smith, Marian W. "The War Complex of the Plains Indians." *Proceedings of the American Philosophical Society* 78 (1937): 425-461. Discusses the culture of and motives for warfare of the Plains tribes.

Trigger, Bruce G. *The Children of the Aataentsic: A History of the Huron People to 1660.* 2 vols. Montreal: McGill-Queen's University Press, 1976. An examination of the social and political worlds of traditional warfare and the effects of European contact.

Wallace, Anthony F. C. *Death and Rebirth of the Seneca.* New York: Alfred A. Knopf, 1973. A study of the mental world of the Iroquois people, carrying their history into the period after their defeat.

Warren, William W.

(May 27, 1825, LaPointe, Mich.— June 1, 1853, St. Paul, Minn.): Author

TRIBAL AFFILIATION: Ojibwa (Chippewa)

SIGNIFICANCE: Educated in both the English and Chippewa languages, Warren wrote a detailed history of the Ojibwa

William Whipple Warren was the son of Lyman Warren, a white blacksmith, fur trader, and Indian agent, and his Chippewa-French wife, Mary Cadotte. As a young boy, Warren attended both the LaPointe Indian School and the Mackinaw Mission School and later studied at the Oneida Institute in New York. Thoroughly schooled in English, he returned to his people as a young man seeking to polish his Chippewa language skills. In 1845, he moved to Crow Wing, Minnesota, where he lived with his wife, Matilda Aiken.

With his considerable command of the Chippewa language, Warren was employed as a U.S. government interpreter. He was elected to the Minnesota State Legislature in 1850, where he earned a reputation for diligence. In 1852, he completed a one-volume history of the Chippewa people containing information he gathered during interviews with many of the tribal elders. Warren died of tuberculosis before finding a publisher for his *History of the Ojibways, Based Upon Traditions and Oral Statements*, published posthumously in 1885.

See also Ojibwa.

Wasco: Tribe
CULTURE AREA: Plateau
LANGUAGE GROUP: Upper Chinookan
PRIMARY LOCATION: The Dalles and lower Columbia River, Oregon

The Wasco and Wishram were contiguous tribes, sharing linguistic and cultural characteristics. The stronger Wasco ultimately absorbed the other group. Both groups maintained themselves through trading and exploiting the resources of the Columbia River and gathering various roots, particularly lomatium. They were noted for their weaving techniques and design in making soft cylindrical blankets.

After the Meriwether Lewis and William Clark expedition of 1805-1806, the first sustained European American contacts were with land-based traders desiring sea otter, beaver, fox, and other furs. The acquiring of European trade goods enhanced the Wasco-Wishram position on the Columbia River, which was the main trade route. The combined population of the Wasco-Wishram in 1937 was 351. Today some of the Wasco live on the Warm Springs and Yakima reservations, employed both on and off the reservations.

See also Wishram; Yakima.

Washakie (c. 1804, Bitterroot Valley, Mont.—Feb. 10, 1900, Bitterroot Valley, Mont.): Tribal chief
ALSO KNOWN AS: Pinquana
TRIBAL AFFILIATION: Shoshone
SIGNIFICANCE: Washakie led the Eastern Shoshone in numerous battles against tribal enemies but remained friendly to whites, offering assistance to settlers and allying with the U.S. Army against hostile tribes

Washakie was born in the southern Bitterroot Valley of Montana to a Flathead father and a Shoshone mother. Following his father's death in a Blackfoot raid, young Washakie roamed with his family among the Lemhi and Bannock Shoshones. Through Washakie's powerful leadership skills against Blackfoot hostility, he soon rose to tribal prominence.

Washakie then joined the Eastern Shoshones, who quickly accepted him as their leader; he soon gained renown for his kind and helpful treatment of white settlers. As Oregon Trail migration escalated during the 1840's, he consistently aided the immigrants, even to the point of recovering stolen property and assisting wagon trains at the Green River crossing. While acknowledging that whites depleted the available game, Washakie vowed never to war against them. For example, Washakie developed extensive relations with the Mormons, who helped achieve peace between him and Walkara, a Ute chief. Such was Washakie's friendship with the Mormons that when the U.S. Army sought his aid to defeat the "treasonous" sect in 1857, Washakie refused. While earning praise for this type of honest loyalty toward whites, he simultaneously became a feared warrior among his Indian enemies.

Washakie's band dominated the Upper Green and Sweetwater rivers in southwestern Wyoming and later laid claim to the Wind River country. Tribal disputes soon arose over this game-rich area. In 1866, the Crow came against Washakie's band in a bloody five-day battle; Chief Washakie emerged from the fight with the Crow chief's heart on the end of his lance and thus gained control of the Wind River Valley.

Two years later, Washakie formalized his claim to the valley by signing a treaty with the U.S. government. In reaction to the treaty and Washakie's friendship with the whites, some tribal warriors began agitating for a new chief. The seventy-year-old Washakie responded by mysteriously leaving his tribe. Two months later he returned with seven enemy scalps and challenged any warrior to better his feat. None accepted the challenge, and Washakie remained chief.

In 1874, Washakie successfully joined with the U.S. Cavalry against the marauding Arapaho; in 1876, he fought with the cavalry against the Sioux. In these campaigns, Washakie's leadership and fighting skills proved invaluable. For his valor, Washakie received high praise and a silver-mounted saddle from President Ulysses S. Grant.

Washakie spent his remaining life encouraging his people to accept the advancing white settlers and to take advantage of government assistance through the reservation system. Prior to his death, Washakie was baptized by John Roberts, an Episcopal missionary who later presided over Washakie's funeral. The highly respected chief was buried with full military honors at Fort Washakie, Wyoming.

See also Bannock; Oregon Trail; Shoshone.

Washita River, Battle of the
DATE: November 27, 1868
PLACE: Oklahoma
TRIBES AFFECTED: Arapaho, Cheyenne
SIGNIFICANCE: Although the U.S. government's Seventh Cavalry did not win a decisive victory in this battle, this engagement pushed the Cheyenne and Arapaho toward final capitulation and removal to a reservation

After widespread raids by Indians into Kansas in the summer of 1868, Major General Philip H. Sheridan initiated a winter campaign to disrupt the raiders' usual pattern of summer raiding and winter quiet. His goal was to compel the Cheyenne and their Arapaho allies, both of whom he blamed for the violence, onto a reservation near Fort Cobb in the northwestern Indian Territory.

Sheridan authorized three columns to converge on the Cheyenne and Arapaho. One of these consisted of the Seventh Cavalry led by Lieutenant Colonel George A. Custer. This force located a large Cheyenne village in the Washita River Valley, near present-day Cheyenne, Oklahoma. This camp was actually on a reservation and the leader, Black Kettle, was trying to cooperate with the army and believed that his protection had been assured by the commander at Fort Cobb. Custer thought otherwise, and he ordered his command to divide into four columns and attack from as many directions at dawn on November 27, 1868.

The initial attack inflicted a large number of casualties on the Cheyenne; among the dead were Black Kettle and his wife, both of whom had survived the Sand Creek Massacre in 1864. Confronted by hosts of warriors from neighboring villages, Custer's attacks stalled and he withdrew that evening. He reported that twenty-one members of his regiment were killed, including a major and eighteen enlisted men, while his troopers had killed more than a hundred warriors. Custer also claimed the Cheyenne had four white captives, two of whom they killed during the fighting.

The Cheyenne loss in manpower may be exaggerated, but Custer's troops did destroy a tremendous amount of food and shelters, and they killed hundreds of ponies. The Seventh Cavalry could not claim a decisive victory, but the damage inflicted did push the Cheyenne and their allies toward capitulation.

See also Arapaho; Black Kettle; Cheyenne; Sand Creek Massacre.

Washoe: Tribe
CULTURE AREA: Great Basin and California
LANGUAGE GROUP: Hokan
PRIMARY LOCATION: West central Nevada
POPULATION SIZE: 1,520 (1990 U.S. Census)

Archaeological evidence and oral tradition suggest that the homogeneous Washoe (also spelled "Washo") culture had origins along the western foothills of the Sierra Nevada slope. Their annual subsistence round successfully exploited plant and animal resources in specialized vegetational zones within a 10,000-square-mile region, ranging from lowland valleys of abundant game, vegetation, and water to high mountain meadows that provided berries, tubers, and seeds. The northern Washoe were largely dependent on acorns, the southern Washoe on pine nuts. Because they used different resources,

A late nineteenth century photograph of a Washoe family, taken near Lake Tahoe. (Library of Congress)

the Washoe enjoyed peaceful relations with neighboring groups, intermarrying and trading freely.

Sustained contact with European Americans began in 1825 with trappers and explorers; in the 1840's, immigrant parties began to arrive in Washoe territory. Conflict with settlers reached a climax in the 1857 "Potato War" and continued with settlers confiscating traditional resource areas. Under the General Allotment Act of 1887, small parcels of barren and nearly waterless land were allotted. In 1917 the government provided funds for purchasing additional small tracts of land near Carson City. Later, 40 acres were donated by a white rancher near Gardnerville, and an additional 20 acres near Reno became the Reno-Sparks Indian Colony.

Some Washoe practiced the peyote religion (Native American Church) in the early 1920's; by 1938 factionalism had developed, partly caused by disagreements over church rituals. The Indian Reorganization Act of 1934 recognized the Washoe as a legally constituted tribe, and they were authorized 795 acres on the Carson River.

Efforts at farming and raising livestock were hindered in the 1950's by poor management, factionalism, and poor relations with the Bureau of Indian Affairs. Ongoing litigation with the government over the loss of 9,872 square miles of aboriginal lands resulted in the 1970 Indian Claims Commission award of approximately $5 million. A Washoe tribal council headquarters and Indian crafts enterprise is located near Gardnerville, where there is a park with camping facilities on the Carson river, and in Dresslerville the tribe operates a Health Center and Senior Citizens' Center. The tribe also supports an aquaculture and construction company.

See also Datsolalee; Great Basin; Hokan language family.

Water and water rights

TRIBES AFFECTED: Pantribal

SIGNIFICANCE: Questions regarding ownership of, and rights to use, natural resources, including water, are among the most crucial issues currently facing American Indian tribes

As European American settlers moved farther and farther west across the continent, Native Americans lost most of their rights to the water they had once used freely. It was not until the twentieth century—and primarily the last two decades of the century—that courts began to recognize Indian rights to the water lying underneath or flowing through their lands. Water is among the most precious of resources in many parts of the United States, notably the Southwest. In 1907, a case known as the Winters decision first recognized the reserved water rights of reservations.

In the 1970's, the protection of water rights began to gain recognition as one of the most important issues faced by American Indian tribes. Debate began to rage, and cases were taken to court, regarding crucial questions of whether a state or a tribe owned various water supplies. In addition to the issue of ownership are questions concerning the uses to which water can be put and regulation of access to water. In 1973, the National Water Commission (created by Congress) criticized

Type	Number	Surface Acres	Length in Miles	Shoreline Miles
Natural lakes and ponds	5,690	1,001,825		5,845
Reservoirs and impoundments	17,537	507,139		4,573
Perennial streams	4,047	384	14,279	6,500
Coastal shorelines	349		39	330

SURFACE WATER ON AMERICAN INDIAN LANDS, 1989

Source: U.S. Department of the Interior, *Bureau of Indian Affairs Natural Resource Information System Inventory and Production Report, 1989.* Washington D.C.: U.S. Government Printing Office, 1989.

Note: Includes only water sources under BIA jurisdiction, not those on privately owned lands.

the government's failure to protect Indian water rights adequately. A number of cases in 1983 affected water rights. For example, the Supreme Court, in *Nevada v. U.S.*, upheld the allocation of water rights to the Pyramid Lake Reservation in Nevada. On the other hand, the Court denied five tribes a requested larger allocation of Colorado River water (*Arizona v. California*), and it ruled in *Arizona v. San Carlos Apache Tribe* that state courts have the authority to decide cases involving Indian water rights (tribes were attempting to establish that only federal courts should have jurisdiction over these matters). In 1989, Secretary of the Interior Manuel Lujan announced that the Working Group on Indian Water Settlements, which would report to the Water Policy Council, would establish principles for guiding settlements and would assist in negotiations with tribes.

Pacific Northwest Issues. A closer examination of water rights issues in the Pacific Northwest provides examples of the difficulties involved in deciding such questions. Rainfall in the Pacific Northwest varies dramatically from the lush western half of the region, with an annual precipitation of up to 35 inches, to the arid Columbia Basin plateau, with an annual rainfall as low as 10 inches in certain parts. Because of the scarcity of this resource in parts of the Pacific Northwest, and a growing population as the West becomes an increasingly popular place to live, water is the most precious resource in the region. Commercial fisheries, sportsmen, farmers, Native Americans, and residential users are all competing for water.

Courts throughout the West are deciding whose claims to the resource are the most legitimate. In the interior Pacific Northwest, for example, several rivers are the lifeblood of Indian society, with the Columbia River affecting the largest number. Pacific Northwest Indians traditionally have relied upon surrounding water resources for a rich fishing harvest, particularly salmon, making it imperative to preserve an adequate in-stream flow. In recent years, water has gained new importance because of irrigation. For example, the Yakimas have irrigation on their reservation and are now one of the parties involved in the adjudication of Yakima River water.

In the last half of the twentieth century, Pacific Northwest Indian claims for either water rights or compensation have met with limited success. In Pacific Northwest rivers, such as the Salmon River, it was evident by the 1950's and 1960's that there was not enough fish for everyone (sport and commercial fishing interests and Native Americans), and state officials decided that Indian fishing would have to be regulated. Before this, states had observed treaty provisions that allowed Indians to fish at "all usual and accustomed grounds and stations" and did not place limits on their catch at off-reservation sites. The tribes contended that the treaty provisions should still be in effect and resisted regulations; protests and arrests occurred at fishing sites.

Court cases ensued, and two cases in 1968, *United States v. Oregon* and *Sohappy v. Smith* (they were consolidated into one), dealt with Indian rights to continue fishing at traditional sites and the assurance that at these traditional sites the Indians would be ensured a catch of salmon and steelhead. The federal judge ruled in favor of the tribes. The tribes have also won in cases regarding accessibility to fishing sites. In the case of *U.S. v. Winans*, the court ruled that Indians could cross private land to reach a traditional fishing site.

The next major case, in 1971, involved tribes in the Puget Sound area. Fourteen tribes argued that the Washington State department of fisheries regulations denied them a fair amount of the salmon and steelhead runs. The case, *United States v. Washington*, was heard by federal judge George N. Boldt, who ruled in favor of the tribes, concluding that they be allotted 50 percent of the fish run. The decision, known as the Boldt decision, was very unpopular, and state officials ignored it. Boldt's ruling was brought before the Supreme Court, which upheld his decision.

Another area of concern for Pacific Northwest tribes has been the damming of rivers, which causes added pressure on the dwindling salmon and steelhead populations. The dams on the Columbia River have been built primarily to supplement irrigation flows, but they have cut the salmon population drastically, as salmon are denied a sufficient in-stream flow or are forced through fish ladders and suffer disorientation as they swim through warm reservoir water. These issues have still not been resolved, as environmental groups, irrigators, and tribes all press their claims. The construction of dams has also threatened traditional fishing sites. The Dalles Dam, built in 1957, flooded Celilo Falls, for which the Yakima Nation was awarded fifteen million dollars. Further debates over water in the Pacific Northwest will include the protection of habitat. If courts continue to find that the tribes are entitled to an equitable share of the fish population, the tribes will need to participate in decisions that affect the whole ecosystem of Pacific Northwest rivers.

See also Fish and fishing; Indian-white relations—U.S., 1934-1995; Resources.

Watie, Stand

Watie, Stand (Dec. 12, 1806, near Rome, Ga.—Sept. 9, 1871, Indian Territory, present-day Okla.): Tribal leader, Confederate general

ALSO KNOWN AS: Dagataga, Degadoga (He Stands on Two Feet)

TRIBAL AFFILIATION: Cherokee

SIGNIFICANCE: Stand Watie helped establish the *Cherokee Phoenix*, was a signer of the treaty accepting removal to Indian Territory, and was a Confederate brigadier general in the Civil War

Born on December 12, 1806, in northwestern Georgia, to a full-blooded Cherokee father and half-blood mother, Watie was called Degataga, but when his parents converted to Christianity, they changed their name from Oo-wa-tie to Watie and renamed their second son Isaac S., which he later turned to Stand. With his older brother Galegina ("Buck"), he attended the Moravian mission schools at Spring Place, Georgia, and Brainerd, Tennessee. While Buck went on to study in Connecticut at the Foreign Mission School and to change his name to Elias Boudinot (one of the school's benefactors), Stand took up farming. At the age of twenty-two, he also became clerk of the Cherokee Supreme Court, and later he became a lawyer. When Boudinot became editor of the Cherokee newspaper, the *Cherokee Phoenix*, Stand Watie sometimes assisted him, and in 1835, he joined him, their cousin John Ridge, and their uncle Major Ridge in signing the Treaty of New Echota, which required the Cherokees to give up their lands in Georgia and "remove" to comparable land in what is now Oklahoma. The signers were liable to the "blood law," which decreed death for anyone selling Cherokee land without the full consent of the nation, and Principal Chief John Ross and his followers, not at New Echota, repudiated the treaty. After President Martin Van Buren had the Eastern Cherokees rounded up and removed west in 1838-1839 on the Trail of Tears, a death march that killed one-third of the tribe, militant followers of Ross murdered the Ridges and Watie's brother Boudinot. Watie himself was marked for death but escaped, offered $10,000 for the murderers of his brother, and became leader of the anti-Ross party.

Before removal, Watie had several wives but no children; in 1843, the widower married Sarah Caroline Bell, by whom he had five children. When the Cherokees joined the Confederacy at the beginning of the Civil War, Watie raised the first regiment of Cherokee volunteers, the "Cherokee Mounted Rifles." As a daring cavalry commander along the border of Indian Territory and at the battles of Pea Ridge and Wilson's Creek, Watie became the most outstanding Indian soldier in history and was promoted to brigadier general. During the war, he got revenge on his enemy John Ross by burning Ross's house. When the majority party of the Cherokees broke their alliance with the Confederate states in 1863, Watie remained loyal to the Confederacy and was elected principal chief by the tribe's southern faction. At the war's end, Watie was the last Confederate general to surrender, on June 23, 1865. After the war, Watie was a member of a Cherokee delegation to Wash-

Stand Watie was one of the Cherokee signers of the Treaty of New Echota; he later raised a Cherokee regiment for the Confederacy. (Library of Congress)

ington, and he then went home to resume farming until his death on September 9, 1871.

See also Boudinot, Elias; Cherokee; Journalism; Removal; Ridge, Major; Ross, John.

Wattle and daub

TRIBES AFFECTED: Primarily tribes in the Southeast
SIGNIFICANCE: Wattle and daub dwellings provided effective shelter in the relatively mild environmental conditions of the Southeast

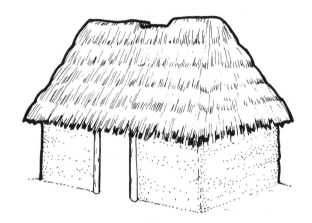

Wattle and daub

The term "wattle and daub" refers to a type of construction that, with variations, was widely used for dwellings in North America, especially in the Southeast. Wattle and daub construction involves a pole framework around which is interwoven a latticework of branches, twigs, or vines (the wattle). The construction is then covered with clay or mud plaster (the daub). The typical wattle and daub dwelling of the Southeast was roughly rectangular in shape and had a thatched roof with a smoke hole. The ancient "jacal" construction which preceded true masonry techniques in the Southwest was similar to wattle and daub; in jacal construction, stone slabs, held in place with adobe, were placed against the bottoms of walls.

See also Architecture—Southeast; Architecture—Southwest; Chickee; Wickiup; Wigwam.

Weapons

TRIBES AFFECTED: Pantribal
SIGNIFICANCE: The demands of daily living, such as hunting and warfare with other tribes and white settlers, required a variety of weapons

American Indian life required weapons for hunting game and, in many cases, for fighting with other tribes (and eventually with white settlers and soldiers). Accordingly, a variety of weapons were developed.

Bow and Arrow. This weapon preceded the arrival of whites in North America. Indian archers were skilled marksmen, and they developed a variety of bows and arrows with a deadly combination of accuracy and power. For example, chain-mail armor worn by the soldiers of the Spanish explorer Hernando de Soto could be pierced by an arrow at 150 paces. Even soldiers wearing plate armor could be felled by arrows through the eyes, mouth, or throat. In less than four years, de Soto lost 250 troops and 150 horses to the bow and arrow. Silent and quickly reloaded, the bow and arrow was universally used by North American Indians for centuries.

Crossbow. It is highly likely that Indians borrowed the crossbow from whites, as the earliest French and Spanish explorers had them. They were used by some eastern tribes (Cherokees, Potawatomis), but it is not known when they first came into use. The crossbow had a gun-shaped grooved stock in which the arrow was placed. The bow was mounted at a right angle at the stock's forward end, and the bowstring was released by a trigger device.

Although very powerful and accurate, the crossbow never attained the popularity and universal use of the bow and arrow—possibly because it was more difficult to carry and slower to reload or because it was developed at about the same time that the bow and arrow began to be supplanted by firearms.

Tomahawk and Lance. The tomahawk was commonly used by the Algonquian tribes of the eastern United States during combat at close quarters. It was made of wood and consisted of a stem or handle about 3 feet long and a head which was a round ball or solid knob of wood. Where the stem pierced the head, a point projected forward which could be thrust like a lance. When the Indians were taught the use of iron and steel, the wooden tomahawk gave way to metal hatchets.

The lance was a long pole to whose end was attached a warhead made of chipped stone, not unlike an arrowhead. It was widely distributed among American Indians and developed into a number of varieties depending on the environment and type of animal hunted. For example, the Inuits developed the greatest variety, in response to an environment characterized by numerous animal forms. The Plains Indians made more extensive use of the lance as a weapon of war than other tribes did, because it adapted well to use from the horse.

Blowgun and Dagger. The blowgun was used by a few tribes, including the Cherokee, Choctaw, and Iroquois, solely for hunting small game—not for war. It was a hollow tube from 6 to 10 feet in length made from plant material such as cane or walnut. Darts, ranging in length from 15 to 26 inches, were placed in the end of the blowgun and expelled with a quick, sharp breath. This was a versatile weapon: Highly accurate at fairly short distances, it could also propel a dart more than a hundred yards.

The dagger was a sharp-pointed instrument used to stab and thrust at close range. Originally made of stone or bone, later versions were of copper, iron, or steel.

Rifle. Muskets were obtained from whites as early as the 1600's by eastern tribes, primarily through fur trading. The Indians became accomplished marksmen and also built their own forges and engaged in gunsmithing. Firearms spread west

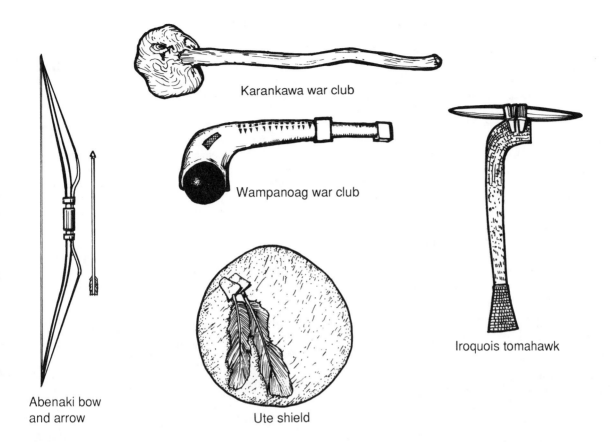

Karankawa war club

Wampanoag war club

Iroquois tomahawk

Abenaki bow
and arrow

Ute shield

and were utilized by many tribes, often with great advantage to the tribes who used them first. For example, the Chippewa became the first in their region to receive firearms from white traders, which enabled them to drive the Sioux from the woodlands in the late 1600's.

The rifle was used at first as a supplement to native weapons rather than as a replacement for them. The bow and arrow was cheap and readily available, and its rapid rate of fire made it an excellent weapon. It was not until the development of the repeating rifle that native weapons gave way significantly to firearms. —*Laurence Miller*

See also Bows, arrows, and quivers; Guns; Lances and spears; Tomahawks; Tools; Warfare and conflict.

Weatherford, William (c. 1780, near Montgomery, Ala.—Mar. 9, 1822, Polk County, Tenn.): Military leader
ALSO KNOWN AS: Lamochattee, Lumhe Chate, Red Eagle
TRIBAL AFFILIATION: Creek
SIGNIFICANCE: As principal leader of the Creek war faction, the Red Sticks, Weatherford fought the Americans during the Creek War, 1813-1814

William Weatherford's father was a Scottish trader, and his mother was chief Alexander McGillivray's sister. In 1811, the Creek peace faction, the White Sticks, refused Tecumseh's appeal for Creek support of his pantribal alliance. Many Red

Stick warriors, including Weatherford, sympathized with and were influenced by Tecumseh.

During the Creek War (1813-1814), approximately one thousand warriors under Weatherford's command successfully assaulted Americans at Fort Mims on August 13, 1813, killing five hundred settlers and releasing their black slaves. Subsequently, federal and state troops were mobilized under the command of General Andrew Jackson. At the Battle of Horseshoe Bend, March 27, 1814, Weatherford's forces suffered their final defeat. After surrendering several days later to Jackson, Weatherford was freed after promising to maintain peace thereafter. He died at his farm near Little River, Arkansas, shortly before the remaining Creeks were forced to relocate to Indian Territory.

See also Creek; Creek War; Francis, Milly Hayo; Menewa; Opothleyaholo; Tecumseh.

Weaving
TRIBES AFFECTED: Pantribal, especially Navajo
SIGNIFICANCE: Textiles were made and used by the American Indian for everyday life as well as for trade and gift giving; the best-known and most prolific weavers were the Navajo

Weaving is the creation of a textile by means of a mechanical device called a loom. Vertical yarns (the "warp") and horizontal (the "weft") are interlaced in a variety of patterns to produce goods such as blankets, cloth, and rugs. Weaving—a very old art, preceded historically by basketry and finger weaving—progressed as different types of looms were developed and put to use.

Pre-contact Textiles. Before Europeans arrived in the Americas, the native populations made fabrics from cotton, milkweed, yucca fiber, bark fiber, strips of fur, twine, and hair. Textiles had utilitarian purposes heavily influenced by regional and climatic considerations. They were generally soft, two-dimensional items, but by 500 C.E. the Anasazi of the Southwest were making woven footwear and bags. By 700, the Anasazi probably had a simple upright loom.

By the time Europeans arrived, weaving was technically quite advanced, having slowly progressed from plaiting, braiding, and finger weaving. Three basic types of loom were in use: elementary one-beam looms for use with unstretched warp yarns, two-beam looms that used stretched warp (the first true loom), and the combination loom on which the warp was stretched over a roller loom. The latter variety, used in the area around Puget Sound, Washington, was a considerable advancement over the simpler methods, producing more even, finished, and wider pieces in less time.

In the early years, color was usually rubbed or painted onto the finished woven piece. Eventually, the fibers were dyed first and then woven. Textiles were decorated with embroidery, applique and beadwork. Beads were sometimes woven into the work.

European Influence. By the nineteenth century, the influence of Europeans had been felt. The settlers brought new materials, such as commercial dyes, and new styles and design concepts to the American Indian weaver—as well as different markets. Spanish settlers and missionaries introduced sheep in the sixteenth and seventeenth centuries, adding wool to the fiber content in blankets and rugs. The use of Shroud cloth (made in Shroud, England, in the early seventeenth century) became widespread except in the Southwest, replacing the majority of native weaving by the mid-eighteenth century.

Regional Centers. While weaving was practiced at some level throughout American Indian culture, some prominent practitioners can be identified. These were the Indians of the

Navajo woman weaving a blanket on a large vertical loom. (W. T. Mullarky, Museum of New Mexico)

Southwest and Great Lakes region, the Tlingit of Alaska, and the Salish of the Puget Sound area.

The Pueblo are known to have been weavers since around 800 C.E., and the Navajo—known for high-quality blankets and rugs—since around 1700. The Great Lakes area was known for the weaving of flat, rectangular wool bags, and the Tlingit weavers of southeastern Alaska produced the prized Chilkat blanket. The Salish of the Northwest Coast area were known for using mountain goat and dog hair to make blankets.

Weavers of the Pueblo culture wove blankets and articles of clothing of cotton; after the Spanish introduced sheep into the area, they began to use wool. In Central America, Mexican serapes and blankets were made in Saltillo and Oaxaca.

Little is known about prehistoric weaving of the Tlingit people, largely because of the ill effects of their climate on the preservation of goods and materials, but it is believed that the Chilkat blankets they made are evidence of the survival of a very old primitive craft. These blankets were produced on a simple "suspension" or "bar" loom using cedar-bark fibers and mountain-goat wool. Each took from six months to a year to complete. Design motifs—all of which were symmetrically balanced and intricately patterned—featured totemic animals, family crests and natural forms in black, white, yellow, and green. Blankets were five-sided and fringed on two or three of the five sides. The Tlingit were also known for making ceremonial dance skirts and robes.

In the Eastern Woodlands areas, Indians made twined medicine bags, storage bags and woven belts with beadwork. In the Plains region, where leather and beadwork were more prevalent than weaving, woven mats were used to cover medicine bundles and as altar cloths for displaying objects. The Cherokee were very active weavers who used the English loom and allowed their weaving to be influenced by social and artistic forces outside their tribal group.

The best-known textiles were produced by Navajo women who made blankets, rugs, clothing, and other household items. They would use a simple loom made of two straight poles hung between two trees or a backstrap loom which had one end attached to a wall or tree and the other anchored at the weaver's waist. On these looms they produced narrow lengths of cloth used for headbands, belts, and sashes.

The development of Navajo weaving was connected to the introduction of sheep-raising. At first, the Navajo used undyed natural wool in white, black, and brown. After 1800, dyed bayeta cloth imported from Spain and England to Mexico made its way into their work; they unravelled the cloth and rewove the yarns into their own designs. Experimentation with dyes and a variety of weaves began about this time as well, although they seldom used more than five colors in addition to black, white, and undyed wool. Designs were simple, using the repetition of a few elements on a plain or striped background. The Chief's Blanket, also popular with the Plains Indians, was considered the best product of the Navajo.

By the mid-1800's, during what is known as the Classic period of Navajo weaving, Navajo weavings were the most valuable product of the Southwest. After 1925, however, because of increased commercialization, the level of quality dropped. More recently there has been a rise in quality with smaller quantities of higher-quality goods generally being produced.

Social Aspects. Social forces exerted an influence in the design and use of woven items. Textiles were highly valued not only for their beauty and utility but also because they represented an interweaving, so to speak, of social, religious, historic, and economic forces. Traditional ceremonial and mythological symbols particular to the tribe were made a part of the design. A variety of statements about social position or wealth, such as the wearing of the Chief's Blanket or Chilkat robe, could be made. Textiles were also used in gift giving, courtship, and intertribal trade as well as commerce with whites, for whom the blanket represented a standard of currency. —*Diane C. Van Noord*

See also Appliqué and ribbonwork; Baskets and basketry; Beads and beadwork; Blankets; Chilkat blankets; Cotton; Dress and adornment; Navajo.

BIBLIOGRAPHY

Conn, Richard. *Native American Art in the Denver Art Museum*. Denver: Denver Art Museum, 1979.

Dockstader, Frederick J. *Weaving Arts of the North American Indian*. New York: Thomas Y. Crowell, 1978.

Kapoun, Robert W. *Language of the Robe*. Salt Lake City, Utah: Peregrine Smith Books, 1992.

LaFarge, Oliver, et al. *Introduction to American Indian Art*. Glorieta, N.Mex.: Rio Grande Press, 1973.

Rodee, Marian E. *Weaving of the Southwest*. Westchester, Pa.: Schiffer, 1987.

Weetamoo (c. 1650, southwestern Mass.—Aug. 6, 1676, near Taunton, Mass.): Tribal chief

ALSO KNOWN AS: Namumpum, Tatapanum

TRIBAL AFFILIATION: Pocasset, a branch of the Wampanoag

SIGNIFICANCE: Weetamoo was a "squaw sachem," or female chief; such chiefs were sometimes found among the Algonquian peoples of New England

Weetamoo was sachem of the Pocasset, whose territory lay east of Mt. Hope Bay in southwestern Massachusetts. When King Philip's War broke out in June, 1675, she resisted the urging of English emissaries to remain neutral and joined Metacomet (King Philip), sachem of the Wampanoag, with whom the Pocasset were affiliated. She provided canoes that allowed Metacomet's people to escape an English force advancing into Mt. Hope Peninsula. Her band spent much of the war in flight, sometimes in the Narragansett country, sometimes with Metacomet's forces. During the war she married the Narragansett sachem Quinnapin. In August, 1676, her band was taken by surprise on the bank of the Taunton River, near Taunton, Massachusetts, and Weetamoo drowned while trying to escape across the river on a raft. Her head was cut off and set on a pole in Taunton.

See also King Philip's War; Metacomet; Narragansett; Sachem; Wampanoag; Women.

Weirs and traps

TRIBES AFFECTED: Pantribal

SIGNIFICANCE: Ingenious traps were used throughout North America for capturing fish and animals

Hunting and fishing were labor-intensive activities, but various inventions permitted the capture of animals with less time and effort. All Indian tribes, including agriculturalists, used these devices both before and after contact with Europeans. Their variety in native North America was tremendous, but they can be divided into three classes: enclosing, arresting, and killing devices.

Enclosing devices prevented an animal—who was unharmed— from escaping. Pits, camouflaged with leaf-covered mats and dug into game trails; and wicker fences on mudflats adjoining estuaries, forming enclosures ("weirs") to trap fish as high tides receded, are examples of enclosing devices.

Arresting devices went one step further, grabbing or entangling an animal. Nets, set between trees to catch birds, or under water to catch fish and aquatic mammals, are one form of this device. Another is the snare, which trapped an animal's leg in a noose. The Montagnais used an ingenious spiked-wheel trap, a tethered hoop of wood with flexible, sharp rods pointing inward like spokes but not quite meeting. A caribou would step into such a trap and be unable to escape.

Killing devices incorporated some means of killing the prey, as when a weight was released by a trigger tripped by the animal (a deadfall). The Tanaina used a complicated torsion trap in which a striker would be held under tension from twisted rawhide until an animal tripped a trigger, releasing the trap on itself. An ingenious, if rather gruesome, killing device used by the Inuit was a sharpened strip of whale baleen, bent double, encased in animal fat and frozen. Left in a place frequented by bears or wolves, it would be swallowed whole by one of these predators and then suddenly spring open after thawing in the animal's stomach, killing it from within.

Indian traps often were cleverly designed to catch only game of a predetermined size. The mesh size of fish nets, for example, was determined by the size of the desired catch, since smaller fish could swim through the mesh and larger fish could not insert their heads far enough to become snagged at the gills. Among the Indians of the Atlantic Coast, mesh gauges were used in making nets so that the desired mesh size would be maintained throughout.

Most traps have left few remains that can be studied, so it is difficult to estimate when traps came into use in North America. Net weights, however, indicate that birds or fish probably were netted in most of eastern North America by 3500 B.C.E. Weirs leave distinctive remains, and the Boylston Street Fishweir under the streets of Boston dates from as early as 2500 B.C.E.; other less well-dated weirs may have predated these by as much as three thousand years.

The European fur trade stimulated Indian fur-trapping, and traditional trap technology was inadequate to the task. The older methods gave way to the use of efficient European iron traps.

See also Fish and fishing; Hunting and gathering; Subsistence; Trade.

Welch, James (b. Nov. 18, 1940, Browning, Mont.): Novelist, poet

TRIBAL AFFILIATION: Blackfoot, Gros Ventre (Atsina)

SIGNIFICANCE: Having published four novels and a book of poetry since 1974, James Welch has gained national recognition as an American Indian writer

Born of a Blackfoot father and Gros Ventre mother, Welch grew up in an Indian environment, and the traditions and religion especially of the Blackfoot inform his writing. He attended the University of Montana, where he received his B.A. degree. As an adjunct professor he teaches writing and Indian studies at the University of Montana.

Much of Welch's fiction pivots on the interaction between the American Indian and white America. In *Winter in the Blood* (1974), Welch presents a nameless protagonist who feels displaced, caught between two worlds, helpless in a world of stalking white men, but unaccepted by Indians—a stranger to both. Similarly, in *The Death of Jim Loney* (1979), Welch portrays a half-blood who is unable to find a place in either world. Different from his first two novels, *Fools Crow* (1986) is a historical novel set in the 1870's which depicts Fools Crow, who attempts to live a traditional Blackfoot life in the context of white settlement and the U.S. government's war against Plains Indians. Welch includes episodes from Blackfoot oral narrative and describes traditional ceremonies. *The Indian Lawyer* (1990) tells the story of an Indian who is torn about how best to help his people: law practice and politics or on the reservations themselves, while his own worst enemy is himself. The poetry collection *Riding the Earthboy 40* (1971) is best for its protest poetry, which often deals with reservation life in Montana.

See also Blackfoot and Blackfeet Confederacy; Reservation system of the United States.

BIBLIOGRAPHY

Wild, Peter. *James Welch.* Boise State Western Writers Series. Boise, Idaho: Boise State University Press, 1983.

Wenatchi: Tribe

CULTURE AREA: Plateau

LANGUAGE GROUP: Salishan

PRIMARY LOCATION: Washington State

POPULATION SIZE: 26 (1990 U.S. Census)

The Wenatchi (also spelled "Wenatchee"), a part of the Salishan family, lived along the Wenatchee River, a tributary of the Columbia River in Washington. Their earliest known homeland was farther inland, perhaps as far east as western Montana. Their name, and the name of the river that was their home, is from the Yakima word *winätshi* ("river issuing from a canyon"). The Wenatchi were probably closely related to the Pisquow. Another, smaller group, the Chelans, spoke the same dialect as the Wenatchi and may have once been a part of the tribe. The Wenatchi lived in villages of varying size. Because

WHITE BUFFALO SOCIETY / 853

they relied on hunting and fishing—salmon was a chief staple of their diet—as well as on gathering roots and berries, they moved throughout the year to find food in different seasons. The Wenatchi were involved in no protracted struggles with their neighbors. The Wenatchi had no continuous contact with whites until the eighteenth century, when they started to feel pressure to vacate their lands. In 1850, a group of fifty Wenatchi were living on the Yakima reservation. By the end of the twentieth century, the Wenatchi were part of the Colville agency.

See also Colville; Plateau; Salishan language family.

Whales and whaling

TRIBES AFFECTED: Clallam, Inuit, Makah, Nootka, Quileute, Quinault

SIGNIFICANCE: Whales provided a primary source of food, grease, and oil for personal use and trade; whales and whaling also fostered a sense of solidarity and provided the basis for religious and magic rituals

The coastal dwelling Inuit (Eskimo) of the Arctic culture area depended exclusively on animals as their food source for much of their history. The spring whale migration was an important source of food and oil, especially in the western region. A successful hunt marked the beginning of a good year and reaffirmed the interrelationship between the two worlds, animal and Inuit. An unsuccessful hunt was inauspicious; it meant further expenditures of energy and time hunting other sea mammals—and the possibility of starvation if the effort failed.

The whale was an integral part of tribal life in the Northwest Coast culture area as well. The Makah, Nootka, Quileute, and Quinault embarked on expeditions to kill humpback, finback, and California gray whale, as they moved up the Olympic peninsula in the spring on their way to summer in the Arctic. The Clallam, on the other hand, hunted whales only if they entered their inland waters. Other tribes, such as the Chinook and Salish, only took dead whales that drifted to shore.

Whaling expeditions were suffused with specialized knowledge, ritual, and ceremony. The Inuit knew the various whale migration routes and schedules in minute detail, and they developed a system to describe the whales themselves in great detail. Magical charms were placed in the whaling boat, which was then launched by ritually selected women who danced and dispensed gifts. The crew sang magic songs to weaken the whale and entice it to the surface. The captain and owner, or *umialik*, exerted religious and economic authority. When the whale was brought to shore the head was severed in order to release the spirit of the whale. The boat owner's wife, herself a type of priestess, would then offer the head a cup of water and thank it for coming, after which the spirit was urged to return to the land of living whales and report how well it had been treated. For the Inuit, who lack a true village-based community, whaling helped to impart a sense of community solidarity.

Among Northwest Coast tribes the harpooner generally owned the boat and equipment and commanded the appropriate magic to ensure success; magical powers were imputed to the harpooner to explain his extraordinary strength and skills.

Songs were sung to bring the whale near, to make it gentle when harpooned, and to bring it safely to shore. The harpooner's share of blubber (whale fat) was placed on display and decorated with feathers to please the whale's spirit; it was believed that otherwise the harpooner might not live to kill another. The ritual ended with the giveaway feast, which was also an occasion for the harpooner to present gifts (usually whale oil) to the tribe and to honor the whales so that they would return the following year.

The depletion of whale populations, their international protection, the movement of tribal members to inland urban cities, and the development of other economies have all reduced the importance of whales and whaling in contemporary tribal life.

See also Clallam; Fish and fishing; Inuit; Makah; Nootka; Quileute; Quinault.

White Bird (c. 1807, Idaho—c. 1882, Canada): Shaman, military leader

ALSO KNOWN AS: Penpenhihi, Peopeo Kiskiok Hihih (White Goose)

TRIBAL AFFILIATION: Nez Perce

SIGNIFICANCE: A skilled negotiator and marksman, White Bird was a major leader in the Nez Perce War of 1877

Along with Joseph the Elder, White Bird refused to sign the Treaty of 1863, by which the Nez Perce would move to the Lapwai Reservation of Idaho. Although originally opposed to war, White Bird became a principal war leader as tensions peaked in 1877 after the Nez Perce were ordered to move to the reservation. As a skilled marksman, White Bird led his warriors against troops commanded by Colonel John Gibbon at the major Battle of Big Hole Valley, Montana, August 9, 1877.

After a six-day siege at the final Battle of Bear Paw, Montana, beginning September 30, White Bird, with approximately twenty other Nez Perce leaders and two hundred followers, retreated to Canada. There they joined Sioux chief Sitting Bull, already in exile after the Battle of the Little Big Horn (1876). Unlike Sitting Bull, however, White Bird remained in exile. He was killed approximately five years later, by the father of two Indian patients who died after White Bird, a medicine man, treated them.

See also Joseph the Younger; Nez Perce; Nez Perce War.

White Buffalo Society

TRIBES AFFECTED: Hidatsa, Mandan

SIGNIFICANCE: The purpose of the all-female White Buffalo Society was to entice buffalo herds to come near the village

The function of the White Buffalo Society, the highest order among women's societies of the Mandan and Hidatsa tribes, was to entice the buffalo herds to come near the village. It was especially used during times of want, when hunting efforts had not proved successful and further measures were deemed necessary. The idea was that if the buffalo were mimicked, they would draw near to the hunters.

This society was an age society with collective purchase: When prospective members were of a certain age, they would buy the right to join the group from the oldest members, whose time it was to leave the group. This purchase provided for the rights to use and practice certain dances, songs, and regalia of the society.

White Buffalo Society members imitated a herd of buffalo. They grouped together in a sort of loose huddle and mimicked the steps and movements of the buffalo with dances and gestures. Each member wore a cap topped with a fan of hawk feathers. The cap itself was high and round, made from the prized skin of an albino buffalo. As they performed their ceremony, the women carried dry branches with tufts of eagle down fastened to the ends of the branches.

See also Buffalo; Gender relations and roles; Hidatsa; Mandan.

White Cloud (c. 1830, Gull Lake, Minn.—1898, White Earth Reservation, Minn.): Tribal chief

Also known as: Wabanaquot

Tribal affiliation: Ojibwa (Chippewa)

Significance: A renowned peace chief, diplomat, and orator, White Cloud was also known for his addiction to alcohol

The son of Wabojeeg, who had been appointed by the U.S. government, White Cloud succeeded his father as chief of the Minnesota Chippewa. He led his people to the White Earth Reservation in 1868, where they adopted sedentary agriculture and settled into a life of peace. White Cloud converted to Christianity in 1871.

Although a renowned politician and diplomat, White Cloud became dependent on alcohol and earned a reputation as a chief who accepted bribes and acted against the best interests of his tribe in favor of his own addiction. He became embroiled in controversy which weakened the tribe and threatened its unity after he sided with an influential white trader, who was liberally supplying him with alcohol, in a dispute against three Indian agents who were loyally serving the Chippewa. For nearly ten years, White Cloud's leadership was challenged and the trade issue was debated in the Chippewa tribal council. At numerous debates, White Cloud's oratory was honed to a fine edge; although he retained tribal leadership, the issue was a divisive one that permanently weakened Chippewa tribal unity.

See also Ojibwa; Trade.

White Deerskin Dance

Tribe affected: Yurok

Significance: This world-renewal ceremony celebrates the continuing cycles of life

The White Deerskin Dance, performed during the fall, lasts from twelve to sixteen days. While essentially a reenactment of the Yurok creation story, it is much more than a retelling: The dance itself is thought to put the world back in order. The ceremony is designed to correct temporary flaws in the relationship of the human community to the natural world and thus to enable the seasonal cycles to continue properly. At the center of the story is the life cycle of the salmon, the main source of sustenance along the rivers of the Yurok homeland.

The name "White Deerskin Dance" was given to this ceremony by non-Indian people and is something of a misnomer. "White" refers to specially prepared deerskins, decorated with feathers, shells, and other materials, that are held up on poles by the dancers during the exoteric portion of the ceremony. The skins are not always white in color.

White, for the Yurok, represents not only a color but also a concept of something pure and clear. It also refers to a tradition of an ancient race of people, called "white" or "clear," who embodied the highest virtues and nobility.

See also Dances and dancing; Yurok.

White Eyes (c. 1730, western Pa.—Nov., 1778, Pa.): Tribal chief

Also known as: Koquethagechton

Tribal affiliation: Delaware (Lenni Lenape)

Significance: White Eyes was an ally of the Americans during the American Revolution

Named for his light-colored eyes, White Eyes played a diplomatic role in the American Revolution after becoming a friend of Colonel George Morgan, Indian agent of the Continental Congress. He signed a treaty in 1778 designed to incorporate the Delaware Nation as the fourteenth state of the United States.

White Eyes became principal chief of the Ohio Delawares in 1776. At the beginning of the American Revolution, he counselled neutrality, but he took up the Patriot cause after the Delaware leader Hopocan sided with the British. In 1778, White Eyes was a party to the first treaty negotiated by the new United States, at Fort Pitt. The treaty was notable because it outlined a plan for a Delaware state with representation in Congress. The plan never materialized.

Two months after signing that treaty, White Eyes was acting as a guide for General Lachlin McIntosh in his expedition against Fort Sandusky. During the expedition, White Eyes was killed by American troops under confusing conditions, possibly by "friendly fire." To cover up the death of an ally, the soldiers reported that White Eyes had died of smallpox.

See also Indian-white relations—English colonial; Lenni Lenape.

White Man Runs Him (c. 1855—c. 1925): Warrior, U.S. Army scout

Also known as: Batsida Karoosh, Beshayeschayecoosis, Miastashedekaroos (White Man Runs Him)

Tribal affiliation: Crow

Significance: White Man Runs Him was Custer's chief scout during the Sioux Wars

Beshayeschayecoosis' father was chased by a rifle-firing white man, thus acquiring the name White Man Runs Him; the young warrior inherited his adult name from his father. Traditionally, the Crow and Sioux were enemies, and White Man Runs Him, in his youth, was a successful warrior who participated in numerous horse-stealing raids against the Sioux. In the 1870's, White Man Runs Him was chief Indian scout in

Crow warrior White Man Runs Him was a scout for Custer in the 1870's. (Library of Congress)

Custer's Seventh Cavalry. While on a scouting foray, White Man Runs Him and four other scouts, in search of Sioux who had left the reservation, spotted them encamped on the banks of the Little Bighorn River. The sighting was reported to Custer, and the stage was set for the Battle of the Little Bighorn. Years later, some of White Man Runs Him's enemies, remembering his scouting activities, used his name derisively. He was often interviewed about his role in the Little Bighorn, but historians are not clear on what function the Indian scouts played during the actual battle. White Man Runs Him died in 1925; he was reburied in the Little Bighorn Battlefield Cemetery in 1929.

See also Crow; Little Bighorn, Battle of the.

White Paper of Canada

DATE: Proposed 1969, withdrawn 1970
TRIBES AFFECTED: Tribes residing in Canada
SIGNIFICANCE: This proposal by the Canadian government to revamp its relationships with, and obligations to, Native Canadians met with the near-unanimous disapproval of native groups

By the late 1960's, it had long been recognized that Native Canadians had failed to share socially and economically in the general prosperity that followed World War II. They were frequently the victims of discrimination and lacked access to the economic, educational, medical, and social benefits available to the majority of Canadians. These issues were frequently lumped together in the popular media and by government bureaucrats as the "Indian problem." The White Paper of 1969 was a policy statement and plan issued by Prime Minister Pierre E. Trudeau to resolve the problem.

Running on the campaign slogan "The Just Society," Trudeau led the Liberal Party to victory in the Canadian national elections in June of 1968. The slogan signified a social consciousness that had been growing among the Canadian populace throughout the 1960's. The White Paper was part of a general attempt by Trudeau and his ministers, following that election, to review and reorder all Canadian social and economic policy.

Trudeau and his followers firmly believed that the special status granted to natives by the Indian Act was at least partly to blame for the discrimination against them. According to the White Paper,

> the separate legal status of Indians and the policies which have flowed from it have kept the Indian people apart from and behind other Canadians. . . . The treatment resulting from their different status has been often worse, sometimes equal and occasionally better than that accorded to their fellow citizens. What matters is that it has been different.

The White Paper recommended the repeal of the Indian Act, the dissolution of the Indian Division of the Department of Indian Affairs and Northern Development (DIAND), and the transfer to the provinces of all responsibility for the delivery of social services to natives.

In order to gain native approval of its proposals, the government facilitated and funded the formation of a variety of native political organizations. The most prominent of these was the National Indian Brotherhood, which later became the Assembly of First Nations. Much to the surprise of the Trudeau government, these native political organizations were nearly unanimous in their rejection of the White Paper proposal. Their objections were many but hinged primarily on the failure of the Trudeau government to recognize native claims of aboriginal rights and sovereignty. These, they believed, would require the acceptance of long-ignored treaty obligations and the settlement of land claims.

Faced with such outspoken and vocal opposition, the Trudeau government withdrew the White Paper in 1970 but continued in various other says to disavow the notion of distinct rights for natives and other cultural minorities. It was later to acknowledge a measure of "existing aboriginal and treaty rights" via the 1982 Constitution Act. Subsequent governments, while implementing some of the White Paper proposals (specifically the transfer of responsibility for social services to the provinces), have also negotiated land claims and aboriginal rights agreements with a number of native political entities.

See also Declaration of First Nations; Delshay; Indian Act of 1876 (Canada); Indian Act of 1951 (Canada); Indian Act of 1989 (Canada); Indian-white relations—Canadian; Land claims; Sovereignty.

Wichita: Tribal group

CULTURE AREA: Plains
LANGUAGE GROUP: Caddoan
PRIMARY LOCATION: Oklahoma
POPULATION SIZE: 1,275 (1990 U.S. Census)

The Wichita people were a confederacy of six or seven subtribes including the Wichita proper, the Tayovaya, Yscani, Tawakoni, Waco, and Kichai. Only the Kichai group spoke a separate Caddoan language; the rest spoke similar dialects of their Caddoan language. The name Wichita is of unknown origin; they refer to themselves as *Kitikiti'sh*, meaning "the people" or "the preeminent people." French traders referred to them as *Pani Piqué*, meaning "Tattooed Pawnee." (They were closely related to the Pawnees.) Other tribes had names for the Wichitas which referred to their distinctive tattooing.

The Wichitas were the fabled people of Quivira whom the Spanish explorer Francisco Vásquez de Coronado encountered in 1541. Their ancestral homeland seems to have been the region of the great bend of the Arkansas River in south-central Kansas. In Coronado's time, this confederacy probably numbered around fifteen thousand; the number was reduced to about four thousand in the eighteenth century. By 1902, there were only 340 members of the Wichita tribe; they have rebounded since.

From the 1600's to 1800's, the Wichitas lived in a number of villages located along rivers, each village having about eight hundred to a thousand grass lodges. These were conical in shape, 15 to 30 feet in diameter, and had the appearance of a haystack. Wichita society was matrilocal—a married couple lived with the wife's family, whose head of household was a grandmother or great-grandmother. The Wichitas were also matrilineal, although no clan system operated in the tribe.

Women farmed to produce corn, beans, squash, pumpkins, and tobacco, while men hunted buffalo, deer, antelope, and bear. There was a seasonal rhythm to Wichita life, with permanent villages occupied in the spring and summer during the planting and harvesting season. In the fall, many left on extended hunting trips, living in portable skin tipis while traveling. Gathered fruits and nuts rounded out the diet. The Wichitas often farmed a surplus and sold it to neighboring tribes that did not engage in agriculture.

By around 1700, the Wichitas had acquired horses, which made buffalo hunting and warfare easier. The Wichitas remained essentially a peaceful people, however, going to war only when provoked. They also retained much of their sedentary farming-oriented culture, rather than becoming solely reliant on buffalo hunting as some other Plains groups did.

In the early 1600's the Osage tribe began to press into Wichita territory, so the Wichitas began moving south into Oklahoma and Texas. By about 1720, the Wichitas began trading with the French, who assisted in establishing peaceful relations between the Wichitas and the Comanche tribe in 1746. The two tribes traded peacefully after 1746 and sometimes allied against Apache invaders in their region. The Wichitas' relationship with the Spanish was much more troubled than their relationship with the French. In the middle-to-late eighteenth century, they were often at war with the Spanish. From that time until the 1900's, warfare with other groups such as the Osage, as well as smallpox and other disease epidemics, took their tool on the Wichita confederacy, and its numbers dwindled. By the 1820's there were also conflicts with American settlers.

In the 1830's, other eastern tribes were being resettled in or near Wichita territory (now called "Indian Territory") by the U.S. federal government. This caused conflicts as well, despite various peace treaties and settlements. During the American Civil War, the Wichitas fled to Kansas but returned to what is now Oklahoma after the war. They were assigned a reservation in Caddo County. The reservation was allotted to individual families and therefore dissolved in 1901. In the late twentieth century, Wichita interest in maintaining their heritage increased as more tribal members learned their songs, dances, and language once more.

See also Caddoan language family; General Allotment Act; Kichai; Osage; Powhatan; Waco.

Wickiup

TRIBES AFFECTED: Apache, Paiute, Ute, other Great Basin tribes
SIGNIFICANCE: The wickiup, a dome-shaped structure, was widely used in the Great Basin culture area

"Wickiup" is the popular name for a dome-shaped dwelling made of a circular framework of poles bent over and tied

Wickiup

together at the top and covered with brush, bark, animal skins, or earth. The name appears to have origins in the Algonquian languages, where the word *Wikiyapi* can mean house, dwelling, or lodge.

The wickiup was used by the mobile hunter-gatherers of the Great Basin culture area—the Apache, Ute, and Paiute in particular—as a temporary residence while moving from area to area in search of food. This type of housing could accommodate from one to several people.

In some cases, an elongated and arched entry, made of the same poles and brush as the domed portion of the structure, was added to form a shaded porch under which people could sit during the heat of the day while eating, talking, or sleeping. When local food supplies were used up, the wickiup was simply abandoned as people moved on to other areas.

See also Architecture—Great Basin; Earthlodge; Pit house.

Wigwam

TRIBES AFFECTED: Northeast tribes
SIGNIFICANCE: The wigwam was a type of dwelling used by tribes in the Northeast

Wigwam is an Algonquian word for a house type that was used throughout the Northeast. The wigwam was an oval or round structure of light poles whose lower ends were stuck in the ground and whose upper ends were bent over and lashed together in the shape of a hoop. Lighter horizontal poles were lashed to the uprights to give the framework strength. Over

Wigwam

this frame large sheets of bark (or, sometimes, mats woven of reeds) were lashed, overlapping like shingles. In one end was a door; a small hole in the roof let out smoke. Daniel Gookin described seventeenth century New England wigwams:

> The best sort of their houses are covered very neatly, tight and warm, with bark of trees. . . . These houses they make . . . some twenty, some forty feet long, and broad. Some I have seen sixty or a hundred feet long, and thirty feet broad. . . . In the greater houses they make two, three, or four fires, at a distance from one another.

Gookin said he "found them as warm as the best English houses." One or two nuclear families lived in the small wigwams; several shared the larger ones.

See also Architecture—Northeast; Longhouse.

Wild rice

TRIBES AFFECTED: Menominee, Ojibwa, Winnebago, other tribes of the Upper Mississippi Valley and Great Lakes regions

SIGNIFICANCE: Wild rice, an abundant grain that requires no agricultural effort, was gathered for food by various tribes of north-central North America

Wild rice grows along the shores of rivers, streams, and lakes from New Brunswick to Manitoba and southward as far as Massachusetts and Nebraska. It is found in greatest abundance around the Great Lakes and in the upper Mississippi Valley, where it forms dense stands covering extensive areas. It is believed that all occurrences outside this area are historic plantings by humans. Most wild rice is of the species *Zizania aquatica*; common names include Indian rice, Canadian rice, water oats, water rice, tuscarora, manomin, and folle avoine.

Wild rice is an annual grass that grows to several feet above water level. It produces several thousand rice grains per plant, each long and black with a starchy core. These are attached to the stem by a very brittle connection, and even a slight breeze can detach the grains and drop them into the water, where they germinate to produce the next generation.

Indian harvesting took advantage of this brittle attachment. The most common method was to glide a canoe into a stand of wild rice as gently as possible and then bend the stems delicately over the canoe and shake them gently, with the ripe grain simply falling into the canoe. Since individual grains mature at different rates, one stand might be visited several times over the two-week ripening period in late summer. An alternate harvesting method involved bundling several stems together with twine while the grains were immature, then returning at maturity and shearing off the entire bundle for threshing on land. Women used distinctive bundle patterns to designate their rights to particular bundles. Either technique permitted enough seeds to escape to ensure a good growth the following year.

After harvesting, the grain was dried in its hulls and could be stored effectively in baskets for a year. Small portions were hulled as needed by heating the grain gently until it split the hull, when it could then be winnowed in baskets. Wild rice was—and is—cooked exclusively by boiling.

It is not known when wild rice was first exploited by Indians. Some hunting-gathering tribes, especially in Wisconsin and Minnesota, depended so strongly on wild rice that they stored large quantities of it and, in the process, became virtually sedentary. Others, especially in more northerly areas, used it as an adjunct to other foods in a seasonal pattern.

In modern times, wild rice has been an important cash crop on some Indian reservations. There, harvesting and sale have been restricted to bona fide members of the tribe using the traditional canoe-harvesting method. Planting and mechanical harvesting of wild rice by commercial concerns, particularly in California, has increased production and lowered prices since the 1980's—adversely affecting the economy of wild-rice producers in the traditional heartland.

See also Hunting and gathering; subsistence.

Wild west shows

TRIBES AFFECTED: Plains tribes

SIGNIFICANCE: Wild west shows, in re-creating events from the American frontier days, fixed the image of the American Plains Indian in the minds of European Americans and the world

From 1883 until World War I, hundreds of North American Indians—primarily from the Plains region—took part in a variety of wild west shows that traveled throughout the United States, Canada, and Europe. Buffalo Bill Cody staged the first one in 1883, and it was immediately joined by many imitators. "Wild wests," usually held outdoors in big arenas, were an entertaining combination of rodeo, circus, and stage play. Their intent was to present "a living picture of life on the frontier," as one poster explained. In addition to trick riders, sharpshooters, and cowboy bands, these shows featured reenactments of famous events from the recent Plains Indian wars, even recruiting as performers some of the Indian people who had participated in the battles and events being portrayed. Many famous Indians of the day who were highly regarded by their own people as warriors, holy men, and wise men took part in these shows. Notable wild west participants included men who not many years before were considered to be "hostiles"—men such as Sitting Bull, Red Cloud, American Horse, Chief Joseph, Geronimo, and Rain in the Face.

Many of the Indians who took part in the shows had already begun to gain notoriety as outspoken critics of federal Indian policy and were able to use the shows for public-relations purposes. Government policy of the time sought to assimilate Indians into mainstream society, reduce their land base, and erase many customs and traditions. Humanitarian Christian reformers and others who believed that Indians should shed their past and accept the civilization of whites vehemently opposed Indian participation in these shows, fearing that they glorified the warrior days and would thereby delay acceptance of the federal government's assimilationist policies. Wild west shows, which emphasized Plains Indian lifeways, were thus

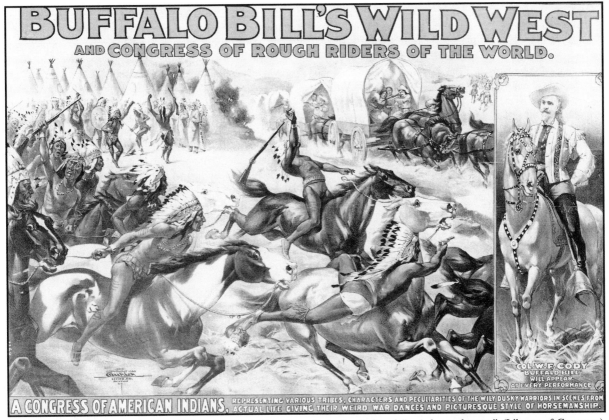

An 1899 poster advertising Buffalo Bill Cody's Wild West Show, featuring Indians' "weird war dances." (Library of Congress)

attractive to many Indians because they placed a value on the older way of life and became a natural forum from which to speak out on Indian issues. Reservation life was difficult in the 1880's and 1890's, and the federal government sought to suppress most traditional cultural and religious expression. Now, suddenly, newspapers were carrying interviews with the Indian performers as they met and spoke with politicians, kings, queens, and presidents. Although Indian policy did not change drastically, an eloquent Indian voice of opposition was heard. The wide popularity of the wild west shows made them influential in more lasting ways, as well. Because most shows recruited their Indian performers from the Sioux reservations, particularly Pine Ridge and Rosebud, the image of the Plains Sioux began to take its place in the popular imagination as the quintessential American Indian.

Even though government officials voiced opposition to wild west shows, the secretary of the interior permitted Indians to tour and enforced a number of regulations to protect the performers, following a number of mishaps. Promoters were compelled to pay performers a fair wage for their time and services, usually fifteen to thirty dollars a month for women and twenty-five to ninety dollars a month for men. Additionally, the shows were required to provide all meals, transportation, and medical expenses. At the end of their contracts, all Indians were to be returned to their reservations at the show's expense. Show owners posted bonds of two to twenty thousand dollars, based on the numbers of Indians employed.

Wild west shows continued until World War I. After the war, films replaced wild wests but for the most part adhered to the image of the Indian the shows had created. The wild west shows were a fascinating chapter in white-Indian relations and contributed many potent symbols that are still prominent in American legend.

See also Indian-white relations—U.S., 1871-1933; Red Cloud; Sitting Bull; Standing Bear, Luther; Stereotypes.

Wildcat (c. 1810, Yulaka, Fla.—1857, Coahuila, Mexico): War chief

ALSO KNOWN AS: Coacoochee

TRIBAL AFFILIATION: Seminole

SIGNIFICANCE: Beginning with the Second Seminole War, Wildcat was the most aggressive of the Seminole chieftains during their crusade against the U.S. Army; he was known for carrying a rifle and a scalping knife

Wildcat was born in about 1810 in central Florida, where the Seminole, or Lower Creeks, had settled in the eighteenth century. A nephew of the Seminole principal chief, Micanopy, Wildcat became the leader of those who strongly opposed white settlement in Seminole territory. When the Second Seminole War began in 1835, Wildcat was at the forefront.

In 1837, Wildcat was captured and put into a jail cell in St. Augustine but soon escaped through a small window 15 feet above the cell floor. Four years later, he was captured again near Fort Pierce. This time he urged his followers, including escaped slaves, or Black Seminoles, to give up the battle. In October, 1841, Wildcat left Florida aboard an American steamer sailing west.

For a brief time after leaving Florida, Wildcat lived with the Cherokee in Oklahoma. Fearing reprisals by the Creeks, however, Wildcat led his followers to Coahuila in northern Mexico, where large land grants were being given by the Mexican government. Wildcat died in Coahuila in 1857.

See also Creek; Micanopy; Osceola; Seminole; Seminole Wars.

Williams, Eleazar (May, 1788, St. Regis, N.Y.—Aug. 28, 1858, near Hogansburg, N.Y.): Missionary

TRIBAL AFFILIATION: Mohawk

SIGNIFICANCE: Williams was an influential missionary who used his position to persuade the Iroquois to establish a new empire west of Lake Michigan

One of thirteen children of Thomas and Mary Rice Williams, Eleazar Williams was placed in the care of Nathaniel Ely at Long Meadow, Massachusetts, where he was trained as an Episcopalian missionary. Between 1809 and 1812, he continued his studies with the Reverend Enoch Hale at Westhampton, Massachusetts. Sponsored by the American Board of Missions, in 1812 he began proselytizing among the Iroquois.

During the War of 1812, Williams served the federal government as superintendent general of the North Indian Department. He was also a scout.

With the Ogden Land Company, fellow missionaries, and the War Department, Williams collaborated in a scheme to relocate the Iroquois empire west of Lake Michigan. After forging Iroquois council members' signatures, Williams left for Wisconsin in 1823, followed by the Oneidas and Mahicans, many of whom he had converted. Scorned by other Iroquois, Williams abandoned his plan in 1832.

Returning east in 1853, Williams claimed to be the lost Dauphin of France, Louis XVII. The Reverend John Hanson wrote *The Lost Prince* in support of Williams' improbable claim.

See also Missions and missionaries; Mohawk; Red Jacket.

Windigo

TRIBES AFFECTED: Cree, Montagnais, Naskapi, Ojibwa (Chippewa)

SIGNIFICANCE: A legendary cannibalistic Algonquian giant, the Windigo personifies the unrelenting forces of winter and starvation that can drive a person to antisocial acts of violence

One of a category of mythic beings found in Northern Algonquian mythology and folklore, the Windigo is usually visualized as an emaciated, filthy, bestial creature of prodigious strength and size that roams the snow-covered boreal forests, seeking to assuage its insatiable hunger for human flesh. Thunderous roars, terrifying whistles, and strange, sparkling lights can all herald its approach, leaving its victim paralyzed with fear. Particularly powerful shamans, however, can defeat a Windigo in "spiritual" combat, whereas native therapists can treat humans in the throes of Windigo transformation—a metamorphosis induced by anthropophagous acts, sorcery, or a vision encounter with a Windigo spirit—through the application of large doses of hot grease, intended to "melt" the patient's icy heart before he or she completely passes from a human state. Windigo symptomatology described in native and non-native oral and documentary accounts have led some anthropologists to hypothesize the existence of a differentiated "windigo psychosis," a rare, psychopathological disorder of the northern Algonquians.

See also Ethnophilosophy and worldview; Religion; Shaking Tent Ceremony.

Winema (c. 1836, Link River, Calif.—May 10, 1932, Klamath Reservation, Oreg.): Interpreter

ALSO KNOWN AS: Toby Riddle

TRIBAL AFFILIATION: Modoc

SIGNIFICANCE: Fluent in English, Winema became an interpreter and mediator during the Modoc War of 1873

Earning a reputation as a brave child, Winema once safely guided her canoe through dangerous rapids to save the lives of several companions. At age fourteen, she led warriors to victory during a surprise attack by a rival tribe.

After marrying Toby Riddle, a white rancher, she was scorned by her tribe, though later her usefulness as an interpreter enabled her to regain her status. On several occasions, she helped diffuse tensions and mediate quarrels between Modocs and whites.

She was shunned by her cousin, Captain Jack, leader of the Modoc Rebellion, after trying to convince him to return to Oregon. In February of 1873, Winema warned a white peace commission of a murder plot by Captain Jack. Ignoring her warning, two members of the commission were killed; Winema rescued a third, Alfred Meacham.

Following the war, Winema became a celebrity, touring cities in a theatrical production about her life. She returned to the state of Oregon in 1890, and she was granted a pension by the federal government, most of which she donated to the Modocs.

See also Captain Jack; Hooker Jim; Modoc; Modoc War.

Winnebago: Tribe

CULTURE AREA: Plains

LANGUAGE GROUP: Siouan

PRIMARY LOCATION: Nebraska

POPULATION SIZE: 6,920 (1990 U.S. Census)

The Winnebago tribe is of Siouan origin. Although the date of its migration westward with other Siouans is unknown, it is believed that the Winnebagos entered what would become Wisconsin during the second of four main Siouan migrations.

Their most closely related kin, therefore, would be the Iowas, Otos, and Missouris. More distant relations include the Crows, Omahas, Osage, and the Dakotas. Tribal tradition regarding Siouan ties is vague. Contemporary Winnebagos, now widely dispersed from the land of their adoption, generally claim that their tribe was originally from Wisconsin, specifically the region around Green Bay, where they were first encountered by Europeans.

Early History and Treaties. It was the Frenchman Jean Nicolet, agent for Quebec governor Champlain, who first reported contacts with the Winnebagos in 1634 in the Green Bay area. Nicolet called them by the name they used for themselves, which was variously translated as "People of the Parent Speech" or "Big Fish people." Winnebago was a name given to them by the central Algonquians (including Miamis, Sauk, and Fox), who inhabited most of the area surrounding them. Fifty years after Nicolet, the Winnebagos had expanded both westward and southward from the Lake Michigan coast, claiming major portions of central and southern Wisconsin.

These claims pitted them against their Algonquian neighbors, and a number of local eighteenth century Indian wars occurred. Sometimes, the French used the Winnebagos as their allies against other Indian groupings, the most notable example being the Fox Wars. This potential source of support for Winnebago predominance disappeared suddenly in 1763, when the French lost their hold on Canada and Britain became the main European power to contend with (at least for the next twenty years, until United States independence). After several decades of relative isolation, clashes with representatives of the American government would begin, ushering in the first stages of Winnebago political and territorial decline.

Winnebago resistance to the presence of white settlers and army forces in their traditional lands peaked during the Blackhawk War of 1832. Their defeat was followed by a thirty-year period of U.S.-imposed treaties that effectively put an end to Winnebago claims over land in Wisconsin and, by removing them in stages farther west into Nebraska Territory, reduced them to full dependence on the government for their very existence.

The evolution of Winnebago treaties with the U.S. government reveals the extent of their territorial losses in less than fifty years. In the first peace treaty of 1816, the Winnebagos were invited to accept the sole protection of the U.S. government and to confirm that any land they had previously given up to the British, French, or Spanish governments was to be considered U.S. public domain. At this time, Winnebago lands still covered most of south-central Wisconsin and portions of northeastern Illinois. By 1828, President John Quincy Adams committed to pay the Winnebagos (and neighboring tribes) some twenty thousand dollars in goods to compensate for "injuries sustained . . . in the consequence of occupation" of land for mining by white settlers.

Within four years, in 1832, President Andrew Jackson agreed to pay the Winnebagos a fixed sum over twenty-seven years for what was considered the fair difference between the value of lands ceded by the Indians (running from Lake Winnebago southward to the Rock River at the Wisconsin-Illinois border) and lands west of the Mississippi (in Iowa) "traded" by the U.S. government. By 1837, the rest of Winnebago land running to the Mississippi in Western Wisconsin was ceded by another treaty.

A Winnebago Agency was created in the northeast corner of Iowa in 1848. By the Treaty of 1846, some 800,000 acres of former Chippewa land in central Minnesota had been granted as additional Winnebago territory, hundreds of miles away from the Iowa Agency. Within nine years, the central Minnesota land was taken back, and a much smaller (18-square-mile) Winnebago Reservation was established on Blue Earth River in southern Minnesota.

The reservation founded in 1857 only functioned for two years before half of it was sold to private settlers for cash "held in trust [by the Government] for Winnebago benefits." An act of Congress in February, 1863, called for the sale of the remainder of the Blue Earth River Reservation.

The crowning acts of U.S. government displacement of the Winnebagos occurred during the Abraham Lincoln presidency. In 1865, the tribe was obliged to cede its reservation in Dakota Territory (which later became part of the Great Sioux Reserve). In return, a section of Omaha tribe land in Nebraska was set aside for the now dwindling population of the Winnebagos, it being agreed that a sawmill and gristmill and fencing be erected on the new site for them. In addition, the government was to provide guns, horses, and oxen, plus some agricultural implements to assist the Winnebagos in their final exile westward to Nebraska Territory.

Archaeology and Traditional Cultural Values. A unique feature of Winnebago archaeology in their homeland in Wisconsin is what is called the effigy mound, first studied in the 1850's by I. A. Lapham. More common conical burial mounds associated with other Siouans are found throughout Wisconsin, but effigy mounds are limited to Winnebago areas. Archaeologists suppose that these structures were meant to represent animals, which were important as symbols of each clan's mythology and served to "stake out" by their physical presence their local territory. Only two effigy mounds portray figures that appear to be human. Their significance remains a mystery.

Despite the disappearance of many traditional social practices once observed by the Winnebagos, many elders remember that clan names not only reflected particular animals but also provided for a division of the Winnebago people into two general groups: "those who are above" (birds) and "those on earth" (land and water animals). In addition to symbolic qualities of association (eagle and hawk are birds of prey, bears represent soldiers), this name dichotomy also seems to have reflected a sort of code for regulating different functions, some practical (including marriage patterns, clan "alignments" while on the warpath) and ceremonial (relationships during

A carefully posed late nineteenth century portrait of a Winnebago named Young Eagle. (Library of Congress)

U.S. STATES WITH THE LARGEST WINNEBAGO POPULATIONS, 1990

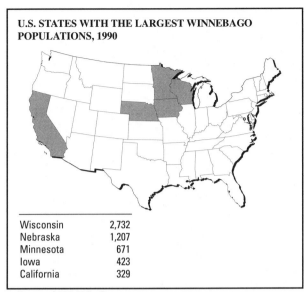

Wisconsin	2,732
Nebraska	1,207
Minnesota	671
Iowa	423
California	329

Source: 1990 U.S. Census.

feast celebrations, proper recognition of roles in ceremonial lacrosse games).

Lacrosse (played differently as a men's or women's competition) combined sport and ceremony among the Winnebagos. A number of other traditional games also existed, including the friendly moccasin "guessing" game and the very rough "kicking game."

Traditional Winnebago religious practices and beliefs were all somehow tied to respect for the preservation of life. Central to their belief system was a concern for the interrelationship between supernatural spirits and the physical domain of nature. In the latter, a stark reality prevails, frequently involving the necessity to kill in order to survive. At the highest and most general level, reverence was offered to spirit deities such as the Earthmaker, the Sun, and the Moon. These gods remained, however, beyond the sphere of daily survival in nature. A distinct set of animal spirits was recognized, therefore, as symbols of the survival cycle. Winnebagos performed a variety of offerings and dance ceremonies involving these animal spirits in order to assure that the spirits of animals that might be killed would be properly appeased, thus allowing for continuity in the necessary life-death cycle.

Certain clans bore the names of the animals who represented these spirits on earth; moreover, key ceremonies throughout the year were dedicated to observance of the animals' importance. The chief feast, accounts of which are less detailed than those covering lesser spirits, was organized around the Thunderbird, usually the symbol of the dominant clan. The Thunderbird chieftain received the food offerings of all other clans, not as a sign of submission to his clan, but as a general act of thankfulness for Thunderbird's overriding importance in the sphere of nature.

Lesser feasts (or fasts) were meant to propitiate the spirits of other key animals. These included (among others) the Bear clan feast in the winter (involving offerings of the favorite berries enjoyed by bears) and the Snake clan feast in the fall (involving four chickens offered to the symbol of the first four snakes created by Earthmaker).

Effects of Dispersal and Population Depletion. Because of the multiple displacements of the Winnebago and the fact that some tribal members stayed behind and were deleted from official records of their whereabouts, it is nearly impossible to reconstitute surviving numbers. Most Winnebagos today live in Wisconsin and Nebraska. Since 1972, representatives of the tribe have published a small newspaper focusing mainly on Winnebago community issues on the Nebraska reservation.

—*Byron D. Cannon*

See also Crashing Thunder; Effigy mounds; Red Bird; Siouan language family; Winnebago Uprising.

BIBLIOGRAPHY

Blowsnake, Sam. *The Autobiography of a Winnebago Indian.* Berkeley: University of California Press, 1920.

Fay, George E., comp. *Treaties Between the Winnebago Indians and the United States of America, 1817-1856.* Greeley: Colorado State College Museum of Anthropology, 1967.

Jones, John Alan. *Winnebago Ethnology.* New York: Garland, 1974.

Radin, Paul. *The Culture of the Winnebago.* Baltimore: Waverly Press, 1949.

_____. *The Winnebago Tribe.* 2d ed. Lincoln: University of Nebraska Press, 1990.

Winnebago Uprising

DATE: June 26-September 27, 1827

PLACE: Prairie du Chien, Wisconsin

TRIBE AFFECTED: Winnebago

SIGNIFICANCE: This uprising against white settlers resulted in the death of several whites, imprisonment and death of the warrior leader Red Bird, and seizure of Winnebago land

A combination of increasing traffic on the Mississippi River and a lead-mining rush in 1821 brought thousands of miners and settlers from the east to Winnebago territory, and hostile incidents and confrontations between whites and Indians began almost immediately. They culminated in June of 1827, when two Winnebagos were arrested for murdering a white family. A false rumor circulated that the two Indians had been turned over to the Chippewa, hated enemies of the Winnebago, and beaten to death by them. Responding to this rumor, Red Bird, a warrior, was asked by tribal leaders to retaliate against the whites. On June 26, 1827, two men and a child were killed. Three days later two crewmen on keelboats were killed, and four wounded.

The government threatened severe reprisals. On September 27, Red Bird surrendered to save his tribe and the Red Bird War or Winnebago Uprising ended. Red Bird died in prison shortly thereafter, and the government used the uprising as a pretext to seize the Winnebagos' lead-mining lands.

See also Red Bird; Winnebago.

Winnemucca, Sarah (c. 1844, Humboldt Sink, present-day Nev.—Oct. 17, 1891, Henry's Lake, Idaho): Political activist

ALSO KNOWN AS: Thocmetony (Shell Flower), Sarah Winnemucca Hopkins

TRIBAL AFFILIATION: Northern Paiute

SIGNIFICANCE: Hopkins is best known for her autobiography and for her determined efforts to gain justice for the Paiutes in their dealings with the federal government

Sarah Winnemucca was born into a rapidly transforming world. Her people, the Northern Paiutes, were pursuing the nomadic hunting and gathering lives common among Great Basin people when their territory was invaded by miners, settlers, and the U.S. Army. Sarah responded to the disruption of the Paiute world by taking on extraordinarily diverse roles, including those of army scout, author, performer, interpreter, political activist, domestic servant, and primary school teacher. Her overriding talent and vocation was that of an intermediary, particularly between Paiutes and non-Indians.

Winnemucca came from a politically and spiritually influential Paiute family, which included her father, Winnemucca, and her grandfather, Truckee (for whom the Truckee River was named). As a young girl, Sarah's family traveled widely to replace the livelihood disrupted by American expansion. In her travels, Sarah acquired an unusual facility with languages and a knowledge of cultural differences. In addition to learning other Indian languages, Sarah learned Spanish during trips to California, where her family found work on ranches. She learned English when she was temporarily "adopted" by an Anglo-American family who treated her as something in between a daughter and a servant.

In 1878, Sarah put her linguistic aptitude to work when she served as an interpreter and scout for the U.S. Army during the Bannock War. She was also intermittently employed as an interpreter for federal Indian agents on the reservations to which the Paiute and neighboring Indian people were being sent. By the early 1880's, the government had scattered the Paiutes among reservations in Washington, southern Oregon, and Nevada, where they were subjected to severe corruption among agents as well as starvation and disease.

In 1880, Winnemucca took her people's plight to the American public. In addition to meeting with numerous government leaders, Sarah delivered lectures to audiences in California and cities throughout the Northeast. She also wrote her autobiography, *Life Among the Piutes: Their Wrongs and Claims* (1883), in which she attempted to gain support for the Paiutes in their struggles for land and freedom. Although her efforts were generally unsuccessful, she became renowned for her determination and resourcefulness.

See also Bannock War; Great Basin; Paiute, Northern; Women.

Wintun: Tribe

CULTURE AREA: California

LANGUAGE GROUP: Wintun (Penutian)

PRIMARY LOCATION: Trinity River, northwestern California

POPULATION SIZE: 2,244 (1990 U.S. Census)

For the patrilineal Wintun, the family was the basic economic and sociopolitical unit. They lived in riverine villages with subterranean lodges. They hunted all large land mammals as well as trapping birds, rodents and insects. Fishing was an important source of food, in addition to seeds and acorns. Numerous plants, roots, and tubers were dug and stored for winter.

The Wintuns' first contact with European Americans occurred in 1826, as recorded by Jedediah Smith and Peter Ogden. From 1830 to 1833, trapper-introduced malaria reduced the Wintun population by approximately 75 percent. The discovery of gold exacerbated white-Indian tensions, resulting in violent incidents, particularly a "friendship feast" given by local whites who poisoned the food and killed a hundred Wintun. Violence against the Indians continued in the form of arson and massacres. In 1859, approximately one hundred Wintun were sent to the Mendocino Reservation. Throughout the 1860's, the Wintun were hunted down, captured, and sent to reservations. By 1871, they had adopted the Earthlodge cult. In the twentieth century, the construction of various dams further dispersed the Wintun, with the Clear Creek Reservation being removed from trust status.

See also California; Penutian language family.

Wishram: Tribe

CULTURE AREA: Northwest Coast

LANGUAGE GROUP: Chinookan (Penutian)

PRIMARY LOCATION: Columbia River, Oregon/Washington coast

The Wishram, a small southern tribe of Northwest Coast Indians, originally lived on the eastern slopes of the Cascade Mountains along the Deschutes River, due south of the confluence of the Deschutes with the Columbia River at The Dalles. Archaeological evidence suggests that Wishram culture was present in the Hood River area toward the Willamette Valley at least nine thousand years ago.

Historic village sites and traditional fishing areas were flooded by the Bonneville, The Dalles, and John Day dams. Many rimrock petroglyphs are now underwater and visible only to scuba divers, though excellent examples are on display at the Winquatt Museum in The Dalles. Tsagigla'lal, an elaborate and impressive petroglyph on the north side of the Columbia River, also remains visible. The site is commonly known simply as "Wishram" and is at the head of Five-Mile Rapids.

In addition to rock carving, Wishram culture was articulated through basketry and storytelling. The Wishram tell a full complement of Coyote tales, including the cycle of Coyote tales going east up the Columbia River. Linguist Edward Sapir's notable *Wishram Texts* (1909) collected many Wishram Coyote tales; more recently, Jarold Ramsey has added to the printed storehouse of Wishram texts.

Wishram culture was diluted in the nineteenth century by the location of the tribe at the western terminus of the Oregon

Trail. It was the poor luck of the Wishram to be situated in superior and coveted farmland. Wishram culture was diluted further in the twentieth century by the federal policy of creating multitribal reservations in areas where tribal bands were small and varied. The Wishram, with nine other tribes, share the Confederated Warm Springs Reservation in north-central Oregon near the southern banks of the Columbia River.

See also Oregon Trail; Penutian language family; Tenino; Wasco.

Witchcraft and sorcery

TRIBES AFFECTED: Pantribal
SIGNIFICANCE: Witchcraft provided a means, although largely a socially unacceptable one, of dealing with offenses that could not be corrected in other ways

The use of witchcraft and sorcery, although considered deviant, was common among American Indians, and it operated along with religion in providing an understanding of everyday life. Within a community, witchcraft was often employed by someone, usually male, who believed that a wrong had been committed against him, especially when that wrong could not be redressed through other socially sanctioned means. A disaffected person would seek the satisfaction that would come with harming or even causing the death of the transgressor. Witchcraft was usually condemned in native cultures, and suspected witches or sorcerers could be killed by members of the community for the offense. It is notable that among the Pueblo, men considered overly ambitious for political power were automatically suspected of witchcraft. In some cultures, datura, or jimson weed, was used as a tonic to determine who was guilty of witchcraft.

Among the Navajo, one who was accused of witchcraft and captured was pressured to confess. If no confession was forthcoming, the accused was executed. If there was a confession, it was believed that the witch would soon die of the same witchcraft he was practicing on his victim.

Witches were seen in some communities as part of a long-term aberrant subculture, with apprentice witches learning their art from an older relative, and employing complicated rituals of membership. Less serious were sorcerers, whose spells were carried out less violently and without all the ritual trappings. Witchcraft directed at a rival community was also considered possible, and along with revenge for deaths, desire for captives, misappropriation of hunting land or other resources, it was considered an appropriate reason for competing groups to go to war. When social constraints such as the need for community harmony or preserving the established leadership structure prevented individuals in native communities from achieving what they perceived as justice, they might resort to witchcraft.

See also Ethnophilosophy and worldview; Religion; Religious specialists; Social control, traditional.

Wiyot: Tribe

CULTURE AREA: California
LANGUAGE GROUP: Algonquian
PRIMARY LOCATION: Northern California
POPULATION SIZE: 450 (1990 U.S. Census)

The patrilineal, socially stratified Wiyot located their villages of split redwood planked, rectangular dwellings on major streams flowing into the Pacific Ocean. Like many central California people, they excelled at basketry. Their redwood canoes permitted effective exploitation of sea mammals and other tidewater resources. When fishing inland waters, they utilized various fish poisons. The Wiyot had numerous complex rites of intensification, particularly the World Renewal, Big Time, Jumping Dance, and White Deerskin ceremonies, whose collective intent was resource renewal, the prevention of natural catastrophe, and a reiteration of the mythical and moral order among the people.

By the time of the initial ethnographic research on Wiyot culture, they had suffered considerable deprivation stemming from contact with European Americans. Whites had slaughtered them in small groups; a massacre at Gunther Island in 1860 killed approximately 250 Wiyot; survivors were forced onto the Klamath and Smith reservations.

See also Klamath; Yurok.

Wolf Mountains, Battle of

DATE: January 1-8, 1877
PLACE: Wolf Mountains, Montana
TRIBES AFFECTED: Cheyenne, Oglala Sioux
SIGNIFICANCE: This battle, the last fight between the U.S. Army and the Cheyenne and Sioux, ended in stalemate but sufficiently weakened the Indians that they sought peace shortly thereafter

After the U.S. Army's resounding defeat at the Battle of the Little Bighorn in June, 1876, the United States redoubled its resolve to defeat the Indians. The Powder River expedition, under the command of General George Crook and Colonel Nelson A. Miles, soundly defeated the Cheyenne in the Wolf Mountains on November 6, 1876. The survivors joined the Oglala Sioux camp under Crazy Horse.

In a series of skirmishes and running battles on January 1, 3, and 7, and a five-hour battle on January 8, 1877, in the Wolf Mountains, Miles was able to drive the Indians out. He was then stopped by fatigue and a shortage of supplies, but the damage to the Indians was already done. Their weakened condition, lack of food, and increasing desire for peace led to negotiations. On May 6, 1877, Crazy Horse and his followers surrendered at the Red Cloud Agency, essentially marking the end of the Plains Indians wars.

See also Cheyenne; Crazy Horse; Indian-white relations—U.S., 1871-1933; Little Bighorn, Battle of the; Sioux.

Women

TRIBES AFFECTED: Pantribal
SIGNIFICANCE: Women have held more central and more powerful roles within Indian communities than outsiders have often realized, although in many cases their power was diminished after tribal contact with Europeans

The lives of Indian women have been as varied as those of any women. Not only have their experiences differed greatly among regions and tribes (and among individuals within those groups), but also Indian women's lives have undergone significant changes historically, both before and after colonization.

Perhaps the most useful generalization one can make about Indian women is that they have often been overlooked and misunderstood by non-Indians. In popular films and novels, when included at all, Indian women typically have been depicted as more passive and less important than Indian men. Indian women have also often been missing from studies authored by historians and social scientists.

The few American Indian women who have gained widespread attention among non-Indians quite often have been those thought to have come to the aid of settlers. Probably the most famous of such women is Pocahontas, who popular legend has credited with saving the life of Captain John Smith and assisting the settlers of the Jamestown colony. In visual images of the colonial era, Pocahontas was used to embody the New World—imagined as a welcoming, feminine, and fertile body. Other women remembered by non-Indians for their aid to whites include Sacajawea of the Shoshone, Winema of the Modoc, and Nancy Ward of the Cherokee—women whose lives were much more complex than one might guess from their popular reputations as charitable maidens and princesses.

Also not very well known is the fact that Indian women were often the most determined to resist European influence. Seventeenth century Huron women, for example, proved far more difficult than Huron men for Jesuit missionaries to convert to Christianity. One of the main reasons the Huron women gave for their resistance was that they could not imagine how they could agree to make a lifetime commitment of marriage. Many Huron women rightly suspected that the missionaries were offering women the possibility of salvation in exchange for less freedom and control over their lives than they had previously enjoyed.

Economic and Social Contributions. Early European and European American accounts of Indians frequently characterized Indian women as subservient drudges, as poor "squaws" who were abused by Indian men. Such characterizations should be understood in relation to the expectation of many European Americans, especially prevalent during the nineteenth century, that in their own societies virtuous women were incapable of and demeaned by physically demanding labor, particularly labor performed outdoors. When European Americans observed native women vigorously hauling firewood, planting and harvesting crops, or tanning hides, they erroneously inferred that Indian women occupied a lowly position in society. Outside observers frequently failed to recognize that women often took great pride in their work and acquired significant respect within their communities as a result of it. Moreover, the work of Indian men was often less visible from the perspective of a village or camp, if, as was often the case, it focused on hunting.

The specific tasks performed by men and women varied

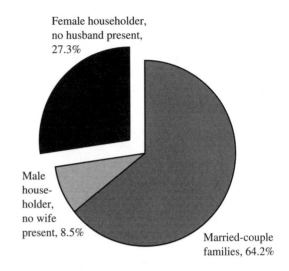

AMERICAN INDIAN HOUSEHOLDS, 1990

Female householder, no husband present, 27.3%

Male householder, no wife present, 8.5%

Married-couple families, 64.2%

Source: Data are from U.S. Bureau of the Census, *We, the First Americans.* Washington, D.C.: U.S. Government Printing Office, 1993.

considerably among tribes, and there were exceptions to the typical patterns—in many Plains societies, for example, there were women who departed from the norm and became known as warriors, hunting big game and leading war parties. In general, however, women tended to have greater responsibilities than men in caring for children and preparing food. Among some groups, such as the Iroquois tribes, women not only prepared food, but were responsible for farming, fishing, and gathering wild plant products valued for medicinal as well as nutritional purposes; many Indian women also maintained the right to distribute any food, even that procured by men.

Throughout Indian history, Indian women have gained great admiration and personal satisfaction from producing and designing objects; in pre-contact societies, much of women's everyday labor involved creative, artistic abilities. In the Southwest, for example, many women were highly skilled potters, who made wares valued for their aesthetic and religious importance as well as for their practical usefulness. Especially among Plains Indians, many women took great pride in decorating leather and designing clothing. In many areas, women wove extraordinarily beautiful and functional baskets. Although in the twentieth century Indian women have much less often produced objects such as pots and baskets for use within their own communities, many Indian women have established successful careers as artists; two of the most renowned include Hopi potter Nampeyo and San Ildefonso potter María Martínez. In parts of the Southwest, pottery and basketry, still made by women more often than men, currently provide significant sources of income for Indian communities as well as a sense of continuity, with designs and techniques handed down among generations of women. In the twentieth century, many native women have also developed artistic skills in fields not typically associated with Indian people—including oil painting, photography, and performing arts such as ballet.

In interpreting early written accounts of Indian women's labor, in addition to considering the possible biases of outside observers, it is useful to consider how perceptions of Indian women as hapless drudges might reflect how women's lives may already have been transformed by interactions with Europeans. For example, during periods when Indian people were trading vast quantities of furs and skins to Europeans, the workloads of many native women increased dramatically. Furthermore, social changes brought about by increased warfare, famine, dependence on trade, and disease epidemics often had a negative influence on the position women occupied within their communities. In the twentieth century, the social problems endemic to many Indian communities have added to women's domestic and economic responsibilities; many Indian women rear families single-handedly. Some researchers have suggested, however, that Indian women's great responsibilities for home and family, while difficult, have also been an important source of strength, stability, and determination.

Religion, Healing, Myth, and Storytelling. Among many Indian communities, past and present, women have been as likely as men to serve as spiritual leaders and doctors. Women have been powerful members of religious societies—some composed of women only, others including both women and men—within tribal communities. Many Indian communities have also held their most powerful and sacred ceremonies centering around female rites of passage, such as a girl's first menstruation. Yet even when indigenous religious practices might appear to be more men's affairs than women's, beliefs about power, deities, and the nature of the universe have tended to emphasize and venerate women. Among Pueblo people in the Southwest, for example, even though women have been excluded from many of the most significant religious activities, the most important deities are female. Many Southwestern Indian people tell sacred stories of female creators and teachers, such as Thought Woman, Changing Woman, Salt Woman, or Spider Woman. Lakota people tell of Falling Star, who on earth became White Buffalo Calf Woman and gave the Lakotas their sacred ceremonies. Similar stories of divine female beings can be found throughout native North America; such beliefs contrast sharply with Christian notions of a single, all-powerful, male creator.

Nevertheless, in many cases Indian women have responded enthusiastically to Christianity, often blending Christian traditions with indigenous ones. They also have taken up powerful positions in many religious revitalization movements that combine Christianity and indigenous beliefs and practices. Among California Indians, for example, women have been among the most prominent leaders in the Bole Maru movement, frequently serving as "Dreamers," a role with political

as well as spiritual dimensions. Women have also held important roles within the Native American Church.

In addition to occupying specialized roles within religious systems, Indian women have an ancient history of passing down knowledge and values as storytellers and as family and community historians. In the twentieth century, many Indian women continue to be especially revered for their formal and informal storytelling. Some have incorporated oral traditions into written literature; writing for Indian and non-Indian audiences, Native women—including Louise Erdrich, Leslie Marmon Silko, and Joy Harjo—have become renowned novelists and poets. Others, such as Ella Cara Deloria and Beatrice Medicine, have made significant contributions to anthropology and history.

Politics and Policies. In precolonial societies, Indian women usually had their own particular ways of exerting political authority. Among the Iroquois, for example, women did not serve on the Council of Elders, but the men who served were appointed and could always be deposed by Iroquois matrons. In Cherokee council meetings, women tended to observe rather then actively contribute, voicing their opinions outside of the public forum. Occasionally, women departed from the usual political roles and occupied leadership positions typically taken by men. In many societies, women's authority was strengthened by matrilineal and matrilocal kinship systems, in which property and land-use rights were inherited through women and which required a man to live with his wife's family after marriage. Kinship and politics were often inseparable, and women often retained the right to arrange marriages for their children; divorces typically could be initiated by men or women.

During the colonial and early reservation periods, the political authority of Indian women was undermined in a number of important ways. Missionary and government agents tended to encourage patrilineal systems of naming and inheritance and often did not recognize the ways in which women had previously influenced political appointments and decisions. For example, in contrast to the way that many Indian Communities traced inheritance and identity through mothers, the Canadian Indian Act of 1876 denied an official native identity to native women and their children who married men from outside their band; native men who married non-native women, however, suffered no similar loss of identity or recognition.

In the late nineteenth and early twentieth centuries, Indian women in the United States and Canada were subject to federal education policies designed to train native women as domestic servants and housekeepers. Among tribes where women had once carried out all the farming, government programs attempted to teach men to farm, while women were trained in such domestic skills as cooking and sewing.

Despite such misguided policies, many Indian women emerged in this period as influential proponents of Indian rights and policy reform. These women included Sarah Winnemucca, who worked as a scout and interpreter for the U.S. Army in the 1870's before writing a book and giving lectures to audiences around the country urging public support for her people, the Northern Paiutes. In the early twentieth century, Gertrude Simmons Bonnin wrote books and articles based on her experiences as a Sioux and devoted much research, writing, and public speaking to issues important to Indian people throughout the United States. Other influential women of this period include writer and administrator Ruth Muskrat Bronson, anthropologist Ella Cara Deloria, and physician Susan La Flesche Picotte.

In the 1960's and 1970's, many women took part in Indian-related activism, such as the Trail of Broken Treaties, the stand-off with the FBI at Wounded Knee, and the occupation of Alcatraz. Although women tended to be less prominent than men in such activities, many women who took part in them went on to become especially influential leaders. One such woman was Wilma Mankiller, who in 1985 became the chief of the Cherokee Nation. Increasingly, native women are being elected to tribal councils and are filling other politically important roles as policymakers, judges, and lawyers.

In the twentieth century, Indian women leaders have been most concerned with issues that pertain to both men and women in Indian communities. Their identities as Indian people—or as members of particular Indian communities—have tended to take precedence over identities as women. Since the 1970's, however, native women have begun to organize politically around concerns specifically identified with Indian women—including their representation in tribal politics, problems with domestic violence, health care, and access to legal services. The Women of All Red Nations (WARN) was formed in 1978; many other native women's organizations have been formed since, both national and local.

Although the polar stereotypes of Pocahontas and lowly squaw continue to survive in non-Indian thinking, they have been continually challenged by Indian women. The stereotypes have also been challenged by a growing body of scholarship and writing, which increasingly is being produced by Indian women themselves. —*Molly H. Mullin*

See also Allen, Paula Gunn; Bonnin, Gertrude Simmons; Bronson, Ruth Muskrat; Deloria, Ella Cara; Gender relations and roles; Harjo, Joy; Harris, LaDonna; Hogan, Linda; Kinship and social organization; La Flesche, Susan; Mankiller, Wilma; Marriage and divorce; Martínez, María Antonía; Pocahontas; Sacagawea; Silko, Leslie Marmon; Stereotypes; Winnemucca, Sarah; Women of All Red Nations (WARN).

BIBLIOGRAPHY

Albers, Patricia, and Beatrice Medicine, eds. *The Hidden Half: Studies of Plains Indian Women.* Washington, D.C.: University Press of America, 1983. A volume of essays offering diverse perspectives on Plains women. The essays cover topics such as women's work, the persistent biases of outside observers, and historical changes in Plains Indian women's lives.

Allen, Paula Gunn, ed. *Spider Woman's Granddaughters: Traditional Tales and Contemporary Writing by Native North American Women.* New York: Fawcett Columbine, 1989. An anthology of works written and told by native women. Informative introduction by Allen, who has written widely on native women's literature.

Anderson, Karen L. *Chain Her by One Foot: The Subjugation of Women in Seventeenth-Century New France.* New York: Routledge, 1991. A study of how Huron and Montagnais women responded to Europeans, particularly Jesuit missionaries, and how religious conversion involved dramatic changes in beliefs about women.

Bataille, Gretchen M., and Kathleen Mullen. *American Indian Women: A Guide to Research.* New York: Garland, 1991. An extensive annotated bibliography of writing and films pertaining to North American Indian women, including more than 1,500 citations.

Bataille, Gretchen M. and Kathleen Mullen Sands. *American Indian Women: Telling Their Lives.* Lincoln: University of Nebraska Press, 1984. Much can be learned about native women's lives from their autobiographies, but it is useful to know something about the context in which these autobiographies were produced. This guide to native women's autobiographical narratives includes an annotated bibliography.

Underhill, Ruth M. *Papago Woman.* 1936. Reprint. New York: Holt, Rinehart and Winston, 1979. The life story of a Papago (Tohono O'odham) woman with particular skills as a healer, born in 1845. Includes songs, stories, and descriptions of tribal life.

Deloria, Ella Cara. *Waterlily.* Lincoln: University of Nebraska Press, 1988. A fictional portrayal of nineteenth century Sioux women. Written in the 1930's by a Sioux historian and anthropologist who devoted her career to combatting popular stereotypes of Indians.

Devens, Carol. *Countering Colonization: Native American Women and the Great Lakes Missions, 1630-1900.* Berkeley: University of California Press, 1992. A study of the diverse ways in which women among the Ojibwa, Cree, and other tribes of the Great Lakes region responded to and were affected by colonization.

Katz, Jane, ed. *I Am the Fire of Time: Voices of Native American Women.* New York: Dutton, 1977. A wide-ranging collection of material, including songs, prayers, and essays, from various tribes and historical periods.

Powers, Marla N. *Oglala Women: Myth, Ritual, and Reality.* Chicago: University of Chicago Press, 1986. A study of Oglala Sioux women, past and present, illustrated with black-and-white photographs. Emphasizes the central role of women in Sioux myth and cosmology and women's perspectives on the important changes in their lives.

Women of All Red Nations (WARN)

DATE: Established 1978

TRIBES AFFECTED: Pantribal

SIGNIFICANCE: WARN works for autonomy among Native American individuals and communities in areas of health care, legal issues, and economic matters

Women of All Red Nations exists for the purpose of achieving autonomy for Native Americans, whatever their tribal affiliation. This Rosebud, South Dakota, association works to establish local chapters across the country.

Many issues of importance to Native Americans fall within the focus of WARN activities. Health care, in particular women's health matters and the misuse of sterilization practices on Indian women, is the group's main concern. Other problems that WARN addresses include children's foster care, adoption, political imprisonment, and juvenile justice. Inequities resulting from abuses of energy resources development on Indian-owned land is another concern.

Since WARN is a grass-roots organization, its efforts also include community education. Its focus is on self-reliance, whether it be for the individual or the local group affiliation. WARN also encourages Native American women to seek positions of leadership, both in and out of governments. WARN issues publications regarding health problems of Native American women and conducts an annual conference.

See also Activism; American Indian Movement (AIM); Harris, LaDonna.

Wooden Leg (1858, Cheyenne River, Black Hills of Dakota—1940, Mont.): Tribal leader, historian

ALSO KNOWN AS: Kummok'quifiokta

TRIBAL AFFILIATION: Northern Cheyenne

SIGNIFICANCE: Wooden Leg's autobiography documents some of the most important events in Cheyenne history

Wooden Leg, camping with Cheyenne and Sioux people near the Powder River in March of 1876, was attacked by troops led by Colonel J. J. Reynolds. Subsequently, he was with those who escaped to the shelter of Sitting Bull's encampment on the Little Bighorn River when Custer attacked. Following Custer's destruction, his family did not follow the ill-fated group led by Dull Knife and Little Wolf; Wooden Leg would live to write of the "Fort Robinson outbreak" by the Cheyenne imprisoned there. He was part of the Ghost Dance movement in 1890.

In his autobiography, he recounts these major historical events and explains the problems of adjusting to reservation living, especially the experience of monogamy and being forced to give up one of his wives. His appearance and survival at such a unique time in American Indian history and his apprehension of the need to record these events earned him an important place in history.

See also Cheyenne; Dull Knife; Ghost Dance; Little Bighorn, Battle of the; Little Wolf; Two Moon.

Woodland: Prehistoric tradition

DATE: 1000 B.C.E.-700 C.E.

LOCATION: Eastern North America

CULTURES AFFECTED: Adena, Hopewell

Copper tools, pearl beads, carved stone tablets, and mica ornaments excavated from burial sites tell the story of ancient moundbuilding peoples, known as the Adena, who lived in eastern North America as early as 1000 B.C.E. The Adena were named for an estate near Chilicothe in southern Ohio, heart-

land of their culture and site of a large burial mound excavated in 1902. Adena culture ranged through the woodlands of present Kentucky, Ohio, West Virginia, Pennsylvania, and New York. These mound builders maintained their way of life for about 1,200 years, coexisting with the Hopewell from around 300 B.C.E. Hopewell culture radiated from its Ohio center throughout the Midwest to the Gulf of Mexico and the Great Lakes. It existed until around 700 C.E. The name Hopewell was used by archaeologists during the 1893 Chicago World's Fair to identify an exhibit of artifacts from thirty mounds on the Ohio farm of M. C. Hopewell.

The Woodland tradition is an archaeological term for these forest-based cultures supported by hunting, gathering, and some agriculture. Pumpkins and sunflowers were a major food source for the Adena, and tobacco was grown for ceremonial use. The Hopewell expanded this agricultural base to include corn. Plentiful food permitted a sedentary lifestyle which allowed the development of large ceremonial centers. There is evidence of a complex, multilevel social organization. Highest status belonged to the priest-chiefs, who guided daily life through ceremonies; then came merchants, warriors, and finally the common people who hunted and farmed to support the community of thousands.

During the many centuries of their existence, mound builders created massive earthworks to honor their deceased leaders, who were buried in ceremonial outfits with bone masks and sacred objects they had used in rituals. Decorated in the unique Woodlands art style, these finely crafted artifacts indicate a preoccupation with death among the Adena and Hopewell. This prevalent theme suggests a possible relationship to the Southern Cult (Southern death cult) found in many cultures in the region of the Gulf of Mexico.

Adena earthworks of geometric shapes often surrounded the burial mounds. The most well-known of these is the Great Serpent Mound in southern Ohio. A low, rounded construction in the form of an undulating snake, it is 20 feet wide and 1,330 feet long and was created by workers carrying thousands of basketfuls of earth under the direction of the priest-chiefs. Hopewell burial and effigy mounds, usually within geometric enclosures, were larger than Adena mounds. Some stood 40 feet high and contained several layers added over long periods of time. Artifacts found at these burial sites were made by skilled artisans who used raw materials from as far away as Canada, Florida, the Rockies, and the Atlantic Coast.

Neither the origin nor the ultimate fate of the Adena and Hopewell is known, although it is thought they may have descended from eastern Archaic or Mesoamerican cultures. Theories about their cultural demise include epidemics, war, or climate changes affecting the food source. At their zenith these cultures represented a complex lifestyle organized around a unifying religious belief. Religion and trade, rather than warfare, linked the Adena and Hopewell network of ceremonial centers across a wide sphere of influence.

See also Adena; Death and mortuary customs; Effigy

mounds; Hopewell; Hunting and gathering; Mounds and mound builders; Prehistory—Northeast; Southern Cult.

Wounded Knee Massacre

DATE: December 29, 1890
PLACE: Wounded Knee, South Dakota
TRIBE AFFECTED: Sioux
SIGNIFICANCE: With this event, in which hundreds of Sioux were killed, the Indian wars ended

In the post-Civil War decades, the United States began an expansion in both land and industry that for speed and scope was unprecedented. Westward migration, in particular, was peaking. Between 1870 and 1890, settlement of the West—the area between the Mississippi and the Pacific Ocean—rose from seven million to almost seventeen million. This expansion brought exploitation of land and mineral resources, in turn increasing demands for a final, complete removal of tribes "in the way" of progress. Through treaties (new or revised) and by military force, tribes were forced onto reservations.

By the mid-1880's, there were some 180 reservations, containing approximately 240,000 American Indians. Among the last to be confined were the Sioux, who fought fiercely to keep their freedom. Nevertheless, a treaty in 1889 created six small reservations in the Dakotas: Pine Ridge, Rosebud, Cheyenne River, Crow Creek, Lower Brule, and Standing Rock. Crop failures in the summers of 1889 and 1890, plus an epidemic of sickness, brought bitterness and poverty to the Sioux, who were ripe for any vision promising them relief.

The Ghost Dance. In Nevada, a messiah appeared, raising hopes of an Indian revival through creation of a happy new world. Wovoka, a Paiute, had lived with a white family in his youth and from them learned about the life and teachings of Jesus. Upon returning to his people, Wovoka preached a hybrid religion, a mix of Christianity and old Indian beliefs.

Wovoka taught that by participating in a particular dance, the Ghost Dance, and by living harmonious, virtuous lives, Indians could bring into existence a paradise, one in which the buffalo would return and in which there would be no sickness. In 1890, delegates from many tribes traveled to visit Wovoka, several Sioux among them. Prominent were Chief Kicking Bear and his brother-in-law, Short Bull; enamored of the Ghost Dance, they brought the new religion to Rosebud, Pine Ridge, and Standing Rock.

Although the Ghost Dance was performed peacefully by

The gruesome aftermath of the Wounded Knee Massacre: innocent victims buried in mass graves. (Library of Congress)

most tribes, among the Sioux it became a rallying cry against the whites. Kicking Bear and Short Bull argued that their people had to assist the Great Spirit in regaining their freedom. A holy shirt was invented, a "ghost shirt" painted with sacred, magic symbols. It was believed that not even bullets could harm a person wearing such a shirt.

The Ghost Dance dominated life on Sioux reservations, greatly disturbing the government agents. There was little or no understanding of the ritual's meaning, and agitated agents and military officers were alarmed at what they perceived to be war preparations. At Pine Ridge, Indian agent Daniel F. Royer, newly arrived in October, 1890, panicked as the people refused his orders to stop dancing. He appealed for soldiers to restore law and order.

Death of Sitting Bull. At Standing Rock in December, 1890, the army attempted to arrest Sitting Bull, a Sioux holy man and staunch champion of traditional ways, thinking that he was behind the Ghost Dance frenzy. Sitting Bull was killed during the attempted arrest, and his death increased tension between Indians and soldiers. Hundreds of Sioux fled Standing Rock, many seeking refuge with Chief Red Cloud at Pine Ridge or with Chief Big Foot (also known as Spotted Elk) at Cheyenne River. Both chiefs were traditionalists, though Big Foot had been earliest in accepting the Ghost Dance. Trying to preserve peace, Red Cloud invited Big Foot and his band to Pine Ridge, a move heartily desired by the army and the Indian Bureau as well.

Big Foot led his people toward Pine Ridge, setting out on December 23, 1890. Their movements were tracked by the army, fearful of treachery. On December 28, only 20 miles from Pine Ridge, a squadron of the Seventh Cavalry, Custer's former command, intercepted the band. Big Foot, ill with pneumonia, persuaded Major Samuel M. Whitside, in command, that he and his people would come peacefully. That night Indians and soldiers camped together beside Wounded Knee Creek. Accounts list 350 Indians, 230 of them women and children, while the Seventh Cavalry counted 500 men.

The Massacre. Colonel James W. Forsyth took command on December 29, his men surrounding the Indian camp. Hotchkiss guns were posted overlooking the camp. Forsyth ordered Big Foot and other leaders to confer with him. He announced that the Indians would be disarmed, and soldiers began entering the tipis, searching for weapons. Yellow Bird, a medicine man, urged resistance, assuring his people that they could not be harmed while wearing their ghost shirts. Black Coyote, said by some Indian witnesses to be deaf, refused to surrender his Winchester rifle; in the ensuing struggle, the gun went off. Both sides began firing, and indiscriminate killing followed. Most of the Indians were unarmed.

Firing fifty rounds a minute, the Hotchkiss guns devastated the Indian camp. Women and children were slaughtered along with the men, few escaping. The fighting lasted less than an hour (or an hour, depending on the sources), but Big Foot and more than half of his people were dead. The army's losses were twenty-five killed and thirty-nine wounded. Surviving Indians were loaded into wagons and taken to Pine Ridge, where some were admitted to the military hospital while most, for lack of space, were housed on the floor of an Episcopal church.

Nationwide, reaction to the Wounded Knee massacre was split: Some people praised the soldiers, others condemned them. In actuality, neither side seems to have plotted the battle or been able to foretell the tragedy. Mutual fear and suspicion were among the underlying causes of the event.

Sioux holy man Black Elk was at Pine Ridge when the massacre occurred. After the fighting ended, he went to Wounded Knee. When he saw the many corpses, he recognized in them the "killing of a dream." It was the end of Indian armed resistance to the United States as well as the end of the Ghost Dance and its promise of a new world. —*S. Carol Berg*

See also Big Foot; Black Elk; Fort Laramie Treaty of 1868; General Allotment Act; Ghost Dance; Indian-white relations—U.S., 1831-1870; Reservation system of the United States; Sioux; Sitting Bull; Wovoka.

BIBLIOGRAPHY

Axelrod, Alan. *Chronicle of the Indian Wars: From Colonial Times to Wounded Knee*. New York: Prentice Hall, 1993.

Brown, Dee A. *Bury My Heart at Wounded Knee*. New York: Bantam Books, 1972.

Mooney, James. *The Ghost Dance Religion and the Sioux Outbreak of 1890*. Annual Report of the Bureau of American Ethnology 14. Washington, D.C.: Government Printing Office, 1896. Reprint.

Prucha, Francis P. *The Great Father: The United States Government and the American Indian*. Lincoln: University of Nebraska Press, 1984.

Smith, Rex A. *Moon of Popping Trees*. New York: Thomas Y. Crowell, 1975.

Wounded Knee occupation

DATE: 1973

PLACE: Pine Ridge Reservation, South Dakota

TRIBE AFFECTED: Teton Sioux

SIGNIFICANCE: The Wounded Knee occupation, an armed skirmish resulting in several fatalities, gave the Pine Ridge Lakota Sioux a national forum for their grievances

The 1973 confrontation involving factions of the Teton Sioux people and European American elements of the Bureau of Indian Affairs (BIA), United States marshals, and the Federal Bureau of Investigation (FBI) on the Pine Ridge Reservation in South Dakota reached a standoff at Wounded Knee.

The elected tribal government at Pine Ridge was headed by Dick Wilson. He was challenged by the traditionalist faction of the tribe led by individuals such as Gerald One Feather. A faction of younger people organized themselves as a chapter of the American Indian Movement (AIM). This was AIM's first reservation-based effort of any scale. AIM had begun as an urban Indian organization in Minneapolis, and it had served as a significant element in the takeover of the BIA headquarters in Washington, D.C., in the fall of 1972.

The difficulties reached a climax at Wounded Knee, the site

of the massacre of Oglala Lakota people in 1890 by the United States cavalry. The people within the Wounded Knee area were armed. They were surrounded by United States marshals, and then both groups were surrounded by the reservation BIA police, an arm of the elected tribal government. Fools Crow, the ceremonial chief of the Teton Sioux, started to talk with representatives of the traditionalists and AIM factions, as well as with the federal authorities, when, without warning, shots were exchanged. Military overflights added to the considerable confusion, and many were injured or killed.

Fools Crow oversaw the process that brought about negotiations, and leaders of the elected tribal government were excluded from the process. An agreement was signed that ended the siege and addressed some of the problems of unemployment, hunger, and poor living conditions on Pine Ridge Reservation. For example, it was estimated that the United States government was spending approximately $30,000 per capita on the reservation, but people were still living in tarpaper shacks, children did not have enough to eat, and the unemployment rate was higher then 60 percent. The Wounded Knee occupation gave the Pine Ridge Lakota Sioux people a national forum for their grievances.

See also Activism; Alcatraz Island occupation; American Indian Movement (AIM); Indian-white relations—U.S., 1934-1995; Pine Ridge shootout; Sioux; Wounded Knee Massacre.

Wovoka (c. 1858, Mason Valley, Nev.—Sept. 20, 1932, Schurz, Nev.): Religious leader

Also known as: Jack Wilson

Tribal affiliation: Northern Paiute

Significance: Wovoka originated the messianic Ghost Dance religion, which was embraced by nearly sixty thousand Indians from 1889 to 1890

Wovoka was born near Walker Lake in western Nevada's Mason Valley. "The Cutter"—the meaning of the name Wovoka—would spend almost his entire life in this isolated valley.

His father was Tavibo, a Northern Paiute shaman and medicine man. His mother's identity is unknown. Orphaned at fourteen, Wovoka was taken in by the family of David and Mary Wilson, white ranchers who had settled in the valley. Devout Christians, the Wilsons introduced Wovoka to their theology. The works and words of the Christian messiah—especially Jesus' teachings about peace, love, and everlasting life in heaven—made an indelible impression upon the Indian teenager.

As a young man, Wovoka spent two years as a migrant worker in Oregon and Washington. In the Northwest, he met numerous Shaker Indians, disciples of a Squaxin religious leader named Squ-sacht-un (known to the whites as John Slocum). The Shakers told Wovoka that Squ-sacht-un, like Jesus, had experienced death and resurrection. He had returned from the spirit world with the message that God would exalt the Indians if they practiced righteousness and abandoned white vices. The testimony of these zealots had a profound effect upon the young Paiute.

Upon returning to his valley home, Wovoka began to identify himself more closely with his own people. When he was twenty, he left the Wilson ranch, moved back into an Indian wickiup, and wed a Paiute woman whom he called Mary. He then cultivated a reputation as a miracle-working religious leader. Using some shamanic techniques learned from Tavibo, he convinced many Paiutes that he had the power to heal the sick and control natural forces.

His reputation as a wonder-worker was further enhanced by a mystical experience he underwent in 1887. One night, he lapsed into unconsciousness and remained in a deathlike state for two days. When he regained consciousness, he claimed that he had been taken up into heaven and had seen God. Angels had urged him to instruct Indians that Jesus was again among them, working miracles and teaching them to love one another and to live at peace with whites.

Wovoka mocked death a second time when he was about thirty. In late 1888, he fell ill with the dreaded scarlet fever and

Wovoka, the Paiute man whose Ghost Dance religion rapidly spread throughout the Great Plains, in an 1892 photograph. (Smithsonian Institution)

appeared to have died. Then, on January 1, 1889, he suddenly revived. The dramatic effect of his recovery was magnified by the fact that it had coincided precisely with a solar eclipse. Wovoka again asserted that he had seen God, who told him that within two years the earth would be regenerated and returned to the Indians, that the whites would disappear, that buffalo herds would re-appear, and that all Indians—including their dead ancestors—would live forever in paradise. In the meantime, Indians must practice pacifism and testify to their faith in Wovoka's prophecy by participating in a sacred ritual, the so-called Ghost Dance, which he taught them.

As a result of this second mystical experience, Wovoka was held in even greater esteem by the Nevada Paiutes. They regarded him as invulnerable to death. His people now called him "Our Father" and revered him as the messiah sent by the Great Spirit to liberate Indians from white bondage.

The Paiutes of Mason Valley danced and soon went out as missionaries to spread Wovoka's gospel to other tribes. Many Great Basin and Plains tribes—including the Arapahos, Cheyennes, Utes, Shoshones, and Sioux—sent emissaries to talk to the Paiute prophet. They returned enthusiastic to start the dance among their own people. Beleaguered tribespeople who had lost hope now found it again in a ritual that promised to usher in a Native American millennium free of white people. By the summer of 1889, the messianic faith had spread beyond the Rockies eastward to the Mississippi.

The phenomenal expansion of the Ghost Dance among the Plains Indians alarmed the white authorities, who feared that militant Sioux chieftains might transform Wovoka's pacifistic religion into a massive Indian resistance movement. In an attempt to suppress the burgeoning revival, the army began to round up many of its promoters, including Big Foot, the leader of a small group of Hunkpapa Sioux. On December 29, 1890, the commander of the Seventh Cavalry started to disarm Big Foot's band of Ghost Dancers near Wounded Knee Creek, South Dakota; someone fired a rifle, and a bloodbath ensued. Trigger-happy soldiers mowed down at least 150 Indians, many of them women and children.

When the report of the massacre reached Wovoka, he was stunned and saddened. He felt partly responsible for the tragedy, because the Sioux had embraced his teachings. After Wounded Knee, the appeal of his religion plummeted. The slaughter of the Sioux Ghost Dancers shattered the faith of tens of thousands in Wovoka's vision of an imminent Indian millennium.

The discredited prophet lived out his remaining forty-two years in Mason Valley as "Jack Wilson." Storekeeper Ed Dyer befriended him, and Wovoka eked out a living by selling ceremonial objects. By 1900, he could no longer find enough disciples to form a Ghost Dance circle; few people continued to call him "Our Father." Nevertheless, Wovoka never aban-

doned his conviction that he had visited heaven and talked to God. In 1932, at the age of seventy-four, he died at Shurz, on the Walker River Reservation in Nevada. —*Ronald W. Long*

See also Big Foot; Ghost Dance; Paiute, Northern; Religious specialists; Slocum, John; Tavibo; Wounded Knee Massacre.

BIBLIOGRAPHY

Andrist, Ralph K. *The Long Death: The Last Days of the Plains Indians*. New York: Macmillan, 1964.

Bailey, Paul. *Wovoka: The Indian Messiah*. Los Angeles: Westernlore Press, 1957.

Marty, Martin E. *Pilgrims in Their Own Land*. Boston: Little, Brown, 1984.

Mooney, James. *The Ghost-Dance Religion and the Sioux Outbreak of 1890*. 1896. Reprint. Chicago: University of Chicago Press, 1965.

Porter, C. Fayne. *Our Indian Heritage*. Philadelphia: Chilton Books, 1964.

Sherer, Joel. "Wovoka." In *Twentieth-Century Shapers of American Popular Religion*, edited by Charles H. Lippy. Westport, Conn.: Greenwood Press, 1989.

Wright, Allen (Nov. 28, 1825, Attala County, Miss.—

Dec. 2, 1885, Boggy Depot, Okla.): Tribal Chief, scholar
ALSO KNOWN AS: Kiliahote (Let's Kindle a Fire)
TRIBAL AFFILIATION: Choctaw
SIGNIFICANCE: A highly regarded scholar, Wright served in several elected tribal offices; he gave Oklahoma its name

Born along the Yaknukni River in Mississippi, Allen Wright relocated to Indian Territory when he was seven years old. His mother died just before the relocation and his father soon after, so missionary Cyrus Kingsbury sponsored the boy's education at local academies. Wright was sent east to continue his education, earning a B.A. at Union College, Schenactady, New York, in 1853 and an M.A. at Union Theological Seminary, New York, in 1855. He became a noted scholar in Latin, Greek, Hebrew, and English.

Ordained by the Presbyterian church in 1865, Wright returned to Indian Territory to work among his people. During the 1870's and 1880's, he translated numerous Indian works into English, including a Choctaw dictionary, and the Choctaw and Chickasaw constitutions and code of laws.

In 1852, he was elected to the tribal house of representatives and to the senate. He was also the tribe's treasurer. After serving the Confederacy during the Civil War, he was elected two terms as Choctaw tribal chief, 1866-1870, during which time he suggested the name Oklahoma for Indian Territory.

See also Choctaw; Indian Territory; Removal.

Wyandot. *See* Huron

Yahi: Tribe
CULTURE AREA: California
LANGUAGE GROUP: Hokan
PRIMARY LOCATION: Upper Sacramento Valley

The Northern, Central, and Southern Yahi had numerous tribelets, each constituting a major village located on an east-west stream. A village had a major chief who inherited his position. Deer was the most important animal for food and by-products, but all other land mammals were hunted and trapped. Women were responsible for gathering and collecting a wide variety of plant products for food and utilitarian use. Many of these subsistence-getting activities were collective, particularly the acquiring of smaller animals and insects.

In 1821, Captain Luis Arguell and approximately fifty-five soldiers became the first Europeans to contact the Yahi. The Hudson's Bay Company, from 1828 to 1846, occupied much of the Yahi territory. In 1837 cattlemen entered the region, and by 1845 the first permanent white settlement was established. The Mexican government granted leases to settlers and cattlemen. The whites introduced new diseases to the Yahi, whose population of 1800 was reduced to thirty-five by 1884. Numerous massacres of Yahi continued until the late 1800's. Ishi, a Yahi Yana, was the last survivor in 1911.

See also Ishi; Yana.

Yakima: Tribe
CULTURE AREA: Plateau
LANGUAGE GROUP: Sahaptian
PRIMARY LOCATION: Washington State
POPULATION SIZE: 7,850 (1990 U.S. Census)

The Yakimas originally inhabited the Columbia Basin Plateau in Washington state. They are identified as Plateau Indians and belong to the Sahaptian language group. Many scholars believe that evidence of human settlement in the Columbia Basin dates back fifteen thousand years. The Yakimas first were exposed to European Americans with the arrival of the Lewis and Clark expedition in 1805.

Although this was the first direct contact the Yakimas had with white people, European American culture had already touched Yakima society, as they were already using horses,

Yakima tribal leaders (chief Thomas K. Yallup is at right) preparing to argue against the state of Washington for their fishing rights in the Columbia River. (AP/Wide World Photos)

and other trade goods were evident. Scholars estimate the introduction of the horse at about 1730. The tribe that would be referred to as the Yakimas was probably composed of other Plateau Indians, such as the Nez Perce and the Palouse (Palus).

The land that they inhabited was arid. Subsistence patterns consisted of hunting, fishing, and gathering berries and roots, particularly camas. Fishing continues to be pursued today, and in the early 1990's the Yakimas were involved in a lawsuit with various irrigators along the Yakima River over water rights.

After the first contact with whites, fur traders and missionaries crossed the Columbia Basin. Finally in 1855, the Yakimas were subjected to treaty negotiations with Washington Territorial Governor Isaac Stevens in which they conceded their claim of approximately ten million acres in the Columbia Basin. The Yakimas, who were one of the few tribes to be ascribed the status of a sovereign nation (hence their title Yakima Nation), were granted 1,250,000 acres on what would be the Yakima Reservation. By the early twentieth century, almost half a million acres had been lost through the provisions of the General Allotment Act, although the Yakima Nation recovered part of this acreage later in the century. The reservation included traditional lands. In addition to the Yakimas, members of the Klikitat tribe moved to the reservation. Dissatisfaction with the treaty grew, however, fueled by the continued traffic of whites across reservation lands, resulting in the Yakima War of 1855.

Although the Yakimas fared well in the initial fighting, internal dissension erupted, caused in part by hostility toward the Yakima leader, Kamiakin, whose father was a Palouse. American troops succeeded in winning the war in 1856, and the Yakimas were forced to accept the terms of the Yakima Treaty, which had been signed by the fourteen confederated tribes of the Yakima Nation on June 9, 1855. The treaty was ratified in 1859. Life on the reservation was difficult for the confederated tribes throughout the nineteenth century. The Yakimas were subjected to Indian agent James Wilbur, a Methodist minister who believed that the future of the Indians lay in their ability to convert to Christianity and learn farming. The Yakimas also had to sustain land losses through allotment. Yet traditional practices continued.

The tribal government that exists today was organized in 1935 and includes a tribal council with fourteen members. During the last half of the twentieth century, the Yakimas pursued claims filed with the Indian Claims Commission for either the return of traditional lands or, in lieu of land, a financial settlement. They have been successful with some of the claims and have received awards in both land and money. Other legal matters include water rights claims on the Yakima River for fishing and irrigation interests.

In the late twentieth century, the reservation's economy relied on farming, grazing, and limited industry. Traditional Yakima culture is still valued and maintained, as evidenced in the persistence of Yakima religious practices and cultural celebrations.

See also Kamiakin; Nez Perce; Palouse; Yakima War.

Yakima War

DATE: 1855-1856
PLACE: South-central Washington State
TRIBES AFFECTED: Cayuse, Umatilla, Walla Walla, Yakima
SIGNIFICANCE: A gold strike in north-central Washington caused a major influx of European gold seekers to encroach on the isolated territories of the Yakima tribe, leading to the Yakima War

The Yakimas lived in an area that was relatively isolated until the mid-nineteenth century—the Columbia River valley in south-central Washington. Conditions changed suddenly, however, when a gold strike in north-central Washington created an influx of white gold seekers. In general, relations between Indians and European-descended residents in the Northwest in the 1850's were characterized by mutual suspicion and dislike, and the latest arrivals made things worse as isolated attacks and retaliations increased.

Isaac W. Stevens, the newly appointed governor of the new Northwest Territory, arrived in Olympia in 1853 to take over his duties. Stevens was determined to persuade all the tribes in the territory to give up their lands and accept being moved to reservations. He ordered his treaty commission secretary, James Doty, to organize a grand treaty council in the Walla Walla area. It was attended by about a thousand Yakimas, including Chief Kamiakin, and members of other area tribes and bands. There was a disagreement among the tribes as to whether to agree to the treaty, but most tribes finally did. Kamiakin was among those leaders who refused. A treaty was signed on June 9, 1855. An Indian agent, Andrew Bolon, was killed by a band of Indians in Yakima country, however, and Major Granville O. Haller was sent to Yakima country from The Dalles. The purpose of his 102-man expedition was to avenge Bolon's death.

The first major battle of the Yakima War occurred at the foot of Eel Trail on Toppenish Creek, where Haller and his forces suffered a substantial defeat. Following this skirmish a full-scale war erupted when several tribes joined with the Yakimas in order to drive the European Americans from their country. Major Gabriel Rains was ordered to avenge Haller's defeat in Yakima country.

Rains's forces pursued the Native Americans to Union Gap (near present-day Yakima). After the Yakimas escaped across the Yakima River, the Union forces proceeded to a nearby Catholic mission and razed it, believing that the mission's Father Pandum had aided and abetted the Yakimas. During the spring of 1856 the fighting resumed with a Yakima attack at a blockade in the Cascades.

Colonel George Wright was in command of the Northwest forces at the time. Wright intensified the campaign against the Yakimas, and a truce was agreed upon in 1856. The volunteers who had participated in the Yakima campaign were dismissed, and with the construction of Fort Simcoe, the U.S. military established control of the Yakima Valley.

By September, 1856, Wright's forces had established control of the area west of the Cascades. Since the original truce was not completely successful, a second Walla Walla Council was organized by Governor Stevens; he demanded unconditional surrender by the Native Americans. In spite of the fact that Chief Kamiakin and other band leaders did not participate, the 1855-1856 Yakima War was essentially terminated at the end of the second Walla Walla Council.

See also Kamiakin; Walla Walla Council; Yakima.

Yakonan language family

CULTURE AREA: Northwest Coast
TRIBES AFFECTED: Alsea, Kuitish, Lower Umpqua, Siuslaw, Yaquina

Yakonan is a language family of the Penutian (or Macro-Penutian) language phylum, which is generally distributed throughout the Northwest Coast culture area, from Yakutat Bay in southern Alaska to Cape Mendocino in Northern California. Yakonan languages were spoken primairly in northern coastal Oregon by the Alsea, Siuslaw, Yaquina, and Kuitish peoples.

The Yakonan family is usually divided into several subdivisions. Its members include Chinookan-Tsimshian (lower and upper, and Cathlamet, Multnomah, and Kiksht), spoken among the lower Columbia River peoples; Takelman (Takelma, Kalapuyan, Tualatin, Yamhill, and Yoncalla), spoken by riverine woodland dwellers in central coastal Oregon; Alsean (Alsea, Yaquina), spoken by the Siuslaw and Lower Umpqua; and Kusan (Miluk, Hanis, Melukitz, and Naseemi), spoken by peoples who lived along the southwest coast of Oregon.

Klamat-Sahaptian (Cayuse, Klikitat, Molala, Nez Perce, Palouse, Umatilla, Walla Walla, Yakima) is a relative spoken along the middle and upper Columbia, and variations on Penutian are spoken in California among the Costanoan, Maidu, Miwok, Wintun, and Yokuts peoples. There appear to be linguistic relatives farther to the south in Mexico and Guatemala as well.

The Yakonan language family is nearly extinct and may have been spoken by no more than a few hundred people even at its peak. Ethnologically it appears to be expressive of cultural elements derived more from southern Salishan and Chinookan speakers and less from those of Penutian-speaking coastal inhabitants.

Writings on this language are minimal. The people who spoke it were the southernmost people to practice head flattening. They did not have a totemic clan system. They lived in small settlements along streams, rivers, and bays with blood relations, and they usually married outside their own immediate group. Their myths and traditional culture show evidence of substantial contact with Californian peoples to the south.

The name of the language appears to come from the name the Yaquina gave the river along which they lived. The people who spoke this tongue and its isolates are said to have lived "south of the Yacon, between the Umkwa and the sea, on the Lower Sayuskla and Smith Rivers." Some nineteenth century writings indicate that it was spoken in various forms among the Tillamooks to the north and the Klamaths to the south, but

whether this was because of linguistic relationship or intermarriage is unclear. Major work in the study of these languages was done by Frachtenberg (in the early twentieth century) and by Melville Jacobs (in his work of 1939 and 1940).

Yakonan has some features in common with Plateau, Californian, and Subartic language families, but has other elements which make it unique among the languages of the world and specific to the coastal cultures of southwestern Oregon. Yakonan is now often referred to as Alsean. This language, like many in the Macro-Penutian Phylum, is considered extinct.

It must be noted that living descendants of the tribes which spoke Yakonan often dispute the assumed relationships between languages and cultures assumed to be true by those in agreement with the classification systems of the dominant culture.

See also Alsea, Coos language, Northwest Coast Umpqua, Siuslaw, Yaquina.

Yamasee: Tribe

CULTURE AREA: Southeast
LANGUAGE GROUP: Muskogean
PRIMARY LOCATION: Georgia, Florida, South Carolina

Little is known regarding the language and culture of the Yamasee tribe, which no longer exists as a distinct entity. The Yamasee spoke a Muskogean language, probably a dialect of Hitchiti. It is assumed by scholars that the Yamasee were culturally similar to the Creeks, another Muskogean people with whom the Yamasee had close relations. The Yamasee may have been the friendly Indians encountered by Hernando de Soto along the Altamaha river in eastern Georgia in 1540. Spanish expeditions to the same area one-half century later made contact with the Yamasee, who were reported as friendly to the Spanish.

In the 1680's, the Yamasee became disenchanted with Spanish efforts to enslave some of the Yamasee. The Yamasee moved north to the English colony of South Carolina; they became trading partners and military allies of the English. In the 1680's, South Carolina induced the Yamasee to attack the Spanish at Santa Catalina. The Yamasee assisted the South Carolinians in a war against the Apalachees of Florida in 1705. In the Tuscarora War of 1711-1713, the Yamasee provided most of the soldiers in the Carolinians' successful war against the Tuscarora.

Following the Tuscarora War, relations between the Yamasee and Carolinians worsened. The Yamasee were angered by their growing dependence upon English trade goods, their indebtedness to English traders, English penetration of Indian lands, and the enslavement of some Yamasee by the English. Deteriorating English-Yamasee relations led to the Yamasee War of 1715-1728, in which the Yamasee were defeated by an army of colonial militia, black slaves, and Cherokee warriors.

The Yamasee were virtually annihilated by the war and subsequently lost their identity as a distinct people. Scattered remnants of the Yamasee settled with the Apalachees,

Choctaws, Creeks, and Seminoles in Georgia and Florida. For a time, some Yamasee maintained their tribal identity under Spanish protection in villages near St. Augustine and Pensacola, Florida. These Yamasee continued to act as allies of the Spanish, helping to defeat an invasion of Florida by Governor James Oglethorpe of Georgia in 1740. By 1761, Yamasee villages in Florida were reduced to fewer than fifty families. By 1773, many Yamasee had been enslaved by the Seminoles.

See also Creek; Hitchiti; Muskogean language family; Slavery; Yamasee War.

Yamasee War

DATE: 1715-1728
PLACE: Florida, Georgia, South Carolina
TRIBES AFFECTED: Cherokee, Choctaw, Creek, Yamasee
SIGNIFICANCE: This largest Indian war of the eighteenth century American South destroyed the Yamasee as a tribe and significantly changed English-Indian relations in the South

Beginning in the 1680's, the Yamasee conducted a large amount of trade with the English in South Carolina, trading deerskins and Indian slaves for English guns and rum. After the Tuscarora War of 1711-1713, however, the ability of the Yamasee to pay for English goods declined. White settlement on Indian lands had ruined the Yamasee deer hunting grounds. The English victory in the Tuscarora War removed most of the tribes from which the Yamasee abducted their slaves. By the 1710's, the Yamasee were heavily indebted to Carolina traders. When they could not pay their debts, Carolina traders started to enslave Yamasee women and children as payment.

The Yamasee made an alliance with the Creeks and Catawbas, who also had trade grievances with the English, and began a war against South Carolina in April of 1715. The Yamasee and their allies attacked Carolina traders and settlements, killing four hundred English and driving the English out of the Port Royal region. The South Carolinians fought back with a hastily constructed army of colonial militia and African slaves, who made up half of the Carolina troops. The English won a decisive advantage after 1717, when they made an alliance with the powerful and abundant Cherokees. The defeated Creeks signed a peace treaty with the Carolinians in November, 1717, and moved westward. The defeated Yamasee retreated to Florida, from which they continued to raid South Carolina for several years, killing whites and stealing black slaves for sale to the Spanish. South Carolina conducted a final expedition against the Yamasee in 1728. The Yamasee were destroyed and subsequently lost their identity as a tribe.

The defeat of the Yamasee and the Creeks opened new lands to white settlement in Georgia and South Carolina. The war induced the Creeks to begin a policy of neutrality toward the English, French, and Spanish, playing the European powers off against one another for maximum advantage. The Cherokees realized that the English were dependent upon them for military success, and began to make greater demands on them.

See also Slavery; Yamasee.

Yana: Tribe

CULTURE AREA: California
LANGUAGE GROUP: Yanan
PRIMARY LOCATION: Between the Sacramento River and Sierra Nevada, bounded by Rock Creek and the Pit River

The Yana were a tribe of Native Americans living in California between the Sacramento River on the west and Lassen Peak and the Sierra Nevada on the east. Rock Creek marked the traditional southern boundary of Yana territory, while the Pit River served as the northern limit of the Yanas' land. Today this area would correspond roughly to the triangle of land between lake Shasta, Mount Lassen (which the Yana called Waganupa), and the city of Chico, about 2,400 square miles. They were bordered on the west by the Wintun tribe, on the north by the Wintun and Achumawi, on the east by the Atsugewi, and on the south by the Maidu.

Most anthropologists agree that there are few if any Yana alive today, and even at their zenith they numbered only fifteen hundred to three thousand. In the Yana language the word "Yana" meant person. There were four distinct divisions among the Yana peoples. The Northern Yana were by far the smallest group. The others were the Central Yana, Southern Yana, and Yahi. The Yahi were the southernmost group. The linguistic anthropologist Edward Sapir made a detailed study of the Yana in the first decades of the twentieth century and found the Yana to belong to the Hokan linguistic family. Each of the four subgroups had its own dialect and usage of the Yana tongue, and communication among the various groups was possible but difficult. Each used two forms of oral communication; one was for women and one was for men.

The Yana/Yahi were hunter-gatherers. They lived on acorns, deer, salmon, rabbit, squirrel, bulbs, and roots. Since they had to move periodically to obtain food, their dwellings consisted of small huts in small villages. Agriculture was not practiced by the Yana. The Yana usually had small families and sometimes were polygamous. All members of the tribes worked according to age, gender, and ability. Both children and the elderly were cherished, and with the exception of the Yahi, who cremated their dead, the Yana buried the deceased in cemeteries near their villages. While raids were not uncommon, true weapons of war were never developed; tools and other everyday implements were used to defend the people.

Following hundreds of years of relatively peaceful and prosperous existence, the Yana were suddenly devastated because of their proximity to the California Trail, the Gold Rush of 1849, and European diseases. The game and food supply of the Yana dwindled as competition from European Americans increased. More significantly, whites, acting from ignorant self-interest, did not recognize the value of Yana culture and considered the Yana nothing more than an obstacle to eliminate. In 1864, for example, a group of miners surrounded a large Yana village and massacred all but about fifty Indians.

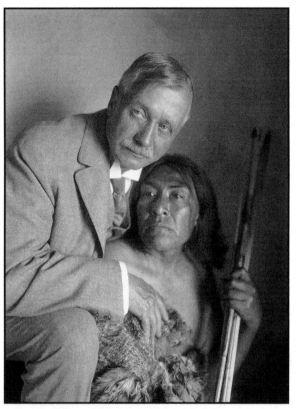

Ishi, the last surviving Yahi, pictured with scholar and archivist Joseph Dixon. (Library of Congress)

Numbers dwindled from that time until 1911, when a fifty-four-year old Yahi man walked into Oroville, California, in search of food. He called himself Ishi, meaning "man" (his true name was never known, since it was too private for Ishi to tell). He was the last living member of his tribe. From 1911 until his death in 1916, Ishi lived and worked at the University of California Museum of Anthropology in Berkeley. While he was there, Alfred Kroeber worked closely with Ishi to salvage a portion of Yahi and Yana culture and language. It is through Alfred and Theodora Kroeber's writings that some aspects of Yana life are known.

See also California; Ishi; Yahi.

Yaqui: Tribe
CULTURE AREA: Southwest
LANGUAGE GROUP: Uto-Aztecan
PRIMARY LOCATION: Sonora, Mexico
POPULATION SIZE: 9,931 in U.S. (1990 U.S. Census), estimated 24,000 in Mexico

After being forced from their lands at the end of the nineteenth century, some Yaquis found their way into present-day Arizona and settled in the environs of Tucson and other parts of the southwestern United States. They were, and continue to be, a fiercely independent tribe. In 1533, Diego de Guzmán suffered defeat at the hands of the Yaqui when he attempted to

enter their territory, and the Spaniards were faced with numerous Yaqui uprisings throughout their three-hundred-year tenure in New Spain.

The fundamental issue for these confrontations was the fact that the Yaqui held communally owned village lands that were a potential source of material wealth and power for the Spaniards and, later, the Mexicans. To the Yaquis, land always meant an ancient, divinely given heritage to be held in sacred trust. This sacredness of the land, the *yo aniya* (enchanted world), had become intricately bound with every aspect of Yaqui life. From 1886 to 1910, General Porfirio Díaz, the last dictator before Mexico's Revolutionary War, sold millions of Yaqui-occupied acres to foreigners at bargain prices. The Yaquis, led by Cajeme, drove back government expeditions sent out to take possession of their land. The resistance was declared an intolerable crime, and the Yaquis were forced to surrender by being starved into submission. Yacqui lands became private landholdings, Cajeme was "tried" and shot in 1887, and thousands of Yaquis were sold like cattle for seventy-five pesos each to rich plantation owners in Yucatán and Quintana Roo. There, unaccustomed to the hot tropical sun, they were worked as slaves in brutal conditions, and, with no hope for the future, died in large numbers. By the 1990's, however, the restless Yaqui spirit had been rekindled in its ancestral homeland and other areas. Timeless rituals were revived to coalesce into ceremonies reflective of the *yo aniya*, the land where all sources of divine power lie.

See also Southwest; Uto-Aztecan language family.

Yaquina: Tribe
CULTURE AREA: Northwest Coast
LANGUAGE GROUP: Salishan
PRIMARY LOCATION: Yaquina River and Yaquina Bay, Oregon

The patrilineal Yaquina were oriented toward the sea and rivers, but they were also dependent upon land animals and plants for food and needed by-products. Their environment provided numerous tidal foods, bird, and waterfowl. They lived in rectangular, multifamily, cedar plank winter houses in autonomous permanent villages. Yaquina society was stratified and wealthy men were often polygamous. Marriage reinforced trading relationships, established status, and redistributed wealth. Slaves, one form of traditional wealth, were usually acquired by raids. They excelled, as did their southern neighbors, the Alsea, in woodworking skills.

The first European American contact in the area was by the American ship *Columbia* in 1788. Unfortunately, little is known of the Yaquina or Alsea people, whose numbers were greatly reduced by early epidemics, particularly smallpox. By 1856 the remaining Alsea and Yaquina had been placed on the Coast Reservation, a small portion of their original territory. The Coast Reservation was split in 1865, and in 1910 only nineteen people who identified themselves as Yaquina remained.

See also Alsea.

Yavapai: Tribe

CULTURE AREA: Southwest
LANGUAGE GROUP: Yuman
PRIMARY LOCATION: Western and central Arizona
POPULATION SIZE: 579 (1990 U.S. Census)

The Yavapai have lived in central and western Arizona since about 1100 C.E., when they arrived from the West. Primarily hunters and gatherers, the Yavapai followed the cycles of nature, moving from one area to another harvesting wild plants. Animals were captured either by hand or by a throwing stick or bow and arrow.

As they migrated, the Yavapai made their shelters in caves and in domed stone or timber huts. Occasionally, hostilities erupted between the Yavapai and the Walapai, Havasupai, Tohono O'odham, Pima, and Maricopa. The Yavapai were most friendly with the Navajo, Hopi, Mojave, Quichan (Yuma), and especially the Apaches, whom they sometimes married.

The first European incursion occurred in the late fourteenth and early fifteenth centuries, when Spanish explorers passed through Yavapai territory. When the Arizona gold rush hit in the 1860's, contact with outsiders, especially European Americans, increased greatly. The Yavapai usually sought peace with these invaders. The Yavapais' numbers dwindled because of various hardships, and in 1865, the two thousand remaining Yavapai were moved to the Colorado River Reservation, the first of many reservations they would be relocated to; others included Fort McDowell, Rio Verde, San Carlos, Camp Verde, Middle Verde, Clarkdale, and Prescott. With the exceptions of River Verde and San Carlos, the Yavapai continue to inhabit these reservations.

Prior to U.S. government intervention, the Yavapai were led by articulate members of the tribe and by shamans notable for their powerful dreams and their healing skills. Past influential Yavapai leaders include Chief Yuma Frank, Chief Viola Jimulla, and Carlos Montezuma.

Modern Yavapais make their living primarily from farming, working for wages, and making and selling traditional crafts. The tribe is governed by an elected board. Contemporary Yavapai spirituality is expressed in a variety of forms, including Christian denominations and the Holy Ground Church, which emphasizes the sacred relationship between humanity and the earth that supports it.

See also Apache; Havasupai; Montezuma, Carlos; Walapai; Yuman language family.

Yaxchilan: Archaeological site

DATE: 200-850?
LOCATION: Chiapas, Mexico
CULTURE AREA: Maya

Yaxchilan was one of the most important Maya centers of the Classic period (150-900). Situated on a series of steep hills and terraces within a tight loop of the Usumacinta River in eastern Chiapas, Mexico, it was home to a powerful dynasty responsible for the erection of temples, palaces, and commemorative carvings. With its strategic and highly defensible location, it rose in prominence through acts of ritual warfare and sacrifice carried out by its leaders. Among the site's most important features are its numerous and well-preserved carvings with hieroglyphic inscriptions depicting the activities of nobility.

The ruling dynasty of Yaxchilan was founded in 320 by an *ahau* (ruler) named Jaguar Penis. He was succeeded by a line of ten descendants who ruled the center until sometime after 808. Yaxchilan was a powerful center of trade and military activities and had important relationships with Piedras Negras, Palenque, Bonampak, and Tikal.

The best documented events in the site's history took place during the reigns of rulers Shield Jaguar and Bird Jaguar, whose raids and ceremonies are commemorated on carved monuments. Shield Jaguar ascended to the throne in 681. At Temple 23, dedicated in 726, the undersides of carved lintels in the doorways depict sacred bloodletting rituals performed by his wife, Lady Xoc. In one, she is shown drawing blood from her tongue using a rope studded with thorns. In another, an ancestor reveals himself to her from the mouth of a supernatural serpent. Shield Jaguar was succeeded by Bird Jaguar in 742. Temple 33 holds a large sculpture of him in an elaborate quetzal feather headdress. A wide step on its basal platform depicts the *ahau* participating in a sacred ball game, in which a captive lord is used as the ball. Lintels over the doorways of this and other structures portray key events in Bird Jaguar's life.

To date, most of our information on Yaxchilan concerns the activities of its most prestigious citizens. Until additional research is undertaken, the site's predynastic history, the size of its population, the nature of the everyday lives of its non-noble inhabitants, and the reasons for its demise can be understood only through comparisons with other, contemporaneous sites.

See also Ball game and courts; Maya; Tikal.

Yazoo: Tribe

CULTURE AREA: Southeast
LANGUAGE GROUP: Muskogean
PRIMARY LOCATION: Mississippi

In 1682 Henri de Tonti found this small tribe living on the Yazoo River, close to the Mississippi River, north of present-day Natchez, Mississippi. The Yazoo tribe was closely associated with the Koroa tribe, resembling them in speech patterns. Both tribes used an "r" sound in speaking, which other tribes in the area did not.

As European trade increased in the lower Mississippi Valley, many of the tribes eagerly sought the goods that could be obtained by trading fur pelts and widely increased their hunting range. The Yazoos took captives, especially the Chawashas, and sold them as slaves to British traders; at times they were made captives themselves (particularly by the Chickasaws), sold into slavery, and sent to Charleston markets. Some were purchased by local planters, but the rest were shipped to the West Indies.

The houses of the Yazoos were round and constructed of poles plastered with a clay-moss mixture. This structure was then covered with cypress bark or palmetto. There was one door, approximately five feet high, but no windows or chimneys. Little is known about tribal customs. After a death, the corpse was carried into the woods, escorted by relatives carrying lighted pine torches that were thrown into the grave before it was covered. Relatives and friends went to cry nightly at the burial site for six months. A post, carved with the figure he painted on his body, marked the head of a chief's grave.

The Yazoos joined with the Natchez Indians in an uprising against the French, who controlled the area along the Mississippi. In 1729 they, along with the Koroas, attacked and destroyed the entire French garrison of Fort Rosalie, a fort not far from the mouth of the Yazoo River, and murdered the French missionary Father Souel, who had settled among them in 1727. Shortly after this event, the Yazoos were attacked and nearly destroyed by the Quapaws; only fifteen Yazoo men were left. The few remaining Yazoos apparently joined with the Chickasaws and Choctaws, and the Yazoos disappeared as a separate tribe.

See also Chickasaw; Choctaw; Natchez; Natchez Revolt; Quapaw.

Yellow Wolf (1856, Wallowa Valley, Ore.—Aug. 21, 1935, Colville Indian Reservation, Wash.): Warrior

ALSO KNOWN AS: Hermene Moxmox (Yellow Wolf), Heinmot Hikkih (White Thunder or White Lightning)
TRIBAL AFFILIATION: Nez Perce
SIGNIFICANCE: Yellow Wolf was an important warrior in the Nez Perce tribe; he exhibited loyalty, courage, and skill during the Nez Perce War of 1877

Yellow Wolf was born in the ancestral Wallowa Valley, Oregon. His mother, Yikjik Wasumwah, was a first cousin of Chief Joseph the Younger, so Yellow Wolf belonged to Young Joseph's band. Yellow Wolf's father, Seekumses Kunnin, was apparently a prosperous tribal member with many horses and cattle. Yellow Wolf remained with his parents until well into adulthood.

Yellow Wolf was not his chosen name, and he always considered it to be a nickname. He was named after the spirit which gave him a promise of its power as a warrior: Heinmot Hikkih (White Thunder). He received the name Yellow Wolf from a dream in which a yellow wolflike form stood in the air in front of him and called itself Hermene Moxmox (Yellow Wolf). Yellow Wolf's calling was as a warrior. The *kopluts*, or war club, he made as a boy, by direction of his spirit, gave him promise of war power because it had the same killing strength as thunder.

This prosperous and contented tribal life ended with the Nez Perce War in 1877, the result of the Wallowa Valley Nez Perce refusing to sign treaties to cede their land to the United States. The war was distinguished by the Nez Perce's masterful march to reach the safety of Canada. The Nez Perce outfought and outmaneuvered the army but were caught within two days of their objective. Yellow Wolf proved to be a loyal, resourceful, and courageous warrior. In September, 1877, Yellow Wolf was moved from a rear guard position to advance guard in order to deal with straggling soldiers before them. This change was recognition from his fellow warriors of their confidence in Yellow Wolf's ability to take care of the enemy singlehandedly.

Yellow Wolf did not attend or participate in the peace negotiations because, according to tribal practice, he had not been a warrior long enough. Yellow Wolf refused to surrender. He and some other warriors escaped and made their way to Sitting Bull's Sioux camp in Canada in October, 1877. Yellow Wolf and other warriors left in June, 1878, to return to Wallowa Valley under the erroneous assumption that the area was now safe. While riding through land that brought back memories of happier times, Yellow Wolf realized that he had no place to go where he was not encircled by his enemies. He returned to the Nez Perce Agency in August, 1878. He was sent to Oklahoma, but the ravages of disease and weather led Yellow Wolf to be resettled at the Colville Indian Reservation in northeast Washington. The reservation provided ample subsistence and Yellow Wolf remained there until his death in 1935.

See also Joseph the Younger; Looking Glass; Nez Perce; Nez Perce War.

Yellowknife: Tribe

CULTURE AREA: Subarctic
LANGUAGE GROUP: Athapaskan
PRIMARY LOCATION: Western Canada

This highly mobile hunting-and-trapping culture was dependent upon the movements of the barren-ground caribou, which involved them in sustained socioeconomic relations with the contiguous Chipewyan and Dogrib groups. Little is known of these people because of a general decline in population caused by introduced communicable diseases and intergroup conflict. At the time of their first contact with whites, the Yellowknife were in constant conflict with the Dogrib, Hare, and Slave; they were even fighting with the Chipewyan. Their winter dwellings were covered with stitched, tanned caribou hides. By the end of the nineteenth century, the Dogrib had expanded their aboriginal territory by defeating the Yellowknife.

The European first contact with the Yellowknife was effected in 1770 by Samuel Hearne. Later, after Arctic explorer Sir John Franklin's 1819-1822 account, most ethnographic data was provided by the Hudson's Bay Company. In 1913, ethnologist J. Alden Mason provided brief descriptions of the Yellowknife whom he met; they were then living in canvas-covered conical lodges at Fort Resolution. By 1914 the Yellowknife had essentially lost their tribal identity, preferring to be known as Chipewyan.

See also Chipewyan; Dogrib; Hare; Slave.

Yokuts: Tribe

CULTURE AREA: California
LANGUAGE GROUP: Yokutsan
PRIMARY LOCATION: Central California
POPULATION SIZE: 2,802 (1990 U.S. Census)

The Yokuts inhabited a south-central portion of California. They hunted, fished, and gathered for subsistence. Yokuts Indians fished throughout the year using nets, spears, and basket traps to catch trout, perch, and chub. Fish not eaten immediately were sun-dried. Men used nets, snares, and wood-tipped arrows to capture deer, rabbit, squirrel, and pigeons. Nets and snares were utilized to capture geese, ducks, and other waterfowl. Seeds, turtles, roots, and shellfish were gathered.

The Yokuts lived in permanent single-family, oval-shaped dwellings covered with tule mats or in long mat-covered structures that housed ten or more families. Water transportation was accomplished with the use of canoe-shaped balsa or tule rafts. Men wore deerskin breechclouts and women wore aprons of the same material. Mudhen or rabbit cloaks were worn in cooler weather.

Tribe members observed a number of superstitions and taboos to preserve health and good luck. Shamans were generally men. They were thought to receive their powers through dreams. Shamans cured the ill and led rituals. Healing methods included sucking out diseases or draining portions of blood. Several shamans used the datura plant, processed into a hallucinogenic drug, to arrive at a diagnosis.

In 1772, Pedro Fages explored Yokuts territory. Other explorers followed but had little direct effect on tribal life. Indians from other tribes fleeing the missions reached Yokuts tribes. Some stayed and introduced their own tribal ways to their Yokuts hosts. Through these visitors the Yokuts learned of the horse, and they wished to join the equestrian ranks. They raided local ranches and missions for horses and soon became known as the "horsethief Indians." Ranchers organized campaigns to recover their livestock and punish the Yokuts.

In 1833, a malaria epidemic devastated the tribe, killing 75 percent its members. Though the Yokuts avoided the infiltration of gold miners suffered by other Californian tribes, numerous whites settlers came into their territory. These settlers met with little resistance from a shrinking Indian population. In the late 1800's, the Yokuts were forced onto reservation lands. They found work on local ranches and in the logging industry, but social problems—including poor education, alcoholism, and poverty—persisted throughout the twentieth century.

See also California; Diseases, post-contact; Indian-white relations—Spanish colonial; Missions and missionaries.

Yonaguska (c. 1760, near the Tuckaseigee River, N.C.— c. 1839, Quallatown, N.C.): Tribal chief

TRIBAL AFFILIATION: Cherokee

SIGNIFICANCE: Under Yonaguska's leadership, a small band of Cherokees successfully resisted removal to Indian Territory and eventually became known as the Eastern Band of the Cherokee

At approximately sixty years of age, Yonaguska fell ill and was mourned as dead. After regaining consciousness a few days later, he claimed to have visited the spirit world and was thereafter regarded by his people as a prophet. As spiritual leader and chief, Yonaguska denounced tribal use of alcohol. He also counselled his people to resist removal to Indian Territory, claiming that if they moved the government would soon desire their new lands.

In 1829, Yonaguska led fifty-one men and their families to a new home at the juncture of the Soco Creek and the Oconaluftee River in western North Carolina. They had separated from the Cherokee Nation through a provision in a treaty that allowed them to settle on an independent reservation. There they made a claim for United States citizenship.

Through the aid of William Holland Thomas, a white lawyer and adopted son of Yonaguska, their small tribe successfully fought removal. Thomas represented his adopted tribe in Washington, using settlements won from treaty violations to purchase land for them. With Yonaguska's death in 1839, Thomas remained the principal advocate for Yonaguska's tribe, acting as its de facto chief. The tribe later became known as the Eastern Band of the Cherokee.

See also Cherokee; Indian Removal Act; Indian-white relations—U.S., 1775-1830; Removal.

Young Bear (c. 1868, Iowa—1933, Tama County, Iowa): Tribal chief

ALSO KNOWN AS: Maqui-banasha

TRIBAL AFFILIATION: Fox

SIGNIFICANCE: During the late nineteenth and early twentieth centuries, when official government policy called for Indian assimilation, Young Bear advocated revitalization of Indian traditions

The last of several Fox chiefs to bear the name, Young Bear was the son of Pushetonequa. Fearing the diminution of Fox culture, Young Bear encouraged his people to restore their tribal customs. To that end, he recorded tribal legends and sponsored a revival of traditional arts and crafts. He bemoaned the U.S. government's intervention in educating Indian children, fearing that white education combined with racial intermarriage would result in the death of Fox culture.

Young Bear died in 1933, a year before President Franklin D. Roosevelt and his commissioner of Indian Affairs, John Collier, instituted a policy of Indian revitalization embodied in the Indian Reorganization Act of 1934.

See also Fox; General Allotment Act; Indian Reorganization Act; Reservation system of the United States.

Young Man Afraid of His Horses (c. 1830-1900, Pine Ridge Reservation, S.Dak.): War Chief

ALSO KNOWN AS: Tasunka Kokipapi (Young Man of Whose Horses They Are Afraid)

TRIBAL AFFILIATION: Oglala Sioux

SIGNIFICANCE: Realizing the futility of further resistance to white expansionism, Young Man worked for improved conditions on the Pine Ridge Reservation

Young Man Afraid of His Horses' name, the same as his father's, is intended to convey the idea that, in war, he is so powerful that even the sight of his horses inspires fear in others. Young Man was instrumental in helping to delay white expansion during the 1860's. Various tribes respected his leadership abilities and, in 1865, the Cheyenne inducted him into their Crooked Lances clan. A realist, Young Man tried unsuccessfully to warn his people of the falseness of the Ghost Dance prophesies. After the massacre at Wounded Knee, Young Man—realizing the hopelessness of any further Sioux resistance—convinced his people to surrender and accept General Nelson Miles's peace terms, which included confinement at Pine Ridge Reservation. In January of 1891, thirty-five hundred starving Sioux men, women, and children—wounded, sick, and demoralized—entered the reservation. Young Man Afraid of His Horses negotiated and won fairer treatment for them. White authorities respected him, but some Sioux felt he was an apologist; other Sioux understood that he was protecting their interests as best he could under the circumstances. He was seventy when he died at the Pine Ridge Reservation.

See also Ghost Dance; Reservation system of the United States; Wounded Knee Massacre.

Yuchi: Tribe

CULTURE AREA: Southeast
LANGUAGE GROUP: Yuchi
PRIMARY LOCATION: Oklahoma
POPULATION SIZE: 430 (1990 U.S. Census)

In the 1540's, Hernando de Soto encountered the Yuchis (also known as the Westos) in present-day eastern Tennessee; by the eighteenth century, the tribe had migrated southward, with the majority of Yuchis settling on the lower Chattahoochee River. Here, the tribe lived as part of the Creek Confederacy.

Though they were similar to other Creek peoples in many aspects of their culture, the Yuchis retained a strong sense of separate identity. They regarded themselves as descendants of the sun and as the original human inhabitants of what is now the southeastern United States. Their language reinforced their sense of distinctiveness—unrelated to any of the languages spoken by other southeastern tribes, Yuchi was difficult for other Indians to master.

From the late eighteenth century, the Yuchis functioned within the context of Creek and Seminole history. Among the most conservative and traditionalist of Creeks, the Yuchis resented the attempt of Muskogee-speakers to dominate Creek affairs. Some Yuchis joined the migration to Florida that eventually gave birth to a distinctive Seminole identity. During the Creek War (1813-1814), the majority of Yuchis supported the traditionalist Red Stick faction against American forces and their Indian allies. After the Red Stick defeat, more Yuchis joined their Seminole kinsmen in Florida. Almost all Yuchis were eventually removed to Indian Territory (modern Oklahoma) either with the Creeks in the 1830's or with the Seminoles in the 1840's. In Indian Territory, the Yuchis settled primarily in the area around Sepulpa in the Creek Nation. Like other traditionalists, they were often opposed to the policies pursued by the more acculturated leaders of the tribal government. During the American Civil War, for example, the Yuchis were predominantly unionist despite the Creek Nation's formal alliance with the confederacy.

The acculturating influences of the twentieth century eventually weakened Yuchi traditionalism. By the 1970's, it was estimated that fewer than fifty speakers of the Yuchi language remained. A small core persisted, however, and in the 1980's an organization of Yuchis petitioned the federal government for formal recognition as a separate tribe.

See also Creek; Indian Territory; Removal; Seminole.

Yuki: Tribe

CULTURE AREA: California
LANGUAGE GROUP: Yuki
PRIMARY LOCATION: Upper Eel River, northwestern California
POPULATION SIZE: 265 (1990 U.S. Census)

The Yuki, Huchnom, and Coast Yuki each spoke a dialect of the Yuki language. They all had tribelets, with the village constituting the main socioeconomic unit, presided over by a chief. They lived in conical dwellings of bark, banked with earth. Subsistence was acquired through hunting, gathering, and fishing; salmon and acorns were their main foods. Trade was primarily with the Pomo and Huchnom, and it involved the exporting of food products in exchange for seafood and various types of shell beads. Dress was minimal, though the women wore a fringed leather apron. Deerskin caps were worn in winter.

The Yukis' first contact with settlers was in 1856, when the Nome Cult Indian Farm, essentially a reservation, was established in Round Valley. Settlers attempted to exterminate the Yuki, who resisted white encroachment and depredation. They recognized and participated in the two waves of the early 1870's Ghost Dance. The Yuki continued to live in the Round Valley area into the twentieth century. By the 1960's, all Round Valley Indians were leading a rural life; problems included sanitation, water supplies, and health care.

See also Coast Yuki; Huchnom.

Yuman language family

CULTURE AREAS: California, Southwest
TRIBES AFFECTED: Cocopa, Diegueño, Hualapai, Kiliwa, Maricopa, Mojave, Paipai, Quechan, Walapai, Yavapai

The Yuman language subgroup is a member of the Hokan family. The geographic distribution of Yuman extends from the lower Colorado River (from Lake Mead in Nevada to Flagstaff, Arizona) southward to the Gila River, and then westward to San Diego, California, and southward to approximately one hundred miles south of Ensenada in Baja California. There were approximately three thousand speakers reported in 1977.

A collection of stories in Yuman languages, *Spirit Mountain*, was published in 1984. Though Yuman languages had no writing system, Walapai (or Hualapai) and Havasupai communities have adopted the official Roman writing systems in the twentieth century. In other communities, orthographies vary widely. In an attempt at phonetic accuracy, scholars have incorporated parts of the International Phonetic Alphabet.

Yuman is among the most studied of American Indian language families. Edward Sapir and Alfred Kroeber were among the many linguists who studied it. It is generally grouped either among the Seri-Yuman subgroup or among the Esselen-Yuman subgroup of the Hokan family.

The "pai" languages are a closely related subgroup of Yuman languages. Havasupai and Walapai are mutually intelligible, acting almost as dialects of the same language. Yavapai has several dialects of its own but is generally mutually intelligible to Havasupai and Walapai speakers. Paipai is slightly intelligible to other "pai" languages.

A second subgroup comprises the River Tribe languages (Mojave, Maricopa, and Quechan). They are relatively different from other Yuman languages. Delta Yuman comprises the languages Diegueño and Cocopa. Kiliwa is distinct from all other Yuman languages and is spoken the farthest south on the Baja peninsula.

Tribes no longer in existence which may also have been Yuman speakers include the Halyikwamai, the Akwa'ala, the Alawisa, the Kohuana, the Kamia, the Yuma (also called Kwichyana), the Halchidhoma, and the Hohuana.

See also Havasupai; Hokan language family; Mojave; Quechan; Southwest; Walapai.

Yurok: Tribe

CULTURE AREA: California
LANGUAGE GROUP: Algonquian
PRIMARY LOCATION: Northeastern California
POPULATION SIZE: 4,296 (1990 U.S. Census)

The sedentary Yurok were a marine-oriented people living in permanent villages of split-plank redwood houses in coastal northwestern Oregon and on the lower forty-five miles of the Klamath River in southwestern Oregon and northwestern California. Close socioeconomic ties were maintained between villages. The major sociopolitical and descent group was the "house," which was neither matrilineal nor patrilineal. Villages owned communal property with exploitation rights to major fishing sites, clamming beaches, berry patches, felled redwood trees, acorn groves, deer-hunting areas, and beached whales. The Yurok excelled at woodworking and basketweaving and had a complex fishing technology. Their society was stratified, with nobles, commoners, and slaves, the latter being established by incurred debt. Traditional forms of wealth and heirlooms were paired obsidian blades, albino deerskins, and dentalium necklaces. Social control was maintained by threats of sorcery, destruction of an accused person's property, liability for injuries, and consensus of opinion.

The Yurok were probably first sighted by Spanish galleons in 1565. The first known contact was in 1828 by Hudson's Bay Company fur traders. Sustained European American contact and incursion commenced in 1850 with gold miners and land developers, usually with considerable violence and killing. Despite numerous attempts by several whites to protect Yurok sovereignty, much of the aboriginal territory was confiscated. By 1939, many of the traditional dances and ceremonies had stopped, particularly the traditional Jumping, Boat, Kick, and Deerskin dances, and the First Salmon Rite. In World War II, during the Battle of the Bulge, a Yurok taught the Brush Dance to his non-Indian unit as a form of exercise. Indian Shakerism was introduced in 1927 and continues to be their most popular religion.

Revivals of the Brush Dance started in 1972, as well as a revitalization of certain traditional skills such as weaving and woodworking. By the 1960's, some young males reinstated the traditional regime of training by using the sweathouse, swimming, and running. Competitive sports, particularly playing shinny or field hockey, are conducted between certain villages. Wage earning primarily involves fishing and logging.

See also Algonquian language family; California; Shaker Church.

Zapotec: Tribe

CULTURE AREA: Mesomaerica
LANGUAGE GROUP: Oto-Manguean
PRIMARY LOCATION: Oaxaca, Mexico

The pre-Hispanic Zapotec kingdom was centered in the Valley of Oaxaca, at the mountaintop site of Monte Albán (estimated population ten thousand). From there, the Zapotec extended their rule over the entire valley and over much of the present-day Mexican state of Oaxaca. The Zapotec were participants in many general Mesoamerican cultural institutions such as the ball game, ceremonial bloodletting, human and animal sacrifice, formal religious art, a hieroglyphic writing system, and the 260-day calendar. Zapotec script is incompletely deciphered.

The origins of Zapotec society can be seen at the Valley of Oaxaca site of San José Mogote. By 1500 B.C.E., small farming hamlets were ubiquitous, but San José Mogote emerged as a unique settlement, as evidenced by a nonresidential public building and by social stratification within the community. Evidence suggests that coercion may have been involved in the rising importance of San José Mogote. By 500 B.C.E., the mountaintop settlement of Monte Albán had been founded, and San José Mogote ceased to grow. Zapotec society expanded rapidly in social, political, and economic complexity throughout the succeeding centuries.

Like most Mesoamerican civilizations, the Zapotec were a highly stratified society. Divine kings topped the social hierarchy, followed by lesser hereditary nobility and priests; craftsworkers occupied an intermediate position. Maize, beans, and squash farmers formed the bulk of the population and were spread throughout the valley, practicing irrigation agriculture. Tribute was paid to the Zapotec kings. Professional warriors controlled Zapotec society and expanded its borders to capture new territory.

The Zapotec portrayed their military conquests on stone slabs at Monte Albán. Conquest slabs depict some thirty spe-

Ruins of the Great Palace at Mitla. Mitla, southeast of Monte Albán, was one of the most important centers of Zapotec culture. (H. S. Rice, American Museum of Natural History)

cific places that were conquered by Monte Albán from around 300 to 500 C.E. Another set of carved tablets, of a type known as Danzantes, are most commonly interpreted as tortured and slain captives, also attesting the militaristic nature of Zapotec society.

The Zapotec kings had a poorly understood political relationship with Teotihuacán, a large and powerful kingdom in central Mexico. As depicted on stone monuments at Monte Albán, Teotihuacán kings paid official visits to the Zapotec kings. There is also a residential area of Teotihuacán known as the Oaxaca Barrio. It appears that Zapotec lived there but retained their identity over hundreds of years—they continued to bury their dead in traditional Zapotec custom and to make their pottery in traditional styles. The Zapotec do not appear to have been ambassadors to Teotihuacán, as their dwellings are modest and are far removed from the central precincts.

For a variety of reasons, Monte Albán declined in power, and by 900 C.E. its population was dispersed throughout the valley. A series of small, independent kingdoms emerged to replace the centralized power of Monte Albán. Beginning in the late 1400's, most Zapotec kingdoms successively fell prey to the expanding Aztec empire. Less than twenty-five years later, the Zapotec kingdoms again fell prey to the Spanish. Today there are an estimated 472,000 speakers of the Zapotec language.

See also Ball game and courts; Maya; Mixtec; Monte Albán; Oaxaca; Teotihuacán.

Zotom (1853, southern Plains—Apr. 27, 1913, Okla.): Artist, warrior, missionary
ALSO KNOWN AS: Podaladalte (Snake Head), the Biter
TRIBAL AFFILIATION: Kiowa
SIGNIFICANCE: Zotom's pictographs on ladies' fans, his model tipis, and his shield covers provide valuable ethnographic and artistic data

Zotom was a warrior who, as a young man, participated in horse-stealing raids in Texas and Mexico. In 1875, he and seventy-one other Indians were captured and exiled to Fort Marion, Florida, for "rehabilitation." There, Zotom discovered his latent artistic talents: He was a graceful dancer, a gifted painter, and an accomplished orator. His decorated ladies' fans were in great demand. His drawing books chronicle Indian activities in the Plains and at the Fort. In 1878, Zotom went to Paris Hill, near Utica, New York, to study for the Episcopalian ministry; he was baptized in October. Ordained deacon in 1881, Zotom returned to Indian territory to convert the Kiowa but was unable to reconcile the cultural dualities he faced, and in 1894 was dropped as a deacon and missionary. His spiritual needs were answered when he joined the Native American Church. Art became his passion and source of income. He made scale models of tipis for the 1898 Omaha exposition. His series of buckskin shield covers provides valuable ethno-graphic and artistic knowledge. Zotom died at age sixty in Oklahoma on April 27, 1913.

See also Arts and crafts—Plains; Kiowa.

Zuni. *See* **Pueblo tribes, Western**

Zuni language
CULTURE AREA: Southwest
TRIBE AFFECTED: Zuni

The Zuni language is spoken at Zuni Pueblo in west-central New Mexico. In the early 1990's there were approximately three thousand speakers of Zuni. Unlike many native languages of North America, Zuni is still being learned by children and is highly viable. The name "Zuni" comes from the Spanish *Zuñi*, which in turn derives from the Keresan name *Sini* ("Zuni Indian"). In the Zuni language, the Zuni call themselves *siwi*.

In the early part of the twentieth century, a large amount of anthropological work was carried out among the Zuni. In the 1930's Ruth Bunxel, working within the ethnographic tradition, published a collection of Zuni texts and the first Zuni grammar; however, it was not until 1965, when Stanley Newman published his grammar, that there was an accurate and precise linguistic description of the language. Newman had previously published a Zuni dictionary in 1958. Later work on the Zuni language has been done by Willard Walker, Julian Granberry, and Carol Stout. Dennis Tedlock investigated Zuni poetics (1972). Overall, however, there is very little material available on the Zuni language.

Linguistic characteristics of Zuni include glottalized consonants, long versus short vowels, aspirated stop consonants, and devoicing of vowels and sonorants at the end of words. Grammatical traits include dual versus plural number distinction, reduplication, and noun incorporation, in which the object is incorporated in the verb. The basic word order of Zuni is subject-verb-object.

Zuni is usually considered a language isolate, since it cannot be proved to be related to any other language. A number of long-distance genetic relationships, however, have been proposed. Edward Sapir tentatively included it with the Aztec-Tanoan group, George Trager thought it also related to Kiowa-Tanoan, and Morris Swadesh tried to relate Zuni to Mixean (this was met with absolutely no acceptance). Finally, Stanley Newman attempted to demonstrate a relationship with Penutian, based on some 123 proposed, but mostly doubtful, cognates as evidence. None of these proposals has been demonstrated satisfactorily.

Zuni shares some linguistic traits, assumed to be attributable to diffusion, with other languages of the Pueblo area (Keresan and Kiowa-Tanoan).

See also Keresan language family; Pueblo tribes, Western; Southwest.

EDUCATIONAL INSTITUTIONS AND PROGRAMS

The following is a select list of institutions with various types of American Indian Studies programs. Tribally controlled colleges are not included.

UNIVERSITIES AND COLLEGES

Alaska, University of
Fairbanks
Native Studies program. Major and minor. Alaska Native Language Center, established in 1972, conducts research and publishes story collections, histories, geographies, dictionaries, and grammars.

Arizona, University of
Tucson
American Indian Studies program. One of only three programs in the United States offering an M.A. in American Studies in 1994 (approval for a Ph.D. degree was pending). Hopi and Tohono O'odham languages taught. Sponsored annual American Indian Language Development Institute in 1994.

Arizona State University
Tempe
Center for Indian Education. Offers courses in Indian education and publishes the *Journal of American Indian Education*. First such center in the United States, established in 1959. Hayden Library houses the National Indian Education Clearinghouse.

Augsburg College
Minneapolis, Minn.
American Indian Support Program.

Bacone College
Muskogee, Okla.
Founded as Indian University in 1880. The college has a special mission to serve American Indian students.

Bemidji State University
Bemidji, Minn.
Indian Studies Department. Major and minor. Minor in Ojibwa language.

Black Hills State College
Spearfish, S.Dak.
Minor in American Indian Studies.

Brandon University
Brandon, Manitoba
Department of Native Studies. Has Native teacher training program and publishes *Canadian Journal of Native Studies*.

British Columbia, University of
Vancouver, British Columbia
First Nations House of Learning. Special programs for Canadian Native students. Publishes the *Canadian Journal of Native Education* in association with the University of Alberta, Edmonton.

California, University of
Berkeley
Native American Studies department. Major.

California, University of
Davis
Native American Studies department. Major (approval for M.A. and Ph.D. degrees was pending in 1994).

California, University of
Irvine
Native American Preparatory School. A five-week summer program for gifted and talented Indian students entering the eighth or ninth grades.

California, University of
Los Angeles
American Indian Studies Center. Publishes *American Indian Culture and Research Journal*.

California State University
Chico
Minor in Native American Studies.

California State University
Fresno
Courses in American Indian Studies.

California State University
Long Beach
American Indian Studies program. Minor, certificate, and concentration.

California State University
Sacramento
Major and minor in Native American Studies.

College of Santa Fe at Albuquerque
Albuquerque, N.Mex.
Sponsored Summer Institute of Linguistics for Native Americans (SILNA) in 1994.

Cornell University
Ithaca, N.Y.
American Indian Program, established in 1981. Publishes the American Indian Studies journal *Akwe:kon*.

Dakota Wesleyan University
Mitchell, S.Dak.
Major and minor in American Indian Studies. Offers Lakota language.

Dartmouth College
Hanover, N.H.
Native American Studies Department founded 1972. Offers B.A. degree. Sponsors annual symposium on Native American subjects. Dartmouth was founded in 1769 to educate Indians using money raised in Great Britain by Samson Occom, a Mohegan.

Fort Lewis College

Durango, Colo.

Offers B.A. degree in Southwest Studies. Navajo language offered. Free tuition for all American Indians and Alaska Natives.

Hampton University

Hampton, Va.

American Indian Educational Opportunities Program. Hampton Normal and Agricultural Institute first accepted Indian students in 1878.

Harvard University

Cambridge, Mass.

Harvard's Native American Program prepares American Indians to fill leadership positions in schools and school systems. Part of Harvard's original 1636 charter was to Christianize Indians.

Haskell Indian Nations University

Lawrence, Kans.

Founded as an Indian boarding school in 1884, Haskell became Haskell Indian Junior College in 1970 and was renamed again in 1993, the same year that a four-year teacher education program was added. Haskell is the only university operated directly by the U.S. Department of the Interior's Bureau of Indian Affairs (BIA).

Humboldt State University

Arcata, Calif.

Offers B.A. and M.A. degrees in Native American Studies. Indian Teacher and Education Personnel Program. Natural Resource, Science, and Engineering Program.

Illinois, University of

Chicago

Native American Studies program. Minor in Native American Studies.

Iowa, University of

Iowa City

Native American law program.

Minnesota, University of

Duluth

Duluth American Indian Teacher Training Program and a variety of other programs serve Indian students.

Minnesota, University of

Twin Cities, Minneapolis

American Indian Studies program. Major and minor. Ojibwa and Dakota languages taught.

Montana State University

Billings

Minor in Native American Studies.

Montana State University

Bozeman

Center for Native American Studies. Minor in Native American Studies. American Indian Research Opportunities (AIRO) program

Morehead State University

Morehead, Minn.

Minor in American Indian Studies.

NACE College

Chicago, Ill.

Offers degree in tribal administration and has site-based programs on reservations in Montana and Wisconsin.

New Mexico, University of

Albuquerque

Native American Studies Center. B.A., M.A., and Ph.D. New Mexico had the only American Indian Studies Ph.D. program in the United States as of 1993.

North Dakota, University of

Grand Forks

Indian Studies Department. Major and minor. Indians into Medicine (INMED) program serving pre-med and medical students.

North Dakota State University

Fargo

Native American Pharmacy Program.

Northeastern State University

Tahlequah, Okla.

Native American Studies program. Major and minor. Center for Tribal Studies. Located on the site of the former Cherokee Female Seminary.

Northern Arizona University

Flagstaff

Four Corners Intertribal Science and Mathematics Summer Program, Native American Forestry Program, and Indian Education Program. Navajo language courses.

Northern State University

Aberdeen, S.Dak.

American Indian Studies minor.

Oklahoma, University of

Norman

Publishes *American Indian Quarterly*. American Indian Institute houses Native American Research Information Service.

Oklahoma, University of

Oklahoma City

Native American Center of Excellence program dedicated to increasing number of Indian physicians.

Pembroke State University

Pembroke, N.C.

Department of American Indian Studies. Major and minor. Founded in 1887 as the Croatan Normal School to serve the Lumbee Indians of North Carolina.

Pennsylvania State University

University Park

American Indian Leadership program. Offers M.A. and Ph.D.

Prescott College

Prescott, Ariz.

Center for Indian Bilingual Teacher Training.

St. Scholastica, College of

Duluth, Minn.

Department of American Indian Studies. Minor.

San Diego State University
San Diego, Calif.
Department of Indian Studies. Minor.

Saskatchewan Indian Federated College
Regina, Saskatchewan
Founded in 1976 in federation with the University of Regina.

Simon Fraser University
Vancouver, British Columbia
Mount Currie Teacher Training program started in 1975 to train teachers for the Lil'wat Band.

South Dakota, University of
Vermillion
Minors in Lakota language and Indian Studies.

South Dakota State University
Brookings
American Indian Studies minor.

Stanford University
Stanford, Calif.
American Indian Program. Provides support for Indian students at Stanford.

Tulsa, University of
Tulsa, Okla.
Certification program in American Indian law.

Washington, University of
Seattle
American Indian Studies Center. Offers B.A. (Individual Studies). School of Medicine's Native American Center for Excellence promotes medical careers for Indian students.

Washington State University
Pullman
Offers B.A. in Comparative American Cultures. Minor in Native American Studies.

Wisconsin, University of
Eau Claire
American Indian Program. Minor.

Wisconsin, University of
Madison
American Indian Studies program.

Wisconsin, University of
Milwaukee
American Indian Studies program. Interdisciplinary degree option.

OTHER EDUCATIONAL INSTITUTIONS AND PROGRAMS

Akwesasne Freedom School
Rooseveltown, N.Y.
Alternative elementary school providing a bilingual Mohawk-English curriculum.

American Indian Graduate Center
Albuquerque, N.Mex.
National nonprofit organization founded in 1969 to enhance the cultural and economic well-being of American Indian graduate students.

American Indian Higher Education Consortium (AIHEC)
Washington, D.C.
Represents thirty-one Indian-controlled colleges in the United States and Canada. Collects data on tribal colleges and sponsors *Tribal College: Journal of American Indian Higher Education*.

American Indian Magnet School
Buffalo, N.Y.

American Indian Science and Engineering Society
Boulder, Colo.
Sponsors various programs to encourage Indian students to major in the sciences and engineering; publishes *Winds of Change* magazine.

Arizona Department of Education, Indian Education Office
Publishes educational material on Arizona Indians.

Blue Quills Native Education Centre
St. Paul, Alberta
Formerly Blue Quills Residential School, the Centre was opened under local control in 1970 to serve students from seven different bands. Offers Cree language courses. Started post-secondary extension courses in 1975.

California Department of Education, American Indian Education Office
Sacramento, Calif.
Publishes American Indian handbook for educators.

Chemewa Indian School
Salem, Oreg.
BIA off-reservation boarding high school founded in 1880.

D'Arcy McNickle Center for the History of the American Indian, Newberry Library
Chicago, Ill.
Sponsors programs to promote the study of American Indian history.

Dene Standardization Project
Yellowknife, Northwest Territories
Started in 1986 to develop a standardized writing system for northern Dene languages for use in schools and other areas of Dene life.

Denver Indian Center, Circle of Learning Pre-K Program
Denver, Colo.
Culturally based preschool classes, home-based instruction, and parent education services for Indian families.

Department of Indian Affairs and Northern Development
Ottawa, Ontario
Funds First Nation schools throughout Canada.

ERIC Clearinghouse on Rural Education and Small Schools (ERIC/CRESS)
Charleston, W.Va.
Federal education clearinghouse serving American Indian education. Publishes digests and monographs on American Indian education.

Flandreau Indian School
Flandreau, S.Dak.
BIA off-reservation boarding high school established in 1893.

Gabriel Dumont Institute
Regina, Saskatchewan
Promotes and publishes research on the Metis and Cree in Canada.

Greyhills Academy
Tuba City, Ariz.
BIA-funded high school with model song, dance, and drama program.

Heard Museum
Phoenix, Ariz.
Sponsors a variety of educational outreach programs focusing on the American Indian.

Heart of the Earth Survival School
Minneapolis, Minn.
Alternative school serving urban Indian students.

Institute of American Indian Arts
Santa Fe, N.Mex.
Government chartered post-secondary school serving the entire United States. Founded in 1962 and chartered by the U.S. government in 1988. In 1991 served two hundred students from seventy different tribes.

James Bay Cree School Board
James Bay, Quebec
Manages Cree schools in Quebec (since 1978).

Kahnawake Education Centre
Kahnawake, Quebec
Offering Mohawk immersion classes since 1979 in primary grades and bilingual Mohawk-English classes in intermediate grades.

Kahnawake Survival School
Kahnawake, Quebec
Since 1978 this high school has emphasized Mohawk history and culture.

Mi'kmawey School
Chapel Island, Nova Scotia
Bilingual/bicultural school opened in 1981 to serve Mi'kmaq Indian children.

Mounds Park All Nations Magnet School
St. Paul, Minn.
Opened in 1991, this public school (kindergarten through eighth grade) offers Indian and non-Indian students an integrated American Indian curriculum.

Mt. Edgecumbe High School
Sitka, Alaska
State-operated magnet boarding school serving Alaska's Native and non-Native population.

Museum of Navajo Ceremonial Art
Santa Fe, N.Mex.
Collection and educational materials focus on traditional Navajo religion.

National Indian Education Association
Washington, D.C.
Lobbies Congress on legislation affecting Indian education, sponsors annual state and national Indian education workshops, and recognizes outstanding Indian educators at its conferences. Founded in 1970.

National Museum of the American Indian
Washington, D.C.
Cultural Resources Center houses library, archives.

Native American Language Issues (NALI)
Choctaw, Okla.
Promotes the maintenance and renewal of American Indian languages through annual conferences and legislative activity.

Navajo Area School Board Association
Window Rock, Ariz.
Works with members at BIA-operated schools.

Navajo Division of Education
Window Rock, Ariz.
Sponsors Navajo tribal scholarships, research on Navajo education, Navajo North Central Accreditation Association, and a variety of other programs.

Navajo Nation Public School Boards Association
Window Rock, Ariz.
Works with members in public schools serving Navajo students.

Navajo Preparatory Academy
Farmington, N.Mex.
BIA-funded high school to train Navajo leaders.

Northwest Indian Head Start Coalition
Fort Washakie, Wyo.
Works to improve Indian Head Start programs.

N'ungosuk Pre-school Project
West Bay, Ontario
Ojibwa preschool begun in 1981.

Office of Indian Education, U.S. Department of Education
Washington, D.C.
Administers programs funded through the Indian Education Act. Programs include educational personnel development, educational services, formula grant, Indian fellowship, Indian gifted and talented pilot, and Indian-controlled schools enrichment. Six regional Indian education technical assistance centers serve the various regions of the United States.

Office of Indian Education Programs (OIEP), Bureau of Indian Affairs, U.S. Department of the Interior
Washington, D.C.
Administers BIA schools and BIA-funded schools. In 1993 there were ninety elementary and secondary schools and six peripheral dormitories (in which students may stay while attending public schools in towns bordering Indian reservations) operated by the BIA; there were eighty elementary and secondary schools and eight peripheral dormitories operated by Indian tribes and tribal organizations under contract or grant with the BIA. These schools served 43,538 students in 1993. OIEP programs include adult education,

bilingual education, Close Up (grades nine through twelve civic education), effective schools, exceptional education, family and child education, higher education grants, Johnson O'Malley funding (assistance to public schools for the education of Indian children), junior achievement, National Indian School Board Association, Principals Leadership Academy, Sandia and Los Alamos National Laboratories (providing training to teachers in math and science), science and math summer workshops, showcase of excellence (showcasing outstanding boarding school programs), Solo Parent (for single-parent high school students), Special Higher Education Grants (funds for Indian students to pursue graduate degrees), summer law, and Whole Language Summer Workshop. OIEP has twenty-six education line officers located around the country.

Peach Springs School District
Peach Springs, Ariz.
Hualapai Bilingual Academic Excellence Program. Publishes a variety of Hualapai curriculum materials.

Riverside Indian School
Anadarko, Okla.
Off-reservation BIA boarding school serving grades two through twelve.

Rock Point Community School
Rock Point, Ariz.
A former BIA boarding school, Rock Point became a locally controlled BIA-funded school in 1977. Rock Point pioneered ESL and Navajo-English bilingual curricula.

Rough Rock Demonstration School
Chinle, Ariz.
First Indian-controlled school in modern times, founded in 1966. Rough Rock Press publishes a variety of Navajo curriculum materials.

San Juan School District
Blanding, Utah
Publishes Navajo curriculum material.

Santa Fe Indian School
Santa Fe, N.Mex.
BIA boarding school opened in 1890 and serving nineteen Pueblo tribes plus Navajo, Mescalero and Jicarilla Apache, and Hopi students.

Sherman Indian High School
Riverside, Calif.
BIA off-reservation boarding school founded in 1902.

Southwest Indian Polytechnic Institute
Albuquerque, N.Mex.
Vocational school run by the BIA.

Wahpeton Indian Boarding School
Wahpeton, N.Dak.
BIA off-reservation boarding school serving grades four through eight.

Wingate High School
Fort Wingate, N.Mex.
BIA boarding school serving Navajo and surrounding tribes.

FESTIVALS AND POW-WOWS

A select calendar, not intended to be inclusive, of annual American Indian gatherings.

JANUARY

Annual Native American Film Festival
Southwest Museum
Los Angeles, California
Kachina Dances
Hopi Cultural Center
Second Mesa, Arizona
San Ildefonso Feast Day
San Ildefonso Pueblo
Santa Fe, New Mexico

FEBRUARY

Lincoln's Birthday Celebration Pow-wow
Warm Springs Tribal Council
Warm Springs, Oregon
O'odham Tash Celebration
Tohono O'odham Nation
Sells, Arizona
Seminole Tribal Fair and Rodeo
Hollywood Reservation
Hollywood, Florida

MARCH

Agua Caliente Indian Market
Palm Springs, California
Epethes Pow-wow
Nez Perce Tribe
Lapwai, Idaho
Mul-Chu-Tha Community Fair
Gila River Indian Community
Sacaton, Arizona
San Jose Feast Day
Laguna Pueblo
Laguna, New Mexico

APRIL

All-Indian Days Pow-wow
Scottsdale Community College
Scottsdale, Arizona
Annual American Indian Days
Chico State University
Chico, California
Annual Pow-wow
Western Washington University
Bellingham, Washington

Annual South Umpqua Pow-wow
Myrtle Creek, Oregon
Annual Spring Pow-wow
University of Wyoming
Laramie, Wyoming
Cocopah Festivities Day
Somerton, Arizona
Institute of American Indian Arts Pow-wow
Santa Fe, New Mexico
Spring Roundup All-Indian Rodeo
White Mountain Apache Tribal Council
Whiteriver, Arizona
University of California, Berkeley, Pow-wow
Berkeley, California
University of Washington Pow-wow
Sandpoint Naval Air Station
Seattle, Washington

MAY

Annual First Peoples Cultural Festival
Capilano Longhouse
North Vancouver, British Columbia, Canada
Annual Intertribal Pow-wow
Trout Lake Community Centre
Victoria, British Columbia, Canada
Annual Pow-wow
Montana State University
Bozeman, Montana
Annual Pow-wow
Stanford University
Palo Alto, California
Chehalis Tribal Day Celebration
Oakville, Washington
Choctaw Annual Rodeo
Jones Academy
Hartshorn, Oklahoma
Louisiana Indian Heritage Association Pow-wow
Folsom, Louisiana
San Carlos Tribal Fair
San Carlos Apache Tribe
San Carlos, Arizona
Spring Pow-wow
Portland State University
Portland, Oregon
Tse-Ho-Tso Intertribal Pow-wow
Window Rick High School
Fort Defiance, Arizona

Tuscarora Nation of North Carolina Pow-wow
Tribal Grounds
Maxton, North Carolina
University of Washington Pow-wow
Seattle, Washington

JUNE

Bear Dance
Ute Mountain Ute Tribe
Towaoc, Colorado
Big Wind Pow-wow
Shoshone and Arapaho Tribes
Fort Washakie, Wyoming
Cherokee Pow-wow
Eastern Band of Cherokee Indians
Cherokee, North Carolina
Cheyenne-Arapaho Pow-wow
Concho, Oklahoma
Osage Tribal Ceremonial Dances
Pawhuska, Oklahoma
Potawatomi Pow-wow
Shawnee, Oklahoma
San Juan Feast Day
Taos Pueblo
Taos, New Mexico
Shoshone Indian Days Pow-wow and Rodeo
Fort Washakie, Wyoming
Stommish Festival
Lummi Indian Tribe
Bellingham, Washington
Warriors Memorial Pow-wow
Nez Perce Tribe
Lapwai, Idaho

JULY

Annual Chumash Intertribal Pow-wow
Santa Ynez, California
Annual Homecoming Celebration
Winnebago, Nebraska
Annual Northern Cheyenne Fourth of July Pow-wow
Lame Deer, Montana
Annual Northern Ute Pow-wow and Rodeo
Fort Duchesne, Utah
Annual Taos Pueblo Pow-wow
Pow-wow Grounds
Taos, New Mexico
Arikara Celebration and Pow-wow
White Shield, North Dakota
Arlee Fourth of July Pow-wow
Pablo, Montana
Coeur d'Alene Pow-wow
Plummer, Idaho

July Fourth Celebration Pow-wow and Rodeo
Window Rock, Arizona
Mescalero Festival
Mescalero, New Mexico
North American Indian Days
Blackfeet Tribal Council
Browning, Montana
Onion Lake Pow-wow
Onion Lake Reserve
Saskatchewan/Alberta, British Columbia, Canada
Poundmaker-Nechi Pow-wow
St. Albert, Alberta, Canada
Santa Ana Feast Day
Santa Ana Pueblo
Bernalillo, New Mexico
Shoshone-Paiute Annual Pow-wow
Owyhee, Nevada
Sisseton-Wahpeton Pow-wow
Sisseton, South Dakota
White Earth Pow-wow
White Earth, Minnesota

AUGUST

American Indian Exposition
Anadarko, Oklahoma
Annual Indian Fair Days and Pow-wow
Sierra Mono, California
Annual Intertribal Indian Ceremonial
Church Rock, New Mexico
Annual Piegan Indian Days
Brocket, Alberta, Canada
Chief Seattle Days
Suquamish, Washington
Crow Fair
Crow Agency, Montana
Kalispel Pow-wow
Usk, Washington
Land of the Menominee Pow-wow
Kenesha, Wisconsin
Little Shell Pow-wow
New Town, North Dakota
Looking Glass Pow-wow
Lapwai, Idaho
Lower Brule Pow-wow
Lower Brule, South Dakota
Ni-Mi-Win Celebration
Duluth, Minnesota
Northern Arapaho Pow-wow
Arapaho, Wyoming
Oglala Nation Pow-wow and Rodeo
Pine Ridge, South Dakota
Ottawa Pow-wow
Miami, Oklahoma

Ponca Indian Fair and Pow-wow
Ponca City, Oklahoma
Rocky Boys Pow-wow
Box Elder, Montana
Rosebud Fair and Rodeo
Rosebud, South Dakota
Shoshone-Bannock Indian Festival and Rodeo
Fort Hall, Idaho
Snake Dance
Hopi Cultural Center
Second Mesa, Arizona
Standing Rock Pow-wow
Fort Yates, North Dakota
Wichita Tribal Pow-wow
Anadarko, Oklahoma

SEPTEMBER

Cherokee Nation Pow-wow
Tahlequah, Oklahoma
Cheyenne and Arapaho Labor Day Pow-wow
Colony Indian Park
Colony, Oklahoma
Cheyenne River Labor Day Pow-wow
Eagle Butte, South Dakota
Choctaw Annual Pow-wow
Arrowhead State Park
Canadian, Oklahoma
Navajo Nation Fair
Window Rock, Arizona
Shoshone Indian Fair
Fort Washakie, Wyoming
Spokane Tribal Fair and Pow-wow
Wellpinit, Washington
Turtle Mountain Labor Day Pow-wow
Belcourt, North Dakota
United Tribes International Pow-wow
Bismarck, North Dakota

OCTOBER

Annual Canadian Thanksgiving Pow-wow
Mt. Currie, British Columbia, Canada
Apache Days
Globe, Arizona
Cherokee Fall Festival
Cherokee Nation of Oklahoma
Tahlequah, Oklahoma

Cherokees of Georgia Gathering and Pow-wow
Tribal Grounds
St. George, Georgia
Chickasaw Nation Annual Day
Chickasaw Nation of Oklahoma, Oklahoma
Four Nations Pow-wow
Nez Perce Tribe
Lapwai, Idaho
Northern Navajo Fair
Shiprock, Arizona
Pow-wow and Fall Festival
Nashville, Tennesee

NOVEMBER

American Indian Film Festival
Palace of Fine Arts
San Francisco, California
Poarch Band of Creeks Pow-wow
Atmore, Alabama
San Diego Feast Day
Jemez Pueblo
Jemez, New Mexico
San Diego Feast Day
Tesuque Pueblo
Santa Fe, New Mexico
Veteran's Day Pow-wow
Nespelem Community Center
Nespelem, Washington
Veteran's Day Pow-wow
Owyhee, Nevada
Veteran's Day Rodeo
San Carlos, Arizona

DECEMBER

Annual All-Indian Rodeo
Colorado River Reservation
Parker, Arizona
Christmas Pow-wow
Portland State University
Portland, Oregon
Christmas Pow-wow
Umatilla Reservation
Pendleton, Oregon
Shalako
Zuni Pueblo
Zuni, New Mexico

MUSEUMS, ARCHIVES, AND LIBRARIES

The following is a list of museums, archives, and libraries in a four-part format: first, museums in the United States; second, museums in Canada; third, libraries and archives in the United States; fourth, libraries and archives in Canada. Each part is arranged alphabetically, first by state, territory, or province, then by city. The list is not intended to be inclusive.

MUSEUMS IN THE UNITED STATES

ALABAMA

Alabama Museum of Natural History
Smith Hall, University of Alabama
Tuscaloosa, 35487-0340
Resource center of Southeastern Indians; ties with Moundville Archaeological Park.

ALASKA

Alaska State Museum
395 Whittier Street
Juneau, 99801-1718
Alaskan Native Gallery; Subarctic and Northwest Coast items.

Totem Heritage Center
601 Deermount
(mailing address: 629 Dock Street)
Ketchikan, 99901
Programs and artifacts in Northwest Coast arts; index to all Alaska totem poles.

ARIZONA

Museum of Northern Arizona
Fort Valley Road
(mailing address: Route 4, P.O. Box 720)
Flagstaff, 86001
Southwest Anglo and Indian art, with Hopi and Navajo emphasis. Harold S. Colton Memorial Library of 24,000 volumes.

Colorado River Indian Tribes Museum
Route 1, Box 23B
Parker, 85344
Artifacts from Mojave, Chemehuevi, Hopi, and Navajo as well as prehistoric cultures.

Heard Museum
22 E. Monte Vista Road
Phoenix, 85004-1480
Southwest emphasis; inventory of 8,200 Native American artists. Library of 40,000 volumes includes Fred Harvey Company documents and photo archives.

Gila River Arts and Crafts Center
P.O. Box 457
Sacaton, 85247
Museum and crafts reflect all tribes of the area.

Arizona State Museum
University of Arizona
Tucson, 85721
Extensive collections from the historic and prehistoric peoples of the area.

Navajo Tribal Museum
Highway 264
(mailing address: P.O. Box 308)
Window Rock, 86515
Four Corners archaeology and ethnography, including re-creation of 1870-1930 era trading post.

ARKANSAS

Arkansas State Museum
P.O. Box 490
State University, 72467
Emphasizes northeastern Arkansas tribes such as the Osage, Caddo, Chickasaw, and others.

CALIFORNIA

Fowler Museum of Cultural History
University of California, Los Angeles
405 Hilgard Avenue
Los Angeles, 90024-1549
Extensive archaeological and ethnographic collections include Native American materials.

Natural History Museum of Los Angeles County
Times-Mirror Hall of Native American Cultures; Hall of Pre-Columbian Cultures
900 Exposition Boulevard
Los Angeles, 90007
Excellent permanent displays, with changing exhibitions on contemporary issues in art and culture. The Pre-Columbian Hall covers cultures form Mexico to Peru.

Southwest Museum
234 Museum Drive
(mailing address: P.O. Box 558)
Los Angeles, 90065
Collections range from Alaska to South America, with permanent displays focusing on the Southwest, Great Plains, California, and Northwest Coast. Braun Research Library contains 50,000 volumes, 100,000 photos, 900 recordings, and archival material.

Maturango Museum
100 E. Las Flores
(mailing address: P.O. Box 1776)
Ridgecrest, 93556
A small regional museum focusing on one of the richest petroglyph areas in the United States at China Lake.

Bowers Museum of Cultural Art
2002 North Main Street
Santa Ana, 92706
Collection of 85,000 items focuses on the fine arts of indigenous peoples, including pre-Columbian and Native American.

COLORADO

Denver Art Museum
100 W. 14th Avenue Parkway
Denver, 80204
Art collection includes Indian clothing, Southwest pottery and kachinas, and Northwest Coast carvings. Frederick H. Douglas Library includes 6,000 volumes.

Denver Museum of Natural History
2001 South Colorado Boulevard
Denver, 80205
Strong on Paleo-Indian culture, including the original Folsom spear point; a 24,000-volume library.

Southern Ute Cultural Center and Gallery
Highway 172
(mailing address: P.O. Box 737)
Ignacio, 81137
Early history; contemporary bead and leather work.

CONNECTICUT

Peabody Museum
Yale University
170 Whitney
New Haven, 06511-8161
Extensive holdings include both archaeological and ethnographic materials of the Americas.

American Indian Archaeological Institute (AIAI)
38 Curtis Road
(mailing address: P.O. Box 1260)
Washington Green, 06793-0260
Continental coverage, but focus is on Northeast Woodlands. Reconstructed Indian village, with Indian Habitats Trail; 250,000 artifacts and a 2,000-volume library.

DELAWARE

Delaware State Museum
316 South Governors Avenue
Dover, 19901
Eastern prehistory; 1,000-volume library; State Archaeological Collection.

DISTRICT OF COLUMBIA

U.S. National Museum of Natural History
Smithsonian Institution
Washington, DC 20560

FLORIDA

Florida State Museum
University of Florida
Gainesville, 32601
Pearsall Collection of ethnographic items ranges from Seminole to Inuit.

Ah-Tha-Thi-Ki Museum
3240 North 64th Avenue
Hollywood, 33024
Artifacts and activities document and preserve Seminole traditions; village, burial site, nature trails.

GEORGIA

New Echota
Route 3
Calhoun, 30701
Restoration of Cherokee capital of 1825-1838. Trail of Tears material.

IDAHO

Nez Perce National Historic Park
Highway 95
(mailing address: P.O. 93)
Spalding, 83551
Prehistoric as well as historic regional items. Park notes sites of Indian-U.S. battles. A 600-volume library and archive of 3,000 photos.

ILLINOIS

Field Museum of Natural History
Roosevelt Road at Lake Shore Drive
Chicago, 60605
Extensive Native American collections, including Pawnee earth lodge replica. Webber Resource Center houses books and audio-visual materials on indigenous cultures.

INDIANA

Eiteljorg Museum of American Indian and Western Art
500 West Washington Street
Indianapolis, 46204
Extensive collection that emphasizes Northeast Woodlands, great Plains, and Southwest culture areas.

IOWA

Putnam Museum of History and Natural Science
1717 West 12th Street
Davenport, 52804
Regional ethnographic collections and important Mississippian materials.

KANSAS

Indian Center Museum
650 North Seneca
Wichita, 67203
Collection reflects Indian art and religion.

KENTUCKY

J. B. Speed Art Museum
2035 South Third Street
(mailing address: P.O. Box 2600)
Louisville, 40201-2600
Collection emphasizes regional materials and the Great Plains, complemented by a 14,000-volume art library that includes the Frederick Weygold Indian Collection.

LOUISIANA

Tunica-Biloxi Regional Indian Center and Museum
Highway 1
(mailing address: P.O. Box 331)
Marksville, 71351
Focuses on descendants of the mound builders. The tribal museum is built in a classic Mississippian style. Collections include colonial Indian-European materials returned to the tribe under the Indian Graves and Repatriation Act.

MAINE

Peary-MacMillan Arctic Museum and Studies Center
Hubbard Hall, Bowdoin College
Brunswick, 04011
MacMillan collection of Inuit and Subarctic material culture.

MASSACHUSETTS

Peabody Museum of Archaeology and Ethnology
11 Divinity Avenue
Harvard University
Cambridge, 02138
Worldwide collection of 2,000,000 artifacts has a North and South American focus; 180,000-volume library.

MICHIGAN

Cranbrook Institute of Science
500 Lone Pine Road
(mailing address: P.O. Box 801)
Bloomfield Hills, 48303-0801
Collection reflects all North American culture areas.

MINNESOTA

Minnesota Historical Society's Grand Mound and Interpretive Center
Route 7
(mailing address: P. O. Box 453)
International Falls, 56649
Burial mounds with extensive exhibits of Woodland, Laurel, and Blackduck cultures.

Mille Lacs Indian Museum
HCR 67
(mailing address: P.O. Box 95)
Onamia, 56359
Ojibwa and Dakota artifacts illustrate traditional lifeways.

MISSISSIPPI

Grand Village of the Natchez Indians
400 Jefferson Davis Boulevard
Natchez, 39120
Artifacts explore the culture of the descendants of the Mississippian mound builders.

MISSOURI

St. Louis Science Center
5050 Oakland Avenue
St. Louis, 63110

MONTANA

Museum of the Plains Indian and Crafts Center
U.S. 89
(mailing address: P.O. Box 400)
Browning, 59417
Northern Plains material culture; reconstruction of 1850's Blackfeet camp.

NEBRASKA

Fur Trade Museum
East Highway 20, HC 74
(mailing address: P.O. Box 18)
Chadron, 69337

Museum of Nebraska History
131 Centennial Mall North
Lincoln, 68508
Anthropology and art of the central Plains tribes.

NEVADA

Lost City Museum
721 South Highway 169
Overton, 89040
Reconstructed pueblo and kiva; archaeological museum; 400-volume library.

NEW JERSEY

Montclair Art Museum
3 South Mountain Avenue
Montclair, 07042
Rand Collection of Native American art. Art history library of 13,000 volumes.

New Jersey State Museum
205 West State Street
Trenton, 08625
Local material as well as Plains, Arctic, Southwest, and Northeast collections.

NEW MEXICO

Maxwell Museum of Anthropology
University of New Mexico
Roma and University, N.E.
Albuquerque, 87131-1201
Extensive Southwest collections. Library of 12,500 volumes and photo archives.

Museum of Indian Arts and Culture
708 Camino Lejo
(mailing address: P.O. Box 2087)
Santa Fe, 87504
Exhibits focus on Pueblo, Apache, and Navajo cultures. A 20,000-volume library on the anthropology of the southwest.

Western New Mexico University Museum
(mailing address: P.O. Box 43)
Silver City, 88061
Eisele collection of classic Mimbres pottery.

NEW YORK

American Museum of Natural History
79th Street and Central Park West
New York, 10024-5192
Exhibitions are especially strong on the cultures of the Arctic and Pacific Northwest.

National Museum of the American Indian
George Gustav Heye Center
Alexander Hamilton Custom House
3753 Broadway at 155th Street
New York, 10032
The first of three planned facilities of the National Museum of the American Indian, part of the Smithsonian Institution, opened in New York in 1994. The largest facility is planned for the National Mall in Washington, D.C., with a projected opening in the year 2000. Much of the extensive New York collection will be moved to Washington.

Seneca Iroquois National Museum
Broad Street Extension
(mailing address: P.O. Box 442)
Salamanca, 14779
Special wampum belt exhibit; typical nineteenth century elm-bark longhouse reconstruction; contemporary art.

NORTH CAROLINA

Indian Museum of the Carolinas
607 Turnpike Road
Laurinburg, 28352
Exhibits feature Southeast cultures and lifeways.

Native American Resource Center
Pembroke State University
Pembroke, 28372
Eastern Woodlands materials; North and South America.

NORTH DAKOTA

Turtle Mountain Chippewa Heritage Center
Highway 5
(mailing address: P.O. Box 257)
Belcourt, 58316
Promotes tribal history and traditions. Contemporary art gallery.

North Dakota Heritage Center
612 East Boulevard
Bismarck, 58505
Plains cultures. A 100,000-volume library on ethnology and history.

OHIO

Cincinnati Museum of Natural History
1301 Western Avenue
Cincinnati, 45203
Good selection of mound builder artifacts from the Ohio Valley.

Cleveland Museum of Natural History
1 Wade Oval Drive
University Circle
Cleveland, 44106-1767
Research fields include archaeology and physical anthropology. A 50,000-volume natural history library.

Oklahoma

Museum of the Great Plains
601 Ferris Avenue
Lawton, 73502
Artifacts, library, and photo archives relating to Plains tribes.

Cherokee Heritage Center
Willis Road
(mailing address: P.O. Box 515)
Tahlequah, 74465
Reconstructed village; contemporary arts and crafts.

The Philbrook Museum of Art, Inc.
2727 South Rockford Road
Tulsa, 74114
Clark Field Basket Collection; Lawson Collection of Indian clothing; Philbrook Collection of American Indian paintings; Lawson Indian library.

Seminole Nation Museum and Library
6th and Wewoka
(mailing address: P.O. Box 1532)
Wewoka, 74884

Oregon

High Desert Museum
59800 South Highway 97
Bend, 97702

Museum of Natural History
University of Oregon
1680 East 15th Avenue
Eugene, 97403-1224
Collection includes 13,000-year-old Fort Rock Cave artifacts.

Pennsylvania

Carnegie Museum of Natural History
4400 Forbes Avenue
Pittsburgh, 15213-4080
Wide coverage, including Arctic and Northwest Coast collections.

Rhode Island

Haffenreffer Museum of Anthropology
Brown University
Bristol, 02809
Arctic and Subarctic materials, including Archaic Period remains of the Red Paint People of Maine.

South Carolina

McKissick Museum
University of South Carolina
Columbia, 29208
Catawba pottery and baskets. Folk Art Resource Center.

South Dakota

Indian Museum of North America
Avenue of the Chiefs, Black Hills
Crazy Horse, 57730

Sioux Indian Museum and Crafts Center
515 West Boulevard
Rapid City, 57709

W. H. Over State Museum
414 East Clark
Vermillion, 57069-2390
Plains material culture and contemporary painting.

Tennessee

Frank H. McClung Museum
University of Tennessee
1327 Circle Park Drive
Knoxville, 37996-3200

Tennessee State Museum
505 Deaderick Street
Nashville, 37243-1120
Strong in prehistoric Mississippian culture.

Texas

Texas Memorial Museum
University of Texas
24th and Trinity
Austin, 78705
Broad focus on the anthropology of the American Indian.

Panhandle-Plains Historical Museum
2401 Fourth Avenue
Canyon, 79016
Hall of the Southern Plains. South and Southwest Indian focus; 10,000-volume library.

Alabama-Coushatta Museum
U.S. Highway 190
Route 3
(mailing address: P.O. Box 540)
Livingston, 77351

Witte Memorial Museum
3801 Broadway
San Antonio, 78209
Samples most North American culture areas.

Utah

College of Eastern Utah Prehistoric Museum
451 East 400 North
Price, 84501
Focuses on Anasazi and Fremont cultures.

Utah Museum of Natural History
University of Utah
Salt Lake City, 84112
Regional, Great Basin, and Southwestern materials.

VIRGINIA

Pamunkey Indian Museum
(mailing address: P.O. Box 2050)
King William, 23086
Contemporary and prehistoric art and artifacts.

Mattaponi Museum
West Point, 23181
Important collection of archaeological materials.

Jamestown Settlement
(mailing address: P.O. Box JF)
Williamsburg, 23187
Reconstruction of Indian village and Powhatan's lodge.

WASHINGTON

Makah Cultural and Research Center
(mailing address: P.O. Box 160)
Neah Bay, 98257
Features remains from the Ozette site, a Late Period pre-contact Makah village buried and preserved in a mudslide. Magnificent Northwest Coast Tradition assemblage of 60,000 artifacts.

The Burke Museum
University of Washington, DB-10
Seattle, 98195
Northwest Coast and Pacific Rim collections.

Seattle Art Museum
100 University Street
(mailing address: P.O. Box 22000)
Seattle, 98122-9700
Excellent collection of Northwest Coast art.

Yakima Nation Cultural Heritage Center
Toppenish, 98948

WEST VIRGINIA

Grave Creek Mound State Park
Moundsville, 26041
Largest mound produced by the Adena ceremonial complex, which flourished around 500 B.C.E. to 100 C.E.

WISCONSIN

Logan Museum of Anthropology
700 College Street
Beloit College
Beloit, 53511-5595
Physical and cultural anthropological materials from the Great Lakes, Plains, and Southwest culture areas.

Neville Public Museum
129 South Jefferson Street
Green Bay, 54301
Archaic Period materials from the Old Copper and Red Ochre cultures.

Lac du Flambeau Chippewa Museum
(mailing address: P.O. Box 804)
Lac du Flambeau, 54538
Eighteenth century dugout canoe, artifacts, and seasonal activities displays.

Milwaukee Public Museum
800 West Wells Street
Milwaukee, 53233
Collections cover North America. A 125,000-volume library.

WYOMING

Anthropology Museum
University of Wyoming
Laramie, 82071

MUSEUMS IN CANADA

ALBERTA

Glenbow Museum
130 Ninth Avenue, S.E.
Calgary, AB T2G 0P3

Provincial Museum of Alberta
12845 102nd Avenue
Edmonton, AB T5N 0M6
Regional materials; Inuit; northern Plains.

BRITISH COLUMBIA

Campbell River Museum
1235 Island Highway
Campbell Island, BC V9W 2C7
Arts of the Indian groups of northern Vancouver Island.

'Ksan Indian Village
(mailing address: P.O. Box 326)
Hazelton, BC B0J 1Y0
A center for the display, preservation, and promotion of Gitksan arts and crafts skills. Seven traditional buildings.

Museum of Northern British Columbia
(mailing address: P.O. Box 669)
Prince Rupert, BC V8J 3S1
Northwest Coast artifacts. Promotes contemporary carving and craft skills.

Museum of Anthropology
University of British Columbia
Vancouver, BC V6T 1Z1
Major Northwest Coast collections. Center for promotion of traditional arts and customs.

Royal British Columbia Museum
675 Belleville Street
Victoria, BC V8V 1X4
Traditional Kwakiutl dance houses; Thunderbird Park totem pole exhibits; art demonstrations.

MANITOBA

Eskimo Museum
La Verendrye Street
(mailing address: P.O. Box 10)
Churchill, MB R0B 0E0
Inuit materials include kayaks dating back 3,000 years. Also, Subarctic materials from Chippewa and Cree cultures.

Manitoba Museum of Man and Nature
190 Rupert Avenue
Winnipeg, MB R3B 0N2

NEW BRUNSWICK

New Brunswick Museum
277 Douglas Avenue
Saint John, NB F2K 1E5
Regional and pre-Algonquian artifacts.

NEWFOUNDLAND

Newfoundland Museum
285 Duckworth Street
St. John's, NF A1C 1G9
Exhibits cover the six major tribal groups of Labrador and Newfoundland.

NORTHWEST TERRITORIES

Northern Life Museum
110 King Street
(mailing address: P.O. Box 420)
Fort Smith, NT X0E 0P0
Arctic and Subartic tools and artifacts.

Dene Cultural Institute
(mailing address: P.O. Box 207)
Yellowknife, NT X1A 2N2

NOVA SCOTIA

Nova Scotia Museum
1747 Summer Street
Halifax, NS B3H 3A6
Artifacts of the Micmac.

ONTARIO

North American Indian Travel College
The Living Museum
RR 3
Cornwall Island, ON K6H 5R7

Museum of Indian Archaeology and Lawson Prehistoric Village
1600 Attawandaron Road
London, ON N6G 3M6
Exhibits cover five phases of culture dating back to Paleo-Indian times. On-site excavation.

Thunder Bay Art Gallery
1080 Keewatin Street
(mailing address: P.O. Box 1193)
Thunder Bay, ON P7C 4X9
Traditional items as well as contemporary art.

Royal Ontario Museum
100 Queen's Park Crescent
Toronto, ON M5S 2C6
Ontario prehistory.

PRINCE EDWARD ISLAND

Micmac Indian Village
(mailing address: P.O. Box 51)
Cornwall, PEI C0A 1H0

QUEBEC

Canadian Museum of Civilization
100 Laurier Street
Hull, PQ J8X 4H2
Spectacular collection of national cultural materials.

McCord Museum
McGill University
690 Sherbrook Street W.
Montreal, PQ H3A 1E9

Abenakis Museum
Route 226
Odanak, PQ J0G 1H0
Displays reflect tribal traditions and lore.

SASKATCHEWAN

Regina Plains Museum
1801 Scarth Street
Regina, SK S4P 2G9
Metis history and the Riel Rebellions are covered in addition to Plains material.

Saskatchewan Museum of Natural History
Wascana Park
Regina, SK S4P 3V7
Native Peoples Gallery focusing on Subarctic tribes.

YUKON TERRITORY

MacBride Museum
(mailing address: P.O. Box 4037)
Whitehorse, YT Y1A 3S9
Artifacts of the Yukon region.

LIBRARIES AND ARCHIVES
IN THE UNITED STATES

ALABAMA

Alabama Department of Archives and History
624 Washington Avenue
Montgomery, 36130

ARIZONA

Smoki People Library
P.O. Box 123
Prescott, 86302
Library of 600 volumes covers North and South American Indian ceremonials and dances.

Tohono Chul Park, Inc.
7366 North Paseo del Norte
Tucson, 85704
Nature center, ethnic art exhibitions, and 800-volume library on Southwest culture and environment.

Western Archaeological and Conservation Center
1415 North Sixth Avenue
(mailing address: P.O. Box 41058, Tucson, 85717)
Tucson, 85705
Focus on Southwest prehistory and ethnography: 17,000-volume library, 100 periodicals, and 160,000-item photo archive.

Navajo Nation Library System
Drawer K
Window Rock, 86515
Collection has 23,000 books, 1,000 manuscripts, and films and tapes. Files of the *Navajo Times*. Two libraries in Window Rock and one in Navajo, New Mexico.

ARKANSAS

Southwest Arkansas Regional Archives (SARA)
P.O. Box 134
Washington, 71862
History of Caddo Indians and Southwest Arkansas.

CALIFORNIA

Malki Museum Archives
11-795 Fields Road
Banning, 92220
Oral history project tapes; field notes of J. P. Harrington and others; manuscript and photo archives.

Native American Studies Library
University of California at Berkeley
103 Wheeler
Berkeley, 94720
Reports of the Bureau of Indian Affairs; Indian Claims Commission materials; special California Indian collection; extensive holdings.

American Indian Resource Center
Public Library of Los Angeles County
6518 Miles Avenue
Huntington Park, 90255
Special collections on Indians of North America; 9,000 volumes.

Rupert Costo Library
UCR Library Special Collections
University of California at Riverside
Riverside, 92517
The 15,000-volume collection is countrywide in scope with a California concentration. Houses the American Indian Historical Society Archives, donated by the Costos. Manuscripts, field notes, and 300 books cover the customs and medicines of the Chinantec Indians of Oaxaca.

Scientific Library
San Diego Museum of Man
Balboa Park
1350 El Prado
San Diego, 92101
Wide coverage of the Americas, including physical anthropology, archaeology, and ethnology.

COLORADO

National Indian Law Library
Native American Rights Fund
1522 Broadway
Boulder, 80302-6296
Documents, periodicals, and 7,500 books on U.S.-Indian relations and law.

Taylor Museum Reference Library
Colorado Springs Fine Arts Center
30 West Dale Street
Colorado Springs, 80903
Art of the Southwest; Hispanic and colonial folk art. Collection houses 30,000 volumes; extensive biographies of folk artists.

Koshare Indian Museum, Inc.
115 West 18th Street
La Junta, 81050
The 10,000-volume Special Koshare Collection focuses on Native America and Western United States.

Ute Mountain Tribal Research Archive and Library
Tribal Compound
(mailing address: P.O. Box CC)
Towaoc, 81334
Includes 2,500 books as well as 30,000 archival items, including tribal government documents.

CONNECTICUT

Mashantucket Pequot Research Library
Indiantown Road
Ledyard, 06339

DISTRICT OF COLUMBIA

American Folklife Center
U.S. Library of Congress
Thomas Jefferson Building - G152
Washington, DC 20540
Biggest collection of early Indian recordings, including the Frances Densmore Collection of 3,600 cylinders and the Helen Heffron Roberts Collection from the Northwest Coast and California.

National Anthropological Archives
Natural History Museum MRC 152
10th and Constitution Avenue
Washington, DC 20560
Extensive collections of recordings, photographs, field notes, and manuscripts of the Bureau of Ethnology.

Natural Resources Library
U.S. Department of the Interior
Mail Stop 1151
18th and C Streets, N.W.
Washington, DC 20240
More than 600,000 volumes and extensive periodicals and archival items, including materials on American Indians.

GEORGIA

Hargrett Rare Books and Manuscript Library
University of Georgia
Athens, 30602

ILLINOIS

Newberry Library
D'Arcy McNickle Center for the History of the American Indian
60 West Walton Street
Chicago, 60610
More than 100,000 volumes, including the E. E. Ayer Collection.

INDIANA

Lilly Library
Indiana University
Bloomington, 47405
Collection includes Indian accounts of Custer's defeat at the Battle of the Little Bighorn.

Fulton County Historical Society Library
Route 3
(mailing address: P.O. Box 89)
Rochester, 46975
Collection houses 4,000 volumes, including coverage of Potawatomi removal to Kansas in 1838 (the Trail of Death).

KANSAS

Mennonite Library and Archives
Bethel College
300 East 27th Street
North Newton, 67117-9989
Includes 26,000 books. Petter Manuscript Collection on the Cheyenne; H. R. Voth Manuscript and Photo Collection on the Hopi.

Mid-America All Indian Center Library
650 North Seneca
Wichita, 67203
Includes 3,000 books and 200 bound periodical volumes on Indian art, history, and culture. Blackbear Bosin Collection of publications and personal papers.

LOUISIANA

Grindstone Bluff Museum Library
(mailing address) P.O. Box 7965
Shreveport, 71107
Contains 6,000 books and 2,000 periodical volumes on regional archaeology and ethnology; emphasis on Caddo Indians.

MASSACHUSETTS

Fruitlands Museums and Library
102 Prospect Hill Road
Harvard, 01451

Mashpee Archives Building
Mashpee, 02649

MICHIGAN

Custer Collection
Monroe County Library System
Monroe, 48161
Contains 4,000 books and archival materials on Custer and the West.

MINNESOTA

Minnesota Historical Society
Divison of Archives and Manuscripts
345 Kellogg Boulevard West
St. Paul, 55102-1906
Materials relating to the Ojibwa and Dakota.

MISSOURI

Missouri Historical Society Library
Jefferson Memorial Building
Forest Park
St. Louis, 63112
Northern Plains; papers of William Clark from Lewis and Clark expedition.

MONTANA

Dr. John Woodenlegs Memorial Library
Dull Knife Memorial College
P.O. Box 98
Lame Deer, 59043-0098
Cheyenne history; oral history collection. Contains 10,000 volumes.

NEBRASKA

Native American Public Broadcasting Consortium Library
P.O. Box 83111
Lincoln, 68501
Special Collection of Native American video programs (171 titles). Audio program "Spirits of the Present." NAPBC quarterly newsletter. Materials available by mail.

Nebraska State Historical Society Library
P.O. Box 82554
Lincoln, 68501
Anderson Collection of Brule Sioux photographs. Library has 70,000 volumes.

Joslyn Art Museum
Art Reference Library
2200 Dodge Street
Omaha, 68102
Native American art covered in collection of 25,000 volumes, 3,000 bound periodicals, and 20,000 slides.

NEW JERSEY

Firestone Library Collections of Western Americana
Princeton University
Princeton, 08544

NEW MEXICO

Mary Cabot Wheelwright Research Library
704 Camino Lejo
Santa Fe, 87502
Contains 10,000 volumes; archives on Navajo religion and sandpainting.

Museum of New Mexico Photo Archives
P.O. Box 2087
Santa Fe, 87504

Millicent Rogers Museum Library
P.O. Box A
Taos, 87571
Registry of New Mexico Hispanic artists, including a number of Indian artists.

NEW YORK

Museum of the American Indian Library
9 Westchester Square
Bronx, 10461
Contains 40,000 volumes; archives.

Akwesasne Library
Route 37-RR 1
(mailing address: P.O. Box 14-C)
Hogansburg, 13655

Iroquois Indian Museum Library
P.O. Box 9
Bowes Cave, 12042-0009
Contains 1,500 volumes; 500 archival items; exhibition catalogs.

Seneca Nation Library
Allegany Branch
P.O. Box 231
Salamanca, 14779
Cattaraugus Branch
Irving, 14981

NORTH CAROLINA

State Archives
109 East Jones Street
Raleigh, 27601-2807

OHIO

Ohio Historical Society Archives and Library
1982 Velma Avenue
Columbus, 43211

OKLAHOMA

Chickasaw Nation Library
Arlington and Mississippi Streets
Ada, 74830

Oklahoma Historical Society
Archives and Manuscript Division
2100 North Lincoln Boulevard
Oklahoma City, 73105
State Indian Agency records; Dawes Commission papers; 125,000 photographs.

Gilcrease Library
1400 Gilcrease Museum Road
Tulsa, 74127
John Ross (Cherokee chief) and Peter Pitchlynn (Choctaw chief) papers; 50,000 volumes.

OREGON

Siletz Library and Archives
119 East Logsden Road, Building II
Siletz, 97380

PENNSYLVANIA

Free Library of Philadelphia
Logan Square
Philadelphia, 19103

University Museum Library
33rd and Spruce Streets
University of Pennsylvania
Philadelphia, 19104
Brinton Collection on Indian linguistics; Delaware materials.

SOUTH DAKOTA

Center for Western Studies
Augustana College
P.O. Box 727
Sioux Falls, 57197
Great Plains history. Collection has 30,000 volumes, 1,500 linear feet of manuscripts.

TEXAS

Fikes Hall of Special Collections
DeGolyer Library
Southern Methodist University
Dallas, 75275

National Archives
Southwest Region
501 Felix at Hemphill, Building 1
P.O. Box 6216
Fort Worth, 76115
Bureau of Indian Affairs records for Oklahoma.

UTAH

Ute Tribal Museum, Library, and Audio-Visual Center
Fort Duchesne, 84026

WASHINGTON

Jamestown Klallam Library
Blyn, 98382

Special Collections
University of Washington
Seattle, 98195

WEST VIRGINIA

ERIC Clearinghouse on Rural Education and Small Schools (CRESS) Library
1031 Quarrier Street
(mailing address: P.O. Box 1348)
Charleston, 25325
Microfiche containing 300,000 documents. Indian/Hispanic issues.

WISCONSIN

Hoard Historical Museum Library
407 Merchant Avenue
Fort Atkinson, 53538
Rare Black Hawk War materials.

Fairlawn Historical Museum
Harvard View Parkway
Superior, 54880
George Catlin lithographs; David F. Berry Collection of Indian photographs and portraits.

WYOMING

McCracken Research Library
Buffalo Bill Historical Center
P.O. Box 1000
Cody, 82414

LIBRARIES AND ARCHIVES IN CANADA

ALBERTA

Canadian Circumpolar Library
University of Alberta
Edmonton, AB T6G 2J8
University of Lethbridge Library
Special Collections
4401 University Drive
Lethbridge, AB T1K 3M4
Native American studies; English literature; education.

BRITISH COLUMBIA

Alert Bay Library and Museum
199 Fir Street
Alert Bay, BC B0N 1A0
Kamloops Museum and Archives
207 Seymour Street
Kamloops, BC V2C 2E7
Interior Salish and Shuswap material.
University of British Columbia Library
1956 Main Hall
Vancouver, BC V6T 1Z1

MANITOBA

Department of Indian Affairs and Northern Development Regional Library
275 Portage Avenue
Winnipeg, MB R3B 3A3
People's Library
Manitoba Indian Cultural Education Centre
119 Sutherland Avenue
Winnipeg, MB R2W 3C9

NEW BRUNSWICK

Education Resource Centre
University of New Brunswick
D'Avray Hall
P.O. Box 7500
Fredericton, NB E3B 5H5

NORTHWEST TERRITORIES

Thebacha Campus Library
Arctic College
Fort Smith, NT X0E 0P0

NOVA SCOTIA

Nova Scotia Human Rights Commission Library
P.O. Box 2221
Halifax, NS B3J 3C4
Rights of indigenous peoples, women, and others; 4,000 books.

ONTARIO

Department of Indian Affairs and Northern Development Departmental Library
Ottawa, ON K1A 0H4
University of Sudbury Library and Jesuit Archives
Sudbury, ON P3E 2C6

QUEBEC

Canadian Museum of Civilization Library
100 Laurier Street
Hull, PQ J8X 4H2

SASKATCHEWAN

Gabriel Dumont Institute of Native Studies and Applied Research Library
121 Broadway
Regina, SK S4N 0Z6
Indian History archives; 30,000 volumes.
Indian Federated College Library
University of Regina
Regina, SK S4S 0A2
Collection has 15,000 volumes. Branch library of 4,000 volumes on Saskatoon Campus.
Saskatchewan Provincial Library
1352 Winnipeg Street
Regina, SK S4P 3V7
Has a 4,000-volume Indian collection. Strong in languages.

ORGANIZATIONS, AGENCIES, AND SOCIETIES

All Indian Pueblo Council
Founded: 1958
P.O. Box 3256
Albuquerque, NM 87190

American Indian Council of Architects and Engineers
Founded: 1976
P.O. Box 230685
Tigard, OR 97223

American Indian Culture Research Center
Founded: 1967
Box 98
Blue Cloud Abbey
Marvin, SD 57251

American Indian Graduate Center
Founded: 1969
4520 Montgomery Boulevard NE
Ste. 1-B
Albuquerque, NM 87109

American Indian Health Care Association
Founded: 1975
245 E. 6th Street
Ste. 499
St. Paul, MN 55101

American Indian Heritage Foundation
Founded: 1973
6051 Arlington Boulevard
Falls Church, VA 22044

American Indian Higher Education Consortium
Founded: 1972
513 Capitol Court NE
Ste. 100
Washington, DC 20002

American Indian Horse Registry
Founded: 1961
Route 3, Box 64
Lockhart, TX 78644

American Indian Liberation Crusade
Founded: 1952
4009 S. Halldale Avenue
Los Angeles, CA 90062

American Indian Library Association
Founded: 1979
50 E. Huron Street
Chicago, IL 60611

American Indian Lore Association
Founded: 1957
960 Walhonding Avenue
Logan, OH 43138

American Indian Movement (AIM)
Founded: 1968
710 Clayton Street
Apartment 1
San Francisco, CA 94117

American Indian Registry for the Performing Arts
Founded: 1983
1717 N. Highland Avenue
Ste. 614
Los Angeles, CA 90028

American Indian Research and Development
Founded: 1982
2424 Springer Drive
Ste. 200
Norman, OK 73069

American Indian Science and Engineering Society
Founded: 1977
1630 30th Street
Ste. 301
Boulder, CO 80301

Americans for Indian Opportunity
Founded: 1970
3508 Garfield Street NW
Washington, DC 20007

Arrow, Incorporated
(Americans for Restitution and Righting of Old Wrongs)
Founded: 1949
1000 Connecticut Avenue NW
Ste. 1206
Washington, DC 20036

Associated Community of Friends on Indian Affairs
Founded: 1869
Box 1661
Richmond, IN 47375

Association of American Indian Physicians
Founded: 1971
Building D
10015 S. Pennsylvania
Oklahoma City, OK 73159

Association of Community Tribal Schools
Founded: 1982
c/o Dr. Roger Bordeaux
616 4th Avenue W
Sisseton, SD 57262-1349

Association on American Indian Affairs
Founded: 1923
245 5th Avenue
New York, NY 10016

Bureau of Catholic Indian Missions
Founded: 1874
2021 H Street NW
Washington, DC 20006

Cherokee National Historical Society
Founded: 1963
P.O. Box 515
Tahlequah, OK 74465

Coalition for Indian Education
Founded: 1987
3620 Wyoming Boulevard NE
Ste. 206
Albuquerque, NM 87111

Concerned American Indian Parents
Founded: 1987
CUHCC Clinic
2016 16th Avenue S
Minneapolis, MN 55404

Continental Confederation of Adopted Indians
Founded: 1950
960 Walhonding Avenue
Logan, OH 43138

Council for Indian Education
Founded: 1970
517 Rimrock Road
Billings, MT 59102

Council for Native American Indians
Founded: 1974
280 Broadway
Ste. 316
New York, NY 10007

Council of Energy Resource Tribes (CERT)
Founded: 1975
1999 Broadway
Ste. 2600
Denver, CO 80202

Crazy Horse Memorial Foundation
Founded: 1948
The Black Hills
Avenue of the Chiefs
Crazy Horse, SD 57730

Creek Indian Memorial Association
Founded: 1923
Creek County House Museum
Town Square
Okmulgee, OK 74447

Dakota Women of All Red Nations (DWARN)
Founded: 1978
c/o Lorelei DeCora
P.O. Box 423
Rosebud, SD 57570

First Nations Development Institute
Founded: 1980
69 Kelley Road
Falmouth, VA 22405

Gathering of Nations
Founded: 1984
P.O. Box 75102
Sta. 14
Albuquerque, NM 87120-1269

Indian Arts and Crafts Association
Founded: 1974
122 La Veta Drive NE
Ste. B
Albuquerque, NM 87108

Indian Heritage Council
Founded: 1988
Henry Street
Box 2302
Morristown, TN 37816

Indian Law Resource Center
Founded: 1978
508 Stuart Street
Helena, MT 59601

Indian Rights Association
Founded: 1882
1801 Market Street
Philadelphia, PA 19103-1675

Indian Youth of America
Founded: 1978
609 Badgerow Building
Sioux City, IA 51101

Institute for American Indian Studies
Founded: 1971
38 Curtis Road
P.O. Box 1260
Washington, CT 06793-0260

Institute for the Development of Indian Law
Founded: 1971
c/o K. Kirke Kickingbird
Oklahoma City University
School of Law
2501 Blackwelder
Oklahoma City, OK 73106

Institute for the Study of American Cultures
Founded: 1983
The Rankin
1004 Broadway
Columbus, GA 31901

Institute for the Study of Traditional American Indian Arts
Founded: 1982
P.O. Box 66124
Portland, OR 97290

Institute of American Indian Arts
Founded: 1962
P.O. Box 20007
Santa Fe, NM 87504

International Indian Treaty Council
Founded: 1974
710 Clayton Street
Number 1
San Francisco, CA 94117

Inter-Tribal Indian Ceremonial Association
Founded: 1921
Box 1
Church Rock, NM 87311

Lone Indian Fellowship and Lone Scout Alumni
Founded: 1926
1104 St. Clair Avenue
Sheboygan, WI 53081

National American Indian Court Clerks Association
Founded: 1980
1000 Connecticut Avenue NW
Ste. 1206
Washington, DC 20036

National American Indian Court Judges Association
Founded: 1968
1000 Connecticut Avenue NW
Ste. 1206
Washington, DC 20036

**National Center for American Indian Enterprise
  Development**
Founded: 1969
953 E. Juanita Avenue
Mesa, AZ 85204

National Congress of American Indians
Founded: 1944
900 Pennsylvania Avenue SE
Washington, DC 20003

National Council of BIA Educators
Founded: 1967
6001 Marble NE
Ste. 10
Albuquerque, NM 87110

National Indian Council on Aging
Founded: 1976
6400 Uptown Boulevard NE
City Centre
Ste. 510-W
Albuquerque, NM 87110

National Indian Counselors Association
Founded: 1980
Learning Research Center
Institute of American Indian Arts
P.O. Box 20007
Santa Fe, NM 87504

National Indian Education Association
Founded: 1970
1819 H Street NW
Ste. 800
Washington, DC 20006

National Indian Health Board
Founded: 1969
1385 S. Colorado Boulevard
Ste. A-708
Denver, CO 80222

National Indian Social Workers Association
Founded: 1970
410 NW 18th Street
Number 101
Portland, OR 97209

National Indian Training and Research Center
Founded: 1969
2121 S. Mill Avenue
Ste. 216
Tempe, AZ 85282

National Indian Youth Council
Founded: 1961
318 Elm Street SE
Albuquerque, NM 87102

National Native American Cooperative
Founded: 1969
P.O. Box 1030
San Carlos, AZ 85550-1000

National Urban Indian Council
Founded: 1977
10068 University Station
Denver, CO 80210

Native American (Indian) Chamber of Commerce
Founded: 1990
c/o Native American Cooperative
P.O. Box 1000
San Carlos, AZ 85550-1000

Native American Community Board
Founded: 1984
P.O. Box 572
Lake Andes, SD 57356-0572

Native American Educational Services College
Founded: 1974
2838 West Peterson
Chicago, IL 60659

Native American Indian Housing Council
Founded: 1974
900 2nd Street NE
Ste. 220
Washington, DC 20002

Native American Policy Network
Founded: 1979
Barry University
11300 2nd Avenue NE
Miami, FL 33161

Native American Rights Fund (NARF)
Founded: 1970
1506 Broadway
Boulder, CO 80302

North American Indian Association
Founded: 1940
22720 Plymouth Road
Detroit, MI 48239

North American Indian Chamber of Commerce
Founded: 1983
P.O. Box 5000
San Carlos, AZ 85550-1000

North American Indian Museums Association
Founded: 1979
c/o George Abrams
260 Prospect Street
Number 669
Hackensack, NJ 07601-2608

North American Indian Women's Association
Founded: 1970
9602 Maestor's Lane
Gaithersburg, MD 20879

North American Native American Indian Information and Trade Center
Founded: 1991
P.O. Box 1000
San Carlos, AZ 85550-1000

Order of the Indian Wars
Founded: 1979
P.O. Box 7401
Little Rock, AR 72217

Pan-American Indian Association
Founded: 1984
P.O. Box 244
Nocatee, FL 33864

Seventh Generation Fund for Indian Development
Founded: 1977
P.O. Box 10
Forestville, CA 95436

Smoki People
Founded: 1921
P.O. Box 123
Prescott, AZ 86302

Survival of American Indians Association
Founded: 1964
7803-A Samurai Drive SE
Olympia, WA 98503

Tekakwitha Conference National Center
Founded: 1939
P.O. Box 6768
Great Falls, MT 59406-6768

Tiyospaya American Indian Student Organization
Founded: 1986
P.O. Box 1954
St. Petersburg, FL 33731

United Indians of All Tribes Foundation
Founded: 1970
Daybreak Star Arts Center
Discovery Park
P.O. Box 99100
Seattle, WA 98199

United Native Americans
Founded: 1968
2434 Faria Avenue
Pinole, CA 94564

United South and Eastern Tribes
Founded: 1969
1101 Kermit Drive
Ste. 302
Nashville, TN 37217

POPULATIONS OF U.S. RESERVATIONS

Alphabetical listing of U.S. reservations and populations; population figures are rounded off.

Reservation	Population	Reservation	Population
Absentee-Shawnee Tribe	1,500	Colville	3,750
Acoma Pueblo	3,100	Comanche Indian Tribe of Oklahoma	4,000
Agua Caliente	200	Coquille Indian Tribe	630
Allegheny	750	Cortina Rancheria	90
Alturas Rancheria	15	Coushatta	295
Apache Tribe of Oklahoma	5,500	Creek Nation of Oklahoma	32,500
Bad River	1,550	Crow Creek	2,500
Barona	330	Crow Indian	5,500
Benton Paiute	68	Cuyapaipe	30
Berry Creek Rancheria	275	Delaware Tribe of Western Oklahoma	1,150
Big Bend Rancheria	110	Devil's Lake Sioux	3,500
Big Cypress	450	Dilkon Community	1,000
Big Lagoon Rancheria	12	Dry Creek Rancheria	30
Big Pine	110	Duck Valley	1,100
Big Sandy Rancheria	55	Duckwater	150
Bishop Indian	1,075	Eastern Shawnee	395
Blackfeet	7,000	Ely Indian colony	350
Blue Lake Rancheria	35	Enterpise Rancheria	20
Bridgeport Indian Colony	90	Fallon Reservation and Colony	700
Brighton	440	Flandreau Santee Sioux	440
Burns Paiute Indian Colony	220	Flathead	3,500
Cabazon	27	Fond du Lac	1,750
Caddo Indian Tribe	1,250	Forest County Potawatomi Community	450
Cahuilla	175	Fort Apache Indian	8,500
Camp Verde	600	Fort Belknap	2,500
Campo	225	Fort Berthold	4,000
Cattaraugus	5,500	Fort Bidwell	200
Cayuga Nation	110	Fort Hall	4,000
Cedarville Rancheria	22	Fort Independence	110
Chehalis	750	Fort McDermitt	710
Chemehuevi	135	Fort McDowell	550
Cherokee	8,800	Fort Mojave	600
Cherokee Nation of Oklahoma	45,000	Fort Peck	5,500
Cherokee Tribe of Virginia	150	Fort Sill Apache Tribe of Oklahoma	380
Cheyenne-Arapaho Tribe	75,000	Gila Bend	300
Cheyenne River	5,500	Gila River	9,750
Chickasaw Nation of Oklahoma	75,000	Golden Hill	5
Chitimacha	310	Goshute	200
Choctaw Indian	3,715	Grand Portage (Pigeon River)	325
Choctaw Nation of Oklahoma	22,000	Grande Ronde Indian Community	640
Citizen Band Potawatomi Tribe	4,500	Hannahville Indian Community	375
Cochiti Pueblo	975	Havasupai	500
Cocopah	550	HOH	75
Coeur d'Alene	850	Hoopa Extension	300
Cold Springs Rancheria	235	Hoopa Valley	2,200
Colorado River	2,400	Hopi	8,500
Colorado River Indian	2,800	Hopland Rancheria	150
Colusa Rancheria	55	Houlton (Maliseet Band)	290

Reservation	Population	Reservation	Population
Houma Indian Communities	2,750	Nooksack	750
Hualapai	1,200	Northern Cheyenne	3,300
Inaja & Cosmit	15	Ojibwa of the Red River	850
Indian Township	395	Omaha	1,500
Iowa	310	Oneida (New York)	1,100
Iowa Tribe of Oklahoma	6,000	Oneida (Wisconsin)	2,700
Isabella	450	Onondaga	1,500
Isleta Pueblo	3,500	Osage Tribe of Oklahoma	6,000
Jamestown S'kallam	250	Otoe-Missouria Tribe of Oklahoma	1,250
Jemez Pueblo	2,000	Paiute Indian Tribe of Utah	600
Jicarilla Apache	2,600	Pajoaque Pueblo	175
Kaibab	250	Pala Indian	395
Kalispel	250	Pamunkey Indian	90
Kaw Tribe of Oklahoma	1,250	Pauma Band of Mission Indians	40
Kickapoo	625	Pawnee Indian Tribe of Oklahoma	2,500
Kickapoo Tribe of Oklahoma	800	Penobscot	1,150
Kiowa Tribe of Oklahoma	4,500	Picayune Rancheria	65
Kootenai	135	Picuris Pueblo	200
Lac Courte Oreilles	2,000	Pine Ridge	14,500
Lac du Flambeau	2,400	Pleasant Point	800
Laguna Pueblo	4,250	Ponca Tribe of Oklahoma	2,500
La Jolla Band of Mission Indians	235	Poospatuck	100
L'Anse (Keweenaw Bay)	950	Port Gamble Indian Communtiy	450
Las Vegas Indian Colony	125	Port Madison	440
Laytonville Rancheria	110	Prairie Island	135
Leech Lake	5,200	Prairie Potawatomi	1,350
Lone Pine	150	Pyramid Lake	850
Los Coyotes	195	Quapaw Tribe of Oklahoma	1,450
Lovelock Indian Colony	175	Quileute	300
Lower Brule	1,100	Quinault	2,200
Lower Elwha Klallam	470	Red Cliff	1,500
Lower Sioux Indian Community	230	Red Lake	4,850
Lummi	3,300	Reno-Sparks Indian Colony	630
Makah	1,250	Rincon	150
Manchester/Point Arena Rancheria	95	Rocky Boy	1,100
Manzanita	25	Rosebud	9,900
Maricopa (Ak Chin)	450	Round Valley	450
Menominee	3,750	Sac and Fox	700
Mesa Grande	70	Sac and Fox Tribe of Oklahoma	1,700
Mescalero Apache	2,750	St. Croix	1,100
Miami Tribe of Oklahoma	1,516	St. Regis Mohawk Indian	6,250
Miccosukee	495	Salt River	3,500
Michigan Bay Mills	395	San Carlos Apache	6,000
Mille Lacs	950	San Felipe Pueblo	2,200
Mississippi Choctaw	4,750	San Ildefonso Pueblo	475
Moapa River Indian	395	San Juan Pueblo	1,100
Morongo	375	San Manuel	55
Muckleshoot	2,500	San Xavier	1,000
Nambe Pueblo	400	Sandia Pueblo	320
Navajo	185,000	Sanostee	550
Nett Lake (Bois Fort)	1,250	Santa Ana Pueblo	1,350
Nez Perce	2,200	Santa Clara Pueblo	2,750
Nisqually Indian	1,400	Santa Rosa	110

Reservation	Population	Reservation	Population
Santa Rosa Rancheria	135	Tohono O'odham (Sells)	7,700
Santa Ynez	100	Tonawanda	675
Santa Ysabel	325	Tonkawa Tribe of Oklahoma	1,500
Santee Sioux	425	Torres-Martinez	90
Sauk-Suiattle Indian	215	Tulalip	950
Sault Ste. Marie Tribe of Chippewa Indians	2,500	Tule River	550
Seminole	500	Turtle Mountain	8,950
Seminole Nation of Oklahoma	4,000	Tuscarora	775
Seneca-Cayuga Tribe of Oklahoma	800	Uintah and Ouray	2,000
Shakopee Sioux community	110	Umatilla	1,750
Shinnecock	375	Upper Sioux Indian Community	150
Shoalwater Bay	100	Upper Skagit Indian	200
Siletz Reservation	800	Ute Mountain	1,600
Sisseton-Wahpeton	4,000	Viejas (Baron Long)	195
Skokomish Indian Reservation	550	Walker River	1,100
Skull Valley Indian Community	85	Wampanoag	550
Soboba Indian	450	Warm Springs	2,750
Sokaogon Chippewa Community	850	Washoe	1,020
Southern Ute	1,200	White Earth	3,200
Spokane	1,200	Wichita Tribe of Oklahoma	700
Squaxin Island	100	Winnebago (Nebraska/Iowa)	1,100
Standing Rock	8,500	Winnebago (Wisconsin)	1,350
Stewarts Point Rancheria	100	Winnemucca Indian Colony	110
Stockbridge-Munsee Community	1,350	Wyandotte Tribe of Oklahoma	500
Sulphur Bank Rancheria	55	Yakima	9,000
Susanville Rancheria	350	Yankton Sioux	2,500
Swinomish	750	Yavapai-Prescott	175
Sycuan	70	Yerrington Indian Colony	430
Table Bluff	218	Yomba	135
Taos Pueblo	1,450	Zia Pueblo	650
Tesuque Pueblo	325	Zuni	7,450

Source: Data are from Klein, Barry T., *Reference Encyclopedia of the American Indian.* 6th ed. West Nyack, N.Y. Todd Publications, 1993.
Note: Some reservations are not listed because they contain no "in residence" population.

RESERVATIONS: UNITED STATES

A listing by state of U.S. American Indian reservations.

ALABAMA
Choctaw Indian
Poarch Band of
   Creek Indians

ARIZONA
Beclabito
Bird Springs
Blue Gap
Broadway
Cameron
Camp Verde
Chilchinbeto
Chinle
Coalmine
Cocopah
Colorado River
   Indian
Copper Mine
Cornfields
Coyote Canyon
Crystal
Dennehotso
Dilkon Community
Forest Lake
Fort Apache Indian
Fort Defiance
Fort McDowell
Fort Mohave
Fort Yuma
Ganado
Gila Bend
Gila River
Greasewood
Havasupai
Hopi
Houck
Hualapai
Inscription House
Jeddito
Kaibab
Kaibito
Kayenta
Kinlichee
Klagetoh
Lechee
Leupp
Low Mountain
Lukachukai
Lupton

Many Farms
Maricopa (Ak Chin)
Mexican Springs
Mexican Waters
Naschitti
Navajo
Navajo Mountain
Nazlini
Oak Springs
Oljatoh
Pascua Yaqui Indian
   Community
Pinon
Red Lake
Red Mesa
Red Rock
Rough Rock
Round Rock
St. Michaels
Salt River
San Carlos Apache
San Xavier
Sanotsee
Sawmill
Shonto
Steamboat
Teecnospos
Teesto
Tohatchi
Tohono O'odham (Sells)
Tolani Lake
Tonto Apache Community
Tsaile-Wheatfields
Tselani
Tuba City
Twin Lakes
White Cone
Wide Ruins
Yavapai-Prescott

CALIFORNIA
Agua Caliente
Alturas Rancheria
Augustine
Barona
Benton Paiute
Berry Creek Rancheria
Big Bend Rancheria
Big Lagoon Rancheria
Big Pine

Big Sandy Rancheria
Big Valley Rancheria
Bishop Indian
Blue Lake Rancheria
Bridgeport Indian Colony
Buena Vista Rancheria
Cabazon
Cahuilla
Campo
Capitan Grande
Cedarville Rancheria
Chemehuevi
Chicken Ranch Rancheria
Cloverdale Rancheria
Cold Springs Rancheria
Colorado River
Colusa Rancheria
Cortina Rancheria
Coyote Valley
Cuyapaipe
Dry Creek Rancheria
Elk Valley Rancheria
Enterprise Rancheria
Fort Bidwell
Fort Independence
Fort Mojave
Fort Yuma
Greenville Rancheria
Grindstone Rancheria
Guidiville Rancheria
Hoopa Extension
Hoopa Valley
Hopland Rancheria
Inaja & Cosmit
Jackson Rancheria
Jamul Indian village
Karok Tribe of California
La Jolla Band of Mission
   Indians
La Posta
Laytonville Rancheria
Lone Pine
Los Coyotes
Lytton Rancheria
Manchester/Point Arena
   Rancheria
Manzanita
Mesa Grande
Middletown Rancheria
Mooretown Rancheria

Morongo
North Fork Rancheria
Pala Indian
Pauma Band of Mission
   Indians
Pechanga
Picayune Rancheria
Pinolville Rancheria
Pit River
Potter Valley Rancheria
Quartz Valley Indian
Ramona Band Cahuilla
   Rancheria
Redding Rancheria
Redwood Valley Rancheria
Resighini Rancheria
Rincon
Robinson Rancheria
Rohnerville Rancheria
Round Valley
Rumsey Rancheria
San Manuel
San Pasqual
Santa Rosa
Santa Rosa Rancheria
Santa Ynez
Santa Ysabel
Scotts Valley
Sherwood Valley Rancheria
Shingle Springs Rancheria
Smith River Rancheria
Soboba Indian
Stewarts Point Rancheria
Sulphur Bank Rancheria
Susanville Rancheria
Sycuan
Table Bluff
Table Mountain Rancheria
Timbisha Shoshone
Torres-Martinez
Trinidad Rancheria
Tule River
Tuolumne Me-Wuk
   Rancheria
Twenty-Nine Palms
Upper Lake Rancheria
Viejas (Baron Long)
Winnemucca Indian Colony
Woodfords Community
Yurok Indian

COLORADO
Southern Ute
Ute Mountain

CONNECTICUT
Eastern Pequot
Golden Hill
Mashantucket Pequot
Schaghticoke Indian

FLORIDA
Big Cypress
Brighton
Miccosukee
Seminole

IDAHO
Coeur d'Alene
Duck Valley
Fort Hall
Kootenai
Nez Perce
Northwestern Band of
    Shoshone Nation
Summit Lake

IOWA
Omaha
Sac and Fox
Winnebago

KANSAS
Iowa
Kickapoo
Prairie Potawatomi
Sac and Fox Tribe of the
    Missouri

LOUISIANA
Chitimacha
Coushatta
Houma Indian Communities
Tunica-Biloxi Indian

MAINE
Houlton (Maliseet Band)
Indian Township
Penobscot
Pleasant Point

MASSACHUSETTS
Grand Traverse
Hannahville Indian
    Community

Isabella
Lac Vieux Desert Band of
    Chippewa Indians
L'Anse (Keweenaw Bay)
Michigan Bay Mills
Sault Ste. Marie Tribe of
    Chippewa Indians
Wampanoag

MINNESOTA
Fond du Lac
Grand Portage (Pigeon
    River)
Leech Lake
Lower Sioux Indian
    Community
Mille Lacs
Nett Lake (Bois Fort)
Prairie Island
Red Lake
Shakopee Sioux
    Community
Upper Sioux Indian
    Community
White Earth

MISSISSIPPI
Mississippi Choctaw

MISSOURI
Eastern Shawnee

MONTANA
Blackfeet
Crow Indian
Flathead
Fort Belknap
Fort Peck
Northern Cheyenne
Rocky Boy

NEBRASKA
Iowa
Omaha
Pine Ridge
Sac and Fox Tribe of the
    Missouri
Santee Sioux
Winnebago

NEVADA
Battle Mountain
Carson Indian Colony
Dresslerville Indian Colony

Duck Valley
Duckwater
Elko Indian Colony
Ely Indian Colony
Fallon Reservation and
    Colony
Fort McDermitt
Fort Mohave
Las Vegas Indian Colony
Lovelock Indian Colony
Moapa River Indian
Pyramid Lake
Reno-Sparks Indian Colony
Ruby Valley (Te-Moak)
South Fort Indian Colony
Summit Lake
Walker River
Washoe
Wells Indian Colony
Yerrington Indian Colony
Yomba

NEW MEXICO
Acoma Pueblo
Aneth
Baca
Becenti
Beclabito
Bread Springs
Burnham
Canoncito
Casamero Lake
Cheechilgeetho
Church Rock
Cochiti Pueblo
Crownpoint
Crystal River
Dalton Pass
Fort Defiance
Huerfano
Isleta Pueblo
Jemez Pueblo
Jicarilla Apache
Laguna Pueblo
Lake Valley
Little Water
Manuelito
Mariano
Mescalero Apache
Mexican Water
Nageezi
Nambe Pueblo
Nenahnezad
Ojo Encino

Pajoaque Pueblo
Picuris Pueblo
Pinedale
Pueblo Plaintado
Puertocito (Alamo)
Ramah Navajo
Red Lake
Red Mesa
Red Rock
Rock Point
Rock Springs
San Felipe Pueblo
San Ildefonso Pueblo
San Juan Pueblo
Sandia Pueblo
Sanostee
Santa Ana Pueblo
Santa Clara Pueblo
Santo Domingo Pueblo
Sheep Springs
Shiprock
Smith Lake
Standing Rock
Sweetwater
Taos Pueblo
Teecnospos
Tesuque Pueblo
Thoreau
Torreon and Star Lake
Tsaile-Wheatfields
Tsayatoh
Two Grey Hills
Upper Fruitland
Ute Mountain
White Rock
Whitehorse Lake
Yanbit
Zia Pueblo
Zuni

NEW YORK
Abenaki Indian Village
Allegheny
Cattaraugus
Cayuga Nation
Oil Spring
Oneida
Onondaga
Poospatuck
St. Regis Mohawk Indian
Seneca Nation
Shinnecock
Tonawanda
Tuscarora

NORTH CAROLINA
Cherokee

NORTH DAKOTA
Devil's Lake Sioux
Fort Berthold
Ojibwa of the Red River
Standing Rock
Turtle Mountain

OKLAHOMA
Absentee-Shawnee Tribe
Alabama-Quassarte Tribe
  Town
Apache Tribe of Oklahoma
Caddo Indian Tribe
Cherokee Nation of
  Oklahoma
Cheyenne-Arapaho Tribe
Chickasaw Nation of
  Oklahoma
Choctaw Nation of
  Oklahoma
Citizen Band Potawatomi
  Tribe
Comanche Indian Tribe of
  Oklahoma
Creek Nation of Oklahoma
Delaware Tribe of Western
  Oklahoma
Eastern Shawnee Tribe of
  Oklahoma
Fort Sill Apache Tribe of
  Oklahoma
Iowa Tribe of Oklahoma
Kaw Tribe of Oklahoma
Kialegee Tribal Town
Kickapoo Tribe of
  Oklahoma
Kiowa Tribe of Oklahoma
Miami Tribe of Oklahoma

Modoc Tribe of Oklahoma
Osage Tribe of Oklahoma
Otoe-Missouria Tribe of
  Oklahoma
Pawnee Indian Tribe of
  Oklahoma
Peoria Tribe of Oklahoma
Ponca Tribe of Oklahoma
Quapaw Tribe of
  Oklahoma
Sac and Fox Tribe of
  Oklahoma
Seminole Nation of
  Oklahoma
Seneca-Cayuga Tribe of
  Oklahoma
Thlopthlocco Tribe of
  Oklahoma
Tonkawa Tribe of
  Oklahoma
United Keetoowah of
  Oklahoma
Wichita Tribe of Oklahoma
Wyandotte Tribe of
  Oklahoma

OREGON
Burns Paiute Indian Colony
Confederated Tribes of
  Coos, Lower Umpqua,
  and Siuslaw Indians
Coquille Indian Tribe
Cow Creek Band of
  Umpqua Indians
Fort McDermitt Reservation
Grande Ronde Indian
  Community
Klamath
Siletz
Umatilla
Warm Springs

RHODE ISLAND
Narragansett Indian

SOUTH DAKOTA
Cheyenne River
Crow Creek
Flandreau Santee Sioux
Lower Brule
Pine Ridge
Rosebud
Sisseton-Wahpeton
Standing Rock
Yankton Sioux

UTAH
Chilchinbeto
Dennehotso
Goshute
Kayenta
Mexican Water
Navajo Mountain
Oljatoh
Paiute Indian Tribe of Utah
Red Mesa
Shonto
Skull Valley Indian
  Community
Teecnospos
Uintah and Ouray
Ute Mountain
Washakie

VIRGINIA
Cherokee Tribe of Virginia
Pamunkey Indian

WASHINGTON
Chehalis
Colville
HOH
Jamestown S'kallam

Kalispel
Lower elwha Klallam
Lummi
Makah
Muckleshoot
Nisqually Indian
Nooksack
Port Gamble Indian
  Community
Port Madison
Puyallup
Quileute
Quinault
Sauk-Suiattle Indian
Shoalwater Bay
Skokomish Indian
Spokane
Squaxin Island
Stillaquamish
Swinomish
Tulalip
Upper Skagit Indian
Yakima

WISCONSIN
Bad River
Forest County Potawatomi
  Community
Lac Courte Oreilles
Lac du Flambeau
Menominee
Oneida
Red Cliff
Sokaogon Chippewa
  Community
Stockbridge-Munsee
  Community
Winnebago

WYOMING
Wind River

Note: List represents 1991 data.

RESERVES AND BANDS: CANADA

A listing by province and territory of Canadian reserves and bands.

ALBERTA
Alexander
Alexis
Athabasca Chipewyan
Bearspaw (Stoney)
Beaver Lake
Bigstone Cree Nation
Blood
Boyer River
Chiniki (Stoney)
Cold Lake First Nations
Cree
Dene Tha' Tribe
Driftpile
Duncan's
Enoch
Ermineskin
Fort McKay First Nation
Fort McMurray First Nation
Frog Lake
Goodstoney (Stoney)
Grouard
Heart Lake
Horse Lake
Janvier
Kehewin
Little Red River Cree Nation
Louis Bull
Lubicon
Montana
O'Chiese
Paul
Piegan Nation
Saddle Lake
Samson
Sawridge
Siksika Nation
Sturgeon Lake
Sucker Creek
Sunchild Cree First Nation
Swan River First Nation
Tallcree
Tsuu T'ina Nation
Whitefish Lake
Woodland Cree

BRITISH COLUMBIA
Adams Lake
Ahousaht
Aitchelitz

Alexandria
Alexis Creek
Alkali
Anaham
Anderson Lake
Ashcroft
Beecher Bay
Bella Coola
Blueberry River
Bonaparte
Boothroyd
Boston Bar
Bridge River
Broman Lake
Burns Lake
Burrard
Campbell River
Canim Lake
Canoe Creek
Cape Mudge
Cayoose Creek
Chawathil
Cheam
Chehalis
Cremainus
Chaslatta Carrier Nation
Clayoquot
Coldwater
Columbia Lake
Comox
Cook's Ferry
Coquitlam
Cowichan
Cowichan Lake
Dease
Dease River
Ditidaht
Doig River
Douglas
Ehattesaht
Esquimalt
Fort George
Fort Nelson
Fort Ware
Fountain Indian
Gitanmaax
Gitanyow (Kitwancool)
Gitlakdamix
Gitsegukla
Gitwangak

Gitwinksihlkw
Glen Vowell
Gwa'sala-'Nakwaxda'zw
Hagwilget
Halalt
Halfway River
Hartley Bay
Heiltsuk
Hesquiaht
High Bar
Homalco
Ingenika
Iskut
Kamloops
Kanaka Bar
Katzie
Kincolith
Kispiox
Kitamaat
Kitasoo
Kitsumkalum
Kittkatla
Kittselas
Kitwancool
Klahoose
Kluskus
Kwakiutl
Kwa-Kwa-A-Pilt
Kwa-Wa-Aineuk
Kwiakah
Kwicksutaineuk-Ah-
   Kwaw-Ah-Mish
Kyuquot
Lakahahmen
Lakalzap
Lake Babine
Langley
Lax-Kw-Alaams
Lillooet
Little Shuswap
Lower Kootenay
Lower Nicola
Lower Similkameen
Lyackson
Lytton
McLeod Lake
Malahat
Mamaleleqala
   Qwe-qwa'sot'enox
Masset

Matsqui
Metlaktla
Moricetown
Mount Currie
Mowachaht
Musqueam
Nadleh Whuten
Nak'azdli
Nanaimo
Nanoose First Nation
Nazko
Nee-Tahi-Buhn
Nemaiah Valley
Neskonlith
Nicomen
Nimpkish
Nooaitch
North Thompson
Nuchatlaht
Ohamil
Ohiaht
Okanagan
Opetchesaht
Oregon Jack Creek
Osoyoos
Oweekeno
Pacheenaht
Pauquachin
Pavilion
Penelakut
Penticton
Peters
Popkum
Prophet River
Qualicum
Quatsino
Red Bluff
St. Mary's
Samahquam
Saulteau
Scowlitz
Seabird Island
Sechelt
Semiahmoo
Seton Lake
Shackan
Sheshaht
Shuswap
Siska
Skawahlook

Skeetchestn
Skidegate
Skookumchuck
Skowkale
Skuppah
Skwah
Skyway
Sliammon
Soda Creek
Songhees
Sooke
Soowahlie
Spallumcheen
Spuzzum
Squamish
Squiala
Stellaquo
Stone
Stony Creek
Sumas
Tahltan
Takla Lake
Taku River Tlingit
Tanakteuk
Tla-O-Qui-Aht First Nations
Tlatlasikwala
Tl'azt'en Nation
Tlowitsis-Mumtagila
Tobacco Plains
Toosey
Toquaht
Tsartlip
Tsawataineuk
Tsawout
Tsawwassen
Tseycum
Tzeachten
Uchucklesaht
Ucluelet
Ulkatcho
Union Bar
Upper Nicola
Upper Similkameen
West Moberly
Westbank
Whispering Pines
Williams Lake
Yakweakwioose
Yale

MANITOBA
Barren Lands
Berens River
Birdtail Sioux

Bloodvein
Brokenhead
Buffalo Point First Nation
Chemawawin First Nation
Churchill
Crane River
Cross Lake
Dakota Ojibway
Dakota Plains
Dakota Tipi
Dauphin River
Ebb and Flow
Fairford
Fisher River
Fort Alexander
Fox Lake
Gamblers
Garden Hill First Nation
God's Lake
God's River
Grand Rapids First Nation
Hollow Water
Indian Birch
Interlake Reserves
Jackhead
Keeseekoowenin
Lake Manitoba
Lake St. Martin
Little Black River
Little Grand Rapids
Little Sask
Long Plain
Mathias Colomb
Moose Lake
Nelson House
Northlands
Norway House
Oak Lake Sioux
Oxford House
Pauingassi First Nation
Peguis
Pine Creek
Poplar River First Nation
Red Sucker Lake
Rolling River
Rosequ River
Sagkeeng
St. Theresa Point
Sandy Bar
Shamattawa First Nation
Shoal River
Sioux Valley
Split Lake
Swan Lake

Valley River
War Lake
Wasagamack
Waterhen
Waywayseecappo First
   Nation
York Factory

NEW BRUNSWICK
Big Cove
Bouctouche Micmac
Burnt Church
Edmundston
Eel Ground
Eel River
Fort Folly
Indian Island
Kingsclear
Oromocto
Pabinequ
Red Bank
St. Mary's
Tobique
Woodstock

NEWFOUNDLAND
First Nation Council of
   Davis Inlet
First Nation Council of
   Northwest River
Maiwpukek

**NORTHWEST
TERRITORIES**
Aklavik
Arctic Red River
Colville Lake
Dechilao'ticouncil
   (Snarelake) Dene
Dene Nation
Dog Rib Rae
Fitz/Smith (Alta-N.W.T.)
Fort Franklin
Fort Good Hope
Fort Liard
Fort McPherson
Fort Norman
Fort Providence
Fort Resolution
Fort Simpson
Fort Wrigley
Hay River
Inuvik
Kakisa Lake

Lac La Martre
Lutsel K'e Dene
Nahanni Butte
Pehdzeh k'i (Wrigley) Dene
Rae Lakes Dene
Rainbow Valley
Sambaa k'e (Trout Lake)
   Dene
Snowdrift
Yellowknives Dene

NOVA SCOTIA
Acadia
Afton
Annapolis Valley
Bear River
Chapel Island
Eskasoni
Horton
Membertou
Millbrook
Pictou Landing
Shubenacadie
Wagmatcook
Whycocomagh

ONTARIO
Albany—Sinclair Island
Albany—Village of
   Kashechewan
Alderville
Algonquin of Golden Lake
Aroland
Attawapiskat
Batchewana
Bearskin Lake
Beausoleil
Beaverhouse
Big Grassy
Big Island
Big Trout Lake
Brunswick House
Caldwell
Cat Lake
Chapleau Cree
Chapleau Ojibway
Chippewas of Georgina
   Island
Chippewas of Kettle and
   Stony Point
Chippewas of Nawash
Chippewas of Rama First
   Nation
Chippewas of Sarnia

Chippewas of Saugeen
Chippewas of the Thames
Cockburn Island
Constance Lake
Couchiching
Curve Lake
Dalles
Deer Lake
Dokis
Eabametoong First Nation
Eargle River
Flying Post
Fort Albany
Fort Severn
Fort William
Garden River First Nation
Ginoogaming First Nation
Grassy Narrows
Gull Bay
Henvey Inlet
Hornepayne
Islington
Kasabonika
Kee-Way-Win
Kingfisher Lake
Lac des Milles Lacs
Lac La Croix
Lac Seul
Lansdowne House
Long Lake No. 58
McDowell Lake
Magnetawan
Martin Falls
Matachewan
Mattagami
Michipicoten
Missanabie Cree
Mississauga
Mississaugas of New Credit
Mississaugas of Scugog
Mocrebec Indian
　Government
Mohawks of Akwesasne
Mohawks of Gibson
Mohawks of the Bay of
　Quinte
Moose Deer Point
Moose Factory
Moravian of the Thames
Munsee-Delaware Nation
Muskrat Dam
Naicatchewenin
New Post
New Slate Falls

Nibinamik
Nickikousemene
Nipigon
Nipissing First Nation
North Caribou Lake
North Spirit Lake
Northwest Angle No. 33
Northwest Angle No. 37
Ojibways of Hiawatha
Ojibways of Onegaming
Ojibways of the Pic River
Ojibways of Walpole
　Island
Oneidas of the Thames
Osnaburg
Pays Plat
Pic Mobert
Pikangikum
Poplar Hill
Rainy River
Rat Portage
Red Rock
Rocky Bay
Sachigo Lake
Sagamok Anishnawbek
Sand Point
Sandy Lake
Saugeen
Saugeen Nation
Seine River
Serpent River
Shawanaga
Sheguiandah
Sheshegwaning
Shoal Lake No. 39
Shoal Lake No. 40
Six Nations of the Grand
　River
Stangecoming
Sucker Creek
Temagami
Thessalon
Wabauskang
Wabigoon Lake Ojibway
　Nation
Wahgoshig
Wahnapitae
Walpole Island
Wapekeka
Wasauksing (Parry Island)
Washagmis Bay
Wauzhushik Onigum
Wawakapewin
Webequi

Weenusk
West Bay
Whitefish Bay
Whitefish Lake
Whitefish River
Whitesand
Wikwemikong
Wunnumin

**PRINCE EDWARD
ISLAND**
Abegweit
Lennox Island

QUEBEC
Abenakis de Wolinak
Abitibiwinni (Algonquin)
Atikamekw De Manouane
Attikameks de
　Weymontachie
Barriere Lake (Algonquin)
Betsiamites
Chisasibi
Eastman (Cree)
Gaspe (Micmac)
Grande Lac Victoria
　(Algonquin)
Huronne-Wendat
Kenesatake
Kipawa (Algonquin)
Kitigan Zibi Anishinabeg
Lac Simon (Algonquin)
Long Point (Algonquin)
Micmacs of Gesgapegiag
Mingan
Mistassini
Mohawks of Kahnawake
Montagnais de la Romaine
Montagnais de les
　Escoumins
Montagnais de Natashquan
Montagnais de Pakua Shipi
Montagnais de Schefferville
Montagnais de Uashat Et
　Maliotenam
Montagnais du Lac St-Jean
Naskapis of Schefferville
Nemaska (Cree)
Obedjiwan
Odanak (Abenaquis)
Restigouche (Micmac)
Temiskaming (Algonquin)
Viger
Waskaganish

Waswanipi (Cree)
Wemindji (Cree)
Weymontachie
Whapmagoostui
Wolf Lake

SASKATCHEWAN
Antahkakoop
Beardy's
Big C
Big River
Black Lake
Buffalo River
Canoe Lake
Carry the Kettle
Cote
Cowessess
Cumberland
Cumberland House Cree
　Nation
Day Star
English River
Fishing Lake
Flying Dust
Fond du Lac
Gordon
Hatchet Lake
Island Lake
James Smith
John Smith
Joseph Bighead
Kahkewistahaw
Kawacatoose
Keeseekoose
Key
Kinistin
Lac La Ronge
Little Black Bear
Little Pine
Lucky Man
Makwa Sahgaiehcan
Mistawasis
Moose Woods
Mosquito Grizzly Bear's
　Head
Muscowpetung
Muskeg Lake
Muskowekwan
Nekaneet
Ocean Man
Ochapowace
Okanese
Okemasis
One Arrow

Onion Lake
Pasqua
Peepeekisis
Pelican Lake
Peter Ballantyne
Pheasant Rump Nakota
Piapot
Poundmaker
Red Earth
Red Pheasant
Sakimay
Sandy Lake
Saulteaux

Shoal Lake of the
    Cree Nation
Standing Buffalo
Star Blanket
Sturgeon Lake
Sweetgrass
Thunderchild
Turnor Lake
Wahpeton Lake
Waterhen Lake
White Bear
William Charles
Witchekan Lake

Wood Mountain
Woosomin
Yellowquill (Nutt Lake)
Young Chipewayan

YUKON TERRITORY
Carcross/Tagish
Champagne/Aishihik
Dawson
Dease River
Kluane First Nation
Kwanlin Dun First Nation
Liard River

Liard River Indian
    Reserve #3
Little Salmon-Carmacks
Na-Cho Ny'a'k-Dun
Old Crow
Ross River
Selkirk First Nation
Ta'an Kwach'an Council
Taku River Tlingits
Teslin
Vuntut Gwitchin (Old
    Crow)
White River First Nation

Note: List represents 1991 data.

TIME LINE

Significant events in American Indian history.

c. 40,000-13,000 B.C.E.	Possible years of migration to the Americas by the ancestors of present-day Native Americans.
c. 27,000 B.C.E.	Estimate of when Paleo-Indians begin to migrate southward through ice-free corridors into the American interior.
c. 15,000 B.C.E.	Clovis Period begins across native North America; centers on hunting mega-fauna, especially the woolly mammoth.
c. 9,000 B.C.E.	Folsom Period emerges, centering on bison hunting.
c. 8,000 B.C.E.	Plano Period replaces Folsom, representing a transitional cultural period culminating in the Archaic.
c. 6,000 B.C.E.	Archaic Period begins, signalling a reliance on a variety of flora and fauna. Cultural innovations such as pottery, the bow and arrow, and the domestication of plants begin to appear across North America.
c. 1,000 B.C.E.	Agriculture appears in the Southwest; it gradually diffuses across North America. Woodland Period emerges in eastern North America.
c. 1-500 C.E.	Complex societies flourish across North America.
c. 825-900	Athapaskan people, ancestors of the Navajo and Apache, invade the Southwest from the north, altering the cultural landscape of the Puebloan people.
c. 1007	Norsemen invade native North America along the eastern seaboard and establish a short-lived colony.
1050-1250	Cahokia, near present-day St. Louis, is established as a great Mississippian trading and ceremonial center. The city may have contained as many as thirty thousand people.
1492	Christopher Columbus lands on Guanahani (the island of San Salvador), launching Europe's exploration and colonization of North America.
c. 1500	European-introduced diseases, warfare, and slavery begin to reduce native populations (from an estimated ten to eighteen million to approximately 250,000 in 1900).
1519-1521	Hernán Cortés conquers the Aztec Empire.
1582-1598	Spanish conquistadores invade and settle in the Southwest.
1585	Roanoke Colony is founded by the British (it lasts only until approximately 1607).
1599	Massacre at Acoma Pueblo. Vincente de Zaldivar attacks Acoma on January 21 because of its resistance to Spanish authority; eight hundred Acomas are killed.
1607	British Virginia Company establishes colony of Jamestown, affecting local indigenous populations.
1609	Henry Hudson opens the fur trade in New Netherlands.
1620	The Pilgrims colonize present-day Massachusetts.

1622-1631	Powhatan Confederacy declares war on the Jamestown colonists.
1629	The Spanish begin establishing missions among the Pueblos, leading to a 1633 revolt at Zuni.
1630	The Puritans colonize New England, carrying with them a religious belief that Native Americans are "children of the Devil."
1636-1637	Pequot War. The Pequot and their allies attempt to defend their homelands against the Puritans.
c. 1640	The Dakota (Sioux), forced in part by hostilities initiated by the fur trade, begin to migrate westward onto the Great Plains.
1642-1685	Beaver Wars. As the supply of beaver is exhausted in the Northeast, the Iroquois Confederacy launches a war against neighboring Native American nations to acquire their hunting territories.
c. 1650	Period of widespread migrations and relocations. Prompted by the diffusion of the gun and the horse, and by the increasing hostility of Europeans, many Native Americans migrate westward.
1655	Timucua Rebellion. Timucuan mission residents rebel against Spanish cruelty in Florida.
1655-1564	Peach Wars. The Dutch launch a war of extermination against the Esophus nation after an Esophus woman is killed for picking peaches.
1670	Hudson's Bay Company is chartered, launching a westward expansion of the fur trade.
1670-1710	South Carolinians in Charleston encourage the development of a Native American slave trade across the Southeast.
1675-1676	King Philip's War. In response to English maltreatment, Metacomet (King Philip) launches a war against the English.
1676-1677	Bacon's Rebellion. Native Americans in Virginia fight a war of resistance but find themselves subject to Virginia rule.
1680	Pueblo (Popé's) Revolt. After decades of Spanish oppression, a Pueblo confederacy expels the Spanish from the Rio Grande region.
1682	Assiniboine and Cree begin to trade at York Factory, initiating European mercantile penetration of the Canadian west as far as the Rocky Mountains.
1689-1763	French and Indian Wars. King William's War initiates conflicts between the French and English that involve Native Americans and disrupt traditional patterns and alliances.
1692	Spanish reconquest of the Southwest (Nueva Mexico).
1695	Pima Uprising. Pimas burn missions in response to Spanish oppression.
c. 1700-1760	The horse diffuses across the Great Plains, prompting massive migrations and a cultural revolution.
1715-1717	Yamasee War. The Yamasee and their allies fight against the English for trading and other abuses.
1729	Natchez Revolt. Resisting French attempts to exact tribute, the Natchez go to war; the tribe is essentially destroyed, and many are sold into slavery.
1730	Articles of Agreement signed between the Cherokee Nation and King George II.

1740	Russia explores the Alaskan coast and begins trading operations.
1755	Some Iroquois settle near the Catholic mission of St. Regis, forming the nucleus of the Akwesasne Reserve.
1763	Proclamation of 1763. The Royal Proclamation of 1763 declares that Native Americans have title to all lands outside established colonies until the Crown legally purchases further land cessions.
1763-1764	Pontiac's War. Ottawa leader Pontiac constructs a multitribal alliance to resist the British.
1765	Paxton Riots (Paxton Boys Massacre). On December 14, 1765, seventy-five Europeans from Paxton, Pennsylvania, massacre and scalp six innocent Conestoga Mission Indians.
1768	Treaty of Fort Stanwix. The Iroquois Confederacy cedes lands south of the Ohio River (a later Fort Stanwix Treaty, 1784, changes the agreement).
1769	The California mission system is established.
1771	Labrador Inuit show missionaries where to build a trading post.
1774	Lord Dunmore's War. Lord Dunmore, the governor of Virginia, leads a fight against Shawnee led by Cornstalk.
1774-1775	The first Continental Congress establishes an Indian Department.
1777-1783	The Iroquois Confederacy is dispersed by the American Revolution.
1787	Northwest Ordinance. The U.S. Congress establishes a legal mechanism to create states from territories.
1789	The Indian Department becomes part of the U.S. Department of War.
1790	First of the Trade and Intercourse Acts enacted; they attempt to regulate trade between Europeans and Native Americans.
1790-1794	Little Turtle's War. Shawnee and their allies under Little Turtle defeat Anthony St. Clair's troops in 1791 but eventually are defeated at the Battle of Fallen Timbers, 1794, by General Anthony Wayne.
1795	Treaty of Fort Greenville. Native Americans of the Old Northwest are forced to treat with the United States after Britain refuses to assist them in their resistance efforts.
1796	Trading Houses Act. On April 18, 1796, the United States establishes government-operated trading houses.
1799	Handsome Lake, the Seneca Prophet, founds the *Gaiwiio*, "the Good Word," also known as the Longhouse religion; it becomes a strong force among the Iroquois.
1803	Louisiana Purchase. The United States acquires 800,000 square miles of new territory.
1804-1806	Lewis and Clark expedition. President Jefferson launches an expedition to collect information of national interest about Louisiana.
1809	Treaty of Fort Wayne. The Delaware are forced to relinquish approximately 3 million acres.
1809-1811	Tecumseh's Rebellion. Shawnee leader Tecumseh leads a multitribal force to resist United States incursions into their lands.
1811	Battle of Tippecanoe. William Henry Harrison and his forces attack and defeat Tecumseh's forces in Tecumseh's absence.

1812	War of 1812. Tribes of the Old Northwest are drawn into the European conflict.
1812	In August, the Hudson's Bay Company establishes the Red River Colony.
1813-1814	Red Stick civil war. Creeks fight a bloody civil war over disagreements about what their political relations with the United States should be.
1817-1818	First Seminole War. U.S. forces under General Andrew Jackson attack and burn Seminole villages.
1821	Sequoyah creates the Cherokee syllabary, the first system for writing an Indian language.
1823	*Johnson v. M'Intosh*. On February 28, 1823, the U.S. Supreme Court rules that Native American tribes have land rights.
1823	Office of Indian Affairs is created within the War Department.
1827	Cherokee Nation adopts a constitution.
1830	Indian Removal Act. At the urging of President Andrew Jackson, Congress orders the removal of all Native Americans to lands west of the Mississippi River. Removal proceeds from the 1830's to the 1850's.
1830	Treaty of Dancing Rabbit Creek. Choctaws cede more than 10 million acres in Alabama and Mississippi.
1830	Upper Canada establishes a system of reserves for Canadian natives.
1831	*Cherokee Nation v. Georgia*. U.S. Supreme Court rules that Native American tribes are "domestic dependent nations."
1832	Black Hawk War. Black Hawk, the Sauk and Fox leader leads a war to preserve their land rights.
1832	*Worcester v. Georgia*. U.S. Supreme Court rules that only the federal government has the right to regulate Indian affairs.
1834	Department of Indian Affairs is reorganized.
1835	Texas Rangers begin raids against the Comanche.
1835-1842	Second Seminole War. The Seminole resist removal to Indian Territory.
1838-1839	Forced removal of Cherokees to Indian Territory becomes a "Trail of Tears" marked by thousands of deaths.
1839	Upper Canadian Judge James Buchanan submits a report suggesting that Canadian natives should be assimilated into larger Canadian society.
1839	Taos Revolt. Taos Pueblos struggle against U.S. domination.
1848	Treaty of Guadalupe Hidalgo. United States acquires southwestern lands from Mexico.
1848-1849	California Gold Rush. Emigrants cross Native American lands, resulting in ecological destruction and spread of diseases.
1849	Metis Courthouse Rebellion. Metis resist Canadian domination.
1850	Period of genocide against California Indians begins and continues for some thirty years; thousands are killed.

1851   First Treaty of Fort Laramie. Great Plains Native Americans agree to allow emigrants safe passage across their territories.

1853   Gadsden Purchase. U.S. government purchases portions of Arizona, California, and New Mexico from Mexico.

1854-1864   Teton Dakota Resistance. The Teton Dakota and their allies resist U.S. intrusions into their lands.

1855   In the Northwest, Territorial Governor Isaac Stevens holds the Walla Walla Council and negotiates a series of treaties with Native American tribes.

1855-1856   Yakima War. Led by Kamiakin, who refused to sign the 1855 treaty, Yakimas fight U.S. forces after the murder of a government Indian agent initiates hostilities.

1855-1858   Third Seminole War. Seminoles react to the surveying of their lands.

1858   British Columbia Gold Rush precipitates large-scale invasion of Indian lands.

1858   Navajo War. Manuelito leads the Navajo against U.S. forces to fight against whites' grazing their horses on Navajo lands.

1860   The British transfer full responsibility of Canadian Indian affairs to the Province of Canada.

1862   Minnesota Uprising. Little Crow carries out a war of resistance against federal authority because of ill treatment.

1863-1868   Long Walk of the Navajo. In a violent campaign, U.S. forces remove the Navajo from their homeland and take them to Bosque Redondo.

1864   Sand Creek Massacre. Colorado militiamen under John Chivington massacre a peaceful group of Cheyennes at Sand Creek.

1866-1868   Bozeman Trail wars. Teton Dakota and their allies resist the building of army forts in their lands.

1867   U.S. government purchases Alaska.

1867   Canadian Confederation. The Dominion of Canada is created.

1867   Commission Act. Legislation calls for the U.S. president to establish commissions to negotiate peace treaties with Native American nations.

1868   Second Treaty of Fort Laramie pledges the protection of Indian lands.

1868   Canadian government adopts an Indian policy aimed at the assimilation of Indians into Canadian society.

1868   Washita River Massacre. A peaceful Cheyenne camp is massacred by the U.S. Seventh Cavalry.

1869   First Riel Rebellion. Louis Reil leads the Metis in resisting Canadian domination; partly triggered by white surveying of Metis lands.

1870   Grant's Peace Policy. President Ulysses S. Grant assigns various Christian denominations to various Indian reservation agencies in order to Christianize and pacify the Indians.

1871   Congress passes an act on March 3 that ends treaty negotiations with Native American nations.

1871   *McKay v. Campbell.* U.S. Supreme Court holds that Indian people born with "tribal allegiance" are not U.S. citizens.

1871   Canada begins negotiating the first of eleven "numbered" treaties with Native Canadians.

1871-1890   Wholesale destruction of the bison on the Plains.

1872-1873   Modoc War. The Modoc resist removal to the Klamath Reservation.

1874   Canadian Northwest Mounted Police move to establish order in the Canadian West.

1874-1875   Red River War. Forced by starvation and Indian agent corruption, Kiowa, Plains Apache, Southern Cheyenne, and Arapaho raid European American farms and ranches to feed their families.

1876   First Indian Act of Canada. The act consolidated Canadian policies toward its indigenous people.

1876   Battle of the Little Bighorn. General Custer and the Seventh Cavalry are annihilated by the Sioux, Cheyenne, and Arapaho camped along the Little Bighorn River.

1877   The Nez Perce are exiled from their homeland and pursued by U.S. forces as they unsuccessfully attempt to escape into Canada.

1877   Battle of Wolf Mountain. The last fight between the Cheyenne and the U.S. Army.

1877-1883   The Northern Cheyenne are forcibly removed to Indian Territory but escape north to their homelands.

1878   Bannock War. Because of settler pressures, the Bannock are forced to raid for food.

1879   Carlisle Indian School, a boarding school with the goal of "civilizing" Indian youth, is founded by Captain Richard H. Pratt.

1880   Canadian officials modify the 1876 Indian Act, empowering it to impose elected councils on bands.

1885   Second Riel Rebellion. Louis Riel leads a second protest, then armed revolt, among the Canadian Metis and Cree; defeated, Riel is executed after the rebellion.

1887   General Allotment Act (Dawes Severalty Act). Provides for the dividing of reservation lands into individual parcels to expedite assimilation. (By the early twentieth century, the allotment policy is viewed as disastrous.)

1890   Wounded Knee Massacre. The Seventh Cavalry intercepts a group of Sioux Ghost Dancers being led by Big Foot to the Pine Ridge Reservation. When a Sioux warrior, perhaps accidentally, fires his rifle, the army opens fire; hundreds of Sioux, most unarmed, are massacred.

1897   Education Appropriation Act mandates funding for Indian day schools and technical schools.

        Indian Liquor Act bans the sale or distribution of liquor to Native Americans.

1903   *Lone Wolf v. Hitchcock.* U.S. Supreme Court rules that Congress has the authority to dispose of Native American lands.

1906   Burke Act. Congress amends the General Allotment Act to shorten the trust period for individual Native Americans who are proven "competent."

1906   Alaskan Allotment Act. Allows Alaska Natives to file for 160-acre parcels.

1910   Omnibus Act. Establishes procedures to determine Native American heirship of trust lands and other resources.

1912   Classification and Appraisal of Unallotted Indian Lands Act. Permits the Secretary of Interior to reappraise and reclassify unalloted Indian lands.

1924   General Citizenship Act. As a result of Native American participation in World War I, Congress grants some Native Americans citizenship.

1928   Meriam Report outlines the failure of previous Indian policies and calls for reform.

1932   Alberta Metis Organization is founded by Joseph Dion.

1934   Indian Reorganization Act. Implements the Meriam Report recommendations, reversing many previous policies.

1934   Johnson-O'Malley Act replaces the General Allotment Act.

1936   Oklahoma Indian Welfare Act. Extends many of the rights provided by the Indian Reorganization Act of 1934 to Oklahoma Indian nations.

1944   National Congress of American Indians is founded to guard Native American rights.

1946   Indian Claims Commission Act. Provides a legal forum for tribes to sue the federal government for the loss of lands.

1950   Navajo and Hopi Rehabilitation Act is passed to assist the tribes in developing their natural resources.

1951   Indian Act of 1951. A new Canadian Indian Act reduces the powers of the Indian Affairs Department but retains an assimilationist agenda.

1951   Public Law 280 allows greater state jurisdiction over criminal cases involving Native Americans from California, Wisconsin, Minnesota, and Nebraska (extended to Alaska Natives in 1959).

1953   Termination Resolution. Congress initiates a policy (which continues into the early 1960's) of severing the federal government's relationships with Native American nations.

1955   Indian Health Service is transferred from the Department of the Interior to the Department of Health, Education, and Welfare.

1961   Chicago Indian Conference, organized by anthropologist Sol Tax, mobilizes Indian leaders to reassert their rights.

1961   National Indian Youth Council is founded by Clyde Warrior and others.

1963   State of Washington rules against Native American fishing rights.

1964   American Indian Historical Society is founded to research and teach about Native Americans.

1966   Hawthorn Report examines the conditions of contemporary Canadian natives and recommends that Indians be considered "citizens plus."

1968   American Indian Civil Rights Act guarantees reservation residents many of the civil liberties other citizens have under the U.S. Constitution.

1968   American Indian Movement (AIM) is founded in Minneapolis by Dennis Banks and Russell Means.

1969   Canadian government's White Paper of 1969 rejects the Hawthorn Report's recommendations, arguing that Canadian natives' special status hinders their assimilation and urging the abolition of the Indian Affairs Department and Indian Act.

1969   Occupation of Alcatraz Island by Native American people begins (continues through 1971).

1971   Alaska Native Claims Settlement Act marks the beginning of the self-determination period for Alaska Natives.

1972   Trail of Broken Treaties Caravan proceeds to Washington, D.C., to protest treaty violations.

1972   Native American Rights Fund (NARF) is founded to carry Indian issues to court.

1972   Indian Education Act enacted; it is intended to improve the quality of education for Native Americans (the act is revised in 1978).

1973   Wounded Knee occupation. More than two hundred Native American activists occupy the historic site to demonstrate against oppressive Sioux reservation policies.

1974   Navajo-Hopi Land Settlement Act facilitates negotiation between the two nations over the disputed Joint Use Area.

1975   Indian Self-Determination and Education Assistance Act expands tribal control over tribal governments and education.

1975   Political violence increases on the Pine Ridge Reservation; two FBI agents are killed in a shootout on June 26.

1975   James Bay and Northern Quebec Agreement is signed; Quebec Cree, Inuit, Naskapi, and Montagnais groups cede tribal lands in exchange for money and specified hunting and fishing rights.

1977   American Indian Policy Review Commission Report is released by Congress, recommending that Native American nations be considered sovereign political bodies.

1978   American Indian Freedom of Religion Act protects the rights of Native Americans to follow traditional religious practices.

1978   Federal Acknowledgment Program is initiated to provide guidelines for and assist tribes seeking official recognition by the federal government.

1978   Indian Child Welfare Act proclaims tribal jurisdiction over child custody decisions.

1978   The Longest Walk, a march from Alcatraz Island to Washington, D.C., protests government treatment of Indians.

1980   *United States v. Sioux Nation*. U.S. Supreme Court upholds a $122 million judgment against the United States for illegally taking the Black Hills.

1981   Hopi-Navajo Joint Use Area is partitioned between the Navajo and Hopi nations.

1982   Canada's Constitution Act (Constitution and Charter of Rights and Freedoms) is passed despite the protests of Indian, Metis, and Inuit groups.

1982   Indian Claims Limitation Act limits the time period during which claims can be filed against the U.S. government.

1985   Coolican Report declares that little progress is being made to settle Canadian native land claims.

1988   Indian Gaming Regulatory Act officially legalizes certain types of gambling on reservations and establishes the National Indian Gaming Commission.

1989   U.S. Congress approves construction of the National Museum of the American Indian, to be part of the Smithsonian Institution.

1989   Violence erupts on St. Regis Mohawk Reservation in dispute over whether to allow gambling; under guard by state and federal law enforcement officers, the tribe votes to allow gambling on the reservation.

1990   The U.S. Census finds the Native American population to be 1,959,234.

1990   In *Duro v. Reina*, the U.S. Supreme Court holds that tribes cannot have criminal jurisdiction over non-Indians on reservation lands.

1990   Canada's proposed Meech Lake Accord (amendments to the 1982 Constitution Act) is sent to defeat in Canada by native legislator Elijah Harper; the accord provided no recognition of native rights.

1991   Tribal Self-Governance Act extends the number of tribes involved in the self-governance pilot project.

1992   Native Americans protest the Columbian Quincentenary.

1992   In a plebiscite, residents of Canada's Northwest Territories approve the future creation of Nunavut, a territory to be governed by the Inuit.

1993   The International Year of Indigenous People.

1994   National Museum of the American Indian opens its first facility in New York's Heye Center (a larger museum is planned for the Mall in Washington, D.C.).

1994   The National Congress of American Indians and the National Black Caucus of State Legislators ally themselves, agreeing that they face similar political and economic forces of oppression.

TRIBES BY CULTURE AREA

ARCTIC
Aleut
Inuit
Yupik

CALIFORNIA
Achumawi
Atsugewi
Cahuilla
Chumash
Coast Yuki
Costanoan
Cupeño
Diegueño
Esselen
Fernandeño
Gabrielino
Huchnom
Hupa
Juaneño
Kamia
Karok
Luiseño
Maidu
Mattole
Miwok
Patwin
Pomo
Quechan
Salinan
Serrano
Shasta
Tolowa
Tubatulabal
Wappo
Wintun
Wiyot
Yahi
Yana
Yokuts
Yuki
Yurok

GREAT BASIN
Bannock
Gosiute
Kawaiisu
Paiute, Northern
Paiute, Southern
Shoshone
Ute
Washoe

MESOAMERICA
Aztec
Carib
Chichimec
Maya
Mixtec
Olmec
Toltec
Zapotec

NORTHEAST
Abenaki
Algonquin
Cayuga
Erie
Fox
Huron
Illinois
Iroquois Confederacy
Kaskaskia
Kickapoo
Lenni Lenape
Mahican
Maliseet
Massachusett
Mattaponi
Menominee
Metis
Miami
Micmac
Mohawk
Mohegan
Moneton
Montagnais
Montauk
    Confederacy
Nanticoke
Narragansett
Nauset
Neutral
Niantic
Nipissing
Nipmuck
Nottaway
Ojibwa
Oneida
Onondaga
Ottawa
Pamlico
Passamaquoddy
Pennacook
Penobscot
Pequot

Petun
Poospatuck
Potawatomi
Sauk
Seneca
Shawnee
Shinnecock
Susquehannock
Wampanoag
Wappinger
Winnebago

NORTHWEST COAST
Alsea
Bella Bella
Bella Coola
Chasta Costa
Chehalis
Chemakum
Chinook
Clallam
Clatskanie
Comox
Coos
Copalis
Cowichan
Cowlitz
Duwamish
Gitksan
Haisla
Kalapuya
Kwakiutl
Lummi
Makah
Muckleshoot
Multnomah
Nisqually
Nooksack
Nootka
Puyallup
Quileute
Quinault
Salish
Samish
Semiahmoo
Siletz
Siuslaw
Skagit
Snohomish
Snoqualmie
Sooke
Squamish
Suquamish

Swallah
Takelma
Tillamook
Tlingit
Tsimshian
Tututni
Twana
Umpqua
Wasco
Yaquina

PLAINS
Apache Tribe of Oklahoma
Arapaho
Arikara
Assiniboine
Atsina
Blackfoot and Blackfeet
    Confederacy
Caddo
Cheyenne
Comanche
Crow
Hidatsa
Iowa
Kansa
Kichai
Kiowa
Mandan
Missouri
Omaha
Osage
Oto
Pawnee
Ponca
Quapaw
Sarsi
Sioux
Tonkawa
Waco
Wichita

PLATEAU
Cayuse
Coeur d'Alene
Colville
Flathead
Kalispel
Klamath
Klikitat
Kutenai
Lake
Lillooet

Methow
Mical
Modoc
Molala
Nez Perce
Okanagan
Palouse
Sanpoil-Nespelem
Shuswap
Spokane
Tenino
Thompson
Tyigh
Umatilla
Walla Walla
Wanapam
Wauyukma
Wenatchi
Wishram
Yakima

SOUTHEAST
Ais
Alabama
Anadarko
Apalachee
Apalachicola

Atakapa
Bayogoula
Biloxi
Calusa
Cape Fear
Catawba
Cheraw
Cherokee
Chiaha
Chickasaw
Chitimacha
Choctaw
Coushatta
Creek
Guale
Hitchiti
Lumbee
Manahoac
Mobile
Nabedache
Natchez
Ocaneechi
Ofo
Pamlico
Powhatan Confederacy
Seminole
Timucua

Tiou
Tohome
Tunica
Tuscarora
Tuskegee
Tutelo
Waccamaw
Yamasee
Yazoo
Yuchi

SOUTHWEST
Apache
Cocopa
Havasupai
Karankawa
Mojave
Navajo
Pima
Pueblo tribes, Eastern
Pueblo tribes, Western
Seri
Tohono O'odham
Walapai
Yaqui
Yavapai

SUBARCTIC
Ahtna
Beaver
Beothuk
Carrier
Chilcotin
Chipewyan
Columbia
Cree
Dogrib
Han
Hare
Ingalik
Kaska
Koyukon
Kutchin
Mountain
Naskapi
Sekani
Slave
Tagish
Tahltan
Tanaina
Tanana
Tsetsaut
Tutchone
Yellowknife

GLOSSARY

Adobe: Unfired brick, usually made of clay and dried in the sun; a structure made with such bricks.

Allotment: U.S. government policy, officially put into effect in 1887, of dividing tribal lands into individually owned parcels, or allotments. The hope of the government and various reformers was that Indians would become typical "American" small farmers and would assimilate into European American society, but the policy ultimately failed.

Amerind: A contraction of "American" and "Indian" that is most often used to refer to pre-Columbian settlers of the Americas, with the exception of Eskimos.

Amulet: An object or artifact that is worn to ward off evil and danger, such as from witchcraft and spirits.

Artifact: Any object found in the context of an archaeological site that was once used by humans; examples include tools, weapons, articles of clothing, and works of art.

Assimilation: The process through which a minority cultural group becomes absorbed into the dominant cultural group. Federal policies toward American Indians have historically bounced back and forth regarding whether attempting to force or coerce Indians to assimilate into mainstream American society is an appropriate policy.

Atlatl: A notched stick used to throw spears, darts, or harpoons.

Band: A tribal subunit, often an extended family; also, in modern Canada, a community of Indians registered under the Indian Act ("status Indians" as opposed to "non-status Indians").

Beadwork: The use of beads (most often of glass) for decorating clothing, bags, and other items; it largely replaced quillwork after trade with Europeans began.

Bear: A common character in stories, a powerful ally in healing that is also admired for its hunting skill.

Bear Dance: A ceremonial dance of medicine societies in many tribes to foster curing or to ask for a long life.

Berdache: Reversal of sex roles, including cross-dressing and assumption of the other sex's occupations. Most North American cultures traditionally accommodated the practice, which is not necessarily homosexual in nature (from the French for "male prostitute").

Bola: A hunting weapon, made of two or more thongs with weights on the end that are attached to a longer thong; when thrown, a bola wraps around the prey's legs or wings, immobilizing it.

Buffalo: A key animal in most midwestern and Great Plains cultures, the buffalo, as a guardian spirit, bestows game on humankind, governs fertility in women, protects unmarried women, mediates in love, rewards the generous, and chastens the stingy.

Bungling host: A common character type in stories throughout North America, marked by his failure to obtain food even when imitating other animals' methods.

Bureau of Indian Affairs (BIA): The U.S. agency established as part of the Department of the Interior in 1824 to manage Indian issues; responsible for overseeing reservation and trust lands and providing Indian education.

Cacique: A prince, chief, or boss; a political system that centers power in such a figure.

Calumet: A sacred pipe; a tobacco pipe made of a reed stem, clay or stone bowl, and feather or carved ornamentation.

Cannibals: Among the most pervasive characters in Indian myths, often in the form of monsters or grotesque humans.

Clairvoyance: Seeing into the future, a belief upon which many cultures relied to diagnose disease or for other purposes.

Clan: A social unit defined by a common lineage from either the female side (matrilineal) or male side (patrilineal).

Clown: In Pueblo cultures, clowns, often acting in ceremonial troupes, entertain by joking or by satirizing individuals or features of society, especially by mocking, burlesquing, displaying backwards or inverse behavior, and simulating gluttony or sexual behavior.

Corn: In mythologies and rituals of corn-growing cultures, corn, often personified as a woman, symbolizes fertility and medicine.

Coup: In some Plains cultures, particularly the Sioux, the points earned during battle for striking or touching an enemy or other acts of bravery; coup increased a warrior's honor and prestige (from the French for "a blow").

Coyote: Among the most common characters in North American myths and story traditions, coyote is the supreme trickster; always male, curious, and imitative, he is sometimes said to be responsible for unpleasant features of culture or life in general.

Cradleboard: A carrier for infants, most often made of wood and leather and worn on the back.

Creation: Although few creation stories start with a cosmic void, as does the creation story in Genesis, most American Indian cultures have stories explaining the beginning of the world and the origin of people, social institutions, animals, plants, and phenomena such as famine and death.

Cremation: A funeral at which the body of the dead person is burned.

Crest: Among Northwest Coast tribes, an artifact made of copper that represents important lineages; ownership of a crest confers prestige.

Crow: An important character in myths, sometimes a trickster.

Culture area: A region in which the indigenous population is more similar than dissimilar; environment, language, physical type, and cultural adaptation are considerations in making such a classification.

Culture hero: A figure in legend or myth who magically performed a feat or taught humans something that inaugurated a distinctive element of culture or feature of nature.

Dance: Dance is an inseparable expression of much Indian ritual, from large-scale public ceremonies (often involving special religious societies) to private rites. Dances can be passed from one generation to the next or invented, usually based upon a vision.

Datura: Jimsonweed, a psychoactive plant whose roots and leaves are used as medicine and whose roots induce visions.

Deer: A common story character, usually female and portrayed as a wife, mother, or sister.

Dialect: A group's distinctive variations in the pronunciation, grammar, and vocabulary of a language; although noticeably different, a dialect can be understood by other groups speaking the same language.

Dirty boy: A common story figure throughout North America; he appears dirty or crippled and is shunned or mistreated, although actually he is a powerful and handsome young man who lavishly rewards those who treat him kindly.

Dog: A significant spirit in myths who is responsible for friendship, faithfulness, and other powers.

Dreams: In Indian belief systems, dreams are portals to the spirit world; they can lead to illness, but they can also heal and initiate new belief systems, rituals, or stories.

Drum: A shamanistic ritual aid of great power; drumming, like dancing, is a central element in many Indian rituals and celebrations.

Earthlodge: A large dome-shaped building with a log frame covered by branches and packed with mud.

Eagle: A frequent figure in myth and ritual who possesses great power in hunting and war.

Earth diver: A type of creation tale common in North America: A primal animal scoops up soil from the bottom of a world-covering sea and fashions the first land from it.

Endogamy: The practice or custom of marrying within a particular group to which one belongs, such as a clan.

Eskimo: A generic term for the Inuit and Yupik peoples of northernmost Alaska and Canada. Its derivation and meaning are debated, but it probably derived from a Montagnais (eastern Canada) word via Basque whalers, and then was adapted into French and English.

Ethnocentrism: The tendency to judge other people's behavior and values on the basis of one's own culture, which is usually considered superior.

Ethnography: The detailed descriptive study of a particular society and its culture.

Exogamy: The practice or custom of marrying outside a particular group to which one belongs, such as a clan.

False face: An English term for the wooden masks and masking ceremonies used to promote healing among the Iroquois.

Fasting: Abstinence from food, especially in preparation for or as part of a ritual.

Federally recognized tribe: A tribe that has official government-to-government relations with the U.S. government and that is eligible for services the government provides to American Indians.

Fetish: An artifact, often a small carved bird or animal, used in rituals and believed to possess power.

Flaking: A technique for shaping stone, such as flint, chert, or obsidian into tools by removing chips.

Gambler: A colorful human or animal character that appears frequently in stories, sometimes as a cannibal.

Gaming sticks: Sticks of wood, reed, cane, or horn used for gambling.

Gorget: A small breastplate worn suspended from the neck as adornment or rank insignia.

Ghost Dance: There was a Ghost Dance of 1870 that involved Great Basin and California tribes as well as one in 1890 that affected the Great Basin and Plains. Both were religious revitalization movements based upon the expected return of the dead, who would drive out white people and establish a paradise.

Ghosts: Stories about spirits, the return of the dead, and beings that help the dead pervade North American cultures; ghosts are sometimes honored with feasts.

Giants: Present in myths in a great variety of forms and specializing in stealing children and wives, although some are helpful.

Girls' puberty rites: The introduction to womanhood upon menarche or soon after often involved seclusion, during which girls learned the responsibilities and privileges of their new status and became eligible for marriage.

Giveaways: Practiced in many cultures, the distribution of one's possessions to members of the community was sometimes a ritual in itself and sometimes part of a larger ritual; examples include the Lakota White Buffalo Ceremony, the Crow Aasshke, the Blackfoot Grass Dance, and, the most widely known, the potlatch of the Pacific Northwest.

Grandmother: A common story character, a solitary old woman who advises a hero about killing monsters, using magic, and escaping dangers.

Grass Dance: In the Plains, a strenuous competitive men's social dance involving much leaping and bending by dancers who wear large amounts of grass tied to belts.

Guardian spirits: Across the northern Plains, young men, and sometimes young women, undertake quests for personal visions by fasting in isolation; the power they gain by the experience assumes the form of a being who can later be called on for help.

Healing: A primary goal of rituals, because illness, often considered a disorder of society or the world, may be corrected by community involvement.

Hogan: A Navajo hut made of wood, sod, mud, or branches.

Human-animal transformations: Shape-changing, from animal to human or vice versa, occurs for a variety of reasons, often evil, in myths and stories.

Igloo: An Eskimo dome-shaped hut made of blocks of compacted snow.

Initiation: A trial of endurance or isolation required for entrance into some societies or a new stage of life.

Jerky: Sun-dried meat strips.

Joking relationships: Teasing and sexual jokes exchanged between people of the opposite sex in some, but not all, family roles, such as between brothers-in-law and sisters-in-law.

Jugglers: Male or female shamans in the Great Lakes and Northeast areas who defanged snakes to display their power over death (from the French *jongleur*).

Kachina: In Pueblo and Southwest cultures, a masked figure or doll representing mediators between the human and spirit worlds.

Keeper: The caretaker of a sacred object who also conducts the rituals and ceremonies pertaining to the object.

Kinnikinnik: The term, of Delaware origin, for a mixture of sumac leaves, the inner bark of dogwood or willow, and other materials smoked in pipes in place of tobacco or mixed with it.

Kiva: In Southwest cultures, most notably Pueblo cultures, a partly subterranean ceremonial council chamber, either circular or rectangular, with an altar.

Kokopelli: In Southwest art, the Humpbacked Flute Player, who appears widely in rock art and ancient pottery and has been revived as a motif in modern pottery and jewelry decoration.

Koshare: Clowns wearing horned headdresses and black-and-white stripes in the Pueblo culture.

Labret: A stone, shell, or bone ornament inserted through the lip.

Lacrosse: A hockey-like field game in which opposing teams try to send a small ball into goals using a hooked stick (from the French *crosse*).

Land cession: Land that Indian tribes gave to Europeans or the United States government as part of a treaty.

Leister: A three-pronged fishing harpoon used by Arctic peoples.

Longhouse: An Iroquoian dwelling in which several family units within an extended family reside; also, a public building for councils or other meetings.

Makai: In the Southwest, medicine men who concern themselves with crops, war, and weather.

Manifest Destiny: A widespread feeling among European Americans, especially in the nineteenth century, that it was the inevitable destiny and right of the United States to stretch from the Atlantic to the Pacific; used to justify seizing Indian lands.

Manioc: A tropical plant, also called cassava, that is a staple of Caribbean Indians; now used to make tapioca.

Manitou: Any of a group of Algonquian spirits and supernatural forces inhabiting all living and inanimate things.

Mano and metate: A set of upper and lower millstones used to grind corn and other grains.

Matrilineal: Any social organization which bases descent or heritage on the female members.

Matrilocal: Any social organization in which husbands move into their wives' households.

Medicine: A term denoting the power in persons, spirits, objects, and activities that can be used for healing, divination, control of nature, or sorcery.

Medicine bundle: A bag or wrapping containing feathers, herbs, stones, animal parts, scalps, pipes, or other objects with special powers or significance.

Metis: The French word for people of mixed blood, specifically those descended from white fur traders who lived with and married Indians; the term is primarily used in Canada, which has a large Metis population.

Military society: A society or club of warriors with special rituals and clothing; most prevalent in Plains cultures.

Moccasin: A soft shoe made of deerskin or other leather.

Moiety: Either of two classes or halves of a tribal group.

Mukluk: A soft Inuit boot made of sealskin.

Native American Church: A pantribal system of rites and celebrations centered on the vision-instilling powers of peyote; officially established in 1918.

Nomadic: A way of life in which people periodically move from one location to another, usually in search of food.

Orenda: An Iroquoian spiritual power or force inherent in all objects; one can communicate with orenda through song.

Paddling: A decorative technique for pottery in which a flat or curved paddle is pressed against the wet clay before firing.

Paleo-Indian: The prehistoric stone age ancestors of modern Indians.

Paleontology: The study of ancient life forms and fossils.

Papoose: The Algonquian word for an infant.

Parfleche: Rawhide with the hair removed, used in garments.

Patrilineal: Any social organization which bases descent or heritage on the male members.

Patrilocal: Any social organization in which wives move into their husbands' households.

Pemmican: Lean meat pounded and mixed with melted fat, forming a paste that is shaped into cakes and flavored with berries.

Petroglyph: A prehistoric carving or inscription on rock.

Peyote: A small cactus, *Lophophora williamsii*, or the button-like structures of the cactus that induce hallucinations.

Pictograph: A prehistoric drawing or painting, often depicting an important event.

Pipestone: A hard red clay or soft stone used to make tobacco pipes.

Pit house: A prehistoric dwelling dug into the ground and generally roofed with tree limbs and mud.

Potlatch: A Northwest Coast (particularly Nootka) feast in which gifts are given to guests in order to increase the host's prestige.

Power: A central concept in Indian religious systems; a spiritual force that gives meaning to, and some measure of control of, life.

Pow-wow: A ceremony, celebration, council, or conference that includes dance contests, group dancing, and giveaways.

Plaiting: A basket or cloth weaving technique in which two different elements cross each other for a checkerboard appearance.

Prayerstick: In the Pueblo culture, a piece of ornamental stone or wood to which is attached a feather or streamer imbued with prayer; it is stuck into the ground so that the streamer can wave in the wind and broadcast the prayer.

Pre-Columbian: All human culture and history in the Americas before Christopher Columbus's voyage of exploration in 1492.

Pueblo: A communal village in the Southwest; also, when capitalized, the cultures that built them (from the Spanish for "town").

Quetzalcóatl: The Toltec and Aztec god of the morning and evening star and patron of priests, represented as a plumed or feathered serpent.

Quilling: Particularly prevalent in the Plains, the art of using dyed porcupine quills, softened in the mouth, to decorate clothing.

Rabbit stick: A curved wooden stick about 70 centimeters long used in rabbit hunts, and possibly as a weapon, in the Southwest.

Radiocarbon dating: The measurement of a substance's age based upon the decay of carbon 14, a radioactive isotope.

Rattles: Percussion instruments fastened to arms, legs, or the waist or held in the hand and used to accompany dancing and singing; individual rattles may have special meaning for a ritual.

Relocation: The U.S. government policy of the 1950's according to which rural Indians were encouraged to move to urban areas to find employment.

Removal: The U.S. government policy of the 1830's-1850's according to which eastern Indians were "removed" to lands west of the Mississippi; the Trail of Tears was the most infamous event of the removal era.

Reservation: An area of land set aside for exclusive Indian use by treaty with the United States government; in the initial reservation era, tribes were forced to live on their assigned reservations.

Revitalization movement: Any of various attempts to restore Indian cultural features lost after contact with Europeans.

Roach: A hairpiece worn on the head as adornment.

Sachem: The overall leader or chief of a Algonquian tribe.

Sagamore: An Algonquian chief subordinate to a sachem.

Scalping: Flaying the skin and hair from an enemy's head as part of coup.

Seine: A fishing net that hangs from the surface of the water on floats and is anchored with weights on the bottom.

Shaking Tent Ceremony: A nighttime conjuring ritual, held in a small hut or tent, in which a conjurer who has been bound sings and beats a drum until spirits release him; thereafter, the spirits divulge information about people or events, which the conjurer translates to his employers.

Shaman: A priest or priest-doctor who consults spirits or magical powers in order to guide or cure others.

Singer: The English term for a Navajo *hataalii*, who conducts rituals and preserves religious lore.

Six Nations: The six tribes—Mohawk, Oneida, Onondaga, Cayuga, Seneca, and Tuscarora—that make up the Iroquois Confederacy.

Snakes: Frequent characters in stories and myths; live snakes are used in some rituals.

Song duel: An opportunity to resolve conflicts among tribal members by ritual exchange of humorous songs; each singer praises himself and makes fun of his opponent's faults.

Sovereignty: Complete national independence; the issue of the sovereignty of Indian tribes or nations has been a perennial problem in Indian-white relations. Under U.S. law, tribes are considered to have distinct but "dependent" governments.

Spirits: Invisible, named entities with distinctive personalities who can influence the human world.

Status Indians: In Canada, Indians who are officially entitled, according to the Indian Act, to be registered by the Department of Indian Affairs and Northern Development.

Storyteller: A highly esteemed person who, from memory, narrates traditional stories, legends, or myths, often as part of a ritual.

Subsistence round: A recurrent migration pattern, usually annual, based on the changing availability of various food sources.

Sun Dance: A yearly summer dance held by many Plains Indians that lasts for three or four days and is considered fundamental to participants' spiritual health.

Sweatlodge: A structure, usually dome-shaped, for sweating, a rite of purification through exposure to heat generated by a fire or by steam from water poured over hot rocks.

Taboo: A restriction or prohibition for reasons of religion or custom.

Thunderbird: In stories, a large bird (or flock) that produces thunder by flapping its wings and personifies thunder.

Tipi: A tent formed of bark, mats, skins, or canvas on a cone-shaped pole frame (also spelled "tepee").

Toboggan: A light sleigh made of thin planks of wood curved at one end.

Tomahawk: An ax, made of a shaft about 60 to 90 centimeters long and a sharpened stone, metal, or horn head, used as a weapon and as a tool in agriculture.

Totem: The term, from an Algonquian word, for a hereditary mark, emblem, or badge of a clan or tribe that takes the image of an animal or other natural object having spiritual powers.

Travois: A sled that consists of a wooden A-frame covered with planks or webbing; pulled by a dog or horse.

Treaty: A formal agreement, pact, or contract jointly agreed upon by a tribe and the United States or Canadian government (or, earlier, by a tribe and a European government).

Tribe: A general term, first applied to Indian societies by Europeans, for a variety of Indian sociopolitical organizations; among the considerations for tribal identity are common ancestry, language, and culture.

Trickster: A widespread type of story character whose principal qualities include cleverness, deception, buffoonish behavior, and misdirection.

Trust lands: Indian lands not classified as reservations that are protected by federal or state governments.

Tule: A bulrush (*Scirpus lacustris* or *Scirpus tatora*) often used as a construction material.

Turquoise: A green-blue semiprecious gem used in Great Basin and Southwest jewelry.

Two-hearts: A common expression denoting a liar or witch.

Underworld: A mythological realm below the earth's surface; frequently it is the place from which the first humans appeared or in which the dead live.

Usufruct: A situation in which a group has access to certain land and its resources, based on a history of usage; no one "owns" the land.

Vision: A direct communication with the realm of spirits.

Vision quest: The ritualized seeking of visions or dreams through self-deprivation, exposure, or hallucinogenic drugs during a rite of passage or other ritual.

Wakan Tanka: Literally, in Lakota Siouan, "the great mystery"; although often translated as "the great spirit," it stands collectively for the spiritual beings and powers in the Siouan belief system.

Walam Olum: The Delaware account of their origin and migrations, painted on sticks in red pictographs.

Wampum: Beads threaded into belts, bracelets, or collars that were used as messages and tribal records as well as ornamentation; the concept of wampum as money is largely a European superimposition.

War bonnet: A headdress containing feathers that symbolize achievements in battle.

Wattle and daub: A construction method that uses a pole frame interwoven with branches and surfaced with mud or plaster.

Weir: A fenced-in enclosure for trapping fish.

Wickiup: A temporary shelter made of grass or brush that was widely used in the Great Basin.

Wolf: An important character in stories and myths; associated with creation, war, and hunting.

MEDIAGRAPHY

A list of select films dealing with American Indians. Documentary films are listed first, followed by feature films.

EDUCATIONAL AND DOCUMENTARY FILMS

Again, a Whole Person I Have Become
Color. 19 min. 16mm.
Shenandoah Film Productions (1982)
Stresses the importance of traditional Indian customs for Indian youth. Three tribal elders speak of the wisdom of the old ways; dances and ceremonies are portrayed. Will Sampson narrates.

Age of the Buffalo
Color. 14 min. 16mm.
National Film Board of Canada (1964)
Shows how the buffalo met the needs of the Indians for food, clothing, shelter, and adventure, and how life changed when the buffalo were gone.

The American Indian
Color. 62 min. VHS.
Library Distributors of America (1993)
A broad view of the origin and culture of American Indians; also examines interactions between Indians and whites.

The American Indian: After the White Man Came
Color. 27 min. 16mm.
Handel Film Corporation (1972)
An extensive examination of American Indians since European discovery of the Americas. Moves to a discussion of the problems facing modern Indians.

The American Indian: Before the White Man
Color. 19 min. 16mm.
Handel Film Corporation (1972)
Comprehensive study of American Indians from the early migration routes to the development of the main tribes of North America. Narrated by Iron Eyes Cody.

American Indian in Transition
Color. 22 min. 16mm.
Atlantis Productions (1976)
An Indian point of view about land and heritage, narrated by an Indian mother who uses Indian chronicles and sayings. Provides a compassionate insight into Indian life and thought.

American Indian Influence on the United States
Color. 20 min. 16mm.
Robert Davis Productions (1972)
Depicts the manner in which life in the U.S. has been influenced by the American Indian economically, sociologically, philosophically, and culturally. Nine dances and ceremonies are authentically portrayed. The graphics used in the film include original Indian illustrations.

The American Indian Speaks
Color. 23 min. 16mm.
Encyclopædia Britannica Educational Corporation (1973)
Members of three Indian cultures state the position and attitudes of American Indians in the twentieth century. Includes remembrances of the Trail of Tears and Wounded Knee.

The American Indian Struggle
Color. 29 min. VHS.
Kent State University (1981)
An examination of several important episodes that contributed to the long history of conflict between American Indians and white settlers. With Kent State University professors James Gidney and Philip Weeks.

American Indians: A Brief History
Color. 22 min. 16mm.
National Geographic Society (1985)
Numerous examples of diverse Indian artistic and cultural traditions. Provides a history of the roots of conflict between the Indians and European settlers. Identifies several settlements and tribes that existed before Columbus arrived in America.

American Indians as Seen by D. H. Lawrence
Color. 14 min. 16mm.
Lewin/Cort (1966)
At the D. H. Lawrence ranch near Taos, New Mexico, his wife Frieda speaks about his beliefs and thoughts. Aldous Huxley presents selections from Lawrence's works.

The Americans: The Buffalo Story
Color. 28 min. 16mm.
O'Laughlin Company (1971)
The great usefulness of the buffalo to the Plains Indians is detailed; it furnished them with food, clothing, and shelter. Buffalo masks convey the spirit of the annual Spring Buffalo Dance.

The Americans: Chief Black Hawk
Color. 23 min. 16mm.
O'Laughlin Company (1971)
Chief White Eagle explains the meaning and logic of sign language and various war paint designs. The story of Black Hawk, war chief of the Sauk Indians, follows, dramatized by paintings and sound effects.

The Americans: Chief Crazy Horse
Color. 26 min. 16mm.
O'Laughlin Company (1971)
Beginning with the Bering Strait migration theory of Indian prehistory, Chief White Eagle moves into a description of Indian cultural evolution, including introduction of horses. Crazy Horse, brilliant leader and military strategist of the Sioux, is profiled.

The Americans: Chief Joseph
Color. 23 min. 16mm.
O'Laughlin Company (1971)

After describing the kinds of horses that Indians used for various purposes and how these horses were trained, Chief White Eagle tells the story of Chief Joseph and the Nez Perce.

The Americans: Geronimo
Color. 25 min. 16mm.
O'Laughlin Company (1971)
The Indians' closeness to nature and ability to forecast weather are discussed. Geronimo is profiled.

America's Indians
Six-part series.
Color. 13 min. each. VHS.
Films for the Humanities and Sciences (1993)
The Indians Were There First
How North American Indians entered the Americas from Asia; various tribes and some of their characteristics.
When the White Man Came
Life among the major tribes before Europeans arrived.
The Bison Hunters
How the Indian became mythologized as the eastern United States became industrialized.
The Trail of Tears
The harm done by explorers and pioneers.
The Warpath
How pioneers moving westward ignored treaties reserving land for Indians.
The Death of the Bison
The many Native American issues that remain unresolved.

Ann of the Wolf Clan
Color. 60 min. VHS.
Rainbow TV Works; Great Plains Instructional TV, University of Nebraska (1982)
A young, middle class Indian girl receives the gift of her Cherokee heritage from her great-grandmother while spending a summer on the reservation.

Apache Indian
Black and white. 11 min. 16mm.
Cort (1943)
Shows the life, ceremonies, and industries of the Apaches. The beauty of their native territory forms the setting for the tribal functions and ceremonies, including a puberty ceremonial and devil dance.

The Apache Indian (Revised version)
Color. 11 min. 16mm. VHS.
Cort (1975)
Acquaints young viewers with the life, culture, and traditions of the Apache of Arizona. Emphasizes the problems that modern living has caused and the Apaches' struggle for education, health care, and economic opportunity.

Arrow to the Sun
Color. 22 min. 16mm.
Texture (1973)
An animated film by Gerald McDermott that illustrates a tale from the Acoma Pueblo of the Southwest. A boy's search for his father leads him to a dazzling voyage on an arrow to the sun.

The Ballad of Crowfoot
Color/black and white. 11 min. 16mm. VHS.
National Film Board of Canada/McGraw-Hill (1968)
Documents the events and problems that characterized the relationship between whites and Indians since whites arrived in the Canadian West in the 1820's. Records Indian traditions and attitudes.

Before the White Man Came
Black and white. 50 min. Silent. 16mm
Northwestern Film Corp. (1921)
Filmed in the Bighorn Mountains of Montana and Wyoming in 1921. In an enactment by Indians, every effort was made to present life as it was before the arrival of whites.

Behind the Masks
Color. 24 min. 16mm.
National Film Board of Canada (1973)
Study of the meaning and myths behind the masks of the tribes of the Northwest Coast. Commentary and analysis by Claude Levi-Strauss, noted French anthropologist.

Black Indians of New Orleans
Color. 33 min. 16mm.
Maurice M. Martinez (1976)
Depicts the activities of highly organized groups of African Americans with mixed Indian ancestry as they prepare for Mardi Gras, with emphasis on their distinctive music, dancing, and costumes.

Boy of the Navajos
Color. 11 min. 16mm.
Cort (1975)
Shows the living habits and activities of a Navajo family in Arizona, with emphasis on the teenage son.

Boy of the Seminoles: Indians of the Everglades
Color/black and white. 11 min. 16mm.
Cort (1956)
Shows the living habits and activities of a teenage Seminole boy and his family in Florida.

Broken Treaty at Battle Mountain
Color. 73 min. 16mm.
Cinnamon Production (1973)
The struggle of the Western Shoshone of Nevada to retain their culture and land is dramatically portrayed. The Shoshone struggle to keep 24 million acres of Nevada land originally promised to them by the U.S. government. Narrated by Robert Redford.

Catlin and the Indians
Color. 25 min. 16mm.
National Film Board of Canada/McGraw-Hill (1967)
Presents biographical material on George Catlin, historian and painter of American Plains Indians. Includes paintings from the Smithsonian's Catlin collection.

Cherokee
Color. 26 min. 16mm.
British Broadcasting Corporation (1976)
Explores the dilemma the Cherokees face in preserving their traditions and captures the beauty of the pageants and

ceremonies performed today. Includes scenes from a pageant play that recounts Cherokee history.

Children of the Eagle: A Tribute to American Indian Children
Color. 28 min. 16mm.
Oklahoma State University
Describes the American Indian family and contrasts contemporary family life with traditional Indian customs. Presents prenatal concerns, parenting behavior, and funeral rituals.

Circle of the Sun
Color. 30 min. 16mm. VHS.
National Film Board of Canada (1960)
Studies the way of life and ceremonial customs of the Blood Indians circa 1960. Pictures the Sun Dance camp and analyzes the feelings of the younger generation about the old Indian customs and the influences of whites.

Contrary Warriors
Color. 60 min. 16mm. VHS.
Rattlesnake Productions (1987)
The Crazy Dogs, one of the original Crow warrior societies, declared themselves "contrary warriors" and pledged to risk death when challenged by outsiders.

Corn Is Life
Color. 11 min. 16mm. VHS.
University of California Extension Media Center (1983)
Shows and explains traditional activities associated with corn that are still an important part of Hopi family and community life. Corn, a major cultural symbol, plays a central role in the life of every Hopi.

Crow Dog
Color. 57 min. 16mm.
Cinema Guild (1979)
Focuses on Leonard Crow Dog, spiritual leader of eighty-nine American Indian tribes and a spokesman for many Indians who wish to retain the beliefs and way of life of their forefathers. Documents the politics and spiritual power of the American Indian Movement.

Custer at the Washita
Color. 26 min. 16mm. VHS.
McGraw-Hill (1966)
An account of the Battle of the Washita River, one of the few decisive battles of the American Indian wars. It signaled the end of freedom for the Cheyenne and planted the seeds of Custer's defeat at the Little Bighorn.

Discovering American Indian Music
Color. 24 min. 16mm. VHS.
Inform (1971)
Introduces the traditional customs, costumes, and dances associated with the music of eleven representative North American tribes, principally of the Plains and Southwest.

The Drummaker
Color. 37 min. 16mm.
Pennsylvania State University Psych Cinema Register (1978)
Presents William Bineshi Baker, Sr., an Ojibwa, one of the last of his people to perfect the art of drummaking. He discusses tradition and his frustration with those who will not take the time to follow it.

End of the Trail: The American Plains Indian
Black and white. 53 min. 16mm. VHS.
McGraw-Hill (1967)
Documents the growth and development of the Plains Indian culture, which culminate with the advent of whites. Illustrates many of the hostile acts inflicted by both sides.

Family Life of the Navajo Indians
Black and white. 31 min. Silent. 16mm.
New York University (1943)
Highlights some of the ways the Navajo child becomes an adult.

Gatecliff: American Indian Rock Shelter
Color. 21 min. 16mm.
National Geographic Society (1973)
Team of amateur archaeologists led by Dr. David Hurst Thomas of the American Museum of Natural History dig in Gatecliff Rock Shelter in Nevada. Layer-by-layer examination reveals information on inhabitants of 5,000 years ago.

Geronimo and the Apache Resistance
Color. 60 min. VU. VB.
WGBH, WNET, KCET (1988)
In 1886, the U.S. government mobilized five thousand men, one quarter of the entire U.S. Army, to capture Geronimo. This profile of Geronimo, believed by his people to have magical powers, highlights the clash of cultures and the legacy of the battles of a century ago. (Part of the PBS series The American Experience.)

Girl of the Navajos
Color. 15 min. 16mm.
Inform/Cort (1977)
A young Navajo girl recalls her feelings of fear and loneliness the first time she had to herd her family's sheep into the canyon alone. Returning to the canyon the following day, she becomes friends with another girl. Filmed on a Navajo reservation.

The Great Movie Massacre
Color. 28 min. 16mm.
United Indians of All Tribes Foundation (1979)
Explores the beginning of the "savage Indian" myth in popular American literature and entertainment, including wild west shows and early motion pictures. Will Sampson narrates. (Images of Indians Series.)

The Great Plains Experience: The Lakota—One Nation on the Plains
Color. 30 min. 16mm. VHS.
University of Mid-America (1976)
Describes the movement of Indians onto the Great Plains and their adaptation to the new environment, focusing on the Lakota in the eighteenth century.

Home of the Brave
Color. 4 min. 16mm.
Pyramid Film and Video (1969)

The five-hundred-year story of a people is documented with great precision in this four-minute encapsulation.

Hopi: Songs of the Fourth World
Color. 58 min. 16mm. VHS.
Newday (no date given)
Study of the Hopi that captures their spirituality and reveals their integration of art and daily life. A farmer, religious elder, grandmother, painter, potter, and weaver speak about the preservation of the Hopi way.

Hopi Indian Arts and Crafts (Revised version)
Color. 10 min. 16mm.
Cort (1975)
Hopis are shown using their ancient tools and knowledge in basketweaving, potterymaking, silverworking, and weaving. Shows how methods of working are changing.

Hopi Indian Village Life
Color/Black and White. 11 min. 16mm.
Cort (1956)
Pictures the Hopi and their mode of living as it existed in the 1950's, emphasizing the changing character of Hopi life and work.

Hopi Kachinas
Color. 9 min. 16mm.
Inform (1961)
The Hopi kachina doll is intended primarily to teach Hopi children to see meaning in religious rituals and dances. Shows an artisan carving, assembling, and painting a doll; also shows Hopi life and dances.

Hopi Snake Dance
Black and White. 10 min. 16mm.
Inform (1951)
Presents the preparations of the dancers, handling of snakes, costumes, and part of a snake dance.

Hopis: Guardians of the Land
Color. 10 min. 16mm.
Inform (1972)
A Hopi living on an Arizona reservation explains the tribal philosophy of seeking peace, brotherhood, and everlasting life by caring for all that is on the land. A nearby power plant and strip-mining operations threaten the union of people and land.

How Hollywood Wins the West
Color. 29 min. 16mm.
United Indians of All Tribes Foundation (1979)
Explores the concept of Manifest Destiny, which encouraged the taking of Indian lands that "nobody owned" by whites in the early nineteenth century.

I Will Fight No More Forever: The Story of Chief Joseph
Color. 106 min. 16mm. VHS.
Wolper Productions (1975)
How Chief Joseph led three hundred Nez Perce braves along with their women and children in the historic running battle against ten separate commands of the army in 1877.

Incident at Oglala
Color. 90 min. VHS.
Miramax (1992)
Reexamines the evidence in the 1975 murder case of two FBI agents on the Pine Ridge Reservation; the conviction of Leonard Peltier for the murders appears to be a travesty of justice. Directed by Michael Apted; narrated by Robert Redford.

Indian Art of the Pueblo
Color. 13 min. 16mm.
Encyclopædia Britannica Educational Corporation (1976)
Introduces the arts and crafts of the Pueblo.

Indian Ceremonial Dances of the Southwest
Color. 11 min. 16mm.
Harold Ambrosch Film Productions (1954)
Presents a number of Southwest dances, accompanied by songs and chants. Includes the Apache crown or devil dance, the Laguna shield dance and the Taos war dance.

Indian Crafts: Hopi, Navajo, and Iroquois
Color. 12 min. 16mm.
BFA Educational Media (1980)
Basketmaking, potterymaking, kachina carving, weaving, jewelrymaking, and mask carving.

Indian Heroes of America
Color. 17 min. 16mm.
Altana Films (1979)
Seven Indian personages are profiled, each representing an aspect of history from the coming of whites to the final confrontations in the late nineteenth century.

Indian Hunters
Black and white. 10 min. 16mm.
Inform (1948)
Shows two Indians seeking new hunting grounds for their band in the wilds of northern Canada.

Indian Musical Instruments
Color. 14 min. 16mm.
University of Oklahoma
Shows big dance drums, rawhide drums, ring and straight beaters, and other Indian musical instruments in the University of Oklahoma museum.

The Indian Speaks
Color. 41 min. 16mm.
National Film Board of Canada (1970)
Presents Indians in parts of Canada who are concerned about preserving what is left of their culture and restoring what is gone.

Indians: The Navajos
Color. 14 min. 16mm.
Hearst Metrotone News (1975)
Examines the winds of change that have been affecting the lives of 140,000 Navajos on the largest Indian reservation in the world.

Ishi, the Last Yahi
Color. 58 min. VHS.
Rattlesnake Productions (1993)
Distributed by Center for Media and Independent Learning, Berkeley, Calif.; Shanachie Entertainment, Newton, N.J.

Award-winning profile of Ishi, a California Indian who came out of hiding in 1911 and lived at the anthropology museum of the University of California at Berkeley until his death in 1916.

Late Woodland Village
Color. 20 min. 16mm.
University of Iowa AV Center (1974)
Excavations of the late Woodland Hartley Fort revealed details of life in a stockaded village of about 900 C.E.

Legend of Corn
Color. 26 min. 16mm.
Films for the Humanities and Sciences (1985)
An Ojibwa legend, dramatized by tribespeople, about how the Great Manitou saved the tribe from starvation.

Life in the Woodlands Before the White Man Came
Color. 12 min. 16mm.
ACI Media (1976)
Dramatizes the daily life, ceremonies, and rituals of Woodlands Indians before whites arrived.

Meet the Sioux Indian
Color. 11 min. 16mm.
Associated Film Artists (1949)
Portrays the nomadic life of the Sioux and shows how they obtained, prepared, and preserved food and made clothing.

Mesa Verde: Mystery of the Silent Cities
Color. 14 min. 16mm.
Encyclopædia Britannica Educational Corporation (1975)
Extensive aerial photography of the ruined cities and multiple-family cliff dwellings of a thirteenth century civilization. Narrated by Jack Palance.

Modern Chippewa Indians
Color. 11 min. 16mm.
Simmel-Miservey (1946)
Shows the life and work of the Chippewa Indians on the Red Lake Reservation in Minnesota.

Nanook of the North
Black and white. Silent. VHS.
Pathé Exchange (1922)
This landmark of documentary filmmaking caused a sensation when it was released. Robert Flaherty spent sixteen months in the Arctic filming an Inuit family. Some events were enacted specifically for the camera, but the portrait of Arctic life is generally realistic.

The Native Americans: How the West Was Lost
Color. 26 min. 16mm.
British Broadcasting Corporation (1976)
Highlights the life of the Plains Indians as it changed with the westward movement of whites. Historical photographs and drawings illustrate the Battle of Little Bighorn and the Wounded Knee Massacre.

Navajo: A People Between Two Worlds
Color. 20 min. 16mm.
Line Films (1958)
A study of the largest Indian tribe in the U.S., including life on the land and tribal government.

Navajo Night Dances
Color. 12 min. 16mm.
Lewin (1957)
Shows a Navajo family going to the Nine Day Healing Chant, feasting, and watching the Arrow, Feather, and Fire Dance.

Navajo Talking Picture
Color. 40 min. VHS.
Women Make Movies (1986)
Documents the life of a grandmother on the Navajo Reservation in Lower Greasewood, Arizona.

Nez Perce: Portrait of a People
Color. 23 min. 16mm.
National Audio Visual Center (No date given)
Tells of the cultural heritage of the Nez Perce and shows how the Nez Perce National Historical Park has influenced and preserved this culture.

North American Indian Legends
Color. 21 min. 16mm.
CBS (1973)
Dramatizes several Indian legends with special-effects photography to emphasize their mythical quality.

Northwest Indian Art
Color. 10 min. 16mm.
Lewin (1966)
Examples of the highly sophisticated art of Northwest Coast Indians collected from six museums.

Now That the Buffalo's Gone
Color. 7 min. 16mm.
Pyramid Film and Video (1969)
Uses group and individual still-photograph portraits, combined with footage from old films, to emphasize the dignity of Indian culture.

Oneota Longhouse People
Color. 14 min. 16mm.
University of Iowa Audio Visual Center (1973)
Archaeological discoveries of longhouses in northwest Iowa. Including a reconstruction of a village and views of how life might have been lived at this site a thousand years ago.

Paddle to the Sea
Color. 25 min. 16mm.
National Film Board of Canada (1967)
The story of a small, hand-carved Indian and a canoe, both called "paddle to the sea." From a book of the same name by Holling C. Holling.

Painting with Sand: A Navajo Ceremony
Color. 11 min. 16mm.
Encyclopædia Britannica Educational Corporation (1949)
Portrays the traditional sand painting and healing rite as performed by a Navajo medicine man for his ailing son.

People of the Buffalo
Color. 14 min. 16mm.
National Film Board of Canada (1969)
Depicts the dependence of western Indians on the buffalo

for food, shelter, and clothing. Shows how the coming of whites and subsequent slaughter of the buffalo herds changed the lifestyle of the Indians.

Potlatch People
Color. 26 min. 16mm.
Document Associates (1976)
With an economy based on the abundant fish of the ocean and rivers, Northwest Coast Indians lived in communal longhouses based on a rigid class system.

Pueblo of Laguna: Elders of the Tribe
Color. 20 min. 16mm.
National Audio Visual Center (No date given)
Describes the dynamic program for taking care of elders on a reservation in Laguna, New Mexico.

Red Sunday: The Story of the Battle of the Little Bighorn
Color. 28 min. 16mm.
Pyramid Film and Video (1975)
An objective account of America's most famous U.S. Cavalry-Indian confrontation. Still photographs, original drawings, paintings, and live action are skillfully blended.

Report from Wounded Knee
Color. 10 min. 16mm.
Sterling Educational Films (1971)
Details the historical events at Wounded Knee using photographic stills.

Sacajawea
Color. 24 min. VHS.
Southerby Productions (1984)
The true story of the young Indian woman who guided the Lewis and Clark expedition.

Seminole Indians
Color. 11 min. 16mm.
University of Minnesota (1951)
Seminole life on the hummocks of the Florida Everglades.

Silent Enemy
Black and white. 88 min. 16mm. VHS.
Blackhawk Films (1930)
A study of the Ojibwas' struggle for food before the arrival of European Americans; filmed on location near Lake Superior.

Sioux Indians: Live and Remember
Color. 29 min. VHS.
Barr Films (1987)
Focuses on the struggle of the Dakota Sioux to preserve their heritage. Shows the Dakota people living in squalid camps in the midst of natural beauty.

Sitting Bull: A Profile in Power
Color. 20 min. 16mm.
Learning Corporation of America (1976)
The heroic but sad saga of relations between the United States and the Indians unfolds through an imaginary dialogue between an interviewer and the charismatic Sioux chief.

Strangers in Their Own Land
Color. 50 min. VHS.
Strangers in Their Own Land (1993)

Records Native American ceremonies, including an emotional Kiowa wedding ceremony and the initiation of a young brave into an ancient warrior society.

The Sun Dagger (Edited version)
Color. 28 min. 16mm. VHS.
Bullfrog Films (1982)
The "dagger," an ancient Indian celestial calendar rediscovered in 1977, is presently the only known archaeological site in the world that marks the extreme positions of both the sun and the moon.

Teaching Indians to Be White
Color. 28 min. VHS.
Films for the Humanities and Sciences (1993)
Shows how schools try to integrate American Indian children into mainstream society and notes problems with turning children away from their families and traditional values.

To Find Our Life: The Peyote Hunt of the Huichols of Mexico
Color. 65 min. 16mm.
University of California Extension Media Center (1968)
Filmed and recorded in the field in December, 1966, by anthropologist Peter T. Furst, this is the first documentary of the annual peyote hunt and ceremonies of the Huichol Indians of Western Mexico.

The Totem Pole
Color. 28 min. 16mm. VHS.
Educational Materials Corporation (1961)
The Kwakiutl and Haida are the Northwest Indians best known for their totem poles. Shows the several types of poles and how they are decorated.

Valley of the Standing Rocks
Color. 24 in. 16mm.
Thomas J. Barbre Productions (1957)
Vividly portrays the life of the Navajos on their reservation in Arizona and Utah.

Walking in a Sacred Manner
Color. 23 min. 16mm.
Stephen Cross (1982)
Using the photographs of Edward S. Curtis, shows how traditional Indian life was centered on the natural world.

Winds of Change: A Matter of Promises
Color/black and white. 58 min. VHS.
PBS Video (1990)
Navajos of Arizona and adjacent states and Lummis of Washington State focus on sovereignty, internal politics, the administration of justice, and relations with the U.S. government.

Winter on an Indian Reservation
Color. 11 min. 16mm.
Inform (1973)
Shows children on a forest reservation in the Great Lakes area; provides an intimate look at both the hardships and joys of Indian life.

Woodland Indians of Early America
Color/black and white. 11 min. 16mm.
Cort (1958)

Depicts a family of hunter-culture Indians, illustrating the migratory nature of such cultures and showing many techniques of hunting, dress, cooking, and home building.

FEATURE FILMS

The depictions of Indians in feature films (often by white actors) have historically been misguided and have engendered considerable outrage. What follows is a select list of films that provide relatively accurate portrayals of Indian life, past and present. In some of the films all Indians are portrayed by Indian actors; in others, white actors fill at least some Indian roles.

Black Robe
Color. 100 min. VHS.
Samuel Goldwyn (1991)
A seventeenth century Jesuit priest is led by a party of Algonquins to a distant mission. Generally accurate depiction of early Indian-white relations as well as intertribal Algonquin, Iroquois, and Huron relations and warfare. From Brian Moore's novel. Lothaire Bluteau, Aden Young, Sandrine Holt.

Cheyenne Autumn
Color. 159 min. VHS.
Warner Bros. (1964)
Renowned director of Westerns John Ford filmed this story of Cheyennes fleeing their reservation to return to their homeland. Not without its flaws, but an early sympathetic look at the situation of western Indians in the late nineteenth century. Richard Widmark, Carroll Baker, Ricardo Montalban, Gilbert Roland.

Dances with Wolves
Color. 181 min. VHS.
Orion Pictures (1990)
A troubled Civil War veteran goes West and finds, in the lifestyle and hunting grounds of the Lakota Sioux, what he has been missing. Generally hailed by critics for its faithful depiction of Indian life and customs; spoken Lakota is dubbed in English. Kevin Costner, Mary McDonnell, Graham Green.

Geronimo: An American Legend
Color. 115 min. VHS.
Columbia Pictures (1993)
The exploits of the Apache leader during the years 1885 and 1886 are effectively dramatized; Geronimo ultimately becomes a larger-than-life hero and an expression of Apache cultural values. Wes Studi, Jason Patric, Gene Hackman.

The Last of the Mohicans
Color. 110 min. VHS.
20th Century Fox (1992)
A sweeping version of the James Fenimore Cooper tale of colonial America during the French and Indian War. Hawkeye (Natty Bumppo) and his Indian brother Chingachgook must rescue hapless colonists who have been captured by Indians. Daniel Day-Lewis, Madeleine Stowe, Russell Means, Eric Schweig.

Little Big Man
Color. 147 min. VHS.
CBS/Fox Video/Hiller Productions, Ltd. (1970)
Jack Crabb, 121-year-old veteran of the Old West and survivor of the Battle of the Little Bighorn, tells his story and stimulates sympathy for Indians along the way. Arthur Penn directed this offbeat epic starring Dustin Hoffman, Faye Dunaway, and Chief Dan George.

A Man Called Horse
Color. 114 min. VHS.
Cinema Center (1970)
In 1825 an English aristocrat is captured by a group of Sioux; he eventually becomes their leader. Relatively realistic, even graphic, portrayal of Indian life and customs, including tribal initiations. Richard Harris, Judith Anderson, Manu Tupou.

Running Brave
Color. 105 min. VHS
Buena Vista (1983)
A sentimental profile of half-Sioux athlete Billy Mills from his childhood on the Pine Ridge Reservation to his victory at the 1964 Tokyo Olympics. (The casting of a white actor in the lead Indian role caused considerable protest when the film was made.) Robbie Benson, Pat Hingle.

Shadow of the Wolf
Color. 108 min. VHS.
Triumph (1993)
A young Inuit hunter sets out to live in isolation in the Arctic wilderness; having killed a white trader, he is pursued by a Canadian mountie. Lou Diamond Phillips, Jennifer Tilly.

Son of the Morning Star
Color. 186 min. VHS.
Republic Pictures Home Video (1991)
A thoughtful look at the life and times of General George Armstrong Custer. Emphasis is on the ill-conceived and disastrous battle against the Sioux at Little Bighorn. Rosanna Arquette, Dean Stockwell, and Rodney A. Grant.

Thunderheart
Color. 118 min. VHS.
Tristar Pictures (1992)
An FBI agent who is part Sioux, sent to investigate a murder on a Sioux reservation, undergoes a personal transformation. The film is noteworthy for its portrayal of contemporary reservation life. Val Kilmer, Sam Shepard, Graham Greene.

BIBLIOGRAPHY

The following select bibliography of works on American Indians is organized into four categories: General Studies and Reference, History, Culture Areas (with eight subsections), and Contemporary Life.

GENERAL STUDIES AND REFERENCE

Bataille, Gretchen M., ed. *Native American Women: A Biographical Dictionary*. New York: Garland, 1993.

Bataille, Gretchen M., and Kathleen M. Sands. *American Indian Women Telling Their Lives*. Lincoln: University of Nebraska Press, 1984.

Bierhorst, John. *The Mythology of North America*. New York: William Morrow, 1985.

Boas, Franz. *Handbook for American Indian Languages*. 3 parts. Bureau of American Ethnology, Bulletin 40. Washington, D.C.: U.S. Government Printing Office, 1911.

Bowden, Henry Warner. *American Indians and Christian Missions*. Chicago: University of Chicago Press, 1981.

Brumble, H. David. *An Annotated Bibliography of American Indian and Eskimo Autobiographies*. Lincoln: University of Nebraska Press, 1981.

Campbell, Lyle, and Marianne Mithune, eds. *The Languages of Native America: Historical and Comparative Assessment*. Austin: University of Texas Press, 1979.

Hamlin-Wilson, Gail, ed. *Biographical Dictionary of the Indians of the Americas*. 2 vols. Newport Beach, Calif.: American Indian Publishers, 1991.

Coe, Michael, et al. *Atlas of Ancient America*. New York: Facts on File, 1986.

Cohen, Felix. *Felix Cohen's Handbook of Federal Indian Law*. 2d ed. Charlottesville, Va.: Michie/Bobbs-Merrill, 1982.

Culin, Stewart. *Games of the North American Indians*. Bureau of American Ethnology, Annual Report 24 (1902-1903). Washington, D.C.: U.S. Government Printing Office, 1907.

Curtis, Natalie. *The Indians' Book*. New York: Harper and Brothers, 1923.

Dawdy, Doris O., comp. *Annotated Bibliography of American Indian Painting*. Contributions from the Museum of the American Indian, Heye Foundation, vol. 21, pt. 2. New York: Museum of the American Indian, Heye Foundation, 1968.

Dobyns, Henry F. *Native American Historical Demography: A Critical Bibliography*. Newberry Library Center for the History of the American Indian Bibliographical Series. Bloomington: Indiana University Press, 1976.

Dockstader, Frederick J. *Indian Art in America: The Arts and Crafts of the North American Indians*. Greenwich, Conn.: New York Graphics Society, 1961.

Driver, Harold. *Indians of North America*. Chicago: University of Chicago Press, 1975.

Eggan, Fred, ed. *Social Anthropology of North American Tribes*. Chicago: University of Chicago Press, 1966.

Erdoes, Richard, and Alfonso Ortiz, eds. *American Indian Myths and Legends*. New York: Pantheon Books, 1984.

Feest, Christian F. *Native Arts of North America*. New York: Oxford University Press, 1980.

Gill, Sam D. *Native American Religions: An Introduction*. Belmont, Calif.: Wadsworth, 1982.

Gill, Sam D., and Irene F. Sullivan, comps. *Dictionary of Native American Mythology*. Santa Barbara, Calif.: ABC-CLIO, 1992.

Green, Rayna. *Native American Women: A Contextual Bibliography*. Bloomington: Indiana University Press, 1983.

Haas, Marilyn L. *Indians of North America: Sources for Library Research*. Hamden, Conn.: Library Professional Publications, 1983.

Hamilton, Charles, ed. *Cry of the Thunderbird*. Norman: University of Oklahoma Press, 1972.

Harris, R. Cole, ed. *Historical Atlas of Canada: From the Beginning to 1800*. Toronto: University of Toronto Press, 1987.

Heard, J. Norman. *Handbook of the American Frontier: Four Centuries of Indian-White Relations*. 3 vols. Metuchen, N.J.: Scarecrow Press, 1987-1992.

Hill, Edward E., comp. *Guide to the Records of the National Archives of the United States Relating to American Indians*. Washington, D.C.: National Archives and Records Service, 1981.

Hirschfelder, Arlene B., et al. *Guide to Research on North American Indians*. Chicago: American Library Association, 1983.

Hirschfelder, Arlene B., and Paulette Molin, comps. *The Encyclopedia of Native American Religions: An Introduction*. New York. Facts on File, 1992.

Hodge, Frederick W., ed. *Handbook of American Indians North of Mexico*. 2 vols. Washington, D.C.: U.S. Government Printing Office, 1907-1910.

Horr, David A., comp. and ed. *American Indian Ethnohistory*. 118 vols. New York: Garland, 1974.

Hoxie, Frederick E., ed. *Indians in American History: An Introduction*. Arlington Heights, Ill.: Harlan Davidson, 1988.

Hoxie, Frederick E., and Harvey Markowitz, comps. *Native Americans: An Annotated Bibliography*. Pasadena, Calif.: Salem Press, 1990.

Hultkrantz, Ake. *The Religions of the American Indians*. Translated by Monica Setterwall. Berkeley: University of California Press, 1967.

Hurt, R. Douglas. *Indian Agriculture in America: Prehistory to the Present*. Lawrence: University Press of Kansas, 1987.

Jenness, Diamond. *The Indians of Canada*. Ottawa: F. A. Acland, 1932.

Johnson, Steven L. *Guide to American Indian Documents in the Congressional Series Set, 1817-1899*. New York: Clearwater, 1977.

Josephy, Alvin M., Jr., ed., and William Brandon. *The American Heritage Book of Indians*. New York: American Heritage, 1961.

Kapplar, Charles. *Indian Affairs: Laws and Treaties*. 2 vols. Washington, D.C.: U.S. Government Printing Office, 1904-1941.

Klein, Barry T., ed. *Reference Encyclopedia of the American Indian*. 2 vols. 4th ed. New York: Todd, 1986.

Krech, Shepard, III. *Native Canadian Anthropology and History: A Selective Bibliography*. Winnipeg: Rupert's Land Research Centre, University of Winnipeg, 1986.

Krupat, Arnold. *For Those Who Come After: A Study of Native American Autobiography*. Berkeley: University of California Press, 1985.

Laubin, Reginald, and Gladys Laubin. *Indian Dances of North America*. Norman: University of Oklahoma Press, 1977.

Leacock, Eleanor Burke, and Nancy O. Lurie, eds. *North American Indians in Historical Perspective*. Prospect Heights, Ill.: Waveland Press, 1988.

Liberty, Margot, ed. *American Indian Intellectuals*. St. Paul, Minn.: West, 1978.

Littlefield, Daniel F., Jr., and James W. Parin. *A Biobibliography of Native American Writers, 1772-1924*. Metuchen, N.J.: Scarecrow Press, 1981.

Littlefield, Daniel F., Jr., and James W. Parin. *A Biobibliography of Native American Writers, 1772-1924: Supplement*. Metuchen, N.J.: Scarecrow Press, 1981.

Marriott, Alice Lee, and Carol Rachlin. *American Indian Mythology*. New York: Thomas Y. Crowell, 1964.

Murdock, George Peter, and Timothy J. O'Leary. *Ethnographic Bibliography of North America*. 4th ed. 5 vols. New Haven, Conn.: Human Relations Area Files Press, 1975.

Nabokov, Peter. *Native American Testimony*. New York: Harper & Row, 1979.

Nabokov, Peter, and Robert Easton. *Native American Architecture*. New York: Oxford University Press, 1989.

Orchard, William C. *Beads and Beadwork of the American Indian*. New York: Museum of the American Indian, Heye Foundation, 1929.

_____. *The Technique of Porcupine-Quill Decoration Among the North American Indians*. New York: Museum of the American Indian, Heye Foundation, 1971.

Prucha, Francis Paul. *A Bibliographical Guide to the History of Indian-White Relations in the United States*. Chicago: University of Chicago Press, 1977.

_____, ed. *Documents of United States Indian Policy*. 2d ed., expanded. Lincoln: University of Nebraska Press, 1990.

_____. *Indian-White Relations in the United States: A Bibliography of Works Published 1975-1980*. Lincoln: University of Nebraska Press, 1982.

Ronda, James, and James Axtell. *Indian Missions: A Critical Bibliography*. Newberry Library Center for the History of the American Indian Bibliographical Series. Bloomington: Indiana University Press, 1978.

Ruoff, A. Lavonne, and Karl Kroeber. *American Indian Literatures in the United States: A Basic Bibliography for Teachers*. New York: Association for the Study of American Indian Literature, 1983.

Schusky, Ernest L., ed. *Political Organization of Native North Americans*. Washington, D.C.: University of America Press, 1980.

Smith, Jane F., and Robert M. Kvasnicka, eds. *Indian-White Relations: A Persistent Paradox*. Washington, D.C.: Howard University Press, 1976.

Snipp, C. Mathew. *American Indians: The First of This Land*. New York: Russell Sage Foundation, 1989.

Snow, Dean R. *The American Indians: Their Archaeology and Prehistory*. New York: Thames and Hudson, 1976.

_____. *Native American Prehistory: A Critical Bibliography*. Newberry Library Center for the History of the American Indian Bibliographical Series. Bloomington: Indiana University Press, 1979.

Spencer, Robert F., Jesse D. Jennings, et al. *The Native Americans*. New York: Harper & Row, 1977.

Stewart, Omer C. *Peyote Religion: A History*. Norman: University of Oklahoma Press, 1987.

Stuart, Paul. *Nations Within a Nation: Historic Statistics of American Indians*. Westport, Conn.: Greenwood Press, 1987.

Sturtevant, William C., gen. ed. *Handbook of North American Indians*. Washington, D.C.: U.S. Government Printing Office, 1978.

Sullivan, Lawrence E., ed. *Native American Religions: North America*. New York: Macmillan, 1987.

Swann, Brian. *Smoothing the Ground: Essays on Native American Oral Literature*. Berkeley: University of California Press, 1983.

Tedlock, Dennis, and Barbara Tedlock, eds. *Teachings from the American Earth: Indian Religion and Philosophy*. New York: Liveright Press, 1975.

Thornton, Russell, and Mary K. Gramsmick. *Sociology of American Indians: A Critical Bibliography*. Newberry Library Center for the History of the American Indian Bibliographical Series. Bloomington: Indiana University Press, 1980.

Tyler, S. Lyman. *A History of Indian Policy*. Washington, D.C.: U.S. Department of the Interior, Bureau of Indian Affairs, 1973.

Ullom, Judith C., ed. *Folklore of the North American Indians: An Annotated Bibliography*. Washington, D.C.: Library of Congress, 1969.

Underhill, Ruth M. *Red Man's Religion*. Chicago: University of Chicago Press, 1965.

Utley, Robert M., and Wilcomb B. Washburn. *The American Heritage History of the Indian Wars*. New York: American Heritage, 1977.

Vogel, Virgil. *American Indian Medicine*. Norman: University of Oklahoma Press, 1970.

Waldman, Carl. *Atlas of the North American Indians*. New York: Facts on File, 1985.

Washburn, Wilcomb E., comp. and ed. *The American Indian and the United States*. 4 vols. New York: Random House, 1973.

Washburn, Wilcomb E. *History of Indian-White Relations*. Vol.4 in *Handbook of North American Indians*. Washington, D.C.: U.S. Government Printing Office, 1988.

HISTORY

Adams, Howard. *Prison of Grass: Canada from the Native Point of View*. Toronto: New Press, 1975.

Axtell, James. *The European and the Indian: Essays in the Ethnohistory of Colonial North America*. New York: Oxford University Press, 1981.

Berkhofer, Robert F., Jr. *Salvation and the Savage: An Analysis of Protestant Missions and American Indian Response 1787-1862*. Lexington: University of Kentucky Press, 1965.

Brown, Dee A. *Bury My Heart at Wounded Knee: An Indian History of the American West*. New York: Henry Holt, 1970.

Brown, Jennifer S. H. *Strangers in Blood: Fur Trade Company Families in Indian Country*. Vancouver: University of British Columbia Press, 1980.

Burt, Larry W. *Tribalism in Crisis: Federal Indian Policy, 1953-1961*. Albuquerque: University of New Mexico Press, 1982.

Calloway, Colin G. *Crown and Calumet: British-Indian Relations, 1783-1815*. Norman: University of Oklahoma Press, 1987.

Cook, Sherburne F. *The Conflict Between the California Indian and White Civilization*. Berkeley: University of California Press, 1974.

Cronon, William. *Changes in the Land: Indians, Colonists, and the Ecology of New England*. New York: Hill & Wang, 1983.

Crosby, Alfred W., Jr. *The Columbian Exchange: Biological and Cultural Consequences of 1492*. Westport, Conn.: Greenwood Press, 1972.

Curtis, Edward S. *In a Sacred Manner We Live*. Barre, Mass.: Barre Publishers, 1972.

Debo, Angie. *The Rise and Fall of the Choctaw Republic*. 2d ed. Norman: University of Oklahoma Press, 1967.

Dickason, Olive P. *The Myth of the Savage and the Beginnings of French Colonialism in the Americas*. Edmonton: University of Alberta Press, 1984.

Dippie, Brian W. *The Vanishing American: White Attitudes and U.S. Indian Policy*. Middletown, Conn.: Wesleyan University Press, 1982.

Fixico, Donald L. *Termination and Relocation: Federal Indian Policy, 1945-1966*. Albuquerque: University of New Mexico Press, 1986.

Foreman, Grant. *Indian Removal: The Emigration of the Five Civilized Tribes of Indians*. Norman: University of Oklahoma Press, 1932.

Fritz, Henry. *The Movement for Indian Assimilation, 1860-1890*. Philadelphia: University of Pennsylvania Press, 1963.

Getty, Ian A. L., and Antoine S. Lussier. *As Long as the Sun Shines and Water Flows: A Reader in Canadian Native Studies*. Vancouver: University of British Columbia Press, 1983.

Green, Michael D. *The Politics of Indian Removal: Creek Government and Society in Crisis*. Lincoln: University of Nebraska Press, 1982.

Hagan, William T. *American Indians*. Rev. ed. Chicago: University of Chicago Press, 1979.

Hanke, Lewis. *Aristotle and the American Indians*. Chicago: Henry Regnery, 1959.

Horsman, Reginald. *Expansion and American Indian Policy, 1783-1812*. East Lansing: Michigan State University Press, 1967.

Hoxie, Frederick E. *A Final Promise: The Campaign to Assimilate the Indians, 1880-1920*. Lincoln: University of Nebraska Press, 1984.

Huddleston, Lee Eldridge. *Origins of the American Indians: European Concepts, 1492-1729*. Austin: University of Texas Press, 1967.

Jackson, Helen Hunt. *A Century of Dishonor: A Sketch of the United States Government's Dealings with Some of the Indian Tribes*. New York: Harper and Brothers. 1881.

Jacobs, Wilbur R. *Dispossessing the American Indian: Indians and Whites on the Colonial Frontier*. New York: Charles Scribner's Sons, 1972.

Jaenen, Cornelius J. *Friend and Foe: Aspects of French-Amerindian Cultural Contact in the Sixteenth and Seventeenth Centuries*. New York: Columbia University Press, 1976.

Jennings, Francis. *The Invasion of America*. New York: W. W. Norton, 1975.

John, Elizabeth A. H. *Storms Brewed in Other Men's Worlds: The Confrontation of Indians, Spanish, and French in the Southwest, 1540-1795*. Lincoln: University of Nebraska Press, 1975.

Jones, Dorothy V. *License for Empire: Colonialism by Treaty in Early America*. Chicago: University of Chicago Press, 1982.

Keller, Robert H. *American Protestantism and United States Indian Policy, 1869-82*. Lincoln: University of Nebraska Press, 1983.

Kennedy, John H. *Jesuit and Savage in New France*. New Haven, Conn.: Yale University Press, 1950.

Little Bear, Leroy, and Menno Boldt, eds. *Pathways to Self-Determination*. Toronto: University of Toronto Press, 1984.

Milanich, Jerald T., and Susan Milbruth, eds. *First Encounters: Spanish Explorations in the Caribbean and the United States, 1492-1570*. Gainesville: University of Florida Press, 1989.

Miller, J. R. *Skyscrapers Hide the Heavens: A History of Indian-White Relations in Canada*. Toronto: University of Toronto Press, 1989.

Mooney, James. *The Ghost Dance Religion and the Sioux Outbreak of 1890*. Bureau of American Ethnology, Annual Report 14 (1892-1893). Washington, D.C.: U.S. Government Printing Office, 1896.

Morrison, Kenneth M. *The Embattled Northeast: The Elusive Ideal of Alliance in Abnaki-Euramerican Relations*. Berkeley: University of California Press, 1984.

Nash, Gary B. *Red, White, and Black: The Peoples of Early America*. Englewood Cliffs, N.J.: Prentice-Hall, 1974.

Priest, Loring Benson. *Uncle Sam's Stepchildren: The Reformation of United States Indian Policy, 1865-1887*. New Brunswick, N.J.: Rutgers University Press, 1942.

Prucha, Francis Paul. *The Great Father: The United States Government and the American Indians*. Lincoln: University of Nebraska Press, 1986.

Ray, Arthur J. *Indians in the Fur Trade: Their Role as Trappers, Hunters, and Middlemen in the Lands Southwest of Hudson Bay, 1660-1870*. Toronto: University of Toronto Press, 1974.

Salisbury, Neal. *Manitou and Providence: Indians, Europeans, and the Making of New England*. New York: Oxford University Press, 1982.

Satz, Ronald N. *American Indian Policy in the Jacksonian Era*. Lincoln: University of Nebraska Press, 1975.

Sheehan, Bernard W. *Savagism and Civility: Indians and Englishmen in Colonial Virginia*. New York: Cambridge University Press, 1980.

_____. *Seeds of Extinction: Jeffersonian Philanthropy and the American Indian*. Chapel Hill: University of North Carolina Press, 1973.

Szasz, Margaret C. *Indian Education in the American Colonies, 1607-1783*. Albuquerque: University of New Mexico Press, 1988.

Trennert, Robert A., Jr. *Alternative to Extinction: Federal Indian Policy and the Beginnings of the Reservation System, 1846-51*. Philadelphia: University of Pennsylvania Press, 1975.

Trigger, Bruce G. *Natives and Newcomers: Canada's "Heroic Age" Reconsidered*. Montreal: McGill-Queen's University Press, 1985.

Utley, Robert M. *The Indian Frontier of the American West, 1846-1890*. Albuquerque: University of New Mexico Press, 1984.

Viola, Herman J. *Diplomats in Buckskin: A History of the Indian Delegations in Washington City*. Washington, D.C.: Smithsonian Institution Press, 1981.

Washburn, Wilcomb E. *The Assault on Indian Tribalism: The General Allotment Law (Dawes Act) of 1887*. Philadelphia: J. B. Lippincott, 1975.

Weaver, Sally M. *Making Canadian Indian Policy: The Hidden Agenda, 1968-70*. Toronto: University of Toronto Press.

White, Richard. *The Roots of Dependency: Subsistence, Environment, and Social Change Among the Choctaws, Pawnees, and Navajos*. Lincoln: University of Nebraska Press, 1983.

CULTURE AREAS

Arctic and Subarctic

Boas, Franz. *The Central Eskimo*. Bureau of American Ethnology, Annual Report 6 (1884-1885). Washington, D.C.: U.S. Government Printing Office. 1888.

Chance, Norman A. *The Eskimo of North Alaska*. New York: Holt, Rinehart and Winston, 1966.

Condon, Richard G. *Inuit Youth: Growth and Change in the Canadian Arctic*. New Brunswick, N.J.: Rutgers University Press, 1987.

Damas, David. *Arctic*. Vol. 5 in *Handbook of North American Indians*. Washington, D.C.: Smithsonian Institution, 1984.

Dumond, Don E. *The Eskimos and Aleuts*. Rev. ed. London: Thames and Hudson, 1987.

Helm, June. *The Indians of the Subarctic: A Critical Bibliography*. Newberry Library Center for the History of the American Indian Bibliographical Series. Bloomington: Indiana University Press, 1976.

_____, ed. *Subarctic*. Vol. 6 in *Handbook of North American Indians*. Washington, D.C.: Smithsonian Institution, 1981.

Krech, Shepard, III, ed. *The Subarctic Fur Trade: Native Social and Economic Adaptations*. Vancouver: University of British Columbia Press, 1984.

Nelson, Richard K. *Hunters of the Northern Forest*. Chicago: University of Chicago Press, 1973.

_____. *Hunters of the Northern Ice*. Chicago: University of Chicago Press, 1969.

Oswalt, Wendell H. *Eskimos and Explorers*. Novato, Calif.: Chandler and Sharp, 1979.

Ray, Dorothy Jean. *Aleut and Eskimo Art: Tradition and Innovation in South Alaska*. Seattle: University of Washington Press, 1981.

VanStone, James W. *Athapaskan Adaptations: Hunters and Fishermen of the Subarctic Forests*. Chicago: Aldine, 1974.

California

Bean, Lowell J. *Mukat's People: The Cahuilla Indians of Southern California*. Berkeley: University of California Press, 1973.

Chartkoff, Joseph L., and Kerry K. Chartkoff. *The Archaeology of California*. Stanford, Calif.: Stanford University Press, 1984.

Grant, Campbell. *The Rock Painting of the Chumash: A Study of a California Indian Culture*. Berkeley: University of California Press, 1965.

Heizer, Robert F., ed. *California*. Vol. 8 in *Handbook of North American Indians*. Washington, D.C.: Smithsonian Institution, 1978.

_____. *The Indians of California: A Critical Bibliography*. Newberry Library Center for the History of the American Indian Bibliographical Series. Bloomington: Indiana University Press, 1976.

Heizer, Robert F., and Albert B. Elsasser, comps. *A Bibliography of California Indians: Archaeology, Ethnography, and Indian History. New York: Garland, 1977.

Heizer, Robert F., and Theodora Kroeber, eds. Ishi, the Last Yahi: A Documentary History. Berkeley: University of California Press, 1979.

Heizer, Robert F., and Mary A. Whipple, comps. and eds. The California Indians: A Source Book. 2d rev., enlarged ed. Berkeley: University of California Press, 1971.

Kroeber, Theodora, and Robert F. Heizer. Almost Ancestors: The First Californians, edited by F. David Hales. San Francisco: Sierra Club Books, 1968.

Ray, Verne F. Primitive Pragmatists: The Modoc Indians of Northern California. Seattle: University of Washington Press, 1963.

Shipek, Florence C. Pushed into the Rocks: Southern California Indian Land Tenure, 1769-1986. Lincoln: University of Nebraska Press, 1987.

Great Basin

Bunte, Pamela A., and Robert J. Franklin. From the Sands to the Mountain: Change and Persistence in a Southern Paiute Community. Lincoln: University of Nebraska Press, 1987.

D'Azevedo, Warren L. Great Basin. Vol. 11 in Handbook of North American Indians. Washington, D.C.: Smithsonian Institution, 1986.

_____, ed. and comp. The Washo Indians of California and Nevada. University of Utah Anthropological Papers 67. Salt Lake City: University of Utah Press, 1963.

Densmore, Frances. Northern Ute Music. Bureau of American Ethnology, Bulletin 75. Washington, D.C.: U.S. Government Printing Office, 1922.

Fowler, Don D., ed. Great Basin Cultural Ecology: A Symposium. Desert Research Institute Publications in the Social Sciences 8. Reno, Nev.: Publications Office of the Desert Research Institute, 1972.

Hopkins, Sarah Winnemucca. Life Among the Piutes: Their Wrongs and Claims. New York: G. P. Putnam's Sons, 1883.

Knack, Martha. Life Is with People. Socorro, N.Mex.: Ballena Press, 1980.

Knack, Martha, and Omer C. Stewart. As Long as the River Shall Run: An Ethnohistory of Pyramid Lake Indian Reservation. Berkeley: University of California Press. 1984.

Laird, Carobeth. Mirror and Pattern: George Laird's World of Chemehuevi Mythology. Banning, Calif.: Malki Museum Press, 1984.

Madsen, Brigham D. The Bannock of Idaho. Caldwell, Idaho: Caxton Printers, 1958.

Steward, Julian H. Basin-Plateau Aboriginal Sociopolitical Groups. Bureau of American Ethnology, Bulletin 120. Washington, D.C.: U.S. Government Printing Office, 1938.

Stewart, Omer C. Indians of the Great Basin: A Critical Bibliography. Newberry Library Center for the History of the American Indian Bibliographical Series. Bloomington: Indiana University Press, 1982.

Northeast

Anson, Bert. The Miami Indians. Norman: University of Oklahoma Press, 1970.

Barnouw, Victor. Wisconsin Chippewa Myths and Tales and Their Relation to Chippewa Life. Madison: University of Wisconsin Press, 1977.

Black Hawk (Ma-ka-tai-me-she-kia-kiak). An Autobiography, edited by Donald Jackson. Urbana: University of Illinois Press, 1955.

Brose, David S., et al. Ancient Art of the American Woodlands Indians. New York: Harry N. Abrams, in association with the Detroit Institute of Arts, 1985.

Clifton, James A. The Prairie People: Continuity and Change in Potawatomi Indian Culture, 1665-1965. Lawrence, Kans.: Regents Press of Kansas, 1977.

Densmore, Frances. Chippewa Customs. Bureau of American Ethnology, Bulletin 86. Washington, D.C.: U.S. Government Printing Office, 1929.

_____. Chippewa Music. 2 vols. Bureau of American Ethnology, Bulletins 45 and 53. Washington, D.C.: U.S. Government Printing Office, 1910-1913.

_____. Uses of Plants by the Chippewa Indians. Bureau of American Ethnology, Annual Report 44 (1926-1927). Washington, D.C.: U.S. Government Printing Office, 1928.

Edmunds, R. David. The Potawatomis: Keepers of the Fire. Norman: University of Oklahoma Press, 1978.

Gibson, Arrell M. The Kickapoos: Lords of the Middle Border. Norman: University of Oklahoma Press, 1963.

Hagan, William T. The Sac and the Fox Indians. Norman: University of Oklahoma Press, 1958.

Hale, Horatio E., ed. The Iroquois Book of Rites. Brinton's Library of Aboriginal American Literature 11. Philadelphia: D. G. Brinton, 1883.

Hickerson, Harold. The Chippewa and Their Neighbors: A Study in Ethnohistory. Prospect Heights, Ill.: Waveland Press, 1988.

Kinietz, W. Vernon. The Indians of the Western Great Lakes, 1615-1760. Ann Arbor: University of Michigan Press, 1940.

Landes, Ruth. Ojibwa Religion and the Mdewiwin. Madison: University of Wisconsin Press, 1968.

_____. Ojibwa Sociology. Columbia University Contributions to Anthropology 29. New York: Columbia University Press, 1937.

Lyford, Carrie A. Iroquois Crafts. Lawrence, Kans.: Haskell Institute Press, 1945.

_____. Ojibway Crafts. Lawrence, Kans.: Haskell Institute Press, 1943.

Mason, Ronald J. Great Lakes Archaeology. New York: Academic Press, 1981.

Morgan, Lewis Henry. League of the Ho-de-no-sau-nee or Iroquois. Rochester, N.Y.: Sage and Brothers, 1851.

Morgan, William N. Prehistoric Architecture in the Eastern United States. Cambridge, Mass.: MIT Press, 1980.

Mountain Wolf Woman. Mountain Wolf Woman, Sister of

Crashing Thunder: The Autobiography of a Winnebago Indian, edited by Nancy O. Lurie. Ann Arbor: University of Michigan Press, 1961.

Quimby, George I. *Indian Life in the Upper Great Lakes: 11,000 B.C. to A.D. 1800*. Chicago: University of Chicago Press, 1960.

Radin, Paul, ed. *The Autobiography of a Winnebago Indian*. University of California Publications in American Archaeology and Ethnology, vol. 16, no. 7. Berkeley: University of California Press, 1920.

Radin, Paul. *The Winnebago Tribe*. Bureau of American Ethnology, Annual Report 37 (1915-1916). Washington, D.C.: U.S. Government Printing Office, 1923.

Ritzenthaler, Robert E., and Pat Ritzenthaler. *The Woodland Indians of the Western Great Lakes*. Garden City, N.Y.: Natural History Press, 1970.

Salisbury, Neal. *The Indians of New England: A Critical Bibliography*. Newberry Library Center for the History of the American Indian Bibliographical Series. Bloomington: Indiana University Press, 1982.

Snow, Dean R. *The Archaeology of New England*. New York: Academic Press, 1980.

Tanner, Helen Hornbeck, et al. *Atlas of Great Lakes Indian History*. Norman: University of Oklahoma Press, 1986.

Tooker, Elisabeth. *The Indians of the Northeast: A Critical Bibliography*. Newberry Library Center for the History of the American Indian Bibliographical Series. Bloomington: Indiana University Press, 1978.

_____, ed. *Native North American Spirituality of the Eastern Woodlands: Sacred Myths, Dreams, Visions, Speeches, Healing Formulas, Rituals, and Ceremonies*. Mahwah, N.J.: Paulist Press, 1979.

Trigger, Bruce G. *The Huron: Farmers of the North*. New York: Holt, Rinehart and Winston, 1969.

_____, ed. *Northeast*. Vol. 15 in *Handbook of North American Indians*. Washington, D.C.: Smithsonian Institution, 1978.

Vennum, Thomas, Jr. *Wild Rice and the Ojibway People*. St. Paul: Minnesota Historical Society, 1988.

Wallace, Anthony F. C. *The Death and Rebirth of the Seneca*. New York: Alfred A. Knopf, 1969.

Webb, William S., and Charles E. Snow. *The Adena People*. Knoxville: University of Tennessee Press, 1974.

Northwest Coast and Plateau

Amoss, Pamela. *Coast Salish Spirit Dancing: The Survival of an Ancestral Religion*. Seattle: University of Washington Press, 1978.

Boas, Franz. *Kwakiutl Ethnography*, edited by Helen Codere. Chicago: University of Chicago Press, 1966.

Codere, Helen. *Fighting with Property: A Study of Kwakiutl Potlatching and Warfare 1792-1930*. New York: J. J. Augustin, 1950.

Drucker, Philip. *Cultures of the North Pacific Coast*. San Francisco: Chandler, 1965.

Fahey, John. *The Flathead Indians*. Norman: University of Oklahoma Press, 1974.

Grumet, Robert S. *Native Americans of the Northwest Coast: A Critical Bibliography*. Newberry Library Center for the History of the American Indian Bibliographical Series. Bloomington: Indiana University Press, 1979.

Haines, Francis. *The Nez Percé: Tribesmen of the Columbian Plateau*. Norman: University of Oklahoma Press, 1955.

Inverarity, Robert B. *Art of the Northwest Coast Indians*. Berkeley: University of California Press, 1950.

Kirk, Ruth, and Richard D. Daughtery. *Exploring Washington Archaeology*. Seattle: University of Washington Press, 1978.

Miller, Jay, and Carol Eastman, ed. *The Tsimshian and Their Neighbors on the North Pacific Coast*. Seattle: University of Washington Press, 1984.

Mourning Dove (Humishuma). *Coyote Stories*, edited by Jay Miller. Lincoln: University of Nebraska Press, 1990.

_____. *Mourning Dove: A Salishan Autobiography*, edited by Jay Miller. Lincoln: University of Nebraska Press, 1990.

People of 'Ksan. *Gathering What the Great Nature Provided: Food Traditions of the Gitksan*. Vancouver: Douglas and McIntyre and Seattle: University of Washington Press, 1980.

Ruby, Robert H., and John A. Brown. *A Guide to the Indian Tribes of the Pacific Northwest*. Norman: University of Oklahoma Press, 1986.

Samuel, Cheryl. *The Chilkat Dancing Blanket*. Seattle: Pacific Search Press, 1982.

Spradley, James, ed. *Guests Never Leave Hungry: The Autobiography of James Sewid, a Kwakiutl Indian*. New Haven, Conn.: Yale University Press, 1969.

Stewart, Hilary. *Artifacts of the Northwest Coast Indians*. Saanichton, British Columbia: Hancock House Publishers, 1973.

_____. *Cedar: Tree of Life to the Northwest Coast Indians*. Seattle: University of Washington Press, 1984.

_____. *Indian Fishing: Early Methods on the Northwest Coast*. Seattle: University of Washington Press, 1977.

Plains

Albers, Patricia, and Beatrice Medicine. *The Hidden Half: Studies in Plains Indian Women*. Lanham, Md.: University Press of America, 1983.

Baird, W. David. *The Quapaw Indians: A History of the Downstream People*. Norman: University of Oklahoma Press, 1981.

Berthrong, Donald J. *The Southern Cheyennes*. Norman: University of Oklahoma Press, 1963.

Black Elk, as told to John G. Neihardt. *Black Elk Speaks*. New York: William Morrow, 1932.

Blaine, Martha R. *The Pawnees: A Critical Bibliography*. Newberry Library Center for the History of the American Indian Bibliographical Series. Bloomington: Indiana University Press, 1980.

Blish, Helen H. *A Pictographic History of the Oglala Sioux, Drawings by Amos Bad Heart Bull.* Lincoln: University of Nebraska Press, 1967.

Bowers, Alfred W. *Mandan Social and Ceremonial Organization.* Chicago: University of Chicago Press, 1950.

Brown, Joseph E. *The Sacred Pipe: Black Elk's Account of the Seven Rites of the Oglala Sioux.* Norman: University of Oklahoma Press, 1953.

DeMallie, Raymond, ed. *The Sixth Grandfather: Black Elk's Teachings Given to John G. Neihardt.* Lincoln: University of Nebraska Press, 1984.

DeMallie, Raymond, and Douglas R. Parks, eds. *Sioux Indian Religion.* Norman: University of Oklahoma Press, 1987.

Densmore, Frances. *Cheyenne and Arapaho Music.* Southwest Museum Papers 10. Los Angeles: Southwest Museum, 1936.

————. *Mandan and Hidatsa Music.* Bureau of American Ethnology, Bulletin 80. Washington, D.C.: U.S. Government Printing Office, 1923.

————. *Pawnee Music.* Bureau of American Ethnology, Bulletin 93. Washington, D.C.: U.S. Government Printing Office, 1929.

————. *Teton Sioux Music.* Bureau of American Ethnology, Bulletin 61. Washington, D.C.: Government Printing Office, 1918.

Dorsey, George A. *The Cheyenne.* Field Columbian Museum Anthropological Series, vol. 9, nos. 1 and 2. Chicago: The Museum, 1905.

Ewers, John C. *The Blackfeet: Raiders on the Northwestern Plains.* Norman: University of Oklahoma Press, 1958.

————. *Blackfoot Crafts.* Lawrence, Kans.: Haskell Institute Printing Department, 1945.

————. *The Horse in Blackfoot Culture.* Bureau of American Ethnology, Bulletin 159. Washington, D.C.: U.S. Government Printing Office, 1955.

Fletcher, Alice C. *The Hako: A Pawnee Ceremony.* Bureau of American Ethnology, Annual Report 22. (1900-1901). Washington, D.C.: U.S. Government Printing Office, 1904.

Fletcher, Alice C., and Francis La Flesche. *The Omaha Tribe.* 2 vols. Bureau of American Ethnology, Annual Report 27 (1905-1906). Washington, D.C.: U.S. Government Printing Office, 1911.

Fowler, Loretta. *Arapahoe Politics, 1851-1978.* Lincoln: University of Nebraska Press, 1982.

Frison, George. *Prehistoric Hunters of the High Plains.* New York: Academic Press, 1978.

Gilmore, Melvin R. *Uses of Plants by the Indians of the Missouri River Region.* Bureau of American Ethnology, Annual Report 33 (1911-1912). Washington, D.C.: U.S. Government Printing Office, 1919.

Grinnell, George B. *The Cheyenne Indians: Their History and Ways of Life.* 2 vols. New Haven, Conn.: Yale University Press, 1923.

Hassrick, Royal B. *The Sioux: Life and Customs of a Warrior Society.* Norman: University of Oklahoma Press, 1964.

Hoebel, E. Adamson. *The Plains Indians: A Critical Bibliography.* Newberry Library Center for the History of the American Indian Bibliographical Series. Bloomington: Indiana University Press, 1979.

Holder, Preston. *The Hoe and the Horse on the Plains.* Lincoln: University of Nebraska Press, 1970.

Hyde, George E.. *Spotted Tail's Folk: A History of the Brule Sioux.* Norman: University of Oklahoma Press, 1961.

Iverson, Peter, ed. *The Plains Indians of the Twentieth Century.* Norman: University of Oklahoma Press, 1985.

Llewellen, Karl N., and E. Adamson Hoebel. *The Cheyenne Way: Conflict and Case Law in Primitive Jurisprudence.* Norman: University of Oklahoma Press, 1941.

Lowie, Robert H. *The Crow Indians.* New York: Farrar and Rinehart, 1935.

————. *Indians of the Plains.* New York: McGraw-Hill, 1954.

————. *Myths and Traditions of the Crow Indians.* Anthropological Papers of the American Museum of Natural History, vol. 25, pt. 1. New York: Order of Trustees, 1918.

————. *Social Life of the Crow Indians.* Anthropological Papers of the American Museum of Natural History, vol. 9, pt. 2. New York: Order of Trustees, 1912.

Lyford, Carrie A. *Quill and Beadwork of the Western Sioux.* Lawrence, Kans.: Printing Department, Haskell Institute, 1940.

Mandelbaum, David G. *The Plains Cree.* Anthropological Papers of the American Museum of Natural History, vol. 37, pt. 2. New York: Order of Trustees, 1940.

Murie, James R. *Ceremonies of the Pawnee.* 2 parts, edited by Douglas R. Parks. 2 vols. Washington, D.C.: Smithsonian Institution Press, 1981.

Newkumet, Vynola Beaver, and Howard L. Meridith. *Hasinai: A Traditional History of the Caddo Confederacy.* College Station: Texas A&M University Press, 1988.

Petersen, Karen D. *Plains Indian Art from Fort Marion.* Norman: University of Oklahoma Press, 1971.

Plenty Coups. *American: The Life Story of a Great Indian, Plenty-coups, Chief of the Crows,* edited by Frank B. Linderman. Chicago, N.Y.: World Book, 1930.

Powell, Peter J. *The Cheyennes, Ma'heo'o's People: A Critical Bibliography.* Newberry Library Center for the History of the American Indian Bibliographical Series. Bloomington: Indiana University Press, 1980.

————. *People of the Sacred Mountain: A History of the Northern Cheyenne Chiefs and Warrior Societies, 1830-1879.* 2 vols. San Francisco: Harper & Row, 1981.

Powers, William K. *Yuwipi: Vision and Experience in Oglala Ritual.* Lincoln: University of Nebraska Press, 1982.

Standing Bear, Luther. *My People the Sioux.* Boston: Houghton Mifflin, 1928.

Stands in Timber, John, and Margot Liberty. *Cheyenne Memories.* New Haven, Conn.: Yale University Press, 1967.

Unrau, William E. *The Emigrant Indians of Kansas: A Critical Bibliography.* Newberry Library Center for the History of the American Indian Bibliographical Series. Bloomington: Indiana University Press, 1979.

Voget, Fred W. *The Shoshoni-Crow Sun Dance*. Norman: University of Oklahoma Press, 1984.

Walker, James R. *Lakota Belief and Ritual*, edited by Raymond J. DeMallie and Elaine A. Jahner. Lincoln: University of Nebraska Press, 1980.

_____. *Lakota Myth*, edited by Elaine A. Jahner. Lincoln: University of Nebraska Press, 1983.

_____. *Lakota Society*, edited by Raymond J. DeMallie. Lincoln: University of Nebraska Press, 1982.

Wedel, Waldo R., ed. *A Plains Archaeology Source Book: Selected Papers of the Nebraska Historical Society*. New York: Garland, 1985.

Weist, Katherine M., and Susan R. Sharrock. *An Annotated Bibliography of Northern Plains Ethnohistory*. Missoula: Department of Anthropology, University of Montana, 1985.

Wildschut, W., and John C. Ewers. *Crow Indian Beadwork*. New York: Museum of the American Indian, Heye Foundation, 1959.

Will, George F., and George E. Hyde. *Corn Among the Indians of the Upper Missouri*. St. Louis, Mo.: William Harvey Minor Co., 1917.

Wissler, Clark, ed. *Societies of the Plains Indians*. American Museum of Natural History, Anthropological Papers, vol. 11., pts. 1-13. New York: The Trustees, 1912-1916.

Wood, W. Raymond, and Margot Liberty, eds. *Anthropology on the Great Plains*. Lincoln: University of Nebraska Press, 1980.

Zimmerman, Larry J. *Peoples of Prehistoric South Dakota*. Lincoln: University of Nebraska Press, 1985.

Southeast

Baird, W. David. *The Chickasaw People*. Phoenix: Indian Tribal Series, 1974.

_____. *The Choctaw People*. Phoenix: Indian Tribal Series, 1973.

_____. *Peter Pitchlynn: Chief of the Choctaws*. Norman: University of Oklahoma Press, 1972.

Blu, Karen I. *The Lumbee Problem: The Making of an American Indian People*. Cambridge, England: Cambridge University Press, 1980.

Densmore, Frances. *Choctaw Music*. Bureau of American Ethnology, Bulletin 136. Washington, D.C.: U.S. Government Printing Office, 1943.

_____. *Seminole Music*. Bureau of American Ethnology, Bulletin 161. Washington, D.C.: U.S. Government Printing Office, 1956.

Edmunds, R. David. *The Shawnee Prophet*. Lincoln: University of Nebraska Press, 1983.

Fogelson, Raymond D. *The Cherokees: A Critical Bibliography*. Newberry Library Center for the History of the American Indian Bibliographical Series. Bloomington: Indiana University Press, 1978.

Gilliland, Marion Spjut. *The Material Culture of Key Marco, Florida*. Gainesville: University Presses of Florida, 1975.

Green, Michael D. *The Creeks: A Critical Bibliography*. Newberry Library Center for the History of the American Indian Bibliographical Series. Bloomington: Indiana University Press, 1979.

Hudson, Charles M., ed. *Ethnology of the Southeastern Indians*. New York: Garland, 1985.

_____. *The Southeastern Indians*. Knoxville: University of Tennessee Press, 1976.

Kidwell, Clara Sue, and Charles Roberts. *The Choctaws: A Critical Bibliography*. Newberry Library Center for the History of the American Indian Bibliographical Series. Bloomington: Indiana University Press, 1980.

King, Duane H., ed. *The Cherokee Indian Nation: A Troubled History*. Knoxville: University of Tennessee Press, 1979.

McReynolds, Edwin C. *The Seminoles*. Norman: University of Oklahoma Press, 1957.

Merrell, James H. *The Indians' New World: Catawbas and Their Neighbors from European Contact Through the Era of Removal*. Chapel Hill: University of North Carolina Press, for the Institute of Early American History and Culture, Williamsburg, Virginia, 1989.

Milanich, Jerald T., and Charles H. Fairbanks. *Florida Archaeology*. New York: Academic Press, 1980.

Mooney, James. *Myths of the Cherokee*. Bureau of American Ethnology, Annual Report 19 (1897-1898). Washington, D.C.: U.S. Government Printing Office, 1900.

_____. *The Sacred Formulas of the Cherokees*. Bureau of American Ethnology, Annual Report 7 (1885-1886). Washington, D.C.: U.S. Government Printing Office, 1891.

Rountree, Helen C. *The Powhatan Indians of Virginia: Their Traditional Culture*. Norman: University of Oklahoma Press, 1989.

Swanton, John R. *The Indians of the Southeastern United States*. Bureau of American Ethnology, Bulletin 137. Washington, D.C.: U.S. Government Printing Office, 1946.

_____. *Myths and Tales of the Southeastern Indians*. Bureau of American Ethnology, Bulletin 88. Washington, D.C.: U.S. Government Printing Office, 1929.

Walthall, John A. *Prehistoric Indians of the Southeast: Archaeology of Alabama and the Middle South*. Tuscaloosa: University of Alabama Press, 1980.

Southwest

Basso, Keith H., ed. *Western Apache Raiding and Warfare, from the Notes of Grenville Goodwin*. Tucson: University of Arizona Press, 1971.

Benedict, Ruth. *Zuni Mythology*. 2 vols. New York: Columbia University Press, 1935.

Bunzel, Ruth L. *The Pueblo Potter: A Study of Creative Imagination in Primitive Art*. New York: Columbia University Press, 1929.

Cordell, Linda S. *Prehistory of the Southwest*. Orlando, Fla.: Academic Press, 1984.

Densmore, Frances. *Papago Music*. Bureau of American Ethnology, Bulletin 90. Washington, D.C.: U.S. Government Printing Office, 1929.

Dobyns, Henry F., and Robert C. Euler. *Indians of the Southwest.* Newberry Library Center for the History of the American Indian Bibliographical Series. Bloomington: Indiana University Press, 1980.

Dozier, Edward P. *Hano: A Tewa Indian Community in Arizona.* New York: Holt, Rinehart and Winston, 1966.

Eggan, Fred. *Social Organization of the Western Pueblos.* Chicago: University of Chicago Press, 1950.

Ferguson, T. J., and Richard E. Hart. *A Zuni Atlas.* Norman: University of Oklahoma Press, 1985.

Foster, Morris. *Being Comanche: A Social History of an American Indian Community.* Tucson: University of Arizona Press, 1991.

Frisbie, Charlotte J. *Navajo Medicine Bundles or Jish: Acquisition, Transmission, and Disposition in the Past and Present.* Albuquerque: University of New Mexico Press, 1987.

Goodman, James M. *The Navajo Atlas: Environments, Resources, People, and History of the Dine Bikeyah.* Norman: University of Oklahoma Press, 1982.

Haile, O. F. M., Fr. Berard, comp. and trans. *Navajo Coyote Tales: The Curly To Aheeddliinii Version,* edited by Karl Luckert. Lincoln: University of Nebraska Press, 1984.

Iverson, Peter. *Carlos Montezuma and the Changing World of American Indians.* Albuquerque: University of New Mexico Press, 1982.

———. *The Navajo Nation.* Westport, Conn.: Greenwood Press, 1981.

———. *The Navajos: A Critical Bibliography.* Newberry Library Center for the History of the American Indian Bibliographical Series. Bloomington: Indiana University Press, 1976.

Kent, Kate Peck. *Navajo Weaving: Three Centuries of Change.* Santa Fe, N.M.: School of American Research Press, 1985.

———. *Prehistoric Textiles of the Southwest.* Santa Fe: School of American Research; and Albuquerque: University of New Mexico Press, 1983.

Kluckhohn, Clyde. *Navaho Witchcraft.* Boston: Beacon Press, 1962.

Laird, W. David. *Hopi Bibliography, Comprehensive and Annotated.* Tucson: University of Arizona Press, 1977.

Lamphere, Louise. *To Run After Them: Cultural and Social Bases of Cooperation in a Navajo Community.* Tucson: University of Arizona Press, 1977.

Leighton, Dorothea, and John Adair. *People of the Middle Place: A Study of the Zuni Indians.* New Haven, Conn.: Human Relations Area Files Press, 1966.

Lister, Robert H., and Florence C. Lister. *Chaco Canyon: Archaeology and Archaeologists.* Albuquerque: University of New Mexico Press, 1981.

Melody, Michael Edward. *The Apache: A Critical Bibliography.* Newberry Library Center for the History of the American Indian Bibliographical Series. Bloomington: Indiana University Press, 1977.

Ortiz, Alfonso, ed. *New Perspectives on the Pueblos.* Albuquerque: University of New Mexico Press, 1972.

———, ed. *Southwest.* Vol. 9 in *Handbook of North American Indians.* Washington: Smithsonian Institution, 1979.

———, ed. *Southwest.* Vol. 10 in *Handbook of North American Indians.* Washington, D.C.: Smithsonian Institution, 1983.

———. *The Tewa World: Space, Time, Being, and Becoming in a Pueblo Society.* Chicago: University of Chicago Press, 1969.

Parsons, Elsie C. *Pueblo Indian Religion.* 2 vols. Chicago: University of Chicago Press, 1939.

Reichard, Gladys A. *Navaho Indian Religion: A Study of Symbolism.* 2 vols. New York: Pantheon Books, 1950.

Stevenson, Matilda C. *The Zuni Indians: Their Mythology, Esoteric Fraternities, and Ceremonies.* Bureau of American Ethnology, Annual Report 23 (1901-1902). Washington, D.C.: U.S. Government Printing Office, 1904.

Tanner, Clara Lee. *Prehistoric Southwestern Craft Arts.* Tucson: University of Arizona Press, 1976.

———. *Southwest Indian Painting: A Changing Art.* 2d ed. Tucson: University of Arizona Press, 1973.

Underhill, Ruth M. *Papago Woman.* New York: Holt, Rinehart and Winston, 1979.

Whitewolf, Jim. *The Life of a Kiowa Apache Indian,* edited by Charles S. Brant. New York: Dover, 1969.

Wills, W. H. *Early Prehistoric Agriculture in the American Southwest.* Santa Fe, N.M.: School of American Research Press, 1988.

CONTEMPORARY LIFE

Ambler, Marjane. *Breaking the Iron Bonds: Indian Control of Energy Development.* Lawrence: University Press of Kansas, 1990.

Berkhofer, Robert, Jr. *The White Man's Indian.* New York: Alfred A. Knopf, 1978.

Deloria, Vine, Jr. *Behind the Trail of Broken Treaties: An Indian Declaration of Independence.* New York: Delta, 1974.

———. *God Is Red.* New York: Grosset & Dunlop, 1973.

Fuchs, Estelle, and Robert Havighurst. *To Live on This Earth.* Garden City, N.Y.: Doubleday, 1972.

Hertzberg, Hazel W. *The Search for an American Indian Identity: Modern Pan-Indian Movements.* Syracuse, N.Y.: Syracuse University Press, 1971.

Highwater, Jamake. *The Sweet Grass Lives On: Fifty Contemporary North American Indian Artists.* New York: Lippincott and Thomas Y. Crowell, 1980.

Hobson, Geary, ed. *The Remembered Earth: An Anthology of Contemporary Native American Literature.* Albuquerque: University of New Mexico Press, 1979.

McNickle, D'Arcy. *The Surrounded.* New York: Dodd, Mead, 1936.

Momaday, N. Scott. *House Made of Dawn*. New York: Harper & Row, 1968.

O'Brien, Sharon. *American Indian Tribal Governments*. Norman: University of Oklahoma Press, 1989.

Red Horse, John, et al. *The American Indian Family: Strengths and Stresses*. Isleta, N.Mex.: American Indian Social Research and Development Associates, 1981.

Rosen, Kenneth. *The Man to Send Rain Clouds: Contemporary Stories by American Indians*. New York: Viking Press, 1974.

Silko, Leslie M. *Ceremony*. New York: Viking Press, 1977.

Waddell, Jack O., and O. Michael Watson, eds. *The American Indian in Urban Society*. Boston: Little, Brown, 1971.

Welch, James. *Winter in the Blood*. New York: Harper & Row, 1974.

RR AMERICAN INDIANS

LIST OF ENTRIES BY CATEGORY

ARCHAEOLOGICAL SITES

Awatovi
Aztalan
Bat Cave
Cahokia
Canyon de Chelly
Chaco Canyon
Chichén Itzá
Copan
Cuello
Danger Cave
El Tajín
Emerald Mound
Etowah
Key Marco
Koster
La Venta
Lehner
Mesa Verde
Middens

Midland
Mitla
Monte Albán
Oaxaca
Ozette
Palenque
Poverty Point
San Lorenzo
Snaketown
Spiro
Tenochtitlán
Teotihuacán
Tikal
Tres Zapotes
Tula
Uxmal
Veracruz
Yaxchilan

ART AND ARCHITECTURE

Adobe
Appliqué and ribbonwork
Architecture—Arctic
Architecture—California
Architecture—Great Basin
Architecture—Northeast
Architecture—Northwest
  Coast
Architecture—Plains
Architecture—Plateau
Architecture—Southeast
Architecture—Southwest
Architecture—Subarctic
Art and artists, contemporary
Arts and crafts—Arctic
Arts and crafts—California
Arts and crafts—Great Basin
Arts and crafts—Northeast
Arts and crafts—Northwest
  Coast
Arts and crafts—Plains
Arts and crafts—Plateau
Arts and crafts—Southeast
Arts and crafts—Southwest
Arts and crafts—Subarctic

Beads and beadwork
Chickee
Earthlodge
Grass house
Hogan
Igloo
Lean-to
Longhouse
Mosaic and inlay
Paints and painting
Petroglyphs
Pit house
Plank house
Pueblo
Quillwork
Sculpture
Shells and shellwork
Symbolism in art
Tipi
Totem poles
Turquoise
Wattle and daub
Wickiup
Wigwam

BELIEFS AND RELIGION

Bundles, sacred
Corn Woman

Ethnophilosophy and
  worldview

Guardian spirits
Kachinas
Kivas
Kuksu rituals and society
Longhouse religion
Manibozho
Maru Cult
Medicine bundles
Medicine wheels
Mother Earth
Native American Church
Peyote and peyote religion
Praying Indians

Quetzalcóatl
Religion
Religious specialists
Sacred narratives
Sacred, the
Sand painting
Shaker Church
Totems
Tricksters
Visions and vision quests
Windigo
Witchcraft and sorcery

CEREMONIES, DANCES, AND FESTIVALS

Bladder Festival
Booger Dance
Buffalo Dance
Chantways
Dances and dancing
Death and mortuary
  customs
Deer Dance
False Face Ceremony
Feast of the Dead
Feasts
Ghost Dance
Gourd Dance
Grass Dance
Green Corn Dance
Hako
Hamatsa
Husk Face Society

Midewiwin
Midwinter Ceremony
Morning Star Ceremony
Okeepa
Potlatch
Pow-wows and contemporary
  celebrations
Puberty and initiation rites
Rite of Consolation
Rites of passage
Shaking Tent Ceremony
Shalako
Snake Dance
Spirit Dancing
Stomp Dance
Sun Dance
Tobacco Society and Dance
White Deerskin Dance

CONTEMPORARY LIFE AND ISSUES

Activism
African American—American
  Indian Relations
Alcoholism
American Indian studies
  programs and archives
Amerind
Art and artists, contemporary
Certificate of Degree of
  Indian Blood
Civil rights and citizenship
Councils, tribal
Courts, tribal
Diseases, post-contact
Education, post-contact
Employment and
  unemployment

Federally recognized tribes
Gambling
Guns
Indian police and judges
Land claims
Medicine and modes of
  curing, post-contact
Pan-Indianism
Pow-wows and contemporary
  celebrations
Ranching
Relocation
Reservation system of the
  United States
Reserve system of Canada
Resources
Stereotypes

Suicide
Tribe
Urban Indians

Voting rights—Canada
Voting rights—United States
Water and water rights

White Paper of Canada
Winnebago Uprising
Wolf Mountains, Battle of
Wounded Knee Massacre

Wounded Knee occupation
Yakima War
Yamasee War

CULTURE AREAS

Arctic
California
Great Basin
Northeast
Northwest Coast

Plains
Plateau
Southeast
Southwest
Subarctic

DRESS AND ADORNMENT

Beads and beadwork
Dress and adornment
Feathers and featherwork
Headdresses
Moccasins

Ornaments
Quillwork
Shells and shellwork
War bonnets

HISTORICAL EVENTS

Acoma, Battle of
Adobe Walls, Battles of
Alcatraz Island occupation
Apache Wars
Articles of Agreement
Bacon's Rebellion
Bannock War
Bear River Campaign
Beaver Wars
Black Hawk War
Bozeman Trail wars
Cayuse War
Cherokee Tobacco case
Cherokee War
Creek War
Declaration of First Nations
Fallen Timbers, Battle of
Fifteen Principles
Fort Mims, Battle of
French and Indian Wars
Gadsden Purchase
Kickapoo Resistance
Kickapoo uprisings
King Philip's War
Little Bighorn, Battle of the
Lone Wolf v. Hitchcock
Long Walk
Longest Walk
Lord Dunmore's War
Manhattan
Meech Lake Accord
Meriam Report
Minnesota Uprising
Modoc War

Natchez Revolt
Navajo War
Nez Perce War
Northwest Ordinance
Pavonia Massacre
Paxton Riots
Peach Wars
Pequot War
Pima uprisings
Pine Ridge shootout
Pontiac's Conspiracy
Powhatan Wars
Proclamation of 1763
Public Law 280
Pueblo (Popé's) Revolt
Red River War
Riel Rebellions
Rosebud Creek, Battle of
Sand Creek Massacre
Saybrook, Battle of
Seminole Wars
Sioux uprisings
Snake War
Tecumseh's Rebellion
Termination policy
Texas Rangers
Thames, Battle of the
Tippecanoe, Battle of
Trail of Broken Treaties
Trail of Tears
Wabash, Battle of the
Wagon Box Battle
Walla Walla Council
Washita River, Battle of the

INDIAN-WHITE RELATIONS

American Indian
Captivity and captivity
  narratives
Indian
Indian Territory
Indian-white relations—
  Canadian
Indian-white relations—
  Dutch colonial
Indian-white relations—
  English colonial
Indian-white relations—
  French colonial
Indian-white relations—
  Norse
Indian-white relations—
  Russian colonial
Indian-white relations—
  Spanish colonial
Indian-white relations—
  Swedish colonial

Indian-white relations—
  U.S., 1775-1830
Indian-white relations—
  U.S., 1831-1870
Indian-white relations—
  U.S., 1871-1933
Indian-white relations—
  U.S., 1934-1995
Journalism
Keetoowah Society
Missions and missionaries
Native American
Oregon Trail
Patents
Railroads
Removal
Santa Fe Trail
Sovereignty
Trading posts
Wild west shows

LANGUAGES

Algonquian language family
Atakapa language family
Athapaskan language family
Beothuk language
Caddoan language family
Chitimacha language
Coos language
Eskimo-Aleut language
  family
Hokan language family
Iroquoian language family
Karankawa language
Keresan language family
Kiowa-Tanoan language
  family
Kutenai language

Language families
Muskogean language family
Na-Dene language family
Penutian language family
Salishan language family
Sign language
Siouan language family
Syllabaries
Timucua language
Tonkawa language
Tunica language
Uto-Aztecan language family
Wakashan language family
Yakonan language family
Yuman language family
Zuni language

LEGISLATION

Alaska Native Claims
  Settlement Act
American Indian Civil
  Rights Act
American Indian Religious
  Freedom Act

Burke Act
General Allotment Act
Indian Act of 1876 (Canada)
Indian Act of 1951 (Canada)
Indian Act of 1989 (Canada)
Indian Child Welfare Act

Indian Citizenship Act
Indian Education Acts
Indian Removal Act
Indian Reorganization Act
Indian Self-Determination and
  Education Assistance Act
Navajo Rehabilitation Act
Navajo-Hopi Land Settlement
  Act
Oklahoma Indian Welfare Act
Trade and Intercourse Acts

ORGANIZATIONS

Alaska Native Brotherhood
  and Alaska Native
  Sisterhood
All-Pueblo Council
American Indian Defense
  Association (AIDA)
American Indian Higher
  Education Consortium
  (AIHEC)
American Indian Movement
  (AIM)
American Indian Policy
  Review Commission
Bureau of Indian Affairs
  (BIA)
Carlisle Indian School
Council of Energy Resource
  Tribes (CERT)
Department of Indian Affairs
  and Northern Develop-
  ment (DIAND)
Determined Residents United
  for Mohawk Sovereignty
  (DRUMS)
Friends of the Indian
  organizations
Hudson's Bay Company
Indian Arts and Crafts Board
  (IACB)
Indian Claims Commission
  (ICC)
Indian Rights Association
Institute of American Indian
  Arts (IAIA)
International Indian Treaty
  Council (IITC)
Keeler Commission
National Congress of
  American Indians (NCAI)
National Council of American
  Indians
National Indian Association
National Indian Youth Council
  (NIYC)
Native American Church
Native American Rights Fund
  (NARF)
Society of American Indians
  (SAI)
Women of All Red Nations
  (WARN)

PERSONAGES

Adair, John L.
Adario
Alford, Thomas Wildcat
Allen, Paula Gunn
American Horse
Annawan
Antonio, Juan
Apes, William
Arapoosh
Arpeika
Asah, Spencer
Atotarho
Auchiah, James
Awa Tsireh
Bad Heart Bull, Amos
Banks, Dennis
Barboncito
Bear Hunter

Bear's Heart, James
Big Bear
Big Bow
Big Foot
Big Tree
Big Warrior
Black Elk
Black Hawk
Black Kettle
Blacksnake
Bloody Knife
Blue Eagle, Acee
Bonnin, Gertrude Simmons
Boudinot, Elias
Boudinot, Elias Cornelius
Bowl
Bowlegs, Billy
Brant, Joseph

Brant, Molly
Bronson, Ruth Muskrat
Bruce, Louis R.
Buffalo Hump
Bull Bear
Bushyhead, Dennis Wolf
Campbell, Ben Nighthorse
Canonchet
Canonicus
Captain Jack
Catahecassa
Charlot
Chisholm, Jesse
Cloud, Henry Roe
Cochise
Colorow
Comcomly
Conquering Bear
Copway, George
Cornplanter
Cornstalk
Crashing Thunder
Crazy Horse
Crazy Snake
Crow Dog
Crowfoot
Curly
Curtis, Charles
Datsolalee
Decora, Spoon
Deer, Ada Elizabeth
Deganawida
Dekanisora
Delaware Prophet
Delgadito
Deloria, Ella Cara
Deloria, Vine, Jr.
Delshay
Dodge, Henry Chee
Dohasan
Donnaconna
Dozier, Edward Pasqual
Dragging Canoe
Dull Knife
Eastman, Charles Alexander
Erdrich, Louise
Eskiminzin
Flat Mouth
Foreman, Stephen
Francis, Josiah
Francis, Milly Hayo
Gall
Ganado Mucho
Garakontie, Daniel
Garra, Antonio
Garry, Spokane

General, Alexander
Geronimo
Gilcrease, William Thomas
Godfroy, Francis
Gorman, R. C.
Grass, John
Great Sun
Hagler
Half-King
Hancock
Handsome Lake
Harjo, Joy
Harper, Elijah
Harris, LaDonna
Hayes, Ira Hamilton
Heat-Moon, William Least
Hewitt, John N. B.
Hiawatha
Hogan, Linda
Hokeah, Jack
Hole-in-the-Day
Hollow Horn Bear
Hooker Jim
Hopocan
Howe, Oscar
Howling Wolf
Hump
Hunt, George
Ignacio
Inkpaduta
Irateba
Isatai
Ishi
Isparhecher
Johnson, Emily Pauline
Jones, Peter
Joseph the Younger
Journeycake, Charles
Kamiakin
Katlian
Kennekuk
Keokuk
Kicking Bear
Kicking Bird
Klah, Hosteen
Konkapot, John
La Flesche, Francis
La Flesche, Susan
La Flesche, Susette or Josette
Lame Deer
Lawyer
Lean Bear
Left Hand the First
Left Hand the Second
Little Crow
Little Priest

Little Raven
Little Robe
Little Turtle
Little Wolf
Logan, James
Lone Wolf
Looking Glass
McGillivray, Alexander
McIntosh, William
McNickle, D'Arcy
McQueen, Peter
Mangas Coloradus
Mankato
Mankiller, Wilma Pearl
Manuelito
Martínez, Crescencio
Martínez, Julián
Martínez, María Antonía
Massasoit
Mato Tope
Matonabbee
Means, Russell
Menewa
Metacomet
Miantonomo
Micanopy
Momaday, N. Scott
Montezuma, Carlos
Mopope, Stephen
Moses
Mountain Wolf Woman
Mourning Dove
Murie, James
Musgrove, Mary
Naiche
Nakaidoklini
Nampeyo
Nana
Natawista
Natiotish
Ninham, Daniel
Ninigret
Occom, Samson
Oconostota
Old Briton
Opechancanough
Opothleyaholo
Ortiz, Simon
Osceola
Oshkosh
Otherday, John
Ouray
Parker, Ely Samuel
Parker, Quanah
Passaconaway
Pawhuska

Peña, Tonita
Petalésharo
Pitchlynn, Peter Perkins
Plenty Coups
Pocahontas
Pokagon, Leopold
Pokagon, Simon
Pontiac
Popé
Popovi Da
Porter, Pleasant
Posey, Alexander Lawrence
Poundmaker
Powhatan
Pushmataha
Queen Anne
Quinney, John W.
Rain in the Face
Red Bird
Red Cloud
Red Jacket
Red Shoes
Reifel, Ben
Renville, Joseph
Ridge, John Rollins
Ridge, Major
Riel, Louis, Jr.
Riggs, Lynn
Rocky Boy
Rogers, Will
Roman Nose
Ross, John
Sacagawea
Samoset
Sassacus
Satanta
Scarface Charlie
Scholder, Fritz
Seattle
Sequoyah
Shábona
Shikellamy
Short Bull
Silko, Leslie Marmon
Sitting Bull
Slocum, John
Smohalla
Spotted Tail
Spybuck, Ernest
Squanto
Standing Bear
Standing Bear, Luther
Stumbling Bear
Sweezy, Carl
Tall Bull
Tallchief, Maria

Tammany
Tarhe
Tavibo
Tawaquaptewa
Tecumseh
Teedyuscung
Tekakwitha, Kateri
Ten Bears
Tendoy
Tenskwatawa
Thorpe, Jim
Tiger, Jerome R.
Tomah
Tomochichi
Tsatoke, Monroe
Two Leggings
Two Moon
Two Strike
Uncas
Victorio
Vizenor, Gerald R[obert]
Waban
Wapasha
Ward, Nancy

Warren, William W.
Washakie
Watie, Stand
Weatherford, William
Weetamoo
Welch, James
White Bird
White Cloud
White Eyes
White Man Runs Him
Wildcat
Williams, Eleazar
Winema
Winnemucca, Sarah
Wooden Leg
Wovoka
Wright, Allen
Yellow Wolf
Yonaguska
Young Bear
Young Man Afraid of His
    Horses
Zotom

PREHISTORIC CULTURE

Adena
Anasazi
Archaic
Ball game and courts
Banner stones
Basketmaker
Beringia
Cíbola, Seven Cities of
Cliff dwellings
Clovis
Dating methods
Desert culture
Dorset
Effigy mounds
Folsom
Fremont
Hohokam
Hopewell
Mimbres
Mississippian
Mogollon

Old Copper culture
Oneota
Paleo-Indian
Patayan
Plano
Prehistory—Arctic
Prehistory—California
Prehistory—Great Basin
Prehistory—Northeast
Prehistory—Northwest Coast
Prehistory—Plains
Prehistory—Plateau
Prehistory—Southeast
Prehistory—Southwest
Prehistory—Subarctic
Projectile points
Serpent mounds
Sinagua
Southern Cult
Thule
Woodland

TRADITIONAL LIFEWAYS

Acorns
Adoption
Agriculture
Astronomy
Atlatl

Baskets and basketry
Beans
Birchbark
Black Hills
Black Drink

List of Entries by Category

Blankets
Boats and watercraft
Bows, arrows, and quivers
Buffalo
Cacique
Calumets and pipe bags
Children
Chilkat blankets
Clans
Clowns
Codices
Corn
Cotton
Coup sticks and counting
Demography
Dogs
Drums
Education, pre-contact
Elderly
Fire and firemaking
Fish and fishing
Flutes
Food preparation and
  cooking
Games and contests
Gender relations and roles
Gifts and gift giving
Gold and goldworking
Hand games
Hides and hidework
Horses
Humor
Hunting and gathering
Incest taboo
Irrigation
Joking relations
Kinnikinnick
Kinship and social
  organization
Knives
Lacrosse
Lances and spears
Maple syrup and sugar
Marriage and divorce
Masks
Mathematics
Medicine and modes of
  curing, pre-contact
Menses and menstruation
Metalwork
Military societies

Money
Mounds and mound builders
Music and song
Names and naming
Oral literatures
Oratory
Parfleche
Pemmican
Pipestone Quarries
Pochteca
Political organization and
  leadership
Pottery
Resource use, pre-contact
Sachem
Salmon
Salt
Scalps and scalping
Secotan
Secret societies
Slavery
Social control, traditional
Societies, non-kin-based
Squash
Subsistence
Sweatlodges and sweatbaths
Tanning
Tattoos and tattooing
Technology
Texas
Tobacco
Tomahawks
Tools
Torture
Toys
Trade
Transportation modes
Tule
Twins
Walam Olum
Wampum
Warfare and conflict
Weapons
Weaving
Weirs and traps
Whales and whaling
White Buffalo Society
Wild rice
Windigo
Witchcraft and sorcery
Women

TREATIES

Dancing Rabbit Creek,
  Treaty of

Fort Atkinson, Treaty of
Fort Greenville, Treaty of

Fort Laramie Treaty of 1851
Fort Laramie Treaty of 1868
Fort Stanwix, Treaty of
Fort Wayne, Treaty of
Guadalupe Hidalgo, Treaty of

Horseshoe Bend, Treaty of
Medicine Lodge, Treaties of
Treaties and agreements in
  Canada

TRIBES

Abenaki
Achumawi
Ahtna
Ais
Alabama
Aleut
Algonquin
Alsea
Anadarko
Apache
Apache Tribe of Oklahoma
Apalachee
Apalachicola
Arapaho
Arikara
Assiniboine
Atakapa
Atsina
Atsugewi
Aztec
Bannock
Bayogoula
Beaver
Bella Bella
Bella Coola
Beothuk
Biloxi
Blackfoot and Blackfeet
  Confederacy
Caddo
Cahuilla
Calusa
Cape Fear
Carib
Carrier
Catawba
Cayuga
Cayuse
Chasta Costa
Chehalis
Chemakum
Cheraw
Cherokee
Cheyenne
Chiaha
Chichimec
Chickasaw
Chilcotin

Chinook
Chipewyan
Chitimacha
Choctaw
Chumash
Clallam
Clatskanie
Coast Yuki
Cocopa
Coeur d'Alene
Columbia
Colville
Comanche
Comox
Coos
Copalis
Costanoan
Coushatta
Cowichan
Cowlitz
Cree
Creek
Crow
Cupeño
Diegueño
Dogrib
Duwamish
Erie
Esselen
Fernandeño
Flathead
Fox
Gabrielino
Gitksan
Gosiute
Guale
Haisla
Han
Hare
Havasupai
Hidatsa
Hitchiti
Huchnom
Hupa
Huron
Illinois
Ingalik
Inuit

Iowa
Iroquois Confederacy
Juaneño
Kalapuya
Kalispel
Kamia
Kansa
Karankawa
Karok
Kaska
Kawaiisu
Kichai
Kickapoo
Kiowa
Klamath
Klikitat
Koyukon
Kutchin
Kutenai
Kwakiutl
Lake
Lenni Lenape
Lillooet
Luiseño
Lumbee
Lummi
Mahican
Maidu
Makah
Maliseet
Manahoac
Mandan
Massachusett
Mattaponi
Mattole
Maya
Menominee
Methow
Metis
Miami
Micmac
Missouri
Miwok
Mixtec
Mobile
Modoc
Mohawk
Mohegan
Mojave

Molala
Moneton
Montagnais
Montauk Confederacy
Mountain
Muckleshoot
Multnomah
Nabedache
Nanticoke
Narragansett
Naskapi
Natchez
Nauset
Navajo
Neutral
Nez Perce
Niantic
Nipissing
Nipmuck
Nisqually
Nooksack
Nootka
Nottaway
Ocaneechi
Ofo
Ojibwa
Okanagan
Olmec
Omaha
Oneida
Onondaga
Osage
Oto
Ottawa
Paiute, Northern
Paiute, Southern
Palouse
Pamlico
Passamaquoddy
Patwin
Pawnee
Pennacook
Penobscot
Pequot
Petun
Pima
Pomo
Ponca
Poospatuck

Potawatomi
Powhatan Confederacy
Pueblo tribes, Eastern
Pueblo tribes, Western
Puyallup
Quapaw
Quechan
Quileute
Quinault
Salinan
Salish
Samish
Sanpoil-Nespelem
Sarsi
Sauk
Sekani
Semiahmoo
Seminole
Seneca
Seri
Serrano
Shasta
Shawnee
Shinnecock
Shoshone
Shuswap
Siletz
Sioux
Siuslaw
Skagit
Slave
Snohomish
Snoqualmie
Sooke
Spokane
Squamish
Suquamish
Susquehannock
Swallah
Tahltan
Tanaina
Tanana
Tenino
Thompson
Tillamook
Timucua
Tiou
Tlingit
Tohome

Tohono O'odham
Tolowa
Toltec
Tonkawa
Tsetsaut
Tsimshian
Tubatulabal
Tunica
Tuscarora
Tuskegee
Tutchone
Tutelo
Tututni
Twana
Tyigh
Umatilla
Umpqua
Ute
Waccamaw
Waco
Walapai
Walla Walla
Wampanoag
Wanapam
Wappinger
Wappo
Wasco
Washoe
Wenatchi
Wichita
Winnebago
Wintun
Wishram
Wiyot
Yahi
Yakima
Yamasee
Yana
Yaqui
Yaquina
Yavapai
Yazoo
Yellowknife
Yokuts
Yuchi
Yuki
Yurok
Zapotec

INDEX

A page number or range in boldface type indicates a full article devoted to that topic. Page numbers in italic type indicate photographs, drawings, maps, tables, charts, and graphs.

Abeel, John. *See* Cornplanter
Abenaki, **1-2.** *See also* Passamaquoddy; Pennacook; Penobscot
Absaroka, 204. *See also* Crow
Acamapichtli, 86
Achumawi, **2**, *2*
Acoma. *See* Pueblo tribes, Western
Acoma, Battle of, **2-3**
Acorns, **3**, *3*, 233, *755*
Activism, **3-6**, 172
Adair, John L., **6**
Adams, Hank, 799
Adario, **6-7**
Adena, **7-8**, 57, 869
Adobe, **8**
Adobe Walls, Battles of, **8**, 388, 579
Adoption, **8-9**, 840
Adzes, 791
African American-American Indian relations, **9-11**
Agriculture, **12-16**, *13, 15*, 757, 771
Agua Caliente, 214
Agwelius. *See* Bruce, Louis
Ahtna, **16**
AIM. *See* American Indian Movement
Ais, **16**
Akimel O'odham. *See* Pima
Akokisa. *See* Atakapa
Akokisa language, 81
Akwesasne Mohawk reservation, 232
Akwesasne Notes, 394
Alabama, **16-17**
Alaska Federation of Natives, 17
Alaska Native Brotherhood and Alaska Native Sisterhood, **17**
Alaska Native Claims Settlement Act, **17-18**, *18*
Alcatraz Island occupation, 4, **18-19**
Alcea. *See* Alsea
Alcoholism, **19-20**; mortality rates, *20*
Aleut, **20-22**, 59, 61, *240*, 360, 753
Aleut language, 60
Aleut League, 22
Alford, Thomas Wildcat, **22**
Algonquian language family, **22-23**
Algonquin, **23-24**
Alibamu. *See* Alabama
All-Pueblo Council, 24
Allen, Paula Gunn, 24
Allotment system, **24-27**, *25*, 129. *See also* General Allotment Act
Almanac of the Dead (Silko), 648
Alsea, **27**
Altithermal, 628
American Horse, **27**, *27*

American Indian, **27-28**
American Indian Athletic Hall of Fame, 294
American Indian Civil Rights Act, **28**, 173
American Indian Defense Association (AIDA), **28-29**
American Indian Fund, 29
American Indian Higher Education Consortium (AIHEC), **29**
American Indian Movement (AIM), 4, **29-31**, *30*, 89, 574, 871
American Indian Policy Review Commission, 19, **31-32**, 376
American Indian Religious Freedom Act, **32**, 174
American Indian studies programs and archives, **32-35**, *33, 34*
American Revolution, 123, 124, 365
Americans for Indian Opportunity (AIO), 317
Amerind, **35-36**
Amerind language family, Greenberg's categorization, 428
Anadarko, **36**
Anasazi, **36-38**, *37*, 57-58, 149, 179, 632, 636, 741
Angpetu Tokecha. *See* Otherday, John
Ani-Yun-Wiya, 152
Animism, 506, 656
Annawan, **38**
Annuity payments, 369
Anpetu Waste. *See* Deloria, Ella Cara
Antonio, Juan, **38**, 295
Apache, **38-41**, 607, *635*, 742; population distribution, *39*
Apache Tribe of Oklahoma, **41-42**
Apache Wars, 40, **42-43**, *43*, 827
Apalachee, **43-44**
Apalachicola, **44**
Apes, William, **44**
Appliqué and ribbonwork, **44-45**
Aquash, Anna Mae, 594
Arapaho, **45-49**, *46, 47*; population distribution, *48*
Arapoosh, **49**
Arateva. *See* Irateba
Arawak, 143
Archaic, **49-50**, 91, 220, 628, 630, 740
Architecture—Arctic, **50-51**
Architecture—California, **51-52**, *52*
Architecture—Great Basin, **52-53**
Architecture—Maya, 467
Architecture—Northeast, **53**
Architecture—Northwest Coast, **53-55**, *54*
Architecture—Plains, **55-56**, *56*
Architecture—Plateau, **56**

Architecture—Southeast, **56-57**
Architecture—Southwest, **57-59**, *58*
Architecture—Subarctic, **59**
Archives, 34
Arctic, **59-63**, *60, 61*, 210
Arctic Slope Regional Corporation, 18
Arctic Small Tool tradition, 625
Arikara, **63**
Arizona v. California, 845
Arizona v. San Carlos Apache Tribe, 845
Arkansa. *See* Quapaw
Arpeika, **63-64**
Arrows. *See* Bows, arrows, and quivers; Projectile points; Weapons
Art, Maya, 466
Art and artists, contemporary, **64-65**
Articles of Agreement, 65
Arts and crafts—Arctic, **66-67**
Arts and crafts—California, **67-68**
Arts and crafts—Great Basin, **68-70**, *69*
Arts and crafts—Northeast, **70**
Arts and crafts—Northwest Coast, **70-72**, *71*. *See also* Totem poles
Arts and crafts—Plains, **72-73**
Arts and crafts—Plateau, **73-74**
Arts and crafts—Southeast, **74-75**
Arts and crafts—Southwest, **75-77**, *76*
Arts and crafts—Subarctic, **77-78**
Asah, Spencer, **78**
Ashishishe. *See* Curly
Assembly of First Nations, 349, 856
Assiniboine, **78-80**, *79*
Assiola. *See* Osceola
Association on American Indian Affairs, 29
Astronomy, **80-81**
Atakapa, **81**
Atakapa language family, **81-82**
Athapaskan, 753
Athapaskan language family, **82**, 632
Atka, 20. *See also* Aleut
Atlatl, **82**, 90
Atotarho, **82-83**, *83*, 224
Atsidi Sani. *See* Delgadito
Atsina, **83-84**, *84*
Atsugewi, **84**
Attakullakulla, 154, 158, 239
Attikamek, 502
Auchiah, James, **84-85**
Avoidance relations, 390
Awa Tside. *See* Dozier, Edward Pasqual
Awa Tsireh, **85**
Awatovi, **85**
Axes, 791
Azapotzalco, 87
Aztalan, **85-86**

Aztec, **86-87**, 161, 242, 505, 824; calendar of, 464; gold and goldworking, 304

Bacon Rind, *563*
Bacon's Rebellion, **88**
Bad Axe, Battle of, *108*
Bad Heart Bear, 5
Bad Heart Bull, Amos, **88-89**
Bagot Commission, 348
Ball game and courts, **89**, 255, 730
Bands, 807
Banks, Dennis, 5, 31, **89**, 799
Banner stones, 82, **89-90**
Bannock, **90**
Bannock War, **90-91**, 371
Barboncito, **91**, 225, 440
Bascom Affair, 42, 181
Basketmaker, 36, 57, **91-92**
Baskets and basketry, **92-94**; California, 67, *93*, 136; Great Basin, 68, *69*; Plateau, 74; Southeast, 74, *169*. *See also* Datsolalee
Bat Cave, **94-95**, 232
Battles and conflicts in the West, 1831-1870, *369*
Battles and conflicts in the West, 1871-1890, *372*
Bayogoula, **95**
Beads and beadwork, **95-97**, 649; Northeast, 70; Plains, 72, *96*; Plateau, 74; Southeast, 74
Beans, **97**
Bear Hunter, **97**
Bear River Campaign, **97-98**
Bear's Heart, James, **98**
Beaver, **98**
Beaver Wars, **98-100**, 842
Beet Queen, The (Erdrich), 260
Belanger, Lance, 64
Belief systems. *See* Religion
Bella Bella, **100**
Bella Coola, **100**, 688; secret societies, 733
Bellecourt, Vernon, *226*
Bennett, Robert, 376
Beothuk, **100-101**
Beothuk language, **101**
Berdaches and berdache societies, 298, 734
Bering, Vitus, 62
Beringia, **101**, 228, 488, *489*, 573
Big Bear, **101-102**, 677
Big Bow, **102**
Big Dry Wash, Battle of, 523
Big Foot, **102**, 871
Big Mouth. *See* Eskiminzin
Big Tree, **102-103**
Big Warrior, **103**
Biloxi, **103**
Bingo, 291
Birchbark, 70, 78, **103-104**; baskets, Subarctic, 77; canoes, 103, 116

Bislahani. *See* Barboncito
Bison. *See* Buffalo
Bison antiquus, 627
Black Coyote, 871
Black Dog, 612
Black Drink, **104**, 738
Black Elk, **104-105**, 765, 871
Black Hawk, **105-107**, *106*, 403
Black Hawk War, **107-109**, *108*
Black Hills, **109-110**, 158, 724
Black Kettle, **110**, 436, 476, 692, 843
Blackfoot and Blackfeet Confederacy, **110-113**
Blackfoot population distribution, *111*
Blacksnake, **113-114**
Blackware pottery, 75
Bladder Festival, **114**
Blankets, **114-115**, *850*
Blatchford, Herbert, 523
Blood. *See* Blackfoot and Blackfeet Confederacy
Blood quanta. *See* Certificate of degree of Indian Blood; Tribe
Bloody Knife, **115**
Bloody Run, 612
Blowguns, 848
Blowsnake, Sam. *See* Crashing Thunder
Blue Eagle, Acee, **115-116**
Blue Highways (Heat-Moon), 320
Blue Jacket, 145, 267, 485, 832
Boas, Franz, 332
Boats and watercraft, **116-117**, *116*, 802
Boldt Decision, 646
Bonnin, Gertrude Simmons, **117-118**, *118*, 504, 522, 560, 868
Booger Dance, **118**
Bosomworth, Mary. *See* Musgrove, Mary
Bosque Redondo, 440, 531
Boudinot, Elias, **118-119**, 155, 393
Boudinot, Elias Cornelius, **118-119**, *119*, 157
Boudinot v. United States. See Cherokee Tobacco case
Bowl, 120
Bowlegs, Billy, 11, **120**, *120*, 705
Bowlegs, Jim, 11
Bows, arrows, and quivers, **120-121**, *121*, 792, 848
Bozeman Trail wars, **121-122**, 653
Brant, Joseph, **122-124**, *123*
Brant, Molly, 122, **124**, 354
Bronson, Ruth Muskrat, **124**, 868
Bruce, Louis R., **125**
Buckongahelas, 832
Buffalo, 46, **125-126**, *125*, 596, *651*, 759; depletion of, *126*
Buffalo Dance, **126-127**
Buffalo Horn, 90
Buffalo Hump, **127**
Bugonegijig. *See* Hole-in-the-Day

Bull Bear, **127**
Bundles, sacred, **127-128**, 608, 734. *See also* Medicine bundles
Burden baskets, 68
Bureau of Indian Affairs (BIA), **128-129**, 344, 368
Bureau of Indian Affairs building, 1972 occupation of, 5
Burke Act, 26, **129**, 374
Bursum Bill, 24
Bushotter, George, 509
Bushy Run, 613
Bushyhead, Dennis Wolf, **130**
Butler, Dino, 31

Cacique, **131**, 192
Caddo, **131-134**, 745; population distribution, *131*
Caddoan language family, **134-135**
Cahokia, **135**, 556
Cahuilla, 38, **135-136**, *135*
California, **136-139**, *137*, 211
Calling Myself Home (Hogan), 324
Calumets and pipe bags, **139**, 595. *See also* Pipes
Calusa, **139-140**
Camp Grant Massacre, 261
Campbell, Ben Nighthorse, **140**, *140*
Canada. *See* Fifteen Points; Hudson's Bay Company; Indian-white relations—Canadian; Indian Act of 1876; Indian Act of 1951; Indian Act of 1989; Reserve system of Canada; Riel Rebellions; Voting rights—Canada
Canada-Ontario Indian Reserve Lands Agreement, 671
Canadian Arctic Producers, 66
Canadian Metis Society, 223
Canarsee, 432, 455
Cannibal Dance. *See* Hamatsa
Cannon, T. C., 64
Canoes, 116, *116, 539, 802*, 803
Canonchet, **140-141**, 409, 520
Canonicus, **141**, 589
Canyon de Chelly, **141**, 179
Cape Fear, **141-142**
Captain Jack, **142**, *142*, 184, 496, 860
Captain John. *See* Konkapot, John
Captain Pipe. *See* Hopocan
Captivity and captivity narratives, **142-143**
Carib, **143**
Carleton, James H., 440
Carlisle Indian School, **143-145**, *144*, 248, *250*
Carrier, **145**
Carron, Thomas. *See* Tomah
Carson, Christopher "Kit," 8, 440
Cartier, Jacques, 238
Carving, 74-75. *See also* Sculpture
Casas Grandes, 498

Cascade War, 417
Casper, 600
Cass Lake convention, 4
Catahecassa, **145**
Catawba, **145-146**
Catlinite, 595
Cayuga, **146**, 385
Cayuse, **146-148**, *147*, 368
Cayuse War, 148
Ceremony (Silko), 716
Certificate of Degree of Indian Blood
  (CDIB), **148-149**
Chaco Canyon, 37, 57, **149**, 179, *631*, 637
Chaco Phenomenon, 149, 481
Chakofa, 57
Champlain, Samuel de, 355
Chantways, **149-150**
Charlot, **150**, *150*
Charlot, Martin. *See* Charlot
Chasta Costa, **151**
Chato, *40*
Chehalis, **151**
Chehaw. *See* Chiaha
Chelans, 852
Chemakum, **151**
Cheraw, **151**
Cherokee, **151-156**, *153*, 607, 800; Articles
  of Agreement and, 65; population
  distribution, *154*
Cherokee, Eastern Band of the, 155
Cherokee Advocate, 394
Cherokee Almanac, 394
Cherokee Nation v. Georgia, 5, 665, 744
Cherokee National Historical Society, 35
Cherokee Phoenix, 118, 393, 846
Cherokee Tobacco case, **157**, 373, 744
Cherokee War, **157-158**
Cheyenne, **158-160**, 608; population
  distribution, *158*
Chiaha, **160**
Chiapas, Mexico, uprising, 425
Chichén Itzá, 89, **160-161**, 467
Chichikam Lupalkuelatko. *See* Scarface
  Charlie
Chichimec, **161**
Chickahominy. *See* Powhatan Confederacy
Chickamauga, 154
Chickasaw, **161-162**, 800
Chickasaw language, 514
Chickee, 57, **162-163**, *163*
Chief Joseph. *See* Joseph the Younger
Chief Little Crow, 724
Chiksika, 773
Chilcotin, **163**
Childbirth, 678
Children, **163-165**, 263. *See also* Indian
  Child Welfare Act
Chilkat. *See* Tlingit
Chilkat blankets, **165-166**, *166*, 241, 851
Chillicothe, Ohio, 7, 328

Chinook, *54*, **166-167**
Chinook jargon, 167, 188, 587
Chinook language, 167
Chipewyan, **167**, *347*
Chippewa. *See* Ojibwa
Chiricahua Apache, 39
Chisholm, Jesse, **167**
Chitimacha, **167-168**
Chitimacha language, **168**
Chivington, John M., 110, 692
Chiwere language, 383, 566
Choctaw, **168-170**, *169*, 220, 799;
  population distribution, *169*; treaties
  affecting, *170*
Choctaw Academy, 248
Choctaw language, 514
Cholera, 235
Christian affiliations of American Indians,
  658
Chumash, **170-171**
Cíbola, Seven Cities of, **171-172**
Circle, symbolism of, 765
Citizenship. *See* Civil rights and
  citizenship; Indian Citizenship Act
Civil rights and citizenship, **172-177**;
  legislation affecting, *174*
Civil War, 369, 403, 577; Osage and, 563
Civilian Conservation Corps, 258
Civilization Act, 367
Clallam, **177**
Clans, **177-178**
Clatskanie, **178**
Cliff dwellings, **178-179**
Cloud, Henry Roe, **179**
Clovis, **180**, 572, 625
Clowns, **180**
Coacoochee. *See* Wildcat
Coahuiltecan, 791
Coast Yuki, **180-181**
Cochise, 42, **181-182**, 454
Cochise culture, 94, 232, 630
Cochiti. *See* Pueblo tribes, Eastern
Cocopa, **182**
Codex. *See* Codices
Codex Dresdensis, 465
Codices, **182-183**, 495
Cody, Buffalo Bill, 858
Coeur d'Alene, **183-184**
Cogewea (Mourning Dove), 509
Collier, John, 28, 343
Colliflower v. Garland, 744
Color symbolism, 766
Colorado. *See* Colorow
Colorow, **184**
Columbia, **184**
Colville, **184-185**
Colville Indian Reservation, 694
Comanche, **185-187**, *186*
Comcomly, **187**
Comox, 187

Conestoga, 584
Connor, Patrick Edward, 98
Conquering Bear, **187**
Contraries, 734
Coos, **187-188**
Coos language, **188**
Cooswootna. *See* Antonio, Juan
Coowescoowe. *See* Ross, John
Copalis, **188-189**
Copan, 89, **189**, 466
Copway, George, **189**
Corchaug, 502
Corn, 12, **189-192**, *191*; areas of
  cultivation, *13*
Corn Woman, **192**
Cornplanter, 192-193, *193*
Cornstalk, 154, **193**, 446
Cortés, Hernán, 87
Costanoan, **193-194**
Cotton, 14, 194; cultivation, *13*
Council of Energy Resource Tribes
  (CERT), **194**
Council of Forty-Four, Cheyenne, 159
Councils, tribal, **194**, *195*
Coup sticks and counting, **196**, 598, 841
Courts, tribal, **196**
Courts of Indian Offenses, 342
Coushatta, **196-197**
Coushatta language, 515
Cow Creek Band, 819
Cowichan, **197**, *461*
Cowlitz, **197**
Coyote the Trickster, 687, 809
Coyotero Apache, 39
Cradleboards, 2, 68, *147*, 163
Crashing Thunder, **197-198**
Crazy Bear. *See* Porter, Pleasant
Crazy Horse, 104, 122, **198-199**, 680, 865
Crazy Snake, **199**, *199*
Cree, **199-201**, *349*, 607, 711; population
  distribution, *200*
Creek, **201-204**, 282, 330, 799; population
  distribution, *203*
Creek language , 515
Creek Mary. *See* Musgrove, Mary
Creek War, 202, **204**, 450
Croatan, 447
Crook, George, 227, 680, 730
Cross cousins, 336
Crow, **204-207**, *667*; population
  distribution, *207*; Tobacco Society, 788
Crow Dog, **207-209**, *208*, 373, 744, 747
Crow Dog, Leonard, 594
Crowfoot, **209**
Crown Lands Protection Acts, 348
Cuello, **209-210**
Culbertson, Madame. *See* Natawista
Culture areas, **210-214**, *211*, 736
Cupeño, **214**
Curing rituals, 474

Curly, **214**, *215*
Curtis, Charles, **214-216**, *216*
Curtis Act, 744
Custer, George Armstrong, 434
Custer Died for Your Sins (Deloria), 227

Dakota, 718
Dances and dancing, **217-220**, *218*
Dancing Rabbit Creek, Treaty of, **220**, 799
Danger Cave, **220-221**, 232
Darkness in Saint Louis Bearheart
    (Vizenor), 829
Dating methods, **221-222**
Datsolalee, **222**
Davis site, 131
Dawes Severalty Act. *See* General
    Allotment Act
Deadose. *See* Atakapa
Death, leading causes of, 470
Death and mortuary customs, **222-223**, 678
Declaration of First Nations, **223**
Decora, Spoon, **223**
Deer, Ada Elizabeth, **223-224**
Deer Dance, **224**
Deganawida, **224**, 321
Dekanisora, 6, **224-225**
Delaware. *See* Lenni Lenape
Delaware Prophet, **225**, 612
Delaware v. Weeks, 6
Delgadito, **225**
Deloria, Ella Cara, **225-227**
Deloria, Vine, Jr., *226*, **227**, 340, 574
Delshay, **227**
Demography, **227-231**, *821*; population,
    1800-1990, *29*; population, 1990 age
    distribution of, *231*; population,
    pre-contact, *228*
Dendrochronology, 221
Department of Indian Affairs and Northern
    Development (DIAND), **231-232**
Descent, patterns of, *411*
Desert culture, 49, 94, 220, **232**
Deskahe. *See* General, Alexander
Determined Residents United for Mohawk
    Sovereignty (DRUMS), **232-233**
Dheghiha language family, 399
Diegueño, **233**, 755
Diseases, post-contact, *176*, 229, **233-236**,
    235
Divorce, 458
Doak's Stand, Treaty of, 645, 799
Dodge, Henry Chee, **236-237**
Dog Soldiers, 127, 733, 767
Dogrib, **237**
Dogs, **237**
Dohasan, **237-238**
Domestic sovereignty, 743
Donehogawa. *See* Parker, Ely Samuel
Donnaconna, **238**
Dorset, **238**, 380, 625

Dozier, Edward Pasqual, **238-239**
Dragging Canoe, 154, **239**
Dreamer religion, 729
Dress and adornment, **239-243**, *240*, *241*
Drum Dance, Caddo, 132
Drums, **243-244**, *243, 512*, 513
Dugout canoes, 116
Dull Knife, **244-245**, 371
Dumont, Gabriel, 676
Dunmore's War. *See* Lord Dunmore's War
Durham, Jimmie, 64, 379
Dutch. *See* Indian-white relations—Dutch
    colonial
Duwamish, **245**, 701

Earth-diver stories, 686
Earthlodge, 55, *56*, **246**, *246*; California, 52
Earthworks, Adena, 7
Eastman, Charles Alexander, **246-247**, *247*
Education, post-contact, **247-252**, *250*; time
    line of, *249*. *See also* American Indian
    studies programs and archives; Carlisle
    Indian School; Indian Education Acts;
    Indian Self-Determination and Education
    Assistance Act
Education, pre-contact, 164, **252-253**, 263
Educational attainment, 1990, *251*
Edwards, "Junior," 233
*Effigy mounds, **253-254**, 861
El Tajín, **255**
Elderly, **254-255**
Elders, religion and, 661
Eliot, John, 624
Elk v. Wilkins, 373
Elm bark, 70
Emerald Mound, **256**
Emergence stories, 686
Emmons, Glenn, 376
Employment and unemployment, **256-260**,
    257
Employment rate, 1990, *258*, 259
Encomienda, 361
Enfranchisement Act of 1869, 829
Epidemics, 1520-1696, *234*
Erasmus, George, 477
Erdrich, Louise, **260**, *260*
Erie, **260**, 386
Eskiminzin, 40, **261**
Eskimo, 59. *See also* Inuit
Eskimo-Aleut language family, 60, **261**;
    Greenberg's categorization, 428
Esophus, 432, 585
Esselen, **261-262**
Etchaottine. *See* Slave
Ethnophilosophy and worldview, **262-265**
Etokeach. *See* Hump
Etowah, **265**, 740
Ex parte Crow Dog, 209, 373, 744
Exposition of Indian Tribal Arts, 85

Factory system, 366
Fallen Timbers, Battle of, **266-267**, *266*, 280
False Face Ceremony, **267**, 334, 734
False Face Society, 685
Farming. *See* Agriculture
Feast of the Dead, **267**, 678
Feasts, **267-269**
Feathers and featherwork, **269-270**
Federal Acknowledgment Program, 173,
    270
Federal Bureau of Investigation, 594
Federally recognized tribes, **270**
Fernandeño, **270-271**
Fetterman, William J., 122
Fetterman Massacre, 653
Fifteen Principles, **271**
Fifteenth Amendment, 831
Fire and firemaking, **271-272**
Fish and fishing, **272**, *273*, 852
Fish-ins, 4, 523
Fisher v. District Court, 6
Fishing rights, 846
Five Civilized Tribes, 152, 168, 368, 738;
    slavery and, 10
Five Nations. *See* Iroquois Confederacy
Flat Mouth, **272-274**, *549*
Flathead, 150, 164, *164*, **274-275**, *275*, 398,
    688
Fletcher, Alice C., 313
Fletcher v. Peck, 425
Flutes, **275**
Folsom, 180, **276**, *276*, 487, 572
Food preparation and cooking, **276-278**,
    277, 401
Fools Crow, 872
Foreman, Stephen, 278
Fort Atkinson, Treaty of, **278**
Fort Belknap Reservation, 84
Fort Greenville, Treaty of, **278-280**, 284
Fort Harmer, 279
Fort Jackson, Treaty of. *See* Horseshoe
    Bend, Treaty of
Fort Laramie Treaty of 1851, 159, **280-281**
Fort Laramie Treaty of 1868, **281**
Fort Mims, Battle of, **282-283**, *282*
Fort Saybrook. *See* Saybrook, Battle of
Fort Stanwix, Treaty of, **283**
Fort Wayne, Treaty of, **283-284**
Four Bears. *See* Mato Tope
Four Lakes, Battle of, 295
Fourteenth Amendment, 340, 831
Fox, 105, 107, **284-287**; population, *285*.
    See also Sauk
Fox Wars, 357
Foxwoods Resort and Casino, 821
Franchise Act in 1885, 830
Francis, Josiah, **287-288**
Francis, Milly Hayo, **288**
Fremont, **288**

French. *See* Indian-white relations—French colonial
French and Indian Wars, 122, **288-289**, 358
French-Fox War, 284
Friends of the Indian organizations, 289, 522
Fur trade, 256;, Canada, 346; Dutch, 350; English, 353; French, 357; trading posts and, 797

Gabrielino, **290**
Gadsden Purchase, **290**
Gall, 115, **290-291**, *291*
Gambling, **291-292**, *291*, 797
Games and contests, **292-294**, *293*
Ganado Mucho, **294-295**
Garakontie, Daniel, **295**
Garcon, 705
Garra, Antonio, 38, **295**
Garra Uprising, 295
Garry, Spokane, **295-296**
Gauntlet, 794
Gender relations and roles, **296-299**, 412; agriculture, 12; hunter-gatherer, 333; Southeast, 736
General, Alexander, **299**
General Allotment Act, **299-300**, 666; farming and, 14. *See also* Allotment system
Geronimo, **300-302**, *301*, 516
Ghost Dance, *47*, **302-303**, 870
Gifts and gift giving, **303**
Gila River Pima, 593
Gilcrease, William Thomas, **303**
Gingaskin, 621
Gitksan, **304**, 811
Godfroy, Francis, **304**
Going for the Rain (Ortiz), 562
Gold and goldworking, **304-305**
Gorman, R. C., **305**
Goshute. *See* Gosiute
Gosiute, **305**
Gourd Dance, **305-306**
Goyathlay. *See* Geronimo
Grand Medicine Society, 486
Grande Ronde, 501
Grass, John, **306**
Grass Dance, **306**
Grass house, **306**
Great Basin, 212, **306-308**, *307*, *308*
Great Depression, 668
Great Lakes region. *See* Northeast; Old Northwest; Prehistory—Northeast
Great Serpent Mound, 7, 254, 708-709, *709*
Great Sioux Reservation, 281
Great Sun, **308-309**, 412, 521
Green Corn Ceremony and Dance, 128, **309**, 738, 751
Green Grow the Lilacs (Riggs), 677
Greenberg, Joseph H., 427

Griever (Vizenor), 829
Gros Ventre. *See* Atsina
Guadalupe Hidalgo, Treaty of, **309-310**, *310*, 368, 440
Guale, **310**
Guardian spirits, **310-311**
Guelle Plat. *See* Flat Mouth
Guess, George. *See* Sequoyah
Guilá Naquitz, 546
Guipago. *See* Lone Wolf
Guns, **311**, 772, 848

Hackensack, 432
Hagler, **312**
Haida, *794*
Haida language, 516
Haiglar. *See* Hagler
Hair, ways of wearing, 242
Haisla, **312**, 421
Hakar Jim. *See* Hooker Jim
Hakataya, 580
Hako, **312-314**
Hako Ceremony, 510
Half-King, **314**
Hamatsa, **314**
Hammers, 791
Han, **314-315**
Hancock, **315**
Hand games, **315**
Handsome Lake, **315-316**, 443
Hano. *See* Pueblo tribes, Eastern
Harakontie. *See* Garakontie, Daniel
Hare, **316**
Harjo, Joy, **316-317**
Harper, Elijah, **317**, 350, 477
Harpoons, 792
Harris, LaDonna, **317**
Harrison, William Henry, 774, 780
Hasanoanda. *See* Parker, Ely Samuel
Hasinai, 779. *See also* Anadarko; Caddo; Nabedache; Texas
Haskell Institute, 179
Hatchootucknee. *See* Pitchlynn, Peter Perkins
Haudenosaunee, 385
Havasupai, **317-318**
Haverstraw, 432
Hawken, 600
Hayes, Ira Hamilton, 318, *318*
Hayo. *See* Francis, Josiah
Headdresses, **319-320**, 839
Heads of household, 1990, *866*
Health. *See* Civil rights; Diseases, post-contact; Medicine and modes of curing, post-contact
Heap of Birds, Edgar, 64
Heat-Moon, William Least, **320**
Heiltsuk, 421
Herbal medicines, traditional, *475*
Hesi ritual, 419

Hewitt, John N. B., **320-321**
Hiawatha, 224, **321**
Hidatsa, **321-323**, *322*
Hides and hidework, **323**
High Forehead, 187
Hispaniola, 336
Hitchcock v. Lee, 6
Hitchiti, **323-324**, 704
Hogan, **324**, *324*
Hogan, Linda, **324**
Hohokam, 57-58, **324-325**, 631, 730, 740
Hokan language family, **325**
Hokeah, Jack, **325-326**
Holatamico. *See* Bowlegs, Billy
Hole-in-the-Day, **326**, *326*
Hollow Horn Bear, **326**, *327*
Homalco, 187
Honanisto. *See* Howling Wolf
Hooker Jim, 142, **328**, *328*
Hoopa. *See* Hupa
Hopewell, **328-329**, 626, 869
Hopi, *191*, *396*. *See also* Pueblo tribes, Western
Hopkins, Sarah Winnemucca. *See* Winnemucca, Sarah
Hopocan, **329**
Horses, **329-330**, 598
Horseshoe Bend, Battle of, 478
Horseshoe Bend, Treaty of, **330**
Hosa. *See* Littel Raven
Hospitalization, leading causes of, *471*
Hothlepoya. *See* Menewa
Hotonga, 493
Houma, 95, 739
Housatonic. *See* Mahican
House Made of Dawn (Momaday), 501
Housing. *See* Architecture
Houston, James, 66
Howe, Oscar, **330**
Howling Wolf, **330-331**
Hualapai. *See* Walapai
Huchnom, **331**
Hudson, Henry, 454
Hudson's Bay Company, **331**, 347, 464, 797
Huitzilopochtli, 86
Human sacrifice, 264
Humor, **331-332**
Hump, **332**
Hunkpapa, 719
Hunt, George, **332**, 509
Hunting, 852
Hunting and gathering, **332-333**, 754, 771
Hupa, 241, **333**
Huron, 99, **333-334**, 386
Huron Confederacy, 606
Husk Face Society, **334**

"I will fight no more, forever," 536
Igloo, 50, **335**, *335*
Ignacio, **335**

Illinois, **335-336**
In Mad Love and War (Harjo), 316
Incest taboo, **336**
Income on reservations, *669*
Indian, **336**
Indian Act of 1876 (Canada), **337**
Indian Act of 1951 (Canada), **337-338**
Indian Act of 1989 (Canada), **338**
Indian Advancement Act, 830
Indian Alcohol and Substance Abuse
    Prevention and Treatment Act, 20, 175
Indian Archives, 35
Indian Arts and Crafts Board (IACB),
    338-339
Indian Bill of Rights, 28
Indian Child Protection and Family
    Violence Prevention Act, 175
Indian Child Welfare Act, **339-340**
Indian Citizenship Act, 28, 340, 831
Indian Civil Rights Act. *See* American
    Indian Civil Rights Act
Indian Claims Commission (ICC), **340-341**,
    341, 668
Indian Country Today, 394
Indian Defense League, 299
Indian Education Acts, 174, 251, **341-342**
Indian Employment, Training, and Related
    Services Demonstration Act, 176
Indian Gaming Regulatory Act, 175, 291,
    797
Indian Health Care Improvement Act, 175
Indian Health Service, 175, 230, 469-472
Indian Higher Education Programs Act, 175
Indian Journal, 614
Indian police and judges, **342**
Indian Removal Act, **342-343**, 367, 665,
    738. *See also* Removal
Indian Reorganization Act, **343**, 375; tribal
    councils and, 194
Indian Resources Act, 175
Indian Rights Association, 289, **343-344**
Indian Self-Determination and Education
    Assistance Act, 173, **344**
Indian studies programs. *See* American
    Indian studies programs and archives
Indian Territory, **344-346**, *345*
Indian Vocational Training Act, 375
Indian-white relations—Canadian,
    346-350. *See also* Fifteen Principles;
    Indian Act of 1876 (Canada)
Indian-white relations—Dutch colonial,
    350-351
Indian-white relations—English colonial,
    351-355
Indian-white relations—French colonial,
    355-358
Indian-white relations—Norse, **358-360**
Indian-white relations—Russian colonial,
    21, 62, **360-361**

Indian-white relations—Spanish colonial,
    361-364
Indian-white relations—Swedish colonial,
    364-365
Indian-white relations—U.S., 1775-1830,
    365-368
Indian-white relations—U.S., 1831-1870,
    368-371
Indian-white relations—U.S., 1871-1933,
    371-374
Indian-white relations—U.S., 1934-1995,
    375-378
Indians of All Tribes, 18
Ingalik, **378**
Initiation rites. *See* Puberty and initiation
    rites
Inkpaduta, **378-379**
Inlay, 505
Inshtatheumba. *See* La Flesche, Susette or
    Josette
Institute of American Indian Arts (IAIA),
    64, 338, **379**
Intercourse Act. *See* Trade and Intercourse
    Acts
International Indian Treaty Council (IITC),
    379-380, 574
Inuit, 59-60, *61*, **380-382**, *381*, 625, 753,
    852; sculpture and carvings, 66
Inuit Circumpolar Conference, 382
Inummaariit, 380
Iñupiat, 380
Inuvialuit, 380
Inuvialuit Regional Corporation, 806
Iowa, **383**
Ipai, 398
Irateba, 383
Iromagaja. *See* Rain in the Face
Iroquoian language family, **383-385**
Iroquois Confederacy, **385-388**, *385*, *386*,
    542, 606. *See also* Beaver Wars; Cayuga;
    Deganawida; Mohawk; Oneida;
    Onondaga; Seneca; Tuscarora
Iroquois population distribution, *385*
Irrigation, **388**; Hohokam, 730
Isanti, 719
Isatai, **388**
Ishi, **388-389**, *389*, 874, 878, *878*
Isleta. *See* Pueblo tribes, Eastern
Isparhecher, **389**
Iyatiku. *See* Corn Woman

Jacal construction, 636
Jackson, Andrew, 330, 342, 367, 705
Jackson, Edna, 64
Jaguar Penis, 879
James Bay and Northern Quebec
    Agreement, 806
Jay's Treaty, 280
Jemez. *See* Pueblo tribes, Eastern
Jemison, Peter, 64

Jerome Commission, 439
Jesuits, 357, 398
Jewelry, 242; Western Pueblo, 77. *See also*
    Gold and goldworking; Metalwork;
    Turquoise
Jicarilla Apache, 39-40
Jimulla, Viola, 560
Johnson, Emily Pauline, **390**
Johnson-O'Malley Act, 251, 343
Johnson v. McIntosh, 5
Joking relations, 332, **390-391**
Jones, Peter, 391
Jones, Sam. *See* Arpeika
Jones, Wilson. *See* Crazy Snake
Joseph the Younger, 391-393, *392, 534. See*
    also Nez Perce War
Journalism, **393-395**
Journeycake, Charles, **395**
Juaneño, **395**

Kabocca, 293
Kachina dances, 218
Kachinas, **396-397**, *396*, 643
Kadohadacho. *See* Caddo
Kahgegwagebow. *See* Copway, George
Kainah, 110
Kalaallit, 380
Kalapuya, **397**
Kalispel, **397-398**, *397*
Kamia, **398**
Kamiakin, **398-399**, 573, 875
Kangi Sunka. *See* Crow Dog
Kansa, *216*, **399-400**
Karankawa, **400**
Karankawa language, **400-401**
Karok, **401-402**, *401*
Kaska, **402**
Kaskaskia. *See* Illinois
Katapu, 145
Katlian, **402**
Kaw. *See* Kansa
Kawaiisu, **402**
Kawchottine. *See* Hare
Kayaks, 117, *802*
Kayenta, 37, 57
Keeler Commission, **402-403**
Keetoowah Society, **403**
Kennekuk, **403**, 407
Keokuk, 105, 108, **403-405**, *404*
Keresan language family, **405**
Keshena, Gordon, 375
Key Marco, **405-406**
Keyser, Louisa. *See* Datsolalee
Kichai, **406**, 856
Kickapoo, **406-407**
Kickapoo Prophet. *See* Kennekuk
Kickapoo Resistance, **407**
Kickapoo uprisings, **407**
Kicking Bear, **407-408**, 870
Kicking Bird, **408**, *408*, 414

Kicking Bull, 102
Kikiallus, 727
Kinaaldá, 634
King George's War, 289
King Hancock. *See* Hancock
King Philip. *See* King Philip's War;
　Metacomet.
King Philip's War, 38, 140, **408-410**, 483,
　520
King William's War, 289
Kinnikinick, **410**
Kinship and social organization, **410-413**.
　See also Clans
Kintpuash. *See* Captain Jack
Kinzua Dam, 193
Kiowa, *96*, 305, **413-414**
Kiowa Apache. *See* Apache Tribe of
　Oklahoma
Kiowa Five, 85, 325
Kiowa language, 414
Kiowa-Tanoan language family, **414-415**
Kiowa Wars, 414
Kite. *See* Crow
Kitksan. *See* Gitksan
Kitsei. *See* Kichai
Kivas, **415**, 595, 636, *657*
Klah, Hosteen, **415-416**
Klahoose, 187
Klallam. *See* Clallam
Klamath, **416-417**, *416*, 496
Klickitat. *See* Klikitat
Klikitat, **417-418**
Knives, **418**, 792, 848
Koasati. *See* Coushatta
Kondiaronk. *See* Adario
Konkapot, John, **418**
Kootenay. *See* Kutenai
Koroa, 879
Koster, **418**
Koyukon, **418-419**
Kroeber, Alfred, 388, 878
Kuksu rituals and society, **419-420**, 581,
　734
Kukulcan, 466
Kumeyaay, 233. *See* Kamia
Kutchin, **420**
Kutenai, *116*, 274, **420-421**
Kutenai language, **421**
Kwakiutl, *218*, 314, **421-422**, 702; dances,
　217
Kwakiutl language, 834

Labor. *See* Employment and unemployment
Lacey Act, 374
Lacrosse, 294, 359, **423**, 863
La Flesche, Francis, **423**
La Flesche, Susan, **423**, 868
La Flesche, Susette or Josette, **423-424**
Laguna. *See* Pueblo tribes, Western
Laguna Woman (Silko), 716

Lake, **424**
Lake Forest Late Archaic, 552
Lake Mohonk Conference of the Friends of
　the Indian, 289, 374, 522
Lakota, 718
Lalawethika, 773. *See* Tenskwatawa
Lallo. *See* Asah, Spencer
La Marr, Jean, 64
Lame Bull, 111
Lame Deer, **424**
Lances and spears, **424-425**, *424*, 848
Land claims, **425-426**; Canadian, 806;
　Narragansett, 520; Paiute, 571;
　Passamaquoddy, 580; Penobscot, 1, 587
Land ownership under allotment system, *26*
Land use, contemporary, *15*
Language families, **426-429**
Language in the Americas (Greenberg), 427
Languages spoken in the home, *165*
Lark, Sylvia, 64
Laurentian language, 384
Lavell, Jeannette, 337
La Venta, **429**
Lawyer, **429-430**, *430*
Lean Bear, 127, **430**
Lean-to, 59, **430-431**, *430*
Leases on Indian lands, *673*
Left Hand the First, **431**
Left Hand the Second, **431**
Left Handed. *See* Klah, Hosteen
Lehner, **431**
Lenni Lenape, **431-434**, *432*; population
　distribution, *432*
Lewis and Clark expedition, 682
Lillooet, **434**
Lindenmeier, 600, 628
Lineage patterns, 410
Lipan Apache, 39
Little Bighorn, Battle of the, 115, 214,
　434-435
Little Carpenter, 154
Little Crow, **435**, 565, 724
Little Mountain. *See* Dohasan
Little Priest, **436**
Little Raven, **436**, 476
Little Robe, **436-437**, *436*
Little Turtle, 266, **437**, 485, 832
Little Wolf, 244, 371, **437-439**, *438*
Livestock, 14, *652*
Llano, 431
Loft, Frederick Ogilvie, 829
Logan, James, **439**
Lololma, 770
Lone Wolf, 8, 102, **439**
Lone Wolf v. Hitchcock, 5, 374, **439-440**
Long Walk, **440-442**, *441*
Longest Walk, 173, **442**, *443*
Longhouse, 53, **442-443**; Artic, 50
Longhouse religion, 315-316, **443-444**
Looking Glass, **445-446**, *445*, 536

Lord Dunmore's War, 439, **446-447**
Love Medicine (Erdrich), 260
Lovelace, Sandra, 337
Luiseño, **447**
Lumbee, **447-448**; population distribution,
　447
Lummi, **448**
Luna, James, 64
Lykins, Johnston, 394
Lyon, John. *See* Ignacio

Macaw. *See* Makah
MacDonald, Peter, 194
McGillivray, Alexander, **449**
McIntosh, Alex C.. *See* Blue Eagle, Acee
McIntosh, William, 202, **449**
McNickle, D'Arcy, **449-450**
McQueen, Peter, **450**
Mahican, **450**, 650
Mahthela. *See* Spybuck, Ernest
Mahtoiwa. *See* Conquering Bear
Maidu, **451**
Maine Indian Claims Settlement Act, 580,
　587
Maize. *See* Corn
Major Crimes Act, 744
Makah, **451-452**, *452*, 568
Makataimeshekiakiak. *See* Black Hawk
Makhpia-sha. *See* Red Cloud
Malecite. *See* Maliseet
Maliseet, 1, **452-453**
Manahoac, **453**
Mandan, 126, **453-454**, 608; Okipa
　ceremony, 551
Mangas Coloradus, 454, *454*
Mangopeomen. *See* Opechancanough
Manhassett, 502
Manhattan, **454-455**
Manibozho, **455**
Manitoba Act, 348, 675-676
Manitou, 656, 684
Mankato, **455**
Mankato mass execution, 723
Mankiller, Wilma Pearl, 155-156, *156*,
　455-456, *456*
Mantae, 432
Manuelito, 225, 440, **456-457**, *457*, 531
Manypenny Agreement, 110
Maple syrup and sugar, **457-458**
Marco Island, 405
Maricopa, 647
Mariposa. *See* Yokuts
Marriage and divorce, **458-459**, *678*; clans
　and, 178
Martínez, Antonio. *See* Popovi Da
Martínez, Crescencio, 85, *459*
Martínez, Julián, *459*
Martínez, María Antonía, **459-460**, 866
Maru Cult, **460**, 610

Masks, **460-462**, *461*; Northeast, 70; Northwest Coast, 72
Massachusett, **462-463**
Massapequa, 502
Massasoit, **463**, *463*, 482, 691, 836
Mathematics, **463-464**; Maya, 466; Olmec, 553
Mathews, Alex, *583*
Matihehlogego. *See* Hollow Horn Bear
Matinecock, 502
Mato Tope, **464**
Matonabbee, **464**
Mattaponi, **464-465**, 620
Mattole, **465**
Maya, 209, **465-467**, 505, 572, 782
Mayan calendar, 80, 464
Mdewakanton, 719
Mdewakanton Sioux, gambling and, 292
Mean Spirit (Hogan), 324
Means, Russell, 5, 31, 379, 442, **467-469**, *468*
Measles, 235
Mecina, 407
Medicine, Beatrice, 867
Medicine and modes of curing, post-contact, **469-472**
Medicine and modes of curing, pre-contact, **472-475**, *473*
Medicine bundles, **475-476**. *See also* Bundles, sacred
Medicine Lodge, Treaties of, 102, *370*, **476-477**, *476*, 654, 696
Medicine men. *See* Religious specialists; Shamans
Medicine societies, 732
Medicine wheels, 55, 80, **477**
Meech Lake Accord, 317, 350, **477**
Mendota, Treaty of, 435
Menewa, **477-478**, *478*
Menominee, **478-480**; population distribution, *479*
Menominee Restoration Act, 480
Menses and menstruation, **480-481**, 634
Meriam Report, 15, **481**, 668
Merric, 502
Mesa Verde, 37, 57, 179, **481-482**, *482*
Mescalero Apache, 39
Mesquakie, 284
Metacom. *See* King Philip's War
Metacomet, **482-483**, 836
Metalwork, **483**
Methow, **483**
Metis, **483-484**, 674, 676
Miami, **484-485**
Miantonomo, 141, **485**
Micanopy, **485**
Miccosukee. *See* Hitchiti
Miccosukee Tribe of Indians of Florida, 704
Michikinikwa. *See* Little Turtle
Micmac, 1, **485-486**, 821

Middens, **486**
Midewiwin, 484, **486**, 550, 660, 733
Midland, **487**
Midwinter Ceremony, 334, **487**
Migrations, 228, **487-490**, *489*, 753. *See also* Beringia
Miles, Nelson A., 301, 865
Military societies, **490**. *See also* Warrior societies
Mills, Billy, 294
Mimbres, **490**
Minitari. *See* Hidatsa
Minneconjou, 719
Minnesota Uprising, 436, 455, **491**
Minsi, 432
Minuit, Peter, 454
Missions and missionaries, 354-355, **491-492**; French 357; in Canada, 348; Russian, 360; Spanish, 361-363
Mississauga, 548
Mississippian, 256, 265, **492-493**, 630
Missouri, **493**, 566
Mistahimaskwa. *See* Big Bear
Mitchell, George, 31
Mitla, **493-494**, *884*
Miwok, **494**
Mixcóatl, 161, 789
Mixtec, **494-495**, 505
Mobile, **495**
Mobilian Jargon, 736
Moccasins, 495, *495*
Modoc, **495-496**
Modoc War, 142, **496-497**, *497*, 699
Mogollon, 57-58, **497-498**, 631, 740-741
Mohawk, *123*, 385, **498-499**; activism, 4; gambling and, 292
Mohawk language, 384
Mohegan, **499**
Mohican. *See* Mahican; Mohegan
Moieties, 410
Mojave, **499-501**, *500*
Moketavato. *See* Black Kettle
Moki, 419
Molala, **501**
Momaday, N. Scott, 414, **501**
Monacan, 453
Moneton, **501**
Money, **501-502**
Monks Mound, 135
Mono, *52*
Montagnais, **502**, 852
Montauk, 502
Montauk Confederacy, **502-503**, 613
Monte Albán, **503**, *546*, *884*
Montezuma, 87
Montezuma, Carlos, **504**, 879
Moor's Charity School, 248
Mopope, Stephen, **504-505**
Morning Star Ceremony, **505**, 590, 658
Mortality rates, *176*; alcoholism, *20*

Mosaic and inlay, **505**
Moses, **505-506**, 729
Mother Earth, 263, **506**
Mounds and mound builders, 7, 506-507, *507*
Moundville, **507-508**, 740
Mountain, **508**
Mountain Wolf Woman, **508**
Mourning Dove, **508-509**
Muckleshoot, **509**
Multnomah, **509**
Mummy Cave, 628
Murie, James, 313, **509-510**
Musgrove, Mary, **510**
Music and song, **510-514**, *512, 639*
Muskogean language family, **514-515**
My People, the Sioux (Standing Bear), 749
Myth. *See* Oral literature

Nabedache, **516**
Na-Dene language family, **516**; Greenberg's categorization, 428
Nahuatl, 86, 824
Naiche, **516**
Na-i-shan, 41
Nakaidoklini, **517**, 523
Nambe. *See* Pueblo tribes, Eastern
Names, translations of, 517
Names and naming, **517**, 678
Nampeyo, **517-518**, *518*, 866
Nana, **518**, *519*
Naniaba Choctaw, 169
Nanih Waiya, 514
Nansemond. *See* Powhatan Confederacy
Nanticoke, 88, **519**, 838
Nanticoke-Lenni Lenape Indians of New Jersey, 519
Narbona, 440
Narragansett, 409, **519-520**, 588
Naskapi, **520**
Natawista, **520**
Natchez, **520-521**
Natchez Revolt, 308, **521**, 548
Natchitoche. *See* Caddo
Natick, 452. *See also* Massachusett
National Archives, 35
National Congress of American Indians (NCAI), 194, **521-522**, 574
National Council of American Indians, 118, **522**
National Indian Association, **522-523**
National Indian Brotherhood, 223
National Indian Council, 223
National Indian Media Association, 394
National Indian Youth Council (NIYC), 4, **523**, 574
National Native News, 394
National Study of American Indian Education, 251
Natiotish, **523**

Native American, **524**

Native American Church, 32, **524**. *See also* Peyote and Peyote religion

Native American Church v. Navajo Tribal Council, 744

Native American Rights Fund (NARF), **524-525**

Native American studies. *See* American Indian studies programs and archives

Nauset, **525**

Navaho. *See* Navajo

Navajo, 195, *195*, 440, *473*, **525-530**, *526*, *693*, 742, *850*; population distribution, *527*; weaving and, 851

Navajo Community College, 33

Navajo-Hopi Land Settlement Act, **530-531**

Navajo Rehabilitation Act, **531**

Navajo Reservation, *528*

Navajo Times, 394

Navajo Tribal Council Reference Library, 35

Navajo War, 457, **531-532**

Navesink, 432

Nawat. *See* Left Hand the First; Left Hand the Second

Neolin. *See* Delaware Prophet

Nesaquake, 502

Nespelem, 694

Nets, 793

Neutral, **532**

Nevada v. U.S., 845

New, Lloyd Kiva, 379

New Echota, Treaty of, 681, 801, 846

New Netherland Company, 350

News from Indian Country, 394

Nez Perce, 391, **532-535**, *533*

Nez Perce War, 393, 446, 535-536, *534, 535*

Niantic, **536**, 537

Nicola, 780

Nine Years' War, 289

Ninham, Daniel, **537**

Ninigret, **537**

Nipissing, **537**

Nipmuck, 409, **537**

Niska, 811

Nisqually, **538**

Nomkahpa. *See* Two Strike

Nooksack, **538**

Nootka, **538-539**, *539*

Nootka language, 834

Norse. *See* Indian-white relations—Norse

Northeast, 213, **540-542**, *540*

Northwest Coast, 210, **542-544**, *543*

Northwest Ordinance, **545**

Northwest Uprising of 1885, 676

Nottaway, 545, 621

Nunavut, 350, 425

Nuu-chah-nulth. *See* Nootka

Oaxaca, 494, **546-547**, *546*, 884

O'Bail, John. *See* Cornplanter

Obsidian hydration dating, 221

Ocaneechi, **547**

Occom, Samson, 354, **547**

Oconee, 703

Oconostota, 158, **547-548**

Odanak, 1

Offerings Lodge, 48

Ofo, **548**

Ofogoula, 548

Ohkom Kakit. *See* Little Wolf

Ohlone. *See* Costanoan

Ojibwa, *257*, **548-550**; population distribution, *548*

Okanagan, **550-551**

Okeepa, **551**

Okipa. *See* Okeepa

Oklahoma Indian Welfare Act, 133, **551**

Old Briton, **551-552**

Old Copper culture, 483, **552**

Old Northwest, 278, 545, 612

Oliphant v. Suquamish Indian Tribe, 744

Olmec, 89, 429, **552-553**, 691, 807

Olsen-Chubbock, 276, 600, 628

Omaha, **553-555**

Oñate, Juan de, 2, 362

One Feather, Gerald, 871

Oneida, 385, *554*, 555

Oneota, 253, **555-556**

Onondaga, 385, **556**

Onondaga language, 384

Opata, 594

Opechancanough, **556-557**, 620, 621

Opothleyaholo, 203, **557**

Oral literatures, **557-560**

Oratory, **560-561**

Ordinance of 1786, 797

Oregon Trail, **561-562**, *561*

Orenda, 684-685

Ornaments, **562**

Ortiz, Simon, **562**

Osage, **562-564**

Osceola, 485, **564-565**

Oshkosh, **565**

Osteneco, 158

Otherday, John, **565-566**

Oto, 493, **566**

Otoe-Missouria. *See* Missouri; Oto

Ottawa, **566-567**

Ouray, 335, **567-568**, 822

Outagami, 284

Owasco, 387, 626

Ozette, **568**, 627

Pacal, 467

Pahvant, 822

Pai, 743

Paints and painting, **569**, *569*

Paiute, Northern, *307*, **569-570**

Paiute, Southern, **570-572**

Paiute Prophet. *See* Taribo

Palenque, 467, **572**

Paleo-Indian, 276, **572-573**, 630, 740

Palouse, **573**

Pamlico, **573-574**

Pamunkey, 88, 465, 620

Panamint, 714. *See also* Shoshone

Pan-Indianism, **574-575**, 664

Pantribalism, 574

Papago. *See* Tohono O'odham

Parfleche, 72, **575**

Parker, Arthur C., 735

Parker, Ely Samuel, **575-577**, *576*

Parker, Quanah, 8, 388, **577-579**, *578*, 654

Pasqual, 647

Passaconaway, **580**, 586

Passamaquoddy, 1, 452, **580**

Pastoralism, 757

Patayan, **580-581**

Patents, **581**

Patterns of descent, *411*

Patwin, 419, **581**

Paul, William, 17

Paviotso. *See* Paiute, Northern

Pavonia Massacre, **581-582**

Pawhuska, **582**

Pawnee, *56*, **582-584**; Wolf Society, 733

Paxton Riots, **584-585**, *584*

Payne's Landing, Treaty of, 704, 801

Peach Wars, 351, **585**

Pecos. *See* Pueblo tribes, Eastern

Peltier, Leonard, 31, 594

Pemmican, **585-586**

Peña, Tonita, **586**

Pend d'Oreille, 397

Pennacook, 1, **586**

Penobscot, 1, **586-587**

Penutian language family, **587**

Peoria. *See* Illinois

Pequot, 499, **588**, 698; gambling and, 821

Pequot War, **588-590**, *589*, 696, 698

Petalésharo, **590**

Petroglyphs, 136, **590-592**, *591*

Petun, 386, **592**

Peyote and peyote religion, 32, **592-593**, 735. *See also* Native American Church

Pezi. *See* Grass, John

Pharoah, David, 503

Philosophies, traditional Indian. *See* Ethnophilosophy and worldview

Piankashaw, 484

Pickawillany, 552

Picotte, Susan La Flesche. *See* La Flesche, Susan

Picuris. *See* Pueblo tribes, Eastern

Piegan, 110, *805*. *See also* Blackfoot and Blackfeet Confederacy

Pilalt, 197

Pima, **593**, 742

Pima uprisings, **594**

Pin Indians, 403
Pine Ridge Reservation, 871
Pine Ridge shootout, **594**
Pipe ceremonies, 312
Pipes, 73, 75, 139, 595
Pipestone, 73
Pipestone Quarries, **594-595**
Pisquow, 852
Pit house, 56, 57, 91, 415, **595**, *595*, 632;
  California, 52
Pit River, 2
Pitchlynn, Peter Perkins, **595-596**
Pizi. *See* Gall
Plains, 212, 240, **596-599**, *597*, *758*; sign
  language, 714
Plains Village period, 628
Plainview points, 627
Plank house, 51, 54, *452*, **599**, *599*
Plano, 180, **599-600**
Plateau, 210, **600-603**, *601*
Pleasant Point, Battle of, 446
Plenty Coups, **603**, *603*
Plenty Kill. *See* Standing Bear, Luther
Plow, 14
Pocagin. *See* Pokagon, Leopold
Pocahontas, **603-605**, *604*, 619, 866
Pocatello. *See* Shoshone
Pochteca, 86, **605**
Point Elliott Treaty, 701
Pojoaque. *See* Pueblo tribes, Eastern
Pokagon, Leopold, **605**
Pokagon, Simon, **605**
Pokanoket, 836
Political organization and leadership,
  605-609
Pomo, 420, 460, **609-610**; basketry, 67
Ponca, **610-611**, 748
Pontiac, 225, *353*, 567, **611-612**, *611*
Pontiac's Conspiracy, **612-613**
Poospatuck, 502, **613**
Popé, *613*, 637
Popovi Da, **614**
Population. *See* Demography
Porter, Pleasant, **614**
Posey, Alexander Lawrence, **614**
Potawatomi, **614-615**
Potlatch, 264, 544, **615-616**, *616*, 622;
  Canadian outlawing of, 349
Pottery, 75-77, *518*, **616-618**; distribution
  of, *617*; Mimbres, 490
Poundmaker, **618-619**, 677
Poveka. *See* Martínez, María Antonía
Poverty, 230, 259
Poverty Point, **619**, 630
Powell, Billy. *See* Osceola
Powhatan, 557, **619-620**, *620*
Powhatan Confederacy, 88, 464, **620-621**
Powhatan Wars, **621-622**
Pow-wows and contemporary celebrations,
  512, **622-624**, *623*

PrairyErth (Heat-Moon), 320
Pratt, Richard Henry, 143
Praying Indians, 248, 354, **624**
Prehistoric demography, 228
Prehistory—Arctic, **624-625**
Prehistory—California, **625**
Prehistory—Great Basin, **625-626**
Prehistory—Northeast, **626**
Prehistory—Northwest Coast, **626-627**
Prehistory—Plains, **627-629**
Prehistory—Plateau, **629-630**
Prehistory—Southeast, **630**
Prehistory—Southwest, **630-632**
Prehistory—Subarctic, **632-633**
Priests, traditional, 661
Principal Dogs, Kiowa, 414
Printmaking, 66
Problem of Indian Administration, The. See
  Meriam Report
Proclamation of 1763, 446, 545, **633**, 804
Projectile points, 625, 627, **633-634**, *633*,
  771, 792; Clovis, 180; Folsom, 276, *276*,
  487; Plainview, 627
Prophetstown, 775, 785
Puberty and initiation rites, **634-636**. *See
  also* Menses and menstruation
Public Law 280, **636**, 744
Pueblo (dwelling type), 57, *58*, 212,
  636-637, *637*, *640*
Pueblo Bonito, 57, *631*, 637
Pueblo (Popé's) Revolt, 362, 637
Pueblo prehistoric period, 37, 91
Pueblo tribes, Eastern, **637-642**, *657*, 742
Pueblo tribes, population distribution, *638*
Pueblo tribes, Western, **643-645**, 742
Pulque, 87
Puritans, 588
Pushmataha, **645-646**, *645*
Puuc, 826
Puyallup, **646**
Pyke, Mathew, 233
Pyramid of the Sun, 778

Qarmaq, 51
Quah Ah. *See* Peña, Tonita
Quahawan, 503
Quapaw, **647**
Quechan, **647**, 770
Queen Anne, **648**
Queen Anne's War, 289
Quelatikan. *See* Moses
Queletemoc, 161, 466, **648**, 789
Quileute, **648**
Quillwork, 70, **648-649**; Subarctic, 77
Quinault, **649-650**, *650*
Quinequan. *See* Quinney, John W.
Quinney, John W., 450, **650**
Quivers. *See* Bows, arrows and, quivers
Quivira, 856

Radiocarbon dating, 220
Railroads, 651, *651*
Rain in the Face, **651-652**, *652*
Ranching, **652-653**, *652*
Rappahannock, 620
Raritan, 432
Rattles, 514
Red Bird, **653**, 863
Red Cloud, 121, **653-654**, *653*, 833, 871
Red Jacket, 123, **654**
Red Leaf. *See* Wapasha
Red Progressive movement, 522
Red River Metis, 484, 676
Red River Rebellion, 676
Red River War, **654-655**
Red Shoes, **655**
Red Sleeves. *See* Mangas Coloradus
Red Sticks, 202, 204, 282, 450, 564, 849
Reifel, Ben, **655**
Religion, **655-659**; California, 138; Great
  Basin, 308; Plains, 598; Plateau, 602;
  Southeast, 738
Religious specialists, **659-662**
Relocation, 376, **662-664**, *663*, 669, 820
Removal, 367-368, **664-665**. *See also*
  Indian Removal Act
Renville, Joseph, **665-666**
Repartimiento, 361
Reservation populations, U.S., *668*
Reservation system of the United States,
  666-670; employment and, 257-259
Reserve system of Canada, **670-671**
Reserves, Canada, acreage of, *670*
Resource use, pre-contact, **671-672**
Resources, **672-673**, 772; Quapaw, 647
Revolving Loan Fund for Indians, 551
Rhoads, Charles J., 481
Ribbonwork, 75
Ricaree. *See* Arikara
Rice. *See* Menominee
Riddle, Toby. *See* Winema
Ridge, John Rollin, 119, **673-674**
Ridge, Major, 119, **674**, 681
Ridge, the. *See* Ridge, Major
Riel, Louis, Jr., **674-676**
Riel Rebellions, 101, 348, 618, **676-677**
Riggs, Florence, 64
Riggs, Lynn, **677**
Rite of Consolation, **677**, 678
Rites of passage, **677-679**
Robideau, Bob, 31
Rock art, 67
Rockaway, 502
Rocky Boy, **679**
Rogers, Will, **679**
Roman Nose, **679**
Rosebud Creek, Battle of, **679-680**, *680*
Ross, John, 119, 155, **680-681**, 801
Ross, William Potter, 394
Rotten Belly. *See* Arapoosh

Royal Proclamation of 1763. *See* Proclamation of 1763
Roybal, Alfonso. *See* Awa Tsireh
Rugs. *See* Weaving
Russian-American Company, 360
Russian colonial period. *See* Indian-white relations—Russian colonial

Sac. *See* Sauk
Sacagawea, **682-684**, *683*
Sachem, **684**
Sacred, the, **684-686**
Sacred Hoop, The (Allen), 24
Sacred narratives, **686-687**
Sagamore, 684
Sagard, Gabriel, 357
Sagoyewatha. *See* Red Jacket
Sahaptin, 532
St. Augustine, 362
St. Clair, Arthur, 266, 279, 832
St. Clair's defeat. *See* Wabash, Battle of the
Saint Regis Mohawk reserve, 232
Salinan, **687-688**
Salish, **688**. *See also* Quinault; Samish; Sanpoil/Nespelem
Salish, Inland. *See* Flathead
Salishan language family, **688-689**
Salmon, 167, 272, **689**, 759
Salt, **689**
Samish, **689-691**
Samoset, *690*, **691**
San Carlos Apache, 39, 41
San Felipe. *See* Pueblo tribes, Eastern
San Ildefonso. *See* Pueblo tribes, Eastern
San José Mogote, 546
San Juan. *See* Pueblo tribes, Eastern
San Lorenzo, **691**
Sand Creek Massacre, 110, **691-693**
Sand Hollow battle, 148
Sand painting, 149, **693-694**, *765*
Sandia. *See* Pueblo tribes, Eastern
Sanpoil-Nespelem, **694-695**
Santa Ana. *See* Pueblo tribes, Eastern
Santa Clara. *See* Pueblo tribes, Eastern
Santa Clara Pueblo v. Martinez, 744
Santa Fe Trail, **695**
Santee, 719
Santo Domingo. *See* Pueblo tribes, Eastern
Sarcee. *See* Sarsi
Sarsi, *277*, 695-696
Sassacus, 499, 588, **696**
Satank, 102, 414
Satanta, 102, 414, 476, **696**, *697*
Sauk, 105, *106*, 107, **696-698**; population, *285*. *See also* Fox
Saulteaux, 548
Sawokli, 703
Saybrook, Battle of, **698**
Scalps and scalping, **698-699**, 840
Scarface Charlie, **699-700**

Scholder, Fritz, 64, **700**
Scrapers, 792
Scuffletonians, 447
Sculpture, **700-701**, *700*; Arctic, 66; Plateau, 74
Sealaska, 18
Seattle, **701**
Secatogue, 502
Secotan, **701-702**
Secret societies, **702**, 733
Sedna, 660
Sekani, **702**
Sekatau, Ella Thomas, 520
Self-Determination, 376
Selfbow, 121
Semiahmoo, **703**
Seminole, *120*, **703-704**, *703*, 801
Seminole Wars, 120, 564, **704-706**, *705*
Seneca, *193*, 385, **706**
Senijextee. *See* Lake
Sequoyah, 155, **706-708**, *707*
Seri, **708**
Serpent mounds, **708-709**, *709*
Serra, Junípero, 138, 363
Serrano, **709-710**
Setauket, 502
Seven Fireplaces, 719
Seven Old Women, 47
Seventh Cavalry, 214, 434, 843
Sevier-Fremont, 288
Sexual relations, 458
Shábona, **710**
Shaker Church, **710-711**, 729
Shaking Tent Ceremony, 201, 660, **711**
Shalako, **711**
Shamans, 472, 474-475, 660
Shanawdithi, 101
Shasta, **711-712**
Shawnee, 446, **712**
Shawnee Prophet. *See* Tenskwatawa
Shawnee Sun, 394
Sheepeater, 90
Sheepeaters War, 371
Sheepherding, 652, 758
Shellfish, 272
Shells and shellwork, **712-713**
Shield Jaguar, 879
Shikellamy, **713**
Shinnecock, 502, **713**
Shinny, 294, 598
Short Bull, **713-714**, 870
Shoshone, 97, **714-715**
Shroud cloth, 850
Shuswap, **715**
Si Tanka. *See* Big Foot
Sign language, **715**
Siksika, 110
Sikyatki, 517
Siletz, **715-716**
Silko, Leslie Marmon, 648, **716**

Sinagua, **716-717**
Sinew, 793
Sinkaietk, 550
Sinkiuse. *See* Columbia
Sinkyone, 465
Sinte Gleska. *See* Spotted Tail
Sinte Glista College, 33
Siouan language family, **717-718**
Sioux, *118*, 281, 491, **718-723**, *720*, *841*; population distribution, *719*; reservations, *721*
Sioux uprisings, **723-724**
Sioux Wars, 721
Sitting Bear, 476
Sitting Bull, 291, 680, **724-726**, *725*, 871
Siuslaw, **726**
Six Nations. *See* Iroquois Confederacy
Skagit, **726-727**
Skallam, 177
Skykomish, 731
Slave, **727**
Slavery, 9-11, 264, 608, **727-729**
Sleds, 802
Sliammon, 187
Slocum, John, 710, **729**
Smallpox, 233, 235; blankets infected with, 352
Smith, Jaune Quick-to-See, 64
Smith, John, 603
Smohalla, **729**
Snake, 730
Snake Dance, **729-730**
Snake War, **730**
Snaketown, **730-731**
Snohomish, **731**
Snoqualmie, **731**
Snowshoes, 802
Snyder Act. *See* Indian Citizenship Act
Social control, traditional, **731-732**
Social organization, 412; California, 138; Great Basin, 308; Northeast, 541; Northwest Coast, 544; Plateau, 602; Southeast, 736
Societies, non-kin-based, **732-735**; Arapaho, 47
Society of American Indians (SAI), 504, 522, 574, **735**
Sodalities, 490
Sohappy v. Smith, 846
Son of the Forest, A (Apes), 44
"Song My Paddle Sings, The" (Johnson), 390
Sooke, **735-736**
Sordo, El, 225
Southeast, 213, **736-740**, *737*
Southern Cult, 265, 493, 508, 740
Southwest, 212, **740-743**, *741*
Sovereignties, 157
Sovereignty, 28, **743-745**. *See also Lone Wolf v. Hitchcock*; Public Law 280

Spanish. *See* Indian-white relations—Spanish colonial

Spears and spearheads, 424, *424*, 792

Spider Woman's Granddaughters (Allen), 24

Spirit dancing, **745**

Spiritual societies, 734

Spiro, 131, 493, 740, **745-746**

Spokane, **746**

Sports. *See* Games and contests

Spotted Elk. *See* Big Foot

Spotted Tail, 209, 373, **746-747**, *747*

Spybuck, Ernest, 747

Squamish, **747-748**

Squanto, 691, **748**

Squash, **748**

Stand Watie. *See* Watie, Stand

Standing Bear, 610, **748-749**

Standing Bear, Luther, 749, *749*

Standing Bear v. Crook, 373, 749

Stephens v. Cherokee Nation, 374

Stereotypes, **749-751**

Stevens, Isaac I., 573, 835

Stillaguamish, 727

Stockbridge, 450. *See also* Mahican

Stomp Dance, **751**

Stone Child. *See* Rocky Boy

Stone masonry, southwestern, 57

Stoney. *See* Assiniboine

Strange Woman religion, 615

Stratigraphic analysis, 221

Stumbling Bear, 408, **751-752**

Stuyvesant, Peter, 585

Subarctic, 210, **752-754**, *752*

Subsistence, **754-759**, *756*

Suicide, **759-760**, *760*

Sumass, 197

Sun Dance, 47, 111, 219, **760-762**

Sunset Crater, 716

Supreme Court cases. See *Cherokee Nation v. Georgia*; *Cherokee Tobacco* case; *Elk v. Wilkins*; *Ex parte Crow Dog*; *Fletcher v. Peck*; *Lone Wolf v. Hitchcock*; *Oliphant v. Suquamish Indian Tribe*; *Standing Bear v. Crook*; *Stephens v. Cherokee Nation*; *United States v. Kagama*; *Winters v. United States*; *Worcester v. Georgia*

Suquamish, **762**

Surrounded, The (McNickle), 450

Susquehannock, 88, **762-763**

Sutaio Cheyenne, 159

Swallah, **763**

Swampy Cree, 200

Swanton, 1

Sweatlodges and sweatbaths, 55, **763-764**, *763*

Swedish colonial period. *See* Indian-white relations—Swedish colonial

Sweezy, Carl, **764**

Swinomish, 727

Syllabaries, 707, *707*, **764-765**

Symbolism in art, **765-766**

Tachi. *See* Yokuts

Tahltan, 255, **767**

Tall Bull, 476, **767**

Tallchief, Maria, **767**

Tammany, **767**

Tanacharison. *See* Half-King

Tanaina, **768**, 852

Tanana, **768**

Tanning, 323, **768-769**

Tanoan. *See* Kiowa-Tanoan language family

Taos. *See* Pueblo tribes, Eastern

Taos Pueblo, *58, 640*

Tappan, 432

Tarhe, **769**

Tatanka Iyotanka. *See* Sitting Bull

Tatotem, 588

Tattoos and tattooing, 242, **769**, 783

Tavibo, **769**

Tawakoni, 856

Tawaquaptewa, **769-770**

Tayovaya, 856

Technology, **770-773**

Tecumseh, 284, 366, 574, 712, **773-774**, *773*, 780, 785

Tecumseh's Rebellion, **774-775**

Teedyuscung, **775**

Tekahionwake. *See* Johnson, Emily Pauline

Tekakwitha, Kateri, **775-776**

Ten Bears, 476, **776**

Tendoy, **776**

Tenino, **776-777**

Tenochtitlán, 86, **777-778**, *777*

Tenskwatawa, 284, 773-774, **778**, 780, 785

Tents, Arctic, 51

Teosinte, 12

Teotihuacán, 160, 161, 547, **778**, 885

Termination Act of 1953, 375

Termination policy, 669, **778-779**

Termination Resolution, 779

Tesuque. *See* Pueblo tribes, Eastern

Tete de Boule Cree, 200

Teton, 719

Tewa language, 414

Tewanima, Louis, 294

Texas, **779**

Texas Rangers, 127, **779**

Texcoco, 87

Textiles. *See* Weaving

Thames, Battle of the, **780**

Thayendanegea. *See* Brant, Joseph

Thlingehadinne. *See* Dogrib

Thom, Melvin, 523, 574

Thompson, **780-781**

Thorpe, Jim, 294, **781**, *781*

Thule, 380, 625, **781-782**

Tiger, Jerome R., **782**

Tigua. *See* Pueblo tribes, Eastern

Tikal, **782-783**

Tillamook, 715, **783**

Timber resources, 673

Timucua, 104, **783**; smallpox epidemic and, 233

Timucua language, 783-784

Tiou, **784**

Tipai, 398

Tipi, 53, 55, 596, **784-785**, *784*

Tipi rings, 55

Tippecanoe, Battle of, 775, **785-786**, *785*

Tiwa language, 414

Tlacopán, 87

Tlallum, 177

Tlingit, 165, 505, 662, **786-787**, *787*

Tlingit language, 516

Tobacco, 14, **787-788**

Tobacco (tribe). *See* Petun

Tobacco Society and Dance, 206, **788**

Tohome, **788**

Tohono O'odham, 742, **788-789**

Tollán. *See* Tula

Tolowa, *241*, **789**

Tolpiltzin, 789

Toltec, 161, **789**, 812

Tomah, **789-790**

Tomahawks, **790**, 792, 848

Tomochichi, **790**

Tongass. *See* Tlingit

Tonkawa, **790-791**

Tonkawa language, **791**

Tonto Apache, 41

Tools, 771, **791-793**, *792*

Torture, **793-794**

Totem poles, 71, *71*, **794-795**, *794*

Totems, **795**

Towa language, 414

Toys, **795-796**

Trade, 352, 737, **796-797**; Artic, 62; "factory system," 366

Trade and Intercourse Acts, 14, 366, **797**

Trade blankets, 114

Trading posts, **797-799**

Trail of Broken Treaties, 4, 172, *798*, **799**

Trail of Tears, 155, 220, 665, **799-802**, *800, 801*

Transportation modes, 771, **802-804**

Traps, 793. *See also* Weirs and traps

Travois, 596, 802, *803*

Treaties. *See* Dancing Rabbit Creek, Treaty of; Fort Atkinson, Treaty of; Fort Greenville, Treaty of; Fort Laramie Treaty of 1851; Fort Laramie Treaty of 1868; Fort Stanwix, Treaty of; Fort Wayne, Treaty of; Indian-white relations—U.S., 1775-1830; Indian-white relations, 1831-1870; Medicine Lodge, Treaties of; Treaties and agreements in Canada

Treaties and agreements in Canada, **804-807**
Tres Zapotes, **807**
Tribally controlled colleges, 29
Tribally Controlled Community College Act, 29, 33, 174
Tribally Controlled School Grants Act, 175
Tribe, **807-809**
Tricksters, 686-687, **809-810**
Trudeau, Pierre E., 856
Tsatoke, Monroe, **810**
Tsattine. *See* Beaver
Tsetsaut, **810-811**
Tsimshian, **811**
Tubatulabal, **811-812**
Tubutama, 594
Tula, 789, **812**
Tule, 601, 812
Tule Lake. *See* Modoc
Tunica, 548, **812-813**
Tunica language, **813**
Tupilak sculptures, 66
Turkey Dance, Caddo, 132
Turquoise, **813**
Tuscarora, 385, **813-814**
Tuscarora War, 813
Tuskegee, **814**
Tustennuggee Emartha, or Jim Boy, 11
Tutchone, **814**
Tutelo, **814-815**
Tututni, **815**
Twana, **815**
Twenty Points, 5, 799
Twins, **815**
Two Leggings, **815-816**, *816*
Two Moon, **816**
Two Strike, **816**, *817*
Tyigh, 777, **816-818**

Uintah Utes, 822
Umatilla, **819**
Umatilla Reservation, 835
Umiak, 117
Umpqua, **819**
Unalachtigo, 432
Unalaska Aleut, 20
Unami, 432
Uncas, 499, **819-820**
Unemployment. *See* Employment and unemployment
United States v. Kagama, 5, 374
United States v. Mazurie, 6
United States v. Oregon, 846
United States v. Washington, 6, 846
United States v. Wheeler, 744
United States v. Winans, 5, 846
Unquachog, 502
Urban Indians, 664, **820-822**; elderly, 255; population statistics, *821*
Ute, *186*, **822-824**, *823*; adoption, 9
Ute War, 371

Utina, 783
Uto-Aztecan language family, **824-825**
Utsini. *See* Timucua
Uxmal, **825-826**, *825*

Ventana Cave, 788
Veracruz, **827**
Victorio, **827-828**, *828*
Visions and vision quests, 598, **828-829**
Vizenor, Gerald R[obert], 829
Voluntary Relocation Program, 662, 820
Voting Rights—Canada, **829-830**
Voting Rights—United States, **830-831**
Voyageurs, 357

Waban, **832**
Wabanaki, 1, 580
Wabanaquot. *See* White Cloud
Wabash, Battle of the, 266, 279, 437, **832-833**
Waccamaw, **833**
Waco, **833**, 856
Wagon Box Battle, **833-834**
Wahiev. *See* Dull Knife
Wahpetunwan, 719
Wakan, 656, 684-685
Wakashan language family, **834**
Walam Olum, 364, **834-835**
Walapai, **835**
Walla Walla, **835**
Walla Walla Council, 391, 573, 819, **835-836**
Wampanoag, 408, **836**
Wampum, **836-837**
Wamsutta, 836
Wanapam, **837**
Wanig Suchka. *See* Red Bird
Wapasha, **837-838**
Wappinger, **838**
Wappo, **838**
War bonnets, 270, 319, **838-839**, *841*
War of 1812, Cherokee and, 155
War on Poverty, 669
Ward, Nancy, 154, **839**
Warden, Cleaver, 509
Warfare and conflict, **839-842**. *See also* Battles and conflicts in the West
Warm Springs. *See* Tenino
Warren, William W., **842**
Warrior, Clyde, 523, 574
Warrior societies, 732. *See also* Military societies
Wasco, **843**
Wasechun-tashunka. *See* American Horse
Washakie, **843**
Washington v. Fishing Vessel Association, 6
Washita River, Battle of the, **843-844**
Washoe, **844-845**, *844*; basketry, 68
Water and water rights, **845-846**
Water on Indian lands, *845*

Water Sprinkling Old Men, 47
Watie, Stand, 119, 157, **846-848**, *847*
Watohkonk. *See* Kicking Bird
Wattan. *See* Sweezy, Carl
Wattle and daub, 57, **848**, *848*
Wayne, Anthony, 266, 279
Wea, 484
Weapons, 771, **848-849**, *849*
Weatherford, William, 282, **849**
Weaving, 77, **849-851**, *76, 115, 850*; Plateau bags, 73
Weawea, 730
Weetamoo, 684, **851**
Weirs and traps, **852**
Welch, James, **852**
Wenatchi, **852-853**
Wenebojo, 686
Westo. *See* Yuchi
Whales and whaling, 451, **853**
Wheat, 14
Wheel, 802
Wheeler-Howard Act. *See* Indian Reorganization Act
White Bird, **853**
White Buffalo Society, **853-854**
White Cloud, 107, **854**
White Deerskin Dance, **854**
White Eyes, **854**
White Man Runs Him, **854-856**, *855*
White Mountain Apache, 39, 41
White Paper of Canada, **856**
White Sticks, 849
Whitman, Marcus, 148
Whitman, Richard Ray, 65
Whitman Massacre, 368
Wichita, **856-857**
Wichita Memory Exhibit Museum, 35
Wickiup, 52, *52*, **857**, *857*
Wigwam, 53, 59, **857-858**, *857*
Wild rice, 14, **858**
Wild west shows, **858-859**, *859*
Wildcat, 485, **859-860**
Williams, Eleazar, 565, **860**
Wilson, Jack. *See* Wovoka
Wilson, Richard, 5, 594, 871
Windigo, **860**
Winema, **860**
Winnebago, **860-863**; population distribution, *863*
Winnebago Uprising, 653, **863**
Winnemucca, Sarah, 560, **864**, 867
Winters v. United States, 5, 84
Wintun, **864**
Wishram, **864-865**
Witchcraft and sorcery, **865**
Witt, Shirley, 523
Wiyot, **865**
Wodziwob, 302
Wolf Mountains, Battle of, **865**
Wolinak, 1

Women, **865-868**; non-kin-based societies and, 734
Women of All Red Nations (WARN), 574, **868-869**
Wonkas. *See* Uncas
Wooden Leg, **869**
Woodland, 552, 628, 630, **869-870**
Woodwork, Subarctic, 78
Worcester v. Georgia, 5, 665
World War I, 340, 374
World War II, 230, 258, 318, 375, 470, 531; Aleut and, 21
Wounded Knee Massacre, **870-871**, *870*
Wounded Knee occupation, 5, *377*, **871-872**
Wovoka, 302, 570, 870, **872-873**, *872*
Wright, Allen, **873**
Wyandanck, 503
Wyandot. *See* Huron

Xehaciwinga. *See* Mountain Wolf Woman

Yahi, **874**, 877
Yakima, **874-875**, *874*
Yakima War, 391, 398, 417, **875-876**
Yakonan language family, **876**
Yakutat. *See* Tlingit
Yamasee, **876-877**
Yamasee War, 44, **876-877**
Yana, **877-878**
Yankton, 719
Yaqui, 742, **878**
Yaquina, 876, **878**
Yavapai, **879**
Yaxchilan, **879**
Yazoo, **879-880**
Yellow Bird, 871
Yellow Feather, 770
Yellow Thunder, Raymond, 4
Yellow Wolf, **880**
Yellowknife, 167, **880**
Yokuts, **880-881**
Yonaguska, 155, **881**

Young Bear, **881**
Young Man Afraid of His Horses, 121, 517, **881-882**
Yscani, 856
Yuchi, **882**
Yuki, **882**
Yukioma, 770
Yuma. *See* Quechan
Yuman language family, **882-883**
Yupik, 59, 62, 114, 380
Yurok, *273*, *763*, **883**

Zapotec, 494, 503, 505, **884-885**, *884*
Zhogaxe. *See* La Flesche, Francis
Zia. *See* Pueblo tribes, Eastern
Zipkoheta. *See* Big Bow
Zitkala Sa. *See* Bonnin, Gertrude Simmons
Zotom, **885**
Zuni, 172. *See also* Pueblo tribes, Western
Zuni language, **885**